CHINA
SHAKES
THE
WORLD

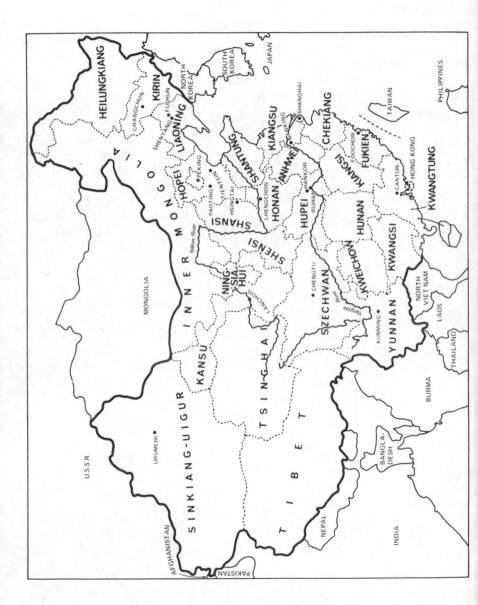

CHINA
SHAKES
THE WORLD

by Jack Belden

Introduction by
Owen Lattimore

(MR)

New York and London

CONTENTS

❦

INTRODUCTION

❦

In the late 1930's and the war years Jack Belden was to me, and I think to quite a number of people who had been in China longer than he had, a legendary figure. He was the man who knew the seamy side of China, where the lice lurked. Most of the rest of us, except for Edgar Snow and Agnes Smedley, were a prosaic lot. Either we had been brought up in China or we had come out to take jobs that had been arranged beforehand, or to study the language on academic fellowships. Jack Belden had worked his way out as an able-bodied seaman and then jumped ship in Hong Kong. After that he knocked about in the seaport cities and made forays into the hinterland. From the beginning he seems to have distrusted the intelligentsia and to have had a fellow-feeling for the disinherited and the down-and-out. He was the man who knew what underemployed peasants, underpaid workers, and sullen soldiery did about sex and drink and drugs.

When the all-out Japanese invasion began in 1937 Jack Belden had already been in China about five years. He had seen a good deal of the country, in the areas where the shock of the Japanese invasion was going to be most brutal, and he knew something of the language. Judging from the indications here and there in his writing, it was more the language of the uneducated and the semi-literate than that of the intellectuals and political hacks. It is also plain, from his writing as a whole, that Belden has an affinity for men of action and is wary of intellectuals. He knows what theory and ideology are, but he is not captivated by them. In a characteristic passage in *China Shakes the World* he describes a man of peasant origin who had gone to middle school and then to a course for training Chiang Kai-shek's gendarmerie. Repelled by the treatment he got there, the peasant had deserted and made his way to Yenan. By the time Belden met him he was a veteran organizer and leader of the guerrillas.

"He was one of the finest examples of a type of man that was by no means rare in Communist areas," Belden writes. "He was that entrancing combination of man of action and intellectual. He had a grave, quiet manner that engendered trust. I often thought that if men of this type gained control of the Communist movement—and the question of power has not yet been completely settled among the Communists—then there would be little to fear from it. If the pure intellectuals gain the upper hand, then cultism may rule China."

Belden reported the early stages of the Japanese invasion. He was the man who broke the story of how the peasants of northern Honan, embittered and crazed by the way they had been racked and taxed and exploited by the army and officials of Chiang Kai-shek, rose up and welcomed the Japanese invaders. (I can remember something similar in the province of Jehol, in 1933, when the Japanese took 100,000 square miles of territory in ten days, When I asked the peasants who were waiting for the oncoming Japanese, who were only a few miles away, what they thought of it all, they said stolidly, "We don't know the Japanese. We know our own governor. If we can eat his liver and drink his blood, that's enough.")

Later Belden saw the great Anglo-American-Chinese defeat in Burma *(Retreat with Stilwell)* and the war in North Africa and the landings in Europe *(Still Time to Die)*. He saw a lot of war. He was one of the great war correspondents, but not as famous as others because his despatches did not get printed in full and because he did not catch the fancy of those at the upper levels of the political and military establishments who had it in their power to make a reporter fashionable.

When he got back to China late in 1946 there was no reporter of any nationality better equipped to record the final civil war between Chiang Kai-shek and the Communists. He knew the country, he knew far more of the language than most correspondents, and he knew and saw through both the conventional military thinking of the Americans and the Chiang clique and the conventional American image of China.

Considering the sour, dense, obstinate refusal of the makers of American policy to look at the facts of a revolution which was going on right under their eyes, and being observed by consuls in many Chinese cities and officers attached to many Chinese military units, not to mention missionaries and the representatives of various relief units, and considering their bewitched belief that the incantation of words like "freedom" and "democracy" (accompanied by the spending of lots of money) could somehow conjure up an Ohio-like or New England-like regime capable of reversing a revolution already in being, we are lucky that the best reports on that revolution have also been written by Americans.

They cover a wide range, and this is not the place to write an essay on all of them, but there are two that must be mentioned if one is writing about Jack Belden's work.

Edgar Snow's *Red Star over China,* published just as the all-out Japanese assault on China began, holds its place as a classic because of the author's own unchallengeable honesty and because he was the first to tell us, more than thirty years ago, what the Chinese Communists were like when they assembled at Yenan at the end of the Long March, and what their leading representatives had to say for themselves and their movement, in their own words. I remember talking to a Communist about Snow, years ago, at a time when adherents of Chiang Kai-shek were denouncing him as nothing but a mouthpiece for Communist propaganda. The Communist shook his head. No, he said, they respected Snow as a completely honest man. His reporting of facts could be relied on. But his *interpretations* did not entitle him to rank as a "spokesman," because he did not really understand Marxism.

Be that as it may, only those who were in China at the time can recall the full impact of Snow's *Red Star over China.* For a decade, the Kuomintang had been alternately reporting the extermination or the approaching extermination of the "Red bandits." From the other side, in Comintern reports and fervid articles in the left-wing journals, which most of us never saw (I myself, in those days, had only a hazy idea that they even existed), came stories of peasant heroes, under the inspiration of "proletarian leadership," battling for the cause of "the masses"; but these heroes, alas, were stereotypes, not real flesh and blood. We foreigners, under the shield of extraterritorial privilege, continued to play polo, go to cocktail parties, picnic in the western hills of Peking, or speculate on the exchange value of the Chinese dollar.

The political vocabulary of most foreigners did not go beyond clichés: the Chinese, especially the peasants, were not interested in politics. Give them law and order and reasonable taxes and they would make no trouble for anybody. Talk of "classes" and "masses" was the jargon of "agitators." What China needed was men of striking personality, "mandate of heaven" types. The great question was whether Chiang Kai-shek was going to prove himself enough of a strong man to subdue "all under heaven"—and at the same time guarantee the interests of the foreign powers. Quite a few foreigners in China thought that the "firm hand" of Japan was a good thing; it might "bring the Chinese to their senses."

It is true, however, that some were worried by the fact that Japan, by carving out huge areas of special interest like "Manchukuo," was breaking the rules of the international club that controlled China by indirection and insured, theoretically, free competition among all the imperialist powers. How could the club continue to demand a standard of law and order while refusing to restrain Japan, a club member, from carrying out a policy of lawlessness and disorder?

In this depressing twilight of political thinking, Snow's *Red Star over China* burst like a fireworks display. It revealed the outlines of things until then unseen or only dimly guessed at. This was not propaganda. It was description. *There was another China.* Snow relayed to us what the Communist leaders had to say, and what they had to say turned out to be not gramophone records reiterating doctrine, but pithy suggestions applicable to the existing problems of China and to the possibility of organizing resistance to Japan. Moreover, *Red Star* is a big book, and its abiding importance rests on much more than quotation of the words of leaders. Snow was the first to describe the Communist-led phase of the Chinese revolution as a movement in which widening circles of voluntary adherence kept spreading out around a nucleus of Communist leadership.

In the days of Sun Yat-sen there had been a similar phenomenon of outer voluntary adherence to the inner core of the Kuomintang, but by the late 1930's the Kuomintang was thinking of itself as an elite, charged with a mission to impose discipline and obedience on the unenlightened masses. For this reason the confrontation between the Kuomintang and the Chinese Communist Party *(Kungch'antang)* is bound to be misunderstood if it is represented as a rivalry between totalitarianisms. The contest was in fact between a self-selected leadership which aimed at imposing control, and a "dialectical" movement in which the Communists, also a self-selected group, sought those principles and methods that would attract voluntary support, while vast numbers of a still inchoate nation were in search of a leadership which they could willingly follow because it represented and served what they felt to be in their own interests—and increasingly, year by year, rejoiced when they convinced themselves that they had found that leadership in the Communist Party.

This feeling for the difference between a movement in which leaders and followers interact is deployed even more consciously, and in great detail, in a second American classic of the Chinese revolution, William Hinton's *Fanshen.* Hinton deals with a limited region in North China. He reaches back in time to give a sketchy account of the region before the Japanese invasion, with spontaneous local resistance crippled at first because too many of the landlords and what was left of the Kuomintang structure of privilege and control collaborated with the invaders. He then discussed the revival of the will to resist, increasingly stimulated not only by the advanced outlying agents and organizers of the Communist Eighth Route Army but—and this marks the difference between a "movement" increasingly generating its own momentum and a "controlled" revolution—by the word of mouth, spread from peasant to peasant, of news and stories of "how to do it," "the right way to do it," and "this is the way 'they' [the Eighth Route Army] do it."

Triumph: The local Japanese withdraw, and from far away comes the news that all the Japanese have surrendered. The people savour the rewards of their own heroism.

Disaster: The troops of Chiang Kai-shek, the landlords, and the Kuomintang place-holders and place-seekers all return. They hunt down the heroes of the Resistance, who are no longer heroes but "subversives."

Liberation: But two things have changed. By reason of what they have done for themselves and learned to do for each other, by reason of their common suffering and common achievements, a significantly large proportion of the peasants are no longer the same old peasants, resigned to being ordered about. And the main function of the Eighth Route Army was no longer to inspire nationalistic resistance to foreign invaders. The Army itself, and the outlying partisans and village militiamen who had more and more closely affiliated themselves to the Eighth Route, were now ready to support the demands of the peasants for a voice in deciding their own fate—demands that led inevitably to class warfare, so that in the end "liberation" came to mean more than pushing an old party aside and putting a new party in power: it meant the destruction of a class system and the transformation of a society.

It is better not to call the demands of the peasants (and others) "democratic," because "democracy" means too many different things to different people. What was involved is illustrated by one of Hinton's stories. For the sake of brevity, I paraphrase his description, and hope that in doing so I do not distort his meaning. The Communists encouraged the villagers to speak out on their grievances and to speak up on what they thought should be done. The Communists, as professional revolutionaries, would then discuss among themselves what the people were saying and demanding. If they adopted as policy what the people were calling for in the heat of the moment, how far would it broaden the movement, and how far might it stiffen opposition? They would then call more village meetings, make it clear that they sympathized in general, but suggest some changes. These exchanges went on and on, back and forth, the Communists not imposing changes and sometimes modifying their own suggestions, if the popular will was firm and clear. From time to time the results of the village debates would be carried, by delegates, to a higher level—a region that included many villages. Hinton once asked a regional official if he didn't think the villagers would get tired of this endless talking and referring back and forth. "They won't get tired. It's their own future they're deciding."

This is where Jack Belden comes in. His area of travel and observation overlaps Hinton's, but is much wider—it includes the Northeast (Manchuria) and the lower Hwai and Yangtze valleys. He also overlaps Hinton in time, dealing in the main with the Liberation War (civil war after the Japanese surrender), but with many references to the past and to the course of the civil war in other regions. His account therefore ramifies much more widely than Hinton's, but while he has a number of intensive descriptions of limited areas and what happened there, he has no long-sustained account centered on a particular area, as Hinton does. He is also measurably more detached than Hinton. He was, after all, a newspaperman; he was observing, not helping, not participating. Hinton was working with students and cadres who had been sent to the villages to promote and participate in *fanshen*—that unique process in which the "mass" overturns the old order, and the individual "converts" himself—and he identified himself very closely with his companions and with the village people.

In one respect, Belden's experience differed both from Snow's and Hinton's. In 1947-48-49, as chaos deepened and Chiang Kai-shek's authoritarian control weakened, an American reporter could slip back and forth between areas that were under full Communist (Eighth Route Army) control; partisan and militia areas that were controlled by the Communists, as far as they were controlled at all, by influence but not by authority; and Kuomintang areas. Belden took advantage of this. The Kuomintang were so deeply dependent on American aid and the hope of more aid to come that they could only partly limit the movement of reporters, even when they distrusted them. As for the Communists, their liberal treatment of reporters is extraordinary evidence of their confidence in themselves and their cause, and their subtle understanding that, things being as they were, the average American would be more sympathetic to what he saw behind the lines than to what he encountered in regions being ravaged by the death-throes of the Kuomintang.

Red Star over China is a long-established classic. *Fanshen* is also an unchallengeable classic. It is, I think (for that period of Maoism), the best revelation of the Maoist "style in action," including the bold principle of allowing mass meetings to call the cadres and Party members before them, question them roughly, and challenge not only their actions and policies, but even their personal integrity. Standing between these two, *China Shakes the World* has until now been a neglected masterpiece. How is this to be explained?

Red Star was published when a decade of frustration was coming to an end—Japanese invasion of Manchuria, Italian invasion of Ethiopia, the Spanish Civil War, renewed Japanese encroachment in China, Munich. The effects of these regional aggressions were clearly converging toward a world war of incalculable sweep, terror, and suffering. Where were the forces which could be rallied against fascism and militarism? Conservatives and untold numbers of "moderates" or "liberals" were paralyzed by German, Italian, and Japanese propaganda describing a Communist world menace; they hesitated and wondered if the fascists and militarists might indeed be holding back a "Red tide of Bolshevism." Suddenly Snow revealed a Communist movement which included untold numbers of non-Communists; which did not stand apart in doctrinal isolation; whose leaders walked about the streets of Yenan without body-guards; who, in the name of national unity, had saved the life of their most embittered enemy, Chiang Kai-shek. Looking back, it is clear that Snow's part in preparing American opinion—and indeed world opinion—for a stand against international aggression in which Communists would be acceptable allies, was of world historical importance.

Fanshen was published long after the period it describes. Hinton returned to America in 1953. The influence of Senator Joe McCarthy, and of Senator Pat McCarran's Senate Internal Security Committee, lay heavy on the land. Hinton's papers were seized and it took years of litigation—costing a lot of money—to get them back, which explains why *Fanshen* was not published until 1967. By then, McCarthy-McCarranism was fading (though it has not altogether faded out, even yet), and a new generation had grown up to read *Fanshen* and, having read it, to ask the probing questions: "If *Fanshen* describes what was really happening in China, then why, at that time, was America being fed with horror tales about Communism being imposed on China by methods of terror directed by a Moscow dictatorship, and why did people believe these tales?" What is the answer?

China Shakes the World supplies at least part of the answer, and the fact that it was not a best-seller when it appeared, and has since then been a neglected masterpiece, has much to do with that answer. Unlike Hinton, who was both participant and observer, but not an on-the-spot reporter, Jack Belden was a working reporter; but he was a reporter at a time when the "China Lobby," which was to become the McCarthy-McCarran cloud, was already smudging the American horizon. More than once he mentions that not a word of some reports he sent to America was published—and mentions at the same time the distorted version of what was going on in China put out by the late Senator Knowland (Republican, California), and the late William C. Bullitt.

It is this aspect of his work that makes it even more important to read Jack Belden at the present time, the time of the Vietnam war, than to read Edgar Snow or William Hinton. Page after page is a reminder that the stupid, obvious, unnecessary mistakes made by the American political and military establishments in China have been made over again, and are still being made, in Vietnam.

How many more times must these mistakes be spelled out, syllable by syllable? Already the American people understand more about what is going on, and what is going wrong, than those in authority, who are trapped in the channels of bureaucracy and precedents, and trammelled by the rules of prescribed behavior. This gap can only be filled by the bulldozer of more pressure from the people on the government. For those who want to know more about the job that has to be done, Jack Belden's account of what went on so long ago and far away in China is invaluable as a general description of the problems of any Asian society, fettered by the colonial heritage of the past and trying to win a foothold in the Twentieth Century; and more than that, it shows why a society blinded by imperialistic preconceptions cannot produce an administration, Democratic or Republican, capable of seeing the facts as they are—let alone dealing with them.

OWEN LATTIMORE

The University of Leeds
January 1970

CHINA
SHAKES
THE
WORLD
❧

PART I

INTO RED CHINA

❧

1. Foreword

WHEN World War II ended, Generalissimo Chiang Kai-shek must have been content.

The Japanese Army, which he had resisted so stubbornly, but so unsuccessfully had just surrendered to him without a fight. The Western powers, with equal docility, had given up their hundred-year role of imperialist aggression, returned the treaty port concessions and recognized China as a fully sovereign state and Chiang as her rightful ruler. Among his own countrymen, Chiang's position appeared even more secure. Under his command, he now had an army of four million men, thirty-nine divisions of which had been American trained and equipped; he had the largest air force any Asiatic mainland power had ever possessed and he held captive or had made innocuous nearly every warlord or politician who had ever opposed him. The only possible challenge to his power was a band of Communist guerrillas whom eight years before he had penned up in the barren loess and cave country of the northwest and all but liquidated.

Emerging from his wartime hide-out at Chungking, China's dictator returned in triumph to his capital in Nanking, ready, willing and seemingly able once more to assume undisputed sway over 450,000,000 people. Outwardly, the generalissimo appeared to have become the most powerful ruler in the last two centuries of Chinese history.

Less than four years later, as I wrote these words, the prospects of Chiang had undergone a cataclysmic change. He had already fled from his capital and sought refuge in his ancestral home, the premier of his government had unblushingly urged the United States to revive the unequal treaties and establish military and naval bases in China and his wife had come to this country to beg American officials to save the shattered fortunes, perhaps, in the long run, the very life of her husband.

In the meantime, these same despised Communist guerrillas have conquered all of Manchuria and North China, captured the capital of Chinese nationalism at Nanking, crossed their Rubicon on the Yangtze and are threatening to overrun the whole country and bring tumbling into ruins, not only the twenty-year reign of Chiang Kai-shek, not only the 100-year reign of Western imperialism in the Orient, but also a way of life that has existed almost unchanged in China for over two thousand years.

Unless all signs are deceiving, it appears likely that just as the Russian Revolution was the greatest by-product of World War I so the Chinese Revolution will be the greatest by-product of World War II.

You will find few such abrupt changes in history—especially if you remember that it involves one-fifth of the world's population. Nor will you find many people who foresaw this dramatic turnabout in China's civil war.

When I returned to China at the end of 1946, I found that among foreign observers there were three general opinions about the outcome of the war between Chiang and his enemies of twenty years' standing.

A small group of Western military men believed that the generalissimo would overrun the Communists within a year and force them to surrender or liquidate them. An even smaller group (considered very radical and leftish) believed, if there were no foreign intervention, that the war would go on for twenty, thirty and even fifty years. The opinion of by far the greatest majority, however, was that Chiang, though not being able to eliminate the Communists entirely, would nevertheless be able to drive them back in the hills, open up the railways and once more unite the country with no one to dispute his control.

In the light of events, these opinions must be considered as ill informed as those of the poll takers who predicted that the American people would vote President Truman out of office. Fundamentally, these prophecies backfired for the same reason—failure to look into the hearts of a number of very common people.

This would seem so trite as to need no further elaboration. But even today, when the Chinese Communists are everywhere victorious over Chiang Kai-shek, the causes of these tremendous events are either ill understood or deliberately blurred. Thus we find such highly placed people as ex-Ambassador William C. Bullitt, Congressman Walter Judd, General Claire Chennault, Alfred Landon, and a strange group of lugubrious mourners at Chiang Kai-shek's bier putting the blame for this supposedly regrettable state of affairs on mistakes in George Marshall's policy, Russian machinations, Communist propaganda and God knows what else. Looking around right and left, casting their eyes heavenward in horror, but never earthward in sympathy, these China experts have discovered every reason for the defeat of Chiang Kai-shek but the right one—the Chinese Revolution. This revolution—and nothing else—is the miracle that has brought China's once proud dictator to his feet in near ruins and has so changed the correlation of forces in the Orient that the whole history of the world is likely to be altered.

This mighty event did not take place overnight and it is still going on; the fact that it ever occurred at all was due to one of the greatest tragedies of modern times—the collision between the capitalist West and the feudal East. The intermingling of these two civilizations resulted in the slow, but nevertheless cataclysmic, proletarianization of nearly the entire Chinese people. Such a process proceeded not along any narrow Marxian path, but unrolled down a broad avenue of almost universal dissolution, with peasant, intellectual and ruler all being dispossessed from their environment. By 1945, this abscessed condition of the Chinese people burst forth once more in renewed civil war and quickly thereafter passed over into revolution.

The premises of the Chinese Revolution, like any other great social revolution were: 1. A disintegrating society, so diseased that it had become incapable of solving the urgent problems of the nation or the living conditions of her people. 2. A bitter hostility to the existing regime plus a revolutionary mood among huge masses of people who were so far gone in despair that they were willing to undergo supreme sacrifices and resort to the most extreme and even suicidal measures to save themselves. 3. Irremedial contradictions within the ruling group which had lost all creative powers and confidence in its ability to get society out of its blind alley. 4 A new group or party which could utilize all the above factors in order to gain control over society and put into practice its own program for saving that society.

All of these factors produced, and are still producing the Chinese Revolution. Undoubtedly, it is in the historic conditions which formed China that one must seek the chief clue to the Chinese Revolution. The changed economic structure of China, as a result of Western penetration, along with the destruction of nearly all previously held life values, produced a conflict of classes within Chinese society which led to the need for revolution.

Between need and possibility, however, there is a wide gulf. For a hundred years the necessity to transform Chinese society by revolution has been imperative. But that revolution never was completed for the simple reason that foreign imperialism was entirely too strong to permit the Chinese people to take control over their own destinies. The Second World War which brought about the defeat of Japan, most dangerous and most powerful of the imperialist countries in the Far East, plus the weakening of western European imperialism, was what made the Chinese Revolution possible and also what changed it in a new direction.

Here again, however, there is also a wide gulf between the possibility of revolution and the success of revolution. It is perfectly clear that without the defeat of Japan, without the weakening of Western capitalism and without those changes which took place inside of China during the Japanese invasion, the Chinese Communists would never have been able to conquer state power. However, it is equally clear, that the Second World War, except in a basic way, cannot account for the immediate events of China's civil war. Nor can the changes in China's economy or the social bases of her classes between 1945 and 1949 account for the twists and turns which that war took. These changes were entirely too insignificant to explain why the Communists were victorious over Chiang Kai-shek just at this moment in world history.

Without wishing to give psychological elements any more weight than they deserve, it is nevertheless impossible to avoid the conclusion that China's dictator was defeated when he was because of the swift and intense changes which took place in the feelings of a decisive portion of the Chinese people between 1945 and 1949.

This change in mass consciousness did not take place in any serene and academic atmosphere, but in one highly charged with emotion. Between 1945 and 1949, it was emotion that played the principal role in China's civil war. That this emotion was produced by previously existing external conditions, the writer does not deny. But it was only when the passions of the Chinese people burst their old confining fetters and in turn reacted on the objective conditions of Chinese society that the Communists and their allies were able to ride to power.

It was passion and principally passion that overwhelmed Chiang Kai-shek. The radiant hopes and murderous hates that the Chinese peasantry poured into the sphere of war and revolution released a flood of emotional energy that exploded with the force of an atomic bomb within Chinese society, nearly dissolving it. The extent and depths of these passions could be felt and seen and heard in the trampling rush of peasant feet toward the landlord's manor; in the dying gasp of a village noble whose body, as well as whose land, was divided by club-swinging peasants; in the flash of a pig knife plunged into the heart of a clan leader whose ancestral tablets the farmers might normally have worshiped; in the shriek of a girl whose mother led Chiang Kai-shek's secret service to chop off her daughter's head and pull out her intestines; in the religious groans of village witches who called down gods to their incense tables and chanted in sepulchral tones: "Chiang Kai-shek comes!" in the snick of scissors wielded by women cutting off the flesh of a village oppressor; in the lamentations of village brides beaten by their husbands and in their murderous cries of vengeance as they organized themselves into Women's Associations and beat, scratched and tore the flesh of their hated lords and masters; everywhere on the good Chinese earth, across the plains, the mountains and the fields, these passions rose up as a new and unconquerable force.

Primarily it was the task of the civil war and the revolution to canalize these tremendous emotions.

There was almost no precedent to follow, no chart by which to steer. Where Chiang Kai-shek had been successful previously in maintaining his rule over the Chinese people, it had been because the despair and the hate of the masses had not been sufficient to stir them out of their traditional apathy. When new conditions arose and the peasantry rose angrily with them, it was necessary that Chiang Kai-shek try to understand both the conditions and the emotions of the peasantry. He failed in both respects; in fact, he did not even try to understand the hearts of his own people. That is part of the inner history of Chiang Kai-shek's defeat and it is also part of the history of American policy in China. Neither the American government, the American press, nor the American people, nor many of their representatives in the Far East in the embassies, the military establishments and the business offices sought to look beyond their own narrow national or personal interests toward the heart of the admittedly ignorant, but terribly emotional, bitter men and women of China.

To all such people, one could justly address the words Mohammed used to denounce the Meccan merchants:

> But ye honor not the orphan
> Nor urge ye one another to feed the poor,

No such words could be addressed to the Chinese Communists. For they themselves were prophets—false or true ones, as the case might be. And in their character of prophets they found a chart—a technique—for navigating through the stormy waves of emotion raised up by war and revolution that was very simple and very old. It was the technique of Amos who brought Yahweh thundering down from the heights to rage against the ruling classes of Israel.

> I hate, I spurn your festal gatherings.
> Even though you offer me burnt offerings,
> And your cereal offerings, I will not accept them
> And the thank offerings of your fatted beasts I will not look upon.
> Take away from me the noise of your songs,
> And to the melody of your lyres I will not listen.
> But let justice roll down like waters,
> And righteousness like a perennial stream.

With such words the prophets of Israel transformed God, and with such words the prophets of Communism have and are transforming Chinese society.

2. The Civil War Begins

WHEN civil war began in China in 1946, I was in the United States, trying like so many other people to put in order a life that had been uprooted by many years of war. I had been away from China for four years, and although, during my absence, great changes had taken place in that country, one thing remained the same. There was no peace. For immediately after the conclusion of hostilities against Japan, the Chinese people had plunged into a civil war that was incomparably more vast, terrifyingly more impassioned and dangerously more important than any conflict they had ever waged in the four thousand years of their tortured history.

The fact that a supposedly pacific people should emerge safely from the purgatory of a brutal foreign invasion only to end up by hurling themselves at each other's throats appeared, on casual glance, shocking. Fighting across the heart of China, both inside and outside the Great Wall, the Nationalists and Reds, after a brief truce engineered by George Marshall, had by the middle of 1946 begun snarling over the bones of Chinese civilization with a ferocity they had seldom shown in fighting the Japanese.

This admittedly horrible phenomenon was attributed by different people to different causes. The Old China Hands ascribed the outbreak of civil war to the barbarous nature of the Chinese people who were incapable of governing themselves, while the New China Hands put it down to corruption of the Chiang government and the intransigent power lusts of the Reds. The Chinese students found the cause in the fact that Chiang's gestapo murdered their professors who were advocating peace; the Chinese intelligentsia found it in the arms America was pouring into Chiang Kai-shek's war machine; and ex-Ambassador William C. Bullitt in the Yalta deal whereby President Roosevelt invited Stalin to come into Manchuria and join the war against Japan. All of these reasons suggested by every variety of personal prejudice may have satisfied their advocates, but in the light of historical facts they appeared quite unconvincing.

Take only one example—the Yalta deal. If we were to believe the logic of Mr. Bullitt, had President Roosevelt not invited Stalin to fight Japan in Manchuria, Chiang Kai-shek would have won complete control over all of China and made the Communists so weak that they either would not have dared to resist China's dictator or they would have been wiped out within the space of a few months. Such a logic, of course, ignored the fact that the Communists had been fighting Chiang Kai-shek for twenty years and had never been wiped out and what is more had fought the Japanese for eight years and instead of growing weaker, as did Chiang, had actually grown stronger. More important, however, if one were searching for causes, was the fact that wars had been going on in China ever since the Western powers blew open the doors of the Orient and produced such fatal contradictions in that ancient Confucian society that they had not been solved to this day. The Opium War of 1840, brought on by the British, the twenty bloody years of the Taiping Rebellion, the Mohammedan Uprising, the Western powers sacking of Peiping, the Boxer Uprising, the Communist-Kuomintang civil wars and the very terrible, but nevertheless true fact that there had been scarcely a single year of peace in China since the 1911 Revolution overthrew the Manchu Empire—all these bloody events were undeniable proof not only that the Russians were not responsible for the civil war in China and had very little to do with it, but were also convincing evidence that this war was practically inevitable.

Therefore, as I sat in America watching the unfolding of still another civil war in China, I was not unduly surprised, but I was sad for I was very fond of the Chinese people. The tragedy of the war was that so many Chinese were against fighting it, not only the common masses, but even some of Chiang Kai-shek's older generals and members of his party — the Kuomintang. These men, however, were lackadaisical in their opposition, and it remained for liberal quarters to raise the loudest voices in favor of peace. The opposition of these liberals was particularly strong during the Marshall truce negotiations when a number of professors tried to stand up against the rightist clique in the Kuomintang which was the most active force in China against peace and for all-out civil war. A vivid picture of this suppression of Chinese intellectuals comes from a quarter where you might least expect to find it. I refer to the writing of an American missionary Dr. James G. Endicott, who spent twenty years in China, was once an adviser to Chiang Kai-shek on social problems, and also a secretary to Madame Chiang Kai-shek. In 1947, Endicott left China and soon made public his reason for doing so. He wrote:

There were increasing signs everywhere that Chiang did not intend to keep his promises [to General Marshall] and was preparing for all-out civil war. At the time he was anxious to silence all liberal opposition. . . . Accordingly in June, 1946, just before he tore up the Marshall truce agreements and launched full-scale civil war, his gestapo was ordered to murder in cold blood this committee of 12 professors [a group of Chinese professors, some educated in the U. S. who were active in trying to promote a middle-way compromise government].

The first one, Professor Li Kung-po was shot down on the street together with his little son. The next day a famous old classical scholar, Wen I-to, was shot while coming away from a meeting. That night all the other 10 of the committee were marked for killing. But one of them got to the U. S. consulate and persuaded the U. S. consul that they were the victims of political persecution. This courageous U. S. consul put on an army uniform, put the U. S. flag on his jeep, and went out and collected nine of the 10 and took them to the consulate for refuge. The 10th took refuge in a high school which had a high wall around it.

The 600 Chinese students manned the walls that night and beat off the gestapo agents who made several unsuccessful attempts to get in. In the end, the U. S. government intervened on behalf of these professors, and they were flown out and given a chance to go in hiding or else leave the country.

The murder of Li Kung-po and Wen I-to was a shock to me for I knew both of them and they were fine men. But like all Chinese liberals, they had no armed forces and they were nearly helpless. Perhaps that is why other scattered groups in China who did have arms refused to give them up to Chiang Kai-shek.

At the conclusion of the Japanese war, the Nanking government had called on the Reds to lay down their arms, but not only had the Reds remained armed, but thousands of peasants and students who had allied themselves with the Communists to fight Chiang Kai-shek also held fast to their arms and prepared to fight any invasion by Chiang Kai-shek's troops of their local areas. Why? What inexorable force drove these non-Communists to support allies that were black-listed by the recognized government of China? Did they really think that with the Japanese gone the rest of Chinese society would support them against the well-armed generalissimo? Even if they were afraid that Chiang might take away some liberties they had won during a painful guerrilla struggle, would it not have been better for them to give up their chimerical loyalty and take their chances with the generalissimo, instead of committing suicide with the Reds?

For at that time, opposition to Chiang Kai-shek did seem suicidal. The generalissimo had an army four times that of the 8th Route Army, with a correspondingly greater fire power in artillery, machine guns and rifles. Moreover he had an air force, railways, gunboats and motor transport while the Reds had none. Chiang had a comparatively potent economy in the fertile fields of the Yangtze Valley and the Canton delta; he held all the big cities and had the most powerful arsenals in Mukden, Shanghai and Hankow. The Communists were isolated in one of the poorer sections of China, had no cities of any size and only a primitive armament industry in the hills. Still more, Chiang held almost the entire seacoast, had access to foreign trade and was recognized by foreign powers, including the Soviet Union, as head of the legitimate government of China, but the Reds were shut up in the interior, carried on trade by bicycle and mule cart between primitive villages and were looked upon as rebels by the outside world. Unquestionably Chiang had the superior-looking war machine.

Even to skeptical Old China Hands, this war machine appeared much more formidable than anything Chiang Kai-shek had possessed before the Japanese war when he was the undisputed ruler of China. Letters from American businessmen in Shanghai sent to me in the United States declared that the Americans had made the generalissimo's army a much different organization than the corrupt one I had known four years before. Well trained, well disciplined and well equipped, it had a high morale. "The Commies don't have a chance," wrote one American businessman. "The war will be over in a few weeks."

Having been with over sixty armies of Chiang Kai-shek, I was very skeptical of this news. But events of China's war as they unfolded in the newspapers seemed to prove my friend right. Everywhere Chiang had victories. With the aid of American ships and planes, he quickly transported his best troops to all the large cities of North China and Manchuria while Red guerrillas raged at the gates. With ridiculous ease he cleared the countryside around Shanghai and Nanking and drove the vaunted Communist troops north of the Yellow River. "The Communists are babies; they don't know how to fight," said one Kuomintang officer. "The war will be over in three months," Chiang's top-ranking generals declared. American publications echoed these sentiments, and with no other news from China, it was hard to believe that the Communists had a chance to resist successfully, much less to win the war.

Then in the middle of 1946 friends began to send me news of an amazing situation that was developing in North China—a situation which was later to culminate in continuous defeats for Chiang Kai-shek and a complete overturn of Chinese society.

Though not very definite, this news consisted of several striking points. The Communists' 8th Route Army, driven back by Chiang Kai-shek, refusing to stand up and give battle, and abandoning all large cities, railway points and fortresses, had nevertheless not only maintained guerrilla bases in Chiang's rear, as it had done in the Japanese war, but was expanding everywhere in the countryside and slowly isolating the Nationalist army. As a result, though Chiang was still winning victories his progress had slowed down and a long war appeared in prospect. Faced by this bleak future, many of Chiang's generals were covertly trying to halt the war, believing it could be decided only by political means. At the same time, hundreds of students, strait-jacketed by Chiang's intellectual terror, were running over to the Communist side and giving leadership to the peasants. More amazing still, businessmen, weighted down by heavy taxes and losing their factories in some cases to Chiang's so-called program of nationalization were becoming so wroth at the national government that they were actively organizing the shipment of American arms and ammunition to the Communists. In the middle of this explosive situation, the Reds, abandoning their ten-year reformist policy, had suddenly hurled a revolution like a bomb at the head of the generalissimo.

There was not a word about this revolution in the papers. It seemed quite incredible. Nor did any of the pronouncements of our government officials, special investigators or China experts contain the slightest mention of this revolution. How, I wondered, could anyone hope to understand the events in China without knowing what the Communists were doing to the people in their areas? The answer was they could not. Not only news, but also policy, it seemed, was being made on entirely false premises. That was depressing.

I knew that the only way to learn anything about this revolution was to go there. I excused myself by saying that life in China was filthy, miserable and boring—all of which was true—and that I was fed up with war, which was also true. Then I thought about the thousands of lives that were being sacrificed in China's civil war, about Li Kung-po and Wen I-to who had been murdered while trying to make peace, and about millions of starving farmers whom the Communists had hurled onto the bitter road of revolution. Could the comfort of one foreign life be better sacrificed than in trying to find out what this war and revolution was all about?

In this somewhat solemn frame of mind, I packed my suitcase, said good-by to my wife and boarded a slow boat to China.

3. China, 1947

IT IS not everyone who can land in a foreign country without a passport. I do not mean to say there is anything to boast about in the accomplishment, but at least it is indicative of conditions in the Far East that I landed in China, not once, but twice without being asked to show my American passport.

The first time, in 1933, I did not have one. I was then an Able-Bodied Seaman on the "President Johnson," an ancient hulk of a ship, built in 1904, with wooden decks that leaked. I had ten cents in my pocket, but being then just twenty-three and of a romantic nature, I jumped ship in Hongkong determined to see the Orient. I planned to stay two weeks, but learning to like the country, remained nine years.

The second time, I really had a passport, but I never used it. We had anchored off Tangku, dirty port of entry for Tientsin after a miserable forty-two-day trip across the Pacific. It was December 1946, and the Chinese dollar, like the temperature, was falling fast, so that the ordinary civilian was not only cold, but hungry, being unable to exchange worthless paper money for either fuel or food. We were not surprised then when a suave customs official, having boarded us from a launch and having announced that he could not possibly take us ashore, as it was against regulations, confided in the same breath that he was the father of many children and was loath to see them starve. His story was long, but lacking in the customary Chinese nuances, so that we quickly grasped his point. When he saw we understood him well, his manner underwent a change and he brusquely demanded from me a leather jacket (which he did not get). He also demanded two hundred American dollars and a gold wrist watch (which he did get) from one of our passengers who had a trunkful of dyes that he valued at one thousand dollars (though I believe they were actually worth fifteen thousand on the dye-short Tientsin market). Then this father of seven, forgetting his customs regulations unceremoniously, dumped us ashore in an empty North China field where neither we nor he would be inconvenienced by any customs or immigration formalities.

That, without any exaggeration, was exactly how I returned to China, after a four-year absence; and that was the first indication I had that the officials of Chiang Kai-shek were still the same old masters of the art of squeeze that they always had been.

Fortunately for us, some American troops bivouacked in the area pitied our condition and took us off to their headquarters in Tangku. There was, if I remember rightly, a company of them guarding a dump of ammunition that was scattered in the fields in the heart of Communist militia country. The soldiers were homesick and disgusted, believing they were being made the suckers for an American policy of which they did not approve. Evidence that their fears were not entirely groundless can be gleaned from the fact that several months later, when they were about to leave China, Communist militia, believing the ammunition was to be handed over to Chiang Kai-shek, attacked the dump, wounding several GI's. American authorities, highly insulted, announced that since the militia had been so premature, the ammunition would not be dumped in the sea, as planned, but would be given to Chiang Kai-shek. This way of spanking the Communists fooled nobody, as nearly everyone was of the opinion that the Americans would have given the ammunition to the generalissimo anyway.

Leaving the homesick Americans at Tangku, I passed through Tientsin to Peiping, entering the crenelated battlements of the Tartar City on the last day of 1946. I had last seen Peiping under Japanese occupation and had left the city in 1939 in company with Colonel Joseph W. Stilwell and his family. Stilwell was then on his way home to report to G-2 with whom he was at loggerheads for their refusal to put much credence in his reports about the rising menace of Japan and the need to give the Chinese help.

That was all long ago, and I only mention it because in 1945, just after the surrender of Japan, when he was still in Okinawa, General Stilwell requested permission of China to pay a last visit to Peiping, but Chiang Kai-shek, making much of an old feud, denied him entrance, so that Stilwell returned home and shortly thereafter died without ever having had the opportunity of seeing again the city he so much loved.

Had he been able to come back with me now, he would have found Peiping in outward appearance little changed. Under the cold and sparkling North China sky, the former capital still glittered with all its old fascination and wonder, and in many imperial parks gaily dressed boys and girls skated on frozen moats so that it was impossible to believe in the China of grinding poverty, civil war and revolution beyond the curving palace roofs. Already, many Old China Hands had returned to the hutungs and, picking up the threads of their former lives, had immolated themselves in quiet gardens, living once again the old lazy life, seemingly quite unaware of the historic drama that was being played in the blood-stained fields of China beyond the city's insulating walls.

And yet, during the New Year holidays, all the defensive masonry of the old Chinese capital could not keep out the atmosphere of war and revolution that hovered over China from Harbin to Shanghai, from the Yellow Sea to Inner Mongolia. In the middle of the Christmas holidays, two American marines allegedly had raped a Chinese girl on the *glacis* outside the old Legation Quarter, and this deed had been enough to set aflame the already exacerbated national feelings of thousands of students then gathered in Peiping.

In 1936, I had seen ten thousand of these students, defiant of the gendarmes' clubbings, parade through the Tartar City shouting in a mighty chorus: "Resist Japan! Reject the demands of Japanese imperialism for the separation of North China." Now, at the end of 1946, beneath these same ancient walls, I was to see another generation of students, undoubtedly the political and spiritual descendants of the first, raise once again the old nationalistic banners and go marching through the streets, but this time they shouted: "GI go home! We are free now. Down with American imperialism!"

The remarkable thing about these two demonstrations was not that they were both made by Peiping students, not that they were both against foreign countries, but that they were both made in defiance of the wishes of the Chiang Kai-shek government. Ten years—two generations of students—and yet both were proclaiming the freedom of the nation in opposition to its leader! There was a lesson here for anyone who had the eyes to read it.

One did not have to be an international spy to discover that many Chinese intellectuals in Peiping, outside of government circles, believed that America was primarily responsible for the continuance of the civil war in China because she was arming Chiang Kai-shek. Nor did one have to be a prophet to conclude that the longer American troops stayed on Chinese soil the easier would it be for the Communists to sell their propaganda line to the people that Chiang Kai-shek had become a tool of the United States.

Because of these and many other factors, the whole American effort to bring about a truce in China's civil war was then crumbling rapidly, and no one seemed to know what to do about it—least of all the American officers of the Executive Headquarters in Peiping. These officers had set up shop in the Rockefeller-founded Peiping Union Medical College and gone to work with such a feverish energy that admiring Chinese scholars soon nicknamed Executive Headquarters the Palace of Ten Thousand Sleeping Colonels.

Whether the colonels slept or not is somewhat immaterial, for by early 1947 the so-called truce in China's civil war had become little more than a ghastly legend. And while Communist representatives were hobnobbing with Chiang Kai-shek's officials in Nanking, Shanghai and Peiping, the soldiers of both sides were ripping one another apart on the fields of Manchuria and North China.

"At the top they drink toasts to one another, but here we plunge the white sword in and drag the red sword out." So went an ancient Chinese saying. Probably it characterized the situation in China in January 1947 better than anything else.

The tragic irony of this farce was not entirely lost on the head of the American truce mission, George Marshall, and in the middle of January 1947, he admitted failure, packed up and went home, leaving behind him a bitter statement which, in effect, said: "a pox on both your camps."

After Marshall's statement, no clairvoyance was needed to see that China's already full-fledged civil war would become an all-out conflict for control of the Asiatic continent. Because the routes might be closed at any moment, I decided to go immediately into the Liberated Areas.[1]

[1] *Chieh Fang,* or Liberated Areas, was a term adopted by the Communists in the Japanese war to indicate all areas free of Japanese troops. It was retained in the civil war and was used as a generic term to indicate all areas which Chiang's troops did not control. The term Communist areas was seldom used.

4. With UNRRA

Just where to go in Communist areas, however, was somewhat of a problem. Ten years before, when Edgar Snow broke the Kuomintang blockade and became the first foreign correspondent to visit Red territory, the Communists had been confined to a very small area in the northwest,[1] and he could, so to speak, put his finger on them. But now the Communists were wandering to and fro across the continent from the borders of the Soviet Union to the Yellow River, and it was hard to decide in all this vast countryside where to contact them.

I could have taken one of the American courier planes which were then still flying to the Communist capital at Yenan, but that cave village had become kind of a tourist center with every foreign correspondent in China hopping over to have a quick look at Mao Tze-tung and Chu Teh, leaders of the Communist party and army, and I had no desire to get mixed up in that circus, fearing it might be very difficult for me to get in close contact with the people, the war or their revolution.

I also might have gone to Manchuria, but the northeast was outside the mainstream of traditional Chinese life; there was no violent struggle against feudalism there, no great land problem and hence no particularly revolutionary situation, and besides, Manchuria, contrary to popular opinion, was not the decisive theater of war in China. I think it was this last that decided me to go elsewhere in the country.

At the moment, the most decisive theater of war lay on the North China Plain, a vast flat pavement, filled with ninety million people, that lay between Chiang Kai-shek's capital in Nanking and his troops in Peiping, Tientsin, North China and Manchuria. Unless the generalissimo could beat his way across this plain and link up his capital with his isolated troops in the north, he could not hope to unify China. Opposing the march of the generalissimo from the south and lying between both his southern and northern forces were two Communist generals, named Chen Yi and Liu Po-cheng. The first of these generals made his head-

---

[1] When the Japanese war began the Communists had only a barren territory in the Northwest with a million and a half people. When it ended they had more than 800,000 square miles with 140,000,000 people. Their lands grew twenty fold and their population nearly 100 times. Of course, they had firm control over neither. Yet, this remarkable fact alone suggests that Communist victory in China had nothing to do with supposed Russian help given the Chinese Reds after the start of the civil war. Actually the Reds won their civil war in the Japanese war.

quarters in the seaboard province of Shantung, north of Shanghai and south of Peiping. The second, one-eyed General Liu Po-cheng, roamed far and wide over the four-province border region of Shansi, Hopei, Shantung and Honan,[2] sometimes operating on the plain and sometimes retiring into the mountains of Shansi Province which dominated the plain on the west. I decided to beard this latter general in his mountain lair, if he was available.

General Liu Po-cheng was not only one of the ablest, but also one of the most colorful of the Red commanders. A former associate of Dr. Sun Yat-sen, he had revolted against Chiang Kai-shek after 1927 and joined Mao Tze-tung in the first Chinese Soviet on the mountain of Chikanshan in South China. At one time, he had been chief of staff of the Red Army. At another time, he had attended the highest military schools in the Soviet Union. He had been in the vanguard of the Red Army's six-thousand-mile Long March in 1934 and had eaten the blood of a chicken with a Lolo tribal chieftain so that the Reds could obtain safe passage through the land of those savage tribesmen. During years of combat a hand grenade had blown out one of his eyes so that he had acquired the nickname of Blind Liu, the One-Eyed General, etc. Sometimes, he was referred to as the One-Eyed Dragon, as, according to Chinese lore, a dragon symbolizes power and cunning. He had also been wounded several other times, but always on the right side, so that sometimes he was also known as the Rightest General. There was in those days a saying among military men in China that there were three and a half strategists in the country. Liu was recognized as one and a half of these.

To get to Liu's headquarters near Hantan, three hundred miles away across the plain from Peiping, I would have to go at least two-thirds of the way by cart, around a few Kuomintang-held cities and by myself, without an interpreter. However, as I spoke quite a bit of Chinese and as I would thus have an opportunity to observe the Communist rear areas without being overseen by a Chinese translator, I did not object to these conditions too strenuously.

Although to get to Liu's headquarters was not so hard, to get into the Liberated Areas in the first place was another matter. To solve this difficulty, some Communists in Peiping had persuaded UNRRA to drop me over the lines by means of one of their ambulances which were about to run supplies into Red areas.

I spent several revealing days with UNRRA people in Tientsin and later during the course of a year, here and there, I came to know a

[2] At this time, there were in the Communist areas, seven border regions, each with their own army and their own elected governments. There was no central government for the whole area. In 1948, however, several of these border regions amalgamated into the North China Liberated Area. This laid the foundations for the Communists to set up a central government of their own, should they so desire.

number of these men and women quite well. As I look back over a long series of fouled-up situations that I have seen in ten years of war, I am inclined to say that UNRRA's work in China was tops on my snafu list. There were Americans, British, Australians, Canadians, Yugoslavs, Frenchmen, Austrians; in fact, the nationals of a score of different countries working for UNRRA in China—and I never found one who was not amazed at the foul and corrupt use made of UNRRA supplies by the Chiang Kai-shek government. What seemed even worse, however, to many of my UNRRA friends was the way the American government toadied to Chiang Kai-shek and let him get away with a monstrous misuse of supplies that had been contributed by the people of fifty-two nations to alleviate the suffering of people made needy and destitute by the war.

To begin with, there was outright discrimination against the suffering people of North China because they happened to be in Communist territories. This was in direct violation of an UNRRA resolution which provided that "at no time shall relief and rehabilitation supplies be used as a political weapon and no discrimination should be made in the distribution of supplies because of race, creed or political belief." In China, however, it was quite obvious that discrimination was being practiced, and deliberately. Of the estimated 266 million Chinese people who had suffered under Japanese occupation, 120 million (150 million, if Manchuria were included) lived in the Communist-led Liberated Areas. If UNRRA supplies were to have been distributed on a fair basis, at least half of the 2,700,000 tons shipped to China would have gone to the Liberated Areas. Actually, 2 per cent went to the people living under the Communists and 98 per cent went to Chiang Kai-shek.

Every device from passive blockade to outright military attack was used to keep UNRRA supplies out of Communist areas. Far worse than this, however, was the way officials became wealthy by means of supplies meant for their own people.

These practices had a demoralizing effect on UNRRA workers. Many of them had volunteered out of idealistic motives for the work, some of them had been sent out under church auspices and received only thirty dollars a month, so it was doubly disillusioning to them to see trainloads of food that were meant to go to China's starving peasants go one thousand miles into the interior and then come one thousand miles back again by truck and boat to be sold by the military on the black market. I shall never forget the American girl who had volunteered to take care of some orphans. UNRRA had sent her supplies to feed her orphans, but Chiang's officers prevented her from getting the food. Many of the children had died while the food that would have saved them was being sold out of a warehouse just around the corner. "This is enough to make a Communist out of me," she had written in a letter to her superiors in Shanghai, who had filed the usual protest, knowing full well that nothing would come of it.

I was surprised, too, at the depth of the feeling of some of the youthful UNRRA workers. Many of them had been in the American Army and some had been members of the European underground against Hitler. They knew what they had fought for; and they were against the way Chiang Kai-shek horned in on an international project and stopped relief supplies from going into North China; that is, to the very people who had suffered most in the war against Japan.

Just now, Tientsin UNRRA was trying to find a route to send medicines and hospital beds across the lines to Communist areas. This was a rather tricky business. The boundaries between the two forces were constantly changing, there were no roads, and soldiers of both sides sometimes took pot shots at UNRRA trucks. Nevertheless, this remained the best way of crossing the lines until Chiang Kai-shek eventually put a halt to all UNRRA traffic and one had to sneak across by oneself.

After a few mild adventures, I made my way down to Tsanghsien, last Kuomintang-held city in this part of North China. There, I ran into George Barkley, a young American, who was just in the process of taking three truckloads of cheap beds over to the Communists. Such a cargo was more than worthless, but Barkley was very conscientious in his duties, taking risks which I am sure were appreciated neither by his superiors, the Communists, nor, of course, by the officials of Chiang Kai-shek.

I told Barkley that I would like to go along with him; that I had to go. He got the idea that I should pose as an UNRRA representative. "Just ride along beside me and keep quiet," he said.

5. Into Red Areas

IT WAS four o'clock in the afternoon, and already the light was turning gray. We knew we would have to hurry to make the thirty miles to Potow, first Communist city on the other side of the lines, before dark. Hastily we threw our cargo of iron cots and medicine boxes aboard the trucks and started out. As we wheeled through the gates of Tsanghsien's walls, a Kuomintang sentry at a barbed-wire barricade signaled us to a halt.

"You know me," said Barkley, smiling down at the sentry who came up to the cab of the truck, gun in hand. "I've been here before."

The sentry nodded.

"Who's that one," he said, jerking his head at me.

"UNRRA, too," said Barkley.

I sat silently in the cab, pretending I did not understand Chinese and trying hard to look like an international relief worker.

Having scrutinized me with casual curiosity, the sentry tapped our medicine boxes once or twice, then drew aside the barricade and motioned us out onto the North China Plain.

Drawing away from the city walls, we crossed the Grand Canal and entered no man's land. Our road was an undulating cart track where we plowed along jerkily, now rising even with the fields, now falling abruptly where metal-wheeled carts had dug deep ruts. On all sides of us, the fields rolled away, flatly, looking bare, brown and decayed in the gloomy winter light.

We went on for ten miles—fifteen—twenty—but there was not a sign of a Communist, not a soldier, not a gun.

Dusk came. The countryside grew gray, the wind cold. The air was boisterous with a leashed-in kind of wildness. The noises of the sky and land were humming as if at any moment they would break into a violent, uncontrollable roar. The wind whistled past our topless truck with crazy laughter; the dust infiltrated around the flanks of our windshield in a dirty cloud and we lurched, rolled and plunged across the plain which fled away everywhere with harsh, monotonous flatness.

We wished the Communists would pick us up quickly. We did not want to be shot at in the dark. We examined the plain to the limits of the horizon, but saw nothing.

It seemed as if the Kuomintang army might have rushed in here and taken all the outposts by surprise.

Turning from the fields, I bent down and lit a cigarette. Suddenly, below me, along the road on the right, there was a kind of stir, then a click, as of snapped rifle bolts, and at last—a terrifying shout. I jumped, as if struck, Barkley slammed down on the brakes, and a dozen armed men sprang onto the truck as if they would tear us from our seats. We came to a grinding halt.

Unconsciously, I put up my arms to ward off blows, but that was not the intention of our boarding party.

"We've been expecting you," said one of the men; "we'll take you into Potow."

The militiamen—for that is who the boarders turned out to be—clambered aboard, some standing on the running boards, others lying flat on the hood of the radiator, and we went forward once more. A sharp crack rent the air and a bullet sang overhead like a bird. Our guards jumped from the truck; again we slammed to a halt. As more bullets whistled by, our guards ran forward, rifles in hand, bodies bent close to the ground, and mouths wide open, howling indistinguishable words. Passwords, we guessed, for the firing ceased, our companions returned to the truck and we went on again.

Coming once more to the Grand Canal, we halted at a bridge while a wooden gate was swung back and then crossed the river and entered Potow, first Communist-held stronghold on the destroyed Tientsin-Pukow Railway.

Inside the town, the streets were dark, there was no life and not a human being could be seen. We parked alongside a stone building; the guards got off and we waited in the trucks to see what would happen. In a moment, doors up and down the street flung open, small shafts of light shot onto the road and patches of men appeared beside the truck.

"Ho . . . Ha!" shouted some voices. Hands reached for the medicine boxes and carried them off in the dark.

A guide appeared and led us into a large room which belonged to the local Chamber of Commerce. In the middle of the room was a pan of charcoal which strove desperately, but without much success, to dispel the cold. In the flickering light cast by two tallow wicks burning in cups of oil, I could make out four men. They introduced themselves as the mayor of Potow, the assistant mayor, the local head of Clara (Communist UNRRA) and the secretary of Public Relations—this last, a shy young man, with the gift of halting English, named Chen. One by one I nodded at them. Someone pushed a stool at me and I sat down. Next I announced that I was an American journalist. At this they looked doubtful.

Had they not been informed of my coming? No, they had not. Was there not an interpreter waiting for me? No, there was not.

I took out a letter of introduction and the pass that General Yeh Chieng Ying, chief of staff of the 8th Route Army, had given me. One by one, the mayor, the vice-mayor, the head of Clara and Mr. Chen went into another room and examined them. The caution they took to look at them in another room made me wonder if there were not secret marks on the letters.

I knew these letters instructed the authorities in Potow to send me on to the headquarters of General Liu Po-cheng, two hundred miles away to the southwest, and I expected that after reading them the men would give me some word of welcome. But instead, they came back into the room, without saying a word, and stared at me. Barkley, presuming on a previous acquaintance, tried to say something on my behalf, but the mayor only grunted and said: "The letters are clear." That was all.

I must confess that this cold reception astonished and, at the time, even angered me. Back in 1939, when I made my first trip to Chinese Communist territory, General Hsiang Ying, commander of the New Fourth Army, had walked ten miles over a mountain so that he could greet me on the trail and personally lead me to his headquarters. Trees and rocks along the paths had even been decorated with signs welcoming me to Communist territory. But now how different everything was! The attitude of these officials seemed plainly to say: "We don't want you." I began to understand from their looks and vague answers to my tentative questions that they were suspicious of me, an American. I was afraid that if I were received everywhere in this fashion my trip might be unproductive.

The next morning, I began to feel even more doubtful. When I got up, Barkley had already gone back to Kuomintang areas, and there was no one else around, so I went out by myself into the streets of Potow. I saw our tea boy poised atop a ladder, busy drawing some Chinese characters beneath a huge portrait of Mao Tze-tung, Communist party chairman, that was painted on the wall of the Chamber of Commerce. I photographed the painting, but a passer-by immediately halted and wanted to know if I had permission to take pictures. I wanted to say: "If you can paint pictures, why can't I take them," but I merely pretended I did not understand Chinese in order not to become involved in an argument.

Taking a turn down the street, I was immediately joined by a small boy who ran alongside of me shouting words that sounded like, "*Mei Kuo fan tung.*" Now, *mei kuo* means America, but *fan tung*, as far as I had ever heard it, means rice bucket, and to call someone a rice bucket is the same as saying he is good for nothing but eating; or another way of saying a man is fat. Since I wore a fur-lined pilot's suit and since I must have looked well padded, I was not inclined to take offense at being called an American rice bucket. However, on walking a few steps further, a group of militiamen who were standing before a wall practicing songs, suddenly turned toward me, grinned and began singing: "First we had the Japanese Devils and now we have the *Mei Kuo fan tung.*" I could not exactly understand it, but the general sense was quite clearly uncomplimentary and it was not long before I realized that I was being called a "*fan tung pai*"; that is, a reactionary. Being the only foreigner in town, I felt rather blue at being publicly ridiculed, but solaced myself with the idea that now I knew how a Chinese laundryman in America feels when children run after him shouting "Chinkee, Chinkee, Chinaman."

As a matter of fact, the treatment I received on my first morning in Communist territory was extremely mild to the receptions that other foreigners sometimes met in Chinese villages. Later as the war became more bitter, as President Truman evolved his anti-Communist policy, and as American-made planes bombed Communist villages, many Chinese peasants crudely insulted all foreigners in their areas.

Feeling lonely and without friends, I went back to the Chamber of

Commerce and engaged our tea boy in conversation. He made more sense than anyone with whom I had yet talked. He said that the Japanese had had a garrison in Potow for nearly eight years. They were bad, he said, because they beat and tortured people. When the Japs left, Kuomintang troops had garrisoned the area for four months. They were no good either. They drank tea without paying for it; looted and broke furniture. Worst of all, in 1946, they broke open the Grand Canal dikes and flooded people's homes. That this was true I had ascertained for myself in a walk outside the town where I saw some homes still underwater and the local match factory filled with mud which the flood had left behind. Later, I was to get a look at Kuomintang flood tactics at firsthand and I learned that Chiang's officers, if they thought it would bring them any military advantage, would break open any river, regardless of the cost to the civilian population.

My companion said he liked the 8th Route Army (Communist-led army) because it did not break open people's homes and did not steal food. Now, there was no 8th Route Army around Potow; the soldiers had gone for several months and there was only the militia. As for Communists—he did not know. Nobody had ever talked to him about Communists and he had never met one.

Something along this line was echoed by the vice-mayor that night over dinner.

"We are no-party-no-clique people," he said. "We don't necessarily want to follow the Russian way."

Thus, by my second night in the Liberated Areas, I had yet to meet my first Communist. I was beginning to wonder why I had come into the region.

During the meal it had been arranged that I would get a cart on the morrow and go to the town of Foutung, thirty-five miles away. There I would pick up another cart and continue on to the next stop and in this fashion proceed to General Liu's headquarters. It was figured I should be able to make the trip in eight or nine days. I thought that optimistic. It is hard for a cart to make more than twenty miles a day; it was snowing and besides it was just approaching Chinese New Year and I doubted if any farmer would want to take his cart out at this season, even for a foreigner.

As I lay down to sleep that night I was not very happy about the prospect for my journey. I would have much preferred to stay around the border areas and join up with some guerrilla outfit operating in no man's land. And while I welcomed the prospect of meeting the legendary One-Eyed Liu, I was not so sure that it made good sense to go wandering off through the countryside when everyone appeared so unfriendly.

Now, it's one thing to understand the reason for the people of one country being unfriendly toward the people of another, but it's quite a different thing to be the subject of that unfriendliness yourself. If people yell anti-American slogans at you, you don't like it, no matter how objective you are. In all justice to the people of the Liberated Areas, I must admit I later was well received, but in those early days I felt very unwelcome indeed.

It was in this somewhat despondent frame of mind that I set out to find General Liu Po-cheng and the headquarters of the Shansi-Hopei-Shantung-Honan Border Region two hundred miles away.

PART II

ACROSS THE GREAT PLAIN

❦

6. Lost in the Snow

"Down with the landlords who drink our blood!"

"Oppose Chiang Kai-shek's betrayal of China to America."

"We did not become slaves of the Japanese militarists; we shall not become slaves of American imperialists."

Under these somewhat disturbing slogans, I arose stiff and cold the next morning, and having changed four hundred thousand of Chiang Kai-shek's dollars for eighty thousand Communist dollars I was ready to start on my journey across the North China Plain.

It was the day before Chinese New Year.

For some days now the frost had been hardening the earth and the night before great black clouds coming from the west had brought snow which fell without interruption during the night and was still coming down as a crowd of children followed me to the outskirts of Potow's walls.

A mule harnessed to a Peking cart waited for me beside the mud wall of a collapsing house. A small boy, carrying a whip, went from one side of the cart to the other, fastening the traces and adjusting the harness. The mule stamped his feet on the ground as if he were cold and drew back his lip and whinnied. My duffel bag was tied on the back of the cart on the outside; my camera case and typewriter placed under the roof of the cart on the inside.

A curtain of interrupted snowflakes constantly sparkled in its descent to the ground. It powdered the heads of the children with fleecy covering. Everything seemed stilled under the silent fall of the snow. Save for the group of children around me, the streets were deserted.

A young man in the uniform of the Potow Peace Preservation Corps appeared, announcing that he was my escort and would take me to the next county seat at Foutung. He walked around the cart checking my bag, the traces and the harness once again. He looked at me for a moment, where I stood, already white with snow, and said to me: "Why not get in the cart? You will be under cover then."

I hastened to do so, entering a small house on wheels, which was protected from the elements by a blue cotton cloth fastened to a wooden frame running in an arch overhead and down the sides. Thus inclosed on three sides, I looked out the front of the cart as through a tunnel.

The floor was covered with some filthy bedding. Sitting on it, I rested against the back and stuck my legs out the front. The cart seemed very small.

The escort climbed aboard, seating himself in front beside my outstretched feet. The driver called:

"Are you ready?"

The children shrieked: "American reactionary, see you again."

We were off. The cart moved slowly for a little way. The wheels were imbedded in the snow; the whole cart groaned with creaking sounds; the mule glistened, puffed and smoked; and the whip of the driver snapped without ceasing, now on this side, now on that, lashing brusquely against the flanks of the mule which put forth its most violent effort and drew us clear.

The day seemed to be growing grayer every minute. The snowflakes fell like a shower of cotton. Almost no light filtered through the great dull clouds which hovered like heavy dumplings in the sky and seemed to presage many hours of snow.

I sat more forward in the cart and looked at my companions in the sad light of the stormy day.

At the front, my escort dangled his feet over the edge of the cart. He was dressed in the darkest blue cotton cloth. A padded long gown, which he did not wear but flung around himself like a cape, added a touch of insouciance to his devilish air. From his peaked uniform cap, his black hair hung in long, loose locks, while across his heavy sensuous lips, a half sneer, half smile ran like a wave. He looked like movie actor John Carradine, but much younger.

He was twenty-four and had for a time been in the 8th Route Army. He handled his Mauser pistol with professional ease. Whenever more than four or five people came across the snow-covered fields, he slipped the gun unobtrusively from its holster and laid it across his knees, not openly, but hid beneath his carelessly flung cloak.

Our driver, with whip in hand, walked beside the mule. He had rosy cheeks, crooked yellow teeth and a sly expression. He was small for his age, being fourteen, but his face was as lined and careworn as a man of thirty-five. In keeping with his size, his whip was of Lilliputian proportions, being made of a stick about two feet long and a thin rope of the same length.

Passing out of Potow, we headed on a cart track directly across the fields. Few people were on the roads. The snow and cold would have been enough to keep all indoors but, in addition, it was New Year's Eve, and the people were inside paying off old debts, doing homage to the Kitchen God or laying plans for a celebration. It was a lonely day to be abroad.

We jounced across a great bare plain. Everywhere the land was flat, the horizon bound only by trees. The earth appeared old and worn, yet there was a certain barren picturesqueness in the leafless trees that raised their "bare ruined choirs" against the sky. The texture of these trees somehow seemed different than those in America, somewhat more delicate—a little feminine, with long slender twigs reaching out from branches like fine hair.

The flakes fell in profusion upon the ugly brown plain until at last there was only a vast white expanse like a cloud beneath our wheels. Once, a flock of birds flew past overhead, on their way to some hidden roosting place, uttering as they flew a clear bell-like chirp; and there was something ethereal in those drops of melodious sound, which fell through the snowy silence like a disembodied song.

This unexpected peace which I had found did not last long; for there was something so vast and overwhelming about this great North China Plain that it assailed the spirit with foreboding. We went so slowly that for hours the scenery never changed. Soon I felt engulfed in the immensity of the plain, lost in gazing upon it as one feels lost in gazing on the sea. I had the feeling of being an alien in a strange world: I knew not where I was nor where I was going. There were no landmarks, no roads, not even a sun to give a sign of progress or direction.

Toward the middle of the afternoon, we stopped in a large village and the driver let his mule eat and drink. We entered a teashop. It was festooned with cobwebs, the dirt floor was sprinkled with manure and the corners of the room were filled with bags of grain, denoting a New Year surplus for the shop owner. Sitting cross-legged on a raised mud platform, we swigged tea out of bowls placed on a tiny table only four inches high.

Behind me I saw incense sticks burning, and going to a corner, I noticed a few bowls of crullers, rice and poor food set before a paper drawing of the Kitchen God. With his long drooping mustache, he looked down in silent benevolence upon the food offered him, but blinked not an eye as the smoke from the incense sticks curled up past his face. I had heard much about the antireligion policy of the Chinese Communists, but here the shopkeeper had put up his paper god, seemingly with no fear that it would be torn from the wall.

We started up again. Toward dusk I witnessed a strange thing. Sitting on the front of the cart with my feet dangling over the side and with my head just under the roof, I saw sudden flashes of fire, first on the right and then on the left, as of lightning, but so close to the ground that it could not be. I sat on the cart and waited for the flashes to be repeated, but saw nothing. Just then from a near-by grove of trees there burst forth an orange ball of light. It flared briefly against the gloomy twilight, then went out leaving the grove of trees blacker than before. I sat up straight and stiffened at this sight. There it was again—a sudden burst of fire and then blackness. In the moment that the lights flared I caught glimpses of figures, darting this way and that. They were all running close to the ground and it was from these figures that the fires seemed to start up and then die.

As we drew close to the grove of trees, I jumped off the cart. Pushing through the outer trees, I saw a number of rounded grave mounds and, in front of them, two men and an old woman. In the hands of each burned a string of paper money. As the flames flared up, they threw the paper on the grave mounds. Then they knelt down on the snow and knocked their heads three times on the ground in front of the tombs. I realized that these people were but doing obeisance to their family ancestors, yet this simple ritual affected me strangely, being alien to my world or my spirit and having all the fascination of the unknown and the mysterious. I turned and went away. As we rode on, I saw more fires flaring from the fields and everywhere men knocking their heads on the ground before their ancestral tombs.

We soon reached a village. Across a narrow alley between two rows of clay houses stretched an arch made of evergreen branches, hung here and there with yellow paper. In the middle of the branches hung four large characters made of paper flowers which said: PROSPEROUS NEW YEAR.

We paused. A farmer asked me from what country I came.

"America," I said.

He grinned in friendly fashion. I looked past his grinning face and I saw behind him some large Chinese characters whitewashed upon a house wall.

WE DID NOT WANT TO BE JAPANESE SLAVES
WE DON'T WANT TO BE AMERICAN SLAVES

I stared at these characters for a long time. It seemed so very strange to see these political slogans in this miserable village, far from America, from George Marshall or from President Truman. Noticing my attitude, my guard smiled.

"It doesn't mean anything," he said. "Don't be alarmed."

I asked the people what they were going to do that night and one man said: "We'll have a play and eat." Then he cut a fancy caper. "We'll jump around."

I wanted to stay there and see how the villagers celebrated New Year's Eve and I wanted to have some fun and jump around myself, but it seemed as if I was only an outcast, doomed for the moment to meet only officials and mule drivers.

It grew dark, the road disappeared, and the cold crept into the cart and made my feet ache with pain. Guiding ourselves toward a fire that gleamed on the horizon, we came to the large village of Chienchao which we entered through a clay wall. There was not a light to be seen anywhere; and it was like going through a wrecked German city in the war.

There being no use in going further, we halted at a carter's inn. The boy led his mule into a yard, undid his harness and gave him grain. A cheerful voice yelled for me to come inside, and I entered a low-ceilinged room. In the feeble light cast by a wick burning in a cup of oil, I made out seven or eight men, peering at me with intense curiosity. Their faces seemed to leap at me straight from the Middle Ages. The innkeeper—a gay old robber with a bearded chin and drooping mustache, bade me to sit down on a bag of grain.

Evidently feeling that this inn was not high toned enough for the "foreign guest," my guard went off to look for a place for me to sleep. For some reason, probably not having been informed who I was, or more probably not understanding just what a correspondent was, he had told the people I was an UNRRA representative, and I was making an inspection trip to Hantan, preparatory to sending in grain and medicine. Such an introduction, I admit, could not have been more calculated to put the people on my side, and I fully expected that they would tell me they were starving and could I not help them out. Instead, to my surprise, they told me they had enough to eat. Because of reduced taxes, they were better off than they had been for fifteen years. The government, they told me, collected only seventeen to eighteen pounds of grain for each mow of land (one-sixth of an acre). Before they had had to pay innumerable surtaxes, including pig-killing taxes, drying-vegetables-on-the-roof taxes, funeral taxes, and besides had to furnish much free labor. They thought there was justice in the present tax system.

My guard returned and led me through the town to a courtyard where a bonfire had been lit specially for my benefit. Several young men and an old patriarch gathered there and demanded that I eat something. My guard, who by this time fancied himself a dictionary of my habits, said with some severity: "He eats only sweet things." Where he obtained this idea, I do not know, but it made little difference; for the food that was brought was a piece of salted pork fat and a bowl of greasy greens. I found it very unappetizing, but seeing that they were poor and had put themselves out for my benefit, I ate as much of it as I could swallow without being sick.

Shortly afterward, a representative of the county government who was posted here at Chienchao came to visit me. Back in 1937, when the Japanese invaded China, he had been a schoolteacher in this, his native village. When the Japanese drove Chiang Kai-shek's troops out, he had formed a guerrilla band with a few of his students. Many other bands had likewise been formed, but most of them, under the name of resisting the Japanese, took advantage of prevailing chaos and became bandits. At one time there had been twelve different commanders in chief, each claiming to be the leader of the resistance movement around the town of Chienchao. In 1938, a battalion of the 8th Route Army passing through on its way from the mountains of Shousi to the sea, had suggested how the local bands could organize themselves, unite together and eliminate bandits. The local villagers, profiting from this advice, soon formed their own government which had led a haphazard existence in the fields for six years. When the Japanese retreated from the area in 1945, this government had moved in and taken over the towns. The young man seemed to be very proud of the government of which he was a member.

"Our government," he said, not without affection, "is composed of Communists, Kuomintang members, liberals, no-party-no-clique people, old and young, men and women."

7. Eating the Landlords' Flesh

THE snow was still coming down as shortly before dawn we set out once again. About ten in the morning we reached the county seat of Foutung where my guard was to drop me. The sight of this, my first goal, was something of a shock. True enough, Foutung was a walled town, but the walls enclosed mostly empty fields. Originally, Foutung had been a town of some five hundred families, but the Japanese retreating from the area in 1945 had deliberately set fire to the houses so that now the town was little more than a cold, bare icebox.

Leaving me to shelter from the snow in a filthy stable, wherein hung an old and dirty picture of Le Ning (Lenin), my guard summoned the district magistrate, a gentle-eyed man who escorted me through the broken shards of the town to his office—a small hovel built of clay and barricaded against the cold by 1939 San Francisco newspapers. How these publications ever reached this primitive town on the North China Plain, whether they were brought in by the Japanese, or whether some rich landlord had come back with them from a journey to the big cities of Peiping and Tientsin was a mystery I could not fathom. From the walls there also stared down at me the bearded visage of Ma Ke SSu (Marx), and pictures of En Ke Le (Engels), Mao Tze-tung, head of the Chinese Communist party and surprisingly enough Dr. Sun Yat-sen, patron saint of the Kuomintang and Chiang Kai-shek. The magistrate informed me that the pictures had come from bookstores in Hengshui, a "warm and busy" city, thirty miles to the south.

Also, a schoolteacher before the war, this magistrate on the arrival of the Japs had settled his wife and baby in a neighbor's house and become a member of the local guerrilla government. "It was bitter then," he said. "We used to move three and four times a day. Government was the same as now, but a little more simple."

His main problem, at the moment, he said, was flood. The year before, many villages near the railway had been submerged, a few people had drowned, some had to eat leaves for a time, but no one had starved and now things were better.

After the flood, some UNRRA supplies had come into the area. Not many and not of much use, either. Torn silk stockings and high-heeled women's shoes. "Maybe your wife or lover could use them," he said grinning, "but not our peasant women." I looked out across the mud and snow and the rambling medieval wall and wondered how many times this silly tale of UNRRA had been repeated all over China.

I liked this young magistrate. He was simple, forward looking, sensible and seemingly close to the people. In the afternoon, after feeding me, he obtained me a cart drawn by two mules and driven by a cheery old farmer with such a childishly rosy face that my lips twisted in a smile as I looked at him.

My escort, a gay young government clerk, ran alongside the cart, chirping encouragingly to the mules. "Go. Trrr——t! Trrr——t!" he cried, shrieking with delight and running along with the mules as they broke into a fast trot. Then he jumped on the front of the cart beside the driver, and flicked a long whip from side to side, giving wild cries, while the driver slapped the rump of the nearest mule smartly with a twig; and we went rocking down the road at a fast clip. Looking across the backs of the swaying mules at the gray sky and feeling the rattling motion of the cart beneath me, I got an impression we were about to leave the earth at any moment.

"That's a pair of fine animals," I said to the driver, looking at the strip of clean red neck showing above his collar.

The old man turned with a wide, pleased grin on his face. "Not bad," he said. "But not to compare with a mule I had before the war. That one could climb mountains like a tiger and swim rivers like a dragon. Would you believe it," he turned to the escort, "it took one's breath away, the rate he flew. He made 150 li [50 miles] in one day, not once, but a dozen times. Only had one fault. Ate too much. You'd think he was a locomotive, the way I had to shovel food into him. But what a mule. When he died,

I didn't eat mule meat. Gave him a burial just like a man. Just think, he lived seventeen years. Healthy. Aiya!"

"There's nothing wrong with your health, old countryman!" I remarked.

The old man, overflowing with health and strength, smiled warmly. "Heavens, no! And why should there be? I get plenty to eat. The government gives me one hundred catties [130 lbs.] of millet a year. My brother peddles beans, my wife and sister make clothes. We get along all right. Will you believe it, we had pork on New Year's Day? We eat well."

"Perhaps you eat landlord's flesh?" I suggested, turning a Communist slogan around.

"You speak strangely, comrade." The driver laid his whip across his knees, removed his glove and wiped his mouth, frowning as though offended. "I don't eat anyone's flesh. Though I won't say there aren't some around here who have tasted the flesh of a landlord. Eh?" he finished, turning to the escort.

"How?" I asked, taking out a cigarette and giving it to the old man.

I waited while he struck a flint on a stone and lit up a piece of wheaten rope which he applied to the cigarette.

"How do they eat the flesh of the landlord?"

"Well, it's the landlords who ate the flesh of the people first. Today it's one man's turn, tomorrow another's. There's Persimmon Valley Village, for instance. Well, there was a landlord named Mu Shih-an there. Did he deal justly with the people? I'll tell you. He was a member of the Kuomintang. When the Jap Devils came, he drafted us for a joint defense corps. He said it was to fight the Japs and the 8th Route bandits. But almost at once he surrendered to the Japs. Then he told the families who had men with the guerrillas to call their sons home. 'I'm afraid the Japs will kill you otherwise,' he said. He promised that no harm would come to anyone who came back. When an 8th Route subcounty leader came back, he killed him and then held a public condolence meeting for him. Oh, he was two-faced, you know. After that no soldiers wanted to come back. So he killed the closest relative of anyone who had a son with the guerrillas. In all he killed one member of each of over one hundred families here. When he saw the Japs were winning, he rounded up thousands of us to carry stones to build Jap blockhouses. Everyone of those stones had our blood on it. And this landlord settled other men's lives as if he was God. One night one of our poor farmers, who had become a militiaman, ducked into the village to see his wife. Third Blossom was her name. Knowing he would leave her at sun-up, she took him to bed at once. We all knew he had come home, but no one said a word except the village chief, who went and reported to the landlord Mu. And Mu—the traitor!—comes and drags him out of his wife's bed and binds him up just as if he was a pig, and takes him off. Well, naturally, the girl tried to beg Mu to release her husband. But she was poor and of course no one interfered on her behalf. She went into the prison all shaking and asked: 'Will you let me see my husband.' And Mu Shih-an's dog leg says: 'Go out on the street and you'll see him.' Well, naturally, she thought he'd been released and she rushed into the street. She saw him, all right. Up on a pole, on the wall of a strong point that Mu had forced us to build with our scratched and bleeding hands—there he was. His head, anyway. All blood and his eyes half gouged. Crazy—that's what she went. Tried to climb on the strong point and get the head, but everyone pulled her off and took her home. That night it rained and the head fell down on the road. The next morning, at cock crow, she was out on the street. She found her husband's head and took it home with her. Three days and three nights she lay on the kang with the head clasped in her arms, kissing and fondling it, as if he were still alive. Like a tiger she was, or a bitch with her pups, she wouldn't let any of us near her. Nothing we did or said made any impression on her, she wouldn't let go of that bloody head for a moment."

The driver had stopped and having put on his glove and picked up the whip, he said angrily:

"Isn't that a shame to the people?" He brought the whip down furiously across the backs of the mules. "Isn't that eating their flesh?"

"But you ate his, too," said the clerk, who had come back to the cart in the middle of the story and listened to the old man's words with a great deal of attention.

"I remember the case of that traitor very well," he continued. "There were over four hundred accusations against him. Twenty thousand people from the whole *chu*[1] came to the Settlement Meeting. Many women with bound feet could not get there, and they led him through the villages first so that everyone would have a chance to take their revenge. I'll never forget that march. I was one of the guards. As we approached the first village, I ran off in advance. And hardly had the traitor passed the first house when a crowd, armed with forks, hoes, pikes and clubs poured toward him. One woman had a pair of scissors in her hand. 'I want to eat traitor's meat,' she cried. When the cadres saw that mob, they knew the traitor would be killed at once before he could even get to the meeting ground. So they made a rule that the people could beat him, but not beat him to death.

"Twenty miles he was taken through village after village, greeted at each by angry crowds. By the rule of the cadres, the peasants had been made to discard their clubs, but they beat him near to death, even as it was. They had kitchen knives and wanted four ounces of his flesh. 'Just four ounces, please,' they said. We had a hard time beating them off.

"At first Mu bore himself well enough. But at one village he stopped

[1] A subdivision of a county.

in the middle of the street, blood and sweat pouring from his face, and cried out in a childish kind of voice:

" 'I worked for you here for eight years. . . . Haven't I even one friend? . . . Isn't there someone here who will give me a handkerchief to wipe my head? . . . Even a dirty handkerchief, a red handkerchief, that will be enough.'

"I hated him, but that voice of his was like a pitiful baby's. He looked around with a hunted expression, seeking for, I suppose, a friendly face. 'Just a piece of cloth, any little rag will do.' He said it again like a child pleading for a piece of millet candy. But all stood there, men and women, and glowered at him. Then someone said: 'Let us give you a ride-the-horse cloth.'[2] At that everyone laughed and fell on him with their fists again. 'Don't hit him too hard.' I shouted, 'he's got to get to the meeting alive.' But I had a hard time dragging him away and one woman even followed us out of the village into the fields, clawing at Mu's face all the while.

"When all the villages had looked at him, we took him to the settlement meeting ground which was near a pine-grove forest. On near-by walls drawings of his history had been painted. And in the forest the names of all those he had killed were listed on papers posted to the trees. That very morning the government had announced that Traitor Mu Shih-an would be executed and as I've said twenty thousand people came to the meeting. No sooner had they put the traitor up on the stage, than ten people rushed at him. 'You killed my son,' cried one. 'Don't talk with him; just beat him,' said another man pushing the first aside. 'That's right, don't talk; just beat him!' I heard hundreds of voices shouting those words and then the crowd started to rush for the stage. The chairman stood up and held up his hand asking for quiet: 'We can only beat him by groups,' he said. 'We must have order.'

"There must have been seven or eight men in that first group to beat him. But others kept running onto the stage and jabbing at him with scissors and knives. I was down front and everyone was yelling: 'don't beat him to death; we want our share.' I felt everyone pushing me from behind . . . forward toward the stage. Aiya, it was . . .'"

The clerk paused.

"Don't forget Third Blossom," exclaimed the driver. "I was at that meeting, too. You may not know me. But I was there, too. I wouldn't eat landlords' flesh. I wouldn't eat any man's flesh. But I was there just the same and I saw everything. I'll never forget Third Blossom on that day. She'd walked thirty li to the meeting. Walked half the night before. What a shy girl she used to be. Never went out of her house alone. But that day—save us!—what a woman! I can still see her as she went right onto the stage before Mu Shih-an.

[2] A rag used after sexual intercourse.

" 'Well, how are you Traitor Mu?' she asked. The crowd had grown still when they saw her—everyone knew her story. In the silence we could all hear his reply.

" 'Badly, as you can see.'

" 'Tell the people how you killed —' she choked and clutched at her breast. I don't know, her next words were a whisper, but they carried to the very edge of the crowd: 'a member of the anti-Japanese forces, my husband.'

" 'No, I didn't kill him.'

" 'Then who was it sent him out of this world?' Third Blossom raised her voice. 'Who was it?'

" 'The Japanese.'

" 'It was you! You killed him. . . .'

"She had taken off her leather belt from her waist and she began to beat that traitor there in front of us all. I don't think I've ever heard such a shrieking. 'Beat him! Beat him!' Every time her strap fell, the crowd yelled and before I knew it I was yelling, too. To see that girl taking her revenge . . . well . . . what a sight . . . she beat Mu Shih-an to his knees. . . . Oh, I shall never forget it. . . ."

The driver shook his head. "No, never. I wouldn't eat landlord's flesh. But Third Blossom, she had reasons."

The old man jumped down off the cart and began to walk beside his mules.

"How did the meeting end," I asked the clerk.

"Well, after that girl beat him, several others rushed on the stage with clubs and knocked him flat. He lay still, pretending he was dead. The meeting had been going on three or four hours, but only forty men had beaten Mu Shih-an. The chairman interrupted things and called out: 'Anyone who has bitterness from this traitor, stand up!' Five hundred people stood up. By that time, it was too hard to keep order. Everyone was trying to rush the stage at once. The cadres did not like the look of things and took Mu out in a field and shot him. They handed his body to his family who covered it with straw sheets. The crowd found out where he was and grabbed the body away from his family, then ripped off the straw sheets and continued to beat him with wooden clubs. One boy with a spear stabbed his corpse eighteen times in succession.

" 'You stabbed my father eighteen times,' he cried, 'and I will do the same.'

"In the end, they tore his head from his body. For days after that, people would come and look at him in the field. Someone said: 'In the past you were a commander in chief and many people came to see you; now you're dead, you can still draw so many people to visit you.' "

When the clerk finished his story, he clicked his tongue.

"Cruel, is it not," he said.

"Cruel!" said the driver, who had dropped back and was walking close beside us. "What's cruel about killing a man that has killed over a hundred of his neighbors. I wouldn't kill any man myself. But how can you blame our people? The landlords all of them have been cruel to us all our lives. But that's the only one we've killed. All the others are living just like us. Cruel. Ah, well, what times we live in."

He grew silent, staring morosely at his mules.

We went on, none of us saying a word. It was growing dusk and we had not yet reached our destination. The wind was bitter cold. I got down from the cart and walked, trying to send some warm blood through my veins. As a village came into view on our right, I said:

"It is too cold. If there is no need for hurry, let's spend the night in that village. Your mules are probably tired, old man, and it will rest them."

We halted for the night in the village. After the freezing wind of the plain the mud hut was homely, comfortable and warm. The earthen floor stank of manure, and the stove, into which an old woman was shoving twigs with one hand and pumping a bellows with the other, smelled of sour burned millet. The old woman replied reluctantly to my questions. She had seen one son killed during the Japanese war and had seen her other son join the 8th Route Army to fight the Kuomintang and her husband join the rising against the landlords. As she started to tell me these things she threw off her reserve and spoke quite bitterly.

"Look what kind of times these are we live in. When the Japs were here my old man couldn't pay the tax and was struck two hundred blows by that dog leg Lu Wa-tsai. They made mincemeat out of his ass. Do you think he learned anything from that lesson? Not a bit of it. When the 8th Route Army comes he wants to join the struggle against the landlords. I said: 'remember your ass; this time it will be your head.' Stubborn old man, do you think he would listen to me. Not at all. We argued the whole night. He became so angry that he beat me black and blue. Is that right to beat his own wife who's trying to keep him out of harm's way?"

"If you opposed his desire to be free . . ." said the clerk.

"Free! Don't you come at me with those high-sounding words, young man. I know all about young men. My first-born was killed by the landlord when the Jap Devils were here. Then when the war was over, my second son wanted revenge. Came here with some *kan pu*[3] . . . When I saw what he was up to, my heart stopped. 'Get out of here, my bad son,' I said. 'Isn't it enough that your elder brother was killed and now you want to be killed too and leave your old mother no way to live.' He

[3] Cadre or staff worker; anybody working in official capacity, such as government, army newspaper, land reform, even an actress. Not necessarily and most often not a member of the Communist party.

laughed at me. My own son laughed at me. As if that wasn't bad enough he went off and joined the army."

"Look, old wife, you don't understand this matter clearly," said the clerk. "We all wanted peace, but Chiang Kai-shek invaded the Liberated Areas. He wanted to kill us all."

"Who is this turtle, Chiang Kai-shek, that he can do with people as he wants." The woman stood up from the fire, her old eyes blinking from smoke. "Why don't you just kill him and make peace? When will this war ever end?"

"Soon. . . . Don't trouble yourself about it."

"Soon! But how soon! Don't you try to quiet me. It wants your very life to live in these times."

"Hush up, old woman, you'll talk us all to death. You'll be giving this foreign guest a bad impression."

"And do you think it's like that in his country?" the old woman retorted.

I compelled them to make peace. After a bowl of millet, the old lady went out to feed her donkey in the next room, and the driver, the clerk and I bundled up on the kang.[4]

I woke up about midnight and lay with open eyes. The driver beside me was making a terrible racket snoring. As I looked at him, my thoughts turned again to his story of Third Blossom, then to the old lady and the county government clerk. At the memory of these things my mind was oppressed by the sadness of the life of the Chinese people. The driver snored interminably and finally I shook him. He groaned, awoke, rubbed his hand across his face.

"Ai! Ai!" he sighed. Then turning over, he went back to sleep and commenced snoring once again.

8. Traveling Companions

IN SPRINGTIME, when the Yellow River and the Grand Canal overflow their banks and the flood water covers all the low-lying water meadows, the North China Plain is like a vast garden where millions of people

---

[4] A large divan made of adobe bricks and heated by a complicated set of flues connected with the primitive kitchen range. Whole families—husband, wife, grandmother and children often sleep together on one of these *kangs*. Because in winter, there is no way to escape the bitter cold in the villages, except by curling up on the kang, North China women often speak of them as "own mother."

live, concealed by the softness of green massed trees, islands upon a softly undulating sea of waving grain.

In the fields an impressive picture of country life unfolds and everywhere you cast your eyes peasants in blue jerkins are at work, methodically, thoughtfully, contentedly.

In the summer, the sun beats down with undiminished force and no wind comes from the sea and the mud roofs in the villages crack and the first rain trickles through in numberless rivulets. In the summer, even at noonday it is quiet, for every man has hidden from the glare of the sun in his mud-brick house.

In the autumn, as the *kaoliang* turns brown, the fields are filled again and there is the sound of winnowing and threshing and the merriment of harvest activity. But in wintertime the plain stands completely deserted, bare, fettered in a cold silence. The serrated edges of the treetops show bleak as telegraph poles against the pallid, wintry sky. Only the rabbits move about the fields, finding a safe haven beneath the untrodden snows.

Across this barren plain, changing carts at every overnight stop, sleeping in peasant homes and with county magistrates, I continued on in a southwesterly direction toward Hantan and the headquarters of the Shansi-Hopei-Shantung-Honan Border Region. On the third day, I reached a suboffice of the Border Region government. Here—already sick of being pulled across the country by a mule at the rate of twenty miles a day—I was overjoyed to find a US Army weapons carrier waiting to take me on to Hantan.

What an old war horse that weapons carrier was! The Americans had brought it from India across Burma into China; then Chiang Kai-shek's troops had taken charge of it and brought it north; and now, having been captured in battle, it was in the hands of the Communists.

By this time, the old campaigner was much frayed from war and travel. The mudguards, cracked and battered, hung perilously close to the ground, the top had long since disappeared and wooden crossbars at the back were flying around at alarming angles, threatening to gouge out the eyes of any passenger.

To navigate this monstrosity there was a whole crew—driver, head mechanic and two subordinates who sat with folded arms, like coachmen, on raised platforms on either side of the front seats.

One hundred villagers came out to see the "foreign hairy devil" ride this "steam chariot." Unparalleled opportunity for sport! and they made the most of it, shouting like maniacs and seeming to say—"Why don't you get a mule?"—when the head mechanic cranked for five minutes without result.

Unable to bear the loss of face, the driver descended from his august perch behind the wheel, donned a pair of gloves, seized the crank from his mechanic and, with a professional whirl, sent the motor roaring into life. The crowd cheered. Doffing his gloves, the driver again ascended to his post behind the wheel. Then he threw out the clutch, threw in the gears, waved gallantly to the crowd, let in the clutch again and raced forward—exactly five yards, where he halted in a stall.

After several false starts, we drew away from the village and climbed up onto a highway built by the Japanese. Though deeply rutted, the road was frozen hard and we soon got up a speed of twenty miles an hour. You might think this slow, but accustomed to making twenty miles a day, I thought we were flying.

"Very fast. Very good," said a voice in a clear Peking accent in my ear.

The speaker was a young political worker, on his way, like me, to the headquarters of General Liu Po-cheng. Dressed in a long gown and a fedora hat, he looked quite out of place in these country regions. As a matter of fact, he confided that the hat sometimes caused him trouble. Peasants, seeing in his dress the likeness of a village boss or a slicker from the Kuomintang-held cities, often hissed at him and called him "traitor." Being stubborn, however, he clung to the hat as to a talisman.

As protection against the wind and flying dust, he donned a pair of goggles. Then he dropped a large scarf over his precious hat and brought it down across his face and neck like a veil. He looked exactly like an American automobilist of the early 1900's.

Seven years ago, my companion had been a student in Peiping National University. In 1940, with one hundred youthful companions, he had run away to the guerrilla areas. Hiding in the wheat by day and crawling through the fields at night, he had reached the Taihang Mountains, filled with tears of joy at his first sight of a Chinese uniform. His tears had hardly dried when the Japanese came thundering into the mountains on one of their burn-all, loot-all, kill-all drives. Nearly every house was destroyed, the cattle slaughtered and the grain carried off. Life was so terrible that he often thought to run back to Peiping. Somehow, he had survived and now here he was doing political work among the peasants.

After many questions, I asked him if he were married. He threw out his arms, laughed bitterly and said hurriedly:

"Well, how could I? What time have we for women? We are always moving, we have no room of our own, no place to meet women, no time to find a lover and no chance to kiss."

This last word he said in English, rolling it around on his tongue as if to savor a delicious foreign food.

"Life is bitter here," he said thoughtfully. "We don't have any energy left for love. Worse than that there are no pretty girls. You won't find a pretty woman doing revolutionary work." His voice grew bitter.

"Someone with bound feet," he said sarcastically, "that is all you can find."

Never, he confided, had he known a woman as a lover. He spoke to me softly, hurriedly, all the time hunching his bowed shoulders, incessantly staring across at me with humble eyes.

"When peace comes," he said, "I'll go to Peiping. . . ." He paused. Something in his gaze was so pitifully lonely, yet so mortally harsh, like the eyes of a stricken animal, that it was painful for me to look at him. He dropped his lashes over his eyes, and smiled forcedly, then suddenly blurted:

"Moon . . . lover . . . kiss!"

He said these words in English as if he had heard them long ago in some movie and stored them up in the secret recesses of his heart which now opened and gushed forth his mournful longing.

Intellectual loneliness and nothing more! I decided harshly, wondering all the time how many more ex-students there were in this backward countryside longing for an idle hour of romance with some svelte girl from the city.

We jogged along through the interminable hours. Once in a while my companion would hum a song. Or maybe he would grow silent with dreaming.

Sometime in the afternoon, we reached Hantan, a town of forty thousand people along the now defunct Peiping-Hankow Railway. Although the first real city I had seen since leaving Kuomintang areas, Hantan was only half alive. "American" planes, the mayor explained, had destroyed the power plant and the city was without lights. Afraid he might lose everything, the mayor had moved the cotton plant, the iron foundry and several small factories along with five hundred workers to safer regions in the mountains.

Along with the industry, the Border Region headquarters had also taken to the hills, so that my journey was not yet ended. Left behind, however, to care for itinerant officials and traveling guests, like myself, was a charming Public Relations official, named Tsai.

"How do you do I am well thank you welcome to Hantan." With these English words said all in one breath, he had greeted me before I had a chance to open my mouth.

Like my truck companion, Tsai was a gentle soul, but no loneliness clouded his busy days. He was married to an attractive girl, whom he called "my lover," and he had a five-year-old son whom his wife had taught to dance the *Yangko* (Planting Song) and to sing anti-Chiang songs. The Tsais had met and married in the guerrilla areas during the Japanese war. A few days after their son was born, the Japanese had closed in on their guerrilla band and both father and mother fled, leaving the child with a friendly farmer. Not until two years later were they able to return and reclaim him.

I was to find that many cadres of the 8th Route Army hid their children in peasant homes, but not all of them had the luck to get them back again. Sometimes the farmer would be killed or he would move and the child could not be found. In other cases, the child, brought up to call the farmer "father," would refuse to recognize his real parents when they came to claim him. Or the farmers, wanting the labor of the extra sons, would be unwilling to give the children back. Finally, some parents, believing revolutionaries could not be burdened with children, surrendered them completely to the farmers.

Hantan, having once been a railway metropolis and a collecting point for the grain from the villages on the plain and the local products from the mountains, and being a town of some size and hence able to offer a few amenities of life, I was afforded the first opportunity of my trip to visit a bathhouse.

When I returned with the mayor from the bathhouse to our hostel, a man in uniform rushed out of a room and accosted us with great excitement. He pointed at a room on our right, hissing out the words— "fa kuo jen!" (Frenchman). The effect on the mayor of these words was startling. Coming close to me, he held out the palm of his left hand and on it with the finger of his right hand traced the character fa (France). Then he mysteriously pointed at his mouth and waved his finger back and forth several times as if to say: "don't talk." A few moments later, somewhat apologetic, he hastened to my room with an explanation. A French representative of UNRRA had just arrived from the south. If he learned that I was going to Liu Po-cheng's headquarters, he might want to come along. That would be embarrassing as the location of the headquarters was secret and only "trusted foreigners" were taken there.

Shortly after this incident, Mr. Tsai brought into my room two glass bottles filled with a substance that looked like blood.

"An American UNRRA doctor, named Harrison," he explained, "died near here two days ago. This is what he spit up before he died. And this is what he spit up after he died."

Holding the bottles for me to see, Tsai looked grave. It was rather gruesome and the mayor hinted that there might be foul play behind Harrison's death.

Later, when I read Harrison's diary, the reason for his death became clearer. Not long before, he had contracted to bring a freight car of supplies to Kaifeng, intending to ship them from there to the Liberated Areas. Kuomintang officials, however, had his freight car shunted onto a lonely siding in the Yellow River flood areas. There was no heat in the car, no food and no populated villages in the area from which he could obtain help. For a week, he huddled in the car, cold and hungry, but afraid to leave his supplies. Friends hearing of his predicament, finally persuaded officials to send the car on to Kaifeng. Weak and ill, but determined to finish his job, Harrison ferried the supplies across the Yellow River to Communist areas. There, however, suffering from exposure and malnutrition, he collapsed and died. Many UNRRA officials carrying supplies to the Liberated Areas were given the run-around like this by Chiang Kai-shek's officials, but Harrison was the only one I heard of that died because of these tactics.

Stopping only overnight I left Hantan early the next morning on a charcoal-burning Japanese truck. Among the passengers was a girl dressed in an 8th Route Army uniform that fitted her like a potato sack. Her name was Jen Chi, and she could speak a lot of English. With us also came a messenger with several million dollars that he carried wrapped loosely in a white cloth. Conditions being peaceful in the area, there was little cause to worry about bandits or robbers, and even if there were, a robber could scarcely have run off with such a bulky bundle.

We left the plain immediately, turned into the foothills of the Taihang Mountains and chugged upward at a slow pace, our truck trailing a thin stream of charcoal smoke behind.

Here, on the terraces necklacing the hills, sprouts of winter wheat shot up from the cold earth. Over the rocky road, sometimes shadowed by cliffs, still lay drifts of snow streaming with moisture. A chill rose from the snow, but this chill was lessened by the sight of the wheat, young and warm with the feel of budding life.

At intervals along the road we ran into mule-cart convoys carrying mountain products to the plains below. Meeting them in narrow ravines slowed us up and caused the carters inconvenience and the animals took fright at the sound of our motors and became tangled in their traces. Once we ran down a cart, caught its wheels in ours, and despite the plaintive protests of the girl, kept on going so that the cart turned over on its side and pulled the mule down on his back. The girl and my Peiping student friend, being intellectuals, complained bitterly to the truck driver that such actions, being unjust, would alienate the civilians from the government, but the proletarian driver merely grunted.

As we went on, our journey was enlivened by some peculiar antics of this driver. Every now and again, he would put the car in low gear, pull down the hand throttle, and jump from his seat to the road. Then, picking up handfuls of snow, he would run alongside the truck and throw the snow in a small tank at the side. Whether this was to cool off the charcoal fire or to put water in the radiator was something I have not discovered to this day.

Gulping snow and belching charcoal smoke, we drew into Wu An, a town set on a plateau between the foothills and the mountain walls further to the west. From the center of the town, a Catholic church and an ancient pagoda raised their spires high above all the other buildings as if competing for the religious affections of the people living thereabouts.

Disdaining both the Catholics and the Buddhists, our truck turned off the road and entered the compound of what had been a Protestant mission. Once the compound might have been neatly kept, but now it was filled with auto wrecks, truck parts, and forty or fifty carts. On the ground, horses, mules and men lay amid fodder and manure.

Our charcoal truck lacking the power to make the grade ahead, we changed into a jeep, loading all our baggage into it and five people besides. Miss Jen sat in the back seat, squeezed between bedrolls on one of which I sat. She held onto my coat so that I would not fall off.

Though almost too good to be true, the girl was not without her interest, and later, as I came to know her better, I even achieved a kind of admiration for her. For a while she was my interpreter in Lin Pocheng's headquarters and I used to question her about her life, some details of which may be mentioned here.

Hantan was her native city and she had been born the daughter of a landlord. In 1937, when the Japanese invaded China she was fifteen years old and a student in a lower middle school in Peiping. Not wishing to study under the Japanese, and Chiang Kai-shek's minister of education having issued a call for all middle school and college students to come to the interior and be educated free, she went home, picked up her younger brother and sister and fled the Japanese areas. For many months she wandered through central China, most often finding that, despite the promises of the Education Ministry, she could not get in a school without money. Evacuating Hankow on a ship with wounded soldiers and refugees on their way nine hundred miles up the Yangtze River to Chunking, she alone, among a horde of rich refugees had been willing to dirty her hands to care for the soldiers. Some Chinese correspondents taking interest in her case recommended her to school authorities and she was able to enter Nankai Middle School.

This, as she described it, was a school for "young nobles," and she had a hard time making friends, constantly being snubbed by the sons and daughters of the rich. Soon she became disgusted at the lack of freedom in the schools and at the spies of the Chiang Kai-shek Youth Corps who went around with clubs and pistols beating up students caught reading any "liberal" books. Attracted by what she had heard of conditions existing in Yenan, the headquarters of the Communist party and the 8th Route Army, she had made her way there in the fourth year of the war. In Yenan, she had, among other things, studied English, which she spoke correctly, but slowly. There she met a young engineer, just returned from England. He had an English wife and child, but he had abandoned them in England at the outbreak of war in 1937 and returned to China and become a Communist. Miss Jen, thinking this sad, promptly fell in love with the engineer.

At the end of the Japanese war, the engineer went to Manchuria with a detachment of troops. Miss Jen had tried to follow him walking across the barren mountains of the northwest to Inner Mongolia seeking a passage through the Great Wall. But she could not get past Chiang's troops and after many months of travel she returned to her home in Hantan.

Dirty with the marks of travel and looking like a tramp in her ragged uniform, she had entered her mother's house. The mother was shocked by her daughter appearing in uniform and, not able to summon up any word of welcome, she blurted out: "You ought to get married."

The land reform was just starting in Hantan and Miss Jen told her mother that they should give up some of their land to the poor. Shocked by this strange daughter, the mother replied: "It is destiny for people to be poor, can I interfere with fate?" But the daughter was persistent. After two nights, during which many tears were shed, the mother finally capitulated, signing away generous portions of her land to peasants who had none.

Now, just turned twenty-six, Jen Chi was very serious about the fight against Chiang Kai-shek. She was not a Communist, but evidently was dying to become one. She wanted to be a heroine and do great things. She had never been kissed and thought the idea revolting. She could not understand the weakness of foreigners concerning these matters. Having once seen a movie in which the women spent a great deal of time fixing up their hair and putting themselves inside strange machines that wiggled their hips, she thought American girls must be horrid and very foolish. "How can they do such things?" she used to ask me. She liked to read books, especially books about war and strong heroes, but when I asked her about Tolstoy's *War and Peace*, she said she did not like that girl Anna (getting mixed with Anna Karenina) because she was too "weak."

Now she was on her way to headquarters, hoping to find some way to get to her lover in Manchuria. So, despite all her pronouncements about heroics and the silliness of American women, she, too, it seems, was slightly infected with the virus of love. After spending three weeks with me, she did leave, trotting away on a donkey on a trip of over a thousand miles toward Harbin. I wish her luck; I hope she got through the lines and found her sweetheart.

By now we were on a very rocky road. At last, it gave out altogether and we turned into a dried-up river bed then through a series of narrow defiles until we came out into a thin valley where all the villages, built of stone, and looking like forts, presented a grimmer aspect than those of the mud villages on the plains below.

At dusk we arrived in Yehtao, military headquarters for the Shansi-Hopei-Shantung-Honan Border Region. General Liu Po-cheng, at the moment, was not around, being off with the troops in west Shantung. General Po Yi-po, vice-commissar of the Border Region came to greet me with his English-speaking secretary, Mr. Li Teh-hua. After a few cursory words of welcome, he asked me my impressions of the Liberated Areas. I told him that I was annoyed at being stopped from taking pictures along the way, and he begged me to forgive them.

"The local officials don't understand what a reporter is. Rest assured that you can take pictures of anything you want in our areas. We have no secrets. We welcome any journalist who comes to see the Liberated Areas. You can write about anything you see and see anything you want."

I was a little skeptical of this carte blanche, but later I was to be amazed at the things the Communists did let me see and the stories, both good and bad, they told me about themselves. As long as I operated in army or commissar channels I found that I had unbelievable freedom to see and investigate anything in the Border Region. It was only when I got out of touch with Communist channels and in the hands of non-Communist, so-called progressive students—especially the English-speaking, chauvinistic ones—that I had trouble.

For the moment, however, there were none of these difficulties. I was given a clean room in a stone house, with a kang to myself, a pan of charcoal, an orderly who had been captured from Warlord Yen Hsi-shan, a mirror, table, chair and a picture of President Truman.

PART III

BIRTH OF AN ARMY

❦

9. Chinese Commissar

ANYONE who was in Paris during the war remembers how several blocks beyond the Etoile were roped off and all the buildings therein requisitioned for Allied Headquarters. The whole area was surrounded by barbed wire and guarded by sentries and no one was allowed through the barricades without proper identification. Thus it was rather breath taking to come into the small mountain village of Yehtao (pop. about two thousand) and find hardly any signs that an army of three hundred thousand regulars and one million partisans was directed from inside its stone walls. Except for a radio aerial over one building, you could not have told this was a headquarters town, for no areas in the villages were restricted and there were no sentries at all outside any of the various military departments.

Perhaps the seclusion of Yehtao in the mountains gave the officials in the headquarters a sense of security they might not have had elsewhere. But whatever the cause, there was no denying that generals and governors moved about like any common soldier or peasant, completely carefree and unguarded. Although most of the time they were extremely busy holding conferences, at more leisurely moments they could be seen sitting on the stone wall overlooking the village pond and chatting with some peasant. Yet these informal officers dressed so poorly in cotton-cloth uniform, were the same men that had directed a war against the Japanese for eight years from these self-same Taihang Mountains. And it was they who had founded the Shansi-Hopei-Shantung-Honan Border Region which was now carrying on one of the main fights against Chiang Kai-shek. Realizing that in the weeks to come, the fate of the war might well depend on this area, I determined to find out as much as I could about it.

What both interested and puzzled me was how a small band of guerrillas, isolated in one of the poorer sections of China, without any outside help, could not only fight an eight-year war behind the Japanese lines, and survive, but come out of that war so strong that they could challenge American-trained and equipped armies of Chiang Kai-shek for control of China. The Kuomintang and even some American congressmen had often declared that the Communists had never fought the Japanese; if that were true—and it might be—then by what methods had they survived and how were they able to fight against Chiang Kai-shek now, if in that eight-year period they had done no fighting against the national enemy?

It was more than a reporter's normal curiosity that made me inquire into these events; I also had a personal interest in finding out how the Reds had lived behind the Japanese lines. In August 1937, after the Japanese captured Peiping, I had sneaked through their lines and after a somewhat adventurous journey joined the troops of Chiang Kai-shek then gathering in North China to do battle. All through the summer of 1937 I had retreated with Chiang's soldiers both across the North China Plain and through the mountains of Shansi. In one terrible retreat through Shansi I had seen the armies of Chiang almost completely collapse, soldiers throw away their weapons and officers grab all available transportation, abandon their troops and rush to the rear. At that time, it had seemed as if China could not possibly resist and as if North China had been completely abandoned into the hands of the enemy. Chiang's soldiers had been driven from the area, and all organized resistance in the north seemed at an end. Yet even while Chiang's troops and I were fleeing the north, the Communists were infiltrating into position behind the Japanese lines where it had appeared to me no Chinese soldiers could possibly operate.

How had they survived?

It seemed to me that here was not only a great story, but a profound human experience. Here also was the answer to the riddle of why Communism was having such great successes in China today. From the epic fight of the people of North China behind the Japanese lines, one also could gain many clues as to who was going to win the war in China— the Communists or Chiang Kai-shek. Finally, it seemed to me that in the history of these years there were many lessons to be learned, not only political and military, but human and philosophic, as well.

To find an answer to these questions, I went to Commissar Po Yi-po who had led a band of students into the Shansi Mountains in 1937 and organized the first guerrilla resistance in the region against the Japanese. Not only had Po fought in these parts for ten years, but he was also a native of Shansi Province, and consequently familiar with the country and its people.

The word commissar to most Americans is a frightening one, conjuring up, as it does, the picture of a ruthless politician, perhaps an inquisitor, with the power of life and death over the mere mortals under him. What a Russian or a European commissar is like, I have no idea; he may be as frightening a personage as everyone says, but Commissar Po, whom I got to know rather well during my stay in Yehtao was a pink-cheeked young man in his late thirties, with a very insouciant manner and an ever-ready smile. He also had a very well organized mind. I had submitted a few very general questions to him such as: "What is the Border Region? How was it formed? What is its history?" On the basis of this very simple outline, he talked for three days, covering such a variety of subjects as guerrilla warfare, famine, the Communist party and the formation of government, without reference to notes, without pausing for breath, except for an occasional cup of tea and, most impressive of all, putting everything in its proper order and context.

I never did get to ask him about his personal life, because shortly after my arrival, the civil war was to erupt in a rather violent way and both he and I became a little too busy to delve into more personal matters. I did hear vague stories that at one time he had been a writer, that he had been arrested and imprisoned by the Kuomintang more than once and that he had a great personal following among many professors in Kuomintang universities. Of none of these things can I speak for sure. Suffice it to say that I found him entertaining, obliging, clear minded and possessing an extremely even temper which was somewhat of a legend among some of the hotter-hearted members of the Border Region staff.

On a cold day, late in January 1947, I sat in a comfortable, plush chair in Commissar Po's residence. This residence was built of stone and had stone floors, curtains and foreign-style chairs and tables so that it probably was a former landlord's house, requisitioned by the government. Seated next to me was Li Teh-hua, a middle-aged secretary to the headquarters Communist party who acted as my interpreter in formal interviews with Po.

Li was a former Yenching University student who had run over to the Liberated Areas shortly after the Japanese war. I don't think he was a Communist, because when I asked him about it, he replied in a somewhat huffy manner, "If you mean am I a member of the Communist party, the answer is no; but if you mean would I like to be a member, I have to answer that I only wish I were worthy."

I was to have a great deal of interpreter trouble in the Liberated Areas, but Mr. Li was ideal for this particular job because, being a native of Shansi, he could understand the Shansi accents of Po, whose language I found quite atrocious. This was more of an advantage than it sounds, for many interpreters from other parts of the country could not understand Po's Shansi speech.

During the several days that followed, Po, Li and I huddled in Po's room over the small charcoal fire—and I wrote until I was ready to fall asleep, but Po seemed as fresh as when we had begun.

Although the main question I had asked Po concerned the story of their eight-year fight behind the Japanese lines and how they had managed to survive, he did not attempt to put this all down to Communist party magic.

"You must know," he said, when we had made ourselves comfortable, "that the natural situation in this region favors us. This Border Region covers an area of two million square kilometers in the heart of North China. If you will look at a map you will see that it has a good strategic unity. It is shaped something like a four-sided box, the bottom of which is the Yellow River, the top of which is the Chengtai Railway and the Shihchiachuang-Techow highway, the left side of which is the Tungpu Railway and the right side, the Tientsin-Pukow Railway.

"For the purposes of administration we have divided the area into five military and government districts. Under these districts are twenty-four subdistricts each with parallel military and government organizations. And under these are 126 (the number constantly changes) county governments and self-defense corps.

"Half of this area contains the biggest plain in China; namely the North China or Yellow River Plain. The other half—the Taihang and Taiyueh area—is all mountains.

"These mountains are of tremendous importance. Native militarists and invading barbarians have always tried to control them, for they dominate the plain. They are continuous and stretch for two thousand miles across China to Tibet. A proverb says: 'Door after door; gate after gate; mountains on the outside; mountains on the inside.'"

If I may rudely interrupt Po at this point, I would like to add a few words about these mountains, the significance of which was never observed by American interventionists who thought that all one had to do to conquer the Communists was to send Chiang Kai-shek a billion United States dollars. The mountains in which Po and I were now sitting were part of the great Kunlun system that extends from the borders of India, across all of China and peters out on the islands of Japan. The military implications of these mountains are staggering. Conceivably, a traveler entering the mountains near the borders of the USSR could journey on hilly trails through a score of provinces, cross the Yellow and the Yangtze rivers and, passing over the roof of the world in Tibet, finally reach India, three thousand miles away, hardly ever descending onto flat ground.

A world in themselves, these mountains offer an ideal hiding place for a hard-pressed army. More than that, if an army controls the passes, it can march up and down their length and debouch almost at will onto the plains against an unsuspecting enemy. To control these mountains completely, of course, is beyond the capacity of any army in the world—a fact that some United States congressmen who think to conquer China for Chiang Kai-shek with a few divisions of American troops might do well to ponder. However, a control only of a small section of the mountains can often be of extreme importance.

But to continue with Commissar Po:

"What I have just told you is a brief description of our Border Region. It is here that the people of North China and the 8th Route Army fought the Japanese for eight years and are preparing to fight the Kuomintang for twenty years, if necessary.

"How can we exist?

"There are three big factors. First, the Border Region has, in the plains of southern Hopei, the largest cotton-producing area in the country. Here grows 36 per cent of all China's cotton. So everyone has enough clothes.

"Secondly, in the Taihang and Taiyueh mountains, there is a surplus of wheat, millet and kaoliang; there is coal, iron and sulfur, useful and abundant enough for present needs.

"Finally, there are seventeen million square acres of cultivated land supporting thirty million people. Most all of these people live in villages. The biggest city the Border Region controls is Tsining with a population of 140,000. In addition there are eight or nine cities of between forty and fifty thousand people.

"These people are of two kinds: the mountaineers and the plainsmen. The mountain people, or the Shansi type, are known as Cow Skin Lanterns, meaning that outside they are dark but inside, bright. For the past two thousand years, their chief characteristics have been frugality, diligence and a capacity to bear hardship. From their outside appearance, they are not bold, but soft, shrinking and timid. In the past, the rest of China has looked down on them, contemptuously calling them 'Old West.'

"In reality, however, these people are far from timid. They are skillful in business and exceptionally far sighted. They do not make plans for one or two years, but for their whole lives. Since the Ming dynasty, for the last five hundred years, Shansi businessmen have controlled banking through many parts of China, and Dr. H. H. Kung is only one of the most recent examples.

"Eight years of war and a guerrilla struggle against the Japanese however has changed these people so that they have become not only frugal, but brave and tough outside, as well as inside.

"The second type of people—the plainsmen of southern Hopei, Shantung and Honan provinces—are of a different order entirely, being healthy and robust in physique and brave and warlike in spirit. Their history has been one of bloodshed and revolt and for the past two thousand years they have always risen against national and alien oppressors to fight for their independence. A proverb says: 'Picks up a stick, then fights.' Another one says: 'Brave in danger; skillful in fighting; never enslaved.' These words accurately describe these people, for they have always been ready to seize a club or stone or any weapon at hand to knock down the officials and raise a people's rebellion.

"In the past, however, these people revolted mostly out of a spirit of revenge and without much purpose. Because of their natural bravery and their spirit of independence, it was easy to get them to rise against the Japanese, but much more difficult to make them organize. We had to teach them that to kill was not enough. During eight years we were able to show them not only how to fight, which they already knew pretty well, but how to fight effectively, and how to retain power once they had taken it in their villages.

"Because of all these things—strategic location, self-sufficient economy and thirty million tough people—what happens to our Border Region and to the one on our flank in eastern Shantung will probably determine the fate of the whole civil war.

"If we can stop Chiang from getting through here, then we can build up bases in Inner Mongolia and Manchuria and thus have a great and safe rear area. But even if Chiang breaks through here, as did the Japanese, we can still maintain the independence of the Shansi-Hopei-Shantung-Honan Border Region by retiring into the impenetrable mountains of the Taiyueh and Taihang ranges.

"Thanks to God," and Po repeated the expression as I looked askance at him, "Thanks to God, the natural situation favors us. The plains and mountains can be used together. The plains produce wheat for the mountains; and the mountains produce what the plains lack and protect them."

10. Formation of a Base

MORE than mountains and plains, however, were needed to create the Shansi-Hopei-Shantung-Honan Border Region. In the beginning, there was no government and only six thousand troops among a population of thirty million people. How these people fought the Japanese for eight years, built up a government of their own, and expanded their army into three hundred thousand regulars is a story not only of great achievement, but a record of unparalleled hardship and determination.

In the early days of China's war against Japan, as I knew, the Japanese swept over North China almost at will. The often leaderless Chinese troops ran away in confusion and the general idea of the Kuomintang command was to get over the Yellow River as fast as possible. Traitors and collaborators sprang up in every town and China was in great peril.

By 1938, the Japanese had cleared North China of nearly all regular opposition except a small force of the Communist-led 8th Route Army.

"In the past," said Po Yi-po, and here we shall let him resume the story, "Chiang Kai-shek called the members of this army bandits, but in the first year of the war against Japan, the only ones who remained behind in North China to fight were just these bandits.

"There were, however, other forces than this army in North China. In the summer of 1937 when the Kuomintang troops began their flight to the Yellow River, underground Communists, who had been in hiding for years and who were completely out of touch with the party, came out into the open and began to pick up arms disbanded by the retreating soldiers. At the same time, the Central Committee of the Communist party issued an order to all members to take off their long gowns, don short coats and pants, take up arms and under no circumstances to cross the Yellow River.

"There was little or no connection between the Central Committee of the party and its underground workers, but messengers and orderlies were dispatched to the large towns to post slogans, distribute handbills and spread the word as best they could. General instructions were for workers, students and farmers to unite, to evacuate the cities immediately and to help organize guerrilla warfare.

"Some party members were reached by this means, but those who were not often adopted independent action of their own. Even before the 8th Route Army appeared in North China, underground Communist workers had organized their own guerrilla units under various names, such as the Hopei Militia or the Dare To Die Corps. Only the leaders of such units were Communists and such groups were primarily of patriotic origin.

"In addition, there were also student groups which took up guerrilla warfare. Some of these groups had been organized before the war because of Warlord Yen Hsi-shan's dissatisfaction with Chiang Kai-shek's continued appeasement of Japan.

"Just before Chiang was kidnaped at Sian, Yen invited me to come down from Yenan and help him train these students.

"When the Japanese invaded Shansi in 1937, Yen tried to attract them to follow him to the south. But I issued a countercall, saying: 'Follow me into the mountains.'

"Most came with me. In the summer of 1937 I led five columns of these students into the Taihang and Taiyueh mountains. Each column was led by a Communist worker, all of whom had only just been released from Chiang Kai-shek's prisons.

"Besides this student army, small groups of railway workers and labor defense units who had spontaneously organized themselves to fight the Japanese followed me into the mountains.

"These bands—you could hardly call them troops—had a United Front complexion and were composed of all those who did not wish to run away and cross the Yellow River with Chiang Kai-shek's forces. As a slogan, I used the words: 'Better to sacrifice to Shansi than be refugees.' Except for the big officials, the big landlords and the government of Yen Hsi-shan, most of the people stayed behind to fight.

"While this movement was going on in the mountains, a parallel movement sprang up on the plains. In Hopei, for example, militia were organized by professors and teachers of North China. Soon a local government, composed of students, a few underground members of the Communist party and liberals, was organized under the leadership of Professor Yang Hsiu-feng who was later to become head of the Border Region government. Similar governments came into being in Honan and in western Shantung.

"Besides these, there sprang up more or less spontaneously nearly a hundred self-defense corps. At this time, all organizations were motivated by a spirit of patriotism, a feeling of horror at Japanese atrocities and an anger at the Kuomintang for retreating so quickly without putting up much of a fight. Altogether, there were perhaps one hundred thousand men.

"This force had little to do with the Communist party and no connection at all with the 8th Route Army. Its strong point was its close relations with the people; its weak point, its lack of unity, central leadership and military experience. Such a force, composed of students who hardly knew how to fire rifles, of professors who knew nothing of tactics and farmers who knew neither tactics nor politics, was in danger of disintegrating for lack of a directing head and of being wiped out for the lack of technique.

"Such was the condition of resistance in North China, when, in November 1937, General Liu Po-cheng led three regiments of the 129th Division of the 8th Route Army from the loess country of Shensi Province on the west, across the Yellow River and into the Taihang Mountains. Here was the military leader we had been waiting for.

"Although Liu had only six thousand men, they were some of the best soldiers in China. All of them had been on the Long March. They were technically skillful, well trained, especially in guerrilla warfare, and politically highly conscious. Members of the three regiments had all fought in Hupeh, Anhui and Honan, north of the Yangtze River against Chiang Kai-shek in the old civil war. They had been originally formed, after the failure of the 1927 Revolution, from a small band of underground Communists, equipped with two rifles. Thus, in a way, it can be said that the 8th Route Army of three hundred thousand men that today occupies this strategic Border Region, was born from two guns. In fact, these troops are illustrative of one of our favorite sayings: 'From smallness to bigness; from nothing to something.'

"These regulars of Liu's were combined with my five student columns and then later sent among the various people's units. The combination of these forces enabled North China to mold a front against the Japanese.

"The force of the people can be compared to water," Po concluded, adopting a famous saying of General Peng Teh-hwai's; "the force of General Liu to fish. Only in the water could the fish swim."

11. Building Resistance

To MOLD a front against the Japanese, however, was a task of Herculean proportions.

With only six thousand troops to face an enemy fifteen times the size of his own in fire power and number, Liu appeared in a position of almost checkmate. If he elected to attack the Japanese, on the theory that the best defense is an offense, he courted almost certain defeat and annihilation. If he decided to remain in the mountains and conserve his forces, the enemy would consolidate their gains on the plain, raise a puppet army for garrison duty and come after him in the mountains at their leisure. Finally, if he scattered his regular army among the people's bands, he would almost certainly destroy his only striking force, he would ruin the unity of the only professional body of troops under his command and, by mixing trained fighters with people's rabble, that is, mixing blood with water, he would run the risk of lowering his soldiers' morale and spoiling the high traditions of the old Red Army.

Liu chose this latter course.

We wish to emphasize this point. Contrary to customary military procedure, Liu did not concentrate his army, but immediately dispersed it. General Liu's destruction (what else was it) of his 129th Division reveals, perhaps, the most remarkable fact about Communist tactics—tactics practiced not only by Liu but by all other Communist commanders. History, indeed affords numerous examples of people's risings and of guerrilla warfare, but few examples of a commander of a cohesive armed force deliberately destroying its unity. Had Liu—or other Communist commanders—failed, their tactics might well have seemed acts of madness. Yet Liu's move was the fruit of deliberate calculation. He had set the fortunes of his army, the future of resistance, life itself, on his plan to get his troops among the people. There was no alternative in his mind, but to spread the war or perish. The measure he adopted greatly increased the chance of success. The idea of direct head-on resistance to the Japanese at this moment would have been chimerical. As it was, by scattering his troops, he deprived the Japanese of any large target.

Perhaps another army, split apart like this behind the enemy's lines, would have become demoralized and disintegrated. But these were no ordinary soldiers. Many years before when they had revolted against the landlords in their own villages, these former tenants had disinherited themselves from the protection of established society. They were used to acting on their own. Under their coarse covering they bore hearts as hard as ever beat in human bosoms. For they were already heroes, when the Japanese war started, veterans of many a hard-fought campaign in the civil war where the odds had been incalculably against them. Now, dispersed and far from their commander's watchful eye, they began to operate on their own.

Descending from the Taihang Mountains, which would have been their best means of security had they chosen to hide among their hilly walls, Liu's regiments entered onto the North China Plain, a region well suited to large-scale military maneuver, but ill endowed by reason of its flatness for guerrilla warfare. Here the troops split into battalions and companies, skirted around Hantan and marched eastward. Traversing the dusty fields of southern Hopei, they threaded their way through the Japanese lines, passing around cities which stood like watchdogs along the railways and holing up at night in small villages or the fields themselves.

Their march was slow and troublesome and many times they had to change direction. The anxiety of their minds, however, made them indifferent to outward annoyances; and they had none, fortunately, to encounter from the local population, for the villagers were amazed to see Chinese soldiers who wanted to fight the Japanese when all they had seen before were soldiers anxious to flee the invader.

Across dusty Hopei, into the crowded villages and green hills of Shantung, the soldiers of Liu and other Communist commanders continued on, marching for many days until they reached the shores of the Pacific Ocean several hundred miles from their starting point. Everywhere behind them had been left companies, squads and platoons to organize guerrilla warfare. And out of every squad had come one or two soldiers to join the various bands that farmers, teachers and even patriotic landlords had raised to fight the Japanese.

Cordially embracing these professional companions in arms, the people soon elevated Liu's erstwhile soldiers to staff positions in their various bands. Even cooks and donkeymen from the old Red Army became company commanders among people's units. The students of Po Yi-po followed where the soldiers had led and before long became political directors in guerrilla organs.

By dispersing his forces and spreading the war Liu had gained a much greater victory than if he had directly attacked and defeated a large Japanese force. For even if he had defeated the Japanese in battle and diminished their forces, he would at the same time have diminished his own. But by adopting the strategy he did, Liu was able to expand to an extent that even he had not thought likely.

Such an expansion was possible in the first place only because General Nakamura, Japanese commander in chief, made the mistake of estimating the strength of Chinese resistance on the number of Communist regulars, because he despised guerrilla warfare and because he did not believe the small people's bands could grow into a large force in his rear without supplies and a supply base. During this period the regular force under Liu multiplied fifteen to twenty times from six thousand men to a mobile force of one hundred thousand men. At the same time, local forces were maintained at one hundred thousand men. In Communist terminology, the regulars were compared to bones, the guerrillas to tissue and the militia to flesh. All combined together to form the body of military force.

So well did the regulars and militia control the North China countryside that in a month's journey by cart and foot from the Tungpu Railway in Shansi to the Tsinpu Railway in Shantung, only three and a half hours were required to detour around three large cities held by the Japanese. Because the three north-south and two east-west railways of North China form a kind of cross and because the Japanese were confined to the railways, the Communists said the Japanese were nailed to the cross during this period. While the Japanese did not dare move out in the countryside, Kuomintang troops, left behind also, did not dare move out against the Japanese. So they either retreated south of the Yellow River or became puppets in this stage of the war.

Parallel with the development of the military organizations went a development of new government in North China. Like many of the armed bands, these governments had often been organized by the people themselves under conditions of universal election. For a while, they were part of Chiang Kai-shek's national government, but maintained their own special system of taxes and finance. In this period, rents were reduced, but landlords were not driven from the land and a kind of United Front government was maintained. With the disappearance of the Kuomintang governing organizations, however, a need was felt to form a more unified, central government in this part of North China. In 1941, five hundred elected delegates from the four provinces, after many weeks of travel across Japanese lines, met in the Taihang Mountains and established the Border Region government, with its own laws, its own money, its own system of taxation and an organization extending through over one hundred counties. The formation of the government coincided with the highest point of expansion of the base.

The events covered in these few bare words are certainly extraordinary. That a small body of men like the troops of Liu Po-cheng should have entered a region already given over to the national enemy, have seized and eliminated bandits that were terrorizing the countryside, have established governments where there were none—that they should have, instead of fighting for their very existence, increased their forces ten and fifteen fold, and have crowned the whole effort by gaining control of nearly all the countryside beyond the cities—that this should have been done, not to a wastrel warlord in the wane of his fortunes, but to a proud and mighty foreign invader at the very height of his power, in the very hour of his victory, when almost all the rest of China was giving way before him—that all this should have been done by a mere handful of peasants and intellectuals who had been born from two rifles is a thing almost too extravagant for the pages of history. It is, nevertheless, literally true.

Yet the very extravagance of the Communist expansion and the very boldness of their raids on Japanese lines of communication soon brought with them difficulties as great as the advantages hitherto gained. For the Japanese, startled at the unlooked-for resistance in areas they had already conquered, took fright at the danger, and suddenly returned to North China with thirty-six divisions, determined to eliminate the threat in their rear.

12. Kill All, Burn All, Loot All!

THE main aim of the Japanese was to wipe out the regular forces of Liu Po-cheng, or to make their existence impossible, to annihilate people's bands and to terrorize the countryside so that the people would abandon both their arms and resistance. In four years of war, they had learned much about Chinese tactics and they now adopted tactics of their own to combat the menace of what had once been their rear, but had now become their main front in China.

Although these tactics were many and varied, I shall mention here only one—"The Prisoner's Cage Tactic." To a Western military ear, this name may sound with a quaint and ridiculous ring, but to the Japanese it meant a particular way of attacking and to the Chinese it meant a matter of life and death. The Prisoner's Cage Tactic was a stratagem designed to bottle up the Chinese in a small area so that the Japanese could move in at will in criss-crossing columns and wipe out all troops caught in their box.

Using cities as locks in this military prison, the Japanese built connecting ditches along railways and roads, twenty feet wide and to the depth of moats. Then across roads and fields about the area they wanted to attack they erected earth walls. So long and numerous were these walls that Po estimated they would go around the earth one and a half times if put end to end. If this seems exaggerated, I can only offer the testimony of my own eyes. Going across the plain, I saw so many pill-boxes, ditches and walls that it is almost inconceivable that the Chinese could have existed in the midst of them. Once the walls were erected, the Japanese would build roads between railway lines and forts all along the roads. Then they would gradually close in on all areas, cutting up the prison like bean curd so that in the end there was no territory anywhere larger than ten miles in which Chinese troops could operate.

Yet the Japanese did not succeed in annihilating the forces opposing them. So, in the winter of 1941 and the spring of 1942, they began to burn and kill everything and everyone in their path. Their slogan was: "Kill all, Burn all, Loot all."

As they moved into an area on their mopping-up campaigns, they killed all young men, destroyed or stole all cattle and broke or made off with all farmers' tools and grain. Their object was to create a no man's land in which nothing could live. At the same time they reinforced their economic blockade, halted all salt and cloth from entering the guerrilla regions and tried to starve the population out of resistance.

How could the Chinese combat such tactics? As the Japanese had had to invent new methods to fight guerrilla warfare so the Chinese also had to invent new methods to fight the Japanese annihilation tactics.

The first line of Chinese resistance was formed by spies and underground workers. Whenever the Japanese started a mopping-up campaign, the Chinese would have word of it beforehand. Their forces would immediately move out of the threatened area and launch an attack on the railways and blockhouses which the Japanese had just left. So the two sides would merely have exchanged positions. The Japanese would find no military force in the area they attacked, but would learn that an attack was being made on the positions they had just left. There was nothing for them to do but return to meet this force. Of course, when they arrived, it was gone.

The most famous method adopted in the area, however, was one known as, "Emptying the House and Clearing Up the Field." It could be called a tactic of attrition. Before the Japanese advanced, furniture, grain, cattle and anything of use to the Japanese would all be moved to caves or buried in a prepared hiding place. All people would evacuate the area. Not a guide could be found. If the attack were in the mountains, militiamen would take up positions on every peak; if in the plains, in underground tunnels.

When the Japanese advanced, they were fired at by snipers from all sides. These were not fortuitous snipers, but the best shots picked out of village units for that purpose. Thus attacked, the Japanese would be afraid to split up. Hearing shots from one mountain, they would say: "There's the 8th Route Army." But when they climbed the mountain with their mortars and heavy equipment, they would find no one. Again, they would move forward, again they would be sniped at from another peak, and again they would sweep and search the hill in vain.

After repeating this process two or three times and finding nothing, they would begin to feel safe. Their scouts would be drawn in and they would move forward swiftly. Just at this time, a regular detachment which had been held back and concealed for the purpose would strike them in force and inflict heavy damage on them before they could recover. In addition, as the Japanese tried to penetrate further into the mountains, they would run into homemade land mines planted all over the hill slopes. If the Japanese were in some strength, the militia would not attempt to attack them, but would content themselves with sniping. But if a small detachment split off from the main group, the people would attack with bird rifles, homemade mortars and anything to hand. Such tactics developed a messy military situation. It might last a week. Then the Japanese would get out of supplies and retreat and the farmers would go back to their homes, dig up buried grain and wait till the next attack.

The war of attrition that is implicit in the phrase "Emptying the House and Clearing Up the Field" is a kind of war that can be carried out only by the co-operation of almost all members of society. This co-operation is seldom found in the industrialized societies of the West and not often in the agrarian villages of China either. But in some areas, especially in the mountains, it was carried on to an almost unbelievable extent, as the following story illustrates.

There is in the Taiyueh Mountains of Shansi a county called Chingyuan in which there are sixty thousand people. The center of the county is a town, bearing the county name, which was once surrounded by a wall that the people knocked down after the Japanese invasion. The residents of this region are independent by nature and during the war were so patriotic that not one traitor or collaborator was found throughout the whole county, a rare thing for China. Chingyuan became a thorn in the Japanese side so, in February 1942, they decided to knock it out of the war. For this purpose, they sent a regiment along a motor highway to occupy the city while another regiment was disposed to the south.

Noting the Japanese advance, the people held a public meeting and gave a pledge never to submit to the enemy. Then the city was immediately emptied of all its inhabitants, grain, livestock and whatever would be of use to the Japanese. In addition, twenty thousand people living along the thirty miles of road of the Japanese advance evacuated their homes and went into the mountains.

Not only the local militia, but all able-bodied young men obtained arms, and with ten thousand rifles they took up positions in the mountains. Those living in the mountains divided their land, cotton and animals with the refugees while all children were distributed around the few available houses. Unable to fight the heavily equipped Japanese, the people decided to lay siege to the city and its supply artery.

The Japanese in typically orderly fashion brought up their supplies to the city by road every other day. The people immediately moved five hundred, then a thousand militiamen to the peaks of a narrow pass known as Sheng Fulin, and every other day rained down a cascade of birdshot on the convoys slowly struggling through the pass. From February to May, this attack was kept up so that, on an average, five Japanese soldiers were killed every day. The pass became so infamous to local Japanese units that anyone put on convoy duty would write a letter to his wife the night before. Finally, Sheng Fulin was known as Ghost Gate in the Japanese Army.

Before evacuating the city of Chingyuan, the people had filled all the wells with earth. Consequently the regiment garrisoned in the city had to obtain their water from the Chin Ho River near by. About this river are high hills, where the people stationed experienced snipers, so that the Japanese had to send a squad of soldiers along with their water carriers. Thus getting water became an engagement. In the city there was no firewood, so the Japanese had to come outside to get their wood. When they climbed trees, they were also picked off by the mountain watchers. When they came out to answer the calls of nature, they were also picked off. In addition, the mountain people would come down in the night and kidnap or kill sentries. Thus, in carrying water, relieving themselves, getting firewood and standing guard, the Japanese lost another additional ten men a day. In the end Chingyuan became too costly for the Japanese to hold.

On the plains of the Border Region, it was even more difficult to maintain the war against the Japs than in the mountains. In southern Hopei Province, for example, any place that did not have Japanese soldiers within six to ten miles was called a "base." Since the Japanese were everywhere, the Chinese could no longer maintain a large mobile army. Units were so dispersed that on the plains there was not a larger echelon than a battalion.

Some of the mud- and plaster-hut villages on this plain are extremely large and often the Japanese would be found living in the western part of the village while Chinese guerrillas lived in the east. Even under these circumstances, the Chinese units were seldom surprised and Japanese attacks did little damage.

This seems incredible, but the Communists lay their ability to exist like this on their work among the people and the puppet troops of the Japanese. In the plains, the guerrillas always knew four hours ahead of time when an attack was coming. Whenever a large mopping-up campaign was coming, the Chinese would be informed by the puppets. Children, pregnant women and wounded men would be sent into the towns and put under the care of puppet families, doctors and nurses. In their attacks on guerrilla villages, the Japanese would always put their puppet troops first and these would fire in the air and shout loudly: "Where is the 8th Route Army?" There was always ample time to get away.

The guerrillas also dug hundreds of trenches across the highways so that Japanese cars had to make constant detours through the fields. The guerrillas, however, could go up and down the trenches at will and escape easily.

Finally, the guerrillas, militia and underground workers in the plains built a vast system of tunnels beneath the fields where units could hide in time of danger and directing organs could carry on work. These tunnels were entered from a carefully concealed hole in the wall or floor of a government worker's house. They extended from two to five miles, coming up not only in different houses, but in different villages. They had many pathways, entrances and exits and many turns at which in time of danger armed guards would always stand in case the Japanese ever got into the tunnels. They seldom did. So the underground government would sit in peace in their houses, not even paying attention to the Japanese if they entered the village. If the Japanese should come to the door of a house, the guerrillas would put up a brief fight and then disappear one by one into the tunnel. Should the Japs enter the house, they would find nothing, except perhaps an old lady sitting quietly in a chair.

The Chinese in this fashion were able to maintain their governments and their fighting organizations, but despite all their heroic efforts, their base grew smaller and the number of regulars in their armed forces was knocked down from one hundred thousand to seventy thousand. The militia force however had grown to over five hundred thousand.

13. Famine, Locusts and Overturned Idols

HERE I cannot even begin to outline the absorbing, yet brutal history of the eight years of the North China people's war behind the Japanese lines—a period that was destined to gain for the Communists the affections of the Cow Skin Lanterns of Shansi and the rebellious plainsmen of Hopei, Shantung and north Honan and thus to be a prelude to the violent civil war that flared up after the defeat of Japan. But despite all the ingenuity of the Communists and the heroism of the people, the Japanese campaigns were not absolute failures. It is true they did not wipe out the forces of General Liu Po-cheng, but they put them completely on the defensive and they created such hardship in North China that resistance was seriously compromised.

But these campaigns, bad as they were, with their emphasis on killing, burning and robbing, were not the worst thing with which the people of North China had to cope in the years between 1941 and 1943.

"Because God did not bless us," say Communists, "we had three successive years of famine."

The drought and crop failure were the most serious in North China in a hundred years. The lack of rain was a heavier blow than the Japanese mopping-up campaigns, for there was little way to fight back. Famine, drought, a locust invasion, plague and a blockade by Chiang Kai-shek threatened to diminish the effectiveness of the Border Region to practically nothing.

To begin with, there was a crop failure in the Taihang and Taiyueh mountains, a flood in southern Hopei and locusts in Honan which soon began to sweep over all four provinces. In addition, one million starving refugees from the Kuomintang-occupied areas of Honan, crossed the Yellow River and invaded the Border Region. Among these refugees, out of ten family members, it was estimated that five had died in their native place. The other five were flocking into the Communist areas to try and save their lives. The Border Region tried to lend food, money and land to the refugees, but with a crop failure in their own area, there was a limit to this relief.

In Honan, the roads to the Taihang Mountains were soon filled with corpses. In the spring of 1942, the buds of all trees were eaten. The bark was stripped from every tree so that the trunks presented a strange white appearance like people stripped of clothes. In some places, people ate the feces of silkworms; in other places, they ate a queer white earth.

61

But such food could only stave off starvation for a few days and the victims quickly died.

Women exchanged their babies, saying: "You eat mine, I'll eat yours." When a man was going to die, he dug a pit and sat inside and asked neighbors to fill in the earth when he was dead. Afterward, however, no one could be found to fill in the pits for all were either dead or too weak to shovel earth. Men sold their children first, then their wives. Those who survived were getting weaker and even in those areas where there was rain, they were too weak to plant or plow. This kind of famine is known in China as successive famine.

In the no man's lands along the borders of the Japanese-occupied areas, one could not find a cat, dog, pig or chicken, so there was no breeding. Many times whole families committed suicide. The head of the family would bury his father, mother, wife and children alive and then commit suicide himself. These conditions did not exist in the Liberated Areas or the rear but in the guerrilla areas on the borders of the Japanese- or Kuomintang-occupied regions.

In order to relieve pressure on the worst parched land, the government moved over one hundred thousand people to new land. The government set up stations every ten miles to receive the hundreds of farmers who were pouring from their homes, weeping bitter tears and carrying pots, bags of grain and household goods on their backs—desolate at leaving their ancestral homes, but seeing no other way to remain alive.

When the drought continued month after month, the people looked at the harsh sun burning up the sky overhead and then at the land cracking beneath their feet and they said: "We are condemned by Heaven."

Some Christians thought they were being punished for their sins; a few thought the earth had too many people and God was calling them back to Heaven; but among most, the general suspicion prevailed that the gods were indulging in one of their periodic wars against human beings.

Whole villages marched in concert to the temples and knelt down before Buddhas, Taoist images and local gods and prayed for rain. Many dressed like prisoners and many clothed themselves in the raiments of religious penitents, putting square boards around their necks and groveling on the ground. Others cut holes in their neck tendons and strung long pieces of string through them, dragging them behind as they walked, as a sign of their penance.

The religious zeal in the villages mounted high, but not all the farmers reverted to ancient superstitions and not all prayed to Heaven. Some of the younger men said: "Manpower can overcome Heaven power." Others said: "God helps those who help themselves." Still others cried:

"Mao Tze-tung is the saving star of the people[1] and he is here; let him save us." Finally, some put their hope in the government and expected help and relief.

As the rain did not fall and as the people grew more hopeless every day, an ideological argument broke out among village officials. At first, they had gone with the people to the temples and prayed for rain like everyone else, but nothing had happened. As the drought grew worse, they had witnessed the barbarous rites of their elders, which they had never seen before, the mutilation of their bodies, and their prostration before wood and clay idols.

Having received some education from the 8th Route Army, their souls sickened at these sights, and at last some of the younger men said: "The gods are bad for the people; we must destroy them." To postpone the deed would be an error in duty. In the enthusiasm of the moment, the younger cadres brushed aside the objections of their more timid companions, forgetting prudence or the dictates of policy.

Meeting little opposition, the more active village officials sprang into the temples, tore the idols from their foundations and broke their heads off with stones. Their fantastic forms and features, conveying a symbolic meaning which had long been forgotten by most and was entirely lost on the younger men, seemed in their eyes only the remnants of a superstition that must die. With unaccustomed energy they rolled the broken idols out of the temples into the streets, amid the misgivings of the village elders. They then consummated the whole by smearing the gods with paint and by smashing them in front of the assembled farmers.

Already having lost a good part of their faith during the drought, the people put up no fight to protect their village idols. And finding their deities incapable of preventing or even punishing this profanation of their shrines, they conceived a low opinion of their power compared to their own village rulers. Only a few old men thought the smashing of the idols would enrage the gods more, but they confined their remarks to dark hints about bitter times to come.

Some villagers reached the conclusion that it was better to depend on themselves and Mao Tze-tung than on a god. They did not at this time replace their deities with Mao, but when the famine was finally broken and good times returned, not a few peasant families put little pictures of Mao in the tiny household shrines where they had formerly kept clay images.

An invasion of locusts magnified the famine almost beyond human endurance. For days on end, for the first two years of the famine, great

[1] A slogan of the Communist party believed in by many superstitious peasants. Edgar Snow in his *Red Star Over China* says: "Don't imagine that Mao Tze-tung can be the saviour of China," but it is interesting to note that the Communists are now saying, "Mao Tze-tung is the saving star of the people."

clouds of these bugs swarmed over the four provinces, blotting out the sun and consuming almost all plant life in their path. The Communist party started a Locust Beating-Down Campaign. Even in small areas, one hundred thousand people were mobilized in the fields to defend the crops against the locusts. As the insects swept toward them, the people with sticks and clubs would stand waiting, drawn up in battle array like an army facing an invader. Also like an army they would dig trenches to block the advance of the locusts. Since locusts can only fly short distances before resting, many of them would light in trenches, like planes landing on refueling bases. As soon as they came down, the people would be on them with sticks and clubs beating and killing. Others would hold woolen bags into which dozens of people would throw the insects, which were then thrown into roaring fires. Still others would excitedly grab up the bugs, take them home and boil them for dinner. In winter and spring, thousands of people were organized to dig up the ground and kill locust eggs. The eggs thus dug up were estimated to weigh nearly three million pounds. During the whole campaign against the locusts, several hundred million labor days were used. In the end, the people won the Insect War and the locusts were defeated.

The years 1941, 1942 and 1943 were the worst in the history of the Border Region, perhaps the worst in the history of North China. That the people were able to emerge victorious with their government and military organizations still intact was probably due mostly to the leadership given by the Communist party. Under orders from the Central Committee of the party, all Communist members and all members of the 8th Route Army became directors of production in the villages. The slogan of the period was "A Good Communist Party Member Is A Good Producer." So soldiers and party workers pitched in with the people, dug canals and wells, plowed the fields, carried water to dried-up fields and took up sticks to beat the locusts. At the same time the rations of party workers, soldiers and government officials were cut in half. Now, instead of two pounds of millet a day, only one pound was allotted to party and government members. Wild plants and leaves were picked in the hills and cooked with the scanty millet ration. Even so, men and women became weak, dizzy, fell down when climbing hills, so that today many of the workers are afflicted with heart disease from overexertion when in weakened condition.

Of all the deeds they accomplished during the eight-year war against Japan, the Communists were perhaps proudest of the way they emerged victorious from these three dark years. Today, they say: "A Good Communist not only has to fight the enemy, but plow and irrigate fields, plant crops, dig wells, eat small rations and fight locusts."

The Communists freely admitted to me that there were desertions from the government, the army and even the party during these three hard years. The second year of the North China famine coincided with a desperate world situation for the United Nations. Stalingrad was nearly in the hands of the Germans. From scanty news published in their mountain newspapers, some few cadres thought the Russians could not hold out. One regiment commander who had been on the famous six-thousand-mile Long March of the Red Army, ten years before, deserted his troops and turned over to the Japanese. The desertion of an officer who had previously stood up so valiantly against every kind of hardship and who was an old party member shocked the leaders of the Border Region. If others followed him there might be a wholesale demoralization of the forces fighting the Japanese in North China.

Party leaders did not try to hide from themselves the dangers inherent in the situation. Some time before, the Central Committee had advocated a new policy of reducing the numbers of the army, simplifying the government and strengthening production. Soldiers released from the army and workers temporarily dismissed from the government could be put to more use in planting, plowing and watering the rain-parched fields. Communist reasoning was simple. During the civil wars against Chiang Kai-shek, as well as during the war against Japan, they had learned that the party could not exist if it left the people. So they decided the party, government and army would have to lighten the people's burden or die.

Besides adopting this economic program, the party carried on intensive work among its cadres to maintain their confidence in final victory. Basic slogans adopted by the Central Committee were carried into the villages and published everywhere, in newspapers, on blackboards and in theaters. The general theme of these messages was: "Democracy Will Win; Fascism Will Fail." Finally in 1943, the party issued a general slogan: "Beat Hitler This Year; Beat The Japs Next Year."

In the meantime, Mao Tze-tung issued secret instructions to all party leaders to make preparations for the worst possible situation. Though it was hard to see how things could possibly get worse, the party prepared for even more disastrous conditions as follows: another famine; no international aid for three more years; the return of the Japs from the Pacific; an anti-Communist attack by Chiang Kai-shek; further desertions from the army and the party. While the party tried to encourage the people and lighten their burden, it harshly told its own cadres to eat bark, to obey directions of the Central Committee and to act as models of frugality for everyone else.

Conditions, however, never reached this last extremity. By 1944, the slogan of the Central Committee of beating Hitler had not been realized, but international conditions had taken a turn for the better and with them conditions in North China also.

The famine was licked and the Japanese mopping-up campaigns had slowed down. The Border Region started a series of partial counter-offensives against Japanese positions. During the Japanese drives, they had learned many new methods of coping with the enemy. Gradually, a few towns and small cities were recovered. Meanwhile, preparations went on for an all-out counteroffensive.

The second stage of the Border Region's war against the Japanese had started with the division of regular army units into small groups so that they would present no large target to the Japanese and could survive. Now the third stage began with the concentration of regulars into larger groups with the intention of building up a sizable striking force. Guerrilla leaders were sent back from the plains and to schools in inaccessible mountain retreats where they were trained in positional and mobile warfare as fought by regular armies.

Hand in hand with the military preparation came a period of political tutelage. In 1943, Mao Tze-tung had directed that every party member must undergo a period of re-education. This was known as the *Cheng Feng* (Correct Wind) Movement. In line with general party directives, Communists in the Four-Province Border Region began to study what should be the relations of the party with the Kuomintang after the Japanese were defeated.

"We also studied the American Communist party," Po Yi-po told me, "so that we would avoid their mistakes."

"You mean," I said, "you studied the attack of Jacques Duclos, the French Communist, on the American Communist party, which led to Earl Browder's being thrown out?"

Po laughed. "Yes, that's what we studied. From it we learned the dangers of an incorrect party policy. If there had been no *Cheng Feng* Movement, we might have been cheated by Marshall's truce maneuvering and surrendered our democracy to the dictatorship of Chiang Kai-shek."

What did Po mean by this statement? As far as I could find out from conversations with him and others in the Border Region, there was such a strong desire for peace throughout the country that the Communist party might have allowed itself to be pushed by popular sentiment into surrendering their arms, in which case they would have found themselves in the same position as other liberals in China, with no freedom, in danger of being jailed and with no voice in the government. In the meantime, thus held captive in the government, all their peasant organizations and local resistance governments would have been completely smashed.

As far as their statements about being "cheated" by Marshall went, I was never able to get from any Communist in the Border Region one clear-cut fact on how they had been cheated. The best answer I could get from anyone was that Marshall was a representative of American policy and therefore could not escape personal responsibility for that policy. If he did not approve of the policy which put him in the curious position of being a mediator between the Communists and Chiang Kai-shek while the American government was supporting and helping Chiang Kai-shek, he should have resigned. As he did not, he could not escape responsibility.

"In this period," he said, "the Chinese Communist party grew from a child to an adult. *Cheng Feng* taught party members to be objective, to be against darkness and ignorance. It taught us to consider the question: Do we dare to win?"

"Do you mean," I asked, "do we dare seize power?"

"No, it was not a question of seizing power. No such period was before us. It was a question of whether we were going to lead the country or whether we were going to be led by Chiang Kai-shek. Finally, *Cheng Feng* taught us that the Chinese Communist party must have its own principles. It was not necessary that we travel the same road as the Soviet Union."

It is not within the scope of this chapter to engage in a polemic discussion; however, a few general comments may not be out of place here.

It seems quite obvious that the Communists had decided before the end of the war with Japan that they could compete on an equal basis with Chiang Kai-shek for power in China. What led them to this belief was not only the tremendous growth in their own strength or the tremendous popular support they had gained in the guerrilla areas, but the almost complete degeneration of economy in Chiang Kai-shek's areas and the gradual dissipation of the political capital with which Chiang had originally entered the war against Japan. The question was, however, not so much one of a personal struggle between Chiang and the Communists, but a struggle between their policies.

Chiang was still upholding the rule of the landlords and village nobles, but the Communists were advocating Dr. Sun Yat-sen's policy of "land to the tiller." In eight years of war, Chiang had neither instituted any effective reforms nor held any popular elections, but the Communists had not only introduced widespread reforms in their areas, but had adopted a policy of elections throughout their villages. Finally, Chiang's printing-press economy was every day becoming more and more tied to the American dollar and native trade and industry was gradually being destroyed. The Communists, on the other hand, had a program of building up a Chinese national industry on a self-sufficient basis.

In short, the Communists believed that Chiang was leading the nation into an inescapable impasse, but more important, they thought the Chinese people would see this and turn against their dictator. Since Chiang, however, still had a reservoir of prestige, especially in the Japanese-occupied areas, there would be no immediate chance of overthrowing him. What could be done was to form a United Front of the Chinese people. This United Front would be different than the one formed against Japan. In that front, the Communists had clearly recognized the leadership of Chiang Kai-shek. Now, however, to recognize that leadership would be to demoralize the people and lose their mass support. Therefore, though willing to make peace with Chiang Kai-shek, they would not subordinate their policies to his. In brief, they had decided that they did, "dare to win."

As far as Soviet Russia went, the Communists, particularly Mao Tze-tung, had long ago come to the conclusion that China could not make a proletarian revolution at the moment since she lacked a large mass of workers to give them a political striking force. Moreover, the Communists were also not sure they wanted to follow the Soviet Union's agrarian path. I was often to be quite astonished while in the Liberated Areas to hear both Communists and non-Communists declare that the Soviet Union had made the peasant the serf of the state. Furthermore, the Chinese Communists were extremely critical of the violence of the Soviet land reform. "We want to avoid that," they would often say to me. "Not only did the Russians make many mistakes, which we don't have to repeat, but also their basic program may not be suited to China."

In the year and a half before the Japanese surrender, preparations for the counterattack went on with increasing acceleration in the Shansi-Hopei-Shantung-Honan Border Region. The regular army was increased from seventy thousand to three hundred thousand. The militia increased to eight hundred thousand. The plan was to make five men out of every hundred of the population a militiaman. The Communist party in the Border Region also became as numerous as the army, increasing its membership to nearly a half a million men (country-wide membership about three million).

In August 1945, when the Russian Red Army invaded Manchuria, the Border Region launched its long-prepared counteroffensive. The plan of the high command of the 8th Route Army was to recover all the important cities of North China and to recapture the Tungpu, Chengtai, Peiping-Suiyuan, Peiping-Hankow and Tientsin-Pukow railways. The first objectives of General Liu Po-cheng's troops, however, were much more limited. They planned to take Taiyuan, Kaifeng, Tuncheng and Shihchiachuang. Thus, they would gain control of Shansi Province and the most strategic points on the Peiping-Hankow and Lunghai railways.

With the slogan: "Push forward to the Japs," General Liu Po-cheng's regular units now moved on the cities while the guerrillas remained behind to mop up. Within a short time, 127 middle- and small-size cities were recovered.

Suddenly, the Japanese surrendered before the power of the atomic bomb. Chiang Kai-shek ordered the 8th Route Army to advance no further. At the same time he got an agreement with Nakamura, Japanese commander in chief in North China, not to surrender to 8th Route Army troops. Finally, scores of puppet troops were overnight declared members of Chiang Kai-shek's army. Yen Hsi-shan, the ancient war lord of Shansi Province, was smuggled back on an armored train by Japanese troops into his capital at Taiyuan, while numerous puppets entrenched themselves in walled towns and cities, waiting for Chiang Kai-shek's troops to arrive.

In the meantime, unknown to the Chinese Communist party, or at least to Communist leaders and their allies in the field, the Soviet Union, a week before V-J Day, signed a treaty of alliance with Chiang Kai-shek. It had always been a nightmare of the generalissimo that after the defeat of Germany the Russians would attack Japan without any understanding with him. He feared that they would then install Chinese Communist guerrillas in power in the wake of their advance into Manchuria. The Kremlin, which seems to have been very skeptical of the postwar possibilities of Mao Tze-tung, chose, instead, to sign a treaty with Chiang which promised to recognize his authority, and his alone, in Manchuria. This treaty, which was not made public until a week after V-J Day, when the 8th Route Army was already on the move toward the cities, forced the Chinese Communists to realize Stalin was committed to support the Kuomintang government. At the same time, MacArthur's headquarters in Japan issued orders that Japanese troops in China should surrender only to the generalissimo, while the United States Navy and Air Force began to transport Chiang's troops to the big cities of Central and North China and Manchuria. These developments completely deprived Mao Tze-tung and his followers of diplomatic support and left them no alternative but to compromise—temporarily.

The Central Committee of the Communist party at Yenan and the leaders of the 8th Route Army immediately decided they could not recover the large cities in North China. Mao Tze-tung issued a statement that the Chinese people after eight years of war needed peace, and ordered the advance of 8th Route Army troops in the field to cease. Then he went to Chungking to confer with Chiang Kai-shek.

In the Shansi-Hopei-Shantung-Honan Border Region at this time, there seems to have been little opposition to Mao's political analysis of the situation and little opposition to the theory that the cities could no longer be recaptured. However, no matter what Mao said or did in Chungking, the leaders and the troops in the Border Region were prepared to beat back any invasion of their area by Chiang Kai-shek's troops. In short, they would not have surrendered the sovereignty of the Border Region to the Kuomintang even at the direction of Mao. There seems to be no doubt on this point, and everyone I talked to about this question—especially non-Communist government officials—declared they would have fought off Chiang's troops no matter what Mao ordered. The war with Japan was now over. There followed a period of armed truce which gradually merged into a civil war.

Looking back on eight years of struggle, Border Region officials were able to congratulate themselves on the following accomplishments.

"From almost nothing," said Po Yi-po, "we built up a new government. It is composed of progressive democrats, enlightened gentry, middle and small landlords, native capitalists and, by law, not more than one-third of Communist party members.

"Through eight long years of war against the Japanese and sometimes against the troops of Chiang Kai-shek, our army has grown from six thousand regulars to three hundred thousand. The militiamen have grown from absolutely nothing to eight hundred thousand.

"Following the Communist party's Agrarian Reform Program, the Border Region has reduced land rent and usurious interest. Out of thirty million farmers, nearly twenty million have become politically self-conscious. Eighty per cent of the people have been emancipated from two thousand years of feudalism. As a result, in this Border Region, the Communist party has become the sole leader of the farmers. A boundless force has been created.

"Finally, paradoxical as it may seem, the standard of 80 per cent of the people has not been lowered despite all the hardships of the Japanese war. This has been due to the redistribution of wealth and to the production campaigns carried out with an intensive vigor, especially during the last two years. Handicrafts have been expanded to a greater extent than at any time since the empress dowager was on the throne in Peking. Landlord and feudalistic capital is being smashed, but commercial, industrial and financial capital is being given preferential treatment. As a result of farm production, capital is rising and not falling.

"We believe all these achievements are so great that they must be safeguarded at all costs, even at the price of civil war, a war which we did not want, but which has been forced upon us."

PART IV

BIRTH OF A GOVERNMENT

❧

14. A Professor Searches His Soul

WHEN I returned to the United States, I was surprised to find that the average American assumed that the war in China was primarily a war between democracy and communism, Chiang Kai-shek representing one side and Mao Tze-tung the other. No one seemed to realize that many Chinese supported the Communists because the Communists were supporting the governments which the people themselves had formed during the Japanese war. Nor did anyone seem to realize that Chiang Kai-shek was losing the war because these people had turned against him for suppressing the very democracy for which he was supposed to stand.

Of course, it was hard for the American people to look on China's civil war in any other manner. Such well-known Americans as Congressman Walter Judd, ex-Ambassador William C. Bullitt, General Claire Chennault and certain prominent members of the Republican party presented the issue in just those lights.

On the other hand, the professional friends of the Chinese Communists went to the other extreme, seeming to believe that a Red soldier merely had to appear in a Chinese village and the peasants would promptly rise up and shout, "Long live the Communist party." Nothing could be more ridiculous.

Somewhere in between these groups were those people who admitted the peasants of China were supporting the Communists, but said it was only because the Communists were sitting on top of them with guns. As a matter of fact, just before I had left Peiping, an American Army officer who had once been in the Communist-led areas of Manchuria voiced just this idea to me.

"You reporters make me sick," he said. "You say the people in the Border Regions like the Communists because they give them freedom and because they allow them to organize their own governments. But how can they say they dislike the Communists when they have a bayonet sticking in their ribs. And what the hell is free or democratic about a government forced on the people by the army?"

This is a serious question and not lightly brushed aside by any gibberish about "proletarian democracy." Yet in wandering about Liberated Area rear lines, I was impressed first of all by the fact that I saw no soldiers of the 8th Route Army anywhere. No army guards hovered before yamen gates, protecting county governments as they did in Chiang Kai-shek's areas, and outwardly, at least, there were no signs that the government was being saved from the supposed wrath of the people by an armed force clamped on them from above.

The second thing that impressed me was that the whole region, save for no man's land, was completely free from bandits and dissident armed farmers that one met so frequently in Kuomintang areas. Travel was so absolutely safe as to be boring. If not an indication of popular government, such conditions pointed at least to a stable government.

Finally, I was surprised to find that of the fifteen or twenty district magistrates I visited nearly all had been schoolteachers before the Japanese war. When the Japs invaded North China and the existing Kuomintang governments fled, these teachers had organized their students, friends and the local farmers into resistance groups which later became local governments. Gradually these coalesced into county, district and regional governments. At this writing, it appears quite probable that these originally primitive groups will form the nucleus of the new national government of China.

That these governments came more under the influence of the Communist party and the 8th Route Army than under the Kuomintang is more a matter of historical development than of armed power. As I discovered, many leaders of the local governments had once followed the Kuomintang and Chiang Kai-shek but had deserted them in favor of the Communists because they found it impossible to fight the Japanese effectively under Kuomintang oppression. The swing of these locally elected leaders to the Communist side for this reason, rather than any Communist arms or Communist propaganda, was one of the big reasons why a full-fledged civil war broke out in China after the defeat of Japan.

I used to wonder while I was in the Liberated Areas how I could possibly explain this phenomenon that had so changed the balance of forces in China and had brought the people of the north over to the Communist side against Chiang Kai-shek. How could I describe the slow disillusionment of men who formerly believed Chiang Kai-shek was the savior of China, yet finally deserted him and went over to the Communists. I could list the bare historic facts as I have done above, but how explain it in more human terms. Then Professor Yang Hsiu-feng, head of the Border Region government, began to tell me something about his life, and as I wrote it down I began to realize that here was not only a personal history, but a record of how the movement against dictatorship in China grew.

I saw quite a lot of Chairman Yang while I was in the Liberated Areas. His government was in a tiny village, about four miles away, up and across a hill, from the village where I lived with the Army. Sometimes, when I had nothing to do, I used to wander over there, hoping he would invite me to dinner— and he always did. Yang had a cook who had been captured from one of Chiang Kai-shek's provincial governors; and though I can't vouch for the cook's political reliability, I can testify that his culinary talents were quite extraordinary. On the spur of the moment from the midst of a peasant's hut, he would whip up five- and six-course dinners that were some of the best I have ever eaten in my life, far surpassing in taste and originality any of the more sumptuous meals for which you had to pay a fortune in Shanghai and Peiping. The cook was particularly expert in eggs, boiling them, rolling them in flour and then baking them. As a matter of fact, he had so many different ways of cooking both eggs and chicken that all the times I was there I don't think he ever repeated himself.

Yang generally just pecked at this delicious food to keep me company, for he had very simple tastes. He dressed in a cotton padded uniform like everyone else in the region, but his shoes were half worn out and patched with leather. He was a rather wizened little man, about fifty, and half deaf, making it very difficult to ask him questions; but since he was a native of Peiping and spoke with a clear Peking accent, it was a pleasure to hear him talk.

One could not always find Yang at home, for it was his custom to mount himself on a donkey and take long trips through the mountains visiting various counties and listening to the complaints of the people. The picture of this frail intellectual, who had traveled widely in Europe and who had once been a highly respected history professor in Peiping— the picture of him jouncing through the mountains like some itinerant friar and dispensing government from the back of a jackass to a crowd of illiterate, suspicious peasants, scarcely emerged from the thirteenth century—this picture, I must confess, always seemed to me highly incongruous. What was this parchment-skinned professor with the quiet voice and the gentle manners doing among a lot of roughneck Communists and former feudal serfs? Why had he, with apparently nothing to gain and everything to lose, suddenly, in middle age deserted to the Communist cause, not as a party member, but as a political ally?

One day we were in his home—a stone affair, for stone was plentiful in these regions—and during dinner and afterward when we sat smoking handicraft-made cigarettes and sipping coarse green tea, Yang began in an unusually quiet, even grave manner to tell me some of his experiences.

"I was forty-one," he said, "when the Japanese invaded China in 1937, and, I suppose, being a history professor, I was even more patriotic than most people. As you probably know, the educated men, representing our higher classes, are so few that there are not many persons who can lead the people in the time of a national crisis. By this you will see how necessary and almost inevitable it was that I should think it my duty to take a particularly active part in the war. All these remarks are only to enable you to understand how I—a middle-aged professor, not a soldier by profession, with little political experience, actuated, I believe, by the highest motives, volunteered my services to the government of Chiang Kai-shek and allowed his military headquarters at Paoting to dispatch me into southern Hopei to arouse our characteristically apathetic, and what I considered ignorant, people to fight guerrilla warfare.

"You may well imagine the surprise engendered in my mind when, on arrival in the guerrilla areas, which Chiang's army had abandoned, I found that the people had already organized several bands of their own and had, with the disappearance of the Kuomintang officials, elected several county governments. Although I was an interloper, I managed to develop some authority with the people, and a year later when thirty counties banded together and formed a Director's Bureau for southern Hopei, I was elected chairman.

"When we had reached this comparatively safe point—safe, at all events, for the moment—the Chiang Kai-shek government, apparently only then realizing for the first time that resistance could exist behind the Japanese lines, suddenly decided to dispatch a Kuomintang member, named Lu Tsung-lin, back to Hopei as governor of the province. This proposal, after they considered that the Kuomintang had let them fight alone for a year, produced such a bad effect on the people that they not only cursed the duplicity of the Kuomintang, but were determined not to recognize Lu as governor.

"I thought it necessary to speak to the people very severely about their attitude. I felt that Chiang Kai-shek was the leader of our country and no matter how bad had been his mistakes in the past, his appointments nevertheless should be honored. After scolding the elected officials in our Director's Bureau all one afternoon, I persuaded them to acknowledge Lu as the governor of Hopei.

"On assuming office, Lu asked me to join his government. I agreed, though making sure that I could continue on with my duties in the Director's Bureau.

"But within a few days, many of Chiang Kai-shek's secret-service men, arriving by foot and mule, began to bring pressure on Lu to abolish the Director's Bureau. Lu called me in and explained his position. While sympathizing with the governor, I had to tell him frankly that I could hardly abolish an organization that the people had formed themselves to fight the Japanese. Anyway, if I tried, the people would not only turn against Lu, but me, too.

"First he demanded that we turn the local guerrilla units into a Peace Preservation Corps. Hardly believing that I had heard him rightly, I answered as calmly as I could: 'If you change these anti-Japanese fighters into provincial guards, you will be destroying their patriotic nature and will ruin their spirit.'

"Next, Lu wanted to change the county magistrates. I opposed this, saying: 'They were elected by the people and they have shown merits against the Japanese. Why demoralize promising young men.'

"Then Lu demanded that all the anti-Japanese associations the people had organized be abolished because they had not been organized under Kuomintang regulations. Wondering how they could have been organized under party regulations when the Kuomintang had not been there when they were formed, I told Lu this measure was reactionary. 'The people,' I said, 'have achieved great things in fighting the Japanese, why should you abolish the very associations they themselves organized to fight the enemy?'

"Finally, Chiang's secret-service men demanded that we abolish the rent reductions and the methods of taxation according to income that the local resistance governments had instituted. Such measures were fundamentally against the common people and these I opposed too.

"After Lu's demands I felt it impossible to go on living as before. Firmly convinced as I was of the righteous nature of the war against Japan, I lost all zest for life after Lu sought to destroy the people's organizations. Only the skeleton of my former enthusiasm remained and the war suddenly seemed to me unexpectedly loathsome.

"Sometimes I thought of giving in to Chiang's secret-service men. I told myself that I would only be compromising my principles temporarily for the national good. But then I was shocked by the thought of how many, like myself, had entered the war with a passionate patriotism, with the love of doing good and of being of service to the people, and had ended up without a bit of good done.

"In my pride I felt that I could no longer compromise on certain points and I determined to maintain an unswerving fight against those who wanted to destroy the patriotic organizations. But I felt myself very much alone in this fight.

"There was a unit of the 8th Route Army not far away, but they did not want to come to my aid. So I had to carry the fight by myself.

"At first, it was not an equal struggle. One day when the Japanese launched an attack near Nankung, I left my office to organize the people in a near-by city for defense. Lu Tsung-lin immediately put up posters, announcing that I had fled and ordering the abolition of the Director's

Bureau. As soon as these posters went up, two hundred representatives of the bureau called a meeting and decided to oppose Lu's order. They reasoned that though Lu had been appointed by Chiang Kai-shek, they had been appointed by the people when none of Chiang Kai-shek's representatives were around.

"However, we did not declare our independence from the Chungking government. We sent telegrams demanding that Lu be replaced, but our telegrams were not answered.

"Since Lu no longer recognized the Director's Bureau, he had to appoint his own county magistrates. For this purpose he called in the troops of General Shih Yu-shan, who escorted the new officials to their offices and guarded them. The people, however, did not recognize these officials and many lawsuits occurred. In the summer of 1939, there were therefore two governments existing side by side, two district magistrates, two county heads and two mayors of each city. Lu and Shih did not recognize the elected government of the people and the people did not recognize the government of Lu and Shih.

"You can imagine how horrified I would have been when I set out from Chiang Kai-shek's headquarters a year or two before to lead guerrilla warfare had I been told that things would reach such an impasse as this.

"I could not have believed it. So I was unprepared for this turn of affairs and did not know just what course to follow. Finally, I wrote down eight Chinese characters and adopted them as my personal guide. 'Co-operate to fight Japanese; improve the people's living.' Whoever opposed this motto, I decided I would fight.

"My ability to fight, however, I guess was mostly in my own mind. I had no force to oppose Shih Yu-shan, whose troops began to kidnap farmers from their homes and drive them into the army. The Director's Bureau sent a note to Shih, saying: 'Tell us how many soldiers you need and we will find them for you. Only stop this kidnaping.' We got no answer. As a consequence, the young men ran away from the villages whenever Shih's soldiers appeared, and it was very difficult to find anyone to fight the Japanese.

"Next, Shih's officials instituted a vicious system of taxation. All coffins were taxed. Vegetables drying on the roofs of the people's homes were taxed. Every time a cow was driven into town, a levy was placed on it. People were forced to contribute gifts to government celebrations. If a kidnaped draftee ran away from the army, his village was fined one hundred suits of cotton clothing to replace the uniform with which the deserter had run off.

"The people petitioned me for help, but I had no force. I felt that I was betraying them. But what could I do? I sometimes felt the 8th Route Army guerrillas near by were too tolerant. I wondered why they did not come and help me. Ineffective and useless to anyone as my life now seemed to me, I felt agitated and irritable. My thoughts would give me no peace. I felt that a terrible situation was developing and I felt powerless to halt it.

"Suddenly, the people took things in their own hands. First they beat up several of Lu Tsung-lin's magistrates. Then they turned on the draft officers of Shih and beat them up, too. Shih sent a representative to me, saying I should control the 'terrible' actions of the people. I answered: 'If you had not oppressed the people so much, they would not be like this now. You are responsible.'

"Since the local guerrilla units supported the local farmers, Shih launched an attack on them, hoping first to wipe them out and then regain control over the people. The guerrillas, however, had good relations with an 8th Route Army battalion in the vicinity and they dared to fight back. So Shih was forced to attack this battalion. Even this did not bring about general fighting, for the 8th Route still remained very tolerant and I must say I sometimes felt annoyed with them.

"It was only when Japanese officers, disguised in the uniforms of Shih Yu-shan's army were found visiting his headquarters that general fighting broke out. Shih was a traitor and had to be attacked. He fled south of the Yellow River and was eventually executed by the Kuomintang. With his military support gone, Lu Tsung-lin, Chiang's appointed governor, also fled. With Lu's departure, his government dissolved and the Director's Bureau became the sole government in southern Hopei.

"The combination of all these events—my own initial pride, my futility, then the brutal attempts to smash the people's organizations and finally the violent reaction of the people—presented itself to me as a profound lesson—vividly, plainly, terribly, and almost as a conversion. What for? Why? What is going on in the world, I had been wont to ask myself with perplexity several times a day. But now all that had previously tormented and puzzled me became clear. I saw it was no longer enough to co-operate with the anti-Japanese elements and I knew I must fight the reactionaries, too. This was the lesson that I, a teacher, in my middle age, had been taught by the people, and it was they who had become the teacher and I the student. This was the profoundest thing I had ever learned in my life: that the true source of knowledge lay in the people's desires and needs and even in their thoughts and hearts. I had to become their servant.

"When I had reached this point in my thinking I was ready to take a further step. I no longer believed that the Kuomintang could lead the war against Japan. I had seen through three hard years of war behind the Japanese lines that the Kuomintang was against the interests of the common people. Perhaps, if in the first place I had been a politician I might not have come to these viewpoints, but I was just a professor with ordinary human feelings and I could not stand what I had seen of the Kuomintang. I was ready to look for new allies against the Japanese. "When the Kuomintang ran away, I found these allies in the 8th Route Army. Since I recognized that the mountains of Shansi on my west could play a great part in helping me fight a war on the plains, I was open to a suggestion that was then made to me that the two areas unite.

"I knew a lot of my former students were in the Taihang Mountains with Po Yi-po and I knew that Jung Wu-sheng who had deserted the government of Yen Hsi-shan was also there. I decided to go over and have a talk with them. After a long journey, I reached the headquarters in the Taihang Mountains and we began to lay plans to form a united government north of the Yellow River."

Yang paused and his eyes and face expressed a fleeting sadness which I could not help remarking.

"I have come—you know—I have come a long way from that professor—well, as you can see—here I am—but what a change—well never mind—"

15. Border Region Bureaucrats

SHORTLY after Professor Yang's journey into Shansi, five hundred delegates from North China, many of whom had come out of guerrilla bands and most all of whom had made perilous trips of many weeks through the Japanese lines, met in the Taihang Mountains and formed a People's Political Council. Yang was elected chairman of this council and Jung Wu-sheng, of whom we shall hear more later, was made vice-chairman.

At this meeting, which lasted forty days, the delegates formally founded the Shansi-Hopei-Shantung-Honan Border Region government and drew up a basic program. This program up to the time of my visit was still the fundamental law of the Border Region. Its main points provided for land reform, taxation according to income, arming of the people, the passage of new marriage regulations, expansion of production and regulations concerning the employment of labor.

According to Yang, the significance of this program at the time lay in the passing of measures that would enable the fight against the Japanese to be carried out most effectively. The arming of the people was forbidden by old law, but "we considered it the highest development of democracy," said Chairman Yang.

"By establishing the equality of man and woman in marriage we broke the hold of feudalism on family life.

"By reducing the rents, we drew the farmers into the fight, but in refusing to meet their demands to divide the land we also prevented the certain alienation of the landlords and the rich farmers.

"Finally, by improving the lot of the workers and at the same time encouraging the development of trade, commercial and industrial capital, we put the war on a sound economic base on which it still exists."

I think Chairman Yang's remarks need several qualifications. There is little doubt in my mind that the Communists have improved the lot of the people in their areas and no doubt at all that they have made tremendous forward strides in giving women equality in marriage. However, though Yang claims it is the fundamental law of the Border Region that land not be divided, this program was entirely abrogated in the middle of 1946 when the Communist party gave directions that landlords' land should be confiscated. It is therefore quite obvious that the government follows Communist policy and that it does not represent the landlords. Therefore, the government which was originally founded to fight a national war has now lent itself to fighting a class war.

The crucial point of this program, however, is the arming of the people. Armed in the Japanese war, these people still possess their arms in the civil war today. This, in a way, is the surest guarantee of their democracy and freedom. Whether or not, in the event that Chiang Kai-shek is defeated, these people will be allowed to keep their arms is a moot question.

The highest political organ in the Border Region, while I was there, was the People's Political Council which was elected by provincial assemblies and which in turn elected Border Region government officials. The political composition of the council, like that of Border Regions elsewhere was fixed by law. No more than one-third of the seats could be occupied by Communist party members; one-third was occupied by representatives of "progressive elements"; one-third by the "middle class."

Under this rule, known as the Three-Thirds System, the Communist party was considered to represent laborers and poor farmers. The "progressives" represented the small merchants, middle farmers, professional people and intellectuals. The "middles" represented the small landlords, merchants and native capitalists.

Lest you get the idea that this government in any way corresponded to American-type government, listen to what Chairman Yang had to say.

"In this government, there is no place for anti-Communists, big landlords or the comprador class. I don't mean the law forbids their holding office or voting. I mean the people just won't elect them. There is a place for Kuomintang members and we have about ten in our standing committee of fifty-one. We have about sixteen or seventeen Communist members. If more than one-third are elected by the people, some Communists give up office to members of another group."

The weak points of this government were obvious. No high court existed and there was no check on the government. The council, however, could impeach the chairman, vice-chairman or any member of the executive branch of the government and cast him out of office by a two-thirds vote.

The Three-Thirds System was also open to question. Border Region officials admitted that some people resigned their party membership so that they might join the government. Also, it appeared obvious that secret party members could get themselves elected to office, if there were any need. Finally, when you came down to fundamentals, this government did not have the controlling power in the Border Region. That was vested in an organization known as the National Salvation Association, which controlled and mobilized the "masses." Of this, more later. It suffices to note here that there was a saying in the Border Region: "The government has the right; the Salvation Association has the power."

The organization of the executive section of the government was perhaps one of the simplest for a government of similar size anywhere in the world. Including the Border Region government, the district, county and village governments, there were only 125,000 men and women on government pay rolls. This number included police, clerks, secretaries, guards, cooks, messengers and mule men in addition to officials.

Of these government functionaries, according to records I saw, 50 per cent were drawn from farmers and laborers; 40 per cent from intellectuals and merchants; 10 per cent from landlords and native capitalists. This was a division roughly equivalent to the division of Chinese society itself.

Of these men, 30 per cent were engaged in administrative work; 20 per cent in the police and law courts; 20 per cent in education; 15 per cent in industry and construction; 10 per cent in work among the masses (land reform, co-operatives, etc.) and 5 per cent in party work. About 90 per cent of these officials could read.

The simple organization of the government was quite a contrast to the top-heavy Kuomintang bureaucracy. For example in the Finance Bureau of the Border Region government there were only sixteen men. Under the Kuomintang in Shansi Province, the Finance Bureau had about 250 members.

The whole number of cadres (they don't like to be called officials) in the central Border Region government only totaled 160 people. One-third of these I found living in the villages near me. The rest were out in the districts, looking into land reform, tax collections and carrying on research.

While I was in the Liberated Areas, Chairman Yang himself made three trips into the countryside within a six-month period. One of these trips he made on mule for two months through the impoverished areas of the Taiyueh Mountains. On such trips Yang wandered around comforting troops, conversing with peasants, studying land reform and, in general, trying to find out whether the laws of the government were effective or should be changed.

These trips had little in common with the baby-kissing junkets of American politicians. Nevertheless, there seemed to be some attempt to impress the local people with the goodness of their government.

"We cannot let the people look on us as different from themselves," said Yang, whose attitude might appear a little too sickish sweet to American politicians, but would find favor among missionaries. "When we go out on the road, we carry grain tickets and cook our own meals. Sometimes, our officials eat worse than the poorest farmers."

When traveling, a government official carried his own bedroll on his back. Seeing this or seeing the patched shoes worn by Chairman Yang, the people got the impression that Border Region officials were somehow different than Kuomintang officials.

Government functionaries had no fixed salaries. They received a ration of twenty-five ounces of grain and three and a half cents a day for vegetables plus a subsidy of three cents a month. Every two years they were given a suit of padded cotton clothing. Cooks, mess attendants, mule men and carters were given an extra suit as their clothing wore out more quickly.

Rent was free to government workers. Three or four functionaries generally lived together in the room of a peasant's house. Although many higher officials lived with their wives, I found that the local officials seldom lived with their families because the grain ration was insufficient to support them. As a consequence, wives and children lived in the ancestral village with in-laws.

Life for a government official in Communist areas was hard and material rewards nonexistent. Opportunities for the time-honored Chinese squeeze simply did not exist. Ordinarily, this might mean that the best brains in the community would not be attracted to government work. However, government members who had originally plunged into official work in order to fight the Japanese remained contented with their small salaries and hard life because they hoped to be recompensed with responsible positions after the victory over Chiang Kai-shek.

I found a small number of government functionaries, particularly among the cooks and mule men, depressed over their dreary living conditions. Higher officials tried to overcome this feeling by teaching them to read and write and broaden their horizons.

Although Communist policies dominated the Border Regions, workers and farmers did not occupy the highest government positions which were almost solely monopolized by literate intellectuals.

Professor Yang was at great pains to point out to me that the intelligentsia had far greater opportunities in the Liberated Areas than the proletariat. The government was continually trying to obtain technicians from the outside world, holding out a subsidy of thirteen hundred pounds of grain a year as lure to all who might want to desert Chiang Kai-shek. University professors who came over from Peiping received a salary of about two hundred American dollars a month which was far more than the Kuomintang paid and of course many times the salary of a regular Border Region official or a Communist cadre. Such preferential treatment of the intellectual merely highlighted the Communists' desperate need for educated men.

An outsider like myself used to wonder how the Border Region could run a government staffed for the most part with officials who had no previous experience. Yang, who up to the age of forty-one was a professor, of course, is a case in point. How could he govern thirty million people without having had any previous experience himself and with a staff equally ignorant of the art of government?

The answer Yang gave me to this question is in a way an answer to those Kuomintang theoreticians who used to declare that the people must be taught democracy, but never said who was going to teach the teachers.

"I am just like a student," Yang told me, "maybe in his first year of middle school. We have no bureaucratic skill. Maybe that is damn hard to learn. The Kuomintang used to laugh at the simple documents of my Director's Bureau. But after a while they thought their simplicity was pretty good. In our courts we go on the same way. Our judges write out simple decisions on slips of paper.

"I feel that the greatest obstruction to my governing well is that I can't get as close to the people as necessary. Sometimes I am too bureaucratic.

"For example, in 1942 we abolished foot binding. We issued an order and adopted a slogan: 'Emancipate feet.' The family of any woman with bound feet was fined. Such bureaucratic methods were not effective. So we canceled the order and adopted propaganda methods and the people emancipated their feet by themselves.

"In 1941, we carried out compulsory education, but this was an intellectual, bureaucratic approach. Parents were too poor to send their children to school and needed their children's labor in the fields. So we abolished that order, too, and tried to better the living of the parents while doing away with the school fee."

In these last ten years, Yang has not only learned something about government, but his whole personal philosophy of life has begun to change.

"An intellectual from an old society finds it hard to work in a new one," he told me.

"When I was fighting guerrilla warfare I thought it better for the government to live in big yamens. Now I find it much more effective to live in this simple house because I am closer to the people that way.

"Before the Japanese war I did not wish to engage in politics. But now I think without political work nothing else is possible.

"A long time ago I was a student in France and I used to enjoy looking at the pictures in the Louvre. But now I've changed. I no longer believe in 'art for art's sake.' "

As this sounded like Marxist doctrine, I asked Yang why he did not join the Communist party.

"If you say I am not good enough to be a Communist, I have no words with which to answer you. But if you say do you want to be a Communist, I can only say I want to try. You can call me a non-party Bolshevik."

"Then is it true," I asked Yang, "that your government is a puppet of the Communist party?"

Yang looked up angrily. "We invite anyone who says that we are puppets of the Communists to come here and see for themselves. If they mean that we are carrying out the program of the Communist party in every major sphere, if they mean we welcome capitalists,[1] back up the land reform and believe in democracy, then they may say we are puppets.

"But the proper way to put the question is whether the Communist party's policy is right for the people. The only way to evaluate any program is on its worth to the people. Our government stands for service to the people. Any visitor who does not like such service need not come here.

"If you want a proper answer to your question," concluded Yang, "you may say we are puppets of the people."

16. Village Democracy

Two revolutionary phenomena have had profound effects on village government in the Communist areas. Land reform by turning the landlords out of village office has killed the peasant's ancient dread of govern-

[1] Present Chinese Communist policy is to eliminate feudalism, encourage capitalism. Landlords are treated ruthlessly, merchants, traders, businessmen and "native capitalists" are encouraged to expand their holdings and get rich. There is, as yet, no abolition of private property.

ment. He no longer regards it with the terror and dismay of the old days. Before his very eyes the peasant has seen village rulers topple from their thrones. Government to him is no longer an invincible force, above, aloof and beyond control.

On the other hand, guerrilla warfare, which often brought the Communist cadre into the peasant's hut seeking refuge, has developed in the farmer a new sense of nearness and familiarity with government. Government has become something close to earth that the peasant can touch, shake by the hand or even slap in the face. Gone are its external trappings, the awe-inspiring uniforms, the fur-lined silk gowns of the officials, the men bearing arms before austere yamen gates. In the villages, the officials dress in cotton jackets and pants like peasants, they talk like peasants, live like peasants. They are mainly peasants. There is nothing about them to distinguish them from anyone else. Nor are they any longer addressed as Officer, Old Master or even Elder Born. Why should they be? They were elevated to office by the votes of the peasants themselves.

But what a strange thing this "new democracy" is! The backward peasant is ill equipped to cope with this instrument that has suddenly been thrust into his hands. Formal, stilted, sometimes even farcical are his village elections. Yet they are going on everywhere in rural areas under Communist control.

When the Communists take over a village from the Kuomintang, they do not immediately start elections and generally do not disturb the village chiefs. But shortly after the land reform and as soon as conditions have settled down, every villager is registered and examined on his right to vote. Any man or woman over eighteen, not insane and not a traitor during the Japanese war, is qualified to vote. The list of all those registered is placed on the bulletin board on the village street. The names of qualified voters are written in black; those unqualified, in red.

An election committee then divides the village into sections according to the points of the compass and each section elects a set of candidates and one or two reserves. The week before election is utilized for campaigning. Candidates generally do not campaign on party platforms, but on individual platforms.

During the Japanese war a typical candidate's plank ran something like this:

    1. I promise to lead you in the fight against the Japanese and get revenge against our village.

    2. I shall lead you in production so that we will be well fed and clothed.

    3. I promise to make your children healthy.

    4. I will organize the militia and guarantee public safety.

Today in the civil war, a campaign promise goes like this:

1. I will protect the results of the overturning movement.
2. I will help us fight effectively against Chiang Kai-shek.
3. I will establish good winter schools.

Pre-election speeches often reflect a struggle between the rich and the poor in the villages.

"If our man is elected," said an old woman in a Shantung village, "there will be more equal distribution of the burden of the village. Our man will maintain public safety, get education for the children and get us profits from production."

A supporter of an ex-landlord, however, spoke in this manner.

"Although our candidate was a landlord, he is a good man. In the past he lent you money at low interest. If he is elected, he will do even better."

Campaign speakers used hand megaphones to draw crowds, went from house to house soliciting votes and published favorable comments on their candidate on the village bulletin board. Although they had few soap box orators, sometimes villagers mounted rollers on the threshing grounds so that everyone could see and hear them. The campaign meetings were not violent, but there were arguments in which words like the following might be distinguished: "Your candidate is no good." "You are a running dog of the landlords." "You are a loafer." And so on.

When the day of election came, the people gathered in the voting place, usually in the schoolhouse or the local temple. The methods of casting votes, due to the inability of many voters to write, were varied and numerous.

One method was to use bowls of different colors, each bowl representing a candidate. Into the bowl representing his choice, the voter put a bean given him by the election committee. In this kind of election, all voters were warned not to bring their own beans. There was a variation of the bowl voting which was more secret. In this type the voter was handed a number of different colored beans, which he placed one by one under overturned bowls set before each candidate. Only one of the beans, say—the red one—however, counted as a vote. The candidate with the most red beans won.

Another method was to put large pieces of paper on a wall with one candidate's name on each paper. The voter, armed with a burning incense stick, approached the papers and, like someone aiming a dart at a target, burned a hole in the paper bearing the name of the candidate of his choice. The candidate with the most holes won in this kind of election.

In another system, all the candidates' names were put on one huge piece of paper and the voters came and drew a circle under their choice.

There was also voting by ballot. One type of ballot was merely a blank piece of paper with the seal of the village office chopped on it. The voter wrote his candidate's name on this ballot and put it in a box. The other kind of ballot gave all names and the voter put a mark beside the one of his choice.

As soon as the voting is finished, votes are counted by an election committee. The result is declared orally at once. Then the list of the successful candidates is put on the wall.

When a village head is elected, the villagers present him with a wreath of red paper flowers. A troop with gongs and drums serenades him at home. When he steps out of doors to greet his well-wishers, he is often placed on a bamboo pole and carried around the town. This pole is known as the Solitary Dragon Pole, signifying that the candidate is the only dragon, or the big noise, in the village now.

The establishment of village democracy was not at all as simple and easy as it sounds. Because communications were poor it took some time to get around to all the villages and institute popular elections. There was little trouble in getting the people to vote, for it was something new in the drab life of the Chinese farmers. At first, everyone was so interested in elections that generally 80 to 90 per cent of a village voted in the first election. Later, when the novelty wore off, some people were apt to begrudge the time they spent in voting as so much labor time lost from their fields.

Because villagers had no long traditions of democracy, they often thought their duty finished when the election was over, and didn't supervise their officials. Also, the lack of trained personnel was a handicap in carrying on local government, for the majority of those governing the Border Region had no past experience in administrative affairs. The officials could only learn through doing.

In a district of Shansi a magistrate wanted to arouse the people to carry on land reform, but did not know just how to go about it. So he called a meeting of all his staff members and ordered one to take the part of a landlord, another the part of a middle class farmer, another a usurer, another a poor farmer and so on. Then they held an informal play and carried on an experiment on how to get in touch with the people.

New officials also had little experience in writing official letters or documents. For example, according to old Chinese official practice, it is customary to address a superior in one way and an inferior in another. Some officials turned these around and wrote to their subordinates: "My exalted Sir," and to their superiors: "I order you."

These were some of the minor everyday difficulties in establishing democracy in a country that has known little of it. But there were more serious problems, too.

Just as in American cities, the villages in the Liberated Areas were sometimes plagued with bosses. Most of these bosses were a hangover from China's feudal society. During the Japanese war, the Communist party did not divide the land and as a consequence the landlords, retaining the economic power in the villages, also retained the political power. Thus in a small village of four hundred people the village chief would continue to be a landlord, while in a larger village of one thousand people he might either be a landlord or one of his agents.

When the elections were first introduced into the villages, the landlords got themselves voted into office merely by threatening to foreclose on peasants' land or threatening to drive sharecroppers from their estates. As the farmers grew more conscious, the landlords used more subtle methods, employing village bullies to scare the voters, placing their agents in strategic vote-counting positions or stuffing the bowls of their candidates with beans.

Such malpractices are described in much detail by Chao Hsu-li, the most popular writer in the Liberated Areas, in his novel the *Ballads of Li Yu-tsai*. The hero of the novel, Li Yu-tsai, is an old shepherd who for years has amused himself and his cronies by making up ballads about the people in his village. When the 8th Route Army announces to the people in Li's village that they have democracy now and should elect their own officers, the village landlord, Yen Heng-yuan, is immediately elected village chief. Every year there is an election, but every year Yen is voted into office. To lampoon these conditions, the Shepherd Li makes up the following verse:

> Hooray for Yen, our village chief, who towers all above us;
> By all the years you've been our boss, it's plain to see you love us,
> Ten autumns now, the polling place has seen the folk in action:
> And each election proves once more that Yen's the big attraction.
> Yet times are getting harder now and labor we'd be saving,
> So I suggest we have your name cut on a wood engraving.
> Each voter then, instead of writing out the famous name,
> Can simply use the chop and the results will be the same.
> Then Yen, who's always first, can take the damn thing home and save it.
> For it will be a hundred years before we re-engrave it.

Embarrassed by Li's ballads, the landlord gives up office, but manages to have one of his own henchmen elected. Thus things continue as before, for the new village chief is at the beck and call of the old. To portray these new conditions the shepherd again makes up another ballad about the landlord and his stooge, the village chief.

Gleefully, the village poor begin to recite Li's ballads. Fearing the shepherd's influence the landlord directs the village chief to exile him from the village. Li is forced to take up an abode in the mountains, but his songs remain in the hearts of the people and eventually they throw the landlord out of office and vote their own man in. Li Yu-tsai comes back to the village and commemorates the victorious election with another ballad.

A simple story? Yes. Propaganda? To be sure. But it is a critical propaganda, propaganda for a noble purpose; for in telling how one village fought against the suppression of democracy, Chao Hsu-li has shown other villages how they, too, can fight off their oppressors and gain democracy. And more—he shows the people how they must fight for equality with their own weapons; they can't just take democracy as a gift from the Communists or the 8th Route Army.

It would be idle to suppose that a perfect form of government exists in Liberated Area villages. And it would be both presumptuous and untrue to think that either the 8th Route Army or the Communist party could come in overnight and found on the ruins of feudalism, a democratic form of government equal to that known in western Europe or America. A low level of culture and a primitive economy must doom the country to backward political forms for a long time to come. However, the lack of experience cannot excuse the Communists for many things they have done in local elections. In many cases, they rode rough shod over elections, with little deference to the wishes of the people. By elevating those who were most active in the land-reform campaigns, they also gave ambitious hooligans the chance to take power. The very fact that in some villages the various planks of all candidates contain a resolution to "Support the Communist party and follow Mao Tze-tung" illustrates clearly enough that the Communists are trying to establish not so much a utopian democracy as a support for themselves. To expect them to do otherwise, in the midst of a war and revolution, however, would be ridiculous. Most of the Communists I talked to on this point were quite frank about their need to create a firm base of support. The so-called liberal and intellectual supporters of the Communists, however, always took great pains to assure me that every village was ruled by the men the people wanted. Such statements are ridiculous. I found not a few villages where the people hated their local officials. I met a farm girl who was very much in love with the Communist party because the party saw to it that women got freedom of marriage and equal rights with men. But this same girl, unlike many who rush to the new power, told me: "I wouldn't marry a cadre. They're all too ambitious. They don't care about the people." You could, of course, find just as many girls on the other side of the fence.

But no matter how distant they may be from a perfect democracy, no matter how exaggerated have been the claims of their misguided friends, the Communists have taken a gigantic step forward awakening millions of Chinese peasants to their rights to elect the men who shall govern them. And surely when a village of five hundred people is governed by the edicts of 150 men and women in the Farmers Association instead of by the whim of one powerful landlord, it must be considered to have taken a mighty progressive step. Despite all the rumors that were circulated about their society, certainly, as far as I saw, the villages in the

Liberated Areas had achieved a form of government so far superior to that practiced in Kuomintang areas that there was no comparison.

The Kuomintang and Chiang Kai-shek always insisted that the people of China were not ready for democracy and that they must undergo a period of tutelage. Leaders in the Liberated Areas scoffed at that theory.

"It is utterly useless to train people for democracy beforehand," Jung Wu-sheng, vice-chairman of the Border Region government, told me. "If the people lead a democratic life, their habits will naturally be transformed. Only through the practice of democracy can you learn democracy."

17. A Beggar Writer

PROPERLY speaking, he doesn't belong in this section of the book on government. But since he walked into my room unannounced, he will have to walk into these pages the same way.

It had been snowing since dawn and I was sitting inside my stone-floored home, feeling blue and lonely, when he came in from the outside —a spectral-looking figure in a long cotton padded gown with a skullcap on his head. Bowing like an old-fashioned schoolteacher, he seated himself on a stool in front of my pan of burning charcoal and greedily warmed his hands. Shivering all the while, he raised his eyes to mine, bent them down again, picked up a watermelon seed from my table, spit it out expertly between his teeth, looked at me tentatively for a moment, then smiled in an embarrassed sort of way. A very shy man! I thought.

But this self-effacing creature who had come to warm his hands at my fire was possibly—outside of Mao Tze-tung and Chu Teh—the most famous man in Communist areas. In fact, he was well known all over China. His name was Chao Hsu-li and he was a writer—the same writer whose verse I have quoted in the last chapter.

I spent two enjoyable days with Chao, but I do not think I ever understood him. He was a peculiar man and he had lived a strange life. Unlike Professor Yang, who came over to the Communists primarily for political reasons, Chao turned toward the 8th Route Army because he had become an outcast in the old feudal society of China. His life, perhaps more than that of Professor Yang, illustrates why the rural intellectuals are turning away from Chiang Kai-shek toward the Communists.

Chao was born in a small town in the Taiyueh Mountains in Shansi, the second son of a poor farmer. With eight family members living off less than three acres of land, he had to scramble hard for his food, foraging in the pits for stray pieces of coal in the wintertime and sweating on the land the rest of the year.

Chao was a boy of insatiable curiosity, who was especially interested in drama and music. At an early age, he learned to beat drums, clang cymbals, clap sticks, blow the flute and sing old-fashioned drama so well that the adults in his village let him become a member of the Eight Sounds Association. Such training stood him in good stead when he later came to write plays for the 8th Route Army.

Chao's grandfather, who was a scholar, gave Chao an education in the classics and also persuaded him to believe in the Three Sects Faith —a religion composed of Buddhist, Taoist and Confucian elements which stressed the doing of good as the means of acquiring a fortune. Chao kept a record of his good and bad deeds, putting white beans in a jar for the former and black for the latter. Repairing bridges and roads counted three white beans and burying human bones two. Bad deeds consisted of being disloyal, unfilial, gaining advantage at the expense of others or burning incense in front of the ancestral tablets without first washing your hands. Chao always had more white beans than black.

Because he believed that the road to position and power was still scholarship, as it had been in the days of the recently overthrown empire, Chao's father sent him to primary school. The school curriculum was still based on the Confucian classics, and Chao, due to his grandfather's patient drills, always stood at the head of his class. He had not the money to go to middle school, but entered a normal school which paid part of his board and keep. Here, from books in the school library, he learned for the first time about the modern world outside his mountains and something about Western countries, including stories of George Washington, the French Revolution and the industrial age. He found some translations of Turgenev and Ibsen and greedily devoured them.

In the meantime, Chao's parents betrothed him to a girl of fourteen, whom he dutifully married. Just as dutifully, he slept with his bride for a few days, then went back to school. After two years, he became a leading figure in a group of twenty students with "advanced thoughts" who believed the curriculum contained too much classical nonsense and not enough science. These rebels accused the principal of raising money to build a science hall, and then "squeezing" so much that there was only a bare room with a few chairs and a table, and absolutely no equipment. In the ensuing scandal, the principal was ousted, but the new principal, evidently acting under instructions from the headquarters of Warlord Yen Hsi-shan, threw Chao and five other students out of school, accusing them of being Communists.

That was in the year 1927, just after the split between Chiang Kai-shek and the Reds at Shanghai. To be called a Communist in the China of those days was even worse than to be called a Communist in the United States of today. And Chao, who had never met a Communist, never read one of their pamphlets or books and had no idea of what Communism meant, had no other course but to return home.

For a while he worked on the farm, then taught monks, then became a teacher in a primary school whose principal was a landlord and the local usurer. About three or four nights every week, peasant debtors, bearing gifts of meat and wine, would feast the principal in the schoolrooms, trying to persuade him not to foreclose on their land. These parties sometimes lasted till three o'clock in the morning, with the result that the principal never showed up for his classes until afternoon. The teachers, becoming demoralized, took to smoking opium.

About this time, Chao's wife died and he went home to bury her. A day after the funeral, agents of Warlord Yen Hsi-shan arrested him and shipped him off to the provincial capital at Taiyuan where he was thrown with a number of students into a special jail for Communists.

In exchange for their freedom, prison officials asked Chao and the others to write some articles against Communism. Chao and his fellow-students were at a loss. None of them had the faintest knowledge of Communism. Cynically the jailers threw some Communist pamphlets in the cell. "Here," they said, "this is Communism. Write something against it."

The jailer might better have thrown Chao the key to his cell. For the pamphlets, though they didn't open the door to freedom, unlocked the boy's soul. "I was attracted," he told me, "by the Communists' vigorous denunciation of the old feudal society of China and their call to build a new one. To me who had felt strangled in the old traditions, their doctrines made sense." So the young outcast lay in jail, starving in body, but feasting his mind.

After a long investigation, Chao was freed. He had never met a Communist, but now, due to cruel treatment and due to the reading matter with which his own jailers had furnished him, he had become a sympathizer. He looked for a real flesh-and-blood "Red bandit," but could find none. Gradually, his thoughts took on a tinge of despair.

Unable to find a teaching job, he became a "beggar writer," doing two weekly newspaper columns for fifty cents a thousand words. His articles were about vagabond characters who ate one day and starved the next, and they contained veiled hints about the bad conditions in society. "I wrote what I knew about," said Chao, "but I could not speak out freely and my style was cramped. Worst of all, I could not make a living." One of the papers, whose editor had written an article criticizing Yen Hsi-shan, was suppressed, and Chao, reduced to penury, went back to the farm. His father was very angry at his failure. Chao replied:

"It's not my fault. If society as a whole changes, then our family fortunes will change. Otherwise, our family will remain destitute."

"My father didn't give a damn for my sayings," said Chao. "He thought I ought to marry again. I didn't care at all about my personal life; it meant nothing to me one way or the other. But the family needed someone to do the housework, so when he suggested marriage, since I had no plans for myself, I just relaxed and let him choose me another wife. I suppose it was a helpless attitude to take, but I couldn't find any other attitude in that ancient society."

Shortly after his marriage, Chao left home again to become a clerk in a friend's bookstore in Kaifeng south of the Yellow River. Here, he hoped to find a measure of economic security, but Chiang Kai-shek's officials, soon after his arrival, broadened the street on which the store was located and tore it down. In despair, Chao started back home.

Now, at this point there occurred one of those amazing incidents which are hard for a Westerner to believe, but which are nevertheless typical enough of the background of Chinese life and explain some of the sources of actions of ordinary Chinese people. On the way home, Chao was halted at the Yellow River bridge by policemen who inspected his bedroll which contained a towel, a basin, a piece of soap and four silver dollars. After this inspection, Chao passed on, halting at a village inn for the night. While lying in bed, he heard four men talking outside his window in a cryptic form of speech used only by members of secret societies. His curiosity aroused, he listened further and was amazed to hear someone speak about the man who had come from Kaifeng with four silver dollars. He concluded the men must be bandits who had obtained their information from the police. Afraid of being kidnaped, he remained in bed three days, smoking a very cheap grade of opium and trying to give the impression he was too poor to be worth the notice of bandits.

His actions, however, aroused the suspicion of the four men and they followed him back to Taiyuan where Chao, very nervous by this time, took up residence with a friend on the campus of Taiyuan University. At night, Chao started to tell his friend about his experiences. Suddenly there was a loud and peremptory rapping on the wall of the room next door. Chao closed his mouth in fright. In the succeeding days, he tried to speak again, but each time there was a rapping and Chao concluded the "clique" men thought he had discovered some of their secrets and were warning him to keep quiet.

It is a remarkable commentary not only on Chinese society, but also on the humbleness and perhaps misguided generosity of Chao's soul, that at this moment, certain he would be tortured or killed, not caring much about his poor life anyway, but above all not wanting to involve his friend in his troubles—at this moment, Chao determined to commit suicide. Without saying a word to anyone, he threw himself in the lake at Taiyuan.

Someone fished him out, and he regained consciousness in the police station, later returning like a whipped dog to the room of his friend. Immediately, the secret society, which had vague connections with Chiang Kai-shek's Special Service Section, spread rumors around the college that Chao was insane and at the same time induced a newspaper to print an article to that effect. The student body was in an uproar, with everyone demanding that Chao's friend get rid of that "crazy man." Feeling his life was doomed anyway and remembering his early religious training not to cause others harm—but to do only good deeds—Chao still made no attempts to deny that he was insane. When an agent of the secret society told his friend that he had a place where Chao could be cured, he meekly allowed himself to be led away.

The agent took him to a barren glen in the hills, swarming with refugees, beggars and bandits, which was known as the Manchurian Tombs. The bandits put Chao up at the home of a baker. "He's a very good cook. You'll like it here with him," they said. With a great show of friendliness, the baker made special bread and cakes for Chao. They were delicious but had a funny smell about them. In a few days, Chao's gums began to bleed. He was convinced he was being fed arsenic. "They used a chemical that decreased the power of the poison," said Chao. "They wanted to kill me slowly so there would be no traces." Every time he ate a funny-tasting cake, the baker would make a record in a notebook. "That's right, eat well," he would say and smile at Chao encouragingly.

The bandits had a secret language of their own. When they were going to kill someone, they said: "A daughter is going to be married." When they fed Chao poison, they indicated the amount by saying to each other: "The price of cotton is ten cents" or "the price of wheat is thirty cents," depending on how much arsenic was in the cakes that day.

Chao had no hope for life and kept on eating. He grew weaker every day, but said nothing. His apathetic stoicism amazed the bandits. They decided such a hopeless man was not worth killing, so one day when they were moving to another headquarters, they let Chao go.

When Chao returned from the Manchurian Tombs, a friend found him a job in a rural normal school. It was just before the Japanese invasion. Patriotic feelings ran high among the intellectuals of Shansi, but Yen would allow no demonstrations or any public anti-Japanese propaganda. Chao now found a real reason for his defiance of the rulers of Chinese society and he also found allies. Every afternoon, Chao and two of his fellow-teachers would lock the gates of the schoolyard and hold forbidden anti-Japanese meetings.

When the Japs invaded China, Chao joined a Sacrifice League organized by Po Yi-po and took to the mountains. He soon found himself alone and deserted in the countryside. All Yen's magistrates had fled and he decided he would become a district officer himself. But his first three days in office, he could find no one to govern. The people had fled to forests and were hiding in caves. Terror-struck at the wild anarchy existing in the retreating army of Chiang Kai-shek, they would not return home. With trembling determination, Chao went among the soldiers who were digging frantically in the ground for the peasants' hidden food stocks. They felt like murdering all the farmers because they had fled. Talking gently, applying some classical maxims, but with his heart in his throat, Chao persuaded the soldiers not to break up any more furniture for firewood and to stop searching for grain. "If you do that," he said, "the people will come back and find it for you." In this manner, he brought people and soldiers together and began to forget his personal troubles.

For two years, he wandered as a guerrilla official, and finally hooked up with the 8th Route Army as a propaganda writer. He liked this job because it gave him a chance to tell soldiers and people to act kindly toward each other and he liked the 8th Route Army because it seemed to him close to the poor people and close to his own life. In 1940, the army established a newspaper and Chao joined the staff. Japanese attacks split the staff in two and for the next four years, Chao was constantly on the run, sometimes writing, sometimes fighting, but never feeling degraded as he had in his days as a "beggar writer." Toward the end of the Japanese war, he had more leisure and began to write a literary column of novelettes and short stories. One of his stories, "The Marriage of Little Black Boy," about a girl and boy who struggled against their parents and their whole village to marry freely, attracted the attention of the Border Region government which published it in book form. This was the beginning of a creative period which resulted in Chao's turning out half a dozen books and a number of plays within the space of a year. It was also the beginning of a fame that soon spread over all the Liberated Areas and then into Chiang Kai-shek's areas where such noted writers as Kuo Mei-jo, Mao Tun and others hailed him as the leader of a new literature.

Chao received no royalties from the sales of his books. To me it seemed that he was little better off than he had been before. I told him so. Chao was amused. "Do you know what it means to be 'a beggar writer' in China? Before the war, you could not get a book published without paying for it. Most authors pay publishers in China, not the other way around. If you had no money, you didn't get published, nor could you ever get anything published about the mass movement. But now the government helps me to publish the very things I want to write about. Furthermore, why should I want to profit in times like these? As there are volunteer soldiers, so are there volunteer culture men. That is why I write plays for the people on a strictly volunteer basis.

"But my material life is also much better than it was before. Besides writing, I also work as an editor in the Border Region Book Publishing Company. We have our own production organization, spinning, weaving, farming and so on, and everyone shares in the work and shares in the proceeds. From the company I get twenty-five ounces of millet a day, a half a catty [little over half a pound] of vegetables and some money for medicine because I am in bad health. I get one cotton padded winter garment and one summer suit every year. Before the war I had only a thin blanket and a few unpadded garments so that I was always cold. Before, I could never sit by a fire, but now I have my own charcoal to burn. Besides, the company gives me enough money for my daughter to go to school. And my wife can raise vegetables and make a pair of shoes a week. She gets the material for five hundred dollars and sells the shoes for two thousand. Such production was impossible before the war because we were overwhelmed with cheap Japanese goods. So now, having almost no burdens, I can devote myself more freely to writing."

Chao, however, had no romantic ideas about becoming a great author, nor did he want to devote all his time to writing. That would take him out of contact with people. "I must join social life," he said. "I want to follow the stages of the revolution. Now, the most important thing is the land reform. Later, it will probably be industrialization. We will need to develop co-operatives and will need American machinery, so I want to go to America. I have the ambition to write big things, and maybe when the civil war is over I will settle down and just do nothing but write for a while. But never will I completely divorce myself from the people.

"Maybe," he said, "some people would find my books boring. Before the war against Japan, authors wrote books about the love of the *petite bourgeoisie*. Such authors are not interested in describing the revolution going on among our farmers. If I tell these people to write books of a political nature, they might be very unhappy and think they were being restricted. But I, who grew from a village, feel no restrictions here. I write exactly as I please. I could not do that before.

"Since I write for village people, I write novels and plays. Formerly I did not use the same language I do now and I had a small circulation among a few intellectuals. Then I began to think that the only books available to farmers were extremely reactionary, teaching them to respect idols, devils and ghosts and to be generally superstitious so that they were at the mercy of witches. I thought I must give these peasants a new knowledge and also entertain them, so I began to write in their own language. I have a standard for the words I use. Whenever I write a line, I read it to my parents, who are farmers, without much education. If they cannot understand it, I change it. I go around to the bookstores and ask what kind of people buy my books, so I can learn if I am reaching a big audience. Since thousands of our farmers can't read I write plays that can be performed for them. Then, sometimes I rewrite these into novels for those who can read. As a result, my writings which previously fell into the hands of only a few literati now are well known among even the poor."

As for Chao's technique, he said he did not like to center a story around just one person, but liked to delineate a whole village and a whole period. For his characters, he made them composites of many people he had known. To find such people he went down into the villages, lived with the farmers, worked in their fields, joined their co-operatives and struggled with them in the land reform.

I translated three of Chao's books. One was about village elections; another about freedom of marriage; a third about wartime life in a village; a fourth called *Fu Kwei* was about a village bum who became a good man during the "overturning" movement. In such a Tolstoyan theme of redemption, one notes traces of Chao's early religious training. However, instead of God reforming man, it is the revolution that does so.

Frankly, I was disappointed in Chao's books. I had heard, if translated, they would make him one of the world's leading literary figures. I cannot agree. His books contained no propaganda. I saw no mention of the Communist party. His descriptions of village life were charming, his humor piquant, his verses highly original and some of his characters were salty. But the plots were mere outlines, the characters often bare types labeled with a name, but possessing no personality, and none of them were fully developed. Worst of all, his stories dealt with outlined events and not with actually felt emotions. Those deep passions which I found out from personal experience were stirring the whole Chinese countryside found no record in his pages.

However, to apply Western critical standards to a Chinese writer, especially one who is not only writing but editing, working on the farm, taking part in the land reform and a half a dozen other movements, would be academic in the extreme. I feel that when the war is over and Chao has more time, he will produce important works and ones that might even interest a Western reader.

PART V

BORDER REGION SOCIETY

❧

18. Death and Taxes

DURING the summer and autumn of 1941, while walking through Honan and Hupeh provinces, from the Yellow River to the Yangtze River, I witnessed the beginnings of that catastrophic famine which has been described in an earlier chapter of this book. It was depressing to walk along the road day after day and see desolate land, fallow fields and empty houses, tumbling with decay. Since, in many places, there had, as yet, been no severe drought, I was puzzled to know why the fields had been abandoned. Then peasants told me they had left their ancestral plots because Kuomintang tax collectors and requisition agents for Chiang Kai-shek's armies were demanding more grain from them than the land could possibly produce. Why work, when not only all the fruits of their labor would be taken from them, but when they would be beaten or imprisoned for not being able to produce the required taxes?

I was ashamed to go from one Kuomintang general to another, eating special delicacies from their well-laid tables, while peasants were scraping the fields outside the yamens for roots and wild grass to stuff into their griping stomachs. But I was more than ashamed—I was overcome with a feeling of loathing—when I learned that these same generals and the Kuomintang officials were buying up land from starving farmers for arrears in taxes and were holding it to wait tenants and rainy days.

As I walked along the road, each day, some peasant would come to my cart crying a new tale of woe and each night some county magistrate would steal quietly into my room and implore me to do something—"for God's sake do something!"—before it was too late and they all starved to death. Well, I tried.

In keeping with promises I made, when I returned to Chungking, shortly before Pearl Harbor, I wrote a story describing the terrible conditions that I had seen with my own eyes, hoping thereby to call these conditions to the attention of the outside world and force Chiang Kai-shek, through either shame or policy, to do something for the lot of his hapless subjects. Much to my disgust, but not surprise, the director of the foreign publicity board, having declared that he had contrary information from missionaries in the interior (who no doubt were not starving), completely censored my dispatch. Yet, from this famine I was supposed to have conjured up out of my imagination, several million farmers died.

What killed those vast numbers of men and women? You will say drought and crop failure, but none of Chiang Kai-shek's officers, landlords or tax collectors died from want of food, nor did the people to the north, in the Liberated Areas where the climate and lack of rain were the same, die in any corresponding numbers. What was the difference? Why did one set of people starve and not another?

The people of Chiang Kai-shek's part of Honan did not die because God sent no rain; they died because of the greed of the men who governed them. Literally, they were taxed to death.

I used to wonder why these people did not revolt. Why didn't they storm into the cities, break open the granaries and take out the food that had been robbed from them by a soldier with a gun or a tax collector with a weighing scale? They were not apathetic; they did not want to die; but since they were going to die anyway, why did they not go down fighting, why did they not rebel against their feudal lords and masters? Well, the answer is, they did. In 1942, when the Japanese invaded northern Honan, thousands of farmers turned on the soldiers of General Tang Eng-po and quite understandably joined hands with the national enemy of China. And after all, why not: could the Japanese be worse than the army of Chiang Kai-shek?

Perhaps this incident was in the mind of the Peiping professor who, in 1947, warned Chiang Kai-shek that Louis XVI was brought down by a corrupt and vicious tax system. "Unless you reform the tax system," prophesied the professor, "a French Revolution will come to China."

There was only one mistake in that professor's remark: the revolution was not about to come to China; it had already come. And partly, it had come because heavy taxes had crushed the peasant to earth so that he was ready to listen to the first one who would lift the terrible burden from his back and let him stand erect again.

Intolerable taxes are nothing new in China. They have existed ever since the Manchus were overthrown and the warlords began to feed their armies with grain taken from the peasant at the point of a gun. But even these crude knights of violence pale into amateur insignificance before the regime of Chiang Kai-shek which has probably squeezed more wealth out of China's farmers than any ruler in Cathay's long and tortuous history.

Although of recent years, the professional apologists of Chiang Kai-shek have been blaming high taxes on the Japanese war, it is curious to note that the Kuomintang government, almost from the day it took power, has been taxing the people out of all proportion to what they can stand.

Even in the so-called halcyon days of Chiang Kai-shek's regime, from 1929 to 1933, there were, according to official investigations, 188 different kinds of taxes to which the Chinese peasantry had to submit. In 1932, when Chiang was supposedly bringing a new and better regime to China, the rate of the land tax in most of the country was four times what it was in the United States.

Far worse than the formal land tax, however, were the surtaxes which were usually ten times the principal tax. In the days of the decadent Manchus, the surtax had never exceeded one-twelfth of the land tax, yet in the days of Chiang's prosperity it was ten times!

Such hitherto unheard-of exploitation of the peasantry, of course, reached even more unprecedented heights during the war against Japan. In order to carry on that struggle, his paper money having become worthless, Chiang was forced to abandon money taxation and to demand the farmer's grain by a tax in kind.

In Szechuan Province, which Chiang made his stronghold during the Japanese war, sometimes as much as 59 per cent of the crop per mow of paddy field was taken by tax collectors; in Hunan, near the Tungting Lake, it was 53 per cent; in Yunan 49 per cent. While the landowners normally bear the burden of increased taxes, they most often shifted this burden to their tenants in the form of increased rent. And where tenants formerly gave half of their rice or wheat crop to the landlord, they now had to give 70, 80 and 90 per cent of that crop. Sometimes, as I discovered on the Chengtu Plain, it was over 100 per cent, so that the tenant had to go out and buy rice to meet his taxes. In other words he might work all year in his paddy fields and yet not have one grain of rice for himself.

The end of the war against Japan, however, brought no relief to the hard-pressed cultivator. Although the Kuomintang government formally exempted peasants in the hinterland and in the areas recovered from Japan from taxes for one year, the farmers actually were forced to donate much more money and grain in special taxes.

Such levies were more or less fixed. Numerous as they were, they failed to tell even half the picture of the peasant's tax burden. This was so because military requisition, an obsolete form of taxation, which long ago ceased to exist in Western nations, never became extinct in China. In fact, owing to the numerous civil wars and to the war against Japan, they have become more prevalent than in many centuries.

The burden of these requisitions for the last quarter-century in China has really been staggering. Because of lack of funds, squeeze among officers, arrears in pay and plain greed, many Chinese troops depended on requisitions to get their food, clothing, housing and a fat bank account. Grain, cattle, carts, homes, money and even human beings have all been grist for the army officers' mill. Such exploitation of the peasantry, however, was not realized without the co-operation of Chiang's officials and the local gentry. As a matter of fact, requisitions have been an institution through which the officials could rob the people and enrich themselves. They did this principally by adding to the requisitions at the time of collection. Thus, an assessment of five catties of flour became eight; five catties of hay, ten; four carts, fifteen; sixty transport carriers, ninety; and one thousand dollars requisitioned by officers was raised to fifteen hundred by gentry and officials. Thus, war, for the officials, was always the swiftest and straightest road to riches.

In 1947, behind the Kuomintang lines in Anyang County in Honan Province, I discovered that requisitions by Chiang's officers, co-operating with the gentry, were often over one thousand times the land tax. But such figures are only academic; for I found requisitions were so bad that often farmers not only lost all their land, grain and clothing, but also had to hand over their children as slaves and their wives as servants and concubines to the tax collectors and requisition officers.

The Kuomintang's taxation-unto-death is ancient history now. But did the Reds bring anything better?

19. Taxes Without Death

THE Communists, surrounded by hostile troops, shut off from trade with the outside world and with practically no income from industry or business, were under an even greater compulsion than Chiang Kai-shek to raise money to wage war. It was imperative that their economy produce enough to feed and equip their armies and run their governments. How could they do that except by outright confiscations, requisitions and taxes even higher than Chiang's?

To get an answer to these questions I went to call on Jung Wu-sheng, vice-chairman of the Border Region government and also head of its finance bureau. Jung was one of the most likable people I met in the Liberated Areas. He had been a prefect official in the government of Warlord Yen Hsi-shan, when war broke out with Japan. Most of the funds to run his prefect came from the revenue of the warlord's opium monopoly bureau.

About a year after the outbreak of war, many of Yen's opium-smoking soldiers had thrown away their arms and become bandits, but a small part of the army took refuge in southern Shansi. Here Yen organized a new "Dare To Die Army," and Jung joined as a political director to instill the troops with patriotism. When Yen showed little stomach for a fight, the new army revolted and rushed away to join General Liu Po-cheng in the Taihang Mountains. After a violent spiritual struggle with himself, Jung followed, leaving home with the blessings of his father, but the curses of his luxury-loving wife who refused to join him in the mountains. In the guerrilla areas, Jung met a girl who was traveling the same "revolutionary road" as he. Obtaining a divorce from his first wife, he married again. In the meantime, five hundred delegates from North China had elected him vice-chairman of the Border Region government.

These experiences had not made Jung stern or forbidding, but had given him a puckish sense of humor. He had none of that depressing fanaticism of the newly arrived Peiping students who were inclined to ruffle up their feathers at the slightest criticism of conditions in the Liberated Areas. Perhaps, because of his broad sympathies, he could discuss with perfect detachment the numerous fights between government and Communist party cadres, while at the same time he was able to relate with good-humored relish the difficulties encountered by backwoods officials when they entered captured cities and got their first glimpses of Western civilization, including machinery and flush toilets.

But the amazing thing about Jung was the extent of his experiences and his knowledge about them. I spent a great deal of time with him, talking about such a variety of subjects as banking, farm production, handicrafts, marriage, opium and a dozen other subjects ranging from the livelihood of mule-cart men to the relationship of wives to revolution. What made Jung's conversation fascinating was that he had in six years held jobs which brought him into direct contact with all these branches of human activity.

He was not necessarily unique, for everyone in the Liberated Areas seemed able to perform more than one job. I remember a cadre[1] of the 8th Route Army who was a political director in a front-line regiment the first time I met him. A week later, after Chiang Kai-shek turned loose the Yellow River into Shantung, I saw this same cadre directing relief work in the flooded areas. Two weeks after that, he was leading land reform in the villages. A month later, he became mayor of a newly

---

[1] Cadre is the translation the Communists give the word *kan pu*—an official of any sort. It is used throughout this book to indicate individuals, not a framework or skeleton of officers.

captured city. Though such versatility was not rare, it never ceased to amaze me, for such talents are seldom found in America, belonging more to the period of the Renaissance than to the capitalist age of specialization. The cadres of the 8th Route Army, it seemed, could do almost anything.

But how could they raise money to run a war in this backward region without excessive recourse to the printing press or without raising taxes to unprecedented heights? That was the question.

I knew that Jung, to make out a budget, assess taxes, finance farm loans, issue money, direct banking and to control the financial affairs of thirty million people, had only sixteen men in his Bureau of Finance. What Jung, himself, knew about finance when he first became head of the bureau, was what he could remember from a few long-forgotten economic lessons he had studied in a provincial school. He had never been in charge of a large bank or a large business firm. Yet here he was financing one part of the largest war China had ever known. "How do you do it?" I asked Jung.

Jung laughed. "That's what I would like to know myself. I don't have any magic formulas. For the first time in history, my budget is unbalanced. I blame this on our stupidity. We thought Marshall was going to bring us peace so we cut down the budget. Now, I have to find three million dollars (US) to cover additional military expenses.

"If we didn't have to wage this war," Jung continued, "we could not only balance the budget, which we'll do in any case, but we could build a self-supporting economy. It would probably surprise you to know how small the budget really is. For this whole area, the expenses for 1947 are only eleven million dollars. Of this sum 70 per cent comes from the land tax, 10 per cent from corporation taxes, 5 per cent from the sale of commodities and customs revenue and the rest from levies on wine, tobacco, public enterprises and business contracts.

"We spend 50 per cent of this revenue for military expenses, 20 per cent for government salaries and administrative expenses, 10 per cent for education, 8 per cent for industrial construction, 5 per cent for public health, 4 per cent for the judicial system and public safety and the remainder for a reserve fund."

"But how can you run a war on eleven million dollars?" I asked Jung. "That doesn't seem possible. You must run it on what you confiscate from the landlords."

Jung laughed. "No, that was how the old Red Army ran their Soviet areas. We can carry on with such a small budget for entirely different reasons.

"In the first place, most all our cadres are working here out of choice. You may take me as an example. I ran over here because I could not stand conditions in Chiang Kai-shek's areas. I left home, my family and a good job. Such acts of renunciation spring from revolutionary motives. All of us can work for almost nothing and we can exist on little food. In the second place, as you've probably noticed, our government is just a skeleton structure. We don't have to support a top-heavy bureaucracy and therefore can keep expenses and taxes low. Thirdly, all of us, not only government cadres, but soldiers too, must engage in some form of production in addition to our regular jobs. Finally, we don't lose all those vast sums of money that the Kuomintang does through squeeze, bribery and corruption. There is almost no chance for squeeze. All payments and collections must go through a supervisory committee so that it's almost impossible to juggle figures. In the villages, the local finance committee must post financial reports on the village bulletin board and anyone has a chance to question these figures. Probably just as important is the fact that we are fighting for idealistic motives. What would be the sense of running away from the corruption of the Kuomintang only to set up the same kind of society here?"

While Jung was talking, it occurred to me that he must have a terrible time collecting taxes with such a small staff. Wouldn't the people be likely to cheat the government and make out false returns.

"Yes," said Jung, "in the beginning we found many farmers who falsely reported the amounts of their land holdings, while merchants and factory owners reported profits of, say, two thousand dollars when they really had profits of five thousand dollars. Having no large staff of tax examiners, we solved this problem by crude democratic methods. Once or twice a year all villages were ordered to hold 'democratic evaluation meetings' at which owner-farmers, tenants and landlords had to state their incomes in public. At these meetings, a village referee stands about the crowd and asks each farmer individually the amount of his harvest. When he gets an answer, he calls out to the farmer's neighbor: 'Right or wrong?' Since everyone in a village knows each other's affairs intimately, wrong statements are corrected on the spot."

With business enterprises, Jung admitted, the discovery of tax evasion was more difficult. But here, too, merchants and shop owners were called together in meetings publicly to report their profits. The system, according to Jung, had on the whole been so successful that the government had been able to get along without a large tax-collecting machine and at the same time had not lost much revenue.

Revenue from business sources were of little importance to the Communists or to their war. The only way you can run a government or prosecute a war in China is to take grain away from the peasants. Without a land tax, no government in China can survive. That is basic and cannot be avoided. The only thing any government can do is try to keep down expenses and take as little as possible from the peasants so that they won't starve or revolt.

In Chiang Kai-shek's areas, sharecroppers had commonly to give from 50 to 90 per cent of their rice or wheat crop to the landlord. In addition, they were forced to pay innumerable surtaxes, to say nothing of the government land tax. Quite apart from anything Border Region officials told me, I found on independent investigations of my own in the villages that the peasants in the Liberated Areas commonly paid from 8 to 15 per cent of their crop to the government. But that's an end of it. There were no rent payments to landlords and few surtaxes. Because of the general mildness of the agrarian reform, there were no mass grain strikes by the farmers against the government. What was slightly incredible was to find women and children winnowing and sifting their grain to get the best they had for the government. Some families even went so far as to invite neighbors in to criticize the grain they were about to send off to the village office. If the neighbors said it wasn't very high grade, they would winnow it again. If this seems impossible to believe, it must be remembered that the people realized the grain wouldn't go into the hands of city merchants or corrupt officials, but would go to the army where their sons and lovers were fighting.

It ought to be made perfectly clear that while the land tax was mild enough and just and while there were no irregular levies and surtaxes, there were nevertheless requisitions of various kinds on the peasantry. Most of these requisitions were of labor.

I have seen peasants conscripted to work on the roads, to plant collectively what land UNRRA tractors had plowed, to furnish carts and mules for transport of grain, to reclaim waste land and to work on various public projects. I think these men may have given even more in labor hours to the Communists than they gave to Kuomintang officials in Chiang Kai-shek's areas.

There was, however, a great difference between this kind of requisition and that practiced in Kuomintang areas. First, labor given in this manner was always for the public good and not for private profit. Secondly, no one was impoverished by requisitions. Any commandeered labor was divided equally among all villagers, whether landlords or tenants. There was no getting out of labor because of political influence, and government workers contributed free labor as did peasants. Thirdly, there were strict limits on all such requisitions. Fourthly, no grain, outside of the land tax, could be requisitioned without grain tickets. Peasants could use these tickets to get back their grain from the government. Finally, and most important of all, the peasants themselves thought the system just and equable. Whether they were fooled by propaganda is something I leave to the moralists.

20. Banking by Moonlight

ONE of the strangest enterprises I came across in the Liberated Areas was that of banking. It was carried on under primitive conditions and with crude methods that would make a Western banker shudder. Yet it seemed to fit the needs of the people well enough to bring into question statements made by those critics who said Communist economy would collapse because of an unsound monetary structure.

Banking was born in North China very much as were guerrilla bands. First there was nothing, then there were co-operatives issuing money, then there were regional banks created by guerrilla bands and guerrilla governments, and finally there was a Border Region bank.

When the Kuomintang armies first retreated from North China, Chiang Kai-shek's national currency was still circulating freely and the Japanese were raking it in to buy foreign exchange. At that time, there were three banks doing business under the auspices of guerrilla governments and they began to issue their own notes to absorb the national currency and keep it out of Japanese hands.

This currency was first issued through co-operatives and factories, but the majority of the people had no confidence in it. A peculiar circumstance tended to increase this distrust. One of the three banks printing money was named Shang Tang Bank—a name taken from a certain district in North China. But the words *"shang tang"* commonly mean in Chinese to cheat or fraud. So when people heard about the Shang Tang notes, they said: "I am not going to be cheated by the Cheat Bank" and refused to honor them. Gradually, however, as they saw they could buy things at the co-operatives, they began to show a little confidence in the new money.

The Kuomintang fought the new currency, forbidding troops to trade with it. Officers told their soldiers to use Shang Tang notes as toilet paper. One model soldier, obediently followed these orders to the letter, using a five-dollar Shang Tang note as he had been instructed. Later, going into a store in a small town, he tendered a ten-dollar national government note to the proprietor in payment for a pack of cigarettes. Much to his astonishment, the proprietor had no national government notes and said: "I must give you change in Shang Tang money." Not wishing to lose anything, the thrifty soldier went back and recovered his own Shang Tang five dollar bill. Having carefully washed it, he took it back to the store and cashed it. When this story, soon acquiring the popularity of a folk legend, was heard by the people, they said: "If you can cash a Shang Tang note after it has been used as toilet paper, it must really be good."

So confidence in the guerrilla money grew.

After 1941, when the Border Region government was formed, the three existing banks were combined into the Chinan[1] Bank which in the next few years established branch offices in every prefecture and county in the Border Region. Only this bank was authorized to print money and it had somewhat the status of a state bank.

The Chinan paper money that I saw was of very inferior quality. Notes were often worn to the point where numerals could not be distinguished. Because of this and because people often could not read, one found half a one-dollar bill pasted together with half of a two-dollar bill. The bank cashed these in at $1.50 apiece. Such a policy added further to the prestige of Chinan money.

The fate of this money, of course, depended on the outcome of the civil war. Vice-Chairman Jung told me: "We have to look on this money as a revolutionary bond. When the revolution succeeds, the bond becomes good."

Even so, Chinan currency did not fare badly in the struggle with Kuomintang money. Originally, the Chinan Bank exchanged the two notes on an equal basis, one for one. But as the civil war sharpened, open circulation of Kuomintang money was forbidden, though landlords were permitted to keep their savings in Kuomintang money. A little later, however, it was forbidden to hoard Kuomintang money and everything had to be changed at the border.

Naturally, there was much smuggling of bank notes between the two areas. Smugglers from the Kuomintang side stuffed coolies' bamboo carrying poles with Chinese national currency and tried to bring it into the Border Region. Other methods were to hide notes in the wooden frames of mule saddles, in a can of kerosene or even in coffins in the mattresses under corpses. The Border Region merely fined merchants who were engaged in this trade for profit, but punished more severely smuggling that had a political aim, even executing "chief conspirators."

Despite all the smuggling, the Chinan Bank soon forged ahead in the war between the two currencies. When I entered the Border Region at the beginning of 1947, I had to pay about five Kuomintang dollars for one Border Region dollar. After several Communist military victories, the exchange rose to eight for one. In the guerrilla areas, however, I found that peasants and militiamen behind the Kuomintang lines were offering as high as ten for one. They were losing confidence in Chiang's army and wanted to be able to buy things in the Liberated Areas. This loss of confidence kept pushing up the exchange rate until in August

[1] *Chi* is the ancient Chinese name for Hopei Province. *Nan* means south. Hence: South Hopei Bank.

1948 it had reached one to fifteen hundred and then in one gigantic leap went to one to ten thousand.

Perhaps these figures illustrate more clearly than anything the difference in living conditions between the Liberated Areas and those governed by Chiang Kai-shek. There is no doubt that there was inflation in Red areas. In the first half of 1948, prices of commodities went up 68 per cent. But this seems like a heavenly economic stability when you know that prices in Chiang's areas rose 1000 per cent in the same period.

To back up its money, the bank had a reserve in cotton, gold, silver and land about equal to the value of its note issue. This was a big advance over the first days when three regional banks existed. All of these banks started from scratch, without capital. While running here and there in the guerrilla areas, they exchanged coupons for gold and silver loaned by friends. Then they obtained some funds from surpluses in government treasuries. Finally, a few officials who revolted against Yen Hsi-shan brought over funds that had accumulated in the warlord's treasuries through the sale of opium.

"I, myself," Jung told me modestly, "brought half a million dollars with me that had accumulated in my prefect from the sale of opium."

Safeguarding the bank's reserve capital was rather an adventurous business in the Border Region. All reserves were buried underground or in caves. Bank branches in guerrilla areas sent all gold and silver immediately to the rear. As a standing rule, whenever the bank had over one thousand ounces of silver or gold in its office, it had to be buried. The same was done with any but small amounts of grain and cotton.

Vice-Chairman Jung was continually poring over maps and searching his memory to find the most inaccessible and wild spots to bury the treasures of the bank. He considered a sparsely populated region most suitable, but such regions were few in crowded China. Jung also took into consideration the patriotism of the people and the political reliability of officials.

"I personally prefer to bury our gold and silver on lonely mountain peaks," he told me, "but other people prefer caves. There is no use in being dogmatic about such a thing, however, and I don't insist on peaks if caves seem safer at the time."

The actual hiding of the gold or silver was secret and took place only at night. Before the burial, there was a long trek by donkey or mule. Of course, only the most reliable mule men were taken on such trips, but even they did not know what cargo they were carrying. Only the bank manager, the treasurer and a dependable party member knew exactly what was on the backs of the mules.

Some bank managers preferred moonlit nights for burial parties, because then it was not necessary to carry lanterns which might attract attention. Others, however, preferred pitch black nights when even a figure against the skyline could not be seen.

When the appointed night came, the manager, the treasurer and the Communist party member, transported the capital close to the chosen spot. Having dismissed the mule men, having made sure that no one else was around and that near-by villagers were asleep, the three men then went to the burial ground and started digging. When the treasure was buried, all three men carefully memorized the surrounding landmarks and departed.

Only these three men actually knew where the bank's treasure was hidden. What if they were killed?

"One killed," said Jung, "okay. Two killed; still okay. Three killed, treasure lost."

In the seven or eight years of its history, the bank only once lost any of its buried capital. That was a time of emergency when only two men were available to bury fifteen hundred pounds of silver. One of these men died, and the other could not remember clearly just where the silver was buried. Since no one is allowed to keep maps, nor any written instructions—such as, "ten paces from the tree and three feet down"—the burier's loss of memory proved serious. Inspectors dug up the general area, but found nothing. Just then the Japanese attacked and, noting the digging, they too sank holes everywhere, but they found nothing either. Just what happened to the silver is still one of the bank's unsolved mysteries.

As the Communist party was very strict about auditing accounts, bank inspectors came once a year to check up on buried treasure. Since the hiding place was uncovered during these bank inspections, a new one had to be found immediately.

Banking in the guerrilla areas was even more peculiar. Because the Japanese and later the Kuomintang troops were very sensitive to banks, no gold or silver was kept behind the enemy lines, but shipped to the rear. There were no safe deposit boxes, either in guerrilla areas or in the rear. "It is troublesome enough to take care of our own business, without taking care of other people's," said Jung.

There were no bank buildings in guerrilla areas. There were no signboards. The bank was generally in an ordinary mud or plaster house. It was found by the use of code names, such as No. 1 or No. 12. In this house, the banker did his business, in a dark room, lit only by a wick hanging from a tiny cup of oil. His equipment consisted of a counting board, a Chinese writing brush, a little paper, some money and the accounts of his clients. People kept accounts with him, for even if he moved away, they could always find him through secret agents.

In reality, a banker in the guerrilla areas could be compared to a grocer's delivery boy. When the enemy came, he packed up his counting board, writing brush, money and accounts in his bedding roll, strapped on a couple of hand grenades and ran away fast, his bank on his back.

Communist victories in 1948 and 1949, however, probably brought an end to the romantic and adventurous aspects of Red banking. As I write, news has just come to hand that all the banks in North China have been amalgamated into one central bank, issuing a unified currency. The base of this new currency is not bullion or precious metal, but commodities, such as foodstuffs and cloth. It is very likely that this bank and its officers will someday take over the main tasks of Chinese finance on a national and maybe a world-wide scale.

Thus, the little paper notes that issued so forlornly from the presses of countryside co-operatives in the dark days of the Japanese invasion have now nearly risen to the stature of a national currency. The revolutionary bond has been made good.

21. Chicken Feathers, Stagecoaches and Telephone Lines

THE most striking thing to an American eye about the economy of the Liberated Areas was its backwardness. Nowhere was this more nakedly revealed than in the field of communications.

These were so primitive that a journey of twenty miles by government mule cart took from sunrise to sunset, a telephone call of the same distance often required a week, a telegram might never be delivered and a letter posted to a destination a few hundred miles away might take forty days.

And yet, during my stay, communications within the Communists' inland empire were better than they had been at any time for the last nine years. A post office had just been established, a military telephone line reached from one end of the border region to the other, and a government-owned transportation company, equipped with motorized trucks, functioned along rocky mountain roads and dirt highways on the plains.

There were, of course, no airplanes in the Border Region. The army had no air force, the government operated no plane service and there were no commercial airlines. Nor were there any railways running in the Border Region. Transport and travel, therefore, was by motor vehicle, cart, animal or foot. At a rough guess, about one-tenth of 1 per cent of transport and travel was by motorcar.

There was very little travel in the Border Region partly because the

Chinese are not great travelers, partly because travel was slow, difficult and pointless, there being no place to go, and because the best means of transport were monopolized in the war by the army and government. I would say, offhand, that no one traveled for pleasure, but only from necessity. Traffic on the roads, therefore, consisted mostly of the transport of army supplies and some mercantile goods.

The transport of mercantile goods was a comparatively easy process, for trade in the Border Region was not highly developed and there was no great bulk of material to be put on the roads. Often a single bicyclist could carry a load of sugar from one town to another, sell it, buy salt and return to his starting place with a profit. Oxcarts made short hauls of vegetables, charcoal and grain between towns. Matches which were scarce and a highly profitable source of income were easy to transport because of their lightness and a cartload of matches sent from one town to another fetched a fancy price.

The transportation of grain, however, was another matter. Large amounts were needed whenever troops were concentrated for battle or to relieve grain shortages in the mountains. The movement of grain in bulk was handled mostly by the government.

Transport was by hired labor, half-paid labor or free labor. Grain needed for the government and for the schools was taken care of by their own transportation teams, but grain for the army and bulk civilian relief had to be moved by organized convoys.

These convoys could be called the freight trains of the Border Region. They were the only system the government had found to move grain in bulk. In 1941, by means of secret convoys, the government transported fifty thousand bushels of grain from the plains of Shantung and Hopei across the Peiping-Hankow Railway and the Japanese lines to famine-stricken areas in the mountains of Honan and Shansi. Some of the grain carts were attacked, but the great majority of them got through.

Before 1943, during the hardest years of the famine, animals and labor were requisitioned by the government without pay. But by 1944, the government had enough grain reserves to feed the requisitioned animals, while half of the existing price for public transportation was paid farmers for convoy duty. On the average, a farmer contributed about ten to fifteen days out of a year to government transport.

Because everyone in the Border Region had to study, educational work was carried on in the convoys. For example, a Chinese character was hung on the back of a mule man so the man behind him might read it. This character was changed every day. Thus a farmer studied while he worked.

Every convoy had a captain and a political or "mass" worker. This last individual generally came from the same village as the farmers and his duty was more or less like that of a YMCA worker. On the road, he told stories, sang songs and related the news of the day or the military situation in the region into which they were going.

With only 150 cars and trucks among thirty million people, motor transport was practically nonexistent in the Four-Province Border Region. To help co-operatives transport their grain and handicraft products to market, the government in 1947 organized a public transport company with fifty of these trucks and three hundred mule carts. Freight rates were excessive, but passenger fares seemed reasonable under the circumstances, a trip of twenty miles costing about eighty cents in American money.

Most trucks burned charcoal or used alcohol. In case of emergency, strong native Chinese wine might pull these latter-type cars for short distances. Gasoline was smuggled in from Tientsin where it was bought on the open market by underground agents. Transport and travel, however, were predominantly by cart and animal.

Sometimes slower, sometimes faster than travel, was the mail service. Actually the Border Region did not get a formal post office system until after the Japanese surrender. As the original postal officials ran away in 1937 and 1938 with Chiang Kai-shek's troops, the Liberated Areas were for some time without any mail service at all. Various guerrilla bands, local governments and newspapers, however, organized their own messenger services and these messengers the Border Region finally took over and organized into a Communications Corps.

This, however, only solved the problem of official letters, and civilians were left without any means of written communication. In the past, it had been customary to paste a chicken feather on a letter that was important. Two feathers meant the message was a matter of life and death and the messenger was duty bound to run as fast as he could. Chicken feathers being bulky and uneconomical, the Communications Corps decided to print Communications stamps so that civilians might also mail letters. Gradually, this became the Post Office Bureau.

By 1947, the Post Office was a going concern, with a small fleet of bicycles, a crew of postal carriers and 336 stations, operating twenty thousand miles of postal lines. Postal carriers wore no uniform, but only ordinary peasant garb. Some had arm bands with the words *Post Office Bureau* sewn on them.

These carriers operated only between towns to established stations. There was no delivery to homes or even to streets. Stations were generally twenty to twenty-five miles apart, with intermediary stop-off points along the way. Messengers on bicycle made a round trip in one day. Those on foot or mule made a round trip every two days, stopping off overnight at each end of the journey.

Most mail was carried by mule or donkey. There was no breakneck speed as with our pony expresses. However, I found three special messengers who could do fifty miles a day on foot. They were given special food and carefully rested between grueling hikes.

In the cities and towns I found postboxes where one might post a letter. A messenger going through would pick it up. In the villages, however, farmers had to leave their letters at the local information post. Every three or four days, these along with official documents would be taken into the towns and left where a passing postman might pick them up.

During the so-called truce of 1946, the Border Region had an agreement with the Kuomintang Post Office authorities whereby each would honor the other's stamps. Later, letters were sent over the lines without stamps and the Kuomintang would stamp them on their side and the Border Region on their side. All that had finished by the time of my arrival.

When a letter was not going into Kuomintang areas, but still had to cross Kuomintang lines, a special, but not secret, system was used. Post Office stations were set up—say on either side of a railway—never more than ten or fifteen miles apart so that a messenger might cross in one night. Only messengers familiar with the routes would be employed on such service. If an important message had to cross the lines, it was written on oil paper and folded into a small pellet that could be carried in the mouth or concealed in the rectum.

Many postmen were peasants who had obtained land, houses and agricultural implements through the land reform and they were quite serious in their duties regarding their jobs as part of the task of striking down Chiang Kai-shek. The zeal which these men showed in the performance of their duties was sometimes amazing. Not only would wind, sleet, hail nor snow fail to keep them from their appointed daily rounds, as the United States Post Office boasts of its carriers, but also rivers, mountains and enemy bullets could not stop them from delivering the mail. One famous postman in the Four-Province Border Region, after crossing the treacherous Yellow River torrent when it was in flood, had to haul his bicycle and mail sacks over four mountain peaks in Shantung in order to by-pass Chiang Kai-shek's lines.

When passing through enemy territory, some of the more ingenious postmen conducted a war of nerves against Chiang's troops, distributing hand bills and writing news of Communist army victories.

Mail in the Liberated Areas, I found, was slow but sure and a far better means of communication than the telephone for the average civilian. Before the Japanese war, the telephone system in Shansi had been military while that in Hopei Province was civilian and mercantile. After the invasion, all telephone service stopped. When it was re-established, it was only over short distances. First, only the military could use the phones, then the government was given lines. Civilians still had a hard time making phone calls when I was there.

Although a phone line extended from one end of the Border Region to the other and though in theory one might make a phone call of 150 miles, in practice, no such thing was possible. Several times, when I was out in the villages, having met trouble with some petty officials, I tried to get in touch with Commissar Po Yi-po by phone, I never succeeded. I could talk with the next county, but no further. One county would transfer my message to the next county on the line, but when a message goes through four or five counties it gets pretty garbled. Telephone service for the ordinary civilian was even worse. If allowed to talk at all, he could not generally make a phone call of more than eight miles.

Because all telephones and equipment were captured from the Japanese or the Kuomintang, because some of the phone sets captured were new, some old, and because some wires were thick and some thin, the telephone system did not work very well. All telephone traffic was carried on a single line strung on short, fragile poles made from every kind of tree in North China. This line, sometimes lying on the ground, sometimes only four feet off it, swaying and dipping through four provinces, was in aggregate seven thousand miles long.

But this single strand of wire represented endless blood and tears for it was collected only through a fierce telephone struggle with the Japanese. Peasants cut down so many telephone poles and stole so much wire that the Japanese used to build stone boxes around the poles and use especially heavy wire that could not be cut. Yet the peasants continued to knock down the poles and steal the wire so that they could build their own telephone system which, especially on the plains, they had to do underground.

The Border Region ran its own schools for telephone, telegraph and radio technicians, but the instructors had no manuals and little apparatus on which to train students, who, therefore, on graduation were not finished technicians.

Such student graduates meeting a telephone different from the one on which they had learned often felt lost. Sometimes they spent five and six hours repairing phones with which there was nothing wrong.

When the 8th Route Army began to enter cities after the Japanese surrender, mechanics seeing electric lights for the first time promptly attached telephone wires to light sockets and, of course, blew out the battery telephone sets.

Some of the 8th Route Army's first contacts with electricity bear the stamp of Don Quixote's tilt with a windmill.

When the army captured the Fengfeng coal mines in Shansi Province, some of the supposedly more educated technicians warned their mechanics about the high-voltage lines connected with the power plant.

"Don't touch the lines with your hands, but only with your feet," the master electricians advised their apprentices.

So the mechanics advanced on the wires with their hands held well back and jumped at them with their feet. After two or three young scientists were thrown thirty feet away by the power lines, the rest decided to wait for more expert advice.

Only a pedant would take these stories as examples of the failure of the Communists to raise the cultural level of the people in their areas. The wonder was, not that the people were so backward, but that these backward people had been able to achieve so much against the Kuomintang which had a monopoly on almost all the Western-educated technicians in the country. Undoubtedly, if the Communists gained power, they would employ these technicians just as the Kuomintang had done. But in the meantime what were the Communists trying to do about the undoubted ignorance of the people in this part of North China?

22. Class Society in the Classroom

I CAN'T remember his name, but the man himself I remember very well. A shaved head; a low tone of speech; a shy manner; frail and tired looking—such is my recollection of the head of the Education Department of the Border Region government, whom I shall call Old Wang.

Wang was a respected teacher of landlords' children until in the middle of the Japanese war he suddenly wearied of the scions of the rich and gave up his home and the presidency of a normal school to stake his future with a guerrilla band. Born in south Hopei, he was the only son of a peasant family. By various sacrifices his parents sent him through middle school. When he wished to continue his studies in Peiping, his father ruefully showed him his empty purse. Wang applied to the family's dearest friend, a rich neighbor, for a loan.

"You have no independent position in society and there is no guarantee you could pay me back," said the rich neighbor and turned down Wang's request.

That a neighbor who was so friendly in normal times should refuse him in his hour of need gave Wang a harsh impression. Believing he had seen "the real face of the rich man," Wang ran away from home, sweated at odd jobs and continued his education until at last he became a teacher. Within a number of years, he became head of a middle school and then president of a normal school.

When the war against Japan broke out, Wang tried to raise his students to fight the Japanese. The sons of the landlords wanted no part of dangerous patriotism; the sons of the poor rushed into the war, many of them sacrificing their lives.

This lesson taught him by his students brought Wang to a crossroad in his life. Believing the rich had but a feeble conception of the nation, but the poor would fight for it, he decided he would be a failure in life if he continued to teach the sons and daughters of the landlords. Abandoning his job, he joined a guerrilla band and became head of a local National Salvation Association.

In the guerrilla areas, Wang continued his teaching, devoting himself particularly to children in the primary schools. Believing they were the future of China, he tried to prevent them from falling into Japanese hands. Without school buildings, he held classes under trees and inside temples. While the children did their lessons on boards held over their knees, Wang kept a weather eye out for the Japanese, dismissing his classes as soon as the enemy approached.

Once, however, he was not quick enough and was caught by the Japanese, beaten and tortured and then thrown into a jail in the Japanese-occupied city of Taming. A famous painter and Wang's eighty-year-old former teacher who were living in the city tried to secure his release. The Japanese demanded a ransom of four thousand dollars. A band of farmers outside the walls raised two thousand dollars and sent it to the Japanese. It was not enough. Through the painter, Wang applied to a rich landlord, the father of one of his former pupils. The landlord sent back word: "I could lend you ten dollars, but anything more, how could you pay it back?"

Indeed how? Wang was in despair, grew weak from many blows and fell sick. One day a stranger came into his cell. A poor man, an ex-vagabond and ex-bandit, he identified himself as the head of the Japanese puppet police bureau in Taming. After a long conversation with Wang, he said: "I know what it is to be poor; I'll try to get the money for you." Within a few days, the stranger raised a thousand dollars. Combined with the money the farmers had raised, it formed an acceptable ransom to the Japanese and Wang was released.

Back in the guerrilla areas, while Wang lay ill, he thought over his latest experiences. Someone who had money had not helped him. But someone he did not even know had given him a thousand dollars. From this Wang concluded: The rich love money and not man; the poor love man and not money. Since then he had shaped his theories of education accordingly.

One day when we were talking, he began to enumerate some of these theories. They were pretty Marxist. "Education is not a way of life in itself," he asserted; "it is only an instrument. Since anyone can use this instrument, it has a class nature. In Chiang Kai-shek's areas, I found that education was used as a tool to forge servile followers for

Chiang Kai-shek. But here in the Liberated Areas, we try to use this tool to make the educated people servants of the masses.

"There is another point. Education cannot be divorced from life, but must be combined with reality. John Dewey says: 'Education is life; school is society.' But we say: 'Life is education; society is a school.' That is why we take the living material around us as subject matter for education. Our education is aimed at the ignorant farmers and the petty bourgeoisie; that is, 90 per cent of the people, and not at the landlords, a very few of the people."

Before seeing how Wang's theories worked out in practice, a few words ought to be said about the difficulties of education in this region of China. Although on the plains, perhaps 90 per cent of the people were illiterate, they were far more culturally advanced to begin with than the primitive people in the mountains. There, some of the people not only believed in fox goddesses, devils and ghosts of all kinds, but they were often in the grip of village witches who fostered in them superstitions and fears that had died out a thousand years ago in other parts of the world. The people had no toothbrushes, hated to wash their hands or faces or cut their nails or hair. No woman could bob her hair and very many had bound feet.

Illiterate, suspicious, somewhat afraid of the outside world, the peasant was interested not in ideas, not in humanity, not in civilization, but only in himself, his own mud-walled little world.

How teach this ignorant human beast of burden anything? How teach him, for example, those terribly complex Chinese characters that the scholars and the wealthy had monopolized for centuries so that they dominated the political and social life of the empire. How drive into the head of a manure-stinking, ghost-believing peasant a bunch of Chinese characters that he did not want to learn and that hitherto he had got along without?

How indeed? It was something the Kuomintang, with all their fine teachers, with their students returned from England, France and America, had not been able to do. A number of years before, James Yen, an American-returned student, had attracted considerable attention because he had established a model mass-education scheme in Tinghsien County in Chiang Kai-shek's areas. But of what use are models, when the problem is to teach millions how to read and write? Not children, but adults.

The Communist solution was both simple and typical. They combined education with life. Instead of drilling the peasant in school (except in winter), the Communists began teaching him how to read by showing him characters connected with his daily life and occupation. Thus a shepherd would be taught the characters for sheep, dog, stick, grass and so on. A farmer would learn the characters for field, millet, wheat, mule and the like. The methods of teaching were also as ingenious as they were pleasant. A school child would go around at the noon recess to the homes of five or six housewives and paste on the front door, the living room table, and the kitchen stove the characters for each of those objects. While continuing to do her work, the housewife would memorize the characters. The next day, the schoolboy would bring three new characters. Or, as I saw, a farmer plowing in his field would put up one character on a big board at each end of the field. Thus, going back and forth all day, even his primitive mind could grasp the complex convolutions.

In village after village I have seen these clods of the soil, hitherto barred from any education, poring over lessons, trooping to the winter schools, watching rural dramatic teams perform on the threshing ground, listening to newscasts broadcast through hand megaphones, and studying the slogans painted on the walls, spelling them out in their tortured but patient way.

While not so dramatic as their accomplishments in adult mass education, the Communists had made advances in educating children in school[1] that might have a more lasting effect. Here, too, the difficulties had been enormous. Since there were no charts or maps to teach geography, the teachers sometimes had to draw them from memory, often with resulting mistakes. Because of the shortage of books, the teachers had to prepare lesson sheets not only for the children but for themselves. In the mountains almost everything had to be mimeographed or stone-block lithographed. Students made their own ink brushes. Paper was short, but due to the revival of handicrafts not so short that students could get out of doing their homework. Professors in the colleges had to teach physics without any apparatus and chemistry without laboratory experiments. Yet, considering the human and physical material they had to work with, it seemed to me that Border Region teachers were accomplishing miracles.

According to Wang, there were 2,200,000 students in the Four-Province Border Region, 65 middle schools, 1500 higher primary schools, 17,162 primary schools, 2 colleges and 1 university. This last—North China University—was not established until 1946 and then in a "borrowed" mission compound in the city of Singtai, from which it was later moved to the mountains in order to avoid bombings. Originally, there were only one hundred students but by the end of 1946, there were thirteen hundred, practically all of whom had run away from Peiping and other cities in Chiang Kai-shek's hands to study in the Liberated Areas.

[1] Under the Border Region system of education there were three sections: institutional, military and social. The first was run by the government, the second by the 8th Route Army and the third by mass organizations.

The life of these students was very hard, but none of them was starving and I never heard of any co-eds forced into prostitution to get funds to continue school, as I know many were in Kuomintang areas. Students were given sixty catties [about 90 pounds] of grain a month (more than government officials) of which they generally used half to feed themselves and the rest to buy books, clothes and school materials. Every one of them had to do some kind of production such as working in the fields or making some useful handicrafts. An example of the strict life of a student can be seen from a special school at Linching where the daily curriculum included four hours of classwork, three hours of "self-study" and five hours of production.

The university had six colleges: medical, economic, engineering, arts and letters, education and government. Of the 240 faculty members, most were from the old Liberated Areas, but there were a few from Kuomintang territory who had run over when they were put on Chiang Kai-shek's black list. Many of the faculty members had no previous experience and were recruited from among cadres. Thus the head of the engineering college was a practical engineer who had never taught before. The teachers in the government and finance colleges were men who had been cadres in the Japanese war. What these men lacked in professional ability, they more than made up for in practical experience.

This university, however, was little more than a luxury. The backbone of the Communist educational system lay in the primary schools, which must have accounted for at least 80 per cent of all the Border Region students. I saw these schools everywhere, in the mountains, in the plains, in large villages and small villages, in temples and in ex-landlords' homes. In Yehtao while I was there I saw children eight and nine years old climb to the peak of a hill and tear down, stone by stone, an ancient temple which the Japanese had used as a lookout post in the war. Laughing and shouting they carried the bricks downhill, piled them up in the schoolyard before their teacher and then the next day began to build themselves a school building.

In another village of four hundred families, which had not had any schools for some years, I found, not one school, but two, with 150 boys and 170 girls. A retired schoolteacher had started these schools on his own initiative. Because parents could not afford to lose the labor of their children in the fields, they at first were cold to the idea of sending their children to study. So the teacher took two boys and one girl and taught them how to spin thread and to make hair nets. The first day the girl brought home five hair nets she had made and gave them to her parents who promptly sold them to village women for fifty dollars (US five cents) apiece. Seeing that their children could earn money and help out with home expenses, even while studying, other parents sent their children to the school. Thus, by unconsciously applying

Wang's theory that education should not be divorced from life, this teacher had not only been able to revive learning in the village, but to guarantee that the farmers would not lose by releasing their children from home and field labor.

What did these children study? Was there any political indoctrination? In the middle schools, yes; in the primary schools, surprisingly little. Two hours each week in middle schools were devoted to a study of current events. Material came from newspapers and from lectures given by county magistrates to teachers and village leaders. The subject matter of these meetings was written in prose and verse on village blackboards. Generally it concerned the course of the war, the assurance of victory and sometimes the causes of the war. It was not uncommon to see a schoolboy telling a group of six or seven women that "our People's Army has crossed the Yellow River" or that "Chiang Kai-shek won't give the people democracy and is a dictator."

But the best way to see what the Communists were teaching the children in their schools and, incidentally, to discover the primary aims of the Communists was to read their school textbooks. Recently I read some six of these books (about fifty lessons, used to teach adults and children how to write Chinese characters) and, while surprised by their wholesome character, there was no doubt that they were using education as a tool to fit their aims. The emphasis in all these books was first and last and always on the need to produce and the advantages and glory of work. A secondary emphasis was on the need to overthrow feudal practices such as foot binding, concubinage and inequality of women. Thirdly, many of the lessons concerned themselves with hygiene, co-operation, good manners and the art of letter writing. In brief, the lessons were aimed at farm children and the necessity for farmers to become self-supporting, modern and healthy. The lessons were notable for their lack of direct political content. In all of them there was not one mention of the Chinese Communist party nor of any Marxist doctrine. There were, however, four or five lesson sections setting out the goodness of society in the Liberated Areas, and one or two references to Border Region leaders. These were tales much like those learned by American children about George Washington and the founding of the United States.

Because these lessons show better than anything else what Chinese children learned in Communist-dominated areas, I include at the end of this chapter some examples taken from the schoolbooks of the Shansi-Hopei-Shantung-Honan Border Region.

One thing sticks out like a sore thumb from these lessons. And that is the poverty of the people. On every page, the talk is about manure, planting date trees, drawing water. Produce! Produce! Produce! That is the constant and ever-recurring exhortation to the farm children of the Liberated Areas. Nothing could more clearly illustrate the primitive nature of Border Region economy than these appeals to the farmer. There is no appeal to proletarians, nothing about industry in all these lessons, but only the talk about the land and how to make it productive.

Clearly, farm production was a matter of life and death to the Communists and the people under them. Let us see how they tried to solve that question.

On the advantages of work

1. Plant beans and you get beans.
   Plant melons and you get melons.
   What you plant that you get.

2. Li Chia Chuang's children's organization
   Started a collect manure competition.
   Whoever collects the most manure
   Is considered as riding in an airplane
   And all little friends want to ride a plane.
   When all have finished classes,
   They shouldered baskets and went to collect manure.

3. Little sisters stay at home;
   I and mother will plant cotton seed.
   Why are you going to plant cotton seed?
   When the seeds are planted, they will grow flowers.
   What happens when the flowers grow?
   We pick the flowers.
   What happens when the flowers are picked?
   We draw and crush them.
   When drawn and crushed, then what?
   We spin into thread.
   Then what?
   We weave into cloth. How very nice.
   When woven into cloth, then what?
   We make it into a new jacket for you.
   It will look nice when I go to grandma's.
   What will you say when you go to grandma's?
   I'll just say: "Mama is planting cotton seed."

On co-operation

1. Little brother does not know how to make shoes,
   So big sister makes shoes for little brother.
   Big sister does not know how to read,
   So little brother teaches big sister to read.

2. When Li Fang was class leader, he liked to fight.
   Teacher said: "Discuss problems reasonably, it is wrong to fight."
   Li Fang would not change. The whole class held a criticism meeting and gave him their opinions, but he would not change. When the classmates saw he would not reform, they held a meeting and deposed him.

On hygiene

1. Long fingernails, three fen long.
   In long fingernails is stored up filth.
   Put in your mouth and your stomach will hurt;
   Scratch itches and you will get boils.
   Quickly cut the long nails;
   Don't leave them to store up filth.

On education

1. When New Year comes, there are holidays.
   Teacher asks what will you do at home?
   Chang Ying says: "In the morning I shall review my lessons.
   And at night I shall teach mama to read."
   Teacher says: "Very good. Very good."

On Communist leaders

Mao Tze-tung is like the sun;
He is brighter than the sun,
Little brother, little sister,
Everyone clap hands, come and sing.

On the Soviet Union

The Soviet Union is our good friend.
In the past many countries deceived us.
Only the Soviet Union helped us.
The Soviet Union is a prosperous, strong and big country.

There everyone has work and everyone food to eat.
While we were fighting Japan,
The Soviet Union helped us.
Only when the Soviet Union attacked
Was Japan defeated.[2]

On government

Teacher said: "Our border region has realized democracy. Whether big things or small things, all has been done in accordance with the mind of the people. We have accomplished reduction of rents and taxes. Poor people and rich people are all producing enthusiastically and many labor heroes have appeared. Here, firstly, there are no greedy and avaricious officials; secondly, there are no overbearing landlords and corrupt gentry; thirdly, there are no bandits, and fourthly, there are no beggars. In fact, the evil phenomenon of the outside areas are all absent here. We not only have regular troops, but also militia. We not only have primary schools and middle schools, but also North China University. The villages also have schools for adults and dramatic troops. The *lao pai hsing* [the common people] are studying at every opportunity and are making progress and enjoying a life of freedom and happiness."

[2] This was the only mention of the Soviet Union in all these lessons. People I questioned about the obvious distortion of history answered: "If I were writing the book, I would have mentioned the United States and England, too."

On bound feet

Old Lady Wang and Young Lady Li have little feet like red peppers. They cannot farm land; they cannot carry water, and they walk one step, sway three times and topple over when the wind blows.

Third Sister Chang and Liu Yu-lin have natural feet that are big. They go down to the river to carry water, go up the mountain to cut kindling, and plow the land to plant crops. They are just like males.

On women's equality

The old society is too dark; men and women are treated differently. The man goes to an office, the woman stays within the compound. The man wears new clothes, the woman dresses in rags. The man eats white flour, the woman, husks and chaff. The man can scold until heaven bursts, the woman seldom opens her mouth. The man reads books, the woman stands at the side of the cauldron. The man three times changes his temperament, the woman swallows into her stomach the words she has to say.

In the new society, a great revolution has taken place. People are free, male and female have equal rights, men and women jointly apply themselves to production, and men and women together enjoy better times.

On religion

People of the world are truly stupid, using money to worship idols. Idols are originally made from mud, and spirits and devils are man-made phenomena.

They make a standing image, but it cannot get up. They make a male image and call it grandfather; they make a female image and call it grandmother. It grows two feet, but cannot walk; it grows two hands, but cannot lift. Its staring eyes cannot see; its mouth cannot open. It is given a nose, but cannot breathe. For two more dollars, give it ears.

Villagers should think it over; it is better to revere people than idols. Save up money for a useful purpose. Buy shares in a co-operative society and set up a business of your own.

23. Are They Slaves to Work?

I WAS once on a walk in the countryside outside the crumbling walls of an ancient county town in Hopei. As I was passing beside a village, I saw a peasant, bent low with a rope over his back, straining in every muscle of his body to pull a small plow, which his sweating wife guided from behind. The bestial nature of the labor shocked me and I paused to talk with the toiling farmer.

"You are eating much bitterness," I said, offering him the time-honored words of sympathy.

"Yes, it is hard work," he said, pausing while both he and his wife raised their work-strained faces to mine.

After mouthing several banal phrases, I ventured to ask the farmer and his wife whether they worked harder in the Liberated Areas than they had worked under the Japanese or Chiang Kai-shek.

"Harder," he said, grinning and mopping at his brow with his sleeve. "Everyone works more."

"Since the 8th Route came, your life's gone back then?"

The man looked up suddenly.

"Back!" he almost spit out the words. "No, indeed. Forward!"

"You do more work. Is that progress?"

"Of course. What else but?"

I stared at the peasant, at the plow, at his toil-worn wife. It seemed so unbelievable that anyone should say that harder work meant progress that I thought I had not heard him rightly. But he was vehement in repeating his assertions and there was no doubt of his meaning.

Later I thought this was just an exceptional outburst of cynicism, a dash of gall on a surging billow of despair. But further experiences in the villages dispelled the supposition soon enough. If I pointed out that the average American thought the aim of society ought to be to give people more leisure and not more work, I was met by reactions that ranged anywhere from astonishment to amused contempt.

"But you work for the capitalists."

"Before we worked for the landlords; now we work for ourselves and keep what we earn."

"You have so many machines. When we have machines, we won't work hard either."

"It is selfish not to work."

It seemed amazing, but there was no doubt about it. The farmer not only worked harder, but often reveled in his longer hours. Why? The answer was that he could keep the fruits of his toil. No more rents to the landlord. No more robbery by the soldiers. Thus he had an interest in working hard. And with that interest and with a new-born pride in work, he became fertile ground for the seeds of propaganda.

"Produce and we can have liberty!"

"Produce and we can overthrow Chiang Kai-shek!"

"Produce and we will end the feudal reign of the landlords."

On village walls, in defiled roadside shrines, in the schoolbooks and on the sides of carts—everywhere—were to be seen these slogans about the necessity and glory of work. And they were effective. Sometimes, however, the enthusiastic cadres went too far. On the long New Year holidays should the cadre try to stir the peasant from his hearth and home, he would be met by vacant stares, well-fed grumblings or good-humored hostility. For not even for the cadres would the peasant give up his fortnight seasonal rest.

Making the peasant sweat harder was for the government and the party a matter of simple logic. Surrounded on every side by hostile troops, living in what amounted to a besieged fortress, threatened on the ground with American guns and in the skies with American planes, the Communists had to make the peasant produce or die.

To perform this task without resort to slave labor appeared impossible. The Communists had no industry and had to depend almost entirely on farm labor. But how could they increase farm production when they were taking labor from the fields and putting it in the army.

I believe the Communists had six main ways of increasing production:

1. Collective labor.
2. Bringing women into the fields.
3. Making every soldier, official and party cadre produce.
4. Dividing the land.
5. Reviving handicrafts.
6. Persuading the people to work longer hours.

In North China there had long been a custom for peasants to get together and do certain jobs collectively. Families would often organize working teams from their surplus labor and send them around to do work for others. Or a man with a mule would plow the field of his neighbor in exchange for help in weeding his own land. These practices never played an important role in Chinese farm production and gradually faded out. The Communists, however, learned about them, refined the old methods and handed them back to the people with the proper propaganda stimulus and efficient organization methods.

Thus came into being labor exchange brigades, mutual work teams and labor co-operatives. With the exception of the guerrilla areas and newly recaptured places, I found few villages without them. In some cases, whole villages worked together on various tasks; in other cases, families pooled tools and draft animals for co-operative work in their own fields or for special jobs like land reclamation or irrigation.

Membership was entirely voluntary, with no punishment either direct or indirect for not joining. But let not the reader conclude from the extent of these mutual work teams that the peasant was joining them without persuasion. Had it been left to him, he would have puttered around feebly, gardening in his own futile and individualistic way. He had to be shown the profits in co-operative labor, that the brigades had a direct economic merit for his own life.

And he was shown.

In Three Wang Village, in the Shansi Mountains, for example, I found a mutual work team of 124 persons, 54 donkeys, 20 oxen, 5 horses and 2 mules. In this group, there was a rich farmer who formerly hired men to work his fields for him. Joining a co-operative and working himself, instead of hiring labor, he saved twenty bushels of wheat a year. In the same village, I came across an opium smoker who hired a man to work his two acres of land for him. Because of the money spent on opium and hired labor, he had barely enough food for himself. Joining the labor brigade, he cured himself of the drug habit, stopped using hired labor and saved two bushels of wheat a year. A poor farmer in the same brigade told me he formerly took sixteen days to weed one-third of an acre of land. Now, with the help of eleven group members, he weeded it in one day.

Although work was done collectively, fields, crops and implements remained private property, so the incentives of collectivism and private ownership were both used to the full. Special methods were worked out whereby more points were given those who contributed animals as well as labor.

Thus a woman, if she could do as much work as a man was counted a full-labor power and was paid accordingly. Old men and children who could not work fast or long enough were counted as half-labor powers. Two persons equaled one mule and a half a person equaled one donkey.

If the reader be shocked at equating animals with men, it ought to be remembered that these were the methods that the people themselves chose to compute the value of what they contributed to the co-operatives. In another village, in the Shansi Mountains, I found a brigade with ninety laborers, eighty-eight half-laborers, eight donkeys and three oxen. Between them they worked sixty acres of land, dividing the produce according to labor and according to the amount of land each family owned. Besides working on their own land, they had reclaimed twenty acres of waste land.

Pitiful efforts, you say. Yes. But there were also larger co-operative ventures. One of the most impressive I came across was in Chihsien County in Hopei Province. Here large tracts of land had been destroyed by floods in 1937, 1939 and 1940 and droughts in 1941 and 1942. The land had lain fallow for some time and everyone thought it would be many years before it could be used again. In August and September, 1947, however, two American farm boys, on loan from a Quaker church to UNRRA, and their Chinese students tractored five thousand mow (eight hundred acres) of this waste land so that it was ready for planting. The Americans expected the land would not be planted for a fortnight.

But in the meantime, unknown to them, fourteen villages had elected committees to divide the land. With pencils and papers and knotted ropes and abacus and stakes they split up the land into fourteen general plots. Then, having obtained seed from the government, on the night the

Americans finished their tractoring, they made the final preparations for planting. That very evening village leaders got up on the roofs with megaphones and shouted for the people to bring rollers, seeders and planters to the fields early the next day.

The following morning, two thousand farmers, men, women and children, appeared in the fields with five hundred mules and four hundred planters. As they fell to work a cloud of dust was raised that could be seen for miles over the countryside. At first the unaccustomed work went slowly, but after an hour the farmers were amazed to see how much land they had planted. They grew elated, began to sing, then competed with each other to see how much ground they could plant. By noon; that is, within four hours of starting, they had completely finished over eight hundred acres of land. So pleased were the villagers over the success of their first community labor that hundreds decided that thereafter they would work in no other way.

To stimulate the formation of labor co-operatives, the Communist party adopted a slogan: "Organized manpower equals a machine: co-operate and get rich!"

But even organized manpower was not able to solve some of the most pressing problems of production in the Border Region. For example, no one had found a way to deal with insects. In the Border Region there were no insecticides, no repellents and no poisons. The only way to fight insects was to catch and kill them.

Almost as hard on crop production was the shortage of farm animals. Although UNRRA shipped thousands of mules to China, few came to the Border Region. None could be bought outside and famine and war had killed off over half the animals. A drive had increased livestock to 70 per cent of normal, but many of these animals had to be used in transport and the situation on the farm remained desperate.

With mules scarce, men were often substituted for animals. Sometimes, man and wife pulled the plow together, but more often four men operated the plow—three pulling at the front, in the place of the mule, and one behind to guide.

Yet men could not equal mules when hooked up to a plow. A good mule could plow an acre of land in a day, but men could plow only half an acre.

Besides the shortage of farm animals, there was also a shortage of men, many of whom were at the front. This brought women into the fields and contributed greatly to the smashing of an old North China custom that women should not be seen outside the home. In harvest time, I saw women, even those with bound feet, and children gathering crops from the fields and working side by side with men. When the idea of mutual help teams was first introduced to the villages, old men and husbands objected violently to women working in the fields; for they were afraid what might happen when their wives and daughters came into contact with other men. Some of the women, however, revolted against their husbands and went to work in the co-operatives of their own accord. Later, when the men saw the money their wives were bringing in, they no longer objected. As more and more women went into the fields and entered handicraft industries, a saying grew up in the villages: "In all times before this, men supported women, but now maybe women can support men."

While the entrance of women into the fields took up part of the slack in production caused by the draft of men into the military service, the army itself took up more slack by turning its troops into producers. As with government cadres, every soldier was required to produce a certain amount of food or cloth or something useful each month. Nearly every company in the army had its own labor brigade, reclaiming waste land or helping farmers with plowing or at harvest time. Sometimes army production was carried to such extremes that whole regiments produced enough to feed themselves, while at other times, such as during General Liu Po-cheng's offensive into the Yangtze Valley, soldiers helped farmers reap harvests right in the middle of a campaign. And it should be admitted these soldiers in passing through Kuomintang cities also helped the poor to help themselves to the grain stores of city merchants and big landlords.

The battle to increase farm production was the most difficult economic problem the Border Region had to solve. Somewhat less important, but hardly less difficult, was the struggle to increase manufactured goods.

When the 8th Route Army first arrived in the Taihang Mountains it found peasants using spinning wheels as fuel and hand looms laid away on the beams of farmers' homes. Oil pressing, paper manufacture and leather tanning were almost lost arts. All those handicrafts, which roused Marco Polo's admiration and which had supplemented the farmers' income from the land, had been destroyed by the influx of Western machine-made goods, for even these rural mountain communities had become linked to the world market.

The Japanese war, however, suddenly cut off imports, and manufactured articles no longer could be found. To supply themselves with cloth and the army with uniforms, the Communists had to seek to revive the old handicrafts. There was no doctrine like Gandhiism behind the mass movement which revived weaving in the villages and introduced spinning into government offices, schools and armies, but only sheer necessity.

So successful was the revival of handicraft industries that the Border Region within a few years became self-sufficient in cloth, produced enough oil for every home to have an oil lamp, made wheat flour and paper and tanned leather enough for every important need.

Over 80 per cent of the industry in the Border Region, according to

Vice-Chairman Jung, went on in the home. Ninety-five per cent of the cloth was produced in village farmhouses.

Economic theorists might find it strange that the home handicrafts did not expand into workshops and weaving mills. The answer was that the mills found it impossible to compete with home industry. Factories need capital; home industries do not. Factories had to feed laborers or guarantee them a wage to buy food; home workers could live off the family's land.

During one of the more optimistic truce periods in 1946, the Border Region officials suddenly drew up an industrial plan. They would build a steel plant, two cotton mills, one woolen mill, two wheat rolling mills, two cement mills, one acid works and two match factories while operating six large coal mines. How would they finance this plan? Vice-Chairman Jung got up before a meeting of the People's Council and made a resolution that American capital be invited to participate in the development of industry in the Border Region. The resolution was unanimously passed. In the meantime, a large cotton mill was brought in from Shanghai.

Suddenly the short-lived truce was over. No funds of course came from America. Afraid of air raids, the government never put up the cotton mill. The big industrial plan was scuttled.

Saddened, but not discouraged, Border Region officials returned to a contemplation of their handicrafts, revising old ones, trying to make new ones. Old looms which could produce sixteen feet of cloth a day were gradually followed by newly invented one-man looms which could turn out forty-eight feet in a day.

What could the Border Region have done with industry? Could they have built up a mighty economy as they had built up a thriving handicraft output? That question, though intriguing to contemplate, would have to wait.

"Now and at this time," rationalized Border Region leaders, "handicrafts are the things for us."

As Lenin said, in the time of revolution, "there is always something backward in a country that is useful for the revolution."

24. Do They Live any Better?

HAVE you ever considered what it means to be a Chinese peasant in the interior of North China? Almost completely outside the influences of modern science and twentieth-century culture, the peasant was a brutal, blundering backwoodsman. He had never seen a movie, never heard a radio, never ridden in a car. He had never owned a pair of leather shoes, nor a toothbrush and seldom a piece of soap. And if he was a mountain man, he perhaps bathed twice in his life—once when he was married and once when he died—not because he so much enjoyed wallowing in the dirt, but because water was scarce and could be spared only for drinking.

Consider the immense implications of such a materially impoverished life. Consider what you as a human being would value most of all in such an environment as this. Is not the answer obvious: food, clothing, shelter, but above all food.

A characteristic North China peasant proverb was the following: "Husks and vegetable peelings are foodstuffs for half a year." Truly startling revelation! It meant the peasant could not even eat grain under the old rule, but only the grain shells or husks.

And the more bitter corollary: "If you don't eat husks for three days, it is hard to maintain the operation of the stomach." Hard indeed! And many people in the old days died for the want of even these husks.

The average consumption of millet, from what peasants in the poorer areas of North China told me, used to be two and four-fifths bushels a year. In the richer grain-producing areas it was only four bushels a year.

Rich area or poor area, the consumption of meat for the average farmer was only one and one-third pounds a year. Just about the weight of a good T-bone steak that you might gobble down at one sitting.

In the cotton-producing areas, farmers used to get two and two-thirds pounds of cotton cloth and the same amount of raw cotton a year per person. In the areas where cotton was not produced, a man got only one pound of cloth and a half a pound of cotton.

Figures. But those figures spelled tragedy for the peasant. A man used to be lucky to have rags. Suits were often shared between two and three people. When a father went out, he would put on the family pair of pants and leave his daughter naked on the bed. A man and wife would split a pair of pants between them. No wonder in north Shansi women did not go out into the fields.

You are stirred and appalled. You overflow with sympathy for such victims of feudal economy. But did the Communist make things any better? Were the labor brigades and the revived handicrafts really means of improving the people's livelihood or were they just subtle traps to snare the peasant into producing for the army? I can only tell you what the peasants told me and what I saw myself. In cotton-producing or non-cotton-producing areas, most of the peasants now had three and a half pounds of cotton a year. Border Region officials said they would soon make it four. Propaganda? Maybe. But for the most part soldiers and the peasants seemed better dressed than I had seen them a number of years before. In some places they were still in rags, but you could seldom find a man and a wife wearing the same pair of pants.

In the past in North China, and in the present in Chiang Kai-shek's areas, the New Year festival, instead of being a time of celebration and happiness, of feasting and merrymaking, as it was for the rich peasant or the landlord, was a period of bitterness and woe, of privation and horror for the poor farmer and the tenant. Flinging themselves out of doors and hiding in the fields, tenants would run from their landlord or his "dog leg" to avoid the New Year settlement day. If he dared not run away or wished to remain in the arms of his family over the holidays, the tenant, in order to pay his debts, would have commonly to strip his house, leaving his loved ones only husks, and sometimes not even that.

In the Liberated Areas when I was there, you could not find a poor peasant enjoying a great banquet over the New Year holidays, but neither could you find him cowering in the fields to avoid his creditors, nor could you find a peasant who gave his daughter as a slave to the landlord or as sleeping companion to the landlord's son in order to fulfill his debts. However, if you go to Kuomintang areas, you will still find these conditions, not as a rare, but as a commonplace, everyday occurrence.

The New Year holidays for hundreds of years have been the periods when the peasants' grain stocks are exhausted. During these periods only the landlord has surpluses. Yet in the New Year holiday fortnight that I traveled across the North China Plain I saw stocks of grain stored in reed-mat containers in many homes. And these were newly liberated areas. In the older areas, the peasant was generally able to get one year's grain surplus out of every three years. This was not without significance. It meant that in time of flood or famine the peasant had a crop reserve to see him through. Perhaps it even meant in the future—distant future, if you will—some new Pearl Buck could not find the conditions on which to base another *Good Earth* (a book written in the prosperous years of Chiang Kai-shek's reign).

In certain sections of North China, it is the custom of the villagers to carry their bowls of food out of doors at New Year's time and eat together. In the past the rich would gather at the east end of the village and eat wheat (a luxury) bread; the poor would gather at the west end and eat a water gruel. True class distinction—one based on points of the compass and food! In the older Liberated Areas I found no such distinctions, for the people all gathered together in the middle of the village and they ate not gruel, not even wheat bread, but meat. And not just at the beginning of the year, but on the Dragon Boat, the Moon, and the New Year festivals.

On the more luxurious side: In the past the great majority of the people thought it a great luxury to be able to smoke two or three cigarettes a year; by 1947 they could afford as much as one cigarette a day. Index of prosperity? No, of course not. But an advance. An indication of health. Due to what? Revived handicrafts that have no fear of being beaten down by the influx of machine-made goods from abroad.

Except once, in a town on the borders of the Kuomintang areas, I did not see any beggars in all my months of travel through the Border Regions. The absence of those creatures that grovel at your feet in Chiang Kai-shek's areas, crying with hideous inferiority—"master, master, a little pity!"—could not but impress an experienced traveler going through Communist areas.

The Communists had not brought tremendous economic benefits to the peasantry, but they had made hitherto unbearable conditions bearable. What they gave the peasant was a chance to live and an improved livelihood. This does not mean the Communists produced perfect conditions everywhere. They did not. You could still find child labor and some horrible examples of it, too. I have seen children of ten and eleven years put in buckets and lowered down fifty feet below the ground into coal pits. I have also seen peasants wheeling over mountain trails wheelbarrows piled with so much pottery that a mule could hardly have carried it. And I have also seen children working in cigarette factories for eight and ten hours a day. Under these circumstances to say that the Liberated Areas had eliminated economic injustice would be to betray the truth.

It would also be betraying the truth to take at face value Commissar Po's statement that the livelihood of 80 per cent of the people in the Border Regions had been improved during the Japanese war. From what I heard and saw, that was patently untrue. Eighth Route Army cadres who had been away from their homes for six and seven years always told me their first impression on going back to their native villages was the terrible poverty. But it was just this poverty that highlighted the Communist contributions to the people's economic welfare. For conditions in areas that had been under Communist control for only two years and those that had been under them for five or six were entirely different. It never failed to impress me that in many small villages the basically poorer mountain areas, conditions were far better than in larger villages on the richer plain. In the first case, the villages had been under Communist control for seven years; in the latter, only since the Japanese surrender.

An interesting feature of life in the older Communist regions was that many farmers, because they had surpluses, because they could make a little profit out of farming and because they had learned to figure, had begun to keep budgets. Here is the budget of a farmer named Shih Yu-li who had a family of six and two acres of land.

Income

8 bushels of grain
2⅖ bushels of Indian corn
4½ bushels of wheat
³⁄₁₀ bushels of beans
33 pounds of peppers
170 pounds of dried millet

670 pounds of cotton
400 pounds of oil seeds (worth $15)
cloth sold for $20
cotton sold for $11
spinning yarn sold for $3.80

Expenses

8 bushels of grain
2⅖ bushels of Indian corn
³⁄₁₀ bushels of beans
80 pounds of salt (costing $4.20)
8 pounds of coal ($5)
medicine ($2)
dyed cloth ($6)
repair house ($10)
miscellaneous $5

For the year, the farmer had a profit of $19.10 plus a four-month millet reserve. To an American, such figures must sound more like the figures for a garden than for those of a farm. But in China these figures spelled the difference between surplus and lack, between a healthy existence and starvation. From these and similar statistics I could only conclude that the farmers of North China would fight hard in defense of their government and in co-operation with the 8th Route Army against Chiang Kai-shek.

By now I had studied the history, government and economy of one Border Region in Communist territory, but in this study, though I had discovered many lessons, I had not discovered anything that added up to victory in the civil war.

For there was no question that the economic and productive machine owned by China's dictator was far superior to the economy of the Liberated Areas. In view of this circumstance, Communist economy could never hope to overcome the economy of Chiang Kai-shek. All the Border Regions could hope to do was to produce enough to keep an army in the fields, to support a government and to clothe and feed the people and keep them content until such time as other factors brought about a change in China's civil war.

What were those factors? They were many, but they could all be combined under one word: revolution.

To understand why Generalissimo Chiang Kai-shek and his well-equipped armies were defeated by the Chinese Communists, I think it is necessary to examine some of the broader aspects of this revolution. Such an examination will take us for a moment out of Red Territory and lead us into a long detour through Chinese history. But perhaps we can return better armed to understand the terror, violence and murders which occupy a great part of the rest of this book.

PART VI

PRELUDE TO REVOLUTION

❧

25. Contradictions in China's Development

THE fundamental features of Chinese life are her tremendous population and the unbroken length of her history, with the economic backwardness, the detailed and deeply rooted social forms and the ingrown conservatism resulting from them.

The population of this gigantic and diverse land, born to fertile plains, great rivers and high mountains, was endowed by nature with both a challenging environment and the prerequisites for a mighty civilization. But the very prodigality of nature defeated these people. They multiplied so greatly that they swarmed over every available piece of cropland and, having reached their natural boundaries, they ceased expanding, shut out the rest of the world, turned to admire themselves and began to rot. Overpopulation brought a bitter struggle for existence; internal wars and nomadic invasion sapped the people's vitality; a primitive written language, monopolized by a bailiff class of scholars, prevented the popularization of culture and successive Asiatic despotisms made impossible political growth and condemned them to economic backwardness.

In the same contradictory way, their long and continuous history was a blessing and a curse to this ancient people. The slow tempo of her development gave China time enough to develop a self-sufficient civilization and the political genius of the race enabled it to unite a country larger and more broken up than the whole European continent. But the very slowness of this development and the very genius for political uniformity with no quickening impulses from outside and no breaks in history from internal revolutions, tended to freeze social forms so that conservatism passed into the marrow of the people and became a racial characteristic. Agriculture, for forty centuries the unchanged basis for development, advanced by intensive means, becoming not farming but gardening. Condemned by the unbroken memories and practices of four thousand years, these ancient people brought with them into modern times an intolerably heavy burden from the past. While European civilization sprang anew from the ruins of Rome, Chinese civilization choked in the weeds of Confucianism and grew old amid a feudalism that had never completely been destroyed.

Neither Buddhism nor Tartar invasion could break this torpor as did Christianity and barbarian rule in the West. The cold paganism of Rome was dissolved in the warm teachings of Christ, but the austere Confucian ethic resisted the gentle corrosion of Buddhism and became a dogmatic weapon for insuring the rule of despots.[1] The Chinese bureaucrats knew neither the spirit of democracy nor much about the idea of the sanctity of the individual. Their faiths were ancestor worship, filial piety and a belief in the Confucian superior man—namely, themselves. With philosophy dominating religion, with everyone turned toward the Confucian grave instead of the Christian manger, toward death instead of birth, the masses became apathetic; the peasants hopeless, the rulers sterile.

In like manner, barbarian invasion, which shattered the political structure of Rome, never destroyed the government system of China. The Tartars, the Mongols and the Manchus simply took over a ready-made apparatus and allowed the Confucian administrators to act as their political lackeys. The alliance between Confucian bureaucrat and alien invader perpetuated an existing political system and made of the native administrators diseased creatures—hateful of the foreign master, but even more fearful of the masses whom they had betrayed. These mixed feelings of dread and guilt have corrupted the soul of the Chinese bureaucrat down to this day.

Thus China developed a kind of paralytic, immortal civilization in which little was learned and nothing forgotten.

Just why this happened is hard to explain and we cannot pretend to seek an adequate solution here. Part of the answer would seem to lie in the struggle for power between the clan chiefs and the early kings which shaped China's later political development.

Power in early China, as elsewhere, seems to have been magical in origin. Tribal elders derived their authority, not from decisions taken by democratic assemblages, but by the performance of magical coercive rites designed to force the hands of the unseen spirits that governed the

---

[1] This is an unavoidable oversimplification of a vast problem. Buddhism, entering China from India, became a religion of the proletariat and was a powerful agent in dissolving the ancient Sinic civilization. But Buddhism never conquered China to the extent that Christianity dissolved the paganism of Rome and western Europe, as is evidenced by the continued sovereignty of numerous local deities and folk gods, widespread animistic beliefs and the prevalence of ancestor worship as the binding ethic in Chinese rural life.

universe.[2] The continuity of life, success in the battle against the malevolent natural world, was preserved by the transmission of certain pious secrets. Control of society came to rest in the hands of those who knew the inner mysteries.[3]

Later, when warrior kings rose, their rule was sanctified by the belief that they and their ancestors possessed *Tien Ming* (Heaven Command)[4] and *Te* (Magical Power).[5] In this way they clothed themselves in a greater mystical prestige than that available to the kings of early Greece and Rome, but probably less than that available to the kings of Egypt. This was a potent factor in enabling them to come off the victor in the political battles with the chiefs of clans where the early Greek rulers lost out.[6] The focal point of Sinic society became not assemblies, as in pre-Christian Greece and Rome, but the monarch on his throne.[7] Thus China early came to a decisive fork in the road which took her down a path that was to lead her to an entirely different destination than the West and that was to stamp her civilization with a political character that perhaps may never be entirely erased.

The increase of royal power was also furthered by the largeness of the community. Sinic society grew by confederation and conquest. The introduction of new tribes into the nation and the mingling of cults and the intermarriage of ancestral gods provided an atmosphere that was

[2] Modern anthropologists incline to the view that primitive societies were neither monarchies, aristocracies nor democracies. It is, of course, not completely safe to apply this view to primitive China and such theses are in conflict with the writings of certain Chinese who depict ancient China as a primitive communist order where government was carried on by deliberative assemblages of the people. These writers would seem to be basing their theories on Engels' origin of the family, property and state. There is no proof that power in primitive China was democratic. Indications are that it was magical in origin.

[3] Knowledge, real or pretended, of occult sciences, has been so closely related to the struggle for power in China that nearly every rebellion against existing authority or state power, right down to that led by Dr. Sun Yat-sen, sprang from some form of secret society.

[4] Some students of the Chinese language believe the character *Tien* (Heaven) originally was an ideograph that represented a great man. Later it acquired the meaning of the "place where great men [the ancestors] dwell."

[5] The *Te* character was later given the connotation of virtue by Confucian scholars. Emperors ruled because they possessed *Te*. They fell when they lost the magic virtue.

[6] The power of the kings was already strong in the Yellow River plain around 1800 B.C. when the Shang dynasty emerged from the era of prehistory. The existence of still earlier dynasties indicates that the kings, though their power was limited, had long before won the battle with the clan chiefs and established a structure and a principle from which China was never able to escape.

[7] *Cf. On Power*, Bernard De Jouvenel (New York: The Viking Press, 1949), p. 90. The victory of the Roman clans led to the creation of the Roman Senate, an institution notably lacking from China, or else so buried in primitive times that it has exercised little influence on the present.

favorable to the accretion of kingly influence. This process reached its height between the eighth and third centuries B.C. when China was a collection of feudal states much like Europe of the Middle Ages. During this time, Confucius, a member of the aristocratic classes, alarmed at the disorders in the lower ranks of society and also fearful of the growth of princely power, raised an anguished appeal for the rulers to go back to the ways of the ancient virtue.[8] He spoke in vain. In the next three hundred years, during the period of the Contending States, the various principalities smashed their own aristocracies, raided the castles of feudalism, released the serfs, turned them into state service and made war on each other until the whole process was consummated when one state finally gobbled up all the others. What came into being with the establishment of the first empire in 251 B.C. was a centralized feudalism in which new feudal lords continued to exist under an all-powerful sovereign.

This primitive universal state concentrated a great deal of power in its hands because it smashed the old nobility,[9] reclassified society, limited slavery and serfdom, established land tenantry and brought a class of free men into the service of the bureaucracy. But it never created the kind of absolute imperium that existed in ancient Egypt; for in spite of its despotic nature, the central power could not completely destroy the clan system, and it was forced to compromise to such an extent that almost all the social authority, such as control of marriage, dispensation of clan justice and the ordinary business of life, remained in the hands of family elders. Political power fell into the hands of the land owning gentry. This class furnished the state with most of its bureaucrats who were chosen for their ability to recite the Confucian dogma—the philosophy of the defeated nobility and the ancient medicine men. In such a manner the damaged aristocracy took revenge on the new state power by limiting to some extent its interference in the social hierarchy.[10]

[8] Confucius, much derided by leftist writers, was a "reactionary," in the sense that he wanted to turn back the clock of history. He seems to have been an opponent of both the princely power and the common people who were tending to form an alliance against the aristocracy of his times. In this sense he was both an opponent of democracy, and also of despotism. His doctrines, seven hundred years later, were used by the state as a weapon of thought control but, in a way, they were also checks on the emperor's power.

[9] Chin Shih Huang Ti, the first emperor of China, destroyed the ranks of the old aristocrats by immolating the Confucian scholars, burning the books of the feudal philosophers and creating a centralized bureaucracy. His actions have been execrated by Chinese scholars and the Chinese traditionally have given as much, if not more, admiration to lords who fought unjust kings as they have given to kings who slew nobles.

[10] The continuity of the priest-sage-scholar-bureaucrat tradition in China is amazing and the continuing prestige of the old aristocrats can be seen from the fact that Dr. H. H. Kung, a direct descendant of Confucius, was but recently premier of China.

The fetters which the aristocrats put on the state in China can also be seen in the double character of the kingly power. Because he was not only a material ruler, but the mystical symbol of the community, the emperor was always hemmed around by ancient ritual and he was never able to play the role of Caesar, leader-adventurer or absolute monarch. In fact, he had often to play the role of sage (as did Chiang Kai-shek) which had been laid out for him by the feudal philosophers. In effect, the emperor was the father of the people and also the Medicine-Man-in-Chief.

This partial compromise between the state system and the old clan system was one of the reasons why Chinese society froze into seemingly immortal forms. Customs and folkways, filial piety and ancestor worship, were more sovereign than the state power.

The repetitious nature of Chinese history finds its most depressing expression in the fact that, though China destroyed formal feudalism over two thousand years ago and though she then built up a higher civilization than any known in the West, yet feudal remnants and a feudal way of life continued to dominate society right up to the present day.

The meagerness of Chinese feudalism is evidenced by the absence of any real medieval productive cities. Though China developed a comparatively complex economic life and created towns larger than any in the world up to the nineteenth century, she did not give birth either to mercantile capitalism or industrial towns.

The craft-guild culture of the West had established itself on a relatively high economic plane by divorcing itself from agriculture and creating its own independent organizations—the cities. Chinese handicraft, however, even where it was located in the towns, was strangled by conservative customs and a network of co-operative agencies, sometimes closely allied with the Confucian family system. Moreover, a large part of the handicraft remained bound either to the governing bureaucracy or to agriculture and thus preserved the character of slave labor or home industry. Chinese cities therefore were not so much centers of production as of administration and consumption. Even Peiping, the center of the empire, was not an industrial city. If urban handicrafts did develop, as in Hangchow, where Marco Polo in the ninth century found twelve thousand workshops, the guilds rarely organized themselves to oppose the government but rather for the sole purpose of guaranteeing industrial secrecy and distributing to a narrow market. They, therefore, restrained free competition, and served as a check on technical progress and market expansion.

These and other factors blocked the development of a merchant-industrial class and insured the survival of a despotic state cemented in the remains of feudalism. Emperors might change, but society did not;

and the landlords, the gentry, and the janizary-dominated court at Peiping became identified in the minds of the people with those clay and wooden images in their temples; that is, they were eternal, they were fate, they were gods. True, they might every couple of centuries or so exercise Mencius' famous "right of rebellion" and change their rulers, just as they beat their idols with sticks when they were displeased, but the earthly as well as the heavenly pantheon remained. The struggle against the state might even be democratic in the extreme, and unfrocked monks, innkeepers and peasant soldiers might rise to the throne in Peiping, but the very fact that dynasties toppled and thrones did not suggests the inner poverty of these peasant rebellions.

What all these popular uprisings needed in order to convert them into a social revolution were the prophets of a new religion dignifying the worth of man and the industrial democracy furnished by well-developed cities. Even a young country such as America, with no burdensome traditions from the past, could not rid the south of slavery without pressure from the northern cities. How then could a tradition-ridden country like China, with no rising merchant or industrial class, free itself from medieval slavery? The people could change their rulers, but to alter the fundamental condition of their lives remained beyond their powers.

The smashing down of China's wall of isolation by the West in the early nineteenth century had a cataclysmic effect and, in the long run, doomed the ancient Chinese society to extinction, because on the one hand it brought Christian ideals and Western concepts of democracy to China while on the other hand it destroyed the self-sufficient feudal economy of the ancient society, broke open the walls of the clans, changed the traditional patterns of "right conduct," and created classes that had hitherto been absent from Chinese life. In the beginning, however, Western penetration of China produced an exactly opposite effect; it did not weaken, but strengthened the feudal power.

In the middle of the nineteenth century, after the Western powers gained a firm foothold in China, there developed in the south a movement of peasants, "long-term" workers and "righteous scholars" known as the Taiping Rebellion. This movement was not unlike the old peasant uprisings against the throne in Peiping, but it had been fertilized by New Testament texts concerning the righteousness of the poor, and it had more of a social basis than the old popular revolts. For this reason it frightened the landed gentry of Central China who had hitherto been in the forefront of the demand for Westernization and who had held aloof from the alien Manchu court. These men soon found it convenient to forget both their modern ideas and their Chinese racial patriotism and to join hands with the foreign dynasty and with the British General Gordon and the American adventurer Ward to put down the rebellion. This triple alliance between Manchu despotism, Chinese feudalism and Western imperialism against the people of China had its counterpart in a triple betrayal. The Manchu court, fearing foreign guns, but fearing more the spread of foreign ideas among their people, betrayed the country to the West. The Chinese landlords, hating the alien dynasty, but fearing the peasants, betrayed their own race. Finally, the foreign powers betrayed their own avowed democratic principles in order to preserve feudalism.

During the next fifty years, the intelligentsia, under the pressure of Western concepts and spurred by the fear of loss of national sovereignty, took up the battle against Manchu despotism. The Westernization of the country became more and more the demand of the scholarly bureaucracy. In 1898, these scholars tried to limit the despotic powers of the Manchus by a series of mild reforms. But these men allied themselves with Confucian ideals and they made no attempts to smash the walls of village clan life and use the released prisoners in the services of a revolutionary power. It is not surprising that the movement remained nothing more than a conspiracy of a few brilliant scholars and collapsed like a house of cards when the Empress Dowager imprisoned the young Emperor Kuang Hsu and seized all the reformists she could and chopped them in half at the waist as traitors. Such was the minor significance of the Reform Movement of Kang Yu-wei.

Even when the Manchu dynasty fell in the 1911 Revolution before the attack of foreign ideas, Chinese society remained pretty much what it had been. There might be ferment among the intellectuals at the top, but in the countryside the peasantry greeted the so-called revolution with little more excitement than his ancestors had greeted the change of emperors. The imperial trappings were gone but underneath still lay the rotten body of medieval life.

More fundamental than the overthrow of the empire was the economic change that was taking place in the country. The requirements of international trade soon gave to the coastal cities a new importance in Chinese life, as the growth of Shanghai, a mud flat before the advent of foreigners, eloquently testified. To act as brokers between foreign and native capital there came into being a class of entrepreneurs—the Chinese compradors, who were often landlords or bureaucrats or both. Over the course of a century, these men became large merchants, city bankers and factory owners; in short, a budding bourgeoisie. Trailing along behind them came the clerks, the accountants, the new shop owners and the lower-ranking army officers—a nascent petty bourgeoisie. And finally, as foreign machine-made goods depressed home handicrafts, a mass of dispossessed peasants flocked into the cities to become factory workers, coolies, thieves and beggars—the proletariat.

Born late, these classes—if you can call such paltry groupings classes —could not repeat the history of Western countries. This was particularly true of Chinese businessmen, merchants and factory owners who could not play the progressive role they played in Europe and America because of the peculiar structure of Chinese industry and the conditions under which it originated. To begin with, Chinese industry was extremely weak, with only a minute segment of the population engaged in it. One of the reasons for this weakness was the agrarian structure of the country. Landlords, who received 50 and 60 per cent of their tenants' crops found agriculture more profitable than industry and were loath to invest in city enterprises. In the West, the city burgher would have led the peasants against the landlords, but in China the compradores were so involved with the big landowners that they dreaded a change of property relations in any form. In addition to its weakness, Chinese industry was concentrated in a narrow strip along the seacoast so that the capitalist was separated from the great mass of the people in the interior. Finally, it must be remembered that modern Chinese business enterprises and industry were all an outgrowth of trade with the West. The proprietors of the principal industrial, banking and shipping companies were foreigners who derived not only profits from China, but also played a political role in Chinese affairs, often opposing the popular wishes of the people, of which the interference in the Taiping Rebellion was but one of many instances.

Thus, the Chinese merchant-industrial class, because of the conditions of its birth, was involved in a double contradiction. For the city bankers and the factory owners had not only failed to cut the cords which bound them to the landlords, but they had also fashioned new chains which bound them to foreign capital. This forced them, even against their will, to put further brakes on the development of Chinese society.

The political isolation of the Chinese merchant-industrial class is best characterized by the events of the 1920's during the rise of Chiang Kai-shek to power. When World War I ended, China's young industry faced a crisis because it could not compete with foreign industry and because the purchasing power of the peasantry was small. Chinese capitalists were anxious to protect what power they had by raising tariffs against foreign imports, but such actions were forbidden by the unequal treaties China had been forced to sign with the foreign nations. The native industrialists wanted a strong national government to contest these treaties and also to put an end to the wars of the provincial warlords. Thus they began to look with favor on the Kuomintang of Dr. Sun Yat-sen which had just such a program of abolishing extraterritoriality and founding an independent nation. However, when the Kuomintang, after the death of Dr. Sun, marched north, under Chiang Kai-shek and in alliance with the Communists, the program included not only the overthrow of imperialist influences but the reduction of rents in the countryside. When the Chinese bourgeoisie saw not only the peasants rising, but the city workers, too, they immediately forgot their anti-imperialist views and joined forces with the foreign powers in Shanghai to quell the popular nature of the movement.

Just as the Manchu court had found strong men[11] in the landed gentry of Central China to crush the Taiping Rebellion, the foreign powers and their agents, the compradors, now found a strong man in Chiang Kai-shek to subjugate the Chinese. In return for promises of financial backing, Chiang Kai-shek immediately obliged his supporters in a particularly sanguinary way. He gave five thousand rifles to the mobsters and gangmen of Tu Yueh-sen, a Shanghai Al Capone who had built his fortune on opium, to smash the workers' organizations and slaughter thousands of disarmed workers in the native city of Shanghai. At the same time, Chiang loosed his soldiers in the countryside to massacre thousands of local peasant leaders. This act once again strengthened feudalism and brought back an Asiatic despotism on top of the Chinese people.

Having divorced itself from the workers in the cities and particularly from the peasant masses in the countryside, the Chinese bourgeoisie lost the capacity for political action. Unable to fight the landlords, as European city merchants once fought manorial barons, the nascent capitalists had no other course but to permit themselves to be dragged like captives behind Chiang Kai-shek's military chariot.

Chiang Kai-shek, himself, having crushed the workers and the farmers and enslaved a weak capitalist class, had to turn for support to the landlords and the gentry. Because he allied himself with medieval elements of Chinese society, he could not solve the basic problem of China— agrarian revolution. It is not surprising that he, therefore, became one of the most contradictory despots in the four thousand years of Chinese history.

But if the Chinese bourgeoisie, captive to both landlords and foreign capital, was too weak to play the role the French bourgeoisie played in the French Revolution, then the Chinese working class was also too weak to play the role the Russian proletariat did in the Russian Revolution. On this hard rock the Chinese Communist party, in fact, the whole Marxist world, cracked its head more than once before it learned any wisdom.

What originally gave the Chinese Communists the idea that they could conquer power through the proletariat was undoubtedly the success of the Russian Revolution itself.

[11] It seems to be an old Chinese custom for the possessing classes to invite foreigners in to crush their own people. Thus in the sixteenth century when a rebellion overthrew the Ming dynasty in Peiping, a Chinese general named Wu San-kwei, guarding the Great Wall passes at Shanhaikwan invited the Manchus in to crush the rebels. The Manchus, having performed this act, were not willing to leave and thereafter overran all of China.

There were, however, important differences between the character and the life conditions of the Russian and the Chinese proletariat. Chinese workers were perhaps more revolutionary than their brothers in the West for the simple reason that they were ferociously oppressed, not only by their native capitalists but by the forces of foreign imperialism and feudal gangsterism. In the semicolonial state of China, there was no economic foundation for social reform such as that existing in western Europe so that the whole working class was predisposed to seek a solution of their dilemma by violent revolutionary methods. They simply had no other way out. But the revolutionary spirit of the Chinese working class could not make up for some of its gravest weaknesses. In the first place, there were only two and a half to three million modern industrial workers in a total population of 450 million. There were perhaps ten to twelve million town handicraftsmen and hired laborers and a large number of rural workers who might be classed among the proletariat but they were entirely too scattered to play the same role they did in the Russian Revolution. Secondly, the Chinese proletariat was very young and inexperienced when compared to the proletariat in Western countries, while its cultural standard was far below that of its enemies in the bourgeoisie.[12] Finally, and very important, three-quarters of all the modern industrial workers in China were concentrated in zones of foreign control and under the menacing guns of foreign warships.

Shanghai provided the classic prototype of this dual control. "Here," in the words of Edgar Snow, "you could see British, American, French, Japanese, Italian and Chinese soldiers, sailors, and police, all the forces of world imperialism combined with native gangsterism and the comprador bourgeoisie, the most degenerate elements in Chinese society "co-operating" in wielding the truncheon over the heads of the hundreds of thousands of unarmed workers."[13]

The Chinese proletariat therefore had to contend not only with one enemy, as did the Russian worker of 1917, but with two: his own nascent bourgeoisie and the entrenched interests of the Western powers. All insurrections in the cities were therefore doomed to failure almost from the start. After the failure of the 1927 Revolution, the Communist party had to fall back on the rural areas and, while retaining the aims of Socialism and the ideology of Communism, assumed in practice the

---

[12] We have been speaking here mainly about the upper or comprador bourgeoisie. The Chinese merchant-industrial class, however, also included elements which were not tied to foreign capital and which various observers have called the "national" or "middle" bourgeoisie. This class controlled by the big landowners and the compradors never held any real political power and therefore under certain circumstances it tended to ally itself with the Communists against Chiang Kai-shek.

[13] Edgar Snow, *Red Star Over China*, Random House.

role of agrarian democrats. In the meantime, Chiang Kai-shek held the cities and his power remained relatively secure.

The Japanese invasion of China, plus World War II, however, produced a striking change in the correlation of forces, not only in China, but all over the world and gave a mighty impetus to the Chinese Revolution.

In the first place, the defeat of Japan, the disarming of Italy, the almost total collapse of French power and the exhaustion of England meant that these powers could not assay any serious adventures in the Pacific even to save the regime of Chiang Kai-shek. Furthermore, the Western powers, as a means of keeping Chiang in the war against Japan, had abrogated all the unequal treaties, agreed to return the foreign concessions and relinquish all military bases; in short, to recognize China as a sovereign nation. This is just what the Kuomintang government had been demanding for twenty years, but in finally putting his stamp of approval on this agreement, Chiang practically signed his own death warrant. For, in effect, this meant that if the Communists ever gained enough power in the countryside so that they could move on the cities, Chiang would be totally without that Western support which had heretofore been an aid in keeping down the workers.

That, of course, could only be the final act of a war between the Communists and Chiang because the Red's 8th Route Army was still very much confined to rural China. But in this countryside itself, great changes had been brought about by the Japanese invasion. Driven into the interior, deprived of its coastal industry and foreign trade, the Chiang Kai-shek despotism during the eight years of the Japanese war came into still sharper conflict with the Chinese people. The comprador bourgeoisie grew more powerful, but its power rested on the ability of the upper bureaucracy to wrest control of important commercial, industrial and banking ventures from native groups in the interior. Also, at the end of the war, the Kuomintang bureaucrats gobbled up many enterprises the Japanese had looted from the Chinese people in Shanghai and Hankow, besides thrusting their way into newspapers, agricultural corporations, shipping companies, banks and many ventures large and small that had hitherto belonged to private interests. Such actions, which alienated native industrialists, merchants and others, tended to isolate the ruling group from quarters that had hitherto supported them. The weight of the petty bourgeoisie, though relatively insignificant, was now also ready to be thrown against the despotism, because government clerks, teachers and army officers, paid in printing press money, felt that their rulers could no longer guarantee their economic livelihood. Finally, the war had brought significant changes in the attitude of the democratic intelligentsia who had become disgusted with the passive attitude Chiang adopted toward the Japanese while suppressing every kind of democratic freedom among his own people. These men, though they had no firm social support, had a great following among the students and they were the most outspoken of all Chiang's critics, some of them even being killed for their views.

In these circumstances, for the Communists to adapt Lenin's program of an immediate proletarian dictatorship to China would have been chimerical. The correlation of forces practically compelled Mao Tze-tung, leader of the Communist party, to advocate a democratic revolution on the broadest possible lines. In switching tactics from proletarian dictatorship to a union of all groups, Mao was certainly closer to the February Revolution in Russia or even in some respects to the French Revolution or a Cromwellian peasant war than to the October Revolution. If that horrified orthodox Marxists, Mao could point out that it was not until the Chinese Communists adopted this program that they began to make any headway. In calling forth a democratic revolution, the Communists hoped to gain the eventual support of nearly the whole mass of the people, except the landlords, the higher army officers, the upper-crust bureaucrats and the very few favored industrialists and compradors tied to Chiang Kai-shek's machine and to foreign capital.

True, they might arouse the antagonism of America, who might see her strategic position threatened, but this opposition would also give to the revolution against Chinese society the nature of a fight for national independence. If Mao could identify himself and his party with the new upsurge of patriotic feeling created by the Japanese war, so much the better.

The Chinese Revolution thus became an extremely complex problem. The central problem of France had been to establish equality and democracy; that of modern Germany, to consolidate into a nation; of Russia, the agrarian revolution. But for China, the problem was to solve all these questions at once. She had to fight for national independence because her status was still that of a semicolonial power under foreign domination; she had to fight for democracy, for she was still under a despotism; and she had to create an agrarian revolution because she was still choking among feudal weeds.

As for the method of conducting that revolution, since the city workers were still so weak and since the Communists were confined to the countryside, it could only be by a peasant war.

Thus, the whole burden of China's future was once again loaded onto the already bent and bowed back of the Chinese farmer.

The essence of China's civil war became a struggle for the affections of the peasant. This simple toiler, caught between two forces, held the destiny of his country in his hands. For whoever won this man's heart was fated to become the ruler of China.

26. The Land Problem

THE Communists could not hope to overthrow Chiang Kai-shek without finding a mighty support in the hearts of the people. Such a support was guaranteed by the land problem.

Early Europeans arriving in China had found agricultural industry, with admitted differences, almost on the same level as it had been several hundred years before in the West. Nevertheless, conditions of land-ownership were already acute. About the time Cromwell was leading his army of artisans and peasants against the English Parliament, the whole area of cultivated land within the limits of the Manchu Empire was 130 million acres. With a population of seventy million, the land problem was plainly critical. But within the next three hundred years, while the area of cultivated land was doubling, the population was increasing over six times! This tremendous overcrowding was made worse by the fact that there was a tendency of public land to become private. Before the 1911 Revolution, Manchurian nobles had already usurped almost all the royal land and after that revolution corrupt bureaucrats and greedy gentry seized vast amounts of temple, educational and military land through illegal sales. No doubt China's contact with modern world commerce was the chief compelling force in bringing about this change from public to private ownership. Such a process, accompanied by increasing concentration, together with archaic methods of farming, automatically sharpened the crisis caused by excess rural population. The peasant, scarcely emerged from the Middle Ages, was doubly trapped because the process was not taking place in medieval times, but under terrible pressure from Western capital and cheap Western products.

Dr. Sun Yat-sen, father of the Kuomintang, and the Communists both realized that China could not be freed unless the peasant were freed and they began preaching a program of land to the tiller—that is to say, they proposed to the peasant that he support them in their northward march against the warlords in exchange for their help in getting him land. This could obviously be achieved only at the expense of the landlords. The peasant did not react to the slogans of unifying the country or overthrowing imperialism, presented him by the Kuomintang bourgeoisie. But he did react, and with impassioned violence, to Dr. Sun's slogan of "land to the tiller," because, choking in his narrow plot, he wanted to throw out the landlord. On this basis, the peasants rose up like a mighty flood, some pouring into Chiang Kai-shek's armies, some joining the peasant unions. On the broad backs of these farmers, Chiang Kai-shek swept to power.

The Chinese bourgeoisie, however, was so tied up with the landlord that it could not abide this ally and turned the peasant soldiers against their brothers in the village associations. Not all the peasants had risen, but those who had were suppressed. Thus the landlords were not settled with despite all the promises of soil to the tillers.

As soon as the mobsters of Tu Yueh-sen's Green Gang had cut down the workers in Shanghai and given the signal for the counterrevolution, the higher army officers, most of whom were large landowners, abandoned all thought of reducing land rents by 25 per cent in accordance with the adopted and passed program of the Kuomintang. Far from reducing rents, the landlords often demanded and received 65 per cent instead of 50 per cent of the tenant's rice or wheat crop. Should the tenant protest, the landlords would simply have their bailiffs throw him in their dungeons. The compensation the peasant received for putting Chiang Kai-shek in power was thus not land or even rent reductions, but threats, curses, blows and sometimes a coffin.

With the party traitor to the program of their founding fathers, the learned economists in Chiang's government began to justify the betrayal by finding that the land problem was a myth and did not exist.

In adopting this attitude, they could conceivably find support if they wished in some very useful figures. On the morrow of Chiang Kai-shek's *coup d'état* in Shanghai all the arable land within China was estimated at one and one-third billion mow.[1] The population of the country was around four hundred and fifty million, of which about three hundred and fifty million were farmers. In effect, and under the most ideal conditions, this meant that the peasant would have to extract taxes, food, fuel, clothing—in fact, everything he would ever use in his life from an iron hoe to a wooden coffin—out of no more than four mow (two-thirds of an acre) of land. This fact by itself suggested that China would have to end feudalism or perish. But Chiang's agronomes now discovered in these figures proof of another sort. "What is the use of dividing the land?" they blandly asked. "There is not enough anyway." As for land concentration, it did not exist and hence there was no cause for revolution. No doubt, the economists wished to rationalize their betrayal of the peasants. But their assumptions not only ignored the wishes of the farmer—as if this flesh-and-blood man were too insignificant to find a place in their figures—but also ignored the process of land concentration which was taking place before their eyes.

People who note the incredibly small plots of Chinese farms are apt to draw the conclusion that there are no large landholdings in China. But small fields, far from showing no land concentration, illustrate the

[1] One mow equals approximately one-sixth of an acre.

backward nature of an economy in which the landlords do not manage large farms for production, but parcel out their land to tenants in order to obtain rents. In Honan, south of the Yellow River, one might ride a donkey cart past scores of villages for a whole day and still be on the same family's land. In Shantung large areas of clan land were monopolized by the descendants of Confucius and in many places the writer came across associations of landlords known as the Hundred Ching Pai, or the Ten Thousand Mow Group. In northern Kiangsu, there was a temple that owned two hundred thousand mow (thirty-three thousand acres) of land.[2] The chief monks, engaged in rent collecting and the practice of usury, maintained big families, including concubines, and had dwellings far grander than even the magistrates. Utterly dependent on the monks for farm tools, the tenants were often conscripted for labor by the armed guards of these ecclesiastical landowners.

Although the national government had no nationwide statistics, there were nevertheless innumerable provincial statistics that formed a most impressive picture of the revolutionary situation engendered by the conditions of landownership. With every desire not to burden this text with figures, I cannot refrain from introducing the statistics of landownership in the home provinces of Chiang Kai-shek, T. V. Soong, H. H. Kung and the brothers Chen Li-ju, and Chen Kuo-fu, party bosses of the Kuomintang.

There is here before us a picture of a nation carrying in its womb a peasant war. In a backward and terribly overcrowded country such as China, where a plot of land often means the difference between life and death, these figures are of far greater significance than they would be in a land-rich country such as the United States.

Generally speaking for the whole of China, landlords and rich peasants forming about 10 per cent of the population occupied 55 to 65[3] per cent of the land. If you do not wish to accept these figures there are those made some years ago, before concentration reached its present height, by the National Land Commission of the Chiang government. This commission, investigating conditions in 11 provinces found that 1500 big landlord families owned on an average over 333 acres per family. Another investigation of over 700,000 peasant families in the same districts showed the average ownership of these families to be 2⅗ acres —130 times smaller than the big landlord families. This remarkable fact alone would suggest the thought that the peasant, impelled by the inequality of landownership and dying on his pitiful plot, must at what-

[2] See *Agrarian China*—published by the Institute of Pacific Relations.
[3] There are no accurate land statistics in China. The Communist party declared 10 per cent of the people held 80-90 per cent of the land. But this seems an exaggeration.

Province	Landlords		Rich Peasants		Middle Peasants		Poor Peasants	
	Per cent of Families	Per cent of Land	Per cent of Families	Per cent of Land	Per cent of Families	Per cent of Land	Per cent of Families	Per cent of Land
Chekiang	3.3	53.0	2.7	8.0	17.0	19.0	77.0	20.0
Tenglu (Shansi)	0.3	24.29	1.82	5.43	68.33	61.43	29.55	8.85
Kwangtung	2.0	53.0	4.0	13.0	12.0	15.0	74.0	19.0
Wusin (Kiangsu)	5.77	47.27	5.68	17.73	20.06	20.83	68.49	14.7

From *Agrarian China*, published by the Institute of Pacific Relations, pp. 3, 4, 8.

ever cost produce an organization able to wrest land from the landlord to give himself a chance to live.

These conditions should have been a warning to both the land-lords and the Chiang Kai-shek government. Chinese rulers, however, are traditionally contemptuous of the masses' ability to interfere in their own fate. Instead of seeking to alleviate these conditions by land reform, the Kuomintang bureaucrats adopted just the opposite policy. During the Japanase war, land became concentrated to an unheard of degree in modern China. Despite the fact that an estimated fifty million mow of land were lying desolate in the provinces of Honan, Hupeh, and Hunan and despite the fact that an estimated ten to fifteen million farmers died of starvation during and after the war, Chiang Kai-shek's bureaucrats using their superior military force and their bureaucratic positions began a gigantic land grab in the interior of China. At the end of the war, the land grab by the Chiang government was even more callous and more open. All the land that the Japanese had robbed from the Chinese people, instead of being turned back to them was taken over by the Kuomintang. Japanese land in Formosa was appropriated by mainland carpetbaggers, while the North China Exploitation Company seized several hundred thousand mow of land in Hopei.

Taking a leaf from the book of their masters, the smaller bureaucrats and the militarists, unable to live on the paper money salaries given them by the Chiang government, also began amassing landholdings as a means of security in times of inflation. Under the concerted drive for land by Chiang's interlopers from the coast, even rich peasants and small land-lords began to lose their holdings. In Szechuan, it was estimated that during eight years of war anywhere from 20 to 30 per cent of the total landlords were new landlords who occupied 90 per cent of the land owned by the old landlords. This explosive bomb directed against the native money-landlords brought forth a bitter reaction. "All land under the sky belongs to the emperor," used to be an old Chinese saying. Now the dispossessed landlords complained: "All land under the sky belongs to Chiang Kai-shek." Such a way of speaking, of course, was mainly symbolic, but it had revolutionary significance.

This creation of a new rural gentry, however, had another side. There was arising from the seized land not only a new rural bourgeoisie but new paupers. The number of peasants dispossessed from their land because of unpaid mortgages and unpaid debts, both in Chiang's areas and in the Japanese-occupied areas, rose by untold thousands during the Japanese war. In the famine periods in North China, peasants who had to give land as security for grain borrowed during the spring, within a space of two or three years would lose everything. It was common for three or four members of a family of seven to starve to death for these reasons. Land concentration thus meant corpses to fertilize the earth, but it also meant thousands of souls for agrarian revolution.

Concentrated ownership of land in crowded China could not help but produce different results from what such a process produced in unpeopled America. In the United States, the way American moneyed barons seized the Western lands was brutal enough, but out of it came railroads, mines, great cattle ranches—all the overflowing gifts of capitalism. But land grabbing in China only filled the granaries of the landlords with grain rents. Thus the process was not productive, but parasitic in nature.

Compared to Prussian junkers or the landed nobility in czarist Russia, the Chinese landlord was a very backward man. While the rich German and Russian peasant leased in land for large-scale farming, the rich Chinese leased out land merely to suck profits from the sweat of his tenants. Reactionary as they were, the kulak and the junker performed at times progressive functions in rural economy; the Chinese landlord performed none. The obverse side of this feudal medal was that the peasant leased in land to maintain a slavelike livelihood. In capitalist countries a landless peasant either goes to the factory or hires himself out as a laborer. But in China there was no industry and no large-scale farming and he had to become a sharecropper in order to live. Thus, while he suffered land hunger, he was at the same time chained to the land.

This semislave type of tenancy was inseparable from the system of usury practiced in China. The most massive and best-built houses in the villages and small towns were always the pawnshops. What the banks were to the rich, these shops were to the poor. The majority of the pawnshop owners were landlords or merchants tied to the landlords. These pawnshops were most often instruments for getting hold of the peasant's land. In Honan, I found a landlord who owned 350 acres of land in a village with only seven hundred acres. Most of this land had been acquired through the pawnshop.

Such deals were possible in the first place only because of the desperate condition of the farmer who had to agree to any rate of interest when in need of food. These rates of interest increased in alarming proportion during the reign of Chiang Kai-shek. In 1932, a peasant borrowing $100 had to pay back at the end of the year $125. By 1936, he had to pay $140 to $160. During the war, the interest jumped to 100 per cent in grain for a three-month period. The severity with which peasant debtors were treated was sometimes unbelievable. The writer came across a farmer in Honan who borrowed a hundred catties of millet from his landlord before planting.[4] At harvest time, according to the agreement, he was to pay back two hundred catties. When he could

[4] One catty=1⅓ lbs.

not raise the amount, he begged for more time and agreed to pay 300 catties at the next harvest. Unable to pay, because of drought, he was then compelled to convert the loan into a mortgage on his land, four mow of which he eventually had to give up. Because of this his mother and two children starved to death. Thus, what originated as a small-grain loan of a hundred catties ended up as a debt of four mow of land and three corpses.

"In good years, the landlord grows crops in the fields. In bad years, the landlord grows money in his house."

This bitter verse of poor Shansi farmers aptly describes conditions whereby drought and famine were often the very instruments landlords and rich peasants used for amassing land and wealth.

In the Japanese areas during the war this process was much accelerated, but in Chiang Kai-shek's areas, the financial organs of the Kuomintang government began to overpower the pawnshops and the local usurers. Formerly, pawnshops had loaned five times the sums the banks loaned to the villages, but by 1946, pawnshops were lending an estimated two-eighths of the amounts loaned out by banks. The usurious character of the loans, however, was maintained. Instead of getting relief, the farmer was only exploited more intensely by Kuomintang banks, which monopolized the operation of farm credit loans and general agricultural finance.

This is explained by the fact that the banks, having muscled in on the usury racket, compensated the landlords by limiting the loans to rural co-operatives organized by the gentry. The county co-operatives would then lend money to village chiefs who would in turn lend it out to farmers. Thus the peasant now had three usurers on top of him instead of one. The process, however, was further complicated by the fact that the local party officials, with the support of the right-wing clique of the Kuomintang, began to expel from the villages rural co-operatives organized by the rural bourgeoisie and partly backed by Dr. H. H. Kung, finance minister of China. This was often done in co-operation with the local military or by party rascals who, when all other measures failed, accused local merchants of being Communists. Giving loans to a small majority of the local party officeholders while discriminating against some of the older gentry and the majority of the farmers was like holding a pistol against the head of the middle peasants and small merchants who had often organized self-help groups of their own during the Japanese war. This produced further contradictions in the villages. The process, however, was greatly accelerated after the Japanese war when Chiang's armies returned to the seacoast and began to drive north against the Communists. Chiang instructed the Farmer's Bank to strengthen control over the co-operative county treasuries. This meant: encourage the gentry and the upper strata of the peasantry to go into usury and convert these rich farmers into a support for the Chiang regime. This lesson was not lost on the peasant who had not seen Chiang's government for eight years, but now quite clearly saw that the Kuomintang was the friend of the landlord and the bailiff. In this attempt to create a firm base of support among the gentry in the reconquered areas, the Chiang regime alienated not only the poor, but also the middle peasant, and in the process committed suicide. For what Chiang created was not so much a new bourgeoisie but thousands of supporters for the Communists' 8th Route Army.

The failure of the Kuomintang, not only to introduce reforms in the villages, but rather to make conditions worse than they ever had been, was not so much a personal failure of evil and greedy men—though these there were in abundance—as it was the failure of the Kuomintang to come to grips with the central problem of Chinese rural civilization: feudalism. That Chiang Kai-shek and his party after twenty years still could not grapple with this problem furnished abundant proof of the terrible contradictions with which their rulership was riven. It was quite clear that the Kuomintang rulers, in addition to leaning on foreign capital, and in spite of their urgent needs to modernize the country, predicated their own rule on the rule of the landlords. In view of this fact, all the pious hopes of President Truman and the bitter blasts of General Marshall calling on the Chiang regime to reform, were just so much wishful thinking. The Chiang regime could not reform as long as it dared not attack the landlords. And it dared not attack the landlords because in essence it represented feudalism itself.

What do we mean by feudalism? Technically speaking, the name is incorrect. And certain learned philosophers, both Chinese and foreign, have taken great pains to point out that feudalism does not exist in China because there is no serfdom; that is, men can sell their labor freely. It is true that China abolished this formal type of feudalism many years ago, just as it is true that the penetration of the West destroyed the self-sufficient natural economy of the centralized feudal society and placed much of Chinese life under the demands of a money economy, though with few progressive results, as we have seen. But this manner of looking at the problem of China is academic in the extreme and takes no cognizance of the feudal remnants that exercise such an important role in the lives, thoughts, customs, habits and emotions of the people. In abolishing serfdom, the Chinese did not entirely do away with the power of the landlord to conscript labor, to jail debtors and to control the life and even death of his tenants; it did not completely abolish child slavery, the custom of buying and selling girls nor the system of concubinage or forced marriage. All of these conditions are irrevocably bound up with the rule of the landlords and the gentry.

The power of the landlords in China was not everywhere the same.

In the provinces along the seacoast and in the Yangtze Valley where foreign capital penetrated and where mercantile and small industrial cities grew up, the power of the rural gentry in many cases had to be shared with city merchants. In the western and northern provinces, however, the landlords had almost unlimited political power because of the thicker atmosphere of precapitalism. Even in northern Kiangsu, along the seacoast and not far from Shanghai, landlords lived like feudal barons in mud castles, surrounded by armed guards and controlling tenants in fifteen or twenty villages. Such castles acted as a trading center for tenants who were completely at the mercy of the landlord or his bailiffs. Not only had the tenant to bring 50 per cent of his crops to the manor, but also his personal and family problems. In Shansi, I found that landlords often governed all wedding ceremonies and funerals, so that no one could get married or be buried without the approval of these feudal lords.

The power of the landlords gave them control over village women, especially the wives of their tenants, with whom they could have whatever relations pleased them. Very often, the tenant and his wife acquiesced in these relations out of fear, but if the tenant should protest, he had little chance to make his protest effective. In a village in western Shantung I came across a landlord whose common practice was to make his tenant go out into the fields and work while he took his pleasure of the tenant's wife. When Li protested, the landlord had him kidnaped by bandits. In order to cover his participation in the kidnaping, the landlord pretended to mediate the affair through puppet troops, preparing a banquet on the tenant's behalf. But observe the cleverness of this plot. The grateful tenant was released and borrowed money from the kindly landlord to pay for the banquet. Of course, a high interest rate was charged, the tenant could not repay his debt, and lost his own small plot of ground. The landlord then consummated the whole affair by taking the peasant's wife as payment of the debt.

Such subtlety as this, however, was often unnecessary. A rich peasant or landlord merely had to wait until a farmer was in the fields and go around to his home and force the farmer's wife to his wishes. Short of murder, which was difficult because of the landlord's guards and because the landlord controlled most of the spears in the village, the farmer had no recourse, especially since the landlord or his henchman was village chief and hence the police power, too.

In another village of western Shantung, I heard of a landlord who had been attracted by the charms of a young neighbor girl, the daughter-in-law of his own cousin. Because the girl was kept behind the mud walls of her house, the landlord had little chance to approach her. The only method was direct assault. So one day, having summoned his village chief and having armed both himself and his bailiff with a pistol and a sword, he made his way to the girl's home and deliberately raped her. No one dared protest—in fact there was no one to whom a protest could be made—because the landlord was the government.

In a village in Anyang County in Honan, I found a young farm wife who told me she was constantly forced to receive the attentions of a local landlord, the head of a Kuomintang militia corps. Neither she nor her husband was able to resist, simply because the landlord was the boss and hence the law in the village.

What more proof does one want that medieval factors still controlled Chinese rural life. The *droit du seigneur* was abolished with the abolition of serfdom in the West, but in the East, though the landlord did not have the right of the first night with his tenant's wife, he nevertheless had the right of many succeeding nights and afternoons, too.

The institutions of slave girls, concubinage and forced marriage were also irrevocably tied to the landlord system. All the fine Kuomintang laws on this subject were meaningless unless landlordism itself were abolished. Slave girls not only worked in landlord homes in the interior, but were bought by merchants and shipped to Shanghai where they were forced to become prostitutes or, if too ugly, factory girls. In this they had no choice, being bound over to the party who had contract to their bodies. Far from helping to end this system, the revolutionary army of Chiang Kai-shek helped to perpetuate it. In various Kuomintang army headquarters I have seen with my own eyes officers call in the local gentry and ask their aid in securing young girls for their use as long as they were in the territory. The girls, so obtained, were not prostitutes, but generally the virgin daughters of poor farmers.

The powers these landed nobles wielded over their tenants even in their personal affairs was sometimes amazing. Often the tenant had to commit degrading acts just to satisfy his landlord's whims. In Peihsien County in northern Shantung I found a landlord's wife who derived pleasure out of forcing her husband's tenant to bite the bound feet of her maid servant. This noblewoman not only took delight in the girl's screams when she was bitten, but also in the tenant's nausea over the odor given off by the bound feet. In another village in this same county there was a landlord who found some masochistic satisfaction out of stuffing wheat into the vagina of a sixteen-year-old girl servant. When he wearied of this sport, he would tie up the maid's hands, put a cat inside her trousers, which he fastened securely with a rope, and then howl with delight as she rolled around in frenzy on the floor. Such were the entertainments in the villages of the old China.

In China, formal feudalism had disappeared almost entirely by the time of Christ—that is, nearly half a millennium before it arose in Europe. But all these medieval remnants—slave girls, *corvée* labor, seigneurial rights, brutal requisitions of labor and property—lingered on for the next two thousand years like a long-drawn-out funeral dirge over the rotten, but not buried corpse of feudalism.

These excrescences on Chinese rural life would have been enough to create thousands of impassioned soldiers for a peasant war, but in themselves they were not decisive. That factor was provided by the decline of Chinese agriculture as a whole.

The end of the Japanese war found the peasantry in this condition. The army had carried away about twelve to fifteen million fieldworkers, famine perhaps another ten million, and there were untold millions of refugees. The landless farmers went under first, the semitenants next. Those dispossessed from the land increased by the hundreds of thousands. During the third and fourth years of the war the middle peasants began to go under. Then some of the rich peasants. By the end of the war small and middle landlords and even large regional landlords began to feel the pressure from Chiang's land-hungry bureaucrats and Japanese puppets. The desolate land ran into millions of acres. Land hunger also spread like the plague. No longer could the peasants live under the system of extortionate land rents. The peasant's holdings had grown so small that he could not afford to pay the traditional 50 per cent, to say nothing of 80, 90 and over 100 per cent, of his main crop. Rents not only used up all his surplus labor, but encroached on the labor necessary to keep him alive. Everyone was asking, "When will these Japanese dwarfs be driven out?" But when the Japanese war ended and a new one started, the peasant found Chiang's new rural bureaucrats even more hostile to him than the Japanese or his old gentry had been. He began to grumble. From grumbling, he passed into banditry. Near the 8th Route Army areas he began to look for allies.

The ruling classes could not help but see that the peasant was going to explode in a violent upheaval. But they kept putting these black thoughts from their minds. Here is what Chen Li-fu, graduate of the Pittsburgh School of Mines, Kuomintang boss and preacher of the Confucian way of life, revealed to one impressed foreign reporter: To divide the land is not necessary because when the head of a Chinese family dies, he divides the land among his sons. Here is what T. V. Soong, after his appointment to the governorship of Kwangtung Province, where he is a large landholder, unveiled to another correspondent: "We are not planning a land reform in Kwangtung because the system we have had here for years is satisfactory." Finally, here is what a liberal professor in a Christian university and at the same time an official of the Shantung government had to say to this writer: "China is not like czarist Russia; we have no large landlords so there is no need for land reform, but only a reform of the officials." (How one of these things was to be done without the other, the Christian professor did not explain.) To introduce a land reform into the countryside thus seemed in the eyes of these party bosses, governors and Christians something alien to the Chinese way of life. It is hardly necessary to remark that such Oriental philosophizing was quite beyond the peasant. He thought there was only one thing to do: throw out the landlord and divide the land. That was the essence of the revolution to the tenant, to the rural worker, to the coolie.

If the villages behind Chiang Kai-shek's lines remained comparatively peaceful, that was only because the peasant was awaiting leadership and an opportunity to rise. He had not forgotten about the land. Nor did the Kuomintang officials, despite their utterances, think he had forgotten either. All their remarks about there being no need for land reform were merely a camouflage for the deep-seated fears that Chinese rulers have always felt toward the peasantry. To the official the thought of this ignorant clod covered with the good Chinese earth rushing into his yamen was like some terrible dream out of the pages of the *Shui Hu Chuan*.[5] Well might the officials tremble!

For this simple man, born to tenant, feudal slavery, to an overworked and crowded plot of ground, stunned into obedience beneath the grasping landlord's hand, dispossessed from his land by crooked deals and savage violence, robbed of his wife's caresses and his children's laughter, suddenly rose with an impassioned thrill and, under the threat of death itself, began to demand land and revenge.

[5] *Water Margin*, one of China's most famous novels, deals with a band of outlaws who revolted against the emperor at Peking and occupied thirty-six counties in west Shantung.

PART VII

LAND AND REVOLUTION

❧

27. The Peasant Speaks

AFTER V-J Day when the Communist party decided it dared struggle against Chiang Kai-shek, it soon appeared that their power resources were insufficient for opposing the Kuomintang state apparatus, and it became necessary for the party to require the almost total participation of the people in the war. In whose name could the Communists make such a demand? In the name of socialism? Communism? Emphatically no. It had to be in the name of the masses themselves. Such an abstract rallying cry, however, could only be effective when it was rooted in a definite material program. This program was found in the Communist land-reform policy.

The words land reform have an academic ring, but few words have ever aroused such tumultuous emotions. When the Communists started out to change land relationships in China, they really began an effort to reform all of Chinese society. The story of the upsetting of land relations in China is a rich cross-section of a new epoch that has dawned in an ancient land, a tale of a whole people in the grip of a mighty passion, an important guide to the future of property, liberty, democracy, religion and marriage in the Communist Orient, a key to the understanding of the Chinese people's sources of action and above all a record of the Communists' drive for power.

The Communist land policy was decisive in the struggle for power in China because it brought hitherto apathetic masses into open revolt against existing society. Land reform shattered the seemingly immortal torpor of the peasant in two revolutionary ways, the one spiritual, the other material, the one acting from within, the other from without. On the spiritual side, the land reform gave to the peasant one emotion that had perhaps hitherto been lacking from his life—hope. On the more material side, the Communist land reform gave to the peasant a method of struggle against his village rulers.

This interaction between politics and passion, technique and emotion, is not easy to trace and any attempt to do so is likely to prove heavy going. Nevertheless, I believe the following paragraphs may furnish a chart of understanding to some of the more violent events that occupy the last part of this book and may give a revealing insight into Communist strategy and just how it weaned rural China away from Chiang Kai-shek. Incidentally perhaps, it is best to remark here that this story of the peasant upheaval in North China was not given me by any high Communist officials, but was pieced together by myself from conversations with local cadres and peasants and from my own experiences.

First of all, in a revolution, it is necessary to understand the peasant, not only as a human being, but as a political animal. Because he is isolated from the rest of the world a peasant generally cannot raise his political horizons beyond the boundary of his fields. For this reason, as Leon Trotsky noted, he is implacable in his struggle against the landlords but most often impotent against the general landlord incarnate in the state. "Hence his need," said Trotsky, "to rely on some legendary state against the real one." These remarks are applicable to China. In olden times the peasantry created such pretenders to the throne as the 108 immortal heroes of the *Shui Hu Chuan,* and during the Taiping Rebellion, they rallied around the idea of a Peaceful Kingdom of Heaven on Earth.[1]

After the recommencement of the civil war, the peasants united under the Communist banner Land and Liberty, sometimes deifying Mao Tzetung as the "saving star" of the people.

These utopian tendencies of all peasants once led many orthodox Marxists to declare that the peasantry cannot make a social revolution by themselves; they must have another class to lead them, such as the Third Estate in eighteenth-century France or the proletariat in nineteenth-century Russia. The experiences of the Russian Revolution caused many of these theoreticians to make it an almost iron-clad law that backward nations today cannot produce a revolution except under the leadership of the workers. The history of the Russian Social Revolutionaries, who got so tangled up in their coalitions that they zealously kept the muzhik away from the land in order not to lose their allies among the bankers, seemed to prove such a thesis. For as a direct result of their failure to come out for land confiscation, the Social Revolutionary party lost the support of the peasantry and collapsed before the Bolsheviks who took power. In like manner, after the kidnaping of Chiang Kai-shek in December 1937, the Chinese Communists, in ex-

---

[1] The leader of the Taiping Rebellion, Hung Hsiu-chuan, a poorly educated scholar of messianic vision, who had met an early Protestant missionary and become a Christian, advocated the overthrow of the Manchus and the establishment of *Tai Ping Tien Kuo*—the Peaceful Kingdom of Heaven.

change for a united front with the Kuomintang and the landlords against the Japanese, abandoned their program of land confiscation. Throughout the whole war they resolutely guarded the land from peasant seizure. Yet, far from losing the support of the peasants and going to pieces, the Communists planted themselves more firmly in the hearts of the farmers and grew stronger. Why? What was the difference?

The answer can be found almost entirely in conditions produced by the Japanese war. Trotskyites were horrified, not at the fact that the Communists submitted to the leadership of Chiang Kai-shek, but that they gave up "the heart of their program" to obtain an alliance. This seemed to them like a complete betrayal of the revolution. But in fighting the Japanese there was no question of making a revolution, there was only a question of existing. Doomed as they were to fight in the heart of enemy territory, surrounded on all sides by hostile forces, the only way the Communists could even remain alive was to find bases among the people. To have started a class war would have endangered these bases.

So the Communists abandoned class war for national war. But this national war, in itself, was revolutionary and often produced more ferment more quickly than the land reform might have done. In drawing hitherto scattered and essentially selfish peasants together, the war taught people the value of co-operation and collective action. The mingling of men and ideas was a revolutionary catalyst in itself. In the barracks, on the training ground and the battlefield, the peasant became familiar with the Communist party and its program in a way that would have been impossible in peacetime. In taking to guerrilla warfare, which depends almost entirely on the people, the peasant also learned to distinguish between friend and foe. Because of all these circumstances, the abandonment of the revolutionary land program did not have such unrevolutionary results as might have been expected from first glance.

Nevertheless, the Communist program did alienate some of the poor peasants, the tenants and the long-term workers. From bitter experience the peasant had learned to distrust any intellectual who came to his village with fine promises. Only if you gave him land did the poor peasant think you meant business. When the Communists abandoned land confiscation and told the tenantry and the rural workers that they must forget about the landlords and fight the Japanese, these dispossessed men saw behind such fine promises nothing but the ancient double cross. "*Fang kuo pi*" ("dog-wind-blowing"), they muttered under their breath and went on their way.

Despite all the importunities of the poor, the Communists resolutely kept the land from the peasants and merely went ahead with a rent-reduction program based on Kuomintang legislation passed in 1926, which cut all rents by one-quarter. Outwardly, this identified the Communists with the Kuomintang. The difference, however, between the Kuomintang official and the Communist cadre was that the cadre tried to enforce rent-reduction regulations. When the peasant saw this, he stopped and turned around. Here was a different kind of official. Even then the peasant did not rush into a struggle to reduce his rents. He was afraid that if the Japanese drove away the 8th Route Army, the landlord might demand back much more than he had been forced to give up. Nor could the Communists themselves enforce rent reductions everywhere. They simply did not have the apparatus. All they could do was seek out a few poor peasants and listen sympathetically to their tales of woe. In a few villages, they suggested that these peasants call meetings and publicly tell their troubles. When one or two villages had done just this, the process by contagion spread from village to village throughout the more firmly established guerrilla areas. As the Communists awakened the peasant to his legal rights, each village held meetings at which tenants publicly accused landlords of violating the regulations for rent reduction. This struggle against peonage conditions of rent and also against the high interest rates of the usurers became during the Japanese war the chief element of the peasant movement. A smaller, but still important place was occupied by the struggle of "long-term" workers which brought them into opposition, not only to the landlords but to the rich peasants. The tenant struggled for the alleviation of conditions of rent, the worker for improvement of conditions of labor.

When these two forces in the villages saw that they could hold landlords accountable for specific deeds of exploitation, they began to go further and demand compensation for other forms of exploitation not necessarily connected with land rents—such as surtaxes, grain levies and labor requisitions. If the landlord saw the ground slipping beneath his feet, there was not much he could do about it. The very farmer who was most active in demanding rent reductions was often an armed militiaman who wanted recompense for the time spent from his fields in guarding the village from the Japanese. Short of turning over to the enemy and calling in his troops, the landlord was, while not powerless, hamstrung.

In the meantime the peasant demand swelled until it shaped into mass movements, centered around Accusation, Speak Bitterness and Struggle meetings. These were destined to become the organs of the Chinese Revolution.

Every social revolution, as distinct from a palace revolt, is truly creative. Out of the urgent necessity to escape from the blind alley where society has cornered them, people in times of revolution invent entirely new forms and methods by which they can struggle to power. So these various organs created by Chinese peasants themselves suggested to the Chinese Communists a way they might most effectively reach the people.

It is impossible to overestimate the significance of these primitive organs of public opinion. They were not unions, not soviets, not even councils. They were merely instruments whereby the peasant could speak his mind in public and pour out his troubles to a host of sympathetic listeners. This in itself was revolutionary. An old saying in Shansi that "a poor man has no right to talk" was literally quite true. A tenant, if he were unaffiliated with a secret society and had no connections with someone of influence, was not a man at all; he was a mere cipher in a landlord's rent equation. Most often, this humble beast did not even have a name, but was called by some aspect of his physical features. Scarface, Crooked Head, Lop Ear—the number of these nameless creatures was legion in the land. For such a man to stand up and speak before his fellow-villagers, both rich and poor, constituted by its very nature a revolutionary break with the past. In the same moment that he burst through the walls of silence that had enveloped him all his life, the peasant also tore asunder the chains that had bound him to feudalism. Awkwardly at first the words crawled from his throat, but once the first word passed his lips, there came gushing forth, not only an unarrestable torrent of speech, but the peasant's soul.

Time and again, in village after village, I have heard these farmers confessing their bitterness to avid listeners. A poor peasant climbs to his feet and tells how his father died of starvation because the landlord took his crops to pay a loan made at an interest rate of 100 per cent. Or a landless widow with two children who makes her living from spinning gets up and says: "Look, I have no man, no land. In one year I cannot harvest two catties of cotton. They say I must pay a levy of five catties. But when I cannot get it, they make me give them my children to work for them. Just look at me! I am a woman, but I must work as a man. But I am weak from hunger and I cannot work well. So I am beaten. . . ." and she breaks into tears. Tears of relief, as well as anguish, I might add; for at last in her own people she has found the priest to whom she can cry out her sorrows.

This psychological medal had its reverse social side. For as one man tells his troubles, another listens and identifies his own troubles with the words of the speaker. "My God!" he says to himself, "that happened to me, too." Or, as often happened, one peasant would interrupt another. "What you say is all well enough; but listen to me, my bitterness is much more." By such methods, the typically selfish peasant began to identify himself with other men. He began to generalize politically, to see himself both as an individual and as a part of society. For the moment, however, he confined himself to struggling against conditions in his own village.

The methods of struggle varied according to local conditions. The methods and forms also changed at various stages of the struggle. But in general the early struggles had two stages. In the first stage the peasant was still testing out his new-found powers of speech. In the next stage, he demanded more sweeping reforms. Both tenant and rural workers had started out by recognizing the landlord as boss, but as soon as they saw the possibility of abolishing all landlords and taking the land, the tenant and the worker ceased to be interested in questions of rent or higher wages. They wanted land of their own. And at once.

During the war, many landlords had gone over to the Japanese and the demands of the people in these villages were particularly insistent. Toward the end of the war, the Communists gave in to some of these demands, but on the whole they were able to keep the peasants in line as long as the Japanese remained near at hand. With the Japanese surrender, however, poorer peasants could no longer be put off with talk. The Communists had awakened them to their rights and they wanted them. This demand spilled over into areas liberated from the Japanese and soon reached a threatening chorus.

28. Revolt of the Slaves

SLAVES generally revolt against their masters under only two conditions: either they see no other way to save their lives or they see a chance of success.

When the Japanese surrendered and retreated from North China, the poorer peasants in the former occupied areas, under pressure from both of these ideas, revolted. The temporary disappearance of all state power gave them the chance for success, and the terrible conditions under which they had been living made a revolt against the landlords imperative.

Though fertilized by ideas and methods of struggle jumping over from Communist areas, this uprising was more or less spontaneous. It had few political aims. The peasants did not think of taking power in the villages. They did not even think of overthrowing the landlord system. All they thought to do was to settle with their traitors who, it just so happened, were most often big landlords.

Not only the tenants and the rural workers, but the rich peasants and even small landlords joined the antitraitor movement. But it was the poor peasant's need for relief that gave the movement its eventual characteristic of a demand for land. The tenants, especially, were nursing bottomless reservoirs of bitterness against the landlords. Not only their grain had been uncovered by the landlords and turned over to the Japanese, but even their seed. Pots, pans, even metal farm tools had been taken to meet the Japanese levies, but half the levy had gone into the landlords' storerooms. "Dog legs"[1] had come into their homes and taken the very cotton out of their quilts to meet fictitious Japanese demands. A peasant in Honan tells how a puppet commander, a landlord's bailiff, threw him in jail and would not let him out until he had given him his daughter. The wife of a middle farmer tells how a landlord forcibly took ten mow of her husband's land and then shot him and threw him in a coalpit outside of town so that no one would be left to take revenge. One hundred and forty peasants tell how a landlord in western Shantung made them roll stones up the side of a mountain for the Japanese while his dog legs walked behind with clubs, and how their legs, arms and backs were broken in the labor. The war had made the poor even poorer. The lack of land and hunger made the neighboring landlords' opulence and luxury especially intolerable. The more destitute of the villages moved into the front of the ranks of the fight. It was they who organized Settlement Meetings and thus gave to the Communists another form of struggle. As impromptu wartime trials got underway in many villages, the peasants' pent-up anger suddenly burst forth in a violent demand for the lands and goods of the traitors in settlement for their suffering. Everything must be paid back, not one robbed cent must be kept. On a cool October morning, the peasants of the village of Likwantun in western Shantung, going from door to door, armed with clubs and pitchforks, called out everybody, small and great, to a meeting against the landlord Maosunpang. "On February 3, you robbed me of three hundred dollars," says one angry peasant. "At that time we had no power. We dared not speak. Your bad behavior is known by everybody. You helped the Japanese rob us of cotton. Now you must pay it back." The crowd shouts: "You must pay! You must pay!" Another tenant struggles up to the front of the meeting. "You killed several members of my family. We are starving. You must give back what you robbed from us." To meet his debt, the landlord has to sell his grove of a hundred oak trees, his furniture, ninety acres of land and seven of his eight houses. The poor leave the landlord only five acres of land and one house.

That particular traitor was lucky. The people at least left him his head. Such was not the case everywhere. In the mountainous part of Shansi that had been occupied by the Japanese, the people settled with their landlords in a particularly violent way. In these mountains, and the adjoining plains where the 8th Route Army had not penetrated during the war, the relics of serfdom had deep roots; the landlords' hold on the land was particularly parasitic; and the poverty of the village most na-

[1] A stooge. Common peasant term for a landlord's agent.

kedly revealed. Bursting out after the retreat of the Japanese, the movement immediately became adorned with acts of terror—the more barbarous because the people were more backward.

In a certain district of Tzehisen County in Shansi, three landlord brothers, who had been responsible for the deaths of eighteen farmers during the war, were hauled before a Speak Bitterness Meeting, during which the passions of the crowd mounted to such heights that cadres who had come to watch the meeting were brushed aside and the landlords strung up to trees. In the Taihang Mountains, the village of Toumachuang seized a dog leg and beat him to death with stones. In another near-by village, peasants took a landlord who had been a puppet commander of the Japanese, hitched him up to a plow, cracked a whip across his back and drove him around the fields. "You treated us like beasts," shouted the peasants, "and now you can be our animal."

Some newly arrived students from Peiping, who had come over to the Liberated Areas with very idealistic thoughts, having no idea of the depths of the peasants' bitterness, tried to keep the movement within bounds. They were brushed aside as so many interfering busybodies. "You intellectuals are useless." Even the newly arrived soldiers often found it impossible to calm the enraged peasants. A soldier in central Hopei told me: "Four of us were taking a traitor to the county government. As we passed a village the Lao Pai Hsing rushed out and crowded around our cart. Soon there were a hundred of them. 'Where are you taking him?' they wanted to know. 'To the government,' we said. 'No you don't,' said they. Well, I ask you. There were a hundred of them. Just four of us. And then what looks they had in their eyes. They meant murder, if it came to that. 'You're not going any further,' said they, 'unless you give us our traitor.' Toma! What could we do?"

The peasant found it easy to make threats because in bringing pressure to bear against the traditional rights of the landlord he had hardly to come in conflict with the state at all. When the Japanese left, many of the puppets fled with them and there were no government organs of any kind. Then the 8th Route Army penetrated only a few of the larger towns and not many of the villages because they were gathering on the borders of the Kuomintang areas. Finally the organs of the Border Region government were too scanty to take over the great majority of the villages. Village committees controlled the militia; there were no courts; the commissars were powerless.

Some of the more inexperienced nonparty cadres—and the majority were inexperienced in this situation—were grieved that the peasants would not submit to the government. But the county commissars were afraid of seeming like defenders of the landlords. In central Hopei cadres who tried to take a traitor away from a village against the people's wishes were sharply reprimanded by their superiors. "You are interfering with the wishes of the people. You mustn't do that. We have to follow the people."

The people—anyway, the poorest and the most active farmers—were hard to follow. They had the bit in their teeth and they moved fast. The antitraitor movement leaped like a flame from village to village. In this not only the poor, but the middle farmers and even the small landlords often participated. The movement thus had a very broad democratic character. That was both its strength and its weakness. When the middle farmer saw the traitors—that is, some of the biggest landlords—going under and the poor being compensated for what had been taken from them, they rushed in for their share, too. But the debts of the traitors were so great that often their whole property could not satisfy their creditors. The small landlord and the rich peasant began to wonder where this would end. He started to hold aloof. But once embarked on settling with the traitors, the resoluteness of the most active poor farmers grew faster even than their numbers. Where some of the largest landlords had fled away with the Japanese the peasants had no way of settlement but to take the nobles' property themselves. Troops of peasant men and peasant wenches, especially when their grain stocks got low, marched on the landlords' homes, drove away the bailiffs, carried off the cattle, took the grain and sealed the houses. In Shantung they began to raid the landlords' granaries, drive out the agents and plunder the storerooms where they very often found their own belongings which the landlords had taken from them under the pretext of satisfying Japanese levies. In one case like this that I know of, the peasants were helped by the landlord's daughter who hated her father for the way he had treated the poor. The peasants justified the seizure of property, saying: "He robbed it from us; now we shall take back what was ours."

There was a limit, however. The Chinese are not wild people. Though there is a Tartar strain in many North China peasants, there is also a thick veneer of civilization. The Chinese pride themselves on their reasonableness. The most common way of halting an argument in China is to say: "Let us speak reasonably." Consequently, many characteristics of the Russian Revolution were lacking to Chinese villages. There were disorders—yes. Looting—yes. But no mass depredations of homes. No smashing of windows, doors, ceilings. No cutting down of orchards. The people wanted to keep these things for themselves. As far as killings went, the peasant wanted his revenge. It was not a case always of private revenge, but collective revenge, a great passionate demand welling up from the depths of whole villages. Since there were no courts, the peasants had to take the job in hand themselves. But that was only one side of the movement, there was another side. Only the most criminal landlords —and not all of these—were settled with by the peasants. There was no attempt to settle with landlords, as such. Thus, the worst, that is, the open and flagrant traitors were done away with, but the men who stood behind the traitors and were still suppressing the people remained. During the Japanese war, the landlords had often appointed a village rascal to be the village chief and do the dirty work of the Japanese against the peasantry. Thus, though the rascal might be punished, the landlord would still remain in power, carrying on endless intrigues against the people.

In Fanchuang in Shantung Province, the Japanese, when they retreated, left behind fifteen thousand catties of grain. Five thousand catties the landlord gave to the people, and the rest he put in his private storeroom. When villagers complained, he said: "Keep quiet. I have friends in the *chu* [sub-county] government." Such a remark in itself was enough to silence the farmer. For all his life the peasant had seen that there was no chance to settle any of his grievances unless he had a relative in the *chu* government. Now, cynical as circumstances had taught him to be, he began to think the government of the 8th Route Army the same as any other government.

While the landlords were playing the peasant off against the cadre, they also sometimes took more drastic means to silence the peasant. In villages where the army had not penetrated—and that meant most villages—the landlords threatened the peasants with dire punishment if they held any settlement meetings. Often the landlord went beyond threats. Sometimes, he kidnaped the most dissatisfied peasants. In other cases, he hired "blackshooters"[2] to kill them.

All these circumstances brought a heavy pressure on the Communist party. Angry peasants settling with a traitor often left the traitor's family no means of living. Such acts, if allowed to continue, would lead inevitably to anarchy and wholesale discontent. On the other hand, landlords were actively suppressing peasants whose need for land was great and whose demands were growing more insistent. Those peasants threatened by the landlords would lose all hope unless steps were taken to relieve them immediately.

But the demand for land threw the Communists onto the horns of a dilemma. They had been practicing a reformist policy for eight years; now the circumstances demanded they put into practice a revolutionary policy. To reverse your field is no more easy in politics than it is in football. If they acceded to peasant demands, the Communists might very well alienate many anti-Japanese landlords who had become leaders in local and even regional governments during the war; they might lose the sympathy of liberals within the Kuomintang and the great reservoir of respect they had built up abroad where they were often looked upon as a cross between enlightened democrats and latter-day saints. But if

---

[2] This term has a double meaning. The first is allegorical and refers to "secret assassins." The second is descriptive and refers to the fact that assassins actually black their faces in order to avoid identification.

they did not accede to the demands of the peasantry, they would lose their mass support.

About this time, the Marshall peace negotiations had begun to break down; civil war was certain. To fight a war without peasant support was impossible for the Communists, and yet—to throw down the gauntlet to a society that had existed for two thousand years, to risk the alienation of everyone but the poor peasants and the rural workers, that, too, seemed difficult.

The Communist party delayed. In the meantime, it called back local cadres and began to collate their experiences, trying to wrest from a welter of details a proper course of action. Autumn 1945 passed. The demands of the peasants grew more urgent. Winter 1946 came and went. Still no decision. Spring came. Time for planting. Time for decision. Still the Communists held back. The delay made everyone feel more keenly the menace of Chiang Kai-shek's armies battering on the threshold of the Border Regions. The Communist party, hovering on the brink of this historic decision, was like a soldier waiting to cross the line into enemy territory. One step forward or one step backward and the thing is over and done with, but it is the waiting that frays tired nerves, starts up uneasy thought and makes one wonder what is on the other side of that line. One longs to go over that line and find out what is there. Just so the Communist party stood on the borderline between the past and the future—and waited. One step back—peace with the land- lords; one step forward—war with feudalism. Truly a terrible decision to make.

In the summer of 1946, messengers brought down to the county com- missars the word: "Divide the land." The party had cast the die. From now on there could be no retreat.

29. Plot and Counterplot

PEOPLE do not revolt against society and commit revolution any more eagerly than a man breaks up a marriage in order to begin a new love affair. In China, the peasant did not always storm the manorial citadels of his own accord; the party often had to lead him by the hand to the as- sault. Nor did the Communist cadre always rush eagerly against the bastions of feudal power; the peasant sometimes had to push him from behind. Peasant and cadre were like a two-man patrol into enemy terri- tory; they went forward into the unknown by a process of mutual encouragement, first one holding back, then the other, then both rushing forward together.

What held back the cadre was his complex character. Although the party laid down the land-reform policy and often helped carry it out, it was the National Salvation Association that directly led the movement in the villages. Teams of four and five nonparty cadres would enter a village and try to arouse it against the landlord. The composition of these teams was contradictory. Very often the cadres were ex-students or intellectuals. As with most intellectuals, they had fine ideas, but drew back when it came to putting the ideas into action. Also, many had become cadres because they could read and write. But anyone in the Chinese countryside who can read and write is generally the son or daughter of, if not a landlord, at least a rich peasant or a middle farmer. Very often the man against whom the cadre had to struggle was the one with whom he had most in common in the way of education and upbringing. Thus, while the cadre's ideas impelled him forward, his inheritance pulled him back from warfare against his own kind. Among the cadres, however, there was a leavening of older, resolute men and also a bitter group of young peasant boys with some education who took the lead in the fight on the landlords.

As for the peasant, his problem was much more critical. Fighting the landlord to him was a simple matter of life or death. He would not have even considered such a struggle had he seen any other way out. Circumstances had put his back against the wall. His neighbors had starved, his family died; he might be next. But to die slowly is much more easy than to die at once; it was far easier for the average peasant to face the prospect of ultimate death by starvation than to face immediate death from a landlord's sword.

Necessity is the god of any revolution. But the old gods often exercise as much, and at first more, influence than the new deity. Not only fear, but also two thousand years of tradition dragged on the peasant's foot as he stepped toward the landlord's mansion.

Man must surrender everything to the future in revolutions. He has to infringe on the traditional morality. The revolution called on the Chinese peasant to do dangerous and blasphemous things, to defy his landlord, to defy a Confucian-made fate, to defy the ethics of his ruler.

None of these things came easily to the peasant. The landlord played on his superstitious mind with all the cunning with which years of overlordship had endowed him. "It is your fate to be poor," said the landlord. The peasant would bow his head: "Yes, I guess I have a bad fate." The landlord would smile and reduce interest by 2 per cent on the peasant's debt.

Tradition had taught the peasant that governments were always on the side of the landlords. Why should the 8th Route Army be any different?

The landlords harped on this idea. Everywhere they tried to discredit the cadres and the government in the peasant's eyes.

In Pingying County in western Shantung, near the end of the Japanese war, the landlords, never having seen the 8th Route Army before, thought the cadres could be bought just like Kuomintang officials. They collected seventy thousand dollars from the people to buy two banners to welcome "the liberation heroes," and at the same time taxed each food stall on the fairgrounds one thousand dollars each in order to buy watermelon seeds and peanuts for the families of the "anti-Japanese fighters." The actual cost of the banners, however, was only twenty thousand dollars while that of the refreshments was but three thousand dollars, the difference being pocketed by the landlords. When a sour note crept into the celebration, the landlords privately told the farmers: "From ancient times till now, every government has grafted; don't entertain any hopes from the 8th Route Army."

Rising to a speech of welcome, made by a village chief, a cadre said: "We understand you have been taxed for this meeting. This money will be returned to you."

Dumfounded by this speech, and having lost face, the landlords realized they had to deal with a different kind of government and they began to play up to the cadres, on the one hand, and to maltreat the people, on the other. When the district government organized by 8th Route guerrillas compelled them to raise the wages of long-term workers, the landlords cut down on the workers' food and refused to give them any oil for their lamps. When militiamen, standing guard outside the village walls, asked for some congee, the village chief scolded them: "Oh you want to eat congee! Next thing you'll want to eat meat!" Then he forced "the congee group" to do transport work for the army. When the peasants grumbled, he called a village meeting and said: "Let's all go to the district government and ask for congee."[1] Seeing that they had nothing to eat and that they were also forced to labor for the army, the people were disgusted with the district government. "We are just eating the Northwest Wind," said they. When the district government sent relief food into the village, the village chief warned the people: "Whoever eats this food will be seized by the army." On this theme, the landlords spread many rumors. "You are all going to meetings, but be careful. You may be taken away by the soldiers." As a consequence many steered clear of the meetings and stayed indoors.

In such ways, the landlord sought to discourage the peasant from rising. The natural suspicions and fears of the peasants themselves also inclined the peasant to go slow. In a village of south Hopei, a group of

[1] Congee is a thin gruel, containing little nourishment. The village chief here is being sarcastic at the district government's expense, meaning even this poor food can't be obtained from the government.

farmers spontaneously decided to settle with their landlord who had grafted five thousand catties of grain. Having seized him, they brought him to the district government and declared: "He killed an intelligence agent of the 8th Route Army and grafted your grain." They were afraid to say that the grain had belonged to the village because they did not think the 8th Route Army would act for the common people.

The farmer was also under great pressure from his family not to struggle against the landlord. In Putsun village, a cadre went home with an active farmer. He was greeted by the farmer's mother with these words: "From what my son says, I know your 8th Route Army is very good, but what will be the last result?" When the cadre left, the father and mother said to their son: "You must take care." Parents were petrified when their sons took the lead in Speak Bitterness Meetings. "Why do you raise your head higher than the rest?" said a farmer in the Taihang Mountains to his son. "Why don't you stay in the common mass and shout slogans in the background?"

Families were also afraid their friends would take part in Struggle Meetings against the landlord. "When my neighbor's house is noisy, how can mine be quiet?" they asked in bewilderment.

These conditions particularly obtained where the army had not penetrated. In such cases, the demands of the farmers were often very small. "If I can eat a potato and two millet seeds, that will be enough," I heard a peasant tell a cadre. Another peasant who had been very badly treated by a landlord told an official: "Let the *chu* cadres arrest me. Then release me. I will say: 'You arrested me and scolded me for not revealing my bitterness.'" Others would get up in a meeting and say: "Now, I speak on behalf of others, but this is not my bitterness."

The remnants of the old servility are hard to shake off. The poor man still bows his head as he passes the landlord in the street. Yet not everybody is looking down now, underfoot. Many are looking forward.

Most important processes are taking place underneath the surfaces, and somehow of their own accord. In the older Liberated Areas, it is a simple matter for the peasants with traditions of struggles to divide the land. The landlords, accustomed to the new regime, hardly put up a fight. In areas occupied by the army, the landlords also go under easily. In the greatest number of villages, however, the struggle moves slowly. The mud hut on the plain and the cave of the poor man in the mountains are the chief forges of the revolution in these days. Here, cadres meet secretly at night with landless farmers. Step by step the cadre convinces the peasant that the landlord is at the root of his poverty. "Yes, if only there were no landlord, life would be bearable," agrees the peasant. "But why don't you settle with him and get land for yourself?" says the cadre. "But how?—he has all the power." "You must organize," says the cadre. "Let me tell you a story . . ." and he tells of a village that has settled with its landlord. Day after day, night after night, the cadre works on the peasant, ridding him of the thought that he is doomed. Before the astonished eyes of his listener, the cadre unrolls a whole new world.

Given a gleam of a livable future, men will undergo any hardship to achieve a sacred goal. So it is with the peasant. Throwing off his last trembling doubts, he agrees that he will take action. "But you mustn't leave me," he adds as an afterthought to the cadre.

Meanwhile, the landlord has not been quiet. Not for nothing is he a landlord. Everything that is going on in the village has come to his ears. He knows all about the secret meetings. Furthermore, he sees the peasant glancing around with a look that says "all the land is mine." Well does the landlord know the value of striking first. He still is the power. At his beck and call are ten or fifteen strong-arm men, with spears and clubs, and he himself has a pistol. What can these young students and that stupid tenant do against him? Such were the landlord's thoughts.

From thought he passed to action. While the tenant was dreaming of a far-off world of peace and plenty, the landlord descended on him in the night, kidnaped him and threw him in his dungeon. In other cases, he cut off the most active farmer's head and stuck it on the village wall as a warning. Or he broke into a small meeting and speared everyone to death on the spot. Nor did the government cadres always escape his attention either. As the cadre was going from village to village, or walking back to the county seat to report, the landlord would set his "dog legs" on him. Often, they would castrate him, trying to make it seem as if he had been killed for raping some village woman. The villagers knew differently but, being afraid, they began to avoid the cadres.

Other strata of the peasantry besides the tenant were also affected. Originally, many of the smaller landlords had joined the people's struggle of their own accord. Not a few of these men were Christians and they had been favorably affected by the strict discipline of the 8th Route Army, the kindliness of the soldiers and also by slogans of justice and equality. Wishing to join the struggles against the biggest traitors, they had come to the cadres with their Bibles, saying: "Look, our Bible says here that it is wrong for a rich man to live off the poor. You see even a rich man is not good according to our Bible."

So long as it was only a question of rent or settling with the traitors, the upper circle of the peasantry had played a prominent role. But when the land began to be divided and when both the landlords and the tenants lashed out in a fury of violence, the rich peasant began to look with distrust and fear at the spread of the movement, not knowing where it would end.

Undoubtedly, landlord terror set the movement back. But sometimes it boomeranged. In the village of Yachiachuang, six landowners and three "dog legs" organized a secret society to oppose the land reforms. A district official walked in the night to remonstrate with the land-owners. "The people here are organizing in a democratic way," said the cadre. "Why oppose them?" The landlords flew into a rage. "I don't care what the people want," one shouted angrily. At the same instant a dog leg hurled his spear and cleaved the cadre's throat from front to back. With a dying shriek for help, the cadre fell to the ground, his life's blood gushing from him. Hearing the fight, farmers ran to neigh-boring villages for help. With picks and shovels a crowd of three hun-dred peasants broke into the meeting place and beat the six landlords to death. The dog legs escaped in the night.

In this fashion, one after another, villages began to fight back against their landlords. New peasants sprang to take the places of murdered ones. In huts and caves, in the plains and in the mountains, secret con-claves went on again. Much blood, however, yet remained to be spilled upon the good Chinese earth.

30. Stone Wall Village

OVERTHROWING a European government by a *coup d'état* at the top, as was done in Czechoslovakia, is perhaps an exact science when done by a sufficient party of trained cadres with arms in hand. But making a revolution from the bottom up, village by village, as was done in China, is an inexact art that guarantees no sure success and that demands a world of patience, an infinitude of cunning and a bellyful of resolution. Such activities, if scrambled at, can become dangerous.

I think I can best illustrate the difficulty of making this type of revolution and incidentally reveal some of the techniques of the Com-munist party by telling the story of how a single village revolted against its landlord. It is a story rather reminiscent of a Greek tragedy in its plot and it concerns Stone Wall Village—a hamlet of five hundred peo-ple located in the southern part of Shansi Province, amid a range of hills, old and redolent of Chinese legend, that are known as the Taiyueh Mountains.

The land in this region is rocky, bare of forest and grudging in its fertility so that the hard-pressed farmers have been forced to build terraces and cultivate the hill slopes nearly to the top of every peak. For many centuries, the peasants have been struggling not only against the parsimonious nature of these mountains, but against the brutal exactions and dark superstitions of a civilization probably very much like that which Christ knew. These people, however, believed in no Supreme God, but rather knew many gods, including the God of Fate who made them poor, and ghosts, devils and evil spirits whom they believed lurked in the rocks, trees and the bodies of the animals which roamed their hills. As a consequence, they were easy prey for the intrigues of village witches who called down spirits to their incense tables and frightened peasants into doing the bidding of the landlords.

The common farmers, always hungry and always in debt, had a verse about their bitter lot which ran like this:

> Harvest every year; but yearly—nothing.
> Borrow money yearly; yearly still in debt.
> Broken huts, small basins, crooked pots;
> Half an acre of land; five graves.

About one hundred families lived in Stone Wall Village, many of them in caves hollowed out of the side of the mountain at the base of which the village was situated. South of the town ran a river, overhung with willows and cedars, on the banks of which was a mill where the people ground their wheat and Indian corn—the two crops raised yearly by Stone Wall Village. The barren aspect of the place was somewhat relieved by small orchards of peach, apricot and pear trees.

Stone Wall Village had one peculiarity that set it apart from most Chinese villages: its women did not raise many children. The reasons for this were manifold. In the first place, many of the farmers were too poor to support a wife and did not marry. Secondly, girl babies were often strangled by their parents at birth because of poverty. Thirdly, the Japanese, who had occupied a strong point on the opposite bank of the river for six years, had raped many of the women, venereal disease had become widespread and many of the women had become sterile.

Politically, Stone Wall Village was in the hands of its village chief, a landlord named Wang Chang-ying. Although his personal characteristics are not germane to this story, it may be mentioned in passing that Landlord Wang was fifty years old, that he wore a small goatee and smoked a long-handled water pipe. In fair weather, it was said that he promenaded on the streets and beat any child who was unfortunate enough to bump into him. At sight of him, many of the village poor would immediately run indoors.

Wang's possessions included sixty-five acres (no one else owned more than three acres) of irrigated land, the riverside mill, a large store of grain, one wife, one son, one daughter, one daughter-in-law and a vengeful nature.

Because of the landlord's comparative wealth, Wang's wife and daughter were the best-dressed women in the village, and for the same reasons the cleanest. During the war against Japan, Chang had coerced his wife and daughter to service the sexual needs of a Japanese platoon leader stationed in the village of Chaopeitsun, two miles away, and from this relationship the family had derived profit, if not pleasure. The platoon leader winked an eye at the share of the Japanese grain levy (exacted from the peasantry) kept by Wang and also brought the family gifts of cloth and furniture gained from his various looting expeditions.

The economic transactions of his father and the sexual ones of his mother and sister did not disturb the son of Landlord Wang, for through these arrangements he was able to avoid being conscripted for hard labor as were the other youths of the village. Twenty-five years old, tall, handsome and with a proud manner, Wang's son used to stride about the village in the daytime in a long black gown and a clean white towel on his head. At night, however, he was a tiger on the prowl, peremptorily knocking on doors and forcing himself on whatever woman took his fancy. If any were bold enough to object, he would threaten them with the Japanese.

Wang's chief friend in the village was a rich farmer named Shih Ping-hua, who acted as the landlord's clerk and assistant. There were two or three other small landlords in the village, but none of them owned more than two acres of land and none had power.

The chief personal enemy of Wang was a tenant farmer named Lee Tien-shang, or Original Fortune Lee. Sixty years old, with a beard down to his chest, his forehead wrinkled like a washboard, his mouth half emptied of teeth, and his eyes radiating crow's-feet, Lee walked around the village, summer and winter, in filthy white rags, his back bent at a forty-five degree angle and his head inclined toward the ground. Lee rented seven mow of land from Wang, but since he had to give half of his crops to the landlord, he was barely able to support his wife and ten-year-old son. There had been another son, but he had died, and the manner of his dying was the principal cause for the enmity between the landlord and the tenant.

During the Japanese war, the landlord used to feast the Japanese platoon leader at frequent intervals, exacting from his tenants all the food necessary for such entertainments. The peasants became incensed at the continued extortions and Lee's son and two militiamen decided to kill the platoon leader, but unfortunately a grenade they threw at him from an overhead cave did not explode. Learning who was behind the plot, the landlord informed the lieutenant who dragged Lee's son and the two militiamen from the fields and slowly bayoneted them to death inside the Three Sects Temple. Thus Lee had come to hate Wang, but he was too afraid and had been too long suppressed to take any action of his own. There were other enemies of the landlord in the village, but here it is not necessary to do any more than note their existence.

In 1945, the Japanese Empire surrendered to the United States, but this meant little to the people of Stone Wall Village. True, they saw the Japanese across the river pack up and leave, and no longer did the platoon leader come to feast with Wang and sleep with his daughter and wife, but the landlord remained the power in the village, his son still blackjacked women into sleeping with him, land rents remained as high as ever and everyone was always in debt.

Such was the condition of Stone Wall Village when the Chinese Revolution suddenly descended on it. There had been vague stories of this revolution in the village; there had been murmurings about the 8th Route Army, about a thing called democracy and about villages where there were no landlords and everyone had an equal amount of land. But the people had listened to these rumors with only half an ear; they were poor and fated to be poor; they did not want to fight anybody, they only wanted to be left alone.

Landlord Wang had also heard these rumors; he did not take them seriously either. But as a precaution, he used to tell the people: "Flesh cut from others won't stick to your own body." The people, however, did not need this warning: they had no intention of moving against Landlord Wang.

Nevertheless, the Revolution came to Stone Wall Village.

It did not come like a flash of swift lightning; for a revolution like everything else moves slowly in China. Nor did it announce itself like a clap of thunder, with the beat of drums, the sound of rifle fire or hot slogans shouted on the country air.

To be more exact, five men brought the Revolution to Stone Wall Village. They were not soldiers nor were they Communist party members. One had been a schoolteacher, another a student, a third a waiter, a fourth a shop assistant and a fifth a farmer. They were all members of the Hohsien County Salvation Association and their job was to "overturn" Stone Wall Village.

"Overturn" is a term of the Chinese Revolution that came into being after the surrender of the Japanese. In Communist terminology it means to turn over the social, political and economic life of every village, to overturn feudalism and establish democracy, to overturn superstition and establish reason. The first step of the overturning movement is to "struggle" against the landlords and divide the land.

To do this sounds easy. You have the guns and the power and you just tell the landlord to give a share of his land to the people. But it is never that easy. In Stone Wall Village, there was no army, there was no militia. The 8th Route Army was far to the south. Even the guerrillas had gone elsewhere. Landlord Wang was the power and the people were afraid of him.

The leader of the Hohsien Salvation team was a thirty-one-year-old cadre, the son of a bankrupt rich farmer, named Chou Yu-chuan. When

Chou and his fellow-workers arrived in Stone Wall Village they posted proclamations of the Shansi-Hopei-Honan-Shantung Border Region government, announcing that every village had the right to elect their own officials and that land rents and rates of interest should be reduced. Then they called a meeting to explain these proclamations, but the people listened only half-heartedly, kept their mouths tightly shut and went home without speaking further to the cadres.

For several days, the cadres went individually among the people asking them about local conditions and their own lives, but no one would talk. Whenever a cadre approached groups of people, they would break apart and move away. One or two men cornered alone admitted they were afraid of the landlord.

Under these conditions, the cadres could not carry on their work, so they decided to seek out one of the poorer men in the village and talk to him alone and in secret.

At this time, Chou and another cadre were living in a cave next door to one occupied by a tenant farmer, named Ma Chiu-tze. Ma had bought his cave before the Japanese war with six dollars earned by his wife in spinning thread. Now, his wife was sick and Ma often came to the cadre's cave and slept on the same kang with them. During the night, the three men always talked.

Ever since the Ching dynasty, Ma revealed, his family had been poor tenants, renting land and never having any of their own. Every year, he raised eight piculs of millet and every year he had to give four of these piculs to Landlord Wang. He could afford no medicine for his wife whom he feared was dying. Two years before, his father had died and he had not been able to buy the old man a coffin, but had to wrap him in straw. Now he was thirty-five and he was still poor and it looked as if he would always be poor. "I guess I have a bad brain," he would say in summing up the reasons for his poverty.

Then the cadres would ask: "Are you poor because you have a bad brain or because your father left you no property?"

"I guess that's the reason; my father left me no property."

"Really is that the reason?" asked the cadres. "Let us make an account. You pay four piculs of grain every year to the landlord. Your family has rented land for sixty years. That's 240 piculs of grain. If you had not given this to the landlord, you would be rich. The reason you are poor, then, is because you have been exploited by the landlord."

They would talk like this for hours and Ma would finally acknowledge that he was exploited by the landlord. Then he would say: "What can I do? Everyone looks down on me. When it's mealtime, the landlord eats inside the house, but I must eat outside, standing up. I am not good enough. Everyone looks down on me."

"And why is that?" said the cadres. "That is because you have no money and because you have no money you have no position. That is why we must overturn so that everyone can have an equal position and no man will look down on another."

Ma agreed that the landlords had to be overthrown before there could be any happiness for the poor, but he was only half convinced of his own statements. There was yet a long distance between words and action and the weight of two thousand years of tradition lay very heavily on Ma as on most Chinese peasants.

For fifteen days, the cadres talked with Ma. In this period they had twenty-three formal talks with him besides the numerous evening talks. They conversed with other farmers in the village, but Ma was the most "active" element. From this it can be seen it is not easy to stir a Chinese peasant.

At last Ma was ready to "struggle" and "settle"—two terms of the Revolution that mean to struggle against the landlord and to settle accounts with him. Still, Ma was a little frightened.

"If we go to work," he said to the cadres, "you must not leave us."

"We will stay until the whole village has turned over," the cadres promised.

Ma Chiu-tze became the Revolution in Stone Wall Village. But one man is not enough to overturn feudalism. More help was needed. So on the sixteenth night of the cadre's stay in the village, Ma brought three of his friends into the cave, including the old farmer Original Fortune Lee.

After offering the farmers cigarettes, the cadres announced they had come to Stone Wall Village to help the people establish a government of their own choosing. "We know you people of Stone Wall Village are eating bitterness," they said. "We, too, in our turn have been oppressed. All the oppressed are from one home. Tell us your sufferings and we shall try to settle them for you. If you don't want to tell us tonight—why—think them over and come and tell us in three or four days."

Under the influence of this talk, the four men began to tell their own private sufferings, sometimes all speaking at once. One of them, a twenty-year-old boy named Liu Kwang, told how Wang had ordered him to go to work in the Japanese labor corps. When he refused, the landlord and his son had lowered him into a well in water up to his neck. When pulled up, he was more dead than alive and could neither work for the Japanese or in his own fields.

A long-term worker named Second Jewel Pao told how the landlord had forced him to dig up grain from a secret hiding place. Finally, Original Fortune Lee told how his son had been bayoneted to death. At this time, the four peasants became so emotional they began to cry. Toward midnight, they reached the conclusion that the time had at last come for their revenge. They swore a solemn oath. "If the Japanese come back tomorrow or if the troops of Chiang Kai-shek come, we will turn over. Even if only for a day, we will turn."

The meeting then broke up with the decision to mobilize more farmers. On the following night, a second meeting was attended by thirteen peasants. It was to prove an unlucky number. In this meeting after the usual "reveal bitterness" talk, it was decided to mobilize more farmers and then hold a mass meeting in which all the villagers could reveal their sufferings.

During the meeting, one or two farmers expressed the fear that Landlord Wang had heard about their talks. Since an ex-puppet militiaman knew of the meeting and since he was sleeping with the landlord's daughter, they surmised the landlord must by now be informed of everything. The cadres made light of the peasants' fears and told them not to worry.

That night, Original Fortune Lee did not come home. As he was an old man and never stayed out at night his wife was worried. When a whole day and then another passed without his appearing, she became frantic and inquired of everyone in the village if they had seen her husband, but no one could give her any information. He had last been seen leaving the meeting and heading for home. His path, it was known, led along a cliff that overhung the river. Whether he had slipped in the darkness and fallen in the water or had just continued walking by his home and left the village was a mystery which no one in the town could answer.

On the third day, a man grinding flour in the water mill beside the river noticed that his water wheel was not turning properly and on investigation he found the body of Original Fortune Lee riding amid the spokes. The old man's mouth was gagged with a cloth, his hands were tied behind him and he had been some time dead.

As no one else would touch him, the cadres extricated the body from the water wheel and carried it up to the Three Sects Temple. Since there is an ancient law in China that the body of a murdered man may not be brought to his home, they left him there and called his wife. Then she came and dressed Original Fortune Lee in funeral white and shed tears on his pock-marked face and moaned over his body. The people saw and they felt sorry, but they went off home and they whispered among themselves: "Better keep quiet, we may be next."

The revolution in Stone Wall Village had been dealt a blow. The counterrevolution had struck first.

* * *

After the murder of Original Fortune Lee the people went about in terror and shut up again like clams. Even those who had attended the second meeting now said: "We haven't begun to struggle with the landlord, but one of us is gone already."

The cadres were very much surprised by the murder. They thought they had been too careless and had not placed enough belief in the peasants' fears. They also thought a hand grenade might be thrown at any time into their meeting cave. Their biggest fear, however, was that the peasants would give up the overturning movement altogether. Therefore they decided to hold a memorial meeting in honor of Original Fortune Lee, and by this meeting to mobilize the people.

On the stage opposite the Three Sects Temple, where semireligious plays were held during festival times, the cadres placed pictures of Mao Tze-tung, chairman of the Chinese Communist party and General Chu Teh, commander in chief of the Communist-led 18th Group Army. Beside these pictures they placed strips of paper saying: WE SHALL TAKE REVENGE FOR THIS PEASANT.

One hundred people of Stone Wall Village attended this meeting, but Landlord Wang did not come. The county magistrate came especially to make a speech and announced: "The government intends to clear up all murders. The people should continue to overturn and to establish a democratic government of their own."

The memorial meeting lasted four hours. After it was over, another meeting was called to decide how to continue "overturning." Only six farmers came to this meeting. No one said directly that he was afraid to attend, but weakly gave the excuse: "I have a little work to do."

These six men, however, decided that because of the murder they would have to "settle" with Landlord Wang immediately.

At the end of five days, thirty farmers mobilized by the other six gathered in the cave for another meeting. Until nearly midnight, they told stories of how they had suffered at the landlord's hands.

Suddenly, someone said: "Maybe Wang will run away."

"Let's get him tonight," said several farmers at once.

After some discussion, they all trooped out of the cave and started a march on Landlord Wang's home. Among the thirty men, there was one rifle and three hand grenades.

The marching farmers separated into two groups. One climbed on top of the cliffs and worked along the cave roofs until they were over the courtyard. The others marched directly to the gate, knocked loudly and commanded the landlord to open up.

Wang's wife answered the door and announced that her husband was not at home. Refusing to believe her, the peasants made a search and discovered a secret passage behind a cupboard. Descending through an underground tunnel, they found Wang cowering in a subterranean cave. They took him away and locked him up overnight.

That night Wang's son fled to the county seat of Hohsien, ten miles away. Here landlords from other villages had organized bandits, former puppet troops, and some of the soldiers of Warlord Yen Hsi-shan into a "Revenge Corps." When the people learned of the flight of Wang's son, they grew anxious and said among themselves: "It is easy to catch a tiger, but it is dangerous to let him go back to the forest."

Nevertheless, they decided to go ahead with the struggle against Landlord Wang. That same day a mass meeting was called in a great square field south of the town, not far from the river. About eighty people came to complain against Wang, while the rest of the village watched—among them Wang's wife and daughter.

In the course of the morning and afternoon, the crowd accused the landlord of many crimes, including betrayal of resistance members to the Japanese, robbing them of grain, forcing them into labor gangs. At last, he was asked if he admitted the accusations.

"All these things I have done," he said, "but really it was not myself who did it, but the Japanese."

He could not have chosen worse words. Over the fields now sounded an angry roar, as of the sea, and the crowd broke into a wild fury. Everybody shouted at once, proclaiming against the landlord's words. Even the nonparticipating bystanders warmed to something akin to anger.

Then above the tumult of the crowd came a voice louder than the rest, shouting: "Hang him up!"

The chairman of the meeting and the cadres were disregarded. For all that the crowd noticed they did not exist.

The crowd boiled around Wang, and somewhere a rope went swishing over a tree. Willing hands slung one end of the rope around Wang's waist. Other eager hands gave the rope a jerk. Wang rose suddenly and came to a halt in mid-air about three feet above the earth. And there he hung, his head down, his stomach horizontal and his legs stretched out—a perfect illustration of what the Chinese call a "duck's swimming form."

About his floating body, the crowd foamed, anger wrinkling their foreheads and curses filling their mouths. Some bent down and spit in the landlord's eyes and others howled into his ears.

As he rose from the ground, the landlord felt a terror which mounted higher as his position became more uncomfortable. Finally, he could bear it no longer and shouted: "Put me down. I know my wrongs. I admit everything."

The spite of the crowd, however, was not so easily assuaged and they only answered the landlord's pleas with shouts: "Pull him up! He's too low! Higher! Higher!"

After a while the anger of the people abated and cooler heads counseled. "If we let him die now, we won't be able to settle accounts with him." Then they allowed him to come down for a rest.

At this point, the wife of Original Fortune Lee came up close to

Wang and said in a plaintive voice: "Somebody killed my husband. Was it you?"

Wang's face which had grown red from hanging in the air slowly was drained of all color. "No, I did not do it," he said.

"Tell the truth," said the crowd. "You can admit everything to us and nothing will happen. But if you don't tell us the truth, we will hang you up again."

"No, it was not me."

These words were hardly out of his mouth before someone jerked on the rope and the landlord flew into the air again. This time the crowd let him hang for a long while. Unable to bear the pain, Wang finally said: "Let me down. I'll speak."

Then, between sobs and sighs, he told how he and his son had seized Original Fortune Lee as he was walking home from the meeting, tied his hands together, held his head under water until he was dead and then had thrown him in the river, thinking he would float away.

A cry of rage went up as Wang finished speaking.

"You've already killed three of our men in the war," said Liu Kwang. "That could be excused. But now your own life can never repay us for the crimes you've done."

Again Wang was hung up and this time many shouted: "Let him hang until he is dead." But others said: "That is too quick; he must first have a taste of the suffering we've had."

At dusk, they let Wang down once more and put him in a cave under guard again.

As soon as the meeting was over, twenty or thirty men went to the landlord's house, drove the wife and daughter out of doors and sealed the house. The two women went to a near-by village to stay with relatives.

That evening the five cadres and those who had taken an active part in the struggle against the landlord walked around the village to listen to the gossip and sample public opinion. Such words were heard as: "Serves him right; he's so wicked. This is too light for him. Just count his sins."

Later that night another meeting of those of the village who wanted to struggle against the landlord was held in a courtyard. This time 120 people attended.

When the cadres asked: "How do you feel? Have you done well?" the answer came back: "Oh fine! Fine!"

But exactly what to do with the landlord was a problem for which the people at first had no solution. Half of these in the meeting thought he should be beaten to death. A few said: "He is too old." Some had no ideas at all. Others thought that his clerk, the rich farmer Shih Tseng-hua, should be bound up with him at the same time in the struggle. This suggestion, however, was voted down when someone pointed out: "You should always collect the big melons in the field first. So we should cut off the big head first."

It was decided that Wang must die for his murders. But how? Should he be sent to the district government to be punished, should the people kill him or what?

"If he is tried before a court-martial for treason," said a farmer, "then there will be only one bullet, and that is too cheap for Wang. We ought to kill him first and report to the government afterward."

"Who dares kill him?" asked a farmer doubtfully.

At this everyone shouted at once: "We dare. We dare. He bayoneted our militiamen to death and we can also do that to him."

Three days after this meeting, the whole village breakfasted early, and shortly after sunrise, seven hundred men and women, including visitors from neighboring villages, many armed with pig knives, hoes, sickles, swords and spears went out to the large field south of town where the landlord was to be killed. The cadres had written down Wang's crimes on large pieces of paper and these, hanging by ropes from the trees, now fluttered in the breeze.

"Traitor Wang Chang-ying killed three militiamen and one active farmer of the village," said one.

"Sinful Landlord Wang grafted money and grain during the War of Resistance," said another.

"Wang Chang-ying shifted the tax burden onto the people and looted the village," said a third.

A shout went up from the crowd as Landlord Wang was led onto the field. Three guards marched him, pale and shaking, to a willow tree where he was bound up. With his back against the tree, the landlord looked once at the crowd but quickly bent his head toward the ground again.

A slight shiver of apprehension went through the audience. They could not believe their enemy was helpless here before them. He was the lamb led to slaughter, but they could not quite believe they were going to kill him.

Ma Chiu-tze stepped before the crowd and called for attention.

"Now the time has come for our revenge," he announced in a trembling voice. "In what way shall we take revenge on this sinful landlord? We shall kill him."

As he said this, he turned around and slapped Wang sharply across the face.

The crack of palm against cheek rang like a pistol shot on the morning air. A low animal moan broke from the crowd and it leaped into action.

The landlord looked up as he heard the crowd rushing on him. Those nearest saw his lips move and heard him say: "Two words, two words please."

The man closest shouted: "Don't let him speak!" and in the same breath swung his hoe, tearing the clothes from the bound man's chest and ripping open the lower portion of his body.

The landlord gave one chilling shriek and then bowed his head in resignation. The crowd was on him like beasts. Their faces had turned yellow and their eyes rolled. A big farmer swung his pig knife and plunged it directly into the landlord's heart. His body quivered—even the tree shook—then slumped, but still the farmer drew his knife in and out, again and again and yet once again.

Landlord Wang was quickly dead, but the rage of the crowd would not abate.

The field rang with the shouts of maddened people.

"It is not enough to kill him."

"We must put him in the open air."

"We must not allow him to be buried for three days."

But such convulsive passions do not last long. They burn themselves out. Slowly, the anger of the crowd cooled. The body of the landlord might rot in the open air and it were better that his wife and daughter be allowed to get him.

That evening, as the sun was going down behind the mountain, the landlord's wife and daughter brought a mule cart slowly across the field to where their husband and father lay. They wept no tears, but silently lifted the mutilated body into the cart and drove away.

Few saw them come and few saw them go. And no one said a word. For there was nothing left to say. The struggle against the landlord was ended.

Stone Wall Village had turned over.

* * *

When the struggle against the landlords of Stone Wall Village ended, an immediate settlement of accounts was begun. According to Communist terminology, this involved the division of the "fruits of struggle." A man who could write was located and established in a cave where he wrote down all the things that were to be divided. Among other things, this included furniture, grain, cotton and cloth, but principally land.

Naturally, this was a complicated process and not everyone at first was satisfied, but after several meetings, all the land taken from Wang Chang-ying was split up in a fashion that satisfied most of the people. When all the land was divided, everyone owned on the average two-thirds of an acre of water land; not much it is true, but far more than the poor had had before. Those whose bitterness had been especially heavy in the past were favored where an exactly equal division was impossible. The families of the four murdered farmers received half an acre more than the others.

Ma Chiu-tze, who previously had owned only one-sixth of an acre of land, now had about an acre and a half for himself and his wife. As soon as the land was his, he gave a feast for his relatives, for those who made out the land credentials, for the county cadres and for those who had helped to turn over Stone Wall Village. Every day, he went out to look at his land and in autumn he weeded, cut grass and plowed the whole day long.

Liu Kwang, no longer afraid of being lowered into a well by the landlord, received a new house from the settlement. Early every morning, his wife got up and swept out the courtyard, she was so happy to be living in a house instead of a cave.

Even stranger things happened which the reader may believe or not, as he likes. In the village, there was an old man who was deaf in one ear. Once he had borrowed four cents from the landlord and he had not been able to repay it, so Wang had boxed him on the ear and he had been deaf ever since. In the overturning movement he acquired two-thirds of an acre of land and he became very happy. One day he remarked to his son: "In the past, I was deaf because I was oppressed by the landlord, but now I am in such high spirits that I can hear with my bad ear again." Shortly after this, the old man looked at the pictures of the Earth and Heaven gods on his wall and angrily said: "I worshiped you for many years, but you did me no good. Now I am going to get rid of you all." So saying, he tore the gods from the wall and threw them in the latrine.

After the struggle against the landlords, the cadres urged the village to organize a Farmers Association and then to elect officers from among the 155 members of whom thirty were women.

Election day proved to be a gala event. The mountains had seen nothing like it in years and people gathered from neighboring villages in a holiday spirit. There had been long and heated discussion in the villages on just how the voting should take place. No one had ever voted before; most could not write. If voting were done by raising hands, there would be no dignity in the first election and it would not be secret. Therefore, it was decided to vote by putting beans in a bowl. Five officers were elected, among them Old Legality Ma, Liu Kwang and Second Jewel Pao. So, with the exception of the murdered Original Fortune Lee, every one of the four members who had attended the original secret meeting was elected.

Shortly after this, the Revenge Corps of Warlord Yen Hsi-shan's army grew increasingly active in the Taiyueh Mountains. Around Stone Wall Village, this corps was composed mostly of landlords and a few of their bailiffs. Sometimes they hired soldiers to make private raids on the villages which had divided their land. At last they struck in the vicinity of Stone Wall Village.

In Chaopeitsun, two miles away, a landlord named Tang Chi-yung and his brother, whose land the peasants had divided, leaving the brothers an equal share with themselves, had fled away to Yen Hsi-shan's area and joined the Revenge Corps. His wife, however, had remained in the village. One day, this wife learned that the village chief, the president of the Farmers Association and the leader of the local militia were holding a meeting about taxation in the village office and she ran away to her husband and told him of the meeting.

Because they did not finish their work till late, the three officials decided to sleep in the office. In the middle of the night Landlord Tang and his brother at the head of fifty armed troops whom they had hired for the occasion returned to the village and bayoneted the cadres to death. The landlord and the soldiers then looted the village granary of all its grain and departed at dawn.

As soon as Stone Wall Village heard the news of what had happened to its neighbor, the farmers called a meeting to discuss the situation.

"We cannot all leave town," said a local cadre, "because the enemy is around. These men were killed because they did not post sentries. We must put sentries outside our village and place our cadres in a well-defended place."

Because there was only one rifle in the village, the Farmers Association decided to appropriate forty piculs of wheat to buy nine rifles and some grenades from a near-by military factory which supplied guerrillas.

These precautions were necessary, for the son of Landlord Wang had not forgotten his father's death and was lurking in the vicinity, looking for revenge. Everyone in the village was of one mind that he would return. They seemed to realize that they had begun an adventure that provoked a sequence, a development and, inexorably, a retribution. Among the more timid, there was a general superstition that anyone who had touched Landlord Wang's property would be sure to die at his son's hands.

Sepulchral rumors floated about the village and it was said that the landlord's son returned in the middle of the night and talked with agents whom he had bribed. One night, a farmer saw a man that looked like Wang's son standing by a gate and he cried out in great alarm. The villagers rushed out of doors and the man took to his heels with the crowd in pursuit. After a chase of three miles, the people lost their quarry and returned home, frustrated and afraid.

A few nights later, Wang's son did in reality return. This time, he came at the head of a hundred armed men. Sentries stationed in the fields caught sight of them while they were still on the march and ran to warn the village which was thrown into pandemonium.

Hastily packing their belongings, the people retired into the ravines back of the village. Cows, donkeys and horses were all led away in the dark. Even those who had not opposed the landlord took their grain with them. The cadres, because they had no adequate weapons to fight with a hundred armed men, retired with all the rest. Not a man nor an animal was left in Stone Wall Village.

When Wang's son returned home, he found no man on whom to spend his revenge and no plunder to carry off. In anger, he set fire to all those houses which would burn. He could not burn the caves, so he smashed the wooden windows, carried out the furniture and threw it into the flames. The people looked at their homes going up in the fire, but they said little, only quietly cursing and once in a while murmuring: "We were lucky we had sentries or we would all be dead men by now."

At dawn, Wang's son and his hired crew of soldiers left. When they were not far distant, the people rushed back to the village and began to throw earth and water on their still burning houses. One by one, the fires were brought under control and put out. There was little weeping and wailing. Those whose homes were too badly damaged to live in went to live with their neighbors. At night, the five county cadres held a private meeting of their own and decided they must make active preparations for a long armed struggle. This was more than an overturning movement; this was war.

Within the next month, eleven people were killed in the near-by villages by marauding bands—bought soldiers, a few village leaders and the landlords in the Revenge Corps. The county government, unable to call on the regulars of the 8th Route Army and the guerrillas who had gone south, sent an open letter to every village to organize its own militia and put guards inside and outside the villages. In addition, volunteers came from the villages and formed a regular force of a hundred men that was at all times under command of the county.

Gradually this force brought peace to the villages. In the meantime, Stone Wall Village continued to "turn over." Taxes were lightened and the people themselves voted the amount of grain to be collected.

The village elected as its new chief a forty-year-old farmer named Ma Ying-hai, who formerly had owned no land of his own, but who had acquired an acre and a half during the land division. Liu Kwang, who had been put down a well by Landlord Wang, became head of the village militia. His wife joined the Women's Association.

The position of women changed greatly. Before, they could not participate in day or night meetings or be seen on the street after dark. Now they participated in meetings with men, day or night. There was not yet time for them to give birth to many children, but maybe the over-turning movement would take care of that, too.

The people began to cast aside their superstitions, no longer believed in ghosts, fox goddesses or a fate unalterable.

The temples remained untouched but no one visited them. The people said: "The Gods brought us no luck, but the 8th Route Army has brought us much luck."

Now the small landlords who fled away have come back and are working their land like common farmers.

The great house of Landlord Wang has been turned into a school. His mill which used to charge the villagers exorbitant prices to grind their grain has become the property of the whole village. Grain is ground free for all local people. Outsiders can use the mill by paying a nominal price. The money goes to pay the expenses of the Farmers Association.

31. Murder, Poison and Seduction

THE revolt against the feudal rulers threatened to become epidemic. Like flood water, the rising swelled and spread, inundating all the districts even to the borders of Chiang Kai-shek's areas. Watching from his manor, the landlord felt he was about to be engulfed.

In order to save himself, the larger landholder abruptly changed tactics, and began to adopt a protective liberal coloring. Instead of opposing the peasant organs, he now took an active, but concealed, part in organizing them. At his command, rascals, loafers and village bullies rushed to form various peasant associations. In this way the landlords hoped to control the farmers and avoid a settlement. Arriving from the county seats, and seeing every conceivable kind of organization in existence, the cadres would congratulate the farmers and go on to some other village. The peasants, finding themselves still under the same old rulers, quickly passed from enthusiasm to bewilderment, then to disgust and fear.

In the village of Huitsaiyu in Hopei Province a farmer came home and told his wife: "We must release ourselves from the landlord." His wife replied: "We are accustomed to be oppressed. We can't speak as fluently as the landlords. We are too slow."

The words of this farm wife expressed the mood of many peasants. The movement fell back again. In vain did the cadres scan the villages for signs of the old enthusiasm. They were no longer to be seen. The peasant wanted land, but the more he struggled, the more he seemed to come under the landlord's grip. Worst of all, the landlord's power was maintained by the very associations which the peasant had formed. The poor farmer was at a loss. The cadre had to take the lead again.

In a certain district of Pingying County in Shantung, there was a village chief named Wang Mao-pin. An opium smoker with a pale blue face, he had formerly operated gambling stalls on village fairgrounds. When the peasants showed signs of restlessness, the landlord called Wang and promised him fifteen mow of land to work on his behalf. Overnight, the gambler organized a Farmers Association and a Workers Union, becoming head of each and later becoming village chief.

When a cadre from the county Salvation Association entered the village, it seemed as if every kind of democratic organization had been formed. On instructions from the landlord, Wang followed the cadre everywhere, performing many services for him. To the peasants, he said: "I'll break the legs of anyone who dares mention the word settlement."

One night seven farmers met secretly with the cadre in a hut. Wang burst in armed with a spear. "What are you doing here?" he shouted at the assembled farmers. Noticing the salvation cadre, he suddenly became quiet, but remained glowering at his fellow-villagers from behind his spear. The farmers hastily rose and left the room, one by one. The cadre went out into the street with the village chief and found himself surrounded by five men with spears. "We must protect you," said Wang, and advised the cadre to leave town. The next day, instead of leaving, the cadre called a meeting and publicly scolded the village chief. The common farmers smiled, but none dared talk.

For some reason, however, the cadre's determined speech frightened the landlord. In the night, he left the village. Before he went, he told his dog leg, Wang: "A settlement is inevitable. But keep my face. Don't settle thoroughly."

Wang came to the cadre. "Look," he said, "I have your interest at heart. The landlord has gone."

"Why did you let him go?" asked the cadre.

"Never mind! Monks flee; temples remain. Rabbits go; holes remain. Let's settle his land."

Summoning twenty men, Wang put guards over the landlord's house and sealed the doors. Then he said: "The landlord has a thousand mow of land, let's harvest his crop." At the same time, he slyly suggested that men be sent to arrest the landlord, but the men who went merely gave the landlord information. The cadre did not know what to do. The village chief came before the people as the enemy of the landlord, but in reality was protecting his interests.

The cadre suggested that thirty thousand catties of grain be divided to pay the debts owed to the farmers. "No, let's take one hundred thousand catties and bust up his house," said Wang. Secretly he told the peasants: "This is enough; let's stop here." But the cadre kept pushing the peasants on. "Let's divide the land," he insisted. "If the landlord comes back, we will settle the account fairly with him."

In the meantime, the village held an election and voted Wang out of office. Shorn of his title, the gambler sent a message to the landlord, saying: "I can't do my duty to you under present conditions."

The farmers, having guaranteed not to kill him, the landlord returned. Relatives of the tenants who had starved to death met the landlord at the entrance to the village and beat him severely. Quaking, the landlord made his way back to a Speak Bitterness Meeting. A farmer told how the landlord and his dog leg, Wang, had dragged him, his wife and children to a dungeon, stripped them naked and whipped them. At this moment, Wang himself rose up and accused the landlord of other evil deeds. Betrayed and disgraced by his own bailiff, the landlord turned to Wang saying, "This is the first time I have ever learned anything from you." Then he kowtowed to the assembled farmers and begged their forgiveness, which was granted.

In such a manner, village by village, trick by trick, the landlords' intrigues were uncovered. Learning by experience, the peasants routed the village bosses from one position after another. As they swept forward, the resolution of the tenants and the rural workers rose by rapid leaps. During the first few months of the movement, bargains were made over seizures of properties. The landlord would say: "You protect me now and I'll protect you when the Kuomintang comes." Or the tenant might say: "You give me your land and I'll give it back when the Kuomintang comes." Now, except on the borders of the fighting areas, this mask fell away. Every step of the movement grew more audacious.

A concerted howl of anguish rose from Kuomintang territory about the barbarous land reform. A foreign correspondent went to Chiang Kai-shek's areas in Shantung and heard from fled-away landlords tales of atrocities. "The revolution," he observed, "is perishing just like the Taiping Rebellion because of terror." But the revolution was not perishing, it was growing stronger on the sorrows of its enemies. A Scripps-Howard correspondent found that it was a myth that the peasants supported the land reform. But this myth was changing all of North China society, and peasants were pouring out their blood and tears to make this legend come true. It is still some time before General Li Tsung-jen, newly elected vice-president of Kuomintang China, will get up in Nanking and say, "We must give the land to the tiller"; and before that date everyone on the Kuomintang side must say that such a program is atrocious.

In the meantime, the peasants had to face a threat from a new direction. Hearing that the land reform had created great inner conflicts among the peasantry, Chiang Kai-shek's secret service had begun to filter through into Communists' areas with the intention of stirring up revolts. But they were too late. By this time the land reform had penetrated very deeply into all sections of North China society and conditions were more or less stabilized. Finding it impossible to foment riots or even stir up public protests in the way the Communists, for example, were able to arouse student strikes and parades in Kuomintang areas, Chiang's agents had to fall back on other tactics. To accomplish their aims, behind Communist lines, they employed the following instruments: assassination, poison, student spies and women agent provocateurs.

The assassinations were carried out by local agents, by the Bureau of Investigation and Statistics and by the Special Service Section, dread terror organs of the Chiang regime. While I was in Communist areas, the biggest case occurred in the city of Tsining where eight assassination groups penetrated the city within six months. During this time, eleven people were wounded, but as far as I know, none were killed.

Carrying credentials written on silk, American-made pistols and gold bars for spending money, the agents filtered across the lines generally disguised as merchants. One such group, headed by two graduates of an American OSS wartime training school in Honan, having crossed the lines into Tsining, took up quarters in a house of prostitution and set out to assassinate General Yang Yun, commander of an 8th Route Army column. The first time, they sniped at General Yang in a theater, but missed. Escaping in the confusion, they returned to the theater some weeks later, again missed their target, but wounded several other people, and were finally caught.[1]

In the beginning, Chiang's killers concentrated almost exclusively on 8th Route Army commanders. But military personnel are hard to kill—especially if in the midst of troops. So the agents began more and more to conspire with landlords—particularly those who had worked with Japanese puppets. As an instance of this, I came across the following.

In the town of Hochien there lived a former commander of a Japanese puppet battalion, named Chun, and several of his officers. When the 8th Route Army entered the town, these men professed repentance and the government did not punish them. To Kuomintang troops ten miles away, however, they promised fertile ground for intrigue. Two Special Service

---

[1] Similar and unsuccessful attempts at assassination probably account for the numerous incorrect stories put out by the Kuomintang of the deaths of Communist army commanders. During the last year, official Kuomintang organs have at one time or another announced the death or wounding of General Lin Piao, Communist c-in-c in Manchuria, General Chen Yi, c-in-c in East China, General Liu Po-cheng and other Communist leaders.

men, having entered the town, persuaded Chun and his followers to set up a local SS station and send reports to the Kuomintang army in Hopei, across the border.

Now it happened that the mother of Chun was the village witch. She called down gods from Heaven, told fortunes and cured sickness. Because of this she had a lot of influence among the superstitious mountain women. At the persuasion of her son, she organized a Common Belief Association, spreading the thought among women that they should make themselves beautiful to attract men. In this way, she got many people—both men and women—to come to her home. Between revels, the witch would pull out her incense table, go into a trance and incant: "The Central Army comes: the Red Army goes. This is Fate. Fate decides. No one can change it. This world belongs to Chiang Kai-shek." Having spread "sky-changing" thoughts among the people, she would then say: "Whoever joins the Common Belief Association won't be killed. So it is decreed." In her home, she incited people to talk against the 8th Route Army. Then, if they still refused to join the association, she would say: "You have talked against the 8th Route Army, I will report you." In such a manner, she built up a following, especially among the town women, who were doubly bound to her because of the affairs they were having with men in her home.

Among these women was one known as Old Lady Peng to whose house the meetings were gradually transferred in order to avoid suspicion. For a time, Mrs. Peng slept without discrimination with the ex-puppets and various other men attracted to the meetings. Feeling, however, that it was inappropriate for a woman of her age to do this, she persuaded her daughter and her daughter-in-law, a girl named Fortunate Flower, to make love with visitors—and especially to entice staff members of the government to the house.

When the government organized a Women's Association and a Women's Evening School, Fortunate Flower joined. Hearing that the 8th Route Army thought women should have equality with men, she began to brood over her actions and think it wrong to partake of her mother-in-law's revels. Although afraid to report her secret to the government, she grew more and more cold to the men Old Lady Peng brought to the house. The SS men could not help noticing her attitude and grew afraid she might give away their secret.

One night Old Lady Peng led Chun and an SS man to her daughter-in-law's room. While they entered, she remained outside, listening at the door. Chun and his cohort seized the sleeping girl by the throat, but she managed to shriek out the one word: "Mother!" Old Lady Peng however, made no attempt to help Fortunate Flower. Stuffing cotton in the terrified girl's mouth, the two men quickly silenced her, then cut off her head and dismembered her body. The head they put in the outhouse of a neighbor, the intestines in the Kuo toilet and the torso they buried in the woods.

Old Lady Peng, to quiet talk over Fortunate Flower's disappearance, said she had run off with a soldier of the 8th Route Army. The girl was quickly forgotten until one day a hired laborer, cleaning the neighbor's outhouse, found the girl's head. At this time, Fortunate Flower's brother, who had been away, returned and by a scar on the girl's cheek identified the head as that of his sister. Neighbors remembering the quarrels of the old lady with her daughter-in-law concluded that she was connected with the murder, and the government put a close watch on the old woman's movements. Government investigators were inclined to think it just an ordinary murder until one day the name list of militiamen posted on the bulletin board of the Farmers Association disappeared. The theft was traced to a farmer who revealed that the ex-puppet Chun had promised him a big reward to murder the captain of the militiamen. With the arrest of Chun, his connection and that of the SS men with the girl's murder was established. But Chun would admit nothing. The whole Peng household was then arrested.

This news spread quickly through the town and a crowd of ten thousand people gathered outside the government office. The government tried to disperse them, but the crowd grew threatening and demanded that the SS men and the whole Peng family be nailed to the walls. Some men ran off to a carpenter shop, brought nails and began to distribute them among the crowd. Only after much pleading were cadres able to persuade the crowd to disperse. The sight of the angry townspeople, however, had frightened Old Lady Peng's maid who had heard Fortunate Flower shriek on the night she was killed. "I'll tell you everything I know," she said, "but the government must promise that I shall never be a maid servant again." With her confession, the whole story came out. A public trial was held before twenty thousand people. The SS man who had killed Fortunate Flower was condemned to death and executed. The fate of the others was still being decided when I left.

Since assassination is an extremely risky business, SS agents turned to poisoning as a safer means of upsetting order and terrorizing people behind the Communist lines.

In the guerrilla regions I came across a village where twenty-eight militiamen had died from poison that had been placed in their wheat-flour stores. In the same district, where there was frequent fighting, the government claimed 350 people had been poisoned, fifty-three of them dying. During the land reform, poison was most commonly put in wells to discourage active farmers from struggling against the landlords. In Honan, I met a girl in the guerrilla regions who had fled from her husband's home because her mother-in-law had poisoned the wells during a settlement struggle. In other places, I found the peasants so incensed by the use of poison that they hated the SS, and consequently Chiang Kai-shek, worse than they did the landlords. Poison thus acted as a political agent in a way its users had not figured.

Besides trying to break down the morale of the common people in the Liberated Areas, the Kuomintang also sent a number of spies to work among the intelligentsia and non-Communist cadres. Many of these agents were unemployed intellectuals and impoverished students whom the Kuomintang had trained in anti-Communist work. Because their families were in Kuomintang areas, the SS thought there was little risk in sending these students over to the Communists, but many were so affected by what they saw that they voluntarily confessed.

Although I can't reveal his name for obvious reasons, I know of just such a boy. Brought up in Mukden under Japanese rule, he nevertheless was patriotically moved by China's war against Japan, and in 1942, having obtained a passport, he came south of the Great Wall and managed somehow to make his way to Chiang Kai-shek areas. Arrested at Tungkwan, he spoke so fervently against the Japanese, that cynical SS men thought he must be a Communist. They sent him to a political reform camp at Sian. After five months' training, he was put in the Three People's Principles Youth Corps, a fascist type organization formed by Chiang Kai-shek to strengthen his domination over Chinese youth. From there he was transferred to a training camp run by Tai Li, then head of all Chiang's secret service and terror organizations. Later he joined a plain-clothes corps. Still later he was brought to Sian and given special training against the 8th Route Army. Having been made to read a lot of books about Marx and Engels, having created a false biography and having also written out a diary as if he were a Communist, he joined many other students who were fleeing Chiang's areas of their own accord, and came into the Shansi-Hopei-Shantung-Honan Border Region. The authorities sent him to the military academy for study as a cadet. In 1947, the cadets were sent to help the peasants in the struggle for the land reform and the boy was much affected by what he saw. Returning to the academy, he went to the principal and confessed that he was a spy. Not only was he not punished, but he was allowed to continue his studies without the other students being told anything of his case.

In trying to subvert the 8th Route Army, the Kuomintang intelligence realized not much could be done with money, but thought Communist soldiers might be overcome by women, as most of them were single. After the Japanese surrender, many girls attached to puppets or daughters of landlords tried to marry into the 8th Route Army. For this reason, authorities, just as with the American Army in Germany, would not let any soldier marry without investigating his prospective wife. Kuomintang girl spies coming into the area, therefore, found it difficult to marry cadres or soldiers openly and adopted covert methods which generally failed with the regulars, but sometimes succeeded in guerrilla areas.

In the summer of 1947, a clerk named Ho Tze-chuan, who had joined the 10th Brigade of the 8th Route Army in August 1946, was wounded while fighting in Shansi Province. As the brigade was advancing he was left behind in a peasant's home to recover. One day while walking on a motor highway near the village of Siaowu, a girl beckoned to him. She was young, had bobbed hair and "emancipated feet." Introducing herself, she told Ho she was from a county fifty miles away and that she had come to seek her husband who was a vice-commander of a company. She had not been able to find him; some people said he had been killed in battle, others said he was missing in action and now all her money was gone and she had no place to go. At the conclusion of her story, she burst into bitter tears. Promising to help her return home, the clerk brought her to the government office who found her lodging in a civilian's house.

Here, Ho often came to see her. During these visits, the girl shed many tears, said she was sure her husband was dead and declared she would rather stay with the troops than go home where things were bad. Finding the girl quite cultured—a rarity in Chinese villages—Ho developed an affection for her which she reciprocated even to the extent of proposing marriage. But Ho refused. "When proof of your husband's death arrives and if the authorities say it is all right, then we can marry, but not now," he told the girl.

But the girl was very passionate. She tried to convince Ho that love was the most powerful thing in the world. "My husband really is dead," she said one afternoon, "I know it. And my home is so poor. I have to be supported. Can't you understand my feelings? Marriage is much more important than revolution."

These words planted a seed of doubt in Ho's mind, and he decided to investigate the girl's home. In the meantime, he pretended to play along with the girl's desires.

Another evening, the girl told him: "I know you can't marry me here, but my uncle is a garrison commander in Chishan [a town on the Kuomintang side]. If you can desert the 8th Route Army, my uncle will make you a company commander."

Convinced that the girl was a spy, Ho took her at once to the district government where she quickly confessed that her whole story had been faked. She had been trained like many other middle-school girls and sent by the Kuomintang into Communist areas to subvert cadres and army officers.

To fully appreciate this story, it is necessary to understand that China under Chiang Kai-shek was a semi-police state with much of the power in the hands of gangsters, secret service men and special agents who exercised the most unholy rights over women, including many of the better-educated and more cultured ones. During the Japanese war, I attended a banquet given by Chinese for American pilots where I met a young Chinese woman with whom I later became quite friendly. This girl told me that she had been raped by one of the top-ranking men in Chiang's secret service and forced to marry him, even against the wishes of her father, a respected professional man. On her wedding day Chiang sent her a present of five thousand dollars, which she said she tried to refuse, but which her husband made her accept. Thereafter, she was constantly thrown in with Tai Li, chief hatchetman for Chiang, and many of his unsavory subordinates. I cannot quite describe the pity I felt for this girl's condition nor the frustration I experienced when she begged me to sneak her onto an American Army plane and help her escape from her husband and his gangster friends. This is far from being the only case that I know of personally. Scores of girls and boys during the last ten years were delivered into the clutches of the Chinese gestapo with little hope of escaping. Men from the very dregs of Shanghai society until recently occupied responsible positions in Chiang's government. Some years ago when I worked for an American news agency in China, a Shanghai loafer with a small-time spy job used to come around to our office and go through our files and intimidate our Chinese employees. During the war, this man obtained an influence with some American Army officers, and because of this and because he could speak English, he rose in the Kuomintang hierarchy. The last time I saw him, in 1947 at a reception in the Shanghai American Club, he was dressed in a full colonel's uniform and hobnobbing with American officials. Seeing me for the first time in years, he was not above boasting and stamped his foot on the floor of the American Club and said, "This is my territory. I control from Soochow Creek to Nantao and from the Bund to Medhurst Road." And indeed, he did, as many arrested men and women who got in his greedy clutches can testify.

But to return to our story. In general the Kuomintang's efforts behind the Communist lines ended in dismal failure. As Communist troops held out and as the Kuomintang SS burrowed into their holes, the peasants, led by the tenants and the "long-term workers," rose still more boldly, not heeding the warning either of the landlords or the rich peasants. By the winter of 1947, outside of the guerrilla areas, scarcely a village could be found without a peasants' association or a settlement committee. Even the middle peasants joined the struggle, while the rich peasants continued to draw further away from the landlord.

Routed from one position after another, the landlord looked around anxiously for allies, but could find none. In desperation, he fell back on the women in his family, trying to use them as an influence among the active farmers to soften the settlement. This became so widespread that it stamped its character on the land reform and continues even to this day. Wives, concubines, daughters and nieces were indiscriminately thrown into the battle for land.

In a village on the outskirts of Hantan, there was a tenant named Wang Chen-teh who was very active in the agrarian movement, and who had a good reputation in the village as a thorough and painstaking worker. His landlord tried to bribe Wang with money not to join the "turning-over" movement. Wang refused. "If the Kuomintang troops come, I won't protect you," threatened the landlord. Wang remained adamant. Seeing that threats failed to move his tenant, the landlord tried soft words. "In the past," he said, "I have wronged you and I want to return what I owe you. Let's you and I make a private settlement." Still the tenant would not agree.

In desperation, the landlord called his niece and said: "You'll have to marry him." At the same time, he persuaded his niece to go to bed with the tenant, saying, "Even if he doesn't want you, he'll have to marry you after sleeping with you." But the tenant, realizing the settlement movement would come to a standstill if he gave in to the landlord, refused to marry the niece.

Afraid Wang would tell the story around the village, the landlord called his followers to kidnap the tenant. Since Wang had been very active in leading the settlement, and since it was rumored that the landlord had tried to find a go-between for his niece, the people immediately suspected the landlord was behind the kidnaping. Searching the village, they found Wang bound and gagged inside a closet and nearly dead. They immediately raided the landlord's home and arrested him.

In Kaoyi village near the Peiping-Hankow Railway, a landlord sent a gift of ten thousand dollars to the head of the Farmers Association and another one to the director of the militia. A few days later he told his wife to go to the government and say: "My husband is no good, he is trying to bribe you." Pretending, in this way, to be very "enlightened," the landlord's wife got close to the farmers most active in the peasant movement. One day, she would make love with one farmer, and the next day she would make love to another staff member of the peasant's association. As a result, each farmer became jealous of the other, no one could agree on anything and the movement came to a halt.

In Wucheng County, a landlord named Li Tsun-lien, lived with his wife and eighteen-year-old virgin daughter. Finding himself helpless in the face of the swelling peasant movement, he ordered his daughter to play up to one of his tenants who was taking a prominent part in the movement. Inviting the tenant to dinner, he ate at a high table with his wife, and placed the tenant with his daughter at a small table at his feet. After a few days, he had the daughter and the tenant eat in a separate room. Within two weeks, the tenant was sleeping with the daughter.

Lying in his arms, the girl said to the tenant, "You now have everything you want so there is no need for you to continue as chairman of the Workers Committee. Don't struggle any more. I can give you anything you lack."

This seemed like a good suggestion to the tenant and gradually he lost his interest in the peasant movement. In meetings, when others proposed certain acts, he would say: "We have millet and clothes to wear. What's the use of struggling any further?"

Becoming suspicious, his fellow-tenants followed him and saw that he was on very good terms with the landlord. "Why," they asked, "are you working so little nowadays and how is it you are so friendly with Li Tsun-lien? And how is it that his daughter, with whom you never dared speak before, is now on such friendly terms with you? You were oppressed before by the landlord, weren't you? What's the matter with you now?"

Pressed on all sides, the tenant finally admitted that he was sleeping with the landlord's daughter. The Workers Committee immediately asked the daughter to come to a meeting. "Why are you sleeping with our comrade?" they asked. "Because my father made me," she said.

The meeting broke up with the shouting of slogans: "We shouldn't be flattered by landlords. We shouldn't be bought by money. We shouldn't be lured by women."

In every Chinese village there is generally at least one woman— usually married—who sleeps with other men, either for pleasure or for money. Such a woman is known as a "broken shoe." Quite often, as might be expected, they are among the most charming women in the village. I met one such woman, named Third Blossom, about whom farmers told me the following story.

Lu Mu-an, the landlord of this village, promised Third Blossom five thousand dollars if she would disgrace the chairman of the Farmers Association. Because, as she later told me herself, she was very poor and had "bad thoughts," she agreed. Telling the chairman that she had a serious problem, she invited him to her home to settle it. When he arrived, Third Blossom prepared some noodles and a little wine. Then she asked the chairman to stay the night. Nothing loath, the chairman leaped into bed. As soon as they had finished making love, Third Blossom ran naked into the street and shouted: "Oh, you chairman of the Farmers Association, you have raped me!" Still shouting, she ran straight to the subdistrict office and made a report to the cadres who summoned a meeting of the whole village next day. During the meeting, Third Blossom, when confronted with the accusations of the chairman, broke down and admitted she had been bribed by the landlord to disgrace the chairman. Though there was no question of rape, the chairman was dismissed by his fellow-farmers, who thought him disgraced enough as it was. Third Blossom, so she said, did not get the five thousand dollars.

Finally, landlords used their concubines to discredit local cadres (farmers holding village office). In Wangtsun, a landlord's concubine lured a tenant into the kitchen, hastily pulled down her pants and yelled rape at the top of her lungs. The landlord then hauled the tenant before a village meeting. As usual the duplicity was discovered.

These crude efforts to stop the onsweep of a mighty social force with the bodies of their womenfolk were the dying gasps of the landlords. Even their own families began to turn against them. In a village in northern Honan, while farmers were organizing themselves, a landlord made his daughter-in-law stand on the roof and keep watch, rain or shine, for anyone who might be coming to kill him. As the farmers grew stronger, the landlord fled, leaving his wife and daughter-in-law alone in the house. Some weeks later, the 8th Route Army having arrived in the city, the Farmers Association asked the people for all their weapons so they could form a militia. When a peasant came to her home, the landlord's wife denied she had any arms. "Oh, yes you have!" said the daughter-in-law who hated both the landlord and his wife. With these words, she pounced on her mother-in-law, tore off her pants, ripped out a pistol concealed between the woman's legs and handed it to the astonished peasant. Such were the final resting places of the landlord's power— between a woman's legs.

Within the Liberated Areas, all the lords of the land collapsed everywhere in the same feeble manner, with the same futile gestures. By the spring of 1947, the more farsighted landowners saw they could not hope to keep their estates. They did not even try to. By summer, almost all the landlords except in the guerrilla regions, had been eliminated—that is to say, all those who had lived off land rents were no longer able to do so, but had to till their own soil. The upheaval was so great and so swift that in the Shansi-Hopei-Shantung-Honan Border Region alone, twenty-one thousand landlords were eliminated within less than a year. The rural possessing classes, despite their murders, their intrigues and the seductive activities of their women, had lost the battle.

32. Land, War and Revolution

THE foregoing account of the struggle between landlords and peasants is not, and does not pretend to be, a scientific treatise on the land reform. The struggle took place over such a wide area, under such varying conditions and between so many people that any report at this time must at best be fragmentary and filled with errors.

Nevertheless, I believe this account presents a reasonably accurate picture of why land reform was necessary, of the techniques used in the struggle and how and why the poorer peasants overcame the landlords. If there is any important distortion in the account I have given it perhaps lies in overemphasizing violence. The violence that accompanied the land reform generally took place on the border of Kuomintang regions, in the guerrilla areas and in the places where the control of the Communist party was not great. In the inner regions of the Communist areas violence was at a minimum. In full justice to the Communists, it must also be clearly stated that the Communist party leadership, as distinct from county commissars and peasants, did not condone violence, nor make it into a system, but actively fought against it. Furthermore, it should also be stated that in newly occupied territories, the Communists did not divide the land, but adopted a go-slow policy of reducing rents and rates of interest (see chapter on Property).

The effects of the land reform on Chinese life, of course, have been far reaching. These effects have not been confined to the system of land-ownership but have produced changes in religion, government, war, art, the status of women and almost all branches of Chinese civilization. Some of these results are examined in a later section of this book, but here I would like to look at some of its more immediate and direct results.

Mao Tze-tung, chairman of the Chinese Communist party, often declared that the party that solved the land question would rule China. He believed that if the Communist policy on land was right, they would definitely win the war. From what I saw—and this is purely my own analysis—the land reform had the following effects on war and revolution.

1. It broke open the remaining castles of feudalism and released the prisoners into services of a new power.

2. Land reform also broke open the peasant's soul and released a flood of mass passions into the sphere of war and revolution. These passions

created a tremendous emotional energy, making both friends and enemies for the Communists, but mostly friends.

3. The land reform posed the question of authority. In thousands of villages it clarified an already existing, but hidden struggle between the landlords and the poor peasants. Because of the land reform the peasant was continually forced to ask himself: "Who is going to rule: the landlord or me?"

4. Thus the peasant became not only self-conscious, but class conscious. In struggling, he found not only a material enemy in his own local landlord, but a spiritual enemy in all landlords. Because the Kuomintang armies supported the landlords, the peasant identified these as his enemies, too. And since the United States was supporting the Kuomintang and Chiang Kai-shek, he often identified America as his enemy also.

5. The land reform gave to the peasant the belief that he was participating in a fight for great human rights. This created a terrific moral force.

6. In struggling for land, the peasant created his own ruling organs— peasant unions, farmers' associations. This meant that the 8th Route Army did not have to hold down territory by force of arms, and could release soldiers for the front and create a pacific rear.

7. The division of land in doing away with landlord rule laid the possibility for elections and thus put village governments in the hands of those favorable to the Communist cause.

8. The elimination of landlords automatically eliminated surtaxes, military requisitions and the time-honored squeeze of the gentry. This meant the abolition of corruption and a well-fed army.

9. The breakdown of traditional landlord authority weakened the landlord ethic of Confucianism, the age-old beliefs in fate and superstitious beliefs in Buddhas, idols and witches. Before, because of gentry propaganda, peasants had thought it was the will of the gods or their fate to be poor. Now, they realized they could get enough to eat by their own efforts.

10. Abolition of the landlords also meant weakening of the paternal system, the break-up of the traditional family and the authority of men over women. Equality for women ended concubinage and resulted in many new freedoms which made women violent supporters of the 8th Route Army.

11. It tended to increase production because men were more willing to work on their own land.

12. It spoke forcibly to the heart of the peasant soldier on the Kuomintang side.

13. Finally, land reform led directly to a people's war which in many counties resulted in the piecemeal destruction of Chiang's armies.

No matter what one thinks of land reform as a social or economic program, whether one thinks it beneficial to human nature or not, there is no denying that in China it was a revolutionary and military tactic almost beyond compare.

There is one other revolutionary aspect of land reform we might amplify here. Land division had a very curious effect on mass consciousness. It not only changed the mind of the peasants in Communist territory, but also shook the thoughts and feelings of the Communists' opponents—especially those in Chiang Kai-shek's army. This change in the collective consciousness of Communist opponents occurred in a very subtle way and often had a semiconcealed character. Materially, the land reform weaned rural China away from Chiang Kai-shek. Since the relative weight of cities in Chinese life is very low, this meant in effect that Chiang Kai-shek's army was gradually isolated from the main currents of Chinese life. The Communist analogy of an army being the fish and the people the water is very applicable here. Land reform not only created an element in which the Communists could live, it also sucked the people away from Chiang Kai-shek's army and left it gasping for breath in a social vacuum.

While Chiang's army was being materially divorced from its environment, the officers and soldiers in the army became psychologically and spiritually disinherited. Because the loss of the countryside deprived it of adequate intelligence reports, Chiang's army became blind, with the result that it could no longer predict events with accuracy and was led into fatal mistakes. This resulted in a tremendous loss of self-confidence. Soldiers and officers came to doubt the things they were fighting for, even the necessity of fighting. Feelings of guilt gnawed away at the soldier's heart, corroding the armor of his soul. Lonely, lost, uncertain, even feeling themselves a little crazy because they had been cast adrift from their social moorings, Chiang's soldiers were ready to take any desperate step to escape the trap in which they were caught. In another society, at a different time and under other conditions, such troubled souls might have sought refuge in religion, the psychiatrist's bench or romantic love; in China, because there was no other way out, they sought it in the revolution.

PART VIII

INTO GUERRILLA COUNTRY

❦

33. On the Road

WHILE I was in the Taihang Mountains, I was continually hearing stories that the farmers in Anyang County in Honan Province, angered by the depredations of Chiang Kai-shek's troops and raiding landlords, were carrying on a vengeful guerrilla warfare behind the Kuomintang lines. This news greatly interested me because I had never seen that kind of warfare. So I determined to go to Anyang to have a look for myself.

A small unroofed cart, with solid wooden wheels, having been obtained for the first stage of the journey, I set out on a cool spring day in 1947. Accompanying me were an interpreter, an orderly and an armed soldier of the 8th Route Army.

The interpreter was a good-looking boy of twenty-six, named Chen. During the Japanese war he had taught school in Chiang Kai-shek areas in Szechuan, had later taken a job in the Executive Headquarters in Peiping and still later come over to the Border Region where he became a reporter for a headquarters' newspaper. Though his English was not as good as that of some other Liberated Area youths, he was a much better interpreter than most because he never tried to propagandize me, never tried to impress me with the "new society," and always translated what I said, a thing you could not count on with some of the more ardent boys who sometimes deliberately mistranslated my too inquisitive questions or my interviewees' too free remarks.

My orderly was a youthful "old soldier" named Liu Ming-chi who had been captured from the army of warlord Yen Hsi-shan. Liu was a likable boy—honest, uncomplaining, decent and modest. He was a good soldier, but did not look like one. He wore a gray army uniform which hung on his short frame like a sack. He brought with him a small cloth bag, a blanket, a towel, a piece of soap, a toothbrush, a small notebook and the chewed stub of a pencil. The bag was slung across his shoulder, the toothbrush stuck out of his left upper pocket and the towel hung at his waist. He was sloppy, no doubt about it, and ugly, too, with a cast in one of his eyes and blemishes on his face. He reminded me somewhat of Sad Sack. Yet for him I felt a friendship I often could not feel for the famous "Little Devils" who also acted as orderlies but who had been so long in the 8th Route Army that they often talked almost wholly in slogans and seemed quite inhuman. I do not mean that Liu did not like the 8th Route Army; obviously he did, but he never made a point of it. He said: "They feed you better and never beat you or make you carry heavy weights," and he let it go at that. He kept a friendly eye on all my wants, laying out soap, towel and basin full of water for me at night, furnishing me with mountain-made cigarettes on the road, and dishing out bank notes for water or tea that we got in roadside stands. Generally, because of his uniform, the vendors would make a show of not taking his money, but Liu always forced it on them. At the end of each day, he would sit close under the oil lamp and total up his expenses, writing in his childish scrawl on a scrap of waste paper, then transferring everything to his precious notebook. Sometimes he could not find a place to sleep—for the villages often were crowded—then he would come and ask me in his shy way if I minded if he bedded down on the kang beside me. Or else he would find a board and lay it across two benches and go to sleep not far away. On the other hand, he seemed to sense when I wanted to be alone and never followed me when I went out exploring by myself, a thing which I often did and in which nobody stopped me.

Though Liu Ming-chi was a sloppy individual, he was a far better soldier than the young boy who had been sent along to guard me from special agents or any stray malcontents who might want to do me harm. Actually, the guard turned out to be quite a dud. He said he was sick and we spent more time taking care of him than he of us. In the end, when we went behind the lines, we shouldered his gun and left him in the safety of a peasant's hut.

Heading south and east through the Taihang Mountains, the first day we journeyed along a dried-up river bed between the enclosing hills of a narrow valley. The river bottom was nothing but a mass of rocks with no flat place for walking. For us the going was unpleasant enough, but for the mule it seemed distinctly painful. At each step, every one of his four hoofs would come down on a teetering rock, so that he went forward at an uneven lurch and with saddened, suffering eyes. Of course, such a road was hard on the cart, and the driver carefully explained that a cart with a normal life of ten years would only last one year on a river bed such as this. As a result, we made little more than two miles an hour.

Despite the state of the road, our journey was enlivened by the sights of China's usually colorful traffic. Now a woman dressed in a red blouse and green pantaloons would pass us, astride a jackass. Next would come a man sitting sidesaddle upon a donkey, his bedding spread beneath him across the animal's back. As for heavy traffic, there were large carts carrying cotton from the plains or else hauling dried persimmons from the mountains down to the towns below. Still other carts were carrying rails into the hills.

These I do not think were being used to build a railway. Probably they were just being taken out of the enemy's reach or perhaps they were to be melted up for ammunition. Nevertheless, there was a railway of sorts being built up in these hills. Just what kind of a railway I could not figure out. The rails were very narrow and on them were little toy carriers, about one foot high and about four feet long. Whether these last were pulled by a toy engine, by mules or men I could not quite fathom.

Toward the end of the day, the valley suddenly broadened out, the rocks ended and we came out on a dirt cart track over which it was a great relief to travel. Night coming on, we halted in a village called Patien where the village chief found us a room in the former house of a landlord. Now it was occupied by two couples, one over sixty years of age and the other about twenty-five. Before the turning-over movement, the old couple had only two mow of land, but now they had six. Despite their years, the old man and his wife were very cheerful and they soon found me some straw, placed it on the kang and made me a bed. The rest of the village, hearing of my arrival, crowded at the front gate, trying to brush their way past Liu Ming-chi and the guard who barred their way. The demands of the crowd being somewhat more than insistent, I went to the door, showed my strange foreign face and said a few inconsequential words which seemed to satisfy everyone as the crowd soon broke up and went away.

That night Liu Ming-chi fetched the old couple two buckets of water from the village well and they, much pleased, gave him a bowl of millet and a flimsy basin in which to wash his feet. Unlucky boy that he was, Liu put his heel through the basin. Mortified at his clumsiness, Liu pressed two hundred dollars into the old lady's hand to pay for the damages, but she would not take the money, saying, "We are all from one home."

We started at dawn the next morning, and after a brisk six-hour walk reached Pengcheng, a town of some ten thousand people, boasting two long, narrow, winding streets, many shops and three bathhouses, located in the heart of a pottery-manufacturing district—one of the oldest, I believe, in China.

At the time of my arrival in Pengcheng, both the distribution and the artistry of the pottery had seriously declined. Because the railways had been torn up and communications with the larger towns destroyed, the pottery industry could find no outlet and many ovens had shut down and the workers gone back to farming. In this, of course, they had been aided by the land reform. What pottery was now being made was of a strictly utilitarian variety, including teapots, wine jugs, cups and plates. Most of the wares, as far as I could see, were transported on huge wheelbarrows over mountain trails, and it was a rather disheartening sight to see a man pushing one of these barrows filled with a load of teapots that would have taxed the strength of a donkey.

The children of Pengcheng, who adopted me as if I were a visiting baseball hero, insisted on showing me the ovens—round, domed, clay-brick houses built over empty pits. When the unfinished pottery, set in molds, was placed inside the houses, the pits were filled with burning coal, the door sealed and the pottery left to cook for a couple of days. The abundance of these ovens in the fields throughout this whole area gave the scenery around Pengcheng a rather unique appearance. In addition, the people, no doubt finding the pottery more sturdy than earthen bricks, had built many of their houses with discarded molds, piling them up like so many jars, one on top of another, and filling the cracks in between with mud. Although from a distance, they looked like charming gingerbread houses, on closer approach these residences appeared more ugly than board and bat shacks in an American tenement district.

Another noteworthy feature of the Pengcheng scenery were the curious flames and fires which kept issuing from unexpected places beneath the ground. The children tried to explain their meaning to me, but I couldn't quite understand them. Perhaps they were natural gas deposits or more likely small coalpits which the people used for crude smelting operations.

Although Pengcheng was only some five or six miles from the Kuomintang army and though the county government of Tzehsien had taken refuge here from the plains below, there were no 8th Route Army troops in town which was guarded solely by locally raised militia. Because of this, you might have thought that Pengcheng was living in an atmosphere of dread and uncertainty. However, far from being gloomy, Pengcheng was in quite a gay and festive mood.

34. Women's Day

We had arrived in Pengcheng on the eve of International Women's Day and all the streets were filled with women and girls from the neighboring villages. In honor of these women, an evening performance of *White Haired Woman* was staged that night in a field in the open air.

The night was bitterly cold, yet a crowd of at least two thousand people came to see the play. County officials, workers from the pottery ovens, clerks from the co-operatives, old peasant women in shawls, girls in uniform and young farm girls in simple jackets and pants all crowded in a great semicircle around the improvised stage which was lit by a glaring pressure lamp. There were a few benches on which some lucky early-comers sat, but most reclined on the ground, the children down front, directly in front of the stage, with others standing in the rear on small elevated humps of ground. Here and there in the audience one could see militiamen with rifles, some of them equipped with bayonets which glinted fitfully in the light.

It would be hard to imagine a more democratic gathering. No tickets were sold, there was no dress circle and no preferred seats. The children in the front, directly below the stage, however, had a hard time seeing. Every once in a while they would climb on one another's shoulders to get a better look at the stage. This blocked the view of those behind who set up a critical clatter. Whenever this happened, one of the actors would reach out with a long stick and bang the offending child gently on the head while yelling out in a loud voice, "Children behave yourself." Sometimes the stage lamp went out. Then a stagehand would fetch a stepladder onto the stage and pump vociferously at the lamp for a few moments until the illumination was restored. Afterward, the actors would pick up their lines as if nothing had happened.

Before the performance, a girl in uniform mounted the stage and through a megaphone shouted out to the audience a synopsis of the play—something entirely unnecessary as, even to me, the story was abundantly clear. The girl had a long, thin body, like a stick, straight black hair, a pale, thin face, and she wore horn-rimmed glasses. Ugly of manner, she was belligerent in voice and she reminded me of the standard caricature of a long-haired radical—the only one of such appearance, incidentally, that I saw in 8th Route Army territory. *White Haired Woman* was a tragic melodrama, but in certain spots it was deliberately funny. Yet when the audience laughed this girl mounted the stage and shouted through her megaphone: "Don't laugh." I told Mr. Chen I did not approve of this practice, but he could not agree with me. "I think it is necessary for us to improve the people and teach them sympathy for the suffering of others," he said. "Perhaps you have something to learn from the people," I replied. "This play is about their own experiences and they know what is funny better than anyone else. If you don't want them to laugh, you should change the play."

Actually, the play needed little changing. Written co-operatively by a great number of writers and constantly rewritten on the advice of farmers, it was by far the best of all the plays that I saw in the Liberated Areas, and was probably the best known. The trouble with most Communist plays, to my way of thinking, was not that they were propaganda, which they undoubtedly were, but that they were too crowded with events, developing none of them fully, so that most of the dramatic impact was lost. Then, the emphasis being on events and themes and not on people, all the characters tended to become cardboard types and not living human beings.

Nothing of the sort, however, could be said of *White Haired Woman*, a story which, no doubt, sounds trite when told here, but was very moving when performed on the stage.

The heroine of the play, as might be expected, is the daughter of a tenant farmer. Seized by the dog legs of the landlord when her father cannot pay his New Year's debts, she is forced to become a maidservant in the landlord's home. There she is constantly beaten by the landlord's wife, a devout, but humorous old Buddhist, and finally raped on a dark night by the landlord's son. Made pregnant (her belly becomes very big, indeed, on the stage) she threatens to reveal her shame to the whole village. The landlord's son, who is about to be married, and the dog leg bind up the girl, throw her in a closet and make ready to murder her. An old woman servant, who many years ago had been brought to the landlord's home under much the same circumstances, releases the girl who flees in the night. The landlord's son and the dog leg pursue her into the mountains.

Wailing a defiant song, the girl evades capture by taking refuge in a rocky glen where she gives birth to a baby, her hair turning white in the process. She is adopted by guerrillas who eventually free her home village and bring the landlord's son before a Speak Bitterness Meeting. The villagers debate what to do with the son. At this juncture, to my utter surprise, many members of the audience stood up in great excitement, shouting "Sha! Sha! Kill him! Kill him!" The boy, showing repentance, however, is merely beaten. The land is divided, the girl gets her share and even the landlord his.

Though melodramatic in the extreme, this play avoided being ludicrous and generated a great amount of excitement, because of the sincerity of the actors and because of a few technical tricks, principally the use of a number of songs. The bitter reality of the play was not lost on the women in the audience many of whom, as I found out, had undergone similar experiences. At several points in the play I saw women, old and young, peasant and intellectual, wiping tears from their eyes with the sleeves of their jackets. One old lady near me wept loudly through nearly the whole play.

Frankly, I was almost as much affected by this play (or by the audience's reaction to it) as were the women. As a matter of fact, the Communists' whole theatrical effort was extremely impressive. While at Yehtao, during a three-day fair, I saw as many as five plays going at one and the same time. The stages were makeshift affairs and the properties the scantiest. Costumes, however, provided no problem as most all the plays concerned everyday people. The actors and actresses made up under a small awning in back of the stage, using flour and axle grease to produce the effects they wanted. Though there were some professional troupes, run by the army or the party, most were groups organized by the villages themselves. If a village had a particularly good troupe it wandered about the county performing on different fair days, without pay and only receiving transportation and food for their services. Until very recently in China, as in Shakespeare's time, all women's parts were played by men, but in the Communist areas, female leads were generally played by women. And it was quite a moving thing to see women with bound feet, who hitherto had not been allowed outside the home, toddling around the stage and acting out the part of an emancipated female.

The next morning being Women's Day, a festival was held on the town's fairgrounds where fifty or sixty women performed a series of group dances with flowers and gaily colored sticks. The spirit of the dances, though the appearance was far different, was somewhat like our Maypole dances. There was nothing particularly athletic about them, certainly nothing militaristic; they were very simple and for that reason all the more impressive. There was no glorification of the body, no upstanding breasts, no sturdy thigh displays, no ruddy, glowing Womanhood, nor any attempt to glorify a national or a class ideal. The whole affair seemed more like a social gathering than an exhibition of mighty women, such as might have taken place in Nazi Germany or Soviet Russia.

At the end of the performance, the women in groups of six and seven, each accompanied by a man piping on a flute and another one beating cymbals, came tripping down the streets of the town, dancing the *Yangko*.

The *Yangko* was perhaps the most enjoyable thing to be seen in the

Liberated Areas. So said all the foreigners who saw these dances and tried to imitate them and so said the youth and maidens themselves as they danced in circles on the streets, and so said even the grown ups who had first frowned on the dance, but later joined in the fun themselves and found them most pleasant! The *Yangko* was danced without any specific partner, either in a circle or in a kind of conga line which primary-school boys and girls often formed on the street as they came home from school.

Just now, a group of women, from six to sixty, had entered the narrow winding main street. Separating into individual groups, they waited for the music to begin. A one-eyed farmer leaned against the side of a house, raised a flute to his lips and piped a note, then a man with a fiddle joined him, and finally a small boy with a pair of cymbals. At the beat of the music a girl of about ten years looked sideways at her companions with a grave air, suddenly crooked her elbows, swung her arms from her sides, bounded forward like a ball, and launched herself in the dance. She glided forward two steps, her swaying body bent slightly at an angle, and, seeming not to notice the mule cart or the spectators that had paused to watch, was dashing straight at them, when suddenly, arms akimbo, she stopped short on the toes of one foot, rocked back on her heel then all the way back on the other foot, stood so a second, then gracefully inclining her body to the other side, sprang forward again. Swiftly following in the circuitous wake described by their leader came the other girls, some awkward, some graceful, some swaying on bound feet, some jumping light-footedly on full-sized flowered slippers. Down the whole length of the narrow thoroughfare circles of girls were revolving in the dance. The flute player, now squatting on his haunches beside the girls' twinkling feet, raised his reed toward the sky and piped merrily on, his one good eye fixed in an unwinking stare. When the music ceased, the girls smiled gravely at each other, brushed back loose wisps of hair, then moved further up the street to repeat the same performance all over again.

I have spent perhaps more words than necessary to describe this dance, because it was symbolic in a way of the nature of the Chinese Revolution. A dance many centuries old, the *Yangko* had been suppressed by rural puritanism. In the same way, Chiang Kai-shek, reviving Confucianism, and Madame Chiang, instituting a New Life Movement, ordered public dancing in the cities to be suppressed. In thus forcing arbitrary and entirely unnecessary codes on their own countrymen, Chiang and his wife became superfluous in the eyes of many Chinese.

The Communists, however, in encouraging the revival of dancing, satisfied a great and heartfelt need of the people for artistic expression. It is a curious fact that most people, especially in times of world-shaking doubt, have a desire to be inspired, to start their lives over again, to become young once more. In this respect, the Chinese Revolution, like any revolution, was memorable. The yearning to dance, to sing, to forget, to dream, to become once more like children became as much a part of the revolution as did the land reform. That, without too much exaggeration, was part of the significance of the *Yangko*.

35. Guerrilla Girl

STAYING only long enough to see the finish of the dancing, we set out once more on the road, this time heading south, toward the Chang River, which here marked the boundary between the Communists and the Kuomintang. As we would have to thread our way around Kuomintang-held towns, we had a guide and seven or eight militiamen as a guard.

Because Chiang's troops held the town of Kwangtai at the main river crossing in this region, we had to double back on ourselves and move westward in order to find a crossing that they could not enfilade with machine-gun fire. This, coupled with the fact that we had started late, delayed us so that we did not reach the river that night, as we had planned, but holed up in a small town called Paicha. As we were not expected, there was some difficulty in finding a room. While Mr. Chen went off to see what he could scrape up, I took refuge in a bathhouse with Liu Ming-chi. A loud crowd soon gathered outside so that even our augmented force was scarcely enough to keep them back. Finding the atmosphere of the bathhouse too close and steamy for comfort, I decided to go out and brave the lesser evil of the crowd. Deliberately I sat on a stone in the center of the street and let the peasants come up and paw me to their heart's content. It made Liu Ming-chi sad to see me so besieged, but I did not mind playing the freak so much, for I found that once I had said a few Chinese words, people ceased to look at me as something strange.

The faithful Mr. Chen, after an hour or so of tedious searching, returned and led us outside of town to a tremendous stone mansion, formerly occupied by a landlord, but at the moment occupied by the owner of the Kwangtai coal mines, a refugee from the Kuomintang. It was not my intention to bring the coal-mine owner into this book, but since returning to America I have been rather surprised by the fact that certain statements of ex-Ambassador William C. Bullitt, given wide circulation by *Time* and *Life* magazines, gained some credence among American congressmen who had no way of knowing differently and consequently had few qualms about throwing a half a billion American dollars into the lap of Chiang Kai-shek.

Mr. Bullitt declared in a letter to *Life Magazine* that refugees fled from Communist areas, but not from those areas controlled by Chiang. While the first statement is true, the last is patently untrue. I personally saw thousands of people flee to the Communists, not out of ideas of romance or adventure, but simply to escape the tax collectors, the draft agents and the mobsters who buried their relatives alive in pits. And not all were poor. Here in this village I was now face to face with a capitalist, a quoter of Confucius, a wealthy man, if you please, who had run away from Chiang Kai-shek.

"Do you think I was a poor man?" he said, smiling sadly. "My father and my grandfather before him managed the coal mines at Kwangtai. I have vast property there. I was rich. But I gave it all up. Why? I was being made poor by Chiang Kai-shek.

"The officers took fifty thousand tons of my coal and sold it for their own personal profit. I moved out what light machines I could and brought them over here because they would have been confiscated for the so-called nationalization. You have been in Chiang Kai-shek's areas. You know what nationalization means. Just looting by private individuals and nothing more. One thousand workers came over here with me. Two thousand stayed behind. But they are constantly running over here, too, because they have no way to live. That's why anyone flees Chiang Kai-shek's area. Because he sees no future with the Kuomintang. Not a particle of hope.

"Sure, I was afraid to come over here. I had been told—who hasn't—that the Communists are nothing but bandits. My friends, the officials, the army officers, all told me the Communists would harm industrialists. But I was helped by them and then I learned their program toward industry and I knew they had nothing against me."

Obviously, this mine owner was quite angry. To calm him down I asked him if he approved of the land reform.

"Yes," he said, "I approve of the agrarian revolution because industry cannot be developed without it. I don't approve of some of the cases of violence that have taken place in the land reform, but I do approve of struggling against the landlords. I am sure no one will struggle against me, for I have never harmed anyone. But if they do, I shall give up all my money. All I care about is developing our China. We must have peace. A man like myself especially needs peace. I can't understand why America deliberately fosters a war by helping Chiang Kai-shek. If America got out of China, there would be peace in a very few weeks. Then I could go back to my coal mines again."

Early the next morning, after a meager breakfast, we set out for the Chang River. It would have been better to cross the river at night, for we would be within artillery range of the Kuomintang garrison at Kwangtai. But there seemed little danger even in the daytime, as there was a hill between the ferry and the Kuomintang guns and, according to the militiamen, the Kuomintang gunners were no good at indirect fire.

All morning we climbed uphill through a narrow twisting canyon. The rocks in this region were numerous and soil extremely scarce; nevertheless the farmers, who were nowhere in evidence, had terraced the slopes nearly to the top of every peak. The plots of ground were extremely small and each one was buttressed by a semicircle of rocks to prevent the earth from sliding away. The terrific labor necessary to build these fields, which could have given but a poor crop, impressed me in a kind of melancholy way.

After an interminable walk, even the fields gave way and we found ourselves marching between sheer rock walls which rose to heights of two and three hundred feet above us. The trail in this canyon doubled and bent back on itself in a most surprising way and it seemed almost as if we were marching through a maze set in an unroofed cave.

Emerging from this canyon, we abruptly came out on the shores of the Chang River, a pale, green, swiftly flowing stream which just at this point emerged from between two rocky hill walls and ran on a straight course toward the plains below. The little village of Yangchen, divided in two by the river, with its gray, flat-roofed houses—on top of which stood a sentry with a rifle looking downstream toward the Kuomintang lines—was just at the water's edge. Upstream, a mile or so toward the west, were two rock cliffs between which ran a wire cable. By means of this cable, men were pulling a flat-bottomed boat hand over hand across the stream. Marching up a rocky beach, we boarded this crude ferry, slowly crossed the river, which ran clear and cool here in the hills, and reaching the other side, set foot in Anyang County.

Resting awhile in the other half of Yangchen, we munched on a few carrots and drank some water at the local outdoor teahouse. Actually, this teahouse consisted of two tables and a few benches placed near a bonfire, and there was nothing so luxurious as tea but only hot water. People here seemed poorer than on the other side of the river. Cotton showed through holes in the black pants and the white jackets worn by the mountain children, and the breasts of the women feeding their babies seemed less full of milk than I had heretofore seen.

The village was very tiny, yet it boasted a school, which I discovered by walking into a tiny temple set near the water. The temple, if it had once owned idols, now had none, but was completely bare save for the pupils' benches. There were no desks; some stone ledges, upon which the idols might formerly have rested, served the purpose. School was not in session, but there were some books lying on the benches and I picked up and read these words:

Sun rises; papa goes to work; child goes to school.
Sun sets; papa comes from work; child comes from school.

I had wandered into the schoolroom alone, but in a moment two young boys and a girl about nine or ten years old entered the room and gazed shyly at me. Having won their friendship by teaching them a game of ticktacktoe—using a stone for a pencil and the earth for paper— I asked the little girl how many people there were in her family. She told me she had a father in the militia, a grandmother and a brother.

"And your mother?" I asked.

"Not here." (Dead.)

"That's too bad," I said.

The girl started crying. One of the boys jerked at my sleeve.

"Her mother *huo mai*," he said.

I didn't understand the words *"huo mai,"*—though in the next few days I got to know what they meant very well—and after a few perfunctory words I went back to the tea tables.

"What's *huo mai* mean?" I asked Mr. Chen.

"Buried alive," he said.

I told Mr. Chen the story and we tried to find the girl, but she had gone. While this had been taking place, our guards had been inquiring the conditions of the road from a few stray militiamen who were operating in and out of Kwangtai. From information they gathered, it seemed that the Kuomintang had stuck a probing finger still deeper into the hills and that we would have to climb back to the west some more and make a detour. As it was already late, we decided to call a halt and rest on the banks of the river for the night.

Having noticed among the militiamen a girl with a pistol and having learned that she was a member of the militia band, I spent a great part of the night interviewing her.

Her name was Misu. She was quite husky and looked almost like a masquerading boy, with stocky legs and heavy shoulders. Possibly nineteen, she had deep red cheeks and straight hair that fell to her shoulders in a bob, and she had a sensuous mouth. She wore a pair of torn gray, cotton pants, stained with recent mud, and a wine-colored jacket, filthy with the drippings from many millet bowls. She was the daughter of a tenant farmer who had gone blind when she was young. Two of her sisters had starved to death in a famine and she had only kept alive by living in the fields with her grandmother and eating raw vegetables.

When Misu was twelve, the chief of her village had conscripted her to work on a road for the Japanese. At the hands of the Chinese overseer, she had suffered daily beatings, traces of which her body still bore.

When she was fifteen or sixteen, she had been betrothed to a boy one year her junior. Because most of her family was starving, she went immediately to her in-laws' house, becoming not so much a wife as a maidservant. She never ate with the others, but only what they left, and that was never much. Whenever she had an argument with her husband, he ran and told his mother and the two of them beat her unmercifully. They beat her on the back, on the legs and on the breasts, all the while telling her that she was a most ungrateful girl.

Her husband worked as a clerk for the Japanese Army and often Japanese officers came to visit her mother-in-law who made her serve the officers tea and cakes. She rebelled against these duties, for the Japanese generally molested her. After one such refusal, she was beaten in a particularly brutal fashion. In despair, she locked herself in her room, tied a rope over a beam and hanged herself. She lost consciousness, but woke up some hours later, the broken rope around her neck and her bed smeared with blood.

Afterward, she was sick and could not work well. As a consequence, she was beaten even more severely and deprived of almost all food. Despairing of her life, she ran home. Her mother- and father-in-law followed and broke into her house. Her grandmother fought viciously to prevent her from being taken away, but was beaten insensible to the ground. Neighbors came to her rescue. From then on she lived at home with her grandmother, the two of them, as before, eking out a starvation diet from the vegetables they grew on their small plot of ground. From time to time, however, her husband and mother-in-law caught her and beat her and she went in constant fear of being kidnaped.

About this time, the Japanese retreated and the 8th Route Army, which had occupied the hills around Kwangtai, entered the town.

One day a girl cadre came to her home and said: "Your neighbors tell me you have suffered much. Now a new day has come for Chinese women and there is no longer any need for you to suffer."

Because no one had ever shown her any sympathy before, Misu was completely won over by the cadre's kindness. She confided her hopes to her grandmother—her only friend. The old woman agreed it would be wonderful if women were the equal of men, but dashed cold water on Misu's hopes. "From ancient times till now," she said, "man has been the Heaven, woman the earth. What chance do we have?"

Misu told her grandmother's words to the cadre. "You must organize," said the cadre. "If we form a Women's Association and everyone tells their bitterness in public, no one will dare to oppress you or any women again."

Much moved, the girl threw herself wholeheartedly into the work of organizing the women on her street. Because of her zeal she was elected head of the Women's Association on her block. Through the aid of this association, she succeeded in obtaining a divorce from her husband. About this time, the civil war started. Kwangtai organized its own militia. The girl used to sit by the militiamen and watch them clean their guns. Soon she was cleaning the gun of each armed man on her street. As a joke, they taught her how to fire a rifle, but always without bullets. In the meantime, the new government to alleviate her poverty gave her some millet. She was very happy.

In 1946, the Kuomintang armies, having entered the North China Plain below, decided to attack and occupy Kwangtai and eliminate any threat from guerrillas in the Taihang Mountains. Many people left the city. Misu went along, helping other women find homes and obtaining cotton for them so that they could spin and make enough money to keep alive.

Later, she returned to within a mile of her native Kwangtai and volunteered her services to a band of militiamen. They laughed at her. She persisted. Finally they allowed her to help with the cooking and to mend clothes. Soon she began to do espionage work, binding up her hair like a married woman, entering the town and gathering information.

On New Year's Eve, she left a note written by the county magistrate in a basket of candy and cigarettes outside a Kuomintang blockhouse. "We know you have been impressed into service," said the note, "so we bear you no enmity. If things get too hard, run over here to us." As a result, two Kuomintang soldiers had come over.

Misu was very proud, but still not satisfied, because she had done no fighting. She trained herself for combat by shooting dogs in the hills. "Wolves," she told all who questioned her. Later, she overcame her fear of hand grenades by standing on rocky ledges and throwing them into the river far below. After that the farmers let her carry arms and go on raids.

Because she knew Kwangtai well, she soon came to plan most of the raids. On such raids, she generally acted as the lookout for the militiamen. Once, however, she climbed over the wall of Kwangtai and participated in a gun fight with members of the Home Returning Corps organized by the Kuomintang. On this occasion two of the enemy were killed. "Maybe I shot one of them; I don't know," she said.

This girl could neither read nor write. She knew nothing of Communism. She had taken up arms, she said, because the soldiers of the 8th Route Army were the first who had ever been kind to the people of Kwangtai. If the 8th Route Army were beaten, her life would not be worth living. After peace came, she had high hopes of a better life. She was not ambitious. She just wanted to be a working girl. She thought China could build up industry and she could work in a factory. That would give her great satisfaction.

In all my years in China, this was the first girl whom I had actually seen carrying a gun on the front. This girl had not joined the guerrillas out of any romantic notions, but to fight for her existence. Plain to the point of ugliness, and with rough hands and coarse features, she was no glamor girl. She had no dresses, but only the clothes she wore upon her back. She had never owned a toothbrush, nor ever brushed her teeth, and by the looks of her, had seldom come in contact with soap, so desperate was her poverty. What she lacked in beauty and dainty manners, however, she made up for with passion and a vital animal energy. I haven't used her real name here because she was engaged in a very dangerous business that would probably only lead to execution if she were caught. For all I know, she may now be dead, but if she isn't I wish her well.

The next day, we proceeded slightly to the north, then south and west around a domed hill within a few thousand yards of Kuomintang positions and picked up a band of farmers who had fled over from Chiang's side. We continued walking over a narrow mountain trail, and at last, sometime after dark reached the headquarters of the Anyang County government.

On waking in the morning, I found myself in a small village extremely clean and in a way quite charming, which was located on a plateau and built half on the side of a hill. The village had about four hundred people, two schools, a couple of wells, no shops, but one street barber.

We were in the heart of the guerrilla area, yet you would never have known it, so peaceful did the village look. Almost the only signs of military activity were the occasional donkeys which passed by with baskets of homemade mines on their way toward the Kuomintang lines. Nevertheless, it was from this village that the county magistrate, an extremely handsome man of about thirty, directed the guerrilla warfare against the Kuomintang. Some miles further off, and much closer to the enemy lines, the assistant magistrate, an ex-schoolteacher of twenty-eight, directed operations behind Chiang's troops. Actually, the county offices of these two and their subordinates were located in farmhouses in whatever territory they happened to land.

Although they did an extraordinary amount of intelligence work, they were not too burdened down with documents, sending most of them to the rear, burying others, and carrying the most important ones with them when they moved, which they often did. On such occasions, the assistant magistrate would pack his things on a donkey, and just take off across the mountains, with one or two of his followers. It was all very simple, but somehow effective.

At the time of my arrival, the city of Anyang on the plains below and about four-fifths of the whole county were occupied by Kuomintang troops and numerous Home Returning Corps organized by the landlords. We were pressed into a very small area of the county between the towns of Kwangtai and Suiyeh, which were held by good-sized Kuomintang garrisons. Between these two towns, from which they sometimes emerged on raids, the Kuomintang had tried to set up a blockade line, but we were continually penetrating through this line into the Kuomintang rear. These penetrations were not made by regular troops, for there were none in the area, but by a group of specially trained guerrilla commandos and above all by roving farmer bands. What was being waged in Anyang County was strictly a people's war.

PART IX

THE PEOPLE'S WAR

❧

36. Burying Them Alive

IN THE West, not much is understood about a people's war. This is strange because the phenomenon has not been entirely unknown to America or Europe. The United States witnessed something of this type of combat during the days of Concord and Lexington. Europe saw it in the nineteenth century when the Spanish and the Russian people raised guerrillas and partisans to fight the regular armies of Napoleon. In more recent times, we have seen partisan warfare spring up during the Russian Revolution, the Spanish Civil War, the Yugoslav national war and the internecine strife in Greece. The spread of this kind of warfare suggests that it may well play a decisive role in any future international conflict.

This is not a prospect to be faced with complete equanimity. People's wars are not romantic. Without a doubt, a people's war is an intensification of the already violent nature of war. When fought in the midst of a national invasion, such a type of combat violates all the so-called rules of civilized warfare. When combined with a civil war, however, a people's war cannot help but take on the nature of a class war. Thus, it becomes more passionate, more savage and more personal than any other type of war yet known. Whether this is salutary for human nature or otherwise is no more readily answered than the question of war itself. For the moment, both questions can be left to the philosophers. What, however, is instructive at this point is how such a war arises.

Nearly a century ago, Clausewitz, who admitted he knew little about the subject, declared that the conditions under which a people's war alone could become effective were the following:

1. That the war is carried on in the interior of the country.
2. That it is not decided by a single catastrophe.
3. That the theater of war embraces a considerable extent of country.
4. That the national character supports the measure.

5. That the country is of a broken and inaccessible nature, either from being mountainous, or by reasons of woods and marshes or by a peculiar mode of cultivation.

All of these conditions existed to an unparalleled degree in China. The war was waged deep in the interior of the country. It had a nebulous, vapory essence, nowhere condensing into a solid body, so that it could not be decided at one stroke. The ground over which the war was waged extended over an area almost as far as from Berlin to Moscow. The peasants, strict individualists, were aptly suited to such a war and the country was decidedly broken up. Yet, as I observed, the Chinese people's war arose and became effective not only for these reasons, but for an additional and extremely important reason which can be summed up under the two words: social conditions. To Clausewitz's five conditions, I therefore would add a sixth:

That the people have a personal stake in the war.

I use the word "personal" here, because in watching the people's war in China, I found that what principally distinguished it from the war fought by regular armies was that the combatants had an immediate and direct advantage always before their eyes. Such is not the case at all with the soldier. Although he may identify his own welfare with the welfare of his unit, with the army and with his country, he usually has not any advantage immediately before him that he can grasp and say: "This is what I get out of the war." A people's war, however, is always waged right around a man's home and close to what he holds most near and dear in life. Unless these things are threatened, I do not believe men will start a people's war; they may join the army, or be drafted into it, but they won't organize a war of their own.

This I found particularly true of Anyang County which offers a striking example of how and why a people's war begins. Anyang, which was the site of the Shang emperor's court, some three thousand years ago, has always occupied an important place in China's civil wars. Many times the broad Chang River has blocked the onward march of troops coming from the south and for months on end soldiers have quartered in the county while the people waited for one side or the other to obtain a decision.

After the 1911 Revolution, as campaign after campaign was fought through the county, arms spread among dissident elements of the population and powerful bandits rose and crushed the people. Becoming landlords, the bandits organized their own feudal fiefdoms, kept large bands of armed retainers and exercised undisputed dominion over many villages. Sometimes the landlord-bandits fought among themselves. Then, to enlist support, they called their organization *chu ti* or "bandit protection corps." The purpose however, was the same—tax collection, usury, local political control.

Between 1938 and 1945, many of these local leaders went over to the Japanese from whom they obtained arms with which to enlarge their organizations. At the same time, they also increased their landholdings at the expense of the poor peasants who mortgaged, then lost their possessions during the famine, which was here quite severe. Near the end of the war, the Japanese retreated from the mountainous parts of the county, and many of the landlords went with them, leaving their affairs in the hands of agents or smaller landlords.

Guerrillas of the 8th Route Army, entering the evacuated places, instituted their program of rent and interest reduction so that many people got back the land that had been taken from them. At the same time, the people formed local governments, militiamen to stand sentry duty, women's associations to fight for women's equality and many other organizations. When peace came, the 8th Route Army had just begun to teach the villagers how to vote.

Now it is a curious and important fact that when the civil war started and the 8th Route Army retreated and gave up nearly all the county to the Kuomintang, almost none of the people went with the Communists, but remained behind to welcome the Kuomintang. Not only did the majority of the farmers remain at home, but also many local cadres, the militiamen and the heads of the women's associations. From what the people in Anyang told me, they did not flee from the Kuomintang because they believed that the reforms the 8th Route Army introduced were merely the reforms that any Chinese government, taking over from the Japanese, would bring. Not wishing to be involved in any further war, they stayed at home.

But when the Kuomintang armies entered the villages, very often there entered with them the former bandits and landlords who had been puppets and sometimes robbers under the Japanese. These men soon became district heads while their bailiffs became village chiefs. Immediately they began a "countersettlement" against the people of their own villages. They either did this directly or "put the finger" on certain men and women who were dealt with summarily by the army or the Special Service Section of the Kuomintang. It was this countersettlement that had fanned into being a people's war that was now raging with undiminished violence throughout the whole country.

The landlords were cruelly subtle. On taking over villages from the Reds, either they or the Kuomintang officers would call a public meeting and declare a general amnesty.

"The Communist policy about the land here was very good," the Kuomintang would say. "We don't want to change anything. We can forgive everyone but the village chief, the head of the militia and the chief of the Communist party in this village. Nobody has anything to fear from us. However, some of you have been led astray by Communist propaganda. If you will just come to the village office and sign a repentance slip, everything will be all right."

And the peasants came. Not knowing any better, they went to the village office and admitted they had joined the women's association or the militia.

Seeing nothing wrong in such actions, the gullible peasants fell into a trap. Wives persuaded their husbands to come back from hiding places in the hills. Then, when it seemed as if all the active peasants were once more in the folds of the village, the Kuomintang rounded up all the self-repenters and publicly executed them.

More brutal than the Kuomintang were the landlords. Very often they buried alive men who had engaged in the struggle for reduction of rents. If they could not find these men, they buried their families. And sometimes they threw living women and children who had no connection at all with the Communists into ditches, pits and wells and covered them with earth.

According to the Anyang County government, up to the time of my arrival, four hundred men, women and children had been killed and buried alive in the 423 villages that had fallen into Kuomintang hands. I have no way of checking these figures, but I have every reason to believe they are not exaggerated. In one village, while I was there, twenty-four bodies, including women and children, were exhumed from a common pit where they had been buried alive and then been partially uncovered and eaten by dogs. In wandering from village to village, I came across numerous people whose relatives had been buried alive.

The worst case of this kind that I saw was in Chintekou, a village of 130 people, on the edge of no man's land. Here, out of twenty-eight families, members from each of twenty-four families had been buried alive or shot by a landlord bandit, named Li Chin-tsang.

When the Japanese evacuated the mountains, Li and the other landlords went with them. The people then got together and divided Li's land. When the Kuomintang returned to the region, Li came back with fifteen armed men. Just before his arrival, all the men in the village fled away.

Seeing the remaining women and children were frightened, Li tried to calm them. "Don't be afraid," he said, "we are all from the same family." Late that night, however, when the village was asleep, Li and his men went around to all but four houses in the villages and took the people out. Ten people, he threw down a dry well and buried alive. Fourteen others, he forced to lie down in a ditch, then he covered them with earth. Among those buried were a two-month-old baby, a boy of ten and a woman of eighty.

Although this was the worst case I personally came across, it was by no means unique. In one *chu*[1] of eighteen villages, local officials told me that forty-six militiamen and local cadres had been killed by the 40th Army, seven being shot, thirty-five buried alive and four forced to hang themselves.

Everywhere I went heard many such stories from the farmers them-selves—stories told in a dreary monotone, with downcast eyes and tightened lips, and with accents of deep hopeless despair. One of the saddest stories of this kind I heard concerned a girl of twenty-two years who was married to a farmer in the village of Tungtachou near the town of Fucheng. Before the arrival of the 8th Route Army, she and her husband barely kept alive by cultivating one-third of an acre of land. During the land reform, the young couple received two-thirds of an acre more. Afterward, the girl became head of the Women's Association in her village and her husband entered the militia, guarding the village against the Japanese. When the Japanese surrendered and the 8th Route guerrillas left, both the girl and her husband stayed behind in the village, not dreaming that they had done anything wrong.

When the Kuomintang entered the village, there came with them the local landlord who went personally and dragged the woman out of her home. Her husband was immediately taken away and shot without the girl's knowledge.

The landlord turned the girl over to the Kuomintang army, saying: "She's 8th Route." "So you're a Communist," said an officer. "You must know how to sing." And with that he led her among Kuomintang soldiers and commanded her to sing. For three days, she was forced to wander from squad to squad, singing what songs she could remember from childhood. Some soldiers manhandled her, but some turned away in shame when they saw her crying. In the evening she was locked up. At night, she was taken to sleep with Kuomintang officers. On the fourth day, she was taken to prison. She was not fed, but her uncle brought her food. One day, the food was left outside her prison cell. From this he knew she had been killed. Searching, he found her mutilated body beneath a near-by bridge with three others. The crime of this girl was that she had believed in the equality of women. In the guerrilla areas, that was Communism.

This is only a little—only a very small part—of the stories I heard from peasants whose mothers, fathers, sons and wives had been killed in that terrible period before the villages organized to defend themselves. Later on, I talked to people behind the Kuomintang lines and they told me stories more pitiful still. They did not like to talk about what had happened to their loved ones, and it was only with great difficulty that I dug stories out of them. One thing was clear, however—their experiences

---

[1] An administrative district somewhat similar to our county, but smaller.

had marked them with deep scars of class hatred that would not be wiped out for the rest of their lives.

Does this mean that when aroused by the Reds that they did not indulge in killings themselves? I do not think so. Later on I will relate the story of how I personally saw these farmers retaliate against one of their landlord tormentors. But first of all let us see in what other ways the peasants had been inflamed in the guerrilla areas.

Officers in Chiang Kai-shek's army were not entirely unaware of the perils of partisan warfare. They made the mistake, however, of thinking they could prevent such a war from occurring by arming a militia corps of their own under various landlord leaders. This only made conditions in the villages much worse and aroused the peasants still more.

Under the slogan of "fighting bandits," the landlords, who in reality were ex-bandits themselves, organized a Home Returning Corps and placed a rifle tax on all the villages. In lieu of a rifle, they collected thirty or forty thousand Border Region dollars from each person or the equivalent in grain or cotton. Though the Kuomintang army tried to sell the tax to the people as a self-defense measure against the bandits, the people could not believe them, because it developed in practice as a get-rich scheme.

In one village of 115 families, I found that taxes had been collected for eighty-three rifles. Actually, the Home Returning Corps bought only nine rifles, the rest of the money being grafted by the landlords, the *pao* leader and an officer in the Kuomintang army. In the 423 fallen villages, the Anyang County government figured that five thousand rifles, or their equivalent in money, had been collected. This would have been enough to form a sizable *gendarmerie*, but the Home Returning Corps defeated their own purposes by pocketing most of the self-defense funds.

On the other hand, Kuomintang officers, finding garrison duty in the Taihang Mountains dreary and seeing little sense in the war in which they had no particular stake, often sold bullets to guerrilla units. Generally the sales were carried on through peasants who paid seventy thousand dollars for a box of ammunition and sold them to the guerrillas for one hundred thousand dollars a box, thus making a profit of thirty thousand for themselves.

This trade used to intrigue me and once I asked a peasant who brought over some ammunition how he got started in the business. According to his story a Kuomintang colonel stationed in his area had asked him to find some opium. The peasant protested he didn't know where there was any opium.

"You wooden head!" said the officer, "I know many of you peasants buried your opium when the 8th Route Army was here. Go find me some."

A few days later the peasant returned and said he had found some opium, but slyly added that it was very expensive.

"Never mind," said the colonel, "take this ammunition, sell it, and bring back the 'black goods.' "

"But nobody here wants the ammunition," said the peasant.

"Take it to the 8th Route Army. They'll buy it."

"Do I dare go over there?" asked the peasant.

"Yes, yes, anything. Only get the black goods."

While the grafting of rifle taxes and the selling of ammunition naturally worked directly in favor of the 8th Route Army, the excessive greed of Chiang officers completely impoverished the people in the guerrilla areas. Levies extracted by the army and the landlords went far beyond even the brutal taxation of which I have already spoken. Because of requisitions, land was being abandoned and whole families were drowning themselves in village wells.

Besides killing, burying alive and terrible taxation, the people of Anyang also had to endure extortion, blackmail and kidnaping. In these activities, Chiang's officers, but more particularly his special agents, often gave the landlords a helping hand. Such blackmail carried on by means of political terror sometimes reached astounding proportions.

Farmers and sometimes their wives were arrested and not released until high ransoms had been paid. They were always arrested on the pretext that they had connections with the 8th Route Army. Whether they had or not, actually made little difference. What counted was their ability to pay.

As I wandered around from village to village in Anyang, every day hearing fresh tales of misery, I sometimes used to get frightened at the implications of this countersettlement. Where would it all end? People just had no safety.

A man never knew when he might be conscripted. Not only by Chiang's 40th Army near by, but by the Home Returning Corps. One night when I was in a village in no man's land nine frightened farmers and their families ran over to our side. According to the story they panted out, the chief of their village had called a meeting and announced that the Kuomintang wanted nine soldiers. Everyone got up to leave the meeting, but found they were surrounded by armed guards of the landlord. No one wanted to volunteer, so lots were chosen and nine men picked. Scarcely waiting for dark, the nine men had gathered their families and headed for the hills.

Another time, I was with the assistant district magistrate, just on the edges of Kuomintang territory, when a student fled over to us. During the Easter holidays he had taken a train from Nanking intending to see his family in North China. At the Anyang station, he had been seized by draft agents and forced to become a clerk in the local regiment.

Serving only one day, he ran away at night and walked up through the hills to us. Once on a trip behind the lines, I came across a village in which there was not one single man below the age of forty. One day the Home Returning Corps had called out all the youths of this village to build defense works and they had gone out on the road with hoes and shovels. Some distance from the village, they were suddenly surrounded by armed soldiers, locked up and then taken away in trucks to Anyang.

As a result, many farmers across the hills from us were mutilating themselves, cutting off their fingers and getting their wives to put out one of their eyes. Not even then could they always avoid conscription, for the agents took the lame, the halt, the blind and the tubercular, as well as the poor.

As might be expected under the terror, the extortion, the taxation and the corruption, the economy and whole livelihood of the people of Anyang had declined even below the subsistence level. So rapacious were the landlords and Chiang Kai-shek's army that they ruined nearly every village they touched.

Though the Communist land "settlement" was sometimes violent, the end result was generally less economic hardship. But after the Kuomintang and landlord countersettlement, the people had no way of subsisting other than by taking up arms. After the burials and the killings, no longer did men and women remain behind when the Kuomintang came. Like a prairie fire, the tale of the brutality of the landlords spread from village to village so that at the first sign of Chiang's troops, all those men and women who had taken an active part in village affairs immediately fled away.

It is a very instructive fact that when the 8th Route Army evacuated most of Anyang, the few cadres huddled up in the western corner of the county were unable to start guerrilla warfare. Yet within a few months of the arrival of the Kuomintang, that guerrilla warfare was being waged on a scale that dwarfed anything seen in the Japanese war. Murders drove some people up in the hills to seek revenge. Extortion, taxes, blackmail drove others over to seek a way of living. Still others fled over to avoid conscription. At the same time, the mountain people, seeing what had happened to their neighbors in the foothills below, out of precaution organized their own militia bands.

Thus, on the one hand were men of desperate resolve who, having lost everything, now wanted revenge; and on the other hand there were men who feared to lose the things they still possessed and held dear and saw no way to save them, but by taking up arms. These men had at last found a stake for which to fight, and on this basis, they emerged from their homes and with crude violence began to fight a people's war.

37. Brother Against Brother

BY THE time I arrived in Anyang, the rising against the landlords and the Kuomintang was spreading like an all-consuming fire. Every village that rose to defend itself, as a matter of course, had to seek to get its neighbor to do the same. Thus, ever new peripheral and protecting groups were built up. Soon the villages learned to co-operate, to succor each other in distress, to fight shoulder to shoulder against the hated bandits and the landlords and even sometimes against the soldiers of Chiang Kai-shek. Yet the steel ring of arms—many of them American, was close about the rising villages. The shadow of destiny was like a brand on men. It was landlord against peasant, bandit against farmer, sometimes brother against brother.

At night I used to sit among the peasants and listen to the stories they told of their villages. Mostly they were brutal stories, told in a flat monotone that failed to convey any sense of life or reality, but always they seemed somewhat sad. One story that has clung to my memory concerns two brothers who fought each other on opposite sides of the lines.

The brothers were sons of a stone worker named Wang, who lived in the east corner of Suiyeh. The gate of their poor home opened out to the countryside. Close by ran the Anyang city road. To the east, a series of steep ravines descended to the plains. On the west rose the Taihang Mountains.

In this environment, the two brothers grew up side by side. But they grew so differently that neighbors said they could not have been born from the same mother. Tungse, the elder brother, was an earnest, hardworking man of twenty-five, with a square face, big eyes and a large nose. Sober and industrious, he worked hard in a cigarette factory to support his wife of whom he was very fond.

Despite the virtues of their elder son, the Wangs preferred the younger boy—Sitze. Sitze was a loafer. He gambled, drank and spent much of his time with whores. A follower of the bandit landlord Ko Tseng-chiang, he kidnaped people for ransom, stole goods and plundered land. When flush, he brought his parents gifts and for this reason they thought him a filial son.

Sitze and his mother were especially close because both believed in gods. On the first and fifteenth of every month, mother and son burned incense before earthen idols. Tungse never joined these rites because he despised his brother and scorned any gods who might listen to him.

The brothers constantly quarreled. Tungse did not approve of his brother's shady transactions nor of the atrocities that were being committed by the landlords who shot and killed many people during the Japanese occupation. Unable to bear the grim life any longer, he fled back into the mountains where the 8th Route Army found him another job in a cigarette factory. Being a native of Suiyeh he became a counselor of the Armed People's Committee. Just before the Japanese surrender, he led the guerrillas back to Suiyeh and even threw hand grenades into the city during the attack. As he was entering the city, his brother was leaving with the landlords and the bandits.

After the liberation of Suiyeh, Tungse became a militiaman, then he was elected chief of the east sector of Suiyeh near the town walls. In struggling against those landlords who had remained behind, he demanded that they give up all their arms. To show his determination, he took four rifles from his own uncle, a man who had many connections with the bandits and bought and sold rifles.

Tungse's determination startled his neighbors. "Your brother is a follower of Ko Tseng-chiang. How do you dare struggle?" they asked. "Never mind," said Tungse, "I am struggling for justice."

In every struggle, in every Speak Bitterness Meeting, in every effort to reduce rents, Tungse was the leader. Yet, he tried to be fair. In order to move the people, he said: "The Communist party wants us to have democracy. When we make a settlement, we must make it reasonably. In the famine, the landlords took our land and houses and left us no way to live, but we shall not do that, we must leave everyone a way to live."

Originally, Tungse's relatives and his mother had thought the younger brother the better of the two sons because he brought them presents. But now, as a result of the settlement, the family got some grain and they began to think the older brother was a capable man.

Just at this point, the Kuomintang army advanced on Suiyeh. With it came Ko Tseng-chiang, a Home Returning Corps and Sitze. The father and mother tried to persuade Tungse to stay behind. "No," he answered, "where the 8th Route Army goes, I follow." Taking his wife with him, he immediately left the city.

On returning to Suiyeh, Ko Tseng-chiang plundered the poor again. Worse, he instituted executions. One of his victims was a fifty-year-old farmer from whom Ko had taken his house a few years before in payment of a debt. During the land reform, the old man had received back his house. Now Ko killed both him and his wife for molesting his property.

In the meantime, Sitze tried to contact his brother who had organized a band of sixty militiamen not three miles outside of Suiyeh. Whenever there was a market day Sitze sent a couple of women messengers to ask him to return home.

Tungse sent back word: "I shall not go back to your side. Even when I die, I shall not come back."

Oddly enough the women messengers encouraged him in this resolve. "The people don't like the Home Returning Corps," they said. "If you come back, your brother can't help you."

By this time, Tungse's clothes were in rags. He sent someone to Suiyeh to beg some cloth. By a young girl, his mother sent him a small bundle of thread. "Tell him," she said, "don't come back. If he has no clothes to wear, I'll make some for him." She begged her younger son for cloth. He would give her none.

Soon, Sitze left home, returning to the plains where life was easier than in the desolate mountains. It was said that he left because he was afraid Tungse would kill him.

The day after Sitze's departure, three hundred men of the Home Returning Corps, summoned from three districts, and some men of the Peace Preservation Corps, organized by the Kuomintang, came out to rob and steal. It was late February and snow still lay upon the ground.

The villages made ready to defend themselves. In wind and cold, the county magistrate himself came to direct operations. In a field west of Suiyeh, he drew up two hundred militiamen and forty men of the 52nd Independent Regiment, these last a group of experienced soldiers organized by the county. Past these sturdy defenses the Home Returning Corps could not go and so they wheeled around to the south, preparing to loot villages in that direction.

Seeing the enemy withdrawing, Wang Tungse impetuously followed with five militiamen. A political director tried to halt him. Tungse shook off the restraining hand.

"We are not regular soldiers," he said. "But we are defending our homes. For a militiaman to sacrifice himself is glorious."

He ran forward into a ditch. His companions, a little to the rear, could see the snow and sand sprinkling down into the shallow gully where he had gone.

As he ran up the ditch, Wang Tungse never saw the machine gun hidden in the temple on his flank. A bullet struck him and he spun around and lay flat on the ground, his face buried in the snow.

His companions tried to rescue him but were driven back. The Home Returning Corps dragged Tungse into their lines. He was not yet dead. He lay in the snow and looked up at his captors.

Hardly moving his lips, he called: "I am Wang Tungse. My home is at the east gate of Suiyeh. I am a village chief." With these words, he died.

Some farmers carried his body to Suiyeh and placed it on the street outside the east gate. The *paochang* called the landlords who came to gloat over their enemy.

Ko Tseng-chiang spit on the corpse.

"Oh, you fine thing!" he said, addressing the dead Tungse. "You said you would not come back. But now you've come."

He gave instructions for the body to be carried in back of the Temple of the God of Fate.

"Don't bury this body," he said. "Let the dogs eat him."

Soon he arrested Tungse's father and mother.

"We have used fifty bullets in attacking your son," he said. "You must repay us."

While his parents were being led off to jail, other relatives gathered secretly near Tungse's body and drove away the dogs. For three days and three nights, they kept watch over the corpse. At last, under public censure, the landlords relented.

"Even the dogs will not eat him," said Ko, and he allowed Tungse's body to be buried.

Wang Tungse had been killed only a short while before I arrived, but already his name had become somewhat of a legend among the mountain people he had led along the road he believed in, the road of revolutionary struggle. He was buried behind the enemy lines, but every now and then a farmer would go across to Suiyeh to look at his grave and see that it had not been disturbed.

38. Counter-Countersettlement

WAGING a war against an enemy equipped as well as you are is a hard enough proposition. Defending yourself against an enemy much your superior in material strength is an affair that tries the soul. But attacking and defeating an enemy that is ten or twenty times as strong as you are seems almost impossible.

The difficulty in the case of Anyang County, as with all half-occupied counties, was that though the people could organize themselves sufficiently to evacuate their homes, to save their goods from plunder and to protect their local officials from murder, they could not develop the military might to drive off the well-armed troops of Chiang Kai-shek by direct assault. Nor, except in isolated cases, could they win the enemy soldiers over by propaganda. Yet, somehow, they had to destroy the forces of Chiang Kai-shek or at least render them harmless.

Since they could not fall upon the larger garrisons Chiang maintained at the front, their only recourse was to operate in his rear, to pick off an isolated outpost one night, to disperse a Home Returning Corps on another night and to free a village on a third night.

Such a way of fighting was not only dangerous, but extremely tiresome and more than slow. Yet these operations, carried on with painstaking patience and over widely scattered areas, were destined in many counties to destroy Chiang's forces piecemeal.

When I arrived in Anyang, this type of warfare had only just begun. Some days before, the county government had managed to break the Kuomintang blockade line between Kwangtai and Suiyeh by infiltrating eighty militiamen past a long row of Kuomintang pillboxes. Though fired on, the militiamen had not stopped to fight, but had continued on ten miles behind the lines. Along the way, two and three militiamen dropped out in each village to do propaganda work. Only thirty men arrived at the main target—a large village housing a Home Returning Corps. In order to give the impression that they were regular troops, the militiamen blew several mighty blasts on their bugles. As hoped, the Home Returning Corps took fright and fled in the night. The militiamen searched out the people and delivered a number of speeches.

"We are from the 8th Route Army," they said. "We want to show you we have not fled. Do not give up hope, we will come back often. From now on anyone who oppresses you will have to deal with us."

The results of this seemingly innocuous raid were more widespread than appears at first glance. As soon as they saw that militiamen were operating behind their lines at night, the soldiers of Chiang, who had little belief in the war, took to their pillboxes and would not come out. Thus, further raids became easier. At the same time, various landlords afraid to sleep in local Home Returning Corps barracks, began to collect in a central location for safety. That left further villages free. Then poor tenants realizing they had allies just across the way began to stand up to the landlords who were scared to be too severe.

Now, on my arrival in Anyang, the raids were spreading ever deeper and wider into Kuomintang territory. Every night small groups of three, five, ten and fifteen men were going behind the lines to gather information, to do propaganda work, to fight with the Home Returning Corps and with stray Kuomintang soldiers.

Very often the militiamen who led the raids were refugees from Chiang's areas. Sometimes they went on the raids to get revenge for relatives who had been killed. Most often, however, the raids were intimately connected with the land reform. Their purpose was to protect the results of the land division, to force the landlords to return what they had taken from the people and generally to encourage the poor. Such operations went under the sinister-sounding name of Counter-Counter Settlement. Although there was often much shooting, the raids did not seem to me to be essentially military. Rather did this kind of warfare seem to be a political and a social combat carried on by armed means. The targets of the raids were not so often strongpoints or even lines of communications, as they were social institutions, government organs and private individuals. Thus, raiding militiamen would free a girl who had been forced into marriage, depose a hated village chief or kidnap a landlord. In brief, this war aimed at people's emotions and sought to conquer hearts and not territory.

I do not mean that propaganda replaced combat, but rather that the guerrilla war was carried on in an entirely different emotional environment than regular war. An example of this is furnished by the way the guerrillas and the militia gathered intelligence. Militiamen, crossing the lines at night, would climb over a house wall, knock on a woman's door and ask: "How are you being treated? How much have you been taxed? What are you getting to eat?" Farmers sneaking over for a day or so to the 8th Route Army side would bring not so much information about Kuomintang dispositions as they would bring the names of peasants who had been conscripted for labor, of women who were being beaten or of children who had lost their fathers.

Time after time I have sat in various villages in no man's land and seen farmers come up to guerrillas and give them information that any regular army officer would have scorned. But such information was extremely useful in this type of warfare. The local guerrillas in learning who was suffering would also learn the name of someone who would probably help them. On the other hand all this information was sent back to the rear where it was collated so that the 8th Route Army could make an effective political and social policy.

While uncovering the suffering of the villagers, the militiamen also uncovered the names of landlords, dog legs and bandits who were treating the people badly. If a landlord took things from the people, the militiamen would send him a letter warning him to return what he had taken. If he did not, they would send him a more peremptory note. If nothing happened, they very often kidnaped him and brought him across the lines in the night.

During a two-month period in Anyang, eighty landlords and members of the Home Returning Corps were brought across the lines in this way. Generally, the subdistrict commissar or the district government head would give them a lecture and then let them go. I don't exactly approve of kidnaping, yet I was sometimes amazed by the patience and forbearance county officials showed toward landlords who had carried arms and fought them.

The operations of militiamen in Kuomintang territory often had a Robin Hood character about them. Since the militiamen were poor men themselves, whenever they found a man or woman in distress they would try to help them out. Undoubtedly the roving farmers in redressing wrongs often committed brutal deeds and to many men they must have appeared as nothing but barbaric murderers. But I have very good reason to know that many poor peasants in Chiang Kai-shek's areas looked on these men who came to them in the night as virtuous outlaws and sometimes as shining Sir Galahads.

Once on New Year's Eve, a small militia band went to the town of Weichang, thirteen miles in the enemy's rear, to deliver a letter to a landlord who had countersettled. On the way, they paused in a village to rest. There was no one on the street, and it was very dark and quiet. While leaning against the side of a house, the militiamen heard the sound of crying coming from within. Climbing over the walls and dropping down into the courtyard, they discovered an old woman sitting on her doorstep weeping bitterly.

At sight of the armed men, the woman grew terrified.

"Do not be afraid," said one of the militiamen, and asked the woman why she had been crying.

"There is a landlord here named Wei Ching-lien," she explained. "During the settlement I got some land and he came and accused me of being a Communist and demanded five tou of millet from me. I didn't have that much millet and couldn't pay him.

"I had prepared a tou of millet for myself and daughter for New Year's Day, but Wei Ching-lien came and took it. I don't know what I am going to do tomorrow. We have nothing to eat."

The militiamen grew angry, but wondered if the old woman's story were true. To find out, they went into four or five houses and asked the people. Everyone said Wei Ching-lien was a wicked man and that the old woman had nothing to eat.

Since the duty of the militiamen was not in this village, they went on to Weichang and delivered their letter. But on the way back, they stopped off again and questioned some more people about the old woman's story. Everything she had told them checked. The militiamen learned where the landlord lived, then borrowed a rope ladder, climbed the wall and jumped down into the courtyard of Wei's house. Everyone was asleep behind bolted doors.

"Is Wei Ching-lien at home?" they called.

A woman answered. "He is not at home." They requested her to open the door, but no one came. The militiamen debated awhile. Finally one said in a loud voice: "Give me a hand grenade."

No one had any grenades, but they hoped to scare the landlord into opening his door. Still no one came.

"Let's blow him up with TNT," said another militiaman.

Though the militiamen, of course, had no such precious substance, these words brought the wife to the door.

The militiamen brushed by. There was Wei in bed.

"Oh you've come back," he said, recognizing he had to deal with 8th Route militia. "If I had known it was you, I would have opened the door."

Without saying a word, the militiamen shot and killed him.

Going out on the street, they shouted: "We have investigated Wei Ching-lien and found that he plundered an old woman's things. He is a sinful landlord and made a countersettlement. We have sentenced him to death. If there is any other landlord who wants to rob the people, then please let him look at Wei Ching-lien."

Not all the raids were so grim as this. Some of them were even funny. A militia band went behind the lines and told a landlord he should give back the things he had taken from the poor. The landlord agreed, but still returned nothing. Again the militiamen went and this time the landlord said: "I am going to give them back right away, but I have to dig them up from the cave where I buried them." Again nothing happened. The third time the militiamen went to the landlord's house, his wife answered the door, saying her husband was not at home. The militiamen walked in and noticed that two people had been sleeping on the kang. Shining their flashlight around the room, they saw the landlord, completely naked clinging to the rafters overhead. When the light shone on him, the landlord trembled so violently that he fell to the floor. It was cold. The militiamen would not let the landlord get dressed.

"Well," they asked, "are you going to give back their things to the poor?"

"Oh, I was just preparing to do so tomorrow," said the landlord.

"Fine," said the militiamen. "When you give back their things, we will give back your clothes," and with these words they walked out with all the landlord's clothing and his blankets.

The militiamen also became mixed up in marital affairs. During the famine, some tenants had lost not only their land, but their wives to landlords and bandits. In the sixth *chu* I heard of a tenant farmer who had struggled against a landlord and received some land in the settlement. When the Kuomintang and the landlord came back, the tenant fled. The landlord kidnaped his wife, saying to neighbors, "He took my property and I'll take his." One night with some militiamen, the tenant returned to his village, climbed over the wall, shot the landlord and took back his wife.

Many as were the personal vendettas, most of the raids behind the lines had more general aims. And they had much more effect than might be imagined. For step by step the militiamen drove the Home Returning Corps from the villages behind Chiang's lines. This meant just so many more people freed from Chiang Kai-shek and just so much narrower an area in which his troops and officials could operate. In the words of one militiaman, these operations showed the people "that the world is ours."

Because of the conditions behind Chiang's lines, thousands of villagers were waiting for the 8th Route Army, and when the militiamen came at night, they received a heartfelt welcome.

Several times, when departing from villages behind Chiang's lines at dawn, I heard farmers remark to militiamen: "Come back quickly again. If you do not, we cannot live on."

39. Guerrilla Commando

THE easiest way for a general to make a people's war more effective is to support the movement by small detachments sent from the regular army. Without support of a few regular troops, the people generally are not encouraged to take up arms.

Such is the classic view of a people's war.

Yet, in Anyang County, the people's war started with little help from the army and primarily because conditions of life had become unbearable. The main fighting force in the county was the militia—that is, farmers with rifles, armed civilians, who came out and fought for two weeks and then went back to their villages to resume farming. Nevertheless, there was a more permanent military force composed of trained soldiers who provided a stiffening to the fighting morale of the untrained farmers.

This force was known as the Armed Working Team. Though there were a few regular soldiers and officers from the 8th Route Army in this outfit, it was by no means a regular army unit, of which there were none in Anyang, and it was completely under the command of the county magistrate. These Armed Working Teams were in a way guerrilla specialists and at the same time they had somewhat the character of commandos, performing jobs that were entirely too big or specialized for the ill-equipped militiamen. Sometimes they would blow up a Kuomintang blockhouse, sometimes derail a train, sometimes join the fight against an especially strong Home Returning Corps. Very often, they came to the rescue of militia units that had become involved in scraps with Kuomintang troops that were too strong for them to handle.

One morning I decided I would like to see one of these teams, so Mr. Chen, Liu Ming-chi, a couple of militiamen and I set out over a mountain trail and after a couple of days' walking reached a small village in the foothills of the Taihang Mountains where a unit of forty men had set up temporary headquarters.

Whether by design or accident, this headquarters was in a rather idyllic spot on the edge of a bubbling brook beneath the overhanging brow of a sheer rock cliff. The Kuomintang troops were only a few miles away, yet I spent a very quiet time here basking in the sun and conversing with my companions about the war.

In aspect, as well as training, these men were entirely different from the militiamen. All of them wore uniforms which were kept spotlessly clean. They seemed healthier than the militiamen and stronger, as if they were particularly well fed. Yet, in all the time I was with them, we never ate anything but millet and a few carrots. Each soldier carried his own millet in a cloth, which he rolled like a sausage and slung over his back in a loop. This grain was given them by the county and no one ever took any food from the civilians, who were in a pretty bad way in this area.

The leader of this particular outfit, Li Yu-ming, was a well set-up man, about thirty-two, slender and wiry, with a bronzed face, and he had a ready but grave smile. He was exceptionally articulate for an army officer and, though normally a quiet man, he used to take me up on the roof of a peasant's home and talk to me for hours about his life. I found it interesting because he was an intellectual who had rebelled against Chiang Kai-shek for reasons quite different than those of the peasants. Yet his revolt was tied up, as almost all such revolts were, with the feudal conditions of China.

He had been born in a good-sized village in the hills of western Shansi Province, not far from the Yellow River. His mother died when he was about ten and his father married again. His new step-mother treated him cruelly and finally forced him to marry a girl with a pock-marked face for whom he had no liking. At the insistence and with the aid of his grandfather, he continued his studies, finally going to middle school in the provincial capital at Taiyuan. There, he was much influenced by his first glimpses of the outside world, glimpses obtained partly from other companions, but mostly from books about Europe and America. He was also deeply moved by various student movements against the Japanese who were then in occupation of Manchuria. For this reason, and also because his money was running out, he was attracted by advertisements of the Nanking government offering scholarships to provincial students in the officer's training school in the national capital.

About 1935, with a number of other students from North China, he journeyed to Nanking and enrolled himself in one of Chiang Kai-shek's military schools. The first morning, he and several hundred other students in the freshman class were greatly surprised when the dean of the school got up and announced that they were to be trained as gendarmes. The dean pointed out that the backbone of any modern country was its police force and its *gendarmerie* and he made numerous references to Italy and Germany to prove his case.

Though the students knew little about Hitler or Mussolini, they were enraged at the way they had been cheated. They had expected to be trained as officers in an army that would eventually fight Japan. Now they found they had been lured from their homes to form an internal police and spy force for Chiang Kai-shek.

Since most of the boys were between seventeen and twenty, they were quite idealistic and the life they were now forced to lead shocked and disillusioned them. Many of the boys had never been away from home before and some cried during the night, but others, especially the northern students, began to run away. As a result, all the new students were forced to hand in their clothes at night and were seldom let out of the compound.

Although they were not in the army, the students were not allowed to resign from the school. They were little better than prisoners. Once, one Honan student was caught running away and the whole school was marched outside the walls of Nanking and made to watch his execution. The students were terror struck, yet the more daring ones continued to flee. In one term, according to Li, nearly three hundred students ran away.

Li, himself, did not flee because he did not want to return home to burden his family which had become still poorer.

One hot summer day when the temperature was over 100, Li's class was sent on a long training march outside the walls of Nanking. In full regalia and with heavy packs on their backs, many of the students, especially those from the north, succumbed to sunstroke and passed out on the road. Li, himself, staggered on. When he walked slowly, he was prodded. When he fell down he was kicked. His eyes staring, his mind reeling, his legs trembling, he at last toppled over.

The next day he regained consciousness in the middle of a hospital courtyard. Drawing the sheet back from his face he saw the bodies of his fellow-students all around him. A nurse came and looked at him in a hard way. She called out: "Here's one that isn't dead." From this he knew that he had been left for dead with about forty of his companions.

He was thrown roughly into a bed where he remained untended for a long time. Next to Li, there was a very sick man who constantly groaned in his sleep. Li used to wake him up with loud curses. The man, however, returned his harsh words with a kindly smile. "It's hard to be away from home when you're young," he said, and Li felt ashamed. Sometimes the man sang songs from Peiping operas and Li cried as he thought of his home in the north.

One night, Li's neighbor became very ill and gasped for water. Li yelled again and again for an orderly, but no one came. In the morning he was awakened by the sound of loud laughter from all the patients.

An orderly was shaking his neighbor. But the man was already dead and the patients were laughing to see the orderly trying to wake a dead man.

The death of his friend drove Li into a state of morbid depression. He thought how terrible it was to die far from home without friends, without family and with people who would laugh when you died. He determined he would never return to the school.

During the training march, Li had slightly injured his leg. He now pretended the leg would not get well. Week after week, he refused to walk. The doctors, puzzled at first, finally announced he had some rare disease. He was dismissed from school.

On crutches and supported by two friends, he made his way to the ferry leading across the Yangtze River. Reaching the other side, he took a deep breath of relief, threw away his crutches and then laughed with joy to find that he was in North China.

Arriving home, he found his father ill in bed. "I knew you were in trouble," said the old man, "and I did not think to live. But now I shall get better."

Li's pock-marked wife was also waiting for him in a subdued, humble way. Although he had been married against his desires and had little affection for his wife, Li treated her well, for she had never done anything bad to him. Then, he had undergone so much bitterness himself, he had not the heart to be unkind to anyone.

For a while he lay in a kind of stupor around the house. Then he began to work in the fields and take long walks in the hills about his home. It seemed to him that the only good thing left in life was nature, a man's family and a few friends. He hated society and had little desire to go out and see the world again. Working in his fields, he made friends with some "long-term" workers and he came to feel that these were much finer people than anyone else in the village.

About this time, one of his former classmates sent him a letter from Yenan, the Communist capital, begging him to come up there to school. After several adventures, Li made his way through the Kuomintang lines and reached Yenan. On his arrival, a cadre warned him that he was in for a hard life, that he would get little to eat and that he would probably be killed in the expected Japanese war or by frost or starvation. Li said he would take a chance.

He enrolled in an anti-Japanese training school. It was the happiest time of his life. Having gone through so much in Chiang Kai-shek's schools, he was surprised to see students walking from classroom to classroom with their arms around each other, singing. He lost his morose depressed attitude and began to open his heart to others.

"You know," he said to me one day, "I've completely changed since then. As you can see, I am always smiling now. But before I was glum, frustrated and unhappy."

Li's idyllic life lasted little more than six months. One day, the schoolteacher came and announced that China was at war with Japan. "You students are not completely trained," said the dean, "but you are needed at the front."

With five or six others, Li went into the Shansi Mountains. He stood on highways and watched the soldiers of Chiang Kai-shek running away in panic through Shansi. Wherever he found a deserting soldier, he tried to get him to go into the mountains and continue resistance. He did not operate as a Communist, which he was not, but as an organizer for the United Front. Except for four or five companions, he operated alone. Gradually he built up a small guerrilla band. He seldom had food. He would go into a village and find a tenant and ask him where the fled-away landlord had buried his grain. The two of them would dig it up and then Li would supply his guerrillas. For months on end, he lived a hunted existence, always surrounded by the Japanese. From one mountain peak to another, he was continually on the move. He ate little, slept less, dressed in rags.

At one time, he joined a United Front government in Shansi. The magistrate was an opium smoker and let Li do all the work. Li tried to lighten the burden of taxes on the peasants. The gentry protested and finally drove him out of office.

Finally he hooked up with a larger guerrilla band, becoming a political director, a duty tantamount to vice-commander. The Japanese savagely attacked the band, wounding many and then bayoneting to death the wounded men before the eyes of Li and his men who were clinging to a higher level of a mountain peak. After a bitter struggle, Li and his men broke through and after a march of many weeks joined a regular 8th Route Army guerrilla outfit.

At the end of the sixth year of the war, Li was sent to the rear to be trained for regular warfare. Nearly all the students and the teachers were hardened fighters and between them they worked out tactical problems. Li came out of this school a finished officer. He wanted no more of guerrilla warfare which he did not find romantic.

He was scheduled with a number of other officers to go to Shantung. But he could not get through the Japanese blockade lines on the plains. So Li was sent once more into guerrilla country—this time in the mountains back of Anyang. Just before he arrived, a patriotic landlord had become involved in a quarrel with several of his neighbor landlords who leaned to the Japanese. The quarrel was over the use of water which flowed through villages occupied by all the landlords. The patriotic landlord was invited to a dinner by the other landlords and was murdered in the middle of a feast. His friends, relatives and villagers wanted revenge. Li undertook the task of organizing and training them. It was a hard job. Li had told the peasants about democracy and everyone took his words so seriously that they would not obey orders. In the middle of a battle, each man would devise his own plan and act accordingly. Then, when they saw fighting was not so much fun, everyone wanted to desert. Li couldn't reprimand anyone, for no one would submit to criticism. He had to take each man aside and lecture him individually. By dint of great patience, he built up an Armed Working Team. Still, he had to lead these soldiers on every occasion, for in danger they were likely to run away. Once, in trying to stem a precipitate retreat, he was wounded and his leg broken. His farmers, however, stood by him and dragged him out of danger.

Because he had a bad limp—this time a real one—he never went on any expeditions that required much walking. Yet, his outfit was now so well trained that they operated well without him. As a matter of fact, Li was very proud of them and it was clear to see that he held them in much greater esteem than the militia.

Li was one of the finest examples of a type of man that was by no means rare in Communist areas. He was that entrancing combination of man of action and intellectual. He had a grave, quiet manner that engendered trust. I often thought that if men of this type gained control of the Communist movement—and the question of power has not yet been completely settled among the Communists—then there would be little to fear from it. If the pure intellectuals gain the upper hand, then cultism may rule China.

I wanted to go behind the lines on a raid with Li's men, for they seemed to me very efficient, but Li was called away and there was no other way to go behind the lines but with a militia outfit. Li had advised me against doing this, as the militiamen were ill trained. But I decided to go anyway.

It would at least be interesting and it would be strictly people's war.

40. The Field Mouse

I SHALL not seek to romanticize the several expeditions I made with militiamen behind Kuomintang lines by pretending that there was anything unusual in rescuing a woman in distress, kidnaping a landlord or killing a bandit. For it was just such numerous groups operating through thousands of Chinese villages that were to enable the poorly armed people of China consistently to beat the troops of Chiang Kai-shek partially armed by America. Nor shall I pretend that there was anything unusual or particularly talented about my companions. They were, with rare exceptions, all farmers. Though none of them were Communists, they supported the Communist cause, because like thousands of other Chinese boys and girls, they saw in the Communists the only hope of rescue from the grim life they were living and into which Chiang Kai-shek was pressing them deeper every day. Whether their views were mistaken or whether they were committing themselves in the long run to a worse dictatorship is something history can decide.

The leader of the particular group to which I attached myself was a sly peasant student of twenty-four, named Tang Wen-liang, and nicknamed, because of his elusiveness, the Field Mouse. He was the head of the Armed People's Committee of the seventh district of Anyang County and he had about 250 militiamen under him who operated in groups of ten, twenty and thirty men.

He was quite a tiny man, not more than five feet tall and about a hundred pounds in weight, with a wind-and-sun-tanned face, and he wore a blue uniform jacket over a pair of peasant pants. Like so many others, he had come into the revolution by way of an unhappy, feudal marriage. When he was fifteen, his father, a man of forty, had locked him in a room with a girl bride he had never seen before and laconically told him to produce a son. For three days and nights, the Field Mouse sat stubbornly on the floor while his bride huddled on the kang, alternately crying and alternately making timid advances which the boy always rejected. On the fourth day, when his father unlocked the door, the boy emerged not only a virgin but an unfilial son.

In the night he ran into the hills back of his town and joined a newly formed guerrilla unit of the 8th Route Army. Because he could read and write, he was immediately made commander of a squad of troops. A doting grandmother harnessed a donkey, pursued the boy and rode to guerrilla headquarters. She found her grandson engaged in military maneuvers on a threshing ground. Before the eyes of his troops, she slid off the donkey, seized the Field Mouse by his jacket collar, curtly asked him a question or two and struck him a blow with a whip between the eyes. Berating the astonished company commander for stealing children from their homes, she then and there secured her grandson's release from the army. Mournfully lowering his head before the snickering of his troops, the Field Mouse followed his grandmother home.

Within a few days his father hired him out as an orderly to the officers of one of Chiang Kai-shek's regiments. Menial tasks and officer blows led him to seek a method of escaping the army. With cunning deliberation, he formed "live-and-die" friendships with each of six different soldiers. One by one, he led these friends to a thicket of trees and, after swapping ancestral names with them, said:

"Now, dear friend, let us both swear to die at the bottom of the blockhouse if we do not succor each other in distress."

A few nights later, one of these carefully selected friends was on sentry duty. The Field Mouse persuaded him to fire into the air as he sneaked out of the encampment. The night was frosty and ringingly icy. The Field Mouse ran straight for a village where his faithful grandmother awaited him with a suit of peasant clothing. Happily, he made his way home.

To his joy, 8th Route Army guerrillas soon occupied his village. The Field Mouse immediately enlisted as a militiaman and stood sentry duty outside the dirt walls. He caught the eye of guerrilla leaders, was singled out for political training and rapidly thereafter became a village cadre.

Determined not to use his position for personal profit, he announced to his neighbors that he was a new type of official and incorruptible. As proof of his devotion to public welfare, he summoned his sister-in-law before a mass meeting, accused her of stealing melons from a neighbor's field and demanded that she reform her character. His wife turned on him. "You did this to my sister because you hate me," she hissed. "There is nothing personal in my actions," said the Field Mouse, but his wife only snarled.

A few days later, to his own and to his whole family's horror, he blundered into a house where his father was making love to another man's wife. In shame and rage, he seized a pistol from a militiaman. "I'll kill you," he shrieked at his father.

With difficulty a fellow cadre disarmed him. The Field Mouse demanded that the county arrest and try his father for immorality.

"This is a shame to me as a cadre," he said, "and a shame to the whole village government."

For a while his whole family hated him. "An unfilial son," they remarked bitterly. The Field Mouse reiterated his previous statement. "There is nothing personal in my actions. If I am to be just I must be the same to my own relatives as to anyone else."

Within a few months the father was a changed man. He went to his son, saying: "I have been a bad father. You have taught me a lesson." The Field Mouse accepted the praise but remained aloof.

Having severed the ties of affection that bound him to his family and the ties of village feudalism that bound him to the past, the Field Mouse was, when I met him, dedicated heart and soul to the Chinese Revolution. Contrary to what might be expected, he was extremely gay and full of pranks. He was a favorite of women, especially voluptuous peasant women, second wives or concubines of rich farmers around the age of thirty, but, though he used them all as messengers and spies and liked to joke with them, he was not attracted to them sexually, claiming that he disliked women and had no time for them outside his work, not even in his dreams.

I mean this quite literally. The Field Mouse claimed that he dreamed that he was leading the land reform, that he was flying an airplane, that he was being battered by artillery shells which burst into his sleep with horrid red glares, but never did he dream of women.

"I don't like them that way," he said. "I got a bad impression from the way my father brought shame to our family."

Yet the Field Mouse did much of his work behind the lines with the aid of peasant women. These women probably liked the Field Mouse because he was so tiny and appeared so helpless, as if he needed mothering. Then, the Field Mouse treated women with a kind of impersonality, which I suppose appealed to them because it was a different approach than either the mealy-mouthed formality or the brutal familiarity practiced by other Chinese males. Finally, the women made alliances with the Field Mouse much as they would with a protector or an avenger.

I discovered this in an accidental sort of way on the night the Field Mouse first took me into the village of Toumachuang. This village was located in the middle of no man's land, which would have made it peculiar enough, but there was the added fact that all the people in the village were related by blood and all had the same family name of Tou. The village had been established nearly half a millennium ago, shortly after the first emperor of the Mings drove the Mongols from the throne in Peiping. In an old temple at the corner of the village, there were the ancestral tablets of twenty generations dating back to the first Tou who had made his way into these hills. Above the door of this temple, there were inscribed the words: WE ARE ALL FROM ONE FAMILY. Yet the members of this family were now killing each other.

It can be imagined that the atmosphere in this village was a little unusual. We had entered after dark and while some militiamen took up outposts on the heights above the village, the Field Mouse, Mr. Chen, Liu Ming-chi and I walked somberly down the one and only street. Depositing me for safety in a house occupied by two women, the Field Mouse went off to gather information.

The sudden appearance of a foreigner in their home must have disconcerted the women, for I found it very difficult to make them talk. There was the added fact that both were wives of a murdered bandit-landlord and I supose that inclined them to reticence with a stranger.

The first wife was about forty-five or fifty, dull and almost incoherent in her speech. The second wife, however, was a comely woman of about thirty, who had an irritating, but attractive way of looking up out of lowered, questioning eyes. While the faithful orderly, Liu Ming-chi, stood watch at the door, I began with the aid of Mr. Chen to question this woman about her life. Since it was bound up with sex and murder, she spoke somewhat reluctantly, but after a while she loosened up and told me the following story.

She had been sent by her parents to Toumachuang when she was seventeen to be the second wife of a rich peasant named Tou Hsikung. She soon displaced the first wife from the bed of her husband and was in turn displaced by a younger third wife. The ministrations of three wives, however, failed to satisfy Hsikung's lusty appetites and about twice a week he used to go boldly into the bed of a poor farmer's wife—a girl named White Flower, who was a native of the village and whom Hsikung had known since childhood.

Possibly the farmer knew White Flower was lying with another man while he was in the fields, but if he did, there was little he could do about it because Tou Hsikung was a powerful man in the village. Tou Hsikung's wives could do nothing either. Only glancing sadly at the embroidered jacket White Flower sent their husband, they kept their silence.

White Flower and the second wife remained on friendly terms, a fact which, in itself, says all that needs to be said about the position of Chinese women. Thus, despite Tou Hsikung's amorous adventures, everything would have been all right if White Flower had not attracted—against her will, it must be admitted—the attentions of a man named Tou Mali.

Now Mali was a partner of Hsikung in a bandit suppression organization that had milked the village pretty dry during the war. Both men had worked harmoniously together in kidnaping people and amassing land, but the sudden lust of Tou Mali for White Flower broke up the happy partnership.

White Flower loved the handsome Hsikung, but she had little affection for the rather ugly Mali, yet Mali, being the most powerful man in the village, forced himself on her pretty much when he pleased. Still, this did not satisfy him.

"Whenever I come," he complained to White Flower, "you look glum, but every time Hsikung comes you look happy."

One night Hsikung was sleeping with his third wife and son in a cave at the back of the village. Mali surrounded the cave with a hundred armed men and opened fire, instantly killing Hsikung's child. Hsikung grabbed his pistol and tried to shoot his way out but was driven back inside. While the whole village huddled indoors, Mali built a fire outside the cave and smoked Hsikung and his third wife to death.

After that Tou Mali became the sole power in Toumachuang, he raped White Flower when he liked and continued to steal land from the people. So severe was this land plunder that I came across one family of eleven people in which seven had starved to death because Tou Mali had taken their land.

These actions of Mali naturally made him many enemies in the village. But perhaps his two worst enemies were White Flower and Hsikung's second wife. And this brings us back to the Field Mouse, the Chinese Revolution and the civil war. For it would be a mistake to think that these sexual intrigues and murders did not have some connection with that revolution. Such affairs could not have happened in the first place —or would have had different results—if it had not been for the feudal nature of Chinese society. As for the Field Mouse's connection with these affairs, it seems to have been pretty much that of a god from the machine.

When the Japanese had retreated from this area, Tou Mali had gone with them. The Field Mouse had then come into the village and begun the land reform. Shortly afterward, the Kuomintang came into Anyang County, the Field Mouse fled and Tou Mali returned. The village, however, remained about midway between the two men, who waged a kind of warfare for the affections of the people.

In this war, White Flower and the second wife of the murdered Tou Hsikung, nursing a bitter hatred, had quite naturally joined forces with the Field Mouse. Secretly, they gave him information when he came to the village. Not only these two women, but many other villagers had also leagued up with the Field Mouse. In a way, it is an indication of the strength and appeal of the Chinese Revolution that most of the people of Toumachuang sided with the Field Mouse, a stranger, against Tou Mali, their own relative.

The struggle between these two men was a rather weird affair. Tou Mali and his Home Returning Corps visited Toumachuang two or three times a week in the daytime. The Field Mouse generally came after dark. Originally, Tou Mali had a much stronger force, but the Field Mouse had whittled it down.

In weakening Mali, the Field Mouse was patient and often subtle. When he had first instituted the land reform in Toumachuang, the Field Mouse had organized a militia band to operate against the Japanese. When the Kuomintang came and he retreated, most of the militiamen had deserted him because they did not wish to leave their families or their land. Some of these militiamen Tou Mali had killed but others he had incorporated into his Home Returning Corps. The Field Mouse used to come into Toumachuang at night to see the wives of these men. In his charming, boyish, but serious way, he would point out to these women the impropriety of having a husband in a Home Returning Corps run by bandits.

"When a bird passes, his music remains; when a man passes, his reputation remains."

Quoting such proverbs as these, of which he had a great many at tongue tip, the Field Mouse would soon have a woman believing that her poor husband's descendants would hold him in loathing and contempt if he did not desert the Home Returning Corps. As a result, many women went to work on their husbands, some of whom deserted while others acted as spies for the Field Mouse.

The Field Mouse had a peculiar affection for his ex-militiamen. He would never take them back in any of his militia corps, yet he bore them no grudge and went out of his way to be kind to them. I remember one of his former militiamen who had been forced into a Home Returning Corps and then had deserted and gone to work in a coalpit. He was living a rather hard life and the Field Mouse heard about it. The next time the Field Mouse came to the village he brought a piece of soap and a towel which he asked the worker's wife to give him. The man was so grateful, he wept and told his wife: "I've treated Old Tang [Field Mouse] so badly and here he sends me presents. It's too much."

Thus, the Field Mouse built up his reputation for kindness and broke down the influence of Tou Mali, head of the Home Returning Corps, among the people. The Home Returning Corps leader was not unaware of this and he began to set traps for the Field Mouse. First, he sent a messenger over to say: "There is no personal enmity between us. If you need anything, just tell me." Then he wanted to arrange a meeting with the Field Mouse.

The Field Mouse was not averse to meeting Mali, but he was afraid of a trap. Finally, he sent back the following word:

"You come into the valley with twenty men and I'll come with twenty men. A li [⅓ of a mile] from each other, we will stop our forces. Then you and I will come out alone. You will carry a gun and I will carry a gun. If you want to talk, we will talk. If you want to shoot, we will shoot."

By way of showing the sincerity of his offer, the Field Mouse ended up with the usual oath: "May I die at the bottom of the blockhouse, if I do not keep my word."

Unfortunately for the local ballad makers, this meeting never came about. Yet, Tou Mali swore he would kill the Field Mouse. Knowing the habit of the Field Mouse to come into Toumachuang in the night, Tou Mali surrounded the village one day just at dusk. He left the path to the village open so that Tang could walk into his trap, but let nobody out that could warn him.

The Field Mouse's friends were greatly worried. One village witch got out her incense table and called down a favorite god to find out what was going to happen.

"Will Old Tang come today?" she asked.

"He is in great danger," answered the god, dodging the question with the agility of all oracles.

"Well, you better warn him," said the witch, "or I will stop burning incense."

Whether this threat caused the god to take action is a question that a poor Western unbeliever such as myself would not dare answer. But whatever the reason, the Field Mouse did not come to the village that night and so was saved.

Another time, Tou Mali sent his chief gunmen with a couple of henchmen to ambush the Field Mouse. Unsuspecting, Tang walked alone into Toumachuang. White Flower flew out of doors and warned him. Beating a hasty retreat, Tang collected a couple of militiamen and set out to capture his would-be assassin. A running gun fight ensued along the hilly paths. When the Field Mouse plugged the chief gunman, the other two turned their hats around in token of surrender and gave up their arms.

The Field Mouse by no means confined his activity to Toumachuang, but roved far and wide in no man's land and behind the Kuomintang lines. In doing this, he made a great many friends, but also some enemies, especially among various Home Returning Corps who chipped together and put up a large reward for his capture, dead or alive. Preferably dead, I should imagine, for the Field Mouse was such a slippery rascal that he undoubtedly would have escaped from any prison.

Some of the Field Mouse's tricks were quite cute and showed an inventive mind. In starting propaganda work in new villages behind the lines, he found that people were scared to open their doors at night, so he had no way to call meetings and get in touch with his public. It was unthinkable that he break into the homes of people he wished to impress, so he devised a peculiar scheme of his own for contacting the people.

One night he took ten of his men to a village that had hitherto denied his ardent night-time wooing. Parking his men in a circle in the middle of the street, he called out in a loud voice: "The meeting is now open." He gave a short speech announcing that he was from the 8th Route Army. Then he asked if anyone had any questions.

Imitating the quavering voice of an old woman, one of his militiamen said: "We know you 8th Route Army are very good, but why don't you come more often?"

When the Field Mouse had answered this question, his men, one by one, imitating farmers or their wives, spoke up so that the villagers in their houses would think a regular meeting was really taking place.

To judge the effect of this trick, which became known as the Meeting at Which Nobody Was Present, the Field Mouse sent one of his militiamen to the village the next day to listen to the gossip. He heard people slyly asking each other:

"Were you at the meeting last night?"

"Oh, no," would come the answer. "But there must have been a lot of people there."

"Are you sure you weren't there?"

Everybody believed everybody else was at the meeting, but was afraid to admit it. As a result, the next time the Field Mouse came, both men and women put on clothes and came outdoors when he called a meeting. In villages, not too far behind the lines, the Field Mouse often opened meetings in the daytime. Such meetings were very simple. Both men and women would gather in a courtyard or in a field and sit in an informal circle while the Field Mouse addressed them. The women most always brought their spinning wheels and also their babies which they breast-nursed during the Field Mouse's speech.

Besides being a propagandist, the Field Mouse was also a literary man of sorts. One day when the two of us were walking along a mountain trail, the Field Mouse suddenly halted and pointed to a small mimeographed newspaper, about five inches square, pasted to a tree. "I have an article in that issue," he said. And sure enough, on going closer, I saw his by-line—Tang Wen-liang—printed under the biggest headline in the paper. It was a rather simple story of some seventy-five characters about a raid behind the lines, but Old Tang seemed rather proud of his effort.

The Field Mouse kept simple notes on all his operations. One day he read from his notebook a summary of a month and a half's activity of one of his militia bands of thirty men, which I give below.

11 defensive engagements; 21 operations behind the lines; four meeting engagements; seven attacks, 11 propaganda meetings; eight intelligence gathering operations; three letters delivered; six mining expeditions; exploded three blockhouses; burned seven village gates and one tower; captured 19 Home Returning Corps members, one Kuomintang captain, one adjutant and an orderly, five documents, four shovels, 17 rifles, two pistols, 30 tou of millet, 40 enemy insignia and $60,000.

A pretty busy record for thirty men, it must be admitted.

Behind the last two items in Tang's notebook hung a story that illustrates the cunning, the daring, perhaps the rashness and even the duplicity of this many-wiled boy.

One night, the Field Mouse had received, through a spy, news that a Home Returning Corps under a landlord named Pan had set up barracks in a large stone mansion in a certain village deep behind the enemy lines. The spy reported that the people were suffering much from the depredations of this corps, which was fairly strong, but which might be successfully attacked and maybe captured if taken by surprise. Armed with this information, the Field Mouse set out at dusk and reached the village around ten o'clock in the evening.

Climbing over a wall surrounding the house, Tang and his men dropped into a courtyard, but found themselves blocked by another wall too high to climb. Immediately they began to dig a hole in this wall, intending to squeeze Tang through. Those inside woke up and the Field Mouse and his men were forced to abandon their surprise tactics and make a direct assault on the gate. Bursting into the inner courtyards, they found that the Pan Corps had already gone. A search revealed one naked member of Pan's Corps under a bed, sixty thousand dollars, and forty insignia—not a very good haul.

Disappointed at his failure, the Field Mouse wanted to pursue the Home Returning Corps, but realized he could not go far as he would be caught behind the lines at daylight. Then a brilliant idea came to him.

"Put on those insignia," he told his peasant-clad militiamen. "We shall be the Pan Corps."

So disguised and with the captured member of the corps now fully dressed and in their ranks as a further aid to dissimulation, the Field Mouse set out deeper into enemy territory. At the first village, some people aroused by the sound of firing were already up.

"We have been attacked by the 8th Route Army," said the Field Mouse. "Have you seen any of them around here? We're from the Pan Corps."

On hearing this, a well-dressed woman came up to the Field Mouse and said:

"My son is in the Pan Corps. Is he with you?"

The Field Mouse thought fast.

"We're from a different section," he said. "We became separated. We're trying to unite. Have you seen any other of our men?"

The villagers directed Tang toward the east. The second village they came to happened to be the native place of one of Tang's militiamen, named Pingtze. Since the whole village knew he was with the 8th Route militia, Pingtze went quickly in the dark to the home of one of his friends. In the meantime, Tang aroused the rest of the village and warned them that the 8th Route Army might come.

Slyly, he asked the members of a few landlord families how they would feel if that happened.

"Oh, we are very afraid of the 8th Route Army," answered a man.

"We hear they rape women," said a rich peasant's wife.

"Don't be afraid," said the Field Mouse, "I'll protect you."

Just at this moment, the villagers saw Pingtze coming out of a house. Again, the Field Mouse thought fast. Pretending to be greatly startled, he advanced in a well-simulated rage on his own militiaman.

"Pingtze!" he said. "You son-of-a-bitch, at last I've caught up with you."

Then turning to two of his militiamen, he said: "Quick, grab him and take him outside and execute him."

The militiamen led Pingtze away. From beyond the village came the sound of a shot.

"That'll teach these pigs not to fool with the Pan Corps men," said the Field Mouse.

Believing that Pingtze had really been executed and seeing that the Field Mouse was apparently a strong, determined man, the rich men of the village began to fawn on him, praising him to the skies and cursing the 8th Route Army. The Field Mouse calmly drank in all their remarks. In the meantime, other elements of the village, who had at first been too scared to come out in front of the supposed Pan Corps men were attracted by the excitement and now came into the street. Among them was a girl who personally knew the Field Mouse.

"What are you doing here with the Pan men," she said, getting him to one side.

"I've been captured," said the Field Mouse sadly hanging his head.

"Oh, you poor boy!" said the woman. "Can I do anything?"

Feeling that he had let this farce go far enough, the Field Mouse mounted a roller and called for attention.

"We have deceived you," he said, his face grim. "We are militiamen of the 8th Route Army."

His words drew a frightened gasp from many of his listeners.

"But you have been deceived about us," continued the Field Mouse. "We are not bandits. We do not rob people and we do not rape women. We have come here tonight to show you what we really are. Some of you have spoken badly of us. Partly because you have not known better, partly because you were afraid. We know many of you have to become two faced in times like these. So we do not hold these remarks against you. But hereafter, when the Kuomintang says something against us, you will know it is a lie. We shall return often now and if you are in trouble we will help you. If the Kuomintang starts a conscription drive run over to us and we will find you jobs so you can keep alive."

Having revealed himself, the Field Mouse left ten of his men behind and went on to a further village. Here, he practiced the same deception again, but when he asked if there were Pan Corps men in the vicinity, he heard that a certain Captain Wei was at that very moment in the house of a girl named Dark Maid, the local "broken shoe."

Tang immediately went to the house. Flashing his light in a room, he discovered the captain in bed with Dark Maid. The captain drew behind the girl in fright.

"Who are you?" he asked.

The Field Mouse shone his light on the Pan insignia one of the militiamen was wearing. The captain laughed: "I thought you were 8th Route; I'm from the Pan Corps, too."

"Arrest that man," said the Field Mouse. His men dragged the captain from bed.

"Don't make a mistake," said the captain. "I'm the same side as you. There are other Pan men here who can prove it."

"Lead us to them," said the Field Mouse, who, in this way, captured four more men. By now it was daylight. Quickly picking up his other militiamen, Tang started back home. After several adventures, including a brief fire fight, Tang safely returned to his own lines.

Such were the exploits of the Field Mouse—a truly remarkable boy. The more I got to know him, the more he intrigued me. He seemed a very contradictory character. Sometimes he appeared like a mother's boy, at other times—a thug. He had the temperament of a propagandist and yet the heart of a poet, too. A cold realist, he was at the same time a dreamer. Gentle, he was also rough; cunning, yet frank; courageous but also cautious; generous yet sometimes greedy. On the surface, he appeared open, simple and frank, yet he defied analysis and his whole character was elusive. At any rate I grew quite fond of him.

But that is enough of the Field Mouse. Here I would like to describe the first expedition I made behind the lines with him. As you will see, this mission was as contradictory as the Field Mouse himself. But then the whole Chinese Revolution was a mass of contradictions.

41. Mission Murder

WE HAD been many days on the road and I was tired and I sat down on a rock beside the trail, arms folded on knees, head bent down, pretending not to breathe hard, and ahead and beyond the cotton-clad figures toiled upward. Their rifles were slung across their backs and the muzzles were stuffed with pieces of green and red cotton cloth as protection against the dust. We were behind the main Kuomintang lines, but well within our own local defense area; there was a mountain between us and Chiang Kai-shek's troops, and no need to have guns at the ready. And so guns were slung on backs and the men, bent low and their hands ever and again reaching out for a hold on a rock or tuft of grass, worked upward.

For a moment I watched them go, then turned my eyes back whence we had come. The mountainside fell steeply down from where I sat, but after a mile or so it rose precipitously up again and I could see the trail lying like a serpent between the walls of the canyon winding up to the pass and the village we had left some hours before. It had been a large village, as villages in the Taihang Mountains went, and the men had come from their fields and the women had abandoned their spinning wheels and gathered on the walls, staring down at me and vocally wondering whether I was a Russian adviser, an American Army officer or a captured spy. Now I did not even remember its name for there had been many villages and the way had been long and one day had been like another, except the trail was ever steeper and more narrow, the food less and the countryside drier and drier.

It was the dryness that was depressing, and the lack of green and no vegetation, as if everything were long dead. There was a break in the walls of the mountains on our right and through a canyon I saw a winding river bed, dry, and the rocks gray and dull even in the spring sunlight.

"Did these rivers ever have water?" I asked.

"No."

"In ancient times, then?"

"Never," he said.

"You are only twenty-four," I said. "Can you remember back to the time of Confucius, then?"

I smiled dryly to myself. It was tiredness that made me needle the Field Mouse who twisted his lip at my words, looked at the treeless mountains and the river bed that held no river and spoke in a shy manner.

"I only went to school a few years and I know little of classical times, but I do know that no stream ever flowed long in these rivers. When it rains—and it doesn't rain often—the water rushes down over the rocks and into the river bed and for a few days there is a stream, but then it is gone and after the going the mud beneath the rocks dries and the earth cracks and the wind blows the dust away and then there are only the rocks and this bitter land again."

"It is all ugly," I said, "but the ugliest are these rivers that are not rivers."

"We call them dry rivers."

"It is a contradiction."

"Yes, it is a contradiction, but our whole life here is a contradiction. The Kuomintang has a brigade of troops, but we not only don't have any troops, we don't even have guerrillas. All we have are these farmers with rifles. If there weren't any contradictions we would have been dead long ago."

"And your revolution," I asked, "is that a contradiction, too?"

"I do not speak in exact figures, but our revolution in Anyang is like one of these dry rivers. One day the water springs forth in a fresh, new stream, and that is the revolution watering the hearts of the people. But the next day there is a blast of withering air, and that is the Kuomintang and it dries up the stream and cracks the heart of the people, and leaves only the hard barren rocks."

"Your revolution, then, is dead?" I asked.

"No," he said angrily, "not dead. This river that passed through here is dry now, but in passing, it nourished the soil. On that nourishment the people still feed and they live in hope. That is why I go night after night behind the lines—to keep that hope alive."

Abruptly, he stopped speaking. He put a finger to his nostril and blew his nose angrily.

"We don't yet have a target for night," he said. "It's time to go. There's much to do."

We started once more to climb. The trail was discernible but rocky and steep and wound around the face of the mountain and then across a peak where was planted a pole with a white flag. Once the enemy came out the flag would be dipped. We passed the summit and started down. The descent was now steeper and more difficult than the climbing, until finally we reached the base of a sheer rock cliff where there was a stream with water in it so clear that one gasped with delight after all the dryness.

"That is very good," I said.

"If they were all like that—" he said. He did not finish his sentence. He was sweating heavily and his lips were twisting as if he were suffering from the climb, for he was not a strong man.

We were now in the foothills of the Taihang Mountains and getting lower all the time. We followed the stream for a while, crossed over in a shallow place on rocks that had been made into a foot bridge, then passed over a low divide and then down into a narrow ravine where sometimes the trail disappeared altogether, and finally toward late afternoon we came out on a ledge and looked down on the North China Plain. The Kuomintang strongholds were below us.

The Field Mouse looked at the rolling country below and the flat fields beyond, and nodded his head as if expressing satisfaction.

"This is better," he said. "Those ravines with no trails arouse one's dislike at night. But here there is no question. The going is easy and quick."

"And for the Kuomintang is it not easy and quick, too?"

His lip twisted in a smile. "He does not dare come out. We can go in the villages and burn down the gates and he will take no notice. He just stays in his pillbox and doesn't shoot unless you bother him."

"How many men has he?"

"A regiment of the 40th Army in that town over there. Just across that rise—a battalion. Another battalion to the north. In between about fifteen to twenty groups of the Home Returning Corps with about forty or fifty men in each group."

"And your men? What is their number?"

"I have five hundred militia under my hand. But only two hundred of them are out at once. The rest are home farming. They change every two weeks. We have thirty-five men in this sector."

"How many rifles?"

"Thirty. And one light machine gun they gave us because you are with us."

"Then it's good if I stay with you a long time, so that you can keep the machine gun."

"It doesn't matter. We can fight with spears."

"Where will we go tonight?"

"I do not know yet. In these next days, we have a new mission. The regular army is coming out of the mountains south of here and will move toward the railway and the Yellow River. All the militia to the north must come out behind the lines and pin down the Kuomintang troops here so that they cannot attack our regulars. We shall also use the opportunity to open up political work, to call meetings behind the lines and let the people know we are their friends. Down there now, in that village over to the east, my column should already have arrived. They will have much information. I go to gather it now."

"Good," I said, standing up.

"No, it is better that you rest here," he said. "That is no man's land. The Kuomintang come today. We come tomorrow. The special agents and spies are many. You are not a target that can be missed. If you come in the daytime, the whole village will know a foreigner has arrived. If the agents don't dare shoot you, yet they may report back to the Kuomintang and that would be bad for our plans. It is better that you come after dark."

I sat down amid my guards and watched the Field Mouse descend the slope. He did not go fast like an ordinary guerrilla and I knew he was not a professional soldier.

But the Field Mouse, I knew, had much experience and knew the country better than any soldier. Still the absence of the army was disquieting. All the soldiers had gone south for the big attack. Then yesterday, the guerrillas had gone, too. Now, I could not help remembering the words Li, the guerrilla leader, had spoken to me before he went.

"To go on an attack behind the lines is nothing," he said. "You understand that."

"Yes, I understand."

"Absolutely nothing. For us."

"How do you mean—for us?"

"For us, it is nothing. We are professionals and Chinese. But for you—it is hard. You are too obvious. But even for you to go with us, it is nothing. You have come seven thousand miles to see how the 8th Route operates and you should see it. That is your right to go with the 8th Route Army."

He trimmed the oil wick on the lamp and smiled at me.

I said nothing.

"You understand that is how it should be done—with the 8th Route Army." He went on looking at me. "That is good. And we welcome you. But with the militia, that is incorrect."

"Why?"

"Why?" he said with an embarrassed smile. "The militia are not regulars. They are very brave," he added hastily and contracted his brows in an earnest manner. "They have their uses. But they have no power. They must be reasonable. They cannot attack strong points. If they meet a force of regulars, they must run away. For them, it is nothing. They bury their rifles and poof! they are just like a farmer. No, it is better that you don't go with these militia."

That was the last I had seen of a regular army uniform, except the one worn by my interpreter, and he was no soldier, but a former student who knew nothing of fighting. So now there were only the militia and they were so unmilitary it sometimes frightened you. There wasn't any use in getting scared, though, or wondering what would happen to you if you were caught. That only made things worse. You either had to trust the people you were with or not go at all. But there was another thing, and that was depressing.

It was the savagery. Ever since I had crossed the Chang River into Anyang County it had hemmed me in like the mountains on all sides and there was no way of escaping it.

There had been that shoemaker who had come across the mountains from the east and down into our village. He had no land and no house and not much of anything but a pretty wife. The landlords of the Home Returning Corps had taken her because the shoemaker could not pay the seventy-five thousand dollars levied on him for the rifle tax. So he had fled to the 8th Route Army.

It was the shoemaker who had given me that verse of the people in Chiang Kai-shek's part of Anyang County.

My land to the pao chang.[1]
My son to old Chiang.
Be an officer, get rich.
Be a soldier, do what you like.
When land is occupied by the Nationalists,
Levies and taxes are like tigers.
All my property sold out.
All my family imprisoned.

[1] The head of 100 families; a local official.

How many times had you heard these stories. But they were nothing. There was worse. That farmer you'd seen two days ago. The one who had dug the pit.

"It was about this high," he said, indicating his chest. "When we'd finished digging, the Home Returning Corps made them get in a hole. There were six. Five men and a girl. They made them stand up and I thought that was strange until they told me to start shoveling in the dirt. They had guns and there was nothing I could do. I threw in the dirt. When it was up to their ankles, that girl started to sing. It wasn't anything I knew. Something about women's equality and the 'world is ours.'

"It was good to hear, but those turtles of the Home Returning Corps didn't like it and one of them said: 'The world is yours, all right. The underworld.'

"He laughed. Then he took my shovel and threw dirt in the woman's face. The men had been silent but now they started to sing. It was very strange. Those turtle landlords felt it and they suddenly were like fools, seizing our shovels and throwing in the dirt themselves.

"They filled the hole. But the necks and heads of those six were still sticking out. They sang for a while, but soon they began to choke as if they couldn't breathe. Then their eyes popped out as big as eggs and blood poured from their seven organs.

"It was most difficult to look at, but those turtles couldn't get enough of looking until they picked up the shovels and beat the heads flat into the earth."

"Let the dogs eat them," I heard one say, "but I didn't wait for any more and went home, leaving my shovel there."

You could hear this story—and I had heard many like it—and the flesh would tighten on your cheeks, but still you could not see it, for it was alien to your world. And if you yourself saw the pits of Chiang, you could not believe them, just as you had seen the concentration camps of Hitler and could not believe them.

And it was no longer an education. You saw it and heard it again and again, but no one ever learned. "Why don't you quit writing fiction?" some wiseacre would say to you in New York months later; that is, if you ever saw New York again. As for yourself, there was no value any longer in this savagery. You saw just so much of it and that was all the system could absorb. At first it was a shock. Then you were horrified. For a while, incredulous. And after that tumultuously angry. But in the end you were depressed.

I sat now on the ground looking at the fields which were more frequent here in the lowlands and, across the path, I noticed there was a plot planted with rows of young wheat. I crossed the path, knelt down beside the wheat and then carefully brushed the dirt away from one shoot, trying, with the curiosity of one city bred to see how deep the roots went. The shoot came away from the earth in my hand and I looked at it and thought: How easy it is to destroy a life, but no matter how much you destroy, new lives keep coming on. No, that was not right, either. If I were to pull up all the wheat in this field, then it would not grow again without someone to plant and tend it.

Since I felt a slight guilt, I scraped a little hole in the earth and then put the wheat back in and patted the earth all around it. Feeling satisfied, I straightened up and saw the Field Mouse coming up the trail. With him was another man, in a dirty white cotton jacket and fading blue pants, wearing broken cloth shoes and white cotton leggings around his ankles. This man had a towel about his head. The two came walking up the slope at a leisurely pace.

"This is Siatze," said the Field Mouse.

"Are you well?" I said to the man with the towel on his head and smiled.

"Well," he said grudgingly. I looked at the man's rough, sunburned face. It was a quiet, solid face that should have been filled with repose, but there was a certain tenseness about the cheek muscles. His eyes could scarcely be seen for the towel came down over one of them and the other kept staring into the distance. He was not tall, nor heavy either, but he was well developed, though slightly stooped. His socks showed out through the holes in his shoes and his fingernails were three-quarters of an inch long and very dirty. He appeared about forty. I liked him.

The Field Mouse nodded his head at this man and smiled.

"We will go to his village tonight," he grinned, then picked at his nose thoughtfully and looked at the man with the towel on his head. "A very good target."

Siatze nodded his head and grunted in reply.

"What kind of a village do you live in?" I asked.

"It was a fine village," Siatze said, "but the old hundred names of my village have suffered in this war." His face grew grave, and he stopped speaking.

"Where is this village of yours?" I asked.

We walked to the ledge and Siatze pointed toward the southeast. "It is over that rise of ground and then some."

"How far from here?" I said.

"Thirty li."

Ten miles, I thought. Eight of it in back of the enemy. "That's pretty far," I said.

"Yes, it is far," he said.

"Are there enemy soldiers in your village?"

"There is a company there. In the daytime, they come to the village. But in the night, they live in five pillboxes outside the village."

"Truly, it is a large target," I said. "And what are the features of the terrain?"

"The village is at the hill's bottom. West, there are the pillboxes I mentioned. East, there is a river."

A perfect trap, I thought. The main Kuomintang lines are to the south. The pillboxes and the company of soldiers block you on the west. The river is on the east and when you go to get out from the north you must run up a hill. A fine business.

I turned to the Field Mouse. "Are all the militia of the district coming with us on this?"

"No, they have their own targets. There will be thirty men on this one. Also Siatze is coming as a guide as is the head of the Farmers Association."

"You are not going to attack these pillboxes with thirty men?"

"No, we shall just burn the city gate and pick up a man there."

"What kind of a man?"

"A sinful landlord."

"You are going ten miles behind the lines with thirty farmers against a company of soldiers just to pick up someone you call a sinful landlord?"

"There is no danger," the Field Mouse grinned. "Besides, he is a sinful landlord."

"Go on."

"He's a grafter," said Siatze, interrupting, "a sexual intercourser with whores, and an oppressor."

"Anything else?"

"He shot my wife, my brother and my baby."

I just stared at him.

"He buried alive four members of my family. My son, my uncle, my nephew and one married daughter who had come home on a visit. One boy—he has six years—got away. They bayoneted him, but the knife slid along his forehead and he didn't die. He lay by his mother, but he didn't cry. When night came he ran back to this side. When I saw him, he was crazy. He's all right now. Goes to school and can write his name."

He stopped speaking, his throat hard and his eyes looking straight ahead. I was silent for a minute, then asked.

"Why was this killing? Was there a connection between you?"

"There was a connection. There was a famine in the village in 1943. We had no food to eat as many others. In the winter he lent me grain. When the fall came I could not pay it back. I had eight mow of land and he took four. He was the bodyguard of the district Japanese puppet leader. He had a pistol and there was nothing I could do. I was without politics, but when the 8th Route Army came and asked our grievances, I told them. They said the poor should not lose their means of living for such reasons and we ought to struggle against the landlords. So I helped lead the struggle. I paid him the debt I owed him, but not the interest, and took back my four mow of land. For this he hated me. Then the Kuomintang came and I knew it was not safe for me and I took to the hills. He was angry to find I had gone. So he killed all of my family members."

I was silent. I could think of nothing to say. You heard the statement of the loss. You did not see the mother lying in the ditch, nor her arms enfolding her frightened children, nor the earth pelting down, nor the terror and the eyes looking up for the last glimpse of the sky. You knew that his family had died but you could only cluck your tongue or look at the ground.

"You will get your revenge," I ventured.

"Yes, I will get revenge," he said, "but will that bring back my family people?"

"Someday you may go home and work the soil again."

"Never. I do not want to go back home now. There is no one there for me. No one. The land lays fallow, no one works the fields and the wild grass grows."

The Field Mouse took Siatze's hand in his as if he were a girl.

"You have not been home for six months," he said. "You may go back tonight."

Siatze looked at the countryside.

"Yes, I shall go back tonight. Just this once. I shall not touch him. But I shall lead you. So that I may go home again. Just this once. To go back home again."

He stared at the fields and my eyes followed his brooding eyes across the rolling country and up the far hill, and then they could go no further but struck the horizon where the twilight was gathering.

Abruptly, Siatze turned on his heel, crossed to the path, then started down. The four guards followed, then the Field Mouse, then I.

The sun was down as we entered no man's land.

* * *

As we came up in the grayness of the twilight, after dropping down from the bluff into the field-parceled valley and moving along it under an eroded earth bank that was tunneled with caves and petered out at the entrance to the village, a man stepped out from the shadow of a mud wall.

"Halt," he said. Then recognizing the Field Mouse, "Who is this with you?"

"An American," the Field Mouse said. "But a progressive one."

"Is it possible?" the guard said, and I grinned as we passed without stopping and turned to the left through a gate and entered a large courtyard.

There were stone buildings on either side of the yard and a high stone screen at the far end on which were written the characters SUPPORT CHAIRMAN MAO! (Mao Tze-tung) The paint of the Mao character was still fresh and, on looking closer, I saw that it had simply been superimposed on the character for Chiang (Chiang Kai-shek), no attempt having been made to wipe out the other characters painted there by the Kuomintang.

A fire made of straw and kaoliang was burning brightly in the courtyard. Hulking about it with their glinting rifles held between their legs were fifteen or twenty farmers. Their clothing was that of peasants, nondescript and completely unmilitary, blue, white, gray and black jackets and pants of the same variety of colors, with towels about their heads or bareheaded. Except for the rifles, there was nothing to distinguish them from ordinary farmers. To a nun they might have looked a hard lot and to a Western military man they might have looked like armed rabble, but what they reminded me of most of all was paintings I had seen of minutemen in the American Revolution.

Against the wall of one of the houses two men were mixing flour and rolling batter. They would take a handful of flour, dash a sprinkling of black cottonseed oil on it, knead it into a lump, then pick the whole mess up and pull it out to the length of their extended arms and, suddenly crossing their hands, whirl it into a figure eight. Then they would slap this down on the board, roll it into a thin, round cake, at least a foot in diameter, and lay the cake in a great black pan set on piled-up stones over a fire made of bushes and small branches.

The wheat cakes looked appetizing and reminded me of giant crêpe suzettes and that made me think of my French wife and I was sick for home. A farmer brought me one of the cakes and a bowl of millet gruel with a pair of chopsticks fashioned out of twigs. I took the cake and the bowl and the twigs and squatted down beside a young boy who was dipping oil out of a bottle with a straw and rubbing it along a bullet. As I sat down, he jabbed me with his finger and passed me the bullet.

"American," he said, "we captured these. They're being used to shoot civilians."

I looked at the bullet. On it was the Chinese character "*mei*," which stands for America in the Chinese language.

"That's not American," I said. "Do you think we would put Chinese characters on our bullets?"

"It says American," he said stubbornly.

"Look," I said, "maybe Chiang put that character on the bullets to make his soldiers think America is sending ammunition to China."

I knew I hadn't satisfied him. These people in the Liberated Areas were convinced America was helping Chiang and there was nothing you could say to the contrary. The children believed it more than anybody. How many times had they come out of the villages and followed me on the trail, running and jumping around me and one or two holding my hand, like children in America might if I had been a baseball hero. And how many times had one of them said, in a quiet hurt manner, "Why is America helping Chiang Kai-shek?"

A few days ago I had stood in a farmer's doorway and watched planes go over. They were bombers and they flew high, beating the sky apart with their motors.

After they had passed, a group had gathered around me and one man had said: "You are not helping Chiang Kai-shek, eh? Where did those planes come from then? Can Old Chiang make planes?"

I had no answer.

Just now there was a group of the militia crowding around me. They were asking me to sing.

"I do not know how to sing," I said truthfully enough.

"Welcome, welcome," they said, laughing and clapping their hands.

They were so insistent that to satisfy their demands I finally croaked through a verse of "My Country Tis of Thee."

"What does it mean?" they said turning to Mr. Chen.

"I don't understand it," he said. "It's probably their national song. Something about mountains and the land and American liberty."

"Do you have liberty?" said a farmer wonderingly.

"Assuredly."

"And democracy like we have in the Liberated Areas."

"We have democracy. Not quite the same as in your Liberated Areas."

"If you have democracy, why do you help Chiang Kai-shek?" said a farmer on the edge of the group.

"I understand nothing of American government policy," I said.

"Then we shall sing you a song so that you will understand," said a farmer.

"Yes, I welcome you to sing," I said.

The boy stood up and turned his face away from us and glanced upward in a theatrical pose.

Chiang Kai-shek has a stubborn heart,

The voice rose harshly, then went on.

America is his father and mother.
He undermines peace and democracy.
And now he fires on us.
And now he fires on us.

"Good," applauded the farmers, and the singer continued:

Comrades, hold fast to your rifle butts
Polish your bayonets.
March on. Destroy the enemy.
Grab the American-made machine guns,
Bazookas, tanks—Hei!
See how bad Chiang is again.

"The words are good, but the voice is very bad," said the Field Mouse, coming over and putting a hand on my arm. He drew me to the fire where three other men and Siatze were standing.

"These are my three column leaders," he said. "You will go with Old Kang here and his third column."

I looked at the man he had indicated. He had a big head with heavy brows that were set in a frown. His eyes, as far as I could see in the firelight, were hard and angry looking. He was a heavy man about six feet tall and his hands and feet were large. His neck was thick and his head set close to his shoulders which were hunched up. The body and the face both seemed set in a scowl.

The Field Mouse looked at this man and smiled.

"He's a hard man," he grinned, then looked up at Kang who was a foot taller than he. "A very big man."

"I can see it," I said. There was nothing I disliked about the man, but there was a brooding quality about him that made him appear unfriendly.

"You will walk behind me," he said.

"Yes," I said.

"Have you ever been out on an attack before?"

"Many times."

"With militia?"

"No."

"That's bad. You can't wear those clothes. You're too big a target."

"Then I shall wear your jacket," I said.

The Field Mouse laughed.

"Take it off, Kang," he said.

The man unbuttoned his jacket and peeled it off. Though he was big, I found I could not get in it. The sleeves were too narrow and the waist too tight. Despite all my walking, I was still fat. Mr. Chen gave me his 8th Route Army coat, which was more loosely made, and I put it on.

"I shall wear my own pants and shoes," I said. "If I were captured in an 8th Route uniform, it would be troublesome."

"No one is going to capture you," said the Field Mouse.

"You will carry a gun," said Kang.

"No, I go unarmed," I said.

Kang scowled and his eyes looked their contempt.

"I understand you," said Mr. Chen, "but don't you want my pistol?"

"No, I go unarmed."

You are a bastard, Jack Belden, I thought. Holding on to your neutrality so that you can truthfully say you are an observer if you are caught. But what of the others who are to protect you? It will be a firing wall or a pit for them. Even my interpreter had a carbine now. I knew he had a pistol under his jacket. He had borrowed it from a schoolmate. It was just to protect me. His superiors had privately given him a warning about protecting me. Particularly against special agents.

"Look out for poison," he said. "If anything happens to Belden, it will be bad for us."

That man might never have given me permission to go on this operation, but he did not know about it. The assistant magistrate had finally agreed to my pleading. I felt sad about that. He would be back there now sweating me out, just hoping nothing happened to me. It was bad for him if it did. Yes, you were a bastard for refusing to protect yourself.

"We will do it this way," said the Field Mouse to the militia that encircled him.

"The first column will go around to the west and get between the pillboxes and the village. You will not fire unless fired on. Even then you won't move until I give the signal. The second column will burn the village gate and the fort at the south end. Kang and the third column will go to the house."

He turned to Kang.

"You have the easiest job. You don't want to waste time. Siatze will lead you to the house. Then just go in and get him. He has a pistol so be careful. If anyone fires on you, don't be courteous. The government will be responsible for your actions."

"If there has to be a sudden retreat I will blow this." He held up a battered bugle decorated with a red rag. "Otherwise, I will blow two blasts on the whistle, then you will all leave quickly.

"One other thing. The password for tonight. 'Chiang Kai-shek,' and the countersign: 'Rotten egg.' "

I smiled. I remembered the time I had invaded Sicily with the First Division. The words that night had been George and Marshall. There had been a photographer with me who had not known the password. Someone kept yelling George at him in the dark. At first he had paid no attention, but then he had become exasperated and said: "Dammit, my name's not George." Now, four years afterward, we were still using passwords. Maybe someday, when there were no more wars you could go walking in the dark and just say hello to anyone you met on the road without fear of being halted for a password. You'd be an old man then and probably wouldn't go walking in the dark. Well, your son, then.

I was nervous now. I was always nervous and irritable before an action. "When do we go?" I asked.

"Now, if you are ready," said the Field Mouse.

He gave the order and the men filed out of the courtyard, the first two columns ahead and then ours, with Siatze ahead of Kang, and I behind and the interpreter behind me.

It was getting cool quickly now and there was a slight filmy mist gathering beneath the stars as we crossed a rocky bed, descended a slope and entered onto a path leading through an open valley. I had not seen such open country in a long while and my first reaction was to look for cover in case of a surprise shot, but there was no shelter—not a tree or a bush anywhere. We were between two low ridges, about a mile apart, and they seemed more to hem us in than give us protection.

We moved fast, strung over a distance of seventy-five yards; Siatze was walking in front of me now, his back bent slightly forward, his towel acting as a marker for me, like a tail light on the car ahead of you. But the night was not black, though there was no moon and a thin mist. From the sky came a faint light from the stars that made the air fuzzy. Through this fuzziness, on either side of us, came another light, flaring gleams as of burning fires or distant cities, and I saw all the men looking toward them and pointing them out to one another.

"Yours?" I asked.

"Ours," Siatze said, but I knew that he could not be sure. They could be a night raiding party of either side. But you always said the fires were ours because it made people feel better. If other militia were out burning down gates you felt you were part of a great force.

"They are ours," Siatze said. "I recognize the direction. Those are all in Kuomintang hands. We have a formidable people's force," he said almost happily.

"Yes."

"And we will win."

"And this going back tonight will help you win?"

"Clearly. If we do not punish this man, then all the others will dare kill as they please."

"And how will you punish him?"

"That is not my affair. As you see I carry no gun."

"Then you will not kill him?"

"He has killed my family. I hate him. Still it is not my duty to kill him. I do not belong to the militia. Everything must be done in the proper way. It is our democratic government that has the right to order his killing. Not I."

"But don't you want to kill him?"

"I could kill him. But it is not my duty. I have never killed anyone. I am not of the sort of Old Kang there."

"He is a killer then?"

"At the orders of the government, he will execute men."

"Will he do so tonight?"

"You may ask him."

I walked up close to Kang and stared at the bulk of his shoulders.

"Old Kang," I said, "how does this affair look to you?"

"It is good."

"And the planning of it is good?"

"The planning is of no consequence. It is never like the plan. But it is good. They will not come out."

"And the objective?"

"Very good. He has a pistol and I can use it."

"And that man? What shall you do with him?"

"We shall seize him."

"And execute him?"

"I cannot say. I obey orders. I do not kill at random."

"You have executed men then?" I asked in the intimacy of the dark.

"Twice."

"How was it with you?"

"It was nothing."

"And your feelings?"

"It was good. I felt good."

He turned his head around.

"I hated them," he spoke savagely. "I only was sorry to waste the bullets. Bullets are scarce."

"You felt no remorse or fear of punishment?"

"They were bad men. Who should I fear?"

"Heaven, maybe."

"I do not believe in gods. Let the rich have gods. The poor only have the 8th Route Army."

"Is it the 8th Route for whom you kill?"

"I fight for myself and the people. We never had any life before. The 8th Route came and they were like our own family. Then we had food and land and a chance to talk. The landlords came back, took the land and killed. Shall we say: 'Please come and kill me?' No, we are free men now."

Somewhere directly ahead a dog barked. Kang ceased talking and quietly cursed the dog. It was the first dog I had knowledge of in many days. The mountain people had killed them all in the Japanese war so the guerrillas could operate. Perhaps this was a Kuomintang dog.

We entered a doorless village gate, passed along a deserted street then came out of a gate on the other end. The dog's barking faded. We climbed a long easy slope, then sat down a moment and rested. One of the farmers lit a cigarette. Mr. Chen and I hissed at him. He looked up, but went on smoking, as if in contempt of such amateurs. "We will rendezvous here," said the Field Mouse. "Now let's go quickly."

We dropped down to a rocky brook bed, and the first two columns continued straight ahead, but ours turned to the right with Siatze in the lead. We crossed the rocks, came out on another path, then walked down a long slope and turned abruptly to the left. Here the path grew wider and dropped in steep turns toward a grove of willow trees the tops of which loomed ahead.

Siatze fell back now and Kang went ahead.

"Slowly. Slowly." Siatze whispered to me, and his hand made a downward motion as if he would restrain my speed.

Kang's rifle was off his shoulder now. The butt in his right hand, the barrel in his left, his arms rigid in front of him, his body tilted slightly forward, his knees bent and his shoulders and arms swaying from side to side, he crept forward. His shadow bulked large and threatening in the gloom.

"Slowly," whispered Siatze again. "It is just here."

Walking carefully downhill, Kang in the lead, three other farmers crouching with rifles swinging from side to side following, Siatze next, I, placing my feet carefully so I would not slip, feeling a rock underfoot and brushing it softly away so that it would not slide downhill and make any noise, seeing the tops of the trees curving inward until the trunks became visible and watching the house tops come into view and then the hay shocks and the mud fences and the indistinguishable objects on the ground and feeling I was in my twenties again and seeing my first battle, we dropped down the curving slope to a point where the path leveled out beside a mud house.

Now Kang halted by a willow tree before the house and he took Siatze's wrist and whispered so low I could hardly hear him, "Is this the house?"

"Just this," said Siatze.

Going forward slowly in the lee of the house wall, we cautiously turned a corner and came out in a yard. I saw stacks of wheat or some stalk and a plow on the ground and then the grinding stones in front of the house.

It was a good house. The mud walls were solid. Heavy wood doors barred the main gate. The roof was high and slanted steeply down and came out over the outer wall of the house about ten feet above the ground.

There was no mist now and I saw the outlines of the village clearly, but still as if in a dream, the tower off the left and the etched outlines of the pillboxes through the trees five hundred yards away on the right, and then Kang standing beneath the roof eaves and Siatze climbing up on his shoulders. The stars shone on him as he reached upward and clutched the straw.

The straw came away in his hands and he let it drop before he reached up again. The edge of the roof furnished no base of support and he ran his hands along it carefully, finding a solid spot, then bracing himself, his feet pressing into Kang's shoulders and his hands pushing on the roof until he was able to get his chest over the edge and resting on it draw up first one leg then another. Then he crept up on hands and knees toward the top.

I saw him straddle the covered ridgepole, then swing over and slide out of sight on the other side. I listened carefully but he made no sound. At the same time I was listening for the Kuomintang soldiers and I was watching beyond the yard for anything to come across the fields. I did not feel afraid but I felt strange to see Siatze dropping down like a cat burglar into the courtyard of the man who had killed his family.

But there was no excitement. It was all calm now.

The gate creaked woodenly. The men gathered around it and clicked back their rifle bolts. Siatze swung the door open and we went in.

We were in a square courtyard. On every side lay a room. All the doors were bolted. Behind what one the sinful landlord lay we did not know.

"Open the door," shouted Siatze, breaking the silence.

From the upper end of the courtyard, where three steps led to a building raised above the others, there came a hoarse woman's whisper.

"Siatze," she said.

"*Huaila*," said a man's voice. "Rotten."

Now we knew where they were and Kang leaped up the steps, banged on the door and roared.

"Open up!"

His voice was a harsh clang on the night stillness and I thought it would rouse the whole village and the Kuomintang soldiers. Those inside the room had the same idea.

"Let us yell," said a woman's voice.

There was a low groan from the man, and I thought: The woman's the brave one here.

"Save life! Save life!"

I jumped as she shrieked and I could feel the skin tightening along my spine.

"Save us! Save life! Save us!"

She would not stop shrieking now and her voice was filled with alarm, fear and an undercurrent of hope.

"Open up!" yelled Kang, trying to drown out the woman's voice. Every time he yelled, the woman yelled back: "Save life."

"*Toma!*" a militiaman said. "What fear is in her voice."

"Since she can do nothing but yell," I said, "don't blame her."

But I was thinking. Sure, make fun of her. But suppose it was you in your bed with your wife and they came around to get you in the middle of the night. Wouldn't you be afraid? Sure you would. That woman's done all right. She's waiting for someone to come to the rescue. She's engaging the enemy. Listen to the little darling.

She had yelled again.

Just then Kang picked up a rock and hurled it at the door. There was a splintering crash, the lock broke and the leaves flew open. We stood at the bottom of the steps and looked through the open door but could see nothing. Inside somewhere and somewhat to the right there was a rustling sound of someone moving.

Then I heard Kang saying: "Stand away!" and I saw him draw back his arm and swing down his wrist and throw a hand grenade through the door. There was a booming crack and I felt the blast from the explosion on my face and the smoke pouring out the door, and at the same time I saw Siatze and Kang going in.

The acrid smoke made one choke and at first it was blinding. By the thin smoke-diffused rays of the flashlight I saw we were in an empty room. There was a doorway on the right and we entered. In the gloom I made out an old woman huddling in a corner and then a woman with a baby in her arms standing by a stone bed. On the bed, face down, lay a naked man. His arm was doubled under his head and he was trembling violently. Kang turned him over roughly and he stared at us wildly.

"Where's your pistol?" said Kang.

The man shook his head and his lips moved, but no intelligible sound came from them. Kang rummaged in the bed and about the room but he could not find any pistol.

"Get up, you turtle's egg!" said Kang, but the man did not move.

"He's been sick for two months," said the young woman. "He cannot move."

"Drag the bastard out," growled another militiaman. "We can't wait half the night."

I thought there was sound military sense in this statement, for it was obvious the man was trying to delay as long as possible in the hope that help would come. I ran out of the courtyard to see what was happening in the village and as I came out the gate, there was a loud whoosh and then a shooting pillar of fire. The Field Mouse had touched off the fort. Now, with the woman's screams, the cracking of the hand grenade and the fire, it was certain that the soldiers in the pillboxes knew we were there.

I ran back in the courtyard and said: "There's a fire."

Reaching down his big hands, and grabbing the man's legs, Kang yanked him off the bed, his body making a dull thud on the floor, then dragged him through the rooms and half pulled, half flung him on the steps.

He lay on his back with his head on one step and his shoulders on another. Lying like that he looked small and weak. His terror made him ugly and it was hard to feel sympathy for him. The woman with the baby knelt beside him and smoothed down his hair.

"Come on, get up," said the militiaman yanking at him.

"He's sick," said the woman pulling on the militiaman's arm. He flung his arm out and the woman tumbled backward.

"Are you going to get up?" said Kang now standing over the man with his rifle idly pointing down at his head.

"Kill me here," said the man and his voice was a babble of words and chattering teeth.

"Get up, you bastard," said Kang.

"Let me die here," said the man.

"The son-of-a-bitch is stalling," said a militiaman. "Let's drag him out."

"Get some clothes for him," Mr. Chen said to the woman in a kindly voice.

She went into the house and came back—her baby no longer in her arms—with a jacket and a pair of pants. The man would not put them on and the militiaman finally lifted up his shoulders and put the jacket on and then drew the pants over his legs.

"Now come on," said Kang.

"Leave me here," said the man. "Just kill me. It will save you trouble. Leave me here."

I was, naturally, in a deadly hurry to be gone, as were the other militiamen. But the man would not move.

"Pick him up," said Kang.

The men put their hands under his armpits, lifted him up and then dragged him out of the courtyard onto the path. The woman ran beside him but she did not cry out or make any sound. The fire was bright now and I saw the trees and the blank mud walls of the house and the haycocks standing in the yards, and then the woman hobbling along on her stockinged feet and the man, now half on the ground, his feet dragging and every once in a while his knees bumping, still trying to delay in the hope that help might come. Strange, there had not been a shot fired. These Kuomintang soldiers must be afraid to come out.

Just then there were two long whistle blasts. The signal for retreat. The sound made one jump and automatically I quickened my steps.

The man was on the ground now and the militiamen were arguing over him.

"We'll have to carry him," said Kang.

Four men picked him up. He jerked his arms and legs trying to get down. I did not wait to see what happened, for a militiaman was tugging at my shoulder and saying: "Come with us."

We climbed hard as we could without looking back. Halfway up the hill, we halted on a bluff and two militiamen went to either side of the path and lay down and covered the path with their rifles where Kang and three others were struggling uphill with the man between them and the woman running alongside. As they came nearer, we got up once more and went ahead. We went very fast now and I thought of nothing but to keep moving. We turned to the right, crossed along the rocks, came out on the other path, then began a long climb up the slope until at last we reached the place of rendezvous and sat down to wait.

In a short while Kang and the others, with the man held like a heavy flour sack between them, came puffing up the hill and deposited their load opposite us. Siatze and I sat looking at him. Since he had dropped over the roof and let us in the courtyard, Siatze had taken no part in the proceedings. He just sat there like a stone now and stared.

I moved across the path and looked down at the man. His lips were moving and I bent down and made out the words. "I'll go. I'll go." He repeated them like a chant, but inside the chant the sound was bubbly and frothy with fear.

The woman sat down beside him and took his head and pillowed it in her lap. Out of decency, I moved away, crossed to the other side of the path and sat down beside Siatze and looked at them.

The sight of the woman, sitting on the hill under the stars, with the head of her terrified husband in her lap, moved me. I knew most Chinese farm women were highly emotional, wept, screamed and often went into incoherent hysterics when something untoward upset their daily existence. But this woman had neither cried, complained nor shown any other feeling than sympathy for her husband. I wanted to ask Siatze what he thought of this woman, but I felt guilty about my sympathy.

You are a sloppy intellectual, said a part of me. This man has shot innocent people and buried others alive. He deserves whatever he gets. Yes, but the woman. One could admire her.

Then Siatze grabbed my arm and pointed and I looked down the hill and saw the Field Mouse coming at the head of the other two columns. He came up breathing hard, but laughing a little.

"That mother of a fort," he said. "It was so high I never thought I would get up."

Abruptly, he stopped speaking and looked at the man and the woman, then at Kang.

"Take the woman away," he said softly.

I felt the flesh crawling on my back.

A militiaman leaned down and touched the woman.

"Come," he said.

She put her husband's head on the ground, but said nothing to him. Then she rose silently and walked down the path with the militia.

The Field Mouse, Kang and I were alone beside the prostrate man. Kang clicked back the bolt on his rifle. I felt a band tightening around my chest and I wanted to reach up and pull it apart.

"Go," said the Field Mouse, walking away.

We walked on. I could hear my boots coming down on the path and I realized I was listening with all my might. My ears seemed about to burst. Then I heard a dull report and a second one. . . .

"How was it?" I asked Kang later.

"He was lying on his back and I stood over him."

"Were his eyes open?"

"Yes, he was staring at me."

"Did he say anything?"

"He said, 'there is nothing worthy of revenge between you and me. I have some treasure left. Take it. I give it to you.' "

"I let him talk. I wanted to find out where his pistol was. I couldn't get anything out of him so I just stood and listened and all the time I was sighting on his forehead. I went up and down like this with the rifle so I'd be sure and hit him. His head split in two. Then I put another in his stomach. I didn't like to use so many bullets."

Now as I heard the firing, I felt it deep inside me. My thoughts were spinning around like a top. I had the feeling of something that had started out as a mild adventure and then brought unlooked-for consequences.

I looked up the path at the militiamen and the woman in front of all at the head of the column. She moved slowly on her shoeless feet and the militiamen prodded her with rifles.

"Faster," they said.

The column only crawled now. I wondered why they didn't put the woman at the end of the column with a guard. Now she was holding us all up. I did not like to see her prodded and pushed. A widow of five minutes should be comforted, not pushed on bare feet across hilly trails.

On impulse, I walked to the head of the column, took the woman by the wrist and gave her a gentle tug to show that she should go faster. Then I made a few moderately swift steps forward, my hand sliding down to hers and giving it a slight squeeze as if to say, "There's a friend here," and she responded immediately, her feet tottering along quickly behind mine.

"*Aiya!*" said a militiaman. "That's the way! Pull her!"

It isn't pulling that makes her go faster, I thought, but sympathy. I was in a rage.

We were walking across the rolling country now and I felt the rise and fall of the path under my boots, felt the woman's quick, stumbling steps behind me, felt her hand tighten against mine and her fingers seeking mine. From the palm of her hand against mine, there came something so intensified, so demanding that it seemed a current moved up my arm and filled my whole body with a desire to comfort her. She drew closer to me, then said something in a low voice that I could not understand. I looked down at her, trying to catch her words. Her face turned up to mine. It was so dark I could distinguish nothing of her features: whether she was ugly or pretty, old or young. She could not tell I was a foreigner. To each other, we were faceless beings in the dark—nameless, without country and without politics. I had never thought that you could respond to a woman in time of danger nor that you could know anybody that you could not see, yet, I responded to this woman and thought I knew her feelings better than those of many women I had known all my life. And though I could not see the expression on her face, it seemed to me that she was looking at me with gratefulness, trust and—hope.

We walked on. The stars faded and now the morning star gleamed alone by itself in the sky. I knew we were safe from pursuit and I slowed my walk and the woman gave my hand a grateful squeeze.

We went on toward the west and the sky grew paler behind us. As we came through the narrow valley and across the rocks to the village from which we had jumped off, it was just growing light. I pressed the woman's hand once, released her and turned to look at her. She was young and pretty and she was smiling at me. If she was startled to see a foreigner, she gave no sign.

The Field Mouse came up and handed the woman a pair of shoes he had obtained from a farmer's house. Quietly, she put them on.

"How do you feel about my executing your husband?" the Field Mouse said.

The question was so sudden and brutal that I flinched. The woman looked up and laughed.

"He was an evil man. He always beat me."

I looked at her. She was smiling. I could not tell whether it was bravado, cunning or honest naturalness.

"You may leave now," said the Field Mouse. "If you cannot support yourself, the 8th Route Army will help you."

She nodded once, smiled and turned back on the path we had just come over. I watched her go with strange and undefined emotions. She will pass her husband's body on the hillside, I thought. What will she do? Throw herself on him and weep? Spit on him and curse? Or walk by and laugh?

I looked east toward the hill over which she had gone and then beyond to the Kuomintang lines. The sun was just peeping over the horizon. It was going to be a lovely spring day.

PART X

THE REVOLT OF WOMEN

❧

42. Gold Flower's Story

I EMERGED from the guerrilla areas of Anyang in a disturbed and confused frame of mind. Many of the things that I had heard and seen in that dark medieval world just would not fit into the usual Westerner's conception of war, revolution or even life itself. The fact that a woman should laugh just after her husband had been murdered on a lonely hillside somehow seemed inexplicable. Was there a connection between that woman's laugh and the Chinese Revolution? I soon came to think so. For it was a curious fact that as I began to mull over in my mind all that I had learned during the land reform and the people's war, I discovered that the Communists' drive for power was touched at almost every point by women, by their feelings, by their relationship to men, by their social status, by their symbol as an object of property, religion and sex. Because of this discovery, I decided that I would make use of the first available opportunity to talk with a Chinese farm woman about her life, her innermost thoughts, her secret feelings.

This I knew would be difficult, for Chinese farm women will not usually talk alone with men, especially foreigners, yet an opportunity of this kind was offered me sooner than I expected.

Having said good-by to Mr. Chen and Liu Ming-chi, I made my way back across the North China Plain and after several days' journey came to Lichiachuang, a small village of about three hundred people in central Hopei. Here I found my further progress halted by the flood waters of the Grand Canal which Kuomintang troops had broken open to block the advance of Communist armies in the area. Not wishing to wander out across the flood waters and offer myself as a target for potshots from either side, I decided to sit down in the village for the moment and await developments. During this period, I tried to persuade several farm women to talk to me about themselves, but they were never willing. After some difficulty, I managed to win the confidence of a

275

peasant girl named Kinhua, whose husband was away in Chiang Kai-shek's areas, and gradually I persuaded her to tell me the story of her life. I found it so interesting that I postponed my departure from the village another week and talked with her every day for eight, nine and ten hours a day. I will try to tell her story here just as she told it to me in a flood of bitter tears, angry imprecations and emotional outbursts of despair, frustration and hope. I am condensing her words but nevertheless I shall tell her story at some length because I think it reveals more clearly than a dozen speeches by Mao Tze-tung just what are some of the techniques of the Chinese Communist party and why they were able to win so many people to their cause.

I should perhaps mention here that I borrowed a young English-speaking professor named Yang Bio, who had come over from Peiping, to translate for me—not that this was necessary, for the girl, despite some peasant inflections and an initial embarrassment, spoke clearly enough for me to understand and in a fashion more articulate than most anyone I met in the Liberated Areas. However, having an interpreter enabled me to copy down everything the girl said and this I did.

At the time I met Kinhua—which translates into English as Gold Flower—she had just turned twenty-one. She was a rather attractive girl, with a pleasant face, embellished by a tiny mouth, an upturned nose and a pair of somber brown eyes. Thin and wiry, she appeared more dainty than the average North China farm woman. She had the slender wrists and ankles that Frenchmen so much admire. Her feet were not bound and her hair was bobbed. We sat and talked in her home —a clay-hut affair of four rooms running in a square around a court-yard—and this is the story she told me.

She had been born in a village ten miles away where conditions were primitive, food scarce, comforts unknown, and she had worked hard ever since she could remember.

When she was fifteen, during the middle of the Japanese invasion, she fell in love with a boy named Lipao, the primary school classmate of her elder brother. He was, to hear her tell it, a distinctly good-looking boy of seventeen years, with a slender, trim body, odd, restful eyes, and a queer deep voice that had the ring of an old bell. It was the voice that got under Gold Flower's reserve: it was so different from the coarse peasant tones to which she was accustomed. Whenever he came to see her brother, Gold Flower would drop whatever she was doing and go and listen to their conversation.

As she heard Lipao talking, his eyes earnest with youthful enthusiasm, his whole body bent forward intent on what he was saying, talking of such grand and, to her, unheard of things as freedom, democracy and the future of China, her heart yearned over him. He was so noble! She wanted to tell him so, but her brother was always present and she never had the opportunity. So she just sat near him, sent him secret smiles and followed his every movement with her eyes.

He soon became aware of her interest, and once, when her brother left the room for a moment, he leaned over close to Gold Flower and said: "I have learned something from your eyes. I know your heart."

Ashamed, yet delighted, Gold Flower was so excited she could make no reply. Later, she longed to have a secret conversation with him. But how?

It is necessary for a North China village girl to give the appearance, if not of disdain for men, at least of disinterest in them, since decorum and dignity rank above love as the virtues most highly prized in China, and girls stay behind the walls of their homes until they are married and even after that. Although there are thousands of authentic instances of Chinese men selling their women into wifery, concubinage or whoredom, there is scarcely any record of a girl indulging a romance with a boy with the consent and knowledge of her parents; and the descent for a girl breaking this rule is very swift, since anyone finding her alone with a boy could accuse her of selling her maidenhood. So hypocritical is Chinese society that while farmers may commit adultery with their tenants' wives without fear of punishment and while every village has and tolerates at least one "broken shoe," a young boy and girl, no matter how innocent their intentions, may neither talk alone together, hold hands nor much less kiss.

Under these circumstances, it must be accounted an act of courage, infatuation, or insanity that Gold Flower, another time, when her brother left the room for a moment, leaned over and whispered in Lipao's ear: "My family will be away tomorrow, will you come?"

The next day, he obtained leave from school, and by nine o'clock was at her gate. She blushed as he entered, and she gave a little affected laugh to keep herself in countenance. Then—so a stray visitor or her family returning would think no one was at home—she led him to her room and immediately closed and bolted the door.

Gold Flower had thought only to have a secret talk with a boy whose intellectual attainments she admired. But her companion mistook her unconventional behavior and the bolted door for an invitation of another sort, and he tried to make love to her. At first shocked, then excited, then frightened, Gold Flower, rebuffed him, half-succumbed to him, then angrily told him to leave. But when he rose to go, Gold Flower's heart was thrown into a turmoil. At one moment she was afraid of not being loved, at another the thought that Lipao wanted her virginity as a kind of medal of conquest tortured her. Had she been sure of his affections, or had she ever had another experience with a man, perhaps she would have let him go, but to lose the friendship of such a boy seemed to her at the moment the worst possible disaster.

Her passion carried her to the point of falling at Lipao's feet and throwing her arms around his knees. She pleaded with him not to try to make love to her—for she would be betrothed to another man—while at the same time she begged him not to desert her for she was lonely. "Be my friend, my elder brother, my lover—in everything but that be my lover," she had cried. Moved by her words and her attitude of humility, the boy overcame his annoyance at being thwarted and agreed to her conditions.

In this way, a romance—childish, but forbidden by Chinese village code—had begun. And so it continued, for when her family returned Gold Flower still contrived ways to meet her lover. Every night when the others were in bed—her three brothers, father and mother, all together on one kang—Gold Flower would tiptoe out her door and softly let back the latch on the front gate. Soon there would be a creaking at the gate and then a shadowy form would flit swiftly across the court-yard and Gold Flower's door would open and then shut again.

During these nightly meetings in Gold Flower's room, the couple poured out much talk from their hearts, but they did not make love, never kissed, only held hands, looked deeply into one another's eyes and swore eternal friendship.

Because her actions were so contrary to village morality, Gold Flower when she first paused to think about her conduct, felt stunned with remorse. But one day when her girl friends gathered in her room to sew flowered shoes she began to feel differently. The girls played the game: "what kind of a man would you like to marry?" and Gold Flower, her cheeks faintly red, replied: "I should like to marry some-one like my neighbor Lipao; he is so handsome and tender."

Then teased to distraction by her friends, and in terror lest her secret be discovered, she shrugged her shoulders and said with an air of worldly wisdom:

"What is the use of talking about what kind of a man we would like to marry, when we have no choice in the matter?"

"Yes," her friends had answered. "How stupid it all is! Our parents arrange everything for us. Like as not we'll get an ugly husband."

The girls wished they had been born in England, France or America, where they heard women married men they loved. They had vague feel-ings that they were living in a "black society," and since in their hearts they were rebels against this society, every one of them thought it all right to have a secret lover.

These conversations gave Gold Flower pleasure, for they clothed her affair with Lipao in a moral garment of which it had hitherto been barren. She even began to revel in her defiance of society and sought proofs that her adventure was making a better woman of her. Some-times she would take her small mirror from under her pillow and look happily at her own face. Never had it seemed more beautiful. "I have a lover! a lover!" she would say, delighting in the idea like a child with a new toy.

The days following passed with new sweetness. The first time Lipao told her he loved her she nearly fell fainting in his arms with ecstasy. Then, because he asked for nothing in exchange for this love, she began to think that generosity, nobility of soul and humanity existed only in this young student.

Lipao taught her how to write a few simple characters. Thenceforth, when she wanted to see him, she wrote the character "come" on a scrap of paper and put it in the hollow of a tree by the village pond. Lipao came to find it and put there another note saying "yes" or "no," or "tonight" or "tomorrow," or "my room" or "your room," for these were nearly all the characters she could read.

Brief as were these notes, Gold Flower guarded them like a treasure, hiding them in a corner of her kang beneath the reed matting, and taking them out every once in a while and tracing the characters Lipao had written over again with her finger.

In fact, the whole art of writing seemed to Gold Flower some powerful black magic. The word "come" often had for her the semblance of a holy and potent incantation, for she only had to write and suddenly —poof!—in answer to her sorcery, Lipao would be in her room.

In other ways, too, the whole horizon of her thoughts and life lifted. Entirely absorbed, before Lipao's coming, with that mass of work which is the lot of any Chinese farm girl, Gold Flower had never thought about passions and love affairs, save in relation to the gossip she had heard in the mouths of other women.

But now these stories began to seem almost as real to her as her own life, and she began to adopt the tricks of every romance of which she had ever heard. Because it was traditional with the heroines of her remembered stories to sew garments for their lovers, Gold Flower began to make Lipao a jacket. Her mother noticed this and became suspicious. Gold Flower put her off, saying:

"His mother has no time to sew, I'll just throw this together carelessly and help her out."

To herself, however, she said: "I must show my love through my work," and she began to make a jacket of which any big city tailor might well have been proud. Instead of the usual five buttonholes, she made thirteen, and around each hole she embroidered a flower. Such buttonholes are known to young boys and girls in this part of China as "the thirteen precious jewels," and Gold Flower was very happy in her work, believing she was having a romance in the best tradition.

Because she had grown very sentimental, she ran with the jacket to

Lipao and insisted that he try it on. All the while she danced around him crying: "Do you like it? Oh, tell me, do you like it?" Her enthusiasm was so captivating and her sentiment so infectious that Lipao had answered just as her heart had wished.

"I love it because it was made by my own true love's hands."

As was the custom, he tried to give Gold Flower money to buy thread to make herself a pair of flowered shoes. At first, she refused, saying, "I don't want anything from you, but your love." But when she saw her refusal saddened him, she took the money, but she never bought anything for herself and spent every dollar to buy cloth, thread and needles to make garments for Lipao.

Gold Flower often thought this was the happiest time of her life—a honeymoon she might have called it had she known the word or been aware of the custom. She would have liked to shout her love for Lipao to the whole village, and though this was impossible, she longed for some friend in whom she could confide. But not only was this denied her, but she had to redouble her caution to prevent the affair from becoming known. By degrees a vague uneasiness took possession of her. She was no longer, as formerly, completely carefree. She began to wonder if she ought not to yield to Lipao, or whether, since she could not completely satisfy his love, cease to see him any more. Her refusal to give herself to him had at first proceeded from strength, but now she found herself wondering if it was not weakness that prevented her from fully consummating their love.

Then she asked herself what would become of her—if her parents would betroth her, and to whom? But Lipao's face always rose before her and she could not picture any other husband. Yet there always rang in her mind that thought: "If you should be betrothed! If you should be betrothed!" At night she could not sleep; she tossed and turned and beat her pillow. Thinking that, after all, it would be worse to give herself to someone she did not know than to Lipao, whom she loved, she promised herself to throw herself in Lipao's arms the next time he came, but when he did come, she could not do it and remained silent.

In the autumn of 1942, Gold Flower was betrothed to a man named Chang, who lived in the village where we were now sitting, and whom she had never seen. At almost the same time, Lipao was also betrothed by his parents to another girl.

As was customary in many Chinese villages, Gold Flower was not informed of her betrothal and only gradually grew aware of it through the frequent visits of the matchmaker, the unwonted preparations in the house and the sly jibes made to her by the neighbors.

It was an unusually lovely autumn. But Gold Flower was miserable most of the time. The matchmaker had told her parents her betrothed was only two years older than her and would make her an excellent husband, but her friends who had seen Chang said he was fifteen years older and had an ugly white face. Gold Flower was depressed. Only with Lipao was she gay. Her tenderness, in fact, grew each day as she thought of her husband-to-be. The more she thought of her real sweetheart, the more she loathed her intended husband. Never had Lipao seemed so desirable to her, and never had marriage seemed more hateful. Never had her parents appeared more disagreeable, society more unfair, life more unjust. She insisted that Lipao come to see her every night, and when he came she decked herself out in her finest clothes. But there came a time when she could not see him any more. Neighbors were constantly in the house, helping with preparations for the wedding, and she had to dance attendance and completely forego her meetings with Lipao.

The wedding was drawing near and Gold Flower grew more tense. She hardly heard what was spoken to her. Her mother had strange fits of anxiety about her daughter. Remembering her own wedding, she wanted to give Gold Flower some words of comfort and advice. But Gold Flower held herself aloof.

She had begun to hate her mother.

* * *

Two nights before her wedding, Lipao came to bid her good-by. Because neighbors were in the house helping with last-minute arrangements for the wedding, Gold Flower hastily and secretly led her lover into the fields. A full moon had just risen and they walked hand in hand across the meadows until they reached the village pond and sat down beneath a tree. Gold Flower saw her lover's face all compounded of shadows and moonlight and she could not bear the thought of leaving him.

"If we were married," she said, "we would be the only happy couple in the world."

The boy abruptly turned toward her. "Let us make this our wedding night," he said. "Take me, love me," he pleaded, grasping her hands in his own.

For a moment she was silent.

"I can't," she said.

"Do take me," he said, and he put his arm around her. But she held herself stiff.

"No—I can't," she said.

"Why?"

"I can't—let us go back."

282   CHINA SHAKES THE WORLD

He dropped his arm and looked across the fields, saying in a low tone, his head held away from her.

"But I love you—and I want you so much—like this, here and now. We may never have the chance again," he said quickly. "Why should you not give yourself to me whom you love? Why to an ugly old man you've never seen?"

This expression of Lipao's jealousy was not unwelcome to Gold Flower, but at the same time she was befogged by his words, by his harping on the fact that she was going into the bed of a man she did not even know. Her eyes began to swell with tears. Mournfully she peered at Lipao. Then she got on her knees and crawled close beside him and put her lips up against his ear and said in a tiny voice:

"Do you know that I can never make a jacket for you again? This is the last time I can talk to you. The last time I can ever give you my words and my heart. Please be kindly with me."

Feeling ashamed, he turned to her, but she held him off with her hands, then stood up crying.

He tried to comfort her. "Don't cry so," he said. "I am desolate that you have to marry such an ordinary man. But do not give up hope. Maybe our marriages will not work out and then someday, somehow, we can get together again. No matter what happens, I will always love you."

Beneath the influence of his kindly words and his voice, which had always affected her, a little fire began to burn up within Gold Flower, and something in her heart sprang alive in consequence. Where his pleadings had left her cold, his kindness now warmed her. She was excited by a mournful happiness, and she could no longer bear to listen to anything. She went close to Lipao, straight to his breast, threw her arms around his neck and for the first time—kissed him. How long she was in his embrace she did not know. But for a moment she forgot everything, but to kiss. While her heart beat against his, Gold Flower felt nothing but rapture. But when their lips parted, division began at once, society crept back between them. And though she kissed him again, her kisses were no longer joyful, for they were too full of pain and parting, and the more she kissed, the sadder she became until her heart swelled up with sorrow and she tore herself away and ran sobbing across the fields.

Gold Flower woke the next day feeling ill. And far off, unreal, seemed last night's romance. The day had turned cold. Toward evening a wind blew in from the north and it began to rain. As darkness descended over the village, Gold Flower's family went out to attend a party given by the neighbors in honor of the coming wedding. Gold Flower stood at the gate and followed them with her eyes until they were swallowed up in the mist which was rising grayly from the ground. In a moment she heard the sound of shouting coming from the party and the clanging of beaten musical instruments and the piping of a flute.

She went back indoors and began pacing from corner to corner in her room, now and then casting hopeful glances toward the door. She was longing for her lover to come and claim her once more and this time she would not deny him. Why had she refused him? It was just cowardice on her part. Perhaps he hates me, she thought with a sudden rush of fear. Why had she failed him? Now he would not come.

Shame at her certain ruin—for she believed her lover could not respect her if she gave her maidenhood to another man—drove her to a desperate step. She resolved to go to Lipao at once, to seek him out in his home and give herself to him.

Bending beneath the rain, she made her way to Lipao's home. Abandoning all caution, she passed through the courtyard and reached Lipao's room. The door was unlocked and she went in without knocking. The room was in darkness, she called her lover's name, but there was no answer. She went up to the bed and ran her hands over it; there was no one there. She ran through every room in the house. It was deserted. The walls around her seemed to be contracting, the ceiling was crushing her, and she ran out, splashing heedlessly in the puddles made by the rain. Swaying drunkenly she reached home.

Leaning against the devil screen in front of the courtyard, she tried to catch her breath. Over the wall came the sigh of a flute and the clanging of gongs. Her wedding music! She put her hands to her ears, then raised her face to the sky. The sky was heavy and dark; down from it came a voluminous splashing of rain. Lost in a stupor and having little consciousness of what she was doing, she wandered about the courtyard.

She was then fifteen. It was her wedding eve. A happy time! But she no longer wanted to live. Quickly, she went to the kitchen and picked up a rope. Groping in the dark, she made her way to her own room, found a bench and dragged it over, near the door. Climbing on the bench, she threw one end of the rope over a beam above the door, tied a slip knot in the rope, stuck her head in the noose, kicked the bench away and hanged herself.

A few moments later, her parents, returning from the party, found her and cut her down. Neighbors, summoned by her parents poured into the house and after two hours' hard work, brought Gold Flower back to life. When she woke, Gold Flower saw her mother weeping with her head on the bed.

Drying her tears, the mother stood up and said solemnly "You must wait for fate."

At these words, which Chinese parents have used for countless generations to badger their daughters into unwanted marriages, an icy chill crept around Gold Flower's heart. So she had not done with this life, she thought, with all this treachery, with this black society, this slavery. She hated it all. When her mother repeated the phrase, Gold Flower felt her gorge rising like a bitter poison in her throat.

"Do you remember the day you were young?" she said. "Was it suitable for you to marry someone fifteen years older than you?" Suddenly she raised herself like a galvanized corpse. "You want to kill me!"

Her mother backed away in astonishment. Feeling she had to struggle, Gold Flower summoned all her strength and, rising from the bed, pushed her mouth into her mother's face.

"I won't obey your commands," she shouted. "You old fool! You stupid woman! You donkey!"

The neighbors, scandalized at this attack, tried to calm Gold Flower, but she would not be still. She soon began spitting like a cat. Her lips became drawn in a snarl. Her limbs were convulsed, her whole body taut as a violin string. She began to scream loudly. She cursed her mother, railed at her, implored her to kill her, and thrust away with stiffened arms anyone who dared approach her.

But finally she exhausted herself. Weeping and choked by sobs that shook her whole body, she collapsed on the bed. She lay at full length, her eyelids closed, her hands open and motionless. Two streams of tears flowed out of her half-closed eyes and fell on the straw matting under head. Once in a while her lips moved in a whisper: "No . . . no." And she savagely gritted her teeth.

The neighbors closed in on Gold Flower and began to offer her words of unwanted comfort and unwanted advice. Gold Flower felt suffocated by the ring of faces above her. But they would not go away. Hour after hour, the neighbors pounded at her. She felt as if a great weight were pressing her down. Not able to marry the man she loved, not able even to kill herself so that she could remain loyal to her lover, completely done in and drained of all strength, she at last fell into a deep stupor.

When Gold Flower awoke, it was her wedding day. The sedan chair was already at the gate. Ruthlessly, she was put aboard.

It was past noon when the sedan chair set her down in the courtyard of her new home, and Gold Flower stepped out and saw her husband for the first time. He was grinning at her appreciatively. But Gold Flower looked at his features with an air of shocked loathing, realizing that her friends had warned her only too well. He appeared twenty years older than she. With the image of Lipao still fresh in her mind, her husband appeared doubly ugly. He had a chalk face, with a mole on one cheek from which hung a long, black hair. His teeth were crooked and of uneven length like tombstones in a graveyard. His nose was flat, his mouth full, his lips loose. A perfect ogre, thought Gold Flower.

With lagging steps, as if she were entering a prison, Gold Flower followed her husband into the house. Her mind was occupied by only one thought: When can I ever escape from here and return to Lipao? Her husband left her alone with his in-laws and curious neighbors. They engaged in fatuous jokes at her expense, pawed her, felt her arm muscles, turned her this way and that, examining her as they might examine a metal pot on the fairgrounds to see if it were worth buying and bringing into the home. Under their handling, Gold Flower froze stiff, feeling that she was no longer a human being, but some kind of a curious, half-dead object.

Night came. She was alone with her husband. She had been wondering about this moment, trying to imagine what would happen, what she would do. When he sat down beside her, she tried to smile at him. When he slid his hand along her arm, she pressed away from him. He took off most of his clothes, and asked her to do the same. She would not. "Why?" he said. "Is not marriage for this?" She felt choked. She crept to a corner of the kang and dissolved in tears. He pulled her out, complimenting her on her good looks, on her youth. Bitterly, she raised her eyes to his face. "You are old and ugly," she said, then bent her head and sobbed. "It won't do you any good to cry," he said. She tried to get off the kang; he pulled her back, slapped her face. Without knowing what she was doing, Gold Flower began to scream. He almost tore her head off with a blow of his fist. Blood ran down Gold Flower's face. He struck her again and again until she was quiet. She lay back exhausted and in a quick fit of passion he raped her.

With a smile of satisfaction, her husband fell asleep. But Gold Flower hardly slept at all. She was thinking, tossing and turning. Her body ached all over, but it was her spirit that had been bruised most of all. She felt that she had betrayed her lover. Some fatal defect in her character had prevented her from giving herself to Lipao until now it was too late. The notion that her husband had taken what belonged to her lover filled her childish soul with a sort of horror. She muttered to herself: "It's awful, what's been done to me—awful!" If it had only been Lipao! How happy that would have made her! Now she could never have him. That was awful! To stay here—more awful still!

Emotion, when you are young and give real vent to it, is sharp, clear, terrifying. And Gold Flower fell asleep, seeing before her the endless stretch of the years. She was caught in a prison and there was no escape. All in one night her life had been ruined.

On the ninth day after her marriage, Gold Flower, as was the local custom, returned to her parents' home. All her vindictiveness poured out on her mother's head.

"You cheated me," she angrily accused her mother. "Do you remember your own marriage? My father was older than you. You, yourself, told me how sad you were. Have you forgotten your own story that you should so carelessly give me—your only jewel—away to a man like that?"

Her mother tried to teach her patience by quoting the old classics. "The wood has been turned into a boat. Everything is fixed. You must remember the old saying: 'A good girl never marries twice.'"

Gold Flower stamped her foot and tears of frustration came to her eyes. Then she softened again, and spoke gently to her mother, because she realized her marriage was not the fault of her parents, but the fault of society itself. Her mother surprised her by saying: "It is not only you who hates society, but me, too."

The next day, while her parents were out, Lipao appeared in her doorway. Almost mechanically, she asked him to enter and sit down. He saw she was unhappy. "You would not believe me when I asked you to give me your love," he said. A bitter retort sprang to Gold Flower's lips. But only for a moment. He sat there, unaltered, just as he had sat there for many nights. The thought that he was about to go out of her life forever hurt her. She wanted to beg her lover's pardon, but she did not know what to say. She was ashamed to look at him; she did not dare make love to him; she thought she had been ruined and no longer deserved such a virtuous young man.

"If I had been brave enough," she admitted, "I would have given myself to you. But now it's too late. I regret my disloyalty."

She watched Lipao rise, say good-by, and go. She called after him: "Work hard, do something for society, forget me." She looked mournfully at his disappearing back, but she did not cry. Already, she was beyond such sentimentality.

Gold Flower tried to build a new life with her husband's family. But there was nothing but hate on which to build. Besides herself and her husband, they had in the house her father and mother-in-law and a younger sister-in-law. The mother-in-law, showing the effects of a hard life, was little more than a living corpse, so Gold Flower did not suffer much from that quarter as did most Chinese brides. But her husband made up for this lack, treating her worse than a dozen mothers-in-law. She had to wait on him, day and night. When he went to sleep she had to take off his shoes and clothing; in the morning, she had to put them on again. She had to light his cigarettes, pour his water, hand him the cup with both hands and with a subservient smile on her face. He struck her daily as a matter of course and beat her unmercifully if she did not obey his commands on the instant.

One night, just before going to bed, Gold Flower brought her husband a bowl of millet broth, some of which slopped over the edge and ran down on his thumb. Immediately, he flew into a rage, picked up a brush from a corner, beat her to the floor and then smashed her about the head. She did not dare scream, but tears came to her eyes. Kneeling on the ground she pleaded with him to forgive her carelessness. She tried to smile in order to soften his heart, but he beat her until he was exhausted. After two hours, he let her crawl back in bed.

Her father-in-law was little better. Gold Flower's mother sent a message that she was sick and wanted to see her daughter. The father-in-law would not let her go.

"Why have we married you?" he asked. "You are here to work for us and you belong to us and not your mother."

Gold Flower pleaded so hard that her father-in-law finally gave her permission to go. When she returned after two days, he ordered her to kneel down in the courtyard and beg his forgiveness for being late. She remained kneeling from noon till evening.

That night as she was taking off her husband's clothes, he asked her: "Tell me the truth. Do you really want to go your own way?"

Gold Flower, fearing further punishment, put on her best face and answered softly:

"I am a girl. I have never been married before. I do not intend to marry again. I shall serve you all my life. When I die, I shall be buried in your tomb."

She put a mask over her face and smiled at her husband. But in her mind she was thinking she was treated like a donkey or an ox, not as a woman. In order to keep her husband quiet, however, she put on her meekest air. She even quoted old proverbs at him.

"Flowers have seeds," she said; "grass has roots, man has heirs. Someday we shall have a baby and I shall raise him for you. We are both young now. But when you are old, I will still be young. Someday, when the harvest is poor and we have to beg, I shall go to the villages and beg for you first. I am a woman and must depend on you. So I must take care of you. If you are captured by bandits, I shall sell all my belongings and even my body to redeem you."

With such words, through three hard years, Gold Flower tried to turn aside her husband's wrath and make her tormented life bearable.

When she was eighteen, the North China famine struck her village. Though her husband and other members of the family still ate millet, Gold Flower had only husks and leaves which she picked from the trees to eat. With conditions growing worse, her husband decided to go to Tientsin and become a merchant. Dutifully, Gold Flower saw him to the gate. No sentimentalist, he did not waste any words on a fond farewell, but snapped out a series of last-minute orders.

"Let my father and sister eat first. If there is anything left, you may eat." Then, turning on her savagely, he warned: "You must preserve my face. If you are irregular in your conduct, I will beat you to death."

Gold Flower's heart sank at these harsh words, but she summoned a smile to her face. "Do not worry," she said, "I want only you."

During this period of her life, a profound change had taken place in Gold Flower. Years so spent always take their toll, nor is there anything more tragic than hopelessness, with its wiping out of the future. Gold Flower, though only eighteen, was already tired of her existence. She hated society, she hated her husband, she hated life itself. She contemplated suicide again, but was restrained by the thought of the sorrow she would bring her mother. When her mother died, she determined she would kill herself.

From her married life, Gold Flower had come to know the truth of the old saying: "Heaven is Man: Earth is Woman." Then, too, she had heard new widows wailing over their husbands' bodies: "Oh, my Heaven! My Heaven!" and her receptive mind had grasped the fact that it was not just her husband but all men who were destined by birth to be the rulers over women.

Gold Flower could not help but accept these laws of society and outwardly she knuckled under to her husband like a slave—meek, obedient, fearful. But in the innermost recesses of her heart, her thoughts were revolving in a different fashion. There, deep down inside her, she was engrossed in one thing only: to pay back, insult by insult, blow by blow, everything she had suffered at her husband's hands. Even as she was saying good-by to her husband at the gate, she was thinking: I will take my vengeance on you someday. Just wait. The day will come.

And as there was a Gold Flower, more or less, beaten and bruised, saddened and soured, in every farm in North China, she became a portent. The Communist party saw her and schemed to serve her and themselves through her. She was that spirit that forgets nothing and forgives nothing. There she stood at her gate, slow-burning revenge incarnate, waiting a better time, waiting an opportunity.

*　　*　　*

In August 1945, a small unit of the 8th Route Army entered Gold Flower's village. They stayed only a few hours and then, having announced they were going to fight the Japanese, passed on. A week later, a county cadre entered the village and called a meeting. Having announced that he represented the government of the 8th Route Army, he declared: "The people and the 8th Route Army belong to the same family." Gold Flower who heard these words said to herself: "That is impossible; you are not even from our village and so how can you be from our family?"

Some time later, the cadre called all the women of the village together and asked them to organize a Women's Association. He declared that every woman had the right to equality with man and he begged all those women who had suffered most to come and meet secretly with him. The words of the cadre excited Gold Flower and gave her much food for thought, but she did not dare go to the secret meeting and besides she did not believe anything would come of it.

"Someone says the 8th Route Army has come to release us," she remarked to her sister-in-law, "but just look: the Japanese have been driven away, yet we two girls in this village still suffer. I think it's just a rumor that the 8th Route helps women."

A few days later when the county cadre went away, without anything extraordinary having happened, Gold Flower felt her suspicions had been fully confirmed. A Women's Association had been formed, but nothing else had happened. "So that's all the 8th Route Army can do," she said to herself. "The poor things."

She was surprised when one of her friends, a girl named Dark Jade, who had been elected a cadre of the local Women's Association came secretly to see her. Since the girls were old friends, they dared speak freely to each other.

"We must release ourselves from the domination of men," Dark Jade told Gold Flower. "But we cannot do it individually, we must all stand together and release ourselves as a unit."

Gold Flower was skeptical. "That's all right for you," she said. "You are a cadre now and are protected by the government. But what about me? Who will protect me?"

"Listen," said Dark Jade, "tell me the truth about your suffering. I will not betray you."

Gold Flower was silent.

"Open your eyes, Gold Flower," said her friend. "This is our day. This means the end of our suffering. The beginning of our hope."

These words, because they were uttered by one of her own friends, kindled a spark in Gold Flower. "Oh, that would be wonderful, if true," she said. "Then the 8th Route Army would really be of our family."

Some days later, Dark Jade returned with a girl named Taowa. Gold Flower questioned them with infinite caution, trying to find out what their strange views of this newly promised life might be. She made up her mind, after rallying the other two on their temerity, that they had confidence in being able to obtain equality for the women in the village. Suddenly she blurted out to the two girls everything she had suffered. Once the words were out she had to use all her self-control. The speaking aloud of what had been going round and round in her mind for so long brought a rush of feeling such as she had not experienced since the days she had known Lipao. She bit her lips to keep back tears and sobs.

Then she was glad to hear her friends promising to do what they could to alleviate her sorry life. There was some difficulty about it, apparently, she was not curious to understand. The girls advised her to stay quietly at home and wait developments.

Within a few days, four women called on Gold Flower's father-in-law.

"Our investigation department has found out that you are treating your daughter-in-law badly," said Dark Jade.

The old man's jaws dropped open. He could not believe what he had heard. Recovering from his first astonishment, he burst out angrily, "Don't interfere with my family. I can do what I want with my daughter-in-law."

For a moment, the women cadres were nonplussed. Then Dark Jade spoke firmly. "We have been polite with you. We are doing this for your own welfare. We are trying to unite your family and make it happy."

Gold Flower's father-in-law jumped up excitedly. "Go away! Get out!" he shouted, gesturing with his arms.

One girl went away. The others fell into silence. In a moment the girl came back with fifteen more women. They were all carrying clubs and ropes. The old man was startled.

"Won't you really change your mind?" asked Dark Jade.

The old man raised his fists. "Nothing! Get out!"

"Bind him up!" shouted Dark Jade.

The old man's arm was just rising up when four women reached for it. The next moment he was caught like a fish in a net, both his arms bound with ropes. Gold Flower looked on amazed. This terror of her life had been overcome with miraculous ease. But when she saw her father-in-law being led through the gate, she experienced a momentary twinge of fear. "I have not suffered," she called. "Don't hurt my dear father."

She ran after the procession. "Father, don't worry," she said. But the old man was thoroughly alarmed. Wriggling his head from side to side, he tried to free himself from the rope. "Don't hurt my father," Gold Flower called, but her insides were turning over with laughter.

The procession went around a corner. Suddenly Gold Flower stopped short in the middle of the street. So this is what happiness is! she thought.

At last she believed in the 8th Route Army.

Gold Flower's father-in-law was held a prisoner for two days in a room in the building of the Women's Association. On the third day a general meeting of all the women in the village was called to decide what to do with him. Groups of women were making their way toward the center of the village. Never had they all come out on the streets before, and Gold Flower realized with a start that there were many women in the village whom she scarcely knew, so close had they heretofore kept indoors. Dark Jade and Taowa sought her out at home and led her to the hall of the Women's Association which had been established in the house of a puppet who had fled away when the Japanese had gone. When they arrived, the meeting was in full swing. Forty or fifty women were crowded into the room and on the steps of the courtyard outside. Up front, behind a table, was a smaller group of women, among them a girl whom Gold Flower had never seen before. Dark Jade went up to the front of the room and called for silence.

"Sisters," she announced, "a cadre from the district will now speak. I ask you to keep order."

The woman whom Gold Flower did not know stood up. From the very first words of her speech the others all came under the spell of her eloquence. She spoke of the feudalism of China, which was making the women slaves of men, of the common interests of brides and maidens, of the necessity to struggle against in-laws who oppressed daughters-in-law, of the need to fight parents who opposed freedom of marriage, of the aims of the 8th Route Army and the Communist party, which were carrying on a struggle against the old black society for the equality of women.

"We stretch out our sisterly hands to the oppressed women, and hope that in our struggle against the dictatorship of Chiang Kai-shek and the landlords we shall find faithful allies among the village women." Her voice sounded like a trumpet to Gold Flower. "At the front the workers and peasants of our democratic army are pouring out their blood against the soldiers of Chiang Kai-shek, armed by the American reactionaries; and in the rear, here in the villages, we must stand together and build a new society. And we shall build it! Hand in hand we shall go into the struggle against those who have enslaved us for two thousand years. And any man, any husband, any father-in-law who opposes us we shall beat to the ground and treat without mercy."

"That's right. Ah, that's right!" Gold Flower said to herself over and over again, as she listened to this woman who seemed to be speaking directly to her heart.

After the cadre finished speaking, Dark Jade, as chairman of the meeting, stood up. Her talk was burdened with clumsy, involved phrases, for she had never made a speech before. But the women listened to her with a great deal of sympathy as she was from their own village and was one of them. Rarely did someone interrupt, and her words found a vivid response.

Suddenly she paused, and Gold Flower felt herself grow weak as Dark Jade looked directly at her and spoke in an intimate way.

"Now," she said, "the time is come to talk of the case of our dearest sister, Gold Flower. Her sufferings are the sufferings of all women. If she is not freed, we cannot be free ourselves. . . ."

"That's true," shouted a voice from the center of the room. "Let us free Gold Flower."

"We must beat that old man," shrieked a voice in Gold Flower's ear. "Beat him. Beat him."

The other women began to take up the cry. Dark Jade pounded on the table with her fist, and the roar died away.

"Sisters! We must take our meeting to be a serious business so that it should not be shameful to the people and so that we should get a good result from our actions. As it is we have been treated unjustly enough by men, but we should not fall into the same error. We must have respect for our Women's Association so that everyone shall respect it. Let us first discuss how we shall treat the old man before we decide on anything."

The meeting finally decided to call in the old man.

Dark Jade threw open the door at Gold Flower's back and her father-in-law, his arms bound to his sides, was led in, guarded by two women. His face was pale and he glanced around the room uncertainly, blinking his old eyes.

"Old man! Be frank. Tell your bad treatment," said Dark Jade, and the rest of the women echoed her shouting: "Be frank!"

"I have done nothing." The father-in-law spoke with deliberate roughness. "If you don't believe me, you can ask my daughter-in-law." His eyes looked over the heads of the other women and fell on Gold Flower with a look that expressed his hostility, and seemed to say: "Be careful."

Looking at him from afar, Gold Flower felt a shiver of apprehension. She saw all eyes were on her. Pressing her fists against her chest, she ran on her toes to the front of the room. Then feeling it was now or never, she summoned all her determination.

"I married into your family—yes!" she hissed into his face. "But there's been no millet for me to eat. No clothes in the winter. Are these not facts? Do you remember how badly you have treated me in these past five years? Have you forgotten the time my mother was sick and you made me kneel in the courtyard for half a day? In the past I suffered from you. But I shall never suffer again. I must turn over now. I have all my sisters in back of me and I have the 8th Route Army."

She shouted these words. His face grew dark and red.

"Is it right for you to treat me like this? There is much that I could say. If I should speak, all these women would beat you to death."

As she said this, a wave of agitation ran through the meeting and a loud shout arose. "Speak!" Then as the roar of the voices sank, a thin girlish shriek pierced the growing quiet:

"Down with those who treat daughters-in-law badly! Long live our Women's Association!"

"You ate wheat flour bread and let me eat husks!" Gold Flower said, growing excited.

"Ai-a-a-ah!" a shout like a bursting shell rose from the women. The crowd groaned. In the heavy swelling voices, the sound of shuffling feet could be heard. Gold Flower felt herself being pushed aside. A fat girl was at her elbow and others were crowding close. "Let us spit in his face," said the fat girl. She drew back her lips over her gums and spat between the old man's eyes. Others darted in, spat in his face, and darted away again. The roar of voices grew louder. The old man remained standing with his face red and his beard matted with saliva. His knees were trembling and he looked such a poor object that the women laughed and their grumbling and groaning grew quieter. Then Dark Jade, pushing the others back, cried:

"Are you ready to reform yourself?"

"I will change." The old man's voice was low and subdued.

"Will you torture your daughter any more?"

"No."

"All women unite," the same girlish voice that had cried from the crowd before shouted out in another slogan.

"Women unite," echoed the crowd.

"Beat down conservatives," cried the voice again.

"Down with conservatives," echoed the crowd.

Now that Gold Flower's father-in-law had confessed his "sins," the meeting was over. But first someone was sent for a guarantor who stood up before all the women and promised:

"If Old Man Chang treats his daughter-in-law badly again, I shall bring him to you."

When Gold Flower's father-in-law had gone, a group of the younger women gathered around to congratulate her.

"My turning over is all due to you," she told them. "I know now that you are powerful. I know, too, that the 8th Route Army has done something for me."

That night when she went home, her father-in-law was so ashamed he could not hold up his head.

"Was this overturning movement your doing?" he asked.

"No, it was not my doing," Gold Flower said. She was still cautious.

"I know you are telling the truth," he said.

"There are sister groups in the village which investigate the bad treatment of women," said Gold Flower. "They know everything."

He looked at his daughter-in-law in fright. Gold Flower smiled to herself.

*   *   *

Although so short a time had elapsed, the Gold Flower who had previously submitted to every kind of evil treatment in her home was a very different girl from the Gold Flower who went about the village after the "reform" of her father-in-law. The very manner of shaking off "Papa" showed it. No longer did she keep her head bowed down and speak only when spoken to. She did not assume, as a matter of course, that her father-in-law was right in everything he said or did, but now argued out any question that displeased her. She ate the same things as did the rest of the family and when her father-in-law took a piece of cloth from a box and said, "Make some clothes for yourself," she began to develop a new pride in her appearance. Because she had always been kept indoors, she made a point of going out at all times of the day. And she would throw out her chest, hold her head high and look at nobody.

Gold Flower, who had never imagined that such freedoms could exist for women, had the sense to see that every woman in the village must be as free as herself before the "struggle" against man's domination could be fully won and the victory guaranteed. Therefore when she was elected head of a group of ten women, she became very zealous in investigating "bad" mothers-in-law and "backward" husbands. All the sly tricks that she had learned to avoid her husband's anger, she now summoned as her aid in the battle against oppressive parents. "Does your daughter-in-law treat you well?" she would say to a woman. "Does she obey your orders?" And the unsuspecting woman would answer: "You know how bad things have become since the 8th Route Army came here. My daughter-in-law goes out when she pleases. You have eyes; you can see." Pretending sympathy, Gold Flower would bid the woman good-by. Then she would hide under a window, all the antennae of her suspicions spreading out to catch word of a family quarrel. Then, having collected her evidence, she would pounce on the hapless mother-in-law and haul her before a "reform" meeting.

In the year 1947, Chiang Kai-shek's offensive pressed hard on North China, and Gold Flower was afraid that the 8th Route Army might be defeated and her new freedoms wiped out with the stroke of a sword. The exhortations of the Communist party to increase farm production fell on her ears like a clarion call. She went about urging women to work in the fields. "We have turned over now and have equality," she would argue. "That means that women do work and don't have to depend on men." Not all the women in the village were convinced. "If we work in the fields," they said, "what shall happen to our work at home? Does turning over mean we shall be worked to death?" "That's wrong," answered Gold Flower. "If we do not work, the fields will produce little; there will be no grain for soldiers at the front. Then we shall be threatened to death by Chiang Kai-shek's army and lose all we have gained. And again we will have to depend on our husbands." The women could not stand up against her arguments.

But there were other considerations. Husbands did not want their women to go into the fields. Gold Flower called on the belle of the village, a girl named White Purity, who agreed to come out and work. "You are too beautiful to work in the fields," her husband said. "What can you do when someone drags you away through the corn?" White Purity laughed. "Yes, I am beautiful," she said. "But does that mean I must stay indoors all my life like a bird in a cage? This is a new society; it is not like the old days. If anyone dares to attack me in the fields I will call our Women's Association to beat him to death." Reluctantly her husband consented, but when he found his income increased by the labor of his wife, he was very pleased. One night he remarked to his wife: "If I ever have to leave home, you can support my whole family." White Purity had been waiting for such a remark. "Yes," she said, "I can support our family now, so you can go off and join the 8th Route Army. You are young and you ought to be ashamed not to be fighting the reactionaries." Perceiving that he had fallen into a trap, the husband refused to go. White Purity would not sleep with him. He threatened to beat her; she threatened him with the Women's Association. Then she said she would kill herself unless he joined the army. Outmaneuvered, the husband at last mounted a donkey and went off to fight Chiang Kai-shek.

Working among the women of her village, Gold Flower discovered new meanings in life. What pleased her most of all was to aid boys and girls to marry freely. Harvest time found her in the fields, wandering among the village boys, trying to match them up with girls of her acquaintance. "Why don't you find yourself a lover?" she would say to a farmer boy. "You are alone and she would probably make clothes for you." "But where can I find such a girl?" the boy would ask. "I'll find her for you," Gold Flower would answer. She arranged meetings in the homes of friends. For it was still impossible for boys and girls to meet openly before their parents. These meetings were stilted, formal and very serious. In them, conversations like the following took place:

Boy: What kind of a lover do you want?

Girl: Someone like you.

Boy: I have a feeling we will make a very good couple. But what about your parents, will they agree?

Girl: We have a new society. The old society will never return. I can threaten them with my Women's Association. If they don't agree, I can pretend to commit suicide. But what about you?

Boy: For me, it's easy. If my family won't agree to my marrying freely, I will threaten to leave home.

Gradually, by such methods, fighting tradition, flouting custom, out-maneuvering parents, the youth of the village won new liberties for themselves. However, girls and boys, set free from the past, found they could not shake everything off all at once. Sexual freedom was practically unknown. A period of three or four months during which couples carefully examined each other usually preceded most marriages. During this period, boys and girls did not make love; they neither kissed, necked, petted nor walked alone on the streets together. Less sex freedom existed than in the United States. There were none of those tremendously challenging ideas that were introduced and then discarded by the Russian Revolution.

With freedom of marriage, a new type of wedding ceremony was introduced into the villages. No longer did the bride's father have to go to the usurer to hire a sedan chair; instead he sent his daughter off to her husband's village on a donkey. Because the old prohibition against marriage within the village had broken down, many girls never left home at all, but married neighbor boys.

Such weddings usually took place in the open fields under a reed shelter and anyone could come. Dressed in cotton suits and millet hats, with colored ribbons around their waists, the bride and groom, instead of kowtowing to the ancestral tablets, as in the past, merely bowed to each other. In more modern marriages, a master of ceremonies made a speech in which he declared: "Now Miss Wang marries Mr. Chou." Then the Prover of the Wedding announced: "This is not a buy-and-sell marriage. It is democratic and desired by both sides and is recognized by the government." The introducer of the couple who was not a paid mediator, as in the past, would then tell how he brought the boy and girl together. Finally, the crowd would shout for the bride and groom to tell their love story. Generally, most were too shy to say anything except, "We are marrying of our own free will." Concluding the marriage, the groom would bow to the three wedding officials and shake the hand of his wife. Couples never kissed in public.

Gold Flower watched all these changes in her village with a sense of triumph. But her mood of exaltation, begotten of personal victory and a sense of public service performed, did not last longer than a few months. For what did all her efforts amount to if she were still tied to a man whom she loathed? Not until she settled affairs with her own husband did Gold Flower think she would be really free.

Suddenly she decided to lure him back home.

When Gold Flower first took part in the Women's Association, her father-in-law said to her: "I have no way to deal with you, but just wait till my son comes back home, he will beat you."

At that time, she had answered: "I do not care. We have our power-

ful Women's Association and we can fight against any kind of enemy."
She now decided to put this theory to the test. Without informing her
father-in-law, she went to a cousin and asked him to write a letter to
her husband which she dictated. With infinite guile, she couched her
letter in terms sweeter than she had ever used before, ending up with
the words: "I miss you. The quicker you come back, the better."

She returned to the farm, working hard in the fields, beating, shouting
at, jerking the mouth of the mule, hoeing the land, turning over the
manure and all the time thinking, brooding, plotting. If her husband
were no better, she decided, she would struggle against him in a meeting
and reform his character. Deep down inside her, however, a passionate
desire for revenge was stirring, and she kept it buried only by throwing
herself into her work.

Twenty days later, her husband, Chang, showed up at her gate. His
face was aglow with pleasure. "As soon as I received your letter," he
said, "I rushed back home." Gold Flower smiled at her husband, but
she could not say if she was glad that he had returned or not. Then as
she saw those old, hated features closer at hand, she knew. She did
not like him. Maybe he had changed, but she did not think so. Even
as she smiled at him, a bitter feeling was gathering in her stomach. She
felt that something desperate was going to happen. Further than that
her imagination could not take her.

She led him to the kitchen and set the kettle on to boil. Her father-in-
law came back from the fields and crouched beside his son, a sullen expression on his face. Gold Flower saw her husband was puzzled by his
father's attitude and wanted to be alone with him. Discreetly, she left
them together and went to her room to spin.

Her mind began to churn with curiosity. What could those two men
be talking about? The father will tell the husband he is dissatisfied with
me, she thought. Feeling she had to be ready for any eventuality, she
crept back to the kitchen and pressed her ear close to the door. She felt
no shame in this act—none at all. Her thoughts were those of a strategist
planning a battle. Her heart beat violently, for it was about her that the
two men were talking.

"It's lucky you've come back," the father-in-law was saying. "Now
you can take your revenge. Your wife has turned bad since the coming
of the 8th Route Army. She is always outside the home, neglects our
own home, pays no attention to me or my daughter."

"Tell me everything you know about my wife," her husband's voice
came to Gold Flower harshly through the doorway. "I have enough
ability to face her. I can beat her to death. If not to death, I'll tear off
two layers of her skin."

Gold Flower straightened up. Her cheeks were unnaturally flushed,
but she was smiling. "Your time has come," she whispered. "You've

fallen into my trap. You just try your business on me. If you touch one of my fingers, I'll give it to you ten thousand times!"

She bent down and listened again.

The old man was talking. "I have a lot of things to tell you. Before the 8th Route Army came, she worked hard for our family. Now everything is changed. Take this so-called overturning movement. Do you understand what it means for a woman to turn over? I'll tell you. It means women become wild, careless, do anything they like. Women's Association! Have you ever heard of such a thing?"

"It's strange for her," Gold Flower's husband said thoughtfully. "She's so brave now. Very strange. Never mind. Leave her to me."

"But you don't know," said the old man. "They bound me up; they spit in my face; they scolded me before a lot of women."

Gold Flower exploded with an inner rage. "You poor old man!" she hissed the words at the half-open door. "So you've told this to your son. Now both you and your offspring shall dance in front of our women."

It was almost dark outside now. Gold Flower saw Dark Jade, the head of the Women's Association, walk into the courtyard and she went to meet her.

"Father and son are talking in there," she said. "You go in and see what you can find out."

Dark Jade went in and greeted Gold Flower's husband. "You've been away so long," she said. "You married such a beautiful wife. How could you be so cruel as to stay away?"

"Since I've been gone," said Chang, "my wife has become worse and neglected my father and sister. I must teach her a lesson."

"This is not the past," said Dark Jade. "Things are different now than when you were here. It is forbidden to say anything like that now."

"Can women really turn over?" Gold Flower's husband sneered. "I don't believe it."

Dark Jade fell silent, then spoke in a thoughtful manner. "Take care of yourself when the time comes. Don't say then that we were not first polite to you."

She rejoined Gold Flower in the courtyard. "He makes me so angry," she said. Suddenly, her manner changed and she looked thoughtfully at Gold Flower. "If he is beaten, would you not be sorry?" she asked.

"What do you mean?" said Gold Flower. "I had already made up my mind to inform the association when you walked in. You think up your way to struggle and I'll think up my own way. His hatred of one woman has now become the hatred of all women as a whole. Sorry? Not at all. I think he should be beaten to death."

"All right," said Dark Jade. "But before the actual struggle, we must hold a meeting where you can stand up and speak your bitterness. In that way we can arouse the hatred of the masses."

Gold Flower agreed.

That evening her husband came to her room and sat on the edge of the kang beside her. Gold Flower felt herself quivering with hatred, but she managed to appear calm, and waited in silence for her husband to make the first move.

"Have you been faithful and correct while I was away?" he asked. Gold Flower spoke belligerently. "If you think I have been unfaithful, try and get evidence. Produce my lover, and I'll confess."

Her husband smiled. "There is no need to say who is your lover." Abruptly his voice became harsh. "You already have a living thing inside you. You called me back because you want to make me believe that child in your body is mine."

Gold Flower stood up. "What a rotten man you are. You think to cheat me this way. But you can't deceive me any more. You say there's something living in my stomach. All right then, we won't sleep together. Let us see what happens then." She broke off, choking. Tears of pure anger came to her eyes. Through a kind of mist, she saw a knife lying on the table. She reached out and picked it up. Her husband drew back in fright. Laughing harshly, she held the knife out to him.

"If you don't believe me, cut me open." She thrust the knife at his face. "Cut open my stomach and see what's there."

Her husband flushed and looked at the knife uneasily.

"But what is the use of your turning over?" he asked lamely.

"It is necessary. For five years you have treated me badly. Do you think I deserve bad treatment? In the past, you could do with me as you liked, but now you can do no harm to me . . . none at all. . . ."

Her husband sneered. "Are you really so brave?"

"Yes, really. But it's not only you. . . . If there were two parents in addition to you, I would not care."

Her husband glared at her. Gold Flower poured out a torrent of words at him.

"If you think it is incorrect for men and women to go to a meeting together, then let us go outside right now and discuss it in front of the masses. You will try to restrain my liberty, try to prevent me from turning over, but you cannot succeed. Here there are only two people. Only us two. Come, let's see how brave you are. Do you dare? Here is a knife. You will tear two layers of skin from my body. Now there are only the two of us. Come on! If you dare!"

Gold Flower was on her feet yelling. "Come on!" she said. "Come on!"

"No," he said. "I won't beat you to death. I will just break your arms and legs and keep you alive, but make you useless. Then you can't go to your meetings. On your broken legs, you won't even be able to crawl."

Gold Flower glowered at her husband with reddened eyes. "You dirty beast," she cried. "I am ready. I have made up my mind to die right in front of your face. But you are afraid."

At last, Gold Flower and her husband both shouted themselves out. That night they slept in the same bed, but did not make love.

Early the next day Gold Flower was up and about, making breakfast, heating water, helping clean the kitchen. Then swiftly, without so much as a word to any member of the family, she hastened to see the head of the Women's Association.

She quickly revealed what had happened the night before in her bedroom.

"It's up to you to call the masses to settle my problem," she said. "Today is the day for me to turn over. My whole life depends on this meeting. I shall fight hard myself, but my sisters must help me struggle against my husband."

"Put your heart at rest," said Dark Jade. "We shall solve this question. All the women united in one body shall be as one sister."

Gold Flower stammered her thanks.

"Remember, sister," Dark Jade said, putting her hand on Gold Flower's arm, "there are times in your life when you've got to be hard. You cannot be soft with him, for the next time he will ruin you completely. You must carry the thing through to the end."

"I can be very hard with my husband," Gold Flower assured her.

"In that case," said Dark Jade, "we must make a plan. First, we shall send our cadres to your husband and try to persuade him to be frank. If he is not frank, we shall drag him by ropes to the meeting."

Within the hour, fifteen women started for Gold Flower's home, led by Dark Jade. Gold Flower's husband met them in the courtyard. "Why are you here, comrade cadres?" he asked. His tone was polite.

"This is a new society," Dark Jade greeted him abruptly and without any preliminaries. "You must tell the truth of how you have treated our sister. If you do not, you may taste our fists."

Chang smiled. His face and manner were courteous and serene. "Has my wife said something about me?" he asked. What he said was perfectly smooth and friendly, but Gold Flower could see his eyes flickering with animosity.

"It is true, your wife has spoken of you," said Dark Jade. "But your evil doings have also been uncovered by our special investigators. The past was the day of man. But now we have our day given us by Comrade Mao and the Communist party. Speak out or we will bind you up."

A slow color rose in Chang's cheeks. He stood there with lips tight and eyes black with contempt. "Do what you like," he shrugged. "I don't care. What can a Women's Association do?"

Dark Jade turned to the other women. "Get a rope," she said.

The women stirred. One of them brought a grass rope. She moved to bind up Chang. He drew back. "Get away!" he said. Dark Jade and another girl rushed at him and slapped his face.

Dark Jade's voice had a hard edge. "If you dare move, we shall beat you to death on the spot."

Gold Flower's husband stiffened in surprise. Swiftly the women bound him. Jerking him with unnecessary roughness, they pulled him down the street and then threw him in a room of the Women's Association. Dark Jade slammed and bolted the door.

"Let him starve there for three days, the pig!" she said.

The next day the women gathered in a solemn conclave in the meeting hall.

"Our comrade, Gold Flower, still suffers the evil treatment of her husband," said Dark Jade. "Comrade Gold Flower's personal affairs should be taken as the affairs of all of us. Alone, she cannot fight. But with us she can fight all bad husbands. Now, are you ready to struggle?"

"Ready," answered the crowd.

"All right," said Dark Jade, "we shall first try to treat this bad husband by reasoning with him. If this does not succeed, we shall no longer be polite."

The women drew up in ranks like soldiers. Gold Flower went to a near-by room. As her husband was led in, various shouts burst from the crowd.

"We have turned over. . . . You cannot treat us badly or we will beat you to death. . . . Tell us the truth. . . . No arguments. . . . If you are frank, you will be treated better; if not, there will be no mercy."

Chang stood before the women listening to their unfriendly greetings with a strained air. "Comrade sisters," he said, "there has been some mistake. Do you know why I married that woman? It was so she could serve us and so she could keep alive. Do you know how badly she has treated our family?"

He looked about with an air of injured innocence.

"All right," said a girl, "tell us what she did to your family."

Chang looked from one face to another, and they were all closed against him. He dropped his eyes in embarrassment. "I am not acquainted with women turning over. . . ."

A hiss went up from the crowd.

"Resolutely oppose that bad husband," shouted a girl.

Amid all the shouting, a cadre said: "Now is the time to bring on Gold Flower."

Gold Flower brushed her way through the women until she stood face to face with her husband.

"Do you know why we have brought you here?" Her voice was harsh.

"Do you recall how you said you would beat me to death? Well, know that all these women are ready to beat you to death. Now I have nothing more to do with you. I leave all my problems with my sisters to settle."

A voice said: "Are you ready to bow to women?"

Chang bowed low. "I bend my head," he said.

"Your bending head is artificial," said Gold Flower. "Therefore you must take an oath and make a resolution."

Chang was silent.

"What are you thinking?" several women shouted at once.

Chang said nothing.

"Well, what shall we do?" Dark Jade asked the crowd.

"Nothing. Just beat him," said a woman. "Hit him. Hit him," shrieked another voice.

As if by a signal, all the women pushed forward at once. Gold Flower quickly went in back of her husband. The crowd fell on him, howling, knocked him to the ground, then jumped on him with their feet. Several women fell with him, their hands thrashing wildly. Those in the rear leaped in, tore at his clothing, then seized his bare flesh in their hands and began twisting and squeezing till his blood flowed from many scratches. Those who could not get close, dove under the rest and seized Chang's legs, sinking their teeth in his flesh.

Chang let out an anguished howl. "Don't beat me! Don't beat me," he bleated in terror. "I'll reform. Don't hurt me any more."

Under the blows of the women, his cries were soon stilled. The women backed off. Gold Flower peered down at her husband. He lay there motionless on the ground, like a dead dog, his mouth full of mud, his clothes in tatters and blood coming in a slow trickle from his nose. "That's how it was with me in the past," Gold Flower thought. Unable to restrain a feeling of happiness, she turned to the other women. "Many thanks, comrade sisters, for your kindness. If it had not been for you, I would not have been able to get my revenge."

"Don't be polite," said a girl. "This is only justice."

Gold Flower's husband groaned. "This is the end," he said.

"Oh, this is nothing," said a fat peasant girl. "Only a light scratch."

"Get up, you pig," said several women at once.

"My leg is broken," said Chang.

"Let me see," said the fat peasant girl, and she ran quickly and jerked Chang's leg from the floor. He shrieked and the girl burst into gales of laughter.

At last Chang stood up. "How do you feel?" Gold Flower asked.

"Never shall I torture you again," he said quickly. "Never again."

"Do you think you deserved this beating?" asked Gold Flower. "If you deserved it, let us beat you some more."

"No more. Please, no more."

"So! No more! Then what oaths will you swear before the masses?" Gold Flower's husband bit his lip. "If I do anything again, then let me be bound up with ropes and brought before the people and cut to pieces."

The women were not satisfied; they demanded written guarantees. With Dark Jade dictating, Chang wrote:

"I was struggled against by the masses. I deserved this struggle. From now on I will never do anything bad again. If I do, my guarantor is responsible."

He and another man, who had been fetched as a guarantor, both affixed their thumb prints to this document. Then the women let Chang go.

"Your husband has been badly beaten today," said Dark Jade. "You better go home, prepare some food for him and take care of him."

Gold Flower agreed.

When Gold Flower arrived home she made her husband a bowl of noodles. He would not touch it.

"Why don't you eat?" she asked.

"I won't eat food prepared by your hands. Maybe you have put poison in it."

"You just watch," said Gold Flower. "I'll swallow this bowl and you see if I die." She bent her head over the bowl and quickly sucked all the noodles down her throat. Then, she threw back her head and laughed at her husband. He lowered his eyes, but he ate the second bowl of noodles which she placed before him. The father-in-law came in from the fields and ate his meal in silence with his head bowed like his son. Gold Flower, fully conscious of her triumph, looked at them with an objectivity she had never before known. They were both ill at ease, but she was perfectly carefree. How light was her heart. How strong was her Women's Association, the Communist party, the 8th Route Army! "The war," she said to herself, "is really doing something for our women."

She was so proud of herself that she could not help challenging her father-in-law. "How do you feel about women beating your son?" she asked.

The old man's lip curled. "It was all his own fault. If he had not done something wrong, he would not have suffered. I told him, but he wouldn't listen. I guess I brought him up wrong. I used to beat him, but I couldn't reform him."

In spite of herself, Gold Flower smiled. "When he was being beaten, my heart ached," she said.

"Yes, it must have been hard for you," said the old man. "But don't feel badly. It was all due to his faulty temperament."

"But how do you feel about the 8th Route Army which is organizing the Women's Associations?" asked Gold Flower.

"Yes. Very good. Just right."

"Why do you say so?"

"Oh, before I had to work alone on my farm. But now you work so hard on the farm."

"So you are glad I work. But what about the clothes you have to give to your daughter-in-law now?"

"That's all right. When anyone sees you in good clothes, they say: 'There goes Old Chang's daughter.' That gives me face. Now, I'm getting old and if you work, it's a help. My life depends on you. My son has done wrong, but for the sake of my old face, you must treat him kindly. I need you both."

Gold Flower stood up. "You know it is not I who fought you. It is the people. They have eyes. If they find wrong, they speak for me. I have some conditions for peace between us. If you guarantee them, I will be quiet. You must realize that our women were turned over by the Communist party and the 8th Route Army. I believe in Mao Tze-tung and you must open your eyes and see he is the reason why we women have been released."

The old man bowed his head. "I know nothing about all that," he said.

Her husband looked up. "What you say is partly true," he said. "I did not believe the 8th Route Army could organize Women's Associations. But now I have been beaten, I know what the 8th Route Army is. I recognize their strength."

Gold Flower examined her husband thoughtfully. So now he was frightened of her as she had been frightened of him. This scared husband bored her.

But that night in bed her husband seemed changed. He seemed to be thinking: I have been beaten and lost face. His brooding air made Gold Flower uneasy. She thought her husband had not really surrendered to the new society with his heart. Her restless mind set out at once in pursuit of an answer.

"Did that beating really teach you a lesson?" she inquired.

Her husband lay on his back and looked up at the ceiling. He spoke in a matter-of-fact tone. "I bowed my head in front of the masses, but not of my own will. There were too many people; I dared not hold my head up."

Gold Flower sat up. "If you do anything bad again, they will beat you to death without mercy."

"That would please you, would it?"

"How can you say that? You must understand this is a new society. You are over thirty. You know character. You have had experience of life. You have been a businessman in Tientsin. What is bad about this society? Shouldn't men be reformed?"

He said: "I don't feel the new society is progressive. I feel no interest in the 8th Route Army. I am not interested in this so-called overturning movement. Can you imagine such conditions in Tientsin? There is no 8th Route Army there and there is no turning-over movement. Women are kept in the old way. Everything is fine."

"You are not interested in the new society? Then what do you like?"

"I am interested in a society such as the one in Tientsin. I believe women must obey the orders of men. But you see in the 8th Route areas women have become crazy. They don't obey men. But there are other things, too. In Tientsin, there is no plundering of the people. There are rich men who dress well. But in the Liberated Areas all property is distributed. The rich become poor. I don't believe in the new society."

Gold Flower sighed deeply. She could not understand why her husband felt the way he did. She tried to be patient, to "explain" things. "Women are given liberties," she said. "They can join social work. The poor who had no food get land enough to keep alive. Everyone has enough to eat and enough clothes to wear. And the people here enjoy liberty."

Gold Flower lay down again. Her husband tried to caress her. She edged away from him. She did not want that. She wanted to talk seriously and see just what was in her husband's heart. "The conditions of the poor here have been reformed," she said. "Mao Tze-tung has built up a new society for the people."

"I don't care about Mao Tze-tung," said her husband. "As for the poor, if they have not enough to eat, let them go. As for the rich, do you think their property was stolen from others?"

Gold Flower was hurt and angry, even puzzled. Everything had seemed so clear to her. But now her husband did not see things her way at all. "You are different now from the meeting," she said. "Then you confessed your belief in the new society. But you are still conservative and backward. Why are the poor destined to have no clothes and no food? And why are the rich destined to live without working? Is it fate? I don't believe in fate any more. Our poor work on the farms to produce wheat and it is the rich who enjoy the fruit of their labor. I believe this is wrong."

But there was nothing Gold Flower could do or say to convince her husband. He was getting as angry as she was. "I am old now," he said. "But if I were young, I would join the Nationalist army. I would become an officer. I would take another wife and let you go."

"So you want another wife. What is wrong with me? You are so old and I am so young. But take another wife. I am ready to divorce you. You are old, but you still dream of being an officer and getting rich. And then you would do evil to the poor. I'll let *you* go. I'll divorce *you!*" Gold Flower spoke in sharp angry bursts. But her husband was just as bitter. "I can't join Chiang Kai-shek's army," he said. "But I'll go back to Tientsin and someday I'll be rich and take a good wife for myself. You go your way. I'll go mine. I don't care."

He turned his back on Gold Flower. Talk ceased. She lay there thinking what she should do. Should she report what her husband had said about going in the Nationalist army? She did not know. Suddenly, he began to caress her again. She drew away. She thought she no longer had anything in common with her husband. He begged her to make love to him. "Why then did we marry?" he asked. His voice grew more gentle, yet more insistent. "This political talk is no use," he said. "You will see; you will feel differently."

Gold Flower was tired. She was exhausted from the Struggle Meeting in the daytime, enervated by the emotional struggle with her husband that had been going on all night. At last she thought: What's the difference? This is the last time. She let him make love to her.

He seemed very pleased with himself. "Do you feel better?" he asked Gold Flower.

"No" she said.

"But I do," he said. He seemed to think that Gold Flower was pretending that she had not enjoyed making love to him.

But now as she lay there, even as she made no attempt to stop his renewed caresses, she knew exactly how she felt about him. She hated him. She did not want him, had never wanted him, nor any man like him. He was just one of those things that society, the old black society had brought on her, and now it and they were going. Good riddance. Nor was her feeling unreasonable. The only thing she and her husband had in common was that old tradition had forced them together. The traditions removed, they had absolutely no means of contact. Their condition was not isolated. It was national.

Gold Flower lay there beside her husband and over and over again she said to herself: "He belongs to the rich. I belong to the poor. He is old and I am young. We are enemies." And though her husband tried again to make love to her, she only lay there, cold to his touch, but burning with anger and hatred.

The next day she got up without saying a word to her husband. All day she brooded. She was cooking the evening meal when suddenly she could contain her rage no longer.

Without warning, she ran to her husband. "You still have an old mind!" Her words came out with a hissing gasp. "You still have not reformed. Do you want some more education? If you don't believe in a classless society, just try our power!"

Chang jumped up in a rage and rushed at his wife. Nimbly she ducked under his arm, then ran as fast as she could toward the Women's Association.

Finding the chairwoman, she yelled at her: "My husband is not yet reformed."

The chairwoman went up to the roof of her house and called through a megaphone. "Comrade women! Come at once! Something of importance!"

Out from nearly every clay hut in the village tumbled a woman. Rushing toward the Women's Association Building, they heard the chairwoman explain: "Gold Flower's husband is bad again! Get ropes and catch him!"

With Gold Flower in the lead, forty howling women ran through the village. But her husband had already fled. The women chased him for three miles through the fields, but in the dark he escaped. Disconsolately Gold Flower returned home. She thanked everyone for helping her.

"Do not be afraid," several women told her. "Someday we shall catch your husband and bite him to death."

The next day Gold Flower reported her husband's flight to the district magistrate. He told her that the government would be responsible for her safety. Then he said: "Comrade Gold Flower, your husband is only one person. You must think of society as a whole. You must go back to your village and unite the women as a piece of iron."

Gold Flower took his words seriously. She had made up her mind that the old society would never come back again. She, personally, would not let it. Shortly afterward, she called the village women together and made a speech.

"Comrade sisters," she said, "we have been released by the Communist party and the 8th Route Army. This is our day! We must produce grain for the armies to fight Chiang Kai-shek and the Nationalist troops. We must oppose America which is helping Chiang to fight the Liberated Areas."

Then she clenched her fist and shouted slogans she had been taught:

"Oppose America! Oppose Chiang Kai-shek! Oppose those fighting the Liberated Areas! Go home and make your husbands participate in the 8th Route Army!"

43. Sex and Revolution

GOLD FLOWER had finished her story. During the latter part of her conversation, I kept wondering what she expected now from life. Had the revolution turned her into a fanatic who sublimated her sexual instincts to the demands of politics? Had she become an ambitious girl who only wanted to be a heroine? Did she think a family, love and affection just so much bourgeois nonsense?

The answer is an emphatic *no*. Gold Flower, at the time of my arrival, was just in the process of getting a divorce, which had been impossible in the old society, and she wanted very much to marry again. What is more, she had very definite ideas on the kind of man she wanted to marry.

"I want to find a progressive," she said, "who will stand amid the working classes. Someone who is not only concerned for himself, someone who will not oppress women and someone who will be responsible in society.

"I want someone about two or three years older than myself, who is cultured, who has suffered much and who has conquered a lot of difficulties.

"I don't want a rich man. I want a worker or a farmer, and someone who is not afraid of death. I don't want anyone with factories or prostitutes or concubines. He only steals from the poor. That's my object— to fight against that kind of man.

"My husband was not rich, but he stood on the side of the rich and he did not have the heart of the poor man and looked down on women."

"What about a teacher?" I asked.

"No, he would not be good. He knows nothing about the new society. Teachers fear death. They teach people to be backward. Although I never went to school, I learned that teachers are bad because I have heard school children say: 'Someday I will be a wealthy man; someday I will be an officer.' That is bad. Then teachers don't teach the children that America is helping Chiang Kai-shek."

An intellectual? "I oppose him," said Gold Flower. "He has a curl in his mind. Of course, there are two kinds of intellectuals. Those who use their brains to oppress the people, and those who use them to help the people. If they say they will help us build factories, I must still study them carefully to see if they mean what they say."

I finally guessed that the ideal husband for Gold Flower would be a cadre. But she surprised me. "No, cadres are loyal to their superiors, but they are just looking for advantages. They do no work. In our village, we had a cadre who was instructed to serve us, but he did nothing, and only got advantages from us.

"A farmer is the best kind of husband for me. He can lead people to produce. He is loyal to the poor from birth. But a cadre is often not loyal to the poor. A peasant is much more resolute than any of these 8th Route Army cadres. He is like a horse or an ox, but he conquers all difficulties and leads his own life. He has done great deeds for our country, although no one knows him."

At last I asked Gold Flower what kind of a temperament she was looking for in a husband. Without even pausing to think, she had an answer ready.

"He should be better educated than me so he could teach me things. For example, he should teach me characters. But if I forget them, he should be patient to teach me again and again. If he has a violent temper, that would be all right, if he employs it in work, to lead people, to arm people. If he had a bad temper, I would help him get rid of it and advise him to use it against landlords, but not against me. I would tell him if he treated me violently that would make our home life unhappy and I would reform him with love. If he were tired, I would take off his clothes and shoes and help him to get to bed, but I would tell him in the morning that I only did so because he was tired, and he could not expect me to do it every night as he would be oppressing women. If he were sad or unhappy, I would put on my cleanest clothes for him, comb my hair and try to make myself look beautiful so that I would be pleasing in his sight. And then I would do that thing which he liked best to do. Thus, with love, I would teach my husband love and I am sure he would not treat me badly, but would love me, too."

I looked at this simple farm girl in amazement. She was crude by Western standards. She wore cotton pants stained with manure from the fields. She could scarcely read, though she was learning from the village school children three characters every day. She spit on the floor in no ladylike fashion. She wiped her nose with the back of her hand. She was no glamor girl. But she was a woman.

I do not wish to make a whole social or political philosophy out of the story of one girl like Gold Flower. She was not a type, but an individual in her own dramatic right. Yet her story has been multiplied to infinity throughout the length and breadth of rural China. The inhuman treatment of Chinese women is well known. But the social, political and religious implications of this treatment, along with its revolutionary significance, has not been given much attention.

For the last three thousand years political power in China has been intimately associated with the control of women. There is, of course, no proof that Chinese society passed through stages in which we now see certain savage communities. Nevertheless, a reference to primitive societies may help clarify the role women have played in the battle for power in China. From everything we know of early man it seems safe to say that the first political and social revolutions in human history were caused by wars—that is, the effort of groups of men to secure for themselves more goods than were within their immediate reach. In savage societies these goods were often women. Freud's Totem and Taboo—the story of the revolt of a band of brothers against a tribal father's monopoly of women—is an exposition in psychological terms of the fact that political power in primitive society was synonymous with control of the female sex. Jouvenel in his book, *On Power*,[1] points out the only form of wealth among Australian savages was their serving maids. These women were so valuable that they were monopolized by the elders whose concubines were always on the increase while the young men had to do without. The absolutist power of the father in clan society came mostly from the possession of women taken in forays against neighboring clans. When young men, chafing at the domination of the Elders, raided enemy tribes for women of their own, their status in their own tribe grew and consequently they altered the balance of political power.

Though vastly more complicated, the patriarchal Chinese society has also rested on the position of the Elders and their possession of women as material sources of wealth. Historically, control of women has been concentrated in the hands of the rural possessing classes. It was the gentry, and not the common peasant, who always had the largest families. The poor peasant seldom had more than one wife, but clan leaders and landlords had numerous wives, concubines and slave girls who not only produced wealth for the landlord by their own labor but also produced numerous sons which gave the gentry local political power. In Honan Province the writer came across a landlord who had a family of sixty-nine members. Through this family, he controlled seven hundred tenant farmers, thirty slave girls, two hundred squatters and seven wet nurses who breast-fed his numerous brood. He was able to buy and sell women because of his wealth and he was also powerful because he possessed women.

Not only Chinese society in general, but even the structure of the state, from the village at the bottom to the throne at the top, was definitely influenced by the status of women as slaves, private property, labor powers and producers of sons for the ruling classes. The family was a training ground for loyalty to state authority. The father was the supreme autocrat in the family. Submission of female to male and of son to father found its natural reflection in submission of peasant to gentry,

[1] *On Power*, Bertrand De Jouvenel, The Viking Press, N. Y., 1949.

tenant to landlord and landlord to state ruler. From the foregoing it should be obvious that any all-out attempt to free women could only result in the upheaval of the whole social pyramid and a tremendous change in the correlation of forces struggling for power. That is why the Communists fought so hard for equality of women and why the more feudal-minded moralists of the Kuomintang never lost an opportunity to inveigh against the Communist "destruction" of the Chinese family. In the first case, the freeing of women was a means of breaking the old power; in the second case, shackling of women was a means of preserving the power.

The inequality of women has also been deeply reflected in Chinese philosophy and religion. Chinese metaphysics recognizes two forces at work in life: the *Yang* or dominant male element and the *Yin* or subordinate female element. Thus the philosophers of the ruling classes made it a law of nature that women should be inferior to man. Chinese ethics have seldom fought against the evil treatment of women. On the contrary, practical Confucianism, in the words of Arthur Smith, a very wise missionary, committed seven deadly sins against women. I paraphrase his words here:

1. Chinese women are provided with no education and their minds are left in a state of nature and millions of them are supposed to have no minds at all.

2. Wives and daughters are sold as readily as cattle and horses.

3. Compulsory marriage of all girls forces Chinese society into cast-iron grooves and leaves no room for individual development.

4. Concubinage is the natural result of the Confucian practice of ancestor worship which demands that sons be raised to worship a man when he is gone.

5. Since women cannot perform the duties of ancestor worship, girl children are often murdered by their parents.

6. The family system has resulted in the suicide of wives and daughters, and the death rolls are convincing enough proof of the woes endured by Chinese women.

7. Finally, the doctrines of ancestor worship and inequality of women help in the overpopulation of the country.

The lowly position of Chinese women not only had a terrible effect on the women themselves, but also succeeded in degrading and debauching all human relations within society. The Chiang Kai-shek government in its twenty-year rule over China produced some improvement, but not much. It is true that Chiang Kai-shek, himself, believed in freedom of marriage and that he was wedded to one of the most charming women in China. It is also true that in Shanghai, Peiping and Hongkong there were Chinese women who had freedoms somewhat approaching those possessed by American women. But in the countryside, particularly the North China countryside, the position of women was little better than it was fifty years ago. In fact, when you considered that the buying and selling of women had increased in alarming proportions during the last decade, it was almost safe to say that the lot of Chinese women was as bad, or worse, than it had ever been. The reason the Chiang Kai-shek regime could not improve the status of rural women, and very often made it worse, was partly because of the ravages of war, partly because the generalissimo revived neo-Confucianism, the philosophic base for women's inferiority, but above all it was due to the fact that the Kuomintang never squarely faced up to the semifeudal land relationships which, unless abolished, guaranteed that farm women would remain serfs and, with them, a great proportion of men, too.

This inferior condition of women, however, was not confined to the countryside. Far from it. In Peiping, the ancient capital of Chinese culture, the numbers of middle and primary school girls who were forced by the press of poverty and the orders of their parents to perform amorous acts for money ran into the untold hundreds. Many such acts were performed with the mother and father outside the door and the girl's bicycle and schoolbooks by the bed. In Chiang Kai-shek's capital at Nanking, in the Futzemiao district, there were row upon row of houses where men openly peddled their wives to stray passers-by. These were not houses of prostitution, but family homes, and if a prospective customer was in a hurry, the husband directed his wife to leave her dinner or the baby she was nursing and go to bed immediately with patrons.

Shanghai, Chiang Kai-shek's financial center, was probably the greatest market place for women in the world. Bought and sold just like merchandise, which is what they were, young females were constantly raked out of the villages and thrown into the Shanghai market in the form of slaves, factory workers, maidservants, concubines and whores. Moreover, many of them had little say in what disposition should be made of them. Despite Madame Chiang Kai-shek's New Life Movement, Shanghai was not only one of the biggest centers of prostitution in the world, but also boasted some of the world's biggest whorehouses. In fact, many Chinese hotels, including the larger ones such as Wing On's, Sincere's, the Yangtze and others, on the main streets of Shanghai, were nothing but glorified whorehouses. Every floor in these hotels had its own quota of girls and sometimes each floor specialized in the women of a certain province. In most cases, these girls were not free, but were owned by men or groups of men and sometimes by women. Most often the girls were too scared or too ignorant to protest about the use to which they were put, but sometimes new arrivals from the country tried to fight back, with the result that they were chained to their beds and burned with lighted cigarettes until they became amenable to the demands of their masters.

The enforced prostitution of women resulted in a material and spiritual cleavage of Chinese society. But it was in the more normal sexual relations in the home that this schism produced its most revolutionary effects. Certain atavistic Westerners have promulgated the theory that Chinese women liked their modest position in society. This is utter nonsense. Chinese women had no love for their galling bonds. They saw no "charm" in their modest life roles, but only the terms of their enslavement.

"Officials depend on seals; tigers depend on mountains; women depend on their husbands."

"If I buy a horse, I can beat it; if I marry a wife, I can do as I like."

"When a woman is angry, her husband beats her; when he is angry, he also beats her."

Such sayings told to me by women in the Taihang Mountains clearly enough reveal that they were perfectly aware of their lowly position in Chinese society and had no liking for it. The well-publicized Chinese family system was, to them, just an institution for oppression of their sex.

So little did the Chinese women think of their position in society that often they wished to be born dogs in the next existence so that they might wander where they chose, instead of being shut inside their husband's home night and day. Almost the only time they could leave their homes was when they were kidnaped or sold.

Marriage was such a terrible prospect for women that in some places they formed sisterhoods, composed of maidens who swore vows to heaven never to get married, believing that their married lives would be miserable and unholy. Until recent years there were cases where bands of maidens committed suicide because one of their number was forced by her parents to be married. Such determined opposition to the laws of society, of course, produced a revolutionary cleavage in that society.

But this schism in the social body extended over into the male population, too. It is no exaggeration to say that men cannot be free until their women are free. The necessity of producing sons for ancestor worship forced boys into early marriage as well as girls. It was by no means uncommon for boys to be married at the age of ten, though fourteen or fifteen was more usual. That the boys liked this little better than the girls is very clearly evident from the story I have already told of the Field Mouse. So often did boys run away from their child brides that it became a very big factor in the formation of the 8th Route Army. More striking than the phenomenon of men running away from unwanted brides was the dreadful fact that society often forced husbands deliberately to mistreat wives they loved. In Tinghu village in Chingyuan

County of Shansi Province, I came across a peasant boy who had to beat his wife on the order of his father. He tried to refuse, but because of the Confucian code of filial piety he could do nothing but beat her insensible almost every day. Had he refused, he could very easily have been thrown into the magistrate's or the landlord's dungeon. Unable to stand his wife's cries or his own spiritual torture, he finally ran away from home. Such incidents only produced another factor into the decay of the Chiang Kai-shek social regime.

Compulsory marriage and other evils related to sex forced Chinese society into cast-iron grooves so that the peasant youth of the country, brought to a hysterical boiling point, was in a mood to shatter their bonds and revolt against society, even against life itself, at the first given opportunity. Such an opportunity came to them with the land reform promulgated by the Communists.

That is part of the significance of Gold Flower. Of course, as in everything else in China, one must speak of this subject with reservations. "Customs change every ten li," says a proverb which is true enough. Therefore, the revolt of women was not always as violent nor as complete as in Gold Flower's village. Yet even the more peaceful and less revolutionary changes in the position of women have exercised a far-reaching effect on family and home, government and agriculture, religion and war. What will be the ultimate effect on Chinese society is something that the writer does not dare predict. Undoubtedly, changes, revolutionary as they are, will come slowly, as does everything in the Orient.

In this connection I would like to tell a story—a short one and the last one—about the previously mentioned village of Tinghu in Shansi Province.

Although this village was located in the mountains where you would expect conditions to be most backward, the women of Tinghu did not have bound feet, but neither did they work in the fields. It was a widespread ambition of these women to marry landlords. "Marriage! Marriage! Clothes to wear; food to eat," was one of their proverbs. However, the women were under no illusions about the joys of marriage, as two other proverbs show. "The thread controls the needle; a husband controls his wife." "Women are like wheelbarrows;[2] if not beaten for three days they cannot be used."

Before the Japanese war, there were only six women in Tinghu who worked in the fields. Of these, all were either widows or wives of soldiers. People laughed at them when they carried hoes on their shoulders through the street, and when the women came back in dirty clothes from the fields, they returned by a roundabout way or after dark in order to

[2] It is necessary to beat the iron rim on the wheel to keep it in shape. So with a woman.

avoid cruel village jibes. The men of the village also looked down on women who worked. In this connection, there was also a proverb! "Man's labor produces everywhere; women can only make water soup."

In Tinghu, there lived a woman named Chan Shu-ying. She had smallpox when she was young and as a consequence her face was rather unattractive. When seventeen, she was married to a farmer, aged thirty-five. Before marriage, the husband had frequent intercourse with other village women. Since Chan Shu-ying was not pretty and very inexperienced, she could not satisfy her husband who continued to go out at night and sleep with other women.

On the New Year's festival when all the others were out in the street singing and dancing the *Yangko*, Chan Shu-ying did not dare participate and was too ashamed even to go and look on.

In 1940, during the rent-reduction movement, the girl entered the Women's Association, much to the dissatisfaction of her mother-in-law. In fact, the mother-in-law came to hate the girl so much that she ate up all the food before Shu-ying could get home from the meeting. When the husband and the mother ate gruel, the girl only got water soup. When she asked for a new suit of cotton clothes, she was told: "A suit of clothes should be divided into three stages: new for three years, old for three years, rags for three years."

In 1941, the government started a production drive and Chan Shu-ying bought a spinning wheel. Through her spinning she earned enough money to buy three new suits of clothes for the family and all the salt the family used. Because of her work, she was elected chairman of the Women's Association. Then she entered the winter schools, learned a few hundred characters and encouraged other women to learn also. Soon, when women became involved in arguments with one another, they came to Chan Shu-ying and asked her to act as mediator. Gradually, her status in the village grew.

When the Japanese war pressed hard on the economic life of the village, Chan Shu-ying led the women to dig up wheat for firewood and to grind the pits of mountain peaches for oil. Later she learned to weave cloth, then to make shoes and finally almost everything needed by her family in the home. As a result, her mother-in-law began to treat her better, having a hot meal ready when the girl came back from her women's meetings. In 1943, Chan Shu-ying was elected the Spinning and Weaving Heroine of Tinghu, and her mother-in-law boasted loudly to everyone of her daughter's accomplishments. Finding that he was married to a woman of great local prestige, the husband of Chan Shu-ying ceased going out at night, desired more and more to sleep with his wife and even bought some medicine that he thought might help her give birth to children.

Women were now a growing power in the village. In 1943, Tinghu held its first election. But the village chief was chosen without a single woman having voted. Chan Shu-ying and other women declared they would not recognize the new village chief. The men laughed and appeared indifferent. But Chan Shu-ying encouraged the women not to sleep with their husbands, and finally the men had to surrender and allow a new election. The voting was extremely heated and the women were so successful in getting out the vote that they captured the office of vice-village chief and also succeeded in getting a woman elected as head of the Education Bureau.

Before the rise of women in Tinghu, there had only been six women working outside the home. By 1941, there were thirteen women engaged in cutting wheat rows, ten in planting new seeds, ten picking young wheat, three water carriers and three wood cutters. By 1943, the number working had increased to 101. In the whole county, that year, according to the county government, there had been two thousand women spinners. By the next year of the eleven thousand women in the county, eight thousand had spinning wheels. With nearly 80 per cent of the women engaged in producing something useful, the economic welfare of the villages rose rapidly.

Such were some of the benefits that the overturning movement brought to the women of Tinghu village. These benefits were spiritual and psychological as well as material, and they all had profound effects on the civil war. In many villages, women exercised more power than men and very often they were much more passionate supporters of the 8th Route Army than were their husbands or their brothers.

This is part of the inner history of the Chinese civil war, just as it is part of the story of the failure of American policy in China. Chiang Kai-shek, in failing to heed the tortured cries of Chinese womanhood, brought on himself a terrible vengeance and a just retribution. The architects of American intervention in China, by ignoring, even being totally unaware of the needs of Chinese women and the part they played in the civil war, evolved theories about that war and tried to force policies on the American and Chinese people that had little relation to reality.

There is nothing farfetched in these statements. It is impossible to understand war and revolution in China in abstract terms. It is necessary to understand human beings. The fact that the pain, anguish and despair of Chinese womanhood has been transmitted by revolutionary fires into new feelings of joy, pride and hope is a phenomenon of tremendous significance for all the world. The revolt of woman has shaken China to its very depths and may shake the foundations of even this strong country. Yet political commentators ignore these peasant women as if they had no part in the drama now being enacted on the stage of world history.

To live and cause to live, to eat food and beget children, these are the primary wants of men, and Chinese are no different from other people in this respect. Significantly, it is to these problems of food and sex that the Chinese Communists have addressed themselves with resolute fury and cunning wisdom. In abolishing the peasant's fear for his food supply and the woman's dread of her sex relationships, the Communists have raised tremendous hopes in the villages and on the waves of these emotions they are riding everywhere to power.

It makes little difference that the Communists may be reforming the relations between the sexes as a means of obtaining power. Their sincerity is of no import at all. The fact remains they have given women a goal toward which they can fight.

At this point, it may occur to the reader that I am overemphasizing the importance of sex in revolution and politics. Perhaps you may think that I am letting my sympathies for women run away with my political judgments. I do not believe so. No social revolution—either good or bad—ever took place without the existence of a great mass of disinherited people who could furnish a new group with a base of support. In the women of China, the Communists possessed, almost ready made, one of the greatest masses of disinherited human beings the world has ever seen. And because they found the key to the heart of these women, they also found one of the keys to victory over Chiang Kai-shek.

PART XI

CIVIL WAR

❦

44. Red War Policies

MORE by accident than by design, my arrival in Communist areas coincided with a decisive turning point in China's civil war. During the several months that I had been wandering around the Liberated Areas, there had taken place three events that had an immediate effect on the military aspects of that war.

The Communist capital at Yenan had been lost. Chiang Kai-shek had closed the breech in the Yellow River dikes and turned loose a flood into the Liberated Areas. And the 8th Route Army had begun to mount a counteroffensive that was ultimately to destroy a good part of Chiang Kai-shek's armies and bring a huge slice of China, from Manchuria to the Yangtze River, under Communist sway.

All of these things greatly surprised me, but especially the counteroffensive. For when I first arrived in the Liberated Areas I could discover almost no outward signs that such a great event was in the offing. On the peasants' huts and on the mud walls of the villages, the slogans were all of a defensive nature. "Restore the lines of the truce agreement." "Beat back the attacks of Chiang Kai-shek and keep our Liberated Areas free." These were two of the most popular slogans at the time of my arrival. Nowhere was there any such exhortation as "Down with Chiang Kai-shek!" At the time, it had all seemed very strange.

When I asked various staff officers in General Liu Po-cheng's headquarters why they were not appealing to the people to overthrow Chiang, I received a variety of answers as amusing as they were unconvincing. "You are a very bad boy," one officer would say to me. Or another one might remark: "Too many people support Chiang; such a slogan would not be appropriate." Or most commonly someone would say: "We don't want to overthrow Chiang; we want to make peace with him and reform his character."

That these hard-bitten guerrilla leaders actually believed in such a

Christian approach to the problem of war and revolution, of course, seemed to me preposterous. One day, when General Liu Po-cheng, himself, told me that the present aim of their civil war against Chiang was to restore the lines of the Marshall truce agreement, I suddenly decided to take the bull by the horns and blurted out:

"Do you mean to tell me that if you have defeated Chiang Kai-shek's army around Suchow and Pengpu and are advancing on Nanking [this is exactly what happened] and if Chiang says at this time: 'Advance no further, go back to the lines of the truce agreement'—do you mean to say under these circumstances, you will suddenly halt your advance, withdraw your forces and make peace with Chiang?"

The one-eyed general looked at me quizzically for a moment. "We have been fighting Chiang for twenty years," he said; "we know him very well. If such a condition as you outline arises, we will not stick our necks out for Chiang to chop off."

I had my answer, and a few days later, I extracted an even more specific one from a staff officer in headquarters. "Look," he said, "this is only a tactic. When the time comes, we will say: 'Down with Chiang Kai-shek' and we will overthrow him."

But what gave the Communists the belief that they could beat Chiang Kai-shek in the first place? On the face of it such ideas appeared presumptuous. Chiang had an army three and a half times that of the 8th Route Army, with a correspondingly greater fire power in artillery, machine guns and rifles. Moreover, while he had an air force, railways, gunboats and motor transport, the Reds had none. Yet, as I soon discovered, the Communists were supremely confident of their ability to beat Chiang—American arms or no American arms. Why?

I had many conversations with 8th Route Army officers on this subject and I soon found out that their belief in victory lay in their analysis of the character of the civil war itself. Their whole viewpoint was perhaps best summed up by Mao Tze-tung in a broadcast on Christmas Day 1947.

"The basic nature of the war," said Mao, "lies in the struggle of the armed Chinese people against feudalism and dictatorship and toward independence and democracy. Under these conditions, Chiang Kai-shek's military superiority and American aid are factors that can play only temporary roles. The unpopular nature of the Chiang regime and the support or opposition of the people, however, will play constant roles."

Officers in Liu Po-cheng's headquarters put it to me this way: "The side with inferior material will overcome the side with superior material; the country will conquer the city; the side without foreign assistance will conquer the side with foreign assistance."

During the war, they believed, China's dictator would alienate most of the Chinese people, most of the officials in his government and a great many officers in his army, so that the road would be open to get rid of him and form a coalition government. That was the political basis for victory.

No doubt the Communists hoped to gain a dominating position in that government. However, there was nothing underhanded in advocating such a program. Quite the contrary, it was wide open to everybody's view and that is why it was such a beautiful strategy. Chiang Kai-shek, in dismissing Red representatives from his capital at Nanking, then declaring that he would not take them in the government at all, put himself in the untenable position of continuing the war when the country wanted peace. Later, he made his position even worse by outlawing the left-wing Democratic League, denying their members positions in the government and even arresting some of them. The Communists, on the other hand, by continuing to advocate coalition government, left the door wide open for all the diverse political elements of China to come over to their side. Such a strategy—whether sincere or not—was definitely appealing.

While they considered China's civil war revolutionary, most of Liu's staff officers believed it was different from other revolutionary wars. Their remarks on this subject are perhaps not without interest and I paraphrase them here.

China's civil war, said staff officers, was not like the Russian civil war because it was primarily a war of farmers with few workers involved. Therefore, land reform and not proletarian support was the decisive factor.

The civil war in China was similar to the American Civil War as it aimed to free the peasants from the landlords as Negro slaves were freed from southern landowners. But it was not a war of an industrial north against an agrarian south, but, according to the Communists, a war of the Chinese people against the "four big families—Chiang Kai-shek, T. V. Soong, H. H. Kung and the Chen brothers, Kuomintang party bosses."

In its opposition to dictatorship, feudalism and foreign intervention, it was like the Spanish Civil War. But the Spanish people fought Franco under the leadership of a popular front, while the Chinese people, though of many parties and groups, were fighting under Communist policies and Communist leadership. Thus, there was a unity of direction and interest that the Spanish Republicans lacked.

Finally, the Communists believed they were fighting quite a different war than they fought against Chiang from 1927 to 1937. There were similarities—the major type of warfare was still mobile war, with guerrilla war to help, and the farmers were still armed to fight the landlords—but the differences were greater.

In 1927, the aim of Red warfare had been the dictatorship of the proletariat and one-party rule; now it was a "new democracy" and coalition government under leadership of the Communists. In 1927, world imperialism was still marching forward. By 1945, however, the imperialist designs of Japan, Italy and Germany had been routed. French and British imperialism were in full retreat. Only America could interfere in China, but being occupied throughout the whole world, she could not play a decisive role in China's war. The fact, however, that many Chinese looked upon Chiang as the man who was selling them out to foreign interests gave the war the character of a war of independence.

Such were the broad outlines of the political and strategic considerations which the Reds believed would bring them victory and a recognized, perhaps dominant position in a coalition government. How did they plan to fight that war? Somewhat differently than before.

Already, on my arrival, Liu Po-cheng had amalgamated his former guerrilla outfits into units analogous to divisions and corps. Though he was still relying on a guerrilla struggle for aid, he planned to use his army in broad-scale mobile maneuvers against Chiang which he had not been able to do against the Japanese.

This was true, not only of Liu Po-cheng, but of all 8th Route commanders. There was nothing particularly secret about these tactics, and they were publicly outlined by Mao Tze-tung, himself, in a Christmas Day speech in 1947 as follows:

1. First strike isolated enemies; later strike concentrated enemies.
2. First take small towns, later cities.
3. Destruction of the enemy's forces and not the capture of cities is the most important objective.
4. In every battle concentrate absolutely superior forces: double, quadruple and sometimes even five or six times those of the enemy. Try for complete annihilation. But don't fight a battle of attrition where the gains cannot equal the losses.
5. Fight only when there is assurance of victory.
6. Fight several engagements in succession without respite.
7. Destroy the enemy while in movement.
8. Wrest all weakly defended cities from the enemy. Wait until conditions mature and then capture powerfully defended cities.
9. Replenish ourselves by the capture of all enemy arms and most of his personnel. Sources of the men and matériel for our army are mainly at the front.
10. Utilize intervals between campaigns in resting, grouping and training troops, but don't let intervals be long or allow the enemy a breathing spell.

"These methods," said Mao Tze-tung, "are well known to Chiang Kai-shek and his American advisers. Many times Chiang has called together his generals and his field officers, issued them our books and sought countermeasures. The American military personnel suggest this and that strategy . . . but our strategy is based on a people's war and no antipopular army can utilize our strategy and tactics."

This outline for victory was to be fulfilled with amazing accuracy in the year following Mao's speech. For the 8th Route Army, having captured small towns, moved against provincial capitals such as Tsinan and Paoting then took great cities, like Mukden, and Tientsin until they finally seized the biggest metropolitan centers at Nanking, Peiping and Shanghai. The country, as my informants had put it, was conquering the city. In other ways, too, time showed Mao to be a sure prophet. Small isolated units, then divisions and finally whole Kuomintang armies were to fall to the Red forces.

Such sudden and sweeping victories, however, were not achieved by force of arms alone. Behind such victories lay some very subtle political stratagems of high-ranking Red commanders. One day, when talking to one-eyed General Liu, I asked him what was the greatest tactical lesson he had learned from a quarter of a century of war. He thought a long while, then answered: "To utilize the contradictions of the enemy. For example, when I have three enemy units before me, I study the history of each commander carefully, try to find out if the commanders have any disagreements among themselves, which commander is the most dissatisfied, which unit the weakest and which soldiers the most depressed. I then try to isolate that unit and attack it." It might be added here that this was also one of the Communists' favorite political tactics.

This tactic was utilized by nearly every high Communist commander throughout the course of the civil war with sometimes astounding results. There was nothing haphazard about the way Red commanders turned the contradictions within the Kuomintang army to their own advantage. Preparations were very detailed. For example, when I was in the Liberated Areas, a Communist force under General Chen Yi decided to attack the City of the White Pagoda. The aim of this operation was not the capture of the city, but the elimination of the Kuomintang 42nd Army Group under General Ho Peng-chu. Now, General Ho once had been a puppet commander under the Japanese. He had surrendered to the Communists and was allowed to keep his army. Then suddenly, in the fashion of the Three Kingdoms, Ho turned over to Chiang Kai-shek. As the Reds prepared to attack Ho, their political directors explained all this to the soldiers of the 8th Route Army. The manner of this precombat political education has been preserved by intelligence agents of Chiang Kai-shek's army itself and I quote from one of its documents.

All troops serving as the spearhead in the attack were given detailed explanations:

a) Of how Ho Peng-chu's troops were puppets; how they had surrendered to the Liberated Army; how the people in the Liberated Army had supported them; how they had been welcomed; how much money they had spent during the last year when they were with the Liberated Army; how many pounds of wheat and flour the army had consumed; how many uniforms they had used; etc. Every item was listed in detail, so that every soldier had a clear understanding of Ho Peng-chu's character and the nature of his army.

b) How during the last year the East China Bureau [of the Chinese Communist party] had sent people to educate Ho's troops; how they had been rejected; how Ho had maintained secret liaison with Nanking. A description was given of the most reactionary elements in Ho's army; the most progressive; and those who did not have much idea one way or the other.

c) Of the combat strength of Ho's army: including the listings of the best equipped battalions, those with the most men, those with the most progressive commanders and those with the most reactionary ones.

Discussions were held in the platoons and companies on the following subjects: a) Are Ho Peng-chu and his army traitors to the people? b) Are Ho Peng-chu and his army traitors to the Communist party? c) How to deal with them? d) How to avenge their wrongs to the people and the party?

After more than three days' discussion in every platoon and company, and after 100 per cent agreement had been reached that Ho Peng-chu and his army must be crushed, the commanders encouraged every soldier to make his personal plan for battle. Every rifle was decorated with some slogan such as: "We are determined to crush Ho Peng-chu." "We advance a foot but never retreat an inch."[1]

It is almost superfluous to remark that poor General Ho could not stand up before this avalanche of political propaganda and was captured within a few days with most of his army intact.

As the war went on, these political tactics of the Reds were to pay huge dividends. For time after time, not only regiments, but divisions and sometimes dissatisfied armies, turned over to the Reds after making only a token resistance.

As a matter of fact, there was in headquarters right at this moment a Kuomintang general named Kao Hsu-hsun who had turned over to the Reds with his whole army. I decided to go see him.

45. Why a General Revolts

NOBODY can understand the Chinese army without understanding something about that fascinating group of half-educated, dispossessed farm boys who suddenly rose from obscurity between 1911 and 1926 and

---

[1] *Important Rules of Communist Bandit Combat,* published by The Kuomintang Military Officers Training Corps, Nanking.

almost overnight became field marshals, generalissimos and warlords, with dominion over regions as large and populous as many modern European states. These quondam rulers of China have had a bad reputation abroad. Many people think they employed their armies merely as weapons to amass wealth, power and concubines, that they fought battles principally with "silver bullets" and that they paid their soldiers in opium. Some of this was true enough of many of the old provincial generals, but many of these petty militarists were not driven by insatiable power lusts, but by high ideals of a romantic, if somewhat confused, nature. Appearing like vaudeville clowns, they were in reality minor actors in one of the greatest tragedies of history—the collision between the East and West. Such a man was General Kao Hsu-hsun, who, having deserted Chiang Kai-shek, now sat before me in a hut in Shansi Province telling me the story of his life.

Now the remarkable thing about General Kao as a study in character development is not that he was a dissolute warlord who was surrounded and cut off by the Communists and surrendered only to save his own life. On the contrary, the uniqueness of his position is this: that this illiterate son of a bankrupt middle farmer, rising to become general of an army when he was still in his twenties, was nevertheless able, when past middle age, to re-create the ideals of his youth, to discard his position of power and finally, in spite of fear of the secret police and the pleadings of his fellow-generals, to disown his loyalty to Chiang Kai-shek and deliberately to bring his whole army over to the Chinese Communists whom he had once thoroughly disliked.

As Kao—a handsome man of fifty, with the open, bronzed, face of a farmer turned soldier—told me about himself, I began to understand with renewed force the tragic necessity that has warped the life of so many men and women during the last thirty-seven years of war and revolution in China. For strange as it may seem, it was the impact of Western capitalism on Chinese life that first set Kao's footsteps on a tortuous road that finally led him into the camp of Chinese Communism.

Kao never went to school as a boy. When sixteen, he came to Peiping. The 1911 Revolution had just occurred, but Kao, though excited by the overthrow of the emperor, was much more concerned by the fact that he could not get a job. Hungry and poorly dressed, he borrowed money from a usurer, bought himself a small tray and peddled cigarettes outside the Chien Men Gate—that forbidding stone battlement that guards the entrance to Peiping's Tartar Walls.

Kao was depressed by the fact that all the cigarettes in his tray were manufactured by foreign concerns. "It irritated me," he said, "to sell cigarettes for foreigners. Why should they get all the profits? Why could not China make cigarettes herself?" He concluded this was because

China was not strong. Looking around at foreign soldiers guarding the embassies in Peking, he decided that the power of a country lay in its army. So he enlisted as a private in the forces of the Christian General Feng Yu-hsiang.

"Under Feng," said Kao, "I came to realize the imperialist designs of the great powers. Worst of all was Japan. Every May 7th, Feng used to assemble all of us on the parade ground and read to us Japan's twenty-one demands. Then he would weep. I was much affected and soon I developed a deep feeling about the necessity for revolution and a great belief in the doctrines of Dr. Sun Yat-sen, especially his principle of nationalism."

In 1926, Kao became commander of Feng Yu-hsiang's 12th Division. When Chiang Kai-shek marched north in 1927, with the slogans of Dr. Sun Yat-sen on his lips and with the intention of throwing out the warlords, Kao's enthusiasm ran very high. The events of 1927 and the despotism of Chiang Kai-shek somewhat disillusioned Kao. "Chiang took up the same old role of the warlords," he said. "I was depressed." His disillusionment, however, was not complete, and Kao still remained ambitious. By 1929, he became commander of the 9th Army under Feng. He went to the far-distant northwest with General Sun Lien-chung with whom he served for twenty years. For a time he was governor of Chinghai Province. Then he fought on Feng's side in a brief but bitter civil war with Chiang. Feng was defeated, and most all of his armies, including Kao's, were incorporated into the national army under Chiang Kai-shek and sent south of the Yangtze River to fight the Communists. Here Kao maintained his position as army commander, but he was unhappy. During his twenty years in the army, he had developed a very bad habit. He had learned to read.

Ambitious and energetic as he had been till now, and swift and successful as had been his rise from jobless wanderer and cigarette peddler to governor and army commander, there had always remained in him a strain of idealism. Influenced by reading, influenced also by many years of war, he gradually came to the conclusion that Chiang Kai-shek had betrayed the principles of Dr. Sun Yat-sen and made of the revolution a thing to mock the hopes of the mass of the people. One day, having read an article about the life of serfs in Czarist Russia, he looked about him and thought that conditions were much the same in China. Embittered when he saw the Kuomintang bureaucrats come in and seize the land of the peasants that he, himself, had freed from the Communists, he thought that Dr. Sun's principle of the "livelihood of the people" existed only in the mouths of officials. Then, too, living among his troops, he wondered why the officials should live so much better than he, who was preserving them in power.

Suddenly he could stand no more, and in the early 1930's without a word to anyone, he gave up his command in the field, and fled to Tientsin. Chiang put out an order for his arrest, but Kao remained safe, hiding in the British Concession. In 1933, he went to Kalgan and joined a movement against the Japanese led by his old commander Feng Yu-hsiang. The movement was quickly suppressed and Kao became head of the Public Safety Bureau of Hopei.

When Japan captured Peiping, Kao led his gendarmes into the countryside to fight a guerrilla war. For five years, he remained behind the Japanese lines, commanding a force of thirty thousand men. The 8th Route Army, expanding everywhere, however, soon left him no place to live and he came across the Yellow River with his troops.

Now, at last safe in the rear lines, Kao went to the then capital of China at Chungking. "I got a headache there," he said. "I was disgusted by what I saw. No government office was doing anything. All the officials were just waiting for Chiang Kai-shek's orders. Everyone was grafting. A needle factory owner invited me to dinner and told me he had to pay the Special Service agents of Chiang Kai-shek one hundred thousand dollars for every worker in his factory so that they would not be conscripted. I was sick."

In anger, Kao went to see General Chen Cheng, chief of staff of the army. Protesting against the corruption and the despotism he had seen in Chungking, Kao angrily burst out: "You may find the Three People's Principles on a wall or in a bookstore, but not among the people. Just show me one county where Dr. Sun's principles have been put in practice."

General Chen flushed, but said nothing. Kao went to see Chiang Kai-shek himself. "I got another headache," he said, and here he got up and gave an imitation of Chiang's "Shanghai-loafer walk," imperceptibly swaggering, nodding his head and saying: "Good! Good!" But Kao got no satisfaction from the generalissimo either.

"I was so angry at what I saw in Chungking," he said, "that I thought there was no way to fight Japan effectively but to kill Chiang Kai-shek."

Such an outspoken critic was not wanted around Chungking and the army found it convenient to ship him back quickly to the front. He arrived just in time to be completely overrun in the battle of Loyang and to see Chinese farmers, angered at the tax collectors, rise in revolt against Chinese soldiers and join the Japanese.

By now, he saw no hope in the Chiang Kai-shek government at all. Meanwhile, the Communists had been watching Kao's antics with much interest. Every time he published a book, Mao Tze-tung sent Kao a copy. Kao began to think nobody could be worse than Chiang and a year before the Japanese surrender he sent a letter by trusted messenger to General Peng Teh-huai, vice-commander of the 8th Route Army and also one to General Liu Po-cheng, suggesting that they arrange further communications. "I dared do this," said Kao, "because I had read a lot of Communist books and because I had over a hundred Communist party members in my army and found they weren't such bad people after all."

Kao's gravitation toward the Communists was soon to have an effect, not only on his own character, but on the course of the civil war. In 1945, after the Japanese surrender, Chiang Kai-shek ordered Kao and two other armies in the vicinity to advance up the Peiping-Hankow Railway and take the town of Sinsiang, preparatory to making a quick dash across the North China Plain and opening up railway communications to Peiping. In Sinsiang, an emissary from General Liu Po-cheng and also two delegates of the Communist party came to see Kao. Kao informed these delegates that he was dispatching his army northward and wanted to know where he could meet the 8th Route Army and come over. This was a terrible decision for Kao. In his own words, though, "It was not an accident but the result of twenty years of experience."

Moving north, Kao wrote One-Eyed Liu asking him not to attack. Liu paid no attention, but let Kao and the other two armies come on and then threw a circling arm about them. "I did not blame Liu," Kao told me. "He was correct."

Kao told the other two army commanders what he was going to do and pleaded with them to come over. They would not. Writing explanatory letters to his wife, his old commanders in the army and to his friends, Kao bid a painful good-by to his fellow-generals and then surrendered with his army to General Liu. Allowed to keep his arms, he sent out a telegram addressed to the whole nation, explaining his attitude and asking every patriotic Chinese to observe three points: "Oppose the civil war, fight for peace and democracy and co-operate with all parties to organize a democratic coalition government."

His sons and daughters in Chiang Kai-shek's hands were immediately arrested, but Kao with the aid of friends rescued them from jail and smuggled one son and his wife across the lines.

Kao's desertion had an important effect on the civil war: it broke the back of Chiang's offensive toward Peiping. This laid the foundation for the Marshall truce negotiations. The effect of his act on Kao's personal life was also somewhat cataclysmic.

"Everything here is different," he told me. "In Chiang Kai-shek's areas, society is distinctly stratified. I know, for I passed up from the bottom through all grades to the top. In Chiang's areas, the important thing is how much money you make, what rank you have or what kind of a house you're living in. Here people ask only one thing: 'Is your work well done?' When I was an army commander on the other side, people used to flatter me, call me Reverend Sir or Elder Born. Nobody does that now, and if I spun thread, I would be just as respected. Before I used to smoke Three Castles, now I smoke grass cigarettes. I used to have central heating in my big house in Tientsin, but now all I have is a pan of charcoal. For twenty years I drank from one to thirty glasses of brandy a day, but now I only drink an occasional cup of *pai kar* [native wine].

"Still this life is appropriate for me because I was born in the country and it seems good to get back to simple standards again. Even in Tientsin, when I had nothing to do, I used to ride out and help the people reap their wheat. But in Tientsin when I rode around in my car with my wife, I saw society from far away. Here, both my wife and I feel very close to life. We like it.

"Well, that's about all," said Kao. "That perhaps explains something about how a man becomes a 'bandit.'" He laughed. "I'm not a Communist, and they won't let me call my army the 8th Route Army. But I think Communist policies are at the moment apropos to the present situation. It's not socialism, but a new democracy, against oppression from outside powers and against despotism from inside."

I certainly was not prepared to take Kao's statements about his feelings toward the Communists at face value. After all what else could he say? Moreover, despite all his protestations of happiness, Kao seemed to me a little sad. I don't know what it was, but as I saw him eating with Red commanders he just appeared out of place—somewhat strained and forcedly gay. Perhaps, the very serious attitude of the Communists depressed him, perhaps the ceaseless political talk bored him. Maybe my impressions were wrong, but that's how I felt.

But actually, the subjective feelings of Kao were not so important as far as the war was concerned. What mattered was that he had deserted Chiang Kai-shek and of his own accord. Just before I said good-by to Kao, he asked me when I returned to the outside world to go and see a very high-ranking officer—whom I can't name here—in Chiang Kai-shek's army. "Give him this message," he said. "Please understand that I came over to this side not for any reasons of personal enmity. And please understand that I had to join the revolution, but still have good friendship with you. Take the lead of all the legitimate forces in North China and we will follow you."

Later, I did as Kao requested. At a party where were present not only a number of high Chinese officials, both in Chiang's government and his army, but also General Wedemeyer, who was then in China on a special mission to see if there were not some way the United States could help Chiang Kai-shek, I told this general I had seen Kao. His reaction was amazing. Right in front of everyone he seized me by the sleeve, drew me close and listened to Kao's message which I delivered. "It's coming, it's coming," he said somewhat cryptically, but with great excitement.

And come it did. The tale of Kao Hsu-hsun was repeated over

and over again, not only on the battlefield, but in government offices and rear-line headquarters all over North China.

But it was not only deserting Kuomintang generals that led to the defeat of Chiang Kai-shek, but also a small matter of the 8th Route Army.

Let's see what kind of an army this was.

46. The 8th Route Army

AMONG world military organizations, the 8th Route Army was probably unique. It owed allegiance to no government, yet fought under a central military command. Its soldiers were volunteers, yet received no salary. Its officers enforced strict discipline, yet had no rank.

So extraordinary was this army that it was probably better known than any fighting force in four thousand years of Chinese history. Not even the Chinese Red Army, from which it sprang, was so loved and hated, so feared and admired, so reviled and praised. The fame of these soldiers had spread so far that you could go almost any place in China, either on the Communist side or the Kuomintang, and merely by holding up your thumb and first finger,[1] signify that you wished to speak about the 8th Route Army. Almost as far traveled as its fame were its soldiers. From the jungles of Burma to the snowy fields of Manchuria, from the mountains of Tibet to the plains by the Yellow Sea, these soldiers had marched back and forth across the continent, fighting over a hundred different armies of the warlords, of Chiang Kai-shek, of the Japanese. They were from all provinces and were in a sense a national army, yet no nation recognized them. In short, they were armed rebels.

Perhaps the best way to approach an understanding of these rebels is statistical. At the start of the civil war the 8th Route Army had about a million men. By the end of 1948, this army totaled nearly three million men, the increase being accounted for partly by recruiting, but mostly by desertions from the Kuomintang. By this time, the Communists had changed the designation of their forces to the People's Revolutionary Army in order to give it the character of a national army. The direction of this army was vested in the five-man Revolutionary

[1] A Chinese way of indicating the figure 8. The use of this sign became as prevalent in China as the V sign in Europe. It, however, was used by friend and foe alike.

Affairs Military Council of the Communist party, headed by Mao Tze-tung.

The very size of this army and the extent of the area in which it operated made it much different from the old Red Army or even than the army which had fought the Japanese. This was particularly so in tactical organization. Previously, the Reds had fought nothing but a partisan warfare and operated in units generally no larger than a regiment. When I was in Communist territory, however, they were just in the process of changing from partisan to mobile and regular warfare and operated in divisions and corps.

War to the Communists not being primarily a military affair, their front-line regiments were often leavened with a large smattering of nonmilitary personnel. In each regiment, there were not only officers and soldiers, but teachers and students, actors and actresses, land reform cadres and farm experts. Thus an 8th Route Army unit was often not only a fighting organization but at the same time a school, theater, labor co-operative and political club.

As for the men themselves, the great majority of them were young peasants. Their average age was much higher than that of the old Red Army and I suppose corresponded somewhat to the age level in our own army. In one regiment that I investigated, the average soldier was twenty-three years old, five feet high and weighed 136 pounds.

In this same regiment, nearly 100 per cent of the soldiers were North China farmers. What southern soldiers remained from the old Red Army days had long since become officers. Of the officers, 71 per cent came from the peasantry, 11 per cent were workers and 12 per cent were students. Only 6 per cent (outside the students) were from the petty bourgeoisie—sons of merchants, intellectuals, small landlords and so on.

The literacy of the soldiers was very much higher than in Chiang's armies and very much higher than the North China peasantry, but compared to Western standards it was still very low. Seventy-three per cent of the soldiers had been illiterate when entering the army, but of these 20 per cent could now read two hundred characters, 23 per cent could read and write three hundred characters, and 30 per cent could read a newspaper. Twenty-three per cent of the soldiers had a primary school education before joining this regiment and of these all could read newspapers and simple books. Soldiers of all regiments were required to study characters when not fighting. Some of these were taught by political directors, some by more educated comrades and some by the platoon commanders themselves.

Soldiers, like their commanders, received no fixed salaries. However, in addition to their food and uniforms, they received a small grain allotment which they generally pooled and traded in for vegetables. After the adoption of the land reform program, every soldier and officer, as well as government member, was entitled to a portion of land equivalent to that given the peasants. This was farmed in his absence by his family or the local Farmers Association.

The officers,[2] except for the top-ranking old-line Communists, were mostly from local areas. A few were from the old Red Army and some were intellectuals who came in from outside during the war against Japan. The average age of these officers was thirty in the regiment, thirty-five in a brigade, forty or over in a division. The oldest commander in the whole army was Chu Teh, next was General Liu Pocheng, who was fifty-five. The youngest division commander was thirty-seven.

Most of the officers had come from the ranks during the Japanese war. Not only did this preclude an officer caste system, but meant that the officer understood both the military and personal problems of the individual soldier far better than if he had been trained in some special academy. As a general rule, each outfit produced its own officers instead of getting them from a central pool. There were few rear line schools—due to the difficulties of communication—and most officer candidates went to schools maintained by columns and brigades in the field. This was not only convenient, but also did away with the kind of replacement depots which so demoralized our young officers during the war.

There was no rank and no confusion on the battlefield because of the lack of it. Saluting was customary among troops, but not around headquarters or in the rear lines.

There was none of that boot-and-polish and asinine discipline that so angered American soldiers in Paris during the war. There were no Courthouse Lees and if one developed, he would soon have been put in his place by the soldiers.

Soldiers committing small offenses were usually talked to by officers or sergeants. Those who continually committed such offenses were criticized at mass meetings of their platoon, company or battalion. Such culprits were told they must "turn over their thoughts." This ideological and social pressure was extremely hard to withstand. More serious offenses were punished by jail. Obvious antiparty activities were presented to mass meetings. Culprits could be shot if the mass meeting so decided. This applied to officers as well as top-ranking commanders.

Soldiers had the right to call meetings to criticize officers and to complain to superior authorities. If judged guilty, the officer generally apologized or repented at a mass meeting. If he disagreed with a com-

[2] Officer is used here in the sense of a commander of a unit, such as a company or a battalion. Officers and soldiers were usually distinguished by the terms "leaders" and "fighters."

plaint, he passed it on to a superior. But he had no right to suppress the complaint or penalize the individual who made it.

There were no clubs for officers or enlisted men, but only army clubs for both together. Possibly, they would have proved dull to American soldiers. Every company, battalion, brigade, division and even head-quarters of the high command had army clubs. Each club had the following committees: food, management, wall newspaper, dramatics and singing and the committee for the survey of activities. The Wall Newspaper Committee had the following sections: current events, questions and answers, woodcuts, cartoons, notices, personal plans. The main emphasis was on the writings of the soldiers themselves, and bore little resemblance to an American Army-managed newspaper such as the *Stars and Stripes*.

Officers were called by their titles, such as Squad Commander Chang or Company Commander Wang. Liu Po-cheng, though a commander in chief, was generally referred to as Division Commander Liu. Because of the growing size of the army, there was some discussion about instituting rank and using insignia so that officers would be recognized, but soldiers and officers were so close that there had not yet been any need for this. If a new officer came from outside, he brought identification papers with him, and soon fitted into the old scheme, despite his lack of bars or eagles or stars. Finally, there were no officer's clubs, no officer wards in hospitals and no officer messes. Idyllic as it may sound, I am afraid it may not last. Most of the officers I met said they certainly did not want to do away with the system as the Russians did, but a few higher-ranking officers confided to me that it was a revolutionary measure and would probably be done away with in peacetime.

The majority of the officers, as well as the soldiers, in the 8th Route Army were unmarried. Those who were married were generally in that state before they entered the army. Local regulars sometimes obtained leave over the New Year holidays to get married. Once he had taken a wife, the soldier got preferential treatment in the way of subsidies. By law, a soldier was guaranteed that his wife could not divorce him while he was on the front. But if the wife did not hear from her husband for three years, she had the right to marry again. This law, I am afraid, sometimes protected the soldier better than it did the wife. I met a girl who was the wife of a brigade chief of staff. She had not seen him for four years and he had taken up with another woman. She wanted a divorce, but did not know what to do about her child.

Many of the officers and soldiers were divorced—that is, they had left their wives and families behind. As a matter of fact, unhappy marriages, I found, were one of the big reasons why both men and women joined not only the army, but the whole revolution. This, of course, was but another way of revolting against feudalism, which forced boys and girls to marry against their wills. Sometimes a soldier would go home on leave to see the girl his family had picked out for him. Having received quite a liberal education in the army and his horizon having been broadened by travel, the soldier would often refuse to marry the girl of his parents' choice.

As far as I could see and learn, the soldiers of the 8th Route Army treated the peasant girls with respect, and the farmers had a far higher opinion of army morality than they did of Chiang's soldiers. One of the reasons 8th Route Army soldiers treated the women so well was that they often fought in their own locality. Kuomintang soldiers were imported from outside and often had no sympathy for the local populace. I even found landlords who had been won to the Communist cause because of the difference between Kuomintang and 8th Route Army officers. In one village, I came across a landlord whose land had been divided and who hated the 8th Route Army because of this. But when the Kuomintang temporarily took over the area, his daughter, being the best-looking girl in the village, as landlords' daughters generally are, was forced to sleep with the local Kuomintang commander. As a result, despite the loss of his property, the landlord much preferred the 8th Route Army.

From the highest commander down to the lowliest soldier, all men of the 8th Route Army dressed alike. The higher the person's job, however, the more privileges. Battalion commanders and up were entitled to a horse or a mule. Army commanders might have a captured jeep. Regiment commanders might have Little Devils (boys who run away from home to join the army) as orderlies. Neither officer nor soldier wore any insignia showing either rank or unit. Commanders were distinguished by their cleaner clothes and sometimes fancy pistol belts. No officer ever went around sporting a row of medals. As a matter of fact, the only medals were worker and soldier medals.

Brave soldiers were rewarded by becoming members of the All Heroes Organization. Their names were published in the newspapers, of which every unit generally had one, or in magazines. For minor deeds of heroism, the soldier was rewarded by having his name placed in his unit's book.

The soldier usually received one winter and two summer uniforms a year. The officers had no fine foreign-style overcoats like Chiang's officers, but the soldiers were far better clad than Chiang's, always having winter uniforms and never being without shoes.

How did the Communists manage to feed, clothe and equip their armies? Here is where the Communist encouragement of production and the revival of handicrafts proved their worth to the army as well as to the economy of the peasant.

As far as armaments went, the United States and Chiang's armies were really their main source of supply. Ninety per cent of all its artillery, machine guns and rifles were from Kuomintang troops. The Border Region could make 80 per cent of the hand grenades and 70 per cent of the shells the army used. The manufacture of shells was a difficult problem. Shells made to fit Chinese- and Japanese-captured guns would not fit the American guns the 8th Route captured from Chiang's troops. Soldiers I saw had mobile American 105s and bazookas with some ammunition. Border Region leaders, when I was there, were debating whether to change the size of their gun barrel to meet their shells or to change the shells to fit the guns. It was a tough problem because they never knew what size guns they were going to capture or whether they would be Chinese, Japanese or American.

As for the individual soldier, he generally had a rifle, two hand grenades, five to ten clips of ammunition, one blanket, an extra suit of underwear, a cake of soap, a rice bowl, a pair of chopsticks, a sewing kit, two pairs of shoes and a notebook. Old soldiers often had fountain pens won as prizes in production campaigns. Seldom did the soldier have a toothbrush and almost never any tooth paste. He wore no charms, carried no Bible, confessed to no chaplain and had few superstitions.

So much for statistics. But really to understand the 8th Route Army it is necessary to understand Chiang Kai-shek's army and the relation of both armies to the Chinese Revolution.

47. Chiang Kai-shek's Army

WHEN civil war broke out in China in 1945, there were three main things wrong with Chiang Kai-shek's army. It had not done any serious fighting for several years; it was at loggerheads with the rest of Chinese society, it had no soul.

Among cynical officers of Chiang Kai-shek, there were several sayings that well characterized the ability of this army to fight. For example, there were the "five discords" between: 1. Government and army; 2. Party and army; 3. People and army; 4. Army and army; 5. Officer and soldier.

There were also the Three Don't Cares: 1. Don't care to fight; 2. Don't care about the people; 3. Don't care about myself.

It is no accident that neither the Japanese war nor the civil war produced a single distinguished military name among Chiang's officers.

Chiang, himself, as commander in chief, was noteworthy only for his stubbornness, his shrill fits of temper and his military errors, as numerous as they were catastrophic. General Ho Ying-chin achieved his high position through intrigue and attention to administrative detail. General Chen Cheng, chief of staff and a half-pint counterpart of the generalissimo, lost nearly every battle he directed in the Japanese and the civil wars. General Li Tsung-jen, more democratic than most, was hamstrung by the generalissimo's distrust of him. General Tang En-po, fellow-provincial of the generalissimo, was more noted for the fact that the people of Honan revolted against his army and joined the Japanese than for the fact that he had once won a small victory at Taierchuang. General Ku Chih-tung, original commander of the Nanking Guard Division— Chiang's own—was distinguished for his passive mandarinism. General Hu Tsung-nan, favorite Whampoa cadet of the generalissimo and so-called King of the Northwest, was famous for the fact that he didn't smoke, drink or play around with women—and also for his blue-shirt organization, his student-filled jails, his concentration camps and his campaign against the Communist capital of Yenan where he lost a good part of his army. General Tu Yu-ming, commander in chief in Manchuria, was sufficiently characterized by foreign military men: "Egotistical, inefficient, jealous, professionally unqualified . . . another failure for the Kuomintang because the generalissimo picks notoriously poor men for important positions." The observer might have added that China's dictator, because he depended on a narrow clique to preserve his despotism, could hardly help but pick his own followers for important jobs.

Of course, not only medieval but also democratic China had its representatives in the officers' corps. The innumerable wars after the 1911 Revolution and the Japanese war poured into the army tens of thousands of idealistic youth in the capacity of officers, clerks, adjutants and so on. Some of the sons of the better-educated peasantry even rose to be commanders of armies, as the phenomenon of Christian General Feng Yu-hsiang or General Li Tsung-jen, the farm boy from Kwangsi, testifies. These circles felt the need for reforms.

There is even the rather pitiful tale told by Captain Wei Sheng-ming, a recent middle school graduate, who wrote as follows in his diary in July 1947:

This is the most shameful day in my whole life. The soldiers were tired after the long journey and I let them rest on the station platform and bought them some watermelon. Colonel —— came and cursed me in front of the whole company. Then, while the soldiers were hastily hiding their watermelons, he slapped me and then kicked me. I have never been so humiliated. The American General Patton is criticized by the American Congress for slapping a soldier. But to what Congress can I turn for help?

This rather inconsequential affair had numerous tragic counterparts.

Impoverished students, as we had seen, were often lured to Nanking by the promises of Chiang's government to train them as army officers. The aim of these schools was simply to make obedient beasts and future slave drivers out of the better-educated young men of China.

The whole Chinese army, from top to bottom, was riven with inhumanity, double-crossing and terror. Officers without influence were always in danger of execution for some minor error in the performance of duty. Ask some of the American officers who were in Burma how Chinese regiment commanders came crawling to them on hands and knees begging that no reports be made about their military mistakes because they would be sent back to China and shot. Or ask even some of the division or army commanders how their life was played out on a stage of doubt and fear. Every army headquarters was a nest of spies. The party secret service, the Bureau of Investigation and Statistics, and the Special Service Section surrounded even war zone commanders with a web of intrigue and jealousy, terrorizing the staff one by one until they had isolated the commander. Staff officers were seized from army headquarters by the SSS without the army commander being able to do anything about it. Further, Chiang made some of the division commanders personally responsible to him so that on the field of battle they could refuse to obey a corps commander's order on the grounds that they were waiting an order from "the highest." Tactics thus were subordinated not to strategy, not to national policy, but to the power needs of a party despot.

The bad feeling between the older democratic officers who still remembered Dr. Sun Yat-sen and the younger generals who knew only Chiang Kai-shek introduced another factor into its decay. The make-up of this army was determined by the make-up of both the old China, which was semifeudal, and the transitional China of Chiang Kai-shek, which was a contradictory hodgepodge of fascism and old-fashioned despotism.

In the latter case, the officer's attitude toward the soldier was sometimes that of a comrade in arms, but mostly it was that of a gang leader toward a petty thief. In the former case, the attitude of the officer toward the soldier was that of landlord toward peasant—that is, the officer, while sometimes paternal, thought the men under him were ignorant villeins who had few human rights. This relationship dominated in the army. It was, however, much more sharply defined in the army than in the villages, and the soldier was undeniably the lowest scum in Chinese society. "You do not make good iron into a nail; you do not make a good man into a soldier." Such was the national tradition of the old Chinese army. This tradition still applied to the army of Chiang Kai-shek because the abortive 1927 Revolution did not change Chinese society as a whole and hence did not change the army.

The fear with which the people looked on the army and the contempt in which the army held the soldier can readily be seen by the way in which the peasant was conscripted for service. The basis of all conscription was graft, bribery and influence. Sons of the rich never entered the army; sons of the poor could never escape. An impoverished widow's only son was always drafted; the numerous offspring of the landlord, never. Since the draftees were the poorest men, they were often the most unhealthy, and it was very common for one-half of a contingent of soldiers to die before they reached the front.

Officers considered it their privilege and right to beat soldiers. During both the Japanese war and the civil war, I saw soldiers beaten on station platforms with bamboo rods, on highways with automobile crank handles, in rooms with iron bars. I once saw a colonel who had been a former consular official in New York City slap a soldier several times across the face because he couldn't find a pack of cards. When I protested, the colonel said: "That's all these dumb beasts understand."

There were some kindly officers who called their troops "my younger brothers" and who adopted a fatherly attitude to the men under them. But on the whole, the life of the ordinary soldier was but one cut above a pig and a cut below a mule. As a matter of fact, mules, on the whole, were better fed and better cared for than men.

Soldiers, if wounded, had small chance of living. Time and again I have seen wounded soldiers thrown off trains because they did not have the price of a ticket, wounded men thrown off half-empty trucks because an officer and his brutal sergeant wanted to transport opium— thrown off, mind you, not in a hospital, but on a mountain road, in the middle of nowhere. In the hospitals, I have seen sick and wounded soldiers piled in latrines and left unattended to die. I have seen them lying in filth, uncared for, like so many prisoners in a concentration camp. So terrible and bestial was the lot of this military slave, so damned his life, so hopeless his existence and almost sure his death, that in his misery he was forced to create "live and die" friends. Thus, if he were wounded or beaten, his sworn brother would take care of him, for neither society nor the army would.

Such was the army of Chiang Kai-shek, based on agrarian gangsterism, semiserfdom and "loyalty to the leader." Throughout the Japanese war and the civil war that followed, this army was continually beaten because it had no soul. Its commanding staff was distinguished by a scorn of the common soldier, by internal jealousy and fear of the secret service, by ignorance of its own trade, by an insidious self-loathing and by an uncontrollable habit of squeeze. The rank and file, submitting to corruption, tyranny and death, was characterized by a philosophy of despair, by a necessity to loot and by a hatred of their own officers and of the common people who pitied, but despised them.

Chinese civilization made the soldier both its slave and its executioner.

American interference in the affairs of the Chinese army in the end produced little change in the status of the soldier. As long as the Americans took an isolated force, trained, equipped and fed it, they might improve the lot of the soldiers, but as soon as this outfit went to war— that is, returned into the mainstream of Chinese life—it reverted to its old ways. Nor—unless the Americans took over almost the whole of China's army and thus created a state within a state—could it be otherwise. For as long as society did not change, the army could not change.

Thus, as for the peasant, so for the soldier, the revolution was the important thing. This observation would seem so trite as to need no further explanation. Yet, despite the fact that war and revolution are unmistakably established as twin movements of our time, the connecting link between the two often passes unnoticed or is deliberately concealed.

I do not pretend to understand much about these two very complex activities, but it seems to me that war and revolution are similar in that they both employ tremendous masses of men for a political purpose. The difference is that people make war only under the compulsion of their rulers to satisfy the aims of the state, but they make revolution under no other compulsion than their bitter life circumstances to overthrow their rulers and win control over their own destinies.[1] War chains the individual to the state; revolution breaks those chains—temporarily.

A revolutionary war resolves these differences by giving hitherto dispossessed classes a stake in the outcome of the fighting. Whether this stake be loot, land or liberty differs according to time, place and circumstance. But as long as the revolting masses get something (or believe they will get something) from you that they did not get from the old rulers, they will fight on your side with all the passion and courage at the command of their admittedly untrained intellects.

Clear as this matter seems to us, some very renowned generals, statesmen and philosophers have found all their theories about war completely confounded during revolutionary times. This is simply because they are so used to seeing history made by their own small clique that they cannot—often will not—analyze events from the standpoint of the revolting slave. Thus, they look everywhere but where they should to discover why one force conquers another.

One hundred and fifty years ago when the monarchs of Europe were falling before the magic of Napoleon and one after another the best armies of the continent saw their methods of war become ineffective, some learned military men found the cause in the wrong conduct of the art of war. But as Karl von Clausewitz, that wise, old Prussian military philosopher aptly noted:

---

[1] I refer here to a large-scale revolution made from the bottom up. Not to a *coup d'état* made at the top as in Czechoslovakia.

The tremendous effects of the French Revolution abroad were evidently brought about much less through new methods and views introduced by the French in the conduct of war than through the changes in statecraft and civil administration, in the character of government, in the condition of the people, and so forth. That other governments took a mistaken view of all these things, that they endeavoured, with their ordinary means, to hold their own against forces of a novel kind and overwhelming strength—all that was a blunder of policy.

In this statement what relates to the changes brought about by the French Revolution is perfectly true of the Chinese Revolution; and what relates to mistakes in policy is true, not only of Chiang Kai-shek, but also, to a degree, true of some of his allies in the United States. The phenomenon of the poorly equipped 8th Route Army defeating the American-equipped forces of China's dictator was attributed by many people to different causes. Thus we find the Kuomintang officials and some of their foreign followers maintaining that Kuomintang defeats were due to Russian help and Russian machinations. The stay-at-home economists found it in the economic collapse brought about by the Japanese war and a lot of mishmash about the high circulation velocity of Kuomintang paper money. The hard-boiled military observers declared the reason lay in the refusal of Chinese armies to obey American advice, in the stupidity of Chiang Kai-shek, in the perfidy of local leaders and so on.

All these reasons may have satisfied their advocates—though even that is doubtful—but they did not satisfy the Chinese soldier in whose heart, had they dared look in such a plebeian place, the theoreticians would have found answers to confound all their neat theorizing.

It is a curious, but nevertheless true, fact that most men are afraid to expose their minds to the shock of revolution. In few people will you find this mental bashfulness more deeply ingrained than in professional army officers. As a result, what passes as a good and even brilliant intellect in a normal war reveals its philosophic inadequacy in a revolutionary war.

An outstanding example of this was furnished by an American general when he stood up before the Congress of the United States and said that the important fact about Chiang Kai-shek was not that he was a despot, which he was, but that he was opposing Communism. We quite sympathize with the fact that the general, isolated behind the walls of military life, had little opportunity to get in touch with common people; we also appreciate his hatred of Communism, but what we find it very hard to understand is that he should fail to correlate intelligence—the mere clerical part of war.

To the Chinese people, the most important fact about Chiang Kai-shek was just the fact that he was a despot. Nobody threw himself with any passion at Chiang's feet because he was fighting the Communists, but many did rush to sacrifice themselves at the Communist altar because the Communists were fighting despotism. As for Chiang Kai-shek's soldiers, their leader's brand of despotism meant blows, kicks, curses, beatings, starvation, chain gangs and executions. It is not surprising that they turned out to be poor defenders of the feudal faith and the "democratic way of life."

48. Revolution and the 8th Route Army

IN ANY social upheaval as vast and violent as the Chinese Revolution, military organizations and concepts of strategy were swept aside as ruthlessly as political institutions and social classes. Just as the French Revolution scrapped the old aristocratic army of the Bourbons and the Russian Revolution abolished the demoralized army of the czars, so the Chinese Revolution destroyed the semifeudal army system of Chiang Kai-shek. There was, however, this significant difference. The French and Russians did not establish a new army until they had seized power; the Chinese established a new army while struggling for state power. This fact alone guaranteed that the revolutionary Chinese army would be much weaker, yet, by force of circumstances, more democratic and more intimately associated with the processes of revolution than either of its earlier counterparts.

In order to promote revolution in Russia, the Bolsheviks had deliberately broken down the morale of the old army, so that when they were forced to fight a civil war they had to re-create this morale by some very undemocratic disciplinary measures, including execution. The French, in carrying Liberty, Equality and Fraternity to the rest of Europe by means of war, also stamped out many gains of the revolution and instituted a levee en masse—that is, universal conscription. The Chinese Communists having neither a Third Estate nor a proletariat had to use their army for revolution. Therefore, in North China where I was, in order to win the peasant to revolution, and to give him the dignity of a personality, they could not conscript him. To do so would have put the Communists on a par with Chiang Kai-shek and given their army no distinction from his. For this reason the 8th Route Army was composed almost entirely of volunteers.

Soldiers were obtained by persuasion, propaganda and local social pressure. Preferential treatment was given to soldier families, the villages guaranteeing to plow a warrior's land and care for his relatives. In Kuomintang areas, peasants considered it a disgrace and a tragedy to be drafted into the army, but in the Liberated Areas, the Communists tried to make it appear an honor to join the army. Instead of being kidnaped from his home by draft agents, the volunteer for the 8th Route Army was given a feast by his whole village, decorated with a banner, set upon a caparisoned mule or even in a flower-decked sedan chair, serenaded by gongs, cymbals and flutes and escorted from the village by all the peasant boys and girls. In this way, the newly enlisted man got the idea that joining the army was not entirely a personal affair, but one in which he represented the whole village.

Though men volunteered for the army, their period of service was not limited to any length of time, but to the duration of the war. Yet, if an enlisted man ran away, he was not put in jail or beaten. A notice was merely sent to his village which would then try to persuade him to go back to the army. If he would not, he was generally shunned. Such social ostracism was generally sufficient to send him back of his own accord. Should he desert three times, he was turned over to the district magistrate for hard labor.

The reform of the draft apparatus had both military and revolutionary effects. For not only did the Communist volunteer fight more spiritedly than the Kuomintang conscript, but many peasants, knowing they would be safe, used to flee over from Chiang Kai-shek's side to the Liberated Areas in order to avoid Kuomintang conscription. Thus the volunteer system built up morale on the Communist side and destroyed it on the Kuomintang side.

It should not be thought, however, that it was easy for a villager to avoid joining the army. The pressures were terrific. In the first place, there was the matter of propaganda. This was usually intimately associated with the land reform. For example, in mass meetings, day-to-day gossip and in discussions and plays, recruiting officers would say:

"The rise of the poor is the result of the struggle of the Communist party and the 8th Route Army.

"In order to protect the fruits of the struggle [land and food received in land reform] the reactionaries must be smashed and our villages defended.

"Let us avenge for our ancestors the exploitation they suffered from corrupt officials and rascal landlords.

"We must create our own freedom and welfare with our own sweat and blood. Everyone join the regular army."

Besides propaganda, family members were mobilized to convince a prospective recruit he should enlist. If this did not work, then the whole people of the village might be mobilized to break down the recruit's resistance and force him to join up.

When a man went off to join the army, the district magistrate served as a groom for the horse of the recruit. When he arrived in a new unit, after a physical examination, he was told the history, reforms and glorious accomplishments of his unit, so that he would feel happy on joining such a distinguished outfit.

As soon as he arrived, old soldiers rushed to pay their respects to the new soldier. Some helped him put on his uniform. Some gave him a haircut, or made him presents of hand towels and soap. A distinct effort was made to make the new soldier feel at home and among friends.

This was not unknown to the officers of Chiang Kai-shek. The Kuomintang intelligence report, which we have previously quoted, sadly noted: "The conscription of our side does not aim to make the people understand, does not carry out educational work, does not convince them ideologically, but only tries to enforce the law. As a result, for ten years the conscription system has been corrupt. To compare our situation with that of the bandits [Communists] is indeed terrifying."

It is almost superfluous to remark that the 8th Route Army treated its soldiers much differently than did the Kuomintang. There were none of those ultrademocratic reforms which were ruthlessly abolished from the early Russian Red Army. Officers were not elected, but appointed. Nevertheless, soldiers were treated with studied kindness. No one was ever beaten. A commander was forbidden to curse his soldiers or even lose his temper when reprimanding them.

The success of these methods, which proved their worth time and again, can be explained in part by the character of the North China peasantry from whose ranks the soldiers were drawn. Thrifty, frugal, frank, single minded, capable of bearing great hardship, the farmer was sympathetic and honest with other people, but extremely vengeful against anyone who did him harm. Self-respecting, he would work hard if encouraged, but would lie down on the job if given bad treatment. "Bear hardship, but not blame," said a proverb. Such a man would not respond to curses. Officers of Chiang's armies beat this peasant and they got a bad instrument. Commanders of the 8th Route Army buttered him up and got a good instrument. For this reason there were few cliques in the 8th Route Army.

Equal pay, equal food, equal treatment, voluntary enlistment—these were all big factors in developing morale in the 8th Route Army. Another factor of great importance was political training. Every unit from the platoon up to the commander in chief of a war zone had a political director or a commissar whose duty it was to raise the morale of troops through political education. If a unit commander was killed, these men took command until another officer was appointed. The duties of these political directors were not, as might be supposed, to spy on military commanders and certainly, as far as I saw, there was no friction between them and purely military officers as there was friction between Chiang's officers and the spies of his secret service. The commanders gave the orders, but the commissars gave the pep talks and led the soldiers into battle.

The purpose of political education, according to the Communists, was to make the soldier believe in victory, to guarantee that victory by the organization of every kind of activity and to carry out the political line handed down from above. In informal meetings, political directors read newspapers to the soldiers, told of the defeats of Chiang Kai-shek in other parts of the country and explained the meaning of the war. Because soldiers do not like to be rebuked by officers, the Communists got each squad to organize a mutual self-help group which criticized the shortcomings of squad members. When a squad moved out of a village, the self-help groups checked to see that everything borrowed from the people had been returned. This was done without the supervision of the commander and for this reason was more effective. Three to five minutes each day were also used by such groups for public self-criticism. Thus one soldier might say: "Today, I dug a ditch poorly." Or another: "I did not fire the machine gun well."

Political education was also used to rid the new soldiers of the fear of death. Old soldiers who had fought the Japanese for eight years would tell their experiences, ending up with a statement something like this: "Cowards die in battle, but brave men live. So run forward quickly and get on top of the enemy before he has a chance to hit you." The commissar would then chime in with a political maxim: "People in Chiang's areas are starving to death because of high taxes. Unless we fight Chiang, we shall die. To fight is to live."

Prior to every battle, the political workers explained to the troops the relation of the battle to the over-all situation, the meaning of this particular battle in the entire Chinese Revolution and the general situation on both sides, with emphasis on the low morale of Kuomintang forces, high prices, revolts in Chiang's rear and so on.

As a matter of fact the aim of all political education in the 8th Route Army was to instill a spirit of class consciousness in the soldier. According to 8th Route Army leaders, this was the surest way of building up morale. Since this is rather a questionable subject, it is perhaps well to insert at this point some words of a conversation I had with the political director of the army in Shansi Province on the whole question of morale.

"To us," said my informant, "war is an emotional struggle carried on through political consciousness. Morale is composed of hatred, love, revenge and confidence in victory. It exists as a social phenomenon and does not lie in the strength of individuals, but in the strength of society. It is decisive in combat and decisive in war.

"The origins of morale lie in the emotions of the people. Our soldiers are farmers in uniform and they bring with them the hearts of farmers. Their social condition therefore determines their morale in fighting. Morale with these soldiers is higher than it was during the Japanese war, because the people hate Chiang Kai-shek more than they did the Japanese, because they have gone through the land reform and because they look on the Liberated Areas as their own nation and feel they have a reason to defend their homes.

"Leadership and education play an important part in raising morale. Leadership depends on the political education of the leader. He must believe in what he is fighting for and he must first of all love his soldiers, attending to their daily wants, their food and their sleeping before anything else. You ask is food, equipment or a political commissar more important for morale. The care of material conditions is a part of leadership. Of course, if troops had no food, a political director would speak empty words.

"Morale can go in waves. In general, with inexperienced troops, a lost battle, fatigue, sickness have bad effects. Raising morale under such circumstances again depends on leadership. Old soldiers are not so influenced by passing circumstances, but they demand more from leadership and so it is important with them too.

"In new outfits, killed friends weakens morale; in old, it toughens morale. All our columns are composed solely of old soldiers. Local regulars are placed in new outfits where they can gradually develop morale.

"Morale is far more important than economic conditions. If we should take economy as a basis for victory, we would have no confidence, as Chiang Kai-shek has a superior economy.

"Our methods of building morale would be of no use in the American army because you have a different kind of society than we do. Our way of building morale depends on class consciousness and hardly could be used except in a revolutionary war."

Examples of the way army political leaders put these theories into practice come readily to mind. Soldiers were told they came from an oppressed class and that the nature of the war they were fighting was to end exploitation. It was explained that the civil war was a war for themselves, for their emancipation and for their protection as individuals. The first lesson the soldier had to learn, therefore, was to cultivate good relations with the people. Incessantly the army dinned into the soldier's head that he could not molest the people, that he had to pay for everything he bought, that he could not loot, that he had to clean up rooms that he had used, that above all he must not make the people feel that the army was crushing their privileges. Naturally, this was of extreme importance, as the people of China have commonly hated all soldiers.

The success of the Communists in this type of political training was amazing to anyone who knew anything about China. Village cadres and local militiamen were often extremely cruel to the people, but rarely could the same thing be said of the 8th Route Army whose soldiers were characterized by an extraordinary pride in their discipline and close relations with the people. Exterior signs of this friendliness could be seen in the special language they adopted toward the peasantry, such as "my big sister," "my younger brother" and so on. Far more revealing than any of these things, however, was to see peasants near the fighting areas carrying pigs and chickens ten and fifteen miles to the front to give the soldiers, to see women sewing shoes for their lovers in the army instead of for their husbands, to see these same women set aside their only beds as rest stations for traveling soldiers, cut up their skirts into bandages and join in celebrations of army victories. Pitiful efforts compared to what America does for her soldiers, but magnificent co-operation of peasantry and army when compared to Chiang Kai-shek's areas.

Lest all the above sound starry-eyed, I should perhaps mention that I have seen the American, British, Burmese, Indian, French, German, Russian and Chinese Kuomintang armies in action, but I have never seen an army quite like the 8th Route Army led by the Chinese Communists. In many ways, it was absolutely unique among the armies of the world. I think this was principally due to the fact that much of it was not created from an old standing army, but out of the people themselves. The very desperateness of their position forced the Communists to form a democratic army. Offhand, the only other army that I know of that was formed in the same way was the Yugoslav partisans of Marshal Tito. But you will not find anyone in Chinese Communist territory who calls himself marshal nor will you find anyone who dresses himself in a fancy uniform and besplatters himself with medals. This, of course, may change now that the Communists are moving toward total power.

Here, I would like to tell about a political tactic that possibly has never been tried before by any army in the world. I refer to the use of the Speak Bitterness Meetings by the army.

Today, the 8th Route Army—or as they are now calling it, the People's Revolutionary Army—is composed of three kinds of soldiers: old soldiers, newly enlisted farmers from the Communist areas and prisoners of war. When a battle takes place and prisoners are captured, the army retires to an open field and holds a vast public meeting. An old soldier gets up and tells how he joined the 8th Route Army, how he fought and what kind of a life he leads. A new soldier tells of his bitterness on the land and how they "turned over" against the landlords and what results they got from the land reform. A prisoner then is persuaded to get up and talk about his life in Chiang Kai-shek's army. He tells how he was dragged from his farm, how he was beaten in the army, how he starved and so on. Some of these tales are so horrible and so filled with suffering that even the most hardened soldiers weep at hearing them.

Each one has a different story. If he has not personally suffered, the soldier tells the sufferings of his parents. Needless to say, it is a tremendous experience for the soldier to be able to cry out his sorrows to a host of sympathetic listeners.

Chinese are philosophical people, and a Chinese soldier is the most philosophical of them all. Like the peasant, the individual soldier thought it was his fate to suffer. But when he saw that everyone had his own store of bitterness, he reached the conclusion that all the poor were from the same family.

These mass confessionals spoke far more forcibly to the heart of the soldiers than did the commanders or the political directors. There was absolutely no way to undermine such teaching. Nor could the method be copied. For had Chiang Kai-shek allowed his soldiers to reveal their bitterness, they might well have risen up against their own officers.

Commissars, of course, took advantage of these meetings to point political lessons to Kuomintang prisoners. They tried to sow dissension between officers and men. They told captives that Kuomintang officers were the sons and brothers of landlords and corrupt officials, that their ancestors had exploited the soldiers' ancestors and that now they had become the slaves of superior officers. "You fight and suffer at the front," political directors told captives, "but nobody even picks up your corpse after you die, while the rich who have authority have a good time in the rear." When a captured soldier blamed an evil village chief for his troubles, the commissar would trace the action up to the magistrate and then to the governor and finally to Chiang Kai-shek. Pretty soon, the soldier came to the belief that his worst personal enemy was not the county chief, but the dictator of China. Thus the commissars taught captured soldiers to generalize politically.

So effective were these new methods that even by the middle of 1947 Kuomintang soldiers captured one day would attend a political meeting the same night, and be fighting in the 8th Route Army the next day. Before 1947, the Communists used to send prisoners to training camps, but the political disintegration in Chiang's armies became so marked that in many places, they no longer felt the need of these camps.

While the Communists welcomed any soldier of Chiang's into the 8th Route Army, at the same time they also released any prisoner who wanted to go back to Chiang's side. As a matter of fact, they even gave prisoners traveling expenses to get home.

There have been too many witnesses to this Communist policy, both Chinese and foreign, to doubt its authenticity. An American Army officer who was captured by the Communists in Manchuria tells how six thousand men of Chiang's 88th Division were brought to a mass meeting and treated as honored guests. An American girl in Shantung tells how she visited a camp for fifty captured Kuomintang generals and saw them getting far better food and living under better conditions than 8th

Route officers. Finally, I myself, when in Kuomintang areas have seen hundreds of prisoners released by the Communists pouring across the lines.

Originally, the Kuomintang had not paid much attention to the political tactics used by the Reds to break down their army. "Just propaganda" was their comment. But as more soldiers began to desert and as the Kuomintang officers learned about Red political undermining, they became terrified. "Upon hearing such things" (Speak Bitterness Meetings), wrote one of Chiang's officers, "how can one help but being heartbroken. Unless we can devise methods of counteraction, it will be simply horrible."

But the army of Chiang Kai-shek was too far gone in dissolution to devise any methods of counteraction. As I was writing these words, there came to hand an Associated Press story out of China describing how General Ma Wen-ting, chief of staff of the 82nd Division, ordered the massacre of five hundred of the soldiers of Communist General Peng Teh-huai.

"Without emotion," says the Associated Press, "the grim-visaged Ma described the mass killing of prisoners. 'We chopped off one head after another with our big broadswords. We finished the others off with hand grenades.' "

Such were the exploits of Chiang Kai-shek's generals. The difference between Kuomintang and Communist treatment of prisoners is too striking to need comment.

Perhaps the difference also accounts in some measure for the different results obtained on the field of battle. Let us look at this battlefield.

49. Chiang Attacks

WAR is only an instrument of policy, but Chiang Kai-shek seems never to have had a war plan. Plans for campaigns—yes; plan for war—no. And throughout the whole conflict with the Communists, we find him ignoring their army and basing his whole hopes for victory on the capture of rail lines, walled cities and strong points.

Let us go back again for a moment to the year 1945 and rejoin Chiang Kai-shek in his rock-ribbed refuge at Chungking.[1] The Japanese have surrendered, but Chiang is fifteen hundred miles away from the seacoast,

---

[1] Chiang established a temporary capital in Chungking during the Japanese war. He returned to the national capital at Nanking after V-J Day.

while his ancient enemies, the Communists, are close by the big cities of North China, demanding entry within their walls. Chiang solves this dilemma by twin strokes: he borrows the American Air Force and Navy to transport his troops to Japanese-held Nanking, Tientsin, Peiping, and Manchuria and he persuades the American government to issue orders to the beaten Japanese not to surrender to the Communist guerrillas at their gates.

This was a clever stratagem, acknowledged by all as a masterpiece—but it was to prove the undoing of China's dictator. For, having isolated these air- and sea-borne divisions in Peiping, Tientsin and Manchuria, he was led on by an inexorable logic to try and link them with his capital at Nanking and his main source of strength, the Yangtze Valley. To do so Chiang had to fight his way on the ground over the North China Plain, the most strategic area on the continent. In this attempt he was to strain his forces beyond their capacities.

Those who wish to gain a clear idea of the North China Plain have only to place, mentally, on the ground, a capital A. The left leg of the A is the Peiping-Hankow Railway, the right one is the Tientsin Pukow Railway, the tie of the A is the Lunghai Railway. The top of the A is Peiping where the headquarters of Chiang's northern army is; the lower left tip is Hankow, where his Central China supply base is; the lower right tip is Nanking, where Chiang Kai-shek and the seat of the Kuomintang government are.[2]

The triangle comprised in the top of the A, between the two legs and the crossbar, is the heart of the plain, where, since 1938, Communists had fought the Japanese. Midway, up the right side of this triangle lies a sacred Buddhist mountain, called Mount Tai, which was once an island in the sea that is now Shantung Province. Down the whole length of the left limb of our A runs a series of mountains which native militarists and invading barbarians have struggled to control for four thousand years and which stretch away for two thousand miles to the roof of the world in Tibet. These mountains dominate the plain.

Emerging west of the mountains and cutting directly across the plain, sometimes north, sometimes south of the crossbar of the A, runs the Yellow River, that great muddy snake that drains half the continent of China.

As for the plain itself, imagine an ancient sea that the Yellow River pumped full of Mongolian loess and made into a vast ocher-colored expanse of ground, flat as a pavement and thickly sown with the villages of ninety million people.

It is the combination of these people, the railways, the river, the mountains and the plain that makes this one of the most interesting and

[2] Strictly speaking Hankow and Nanking lie just south of the Great Plain.

important maneuver grounds for decisive battle in the world. The North China Plain, sometimes known as the Yellow River Plain, is the key to the whole country and he who holds it can open the door to victory. Recognizing this, Chiang Kai-shek, in October 1945, rashly tried to take the area by a series of quick marches, hoping to make secure the overland route between the Yangtze and the north. Using what troops he had in the vicinity and allying himself with the troops of Warlord Yen Hsi-shan, he dashed into the mountains of Shansi Province with fifty thousand men and at the same time ran three corps into the plains of Hopei Province on the east. His move was characteristically opportunistic and had fatal consequences.

For the Communists in the Taihang Mountains, west of the plain, watched his move and recognized its vulnerability. General Liu Po-cheng, debouched from the mountains with fifty thousand troops of his own, picked up fifty thousand more civilians on the way, and within a week wiped out thirty thousand of Chiang's troops in Shansi and captured one army and twelve division commanders. Turning back through the mountains and marching east, Liu, within another week, lured the three corps on the plain into a trap, persuaded General Kao Hsu-hsun, with whom he had been in written communication for a year, to surrender without a fight, wiped out a second corps on the banks of the Chang River, and drove the third back south.

Liu's quick victory was no major action in itself and observers paid it but scant attention; but it brought Chiang to cold-eyed alertness with a shock of recognition: these Communists were no longer the half-starved guerrillas he had driven from the Yangtze Valley twelve years before, but a serious menace. It was this defeat that underlay the short-lived Marshall truce of 1946. The truce was, for Chiang Kai-shek, a period of reflection and consideration. His decision was all-out war. In July 1946, Chiang assembled 200 of his 250 brigades for front line duty and set out on the great drive against the North China Plain with the avowed attention of reaching his isolated troops in the north and ending the war by weight of matériel within three to six months.

Why did Chiang begin an all-out war? The answer is obvious: he thought he could win. The figures seemed to prove it. The opposing sides lined up something like this:

	Chiang	Communists
Population	340,000,000	110,000,000
Army	4,000,000	1,200,000
Irregulars	1,000,000	1,500,000

Despite its several advantages in morale and mobility, the 8th Route Army had to give ground before Chiang's attacks which at first brought rapid and seemingly conclusive successes. Quickly Chiang cleared the area around the nation's capital at Nanking and her chief city at Shanghai and drove Communist General Chen Yi up the seacoast and into Shantung where he took refuge in sacred Mount Tai. With another swift blow, and almost ridiculous ease, he captured Kalgan, the only large North China city in Communist hands.

Success was so easy that Kuomintang officers said: "The Communists know nothing about tactics. They fight like babies." Chen Cheng, army chief of staff, declared the war would soon be over.

Everywhere, Chiang had nothing but victories. But he captured few enemy troops. In a few months his progress slowed down. Chiang captured cities, but the Communists remained in the countryside, sitting athwart his communications. In late 1946, Chiang began to find that the temporary, but necessary, occupation of towns along his supply routes required more forces than he could afford.

Unable to finish off the war quickly, Chiang, who had been waging offensives on four northern fronts at once, was forced to reduce his commitments and concentrate on one main front. By 1947, he drew up a new plan to conquer North China. Around the important railway junction of Hsuchow he massed half a million men and began a drive through Shantung Province, the road to Peiping and Manchuria. This front far outstripped the more publicized Manchurian front and soon became of nationwide importance.

At this time, I was in Communist territory and I saw Red strategists make a decision which was to have profound effects on the course of the war. They decided to halt their retreats and stand up and fight.

"I have noted," General Liu Po-cheng told me, "that while Chiang can still gain local victories, he can no longer keep his offensives rolling because of lack of reserves. We think his manpower is running low and he can't fight big battles any more.

"We have destroyed fifty brigades and when we destroy another fifty we think we can go on the offensive."

In the light of this theory, the Communists laid their plans. General Chen Yi, basing himself on Mount Tai, and one-eyed General Liu, operating against Chiang's flanks on the east, decided to stand up in Shantung, slug it out and see what happened.

At first, they had to give ground, but in exchange, they soon began to get large bags of prisoners. In January 1947, the whole American-equipped 26th Division surrendered with its commander who savagely told his Communist captors that his debacle was due not to clever tactics on their part but to the stupidity of the generalissimo who stubbornly pushed him forward against his will. It was curious, however, that the troops had thought so little of their cause that they had not bothered to destroy one bit of their equipment, which was now taken over by the 8th Route Army and turned around on the Kuomintang.

Chiang did not heed this sign, but pushed on. Bringing another army group over from the American naval base at Tsingtao and sending them south, he tried to catch the Communist forces in Shantung in a pincer. General Chen Yi, instead of waiting for the jaws of this trap to close on him, suddenly retreated from the southern force and from the eminence of Mount Tai threw down all his strength at the group army coming at him from the north. The results were electric. Within a few days, thirty thousand prisoners were taken and Chiang's offensive was completely dislocated.

In desperation, Chiang switched commanders, changing in rapid succession from Liu Chih, the northern general, to Hsueh Yueh, the Cantonese commander, to Tang En-po, his fellow-provincial, and then to Ku Chih-tung, the Kiangsu commander. The results were always the same: terrific losses.

Morale among Kuomintang officers began to drop sharply. Those who wanted to continue and those who wanted to halt the war formed cliques in every unit. The older generals, no longer loyal to "the leader," openly criticized the generalissimo. Officers in their middle thirties, who had previously wanted nothing better than to fight the Communists, now thought the war suicidal. Only the heel-clicking and rabid younger officers wanted to continue, and even they were heartsick.

The soldiers, subjected to inhuman treatment and frequent beatings by their officers, were demoralized by the casualties and often would not attack unless their officers got in front and led them. Offensives that were meant to roll quickly were sabotaged by soldiers who had no desire to fall into a Communist ambush. Though they were told they were fighting bandits the soldiers knew they were fighting the legendary 8th Route Army where rank and officer privileges did not exist. They also became aware that the Communists were giving the peasants land and they began to wonder why they were fighting and many began to desert.

The astonishment and alarm which these events produced among the followers of Chiang Kai-shek were naturally great, but they had at the same time to cope with disasters of another nature. On the island of Formosa, far from the scenes of the fighting, the Taiwan people, angered beyond endurance by the excesses of Chiang Kai-shek's carpetbaggers, turned on the government and revolted. The generalissimo dispatched a division of troops from the mainland to quell the rebellion. Acting either on his own initiative or on instructions from above, the Chinese commander turned his soldiers loose on the civilian population and within the space of a few weeks slaughtered five thousand unarmed men, women and children, many of them being killed before the eyes of Western businessmen, missionaries and consular officials. At the same moment, Manchurians, also driven to desperate straits by Chiang's greedy looters, terrorists and executioners, began to run over to the

8th Route Army. Worse still, in the mountains of Shansi and Honan and in the plains of Shantung, Hopei and Kiangsu, in areas where Chiang's control was supposedly unchallenged, there suddenly burst forth the violence of peasant uprisings.

Kuomintang officers and absentee landlords, returning to the villages from the cities, levied taxes of such a ferocious nature on the people that they were in many cases deprived of their means of existence and starved to death.

As we have seen, the effects of such actions were not to make the people of North China droop, but rage; for when Kuomintang soldiers, and especially landlords and village gangsters armed by the Kuomintang, tortured, murdered and buried alive peasants in common pits, terror was not only raised in the bravest hearts, but this terror produced the reverse of submission to the Kuomintang army and to the landlords. It was seen that rich farmers and middle peasants, friends of Chiang's cause, as well as the landless farmers and the tenants who were his natural enemies, were also liable to be the victims of plunder, robbery and brutal treatment; and thus the people of North China had no choice of action; they had no means of security left but of taking up arms. Thousands who were heretofore neutral in the war saw the necessity of becoming temporary soldiers or militiamen, and thus a farmer army poured forth from the Shansi Mountains on the west and the plains of Hopei, Honan and Shantung on the east.

With recruits, long accustomed to the use of arms, entering into the village and county militia, there soon developed a warfare which added to the already existing weapons of artillery, bazookas and American B-25s such arms as spears, pig knives, sickles, hammers, rabbit rifles and scissors wielded by women who had become like hyenas. And once such arms had been raised, they were never to be put down until rage, revenge and hate had exhausted their users.

The immediate military effect of this kind of war was to tie down troops and make Chiang's rear unsafe. How annoying this can be is to be seen from the village of Paicha in the Taihang Mountains. Having been aroused by the constant looting expeditions of Kuomintang soldiers, the villagers obtained rocks from a near-by hill, built head-high barricades across all their streets, stoned up their windows and ambushed the next Kuomintang foraging group that came to town. Then, armed with a few rifles, they organized a militia. Soon the villages thereabouts followed this example until the whole countryside was up in arms against the local Kuomintang regiment.

Meanwhile, on the flood of passion created by the land reform, a horde of poor peasants, tenants and agricultural workers poured into the Communist camp, while on the other side, landlords and some rich farmers joined the Kuomintang. Since the poor are more numerous than the rich, it is easy to see that the Communists benefited by this state of affairs.

Now, here were conditions that should have given even the rashest of commanders pause. But they seem to have affected the Kuomintang hierarchy so little at this time that even two and three months later, in the summer of 1947, when things were much worse, Kuomintang spokesmen were claiming that 70 per cent of the war was over and only mopping-up campaigns remained.

It is hard to account for this optimism unless one looks on it as a gallows joke.

50. The Communists' Counteroffensive

IN THE spring of 1947, though the loyalty of his troops was shaky and the morale of his officers low, though his reserves throughout the country were getting closer to the bone, though rebellions were springing up in his rear and devouring troops that he could ill spare, though a people's war was spreading around his front line troops and though General George Marshall had returned to the United States and given every indication of abandoning him to his fate, Generalissimo Chiang Kai-shek, instead of learning caution from his straitened circumstances, at his headquarters in Nanking, rashly gave sanction to a plan of grandiose proportions, yet of a dangerous and terrible nature.

To his cause he summoned the treacherous nature of the Yellow River. The Yellow River over several thousand years has shifted its course from time to time, flowing now into the Pacific Ocean through Shantung, now through north Kiangsu. To tamper with the river is like tampering with China itself and, to Chinese, almost like defying God. In 1938, Chiang had cut its massive dikes and diverted the river south across the path of the invading Japanese to halt them before the town of Chengchow. In doing this he submerged eleven cities and four thousand villages and made two million peasants homeless, but he stopped the Japanese.

Now Chiang wished to repair the breach he had made in the dikes and to send the river back once again to the north—that is, into Communist-held areas. No matter what was the real intention of such a move, its military effect would be to place a wall of water between the two main Communist armies in North China—those of General Chen-yi and Liu Po-cheng—and split them apart. If Liu Po-cheng's raiders were immobilized with water, Chiang could also release enough troops for an attack on the Communist capital at Yenan. Finally, the switching of the course of the Yellow River at this time would deal a heavy blow to Communist economy in Shantung Province and might create an environment of flood and misery.

UNRRA had been co-operating with Chiang Kai-shek in 1946 in the engineering work necessary to repair the broken dikes on the completely valid understanding that the restoration of the old channel was necessary to heal China's war wounds. Even the Communists had agreed to co-operate in the work. But all three groups—UNRRA, Communists and Chiang—were parties to an agreement that the river would not be diverted back to its old channel till provision had been made for the peasants who were tilling the dry bed where the river had flowed before 1938. There were some four hundred thousand of these Shantung farmers cultivating eight hundred thousand acres of land in what had once been river bottom —and most of them lived in Communist areas.

During 1946, the dike might have been closed, but Nationalist generals were transporting troops north through Honan on a railway over the dried-up river bed and they interfered with UNRRA's work.[1] By 1947, however, the front had shifted to the east, the government troops no longer had need of the railway, and they brought heavy pressure on UNRRA to close the gap.

Informed of Chiang's intentions, the Communists requested UNRRA to stick to the tripartite agreement. UNRRA wavered. Chiang's generals immediately moved to close the breach. At the same time, his pilots bombed UNRRA ships carrying dike-repair and relief materials to Shantung and his American fighter planes strafed farmers erecting dikes near their native villages.

Each time a bombing occurred, shipping was paralyzed for weeks. The people of Shantung, under the threat of flood, were deliberately deprived of means to fight that flood. Though protesting Chiang's bombings, UNRRA did not break off relations with the generalissimo.

Whether Chiang himself meditated on the political effects of what he was to undertake is something we do not know. China's dictator was accustomed to gaze steadily at war, he never added up the sorrowful details.

He seems to have suffered no alarm at the possible consequences of his act. He played with the Yellow River as if he were a god playing with a garden hose.

[1] Cf. UNRRA monthly report for November 1946. "Military objections which had hampered the work in the spring [1946] because of the danger to the Nationalist military supply line to Hsien Hsiang by rail across the dry bed, were withdrawn and replaced by demands for rapid closure." What military demands had to do with a land reclamation project the report does not disclose.

He gave the order for the breach to be closed.[2]

"China's Sorrow," the peasants of many centuries have called the Yellow River, and China's Sorrow, indeed, it is. Within a short time of the closure of the breach, nearly five hundred villages were inundated, over one hundred thousand people were rendered homeless and, according to the Communists, almost five million mow of crop land were destroyed.

The tale of disaster was not finished at one blow. Besides those districts immediately flooded, the rising waters threatened to engulf twelve hundred river-bed villages and the four hundred thousand people living in them. Worse, still, it was just the time of the wheat harvest and the people had to abandon their fields and turn to halting the flood.

North China had stood up against Chiang's armies, but now it seemed about to fall to the Yellow River. Two things, however, were of importance here: the Communists' organizing ability and the feelings of the Chinese people in Shantung Province.

A picture of the fight the Liberated Area governments waged against the flood is given by an UNRRA official traveling through the region at the time.

"Everywhere, I had the impression that dike repair was by far the most important concern. . . . One hundred thousand workers were employed in the Po Hai region alone. In south Hopei and west Shantung, three hundred thousand men built a dike within twenty-five days. Ninety-six workers were killed by planes and artillery, but the people, chased away in the daytime, came back at night to build the dikes. Government officials would never allow discussion in terms of what the situation would be if the dike repair were unsuccessful. It simply had to be successful. . . . They would have built the dikes higher but for lack of food for the workers. . . . A major problem has been that the enormous amount of dike work has been a drain on their manpower for agricultural work and it has been necessary to organize women and children to fill the gap as much as possible."

As for the effects of the flood on civilian morale, I myself had ample

[2] March 1947 report of UNRRA's Agricultural Division gives a more cold-blooded account of this whole affair. In part it declares that the closing of the breach "was carried out by the Yellow River Commission with UNRRA equipment, foodstuffs and construction materials and with the assistance of UNRRA engineering and mechanical personnel. . . . The final closure operations had been rushed under strong Nationalist military pressure and in disregard of agreements previously made with UNRRA and Border Region representatives. . . . Its immediate effect would be to divide the movements of their armies concurrently with Nationalist military drives in that province, and in the high-water season would flood the agricultural lands in the river bed. Plans which UNRRA, CNRRA and Border Region personnel had made to alleviate the adverse economic effects of the river diversion . . . had not been carried out. Dike work was made difficult by frequent Nationalist air attacks upon the dike workers."

opportunity to observe them. By a curious coincidence, I was with Chiang's troops when he broke the dikes in 1938 and I was in Communist territory when the river was sent back again in 1947. But whereas the first flood had been for the peasants a cause of sorrow, this last flood was a cause of rage. Chinese peasants, who are among the most friendly people in the world, even refused to talk to me because they knew it was American planes that had bombed them while they were repairing the dikes.

One woman, whose nine-year-old boy had been drowned in the flood, when I asked her to tell me her story, answered: "I hate you. Why should I tell you my bitterness?"

Other farmers, more friendly and more worldly, who had labored eight years to reclaim the land around the river mouth, said to me: "Old Chiang did this. How do you think we feel?"

The people's anger and its political consequence perhaps had not entered into Chiang's calculations; but, even worse, those military calculations he had made were to betray him yet further.

By hurling the Yellow River between General Chen Yi in the east and General Liu Po-cheng in the center, the generalissimo may or may not have thought to immobilize Liu. Anyway he denuded his own central front before the one-eyed general and transported his troops far to the west for an attack on Yenan, the Communist capital in desolate Shensi Province.

Again, we must ask: Why? And this time our puzzlement is great.

To take an enemy's capital can often be of decisive importance in war. Capture Paris and you have France. Take Berlin and you conquer Germany. But if the capture of a capital city is to ruin the power of an adversary to resist, that capital should not only be the center of the power of the state but, in addition, at least the seat of political assemblies and factions. But Yenan was none of these things. It certainly was not the center of a state, for no Communist state as such existed, and any one of seven Border Regions, with their own governments and their own military forces, was stronger than Yenan. Moreover, Yenan, a mere cave village, lay on no important communication route, and was a headquarters camp, ready to be struck at a moment's notice. The heart of the resistance to Chiang Kai-shek did not lie here, but down on the plains among eighty million peasants, militia and troops from Manchuria to the Yellow River.

For Chiang to take Yenan was like a man spending a great part of his fortune on a diamond necklace that glitters, but turns out to be paste.

Why then did he attack it? His reasons seem to have been those mostly connected with prestige. For many months he had not been able to present either his own people or the outside world with any decisive victory. His people were tired of the war and there was still pressure from abroad and from within for him to make peace. At this time, the Big Four was holding a conference in Moscow. President Truman's anti-Communist speech was in the making. Greece was to be given or had been given American help. Chiang wanted to impress his own people, impress the world and get American help to fight Communism. The only thing impressive within reach was Yenan.

Having dismissed his enemy's representatives from his own capital at Nanking, Chiang marched on the capital of Chinese Communism. Behind the dust raised by his soldiers' feet, had he the eyes to see, the generalissimo might have discerned the faint signs of a threatening storm.

Yenan was empty. Long before, the Communists had sent their schools, their hospitals, even their troops elsewhere. For their precious capital they put up no fight. Mao Tze-tung, chairman of the Communist party, and General Chu Teh, commander in chief of the army, and other high party leaders left the city without a murmur. Even elsewhere the loss of Yenan created no great stir. Communists and peasants, alike, both shrugged their shoulders.

The Communists hardly paused in the hills behind Yenan, but continued north, apparently in precipitate flight. Ever deeper they went into the mountains, ever further they got away from the main battleground of the Yellow River Plain. Chiang's troops followed.

The turning point in the war had come.

The Communists, like Joe Louis, are counterfighters. When they see an opening they strike. Like the old-time baseball player, Willie Keeler, they "hit 'em where they ain't."

Between Shantung and Shensi, Chiang had denuded his own center in Honan. It was as if he had opened the door to his own house in the Yangtze Valley and invited the Communists in. We might almost say that the coming disaster originated in Chiang Kai-shek's own brain. The Communists poured, not the waters of the Yellow River into the gap in Honan, but the columns of the One-Eyed Dragon, Liu Po-cheng.

This move caught Chiang Kai-shek off balance. Chiang did not believe the Communists could launch an offensive. Nor did his American advisers. Early in the war, a few of the wiser American military men had told Washington that if there were no outside intervention, the civil war in China would go on for twenty, thirty and even fifty years. These views were considered radical, for most Americans thought Chiang could at least open the railways and nominally unify the country. But even the most radical observers, noting that the Communists had no supply bases, no modern transportation corps and no heavy equipment, flatly declared that Communists could not launch an offensive. Even months later, after I had seen this offensive launched, some American military men laughed at me. "Forget it," they said, "the Communists will never be able to attack."

The Communists, however, had reached a different view. "This war has a revolutionary nature," they said, "and is governed by a special set of conditions. The Japanese war had three stages, but this war will have only two stages. There will be no long period of stalemate."

Along the Yellow River, the Communists now put this theory to the test. They attacked.

Their first step was one of preparation and concealment. This was carried out by the militiamen and the guerrilla forces (whose actions in Anyang I have already described). The purpose of these raids was to screen the movement of a larger regular armed force which now moved into southern Shansi and northern Honan, and began to take over the ill-garrisoned towns which Chiang had abandoned to make his attack on Yenan. Abruptly Liu halted his attack, and it seemed as if he had been beaten. But Liu had not been beaten, he had achieved his main purpose of opening a mountain corridor for the passage of the troops of General Chen Kang, into position near the Yellow River.

At the same time, over on the east near Shantung Province, similar preparations went on. Liu already had a force of guerrillas across the Yellow River and south of the Lunghai Railway behind Kuomintang lines. When Chiang had changed the course of the Yellow River, Liu had calmly ordered these guerrillas to stay where they were, and they had remained in Honan, wandering around, half starving, in the deserted areas of the old flooded regions, gathering information and lying low until they were needed.

In the meantime, Liu collected his main force for the crossing of the Yellow River. There were about fifty thousand of them. They formed a front a hundred miles in length. They were divided into many columns perhaps five thousand men each and they had behind and with them a number of men and women—government officials, district magistrates, land reform workers. Only the most healthy young people were allowed to go on this first crossing, for Liu was going far through enemy country and he did not wish to be slowed up. The men gathered in the mud villages near the river wore gray uniforms and gray peaked caps that matched the ancient dust rising from the plain baking under an early summer heat. In June, Liu addressed his columns, telling them that the long-awaited counterattack was about to begin. The soldiers remained near the bank of the river watching plays performed by their regimental combat teams and drawing the biggest supply of ammunition they had ever been issued. At the same time, behind them the old whitewashed slogans began to come off the mud walls of peasant homes. In their places, overnight, appeared the words: "Strike down Chiang Kai-shek. Get to Nanking and capture Chiang Kai-shek alive!"

On the night of June 30th, One-Eyed Liu broke open a front a hundred miles long and slid across the river in boats. At the same time, many miles to the west, General Chen Kang, coming out of Shansi, crossed the river and seized the western half of the Lunghai Railway. This move bottled up four hundred thousand troops of Chiang Kai-shek's army of the northwest behind Tungkwan Pass, deprived them of all rail communications with the rest of China and deprived Chiang of a source of quick help should he ever need it in Nanking. The spectacular move, however, was made by Liu himself.

I have seen a great deal of war, but I don't think I have ever seen anything more brilliant than these and subsequent moves the Communists made across the Yellow River. The brilliance lay not so much in the execution, even though all would have been in vain without it, but in the conception—the daring, the single-mindedness, and above all the creative imagination of it. Chinese Communist military leaders are great masters of one thing: they know how to discard what is not essential and strike directly for what is essential. Liu Po-cheng, for example, as he departed from his old bases in North China left a number of towns garrisoned by Kuomintang troops in his rear. He had been doing this for almost two years, often with the disapproval of his subordinates who wanted to wipe out the weaker of these garrisons, because, as he explained to me, they could do him no harm and the men they might lose in such attacks would not be worth the possible gains.

Now Liu, as he crossed the Yellow River, fought as few battles as he could, for it was his mission to head toward the Yangtze Valley, Chiang Kai-shek's stronghold. Once there, he was to attract as many of Chiang's troops as he could so that other Communist forces, following behind him, might also cross the river and establish themselves in Central China. The whole idea behind this plan was to open up a new theater of war and strike directly against Chiang's bases of power.

Down along the Yangtze River, between Nanking and Hankow, lies a range of hills known as the Ta Pieh Mountains. During the Japanese war a small band of guerrillas who had allied themselves with the Communist New Fourth Army had established bases here. Later they had been driven out by Chiang Kai-shek, but on their departure, they had left underground workers behind, who now began to prepare for Liu's arrival.

Liu's mission being not to stop and fight, but to get into the Yangtze Valley some 200 miles away, his attack, unsupported by follow-up columns and unsupplied from the rear, had somewhat the character of a parachute drop or a cavalry raid deep into enemy territory. It was, however, more than a raid, for Liu planned to build up a new society where he was going.

After Liu had crossed the Yellow River, he made a series of distracting maneuvers. Guided by the guerrillas he had left behind, he crossed the Lunghai Railway east of Hsuchow, entered the lightly held town of Suiteh, stocked up on arms, gathered a few recruits and then turned west and south. He was in the clear with nothing but local troops in his way and he moved fast.

For several days he marched across a barren desolate area where whole villages had been wiped out during the flood of 1938; then he entered the green hills of Anhui, crossed over into Hupeh Province and came out of the millet lands of North China into the rice fields of the Yangtze Valley.

In town after town, Liu's troops broke open the official grain stores of the Kuomintang, replenished their own stocks and distributed the remainder to the poor as a propaganda measure. Local rifles fell into his hands without a struggle. Pauperized tenants, landless peasants, adventure-seeking boys flocked to join him. With his forces increased by many thousands Liu pressed south.

"General Liu Po-cheng," said Kuomintang papers, "is trapped below the Yellow River and is fleeing south."

Liu fled on.

Liu reached the Ta Pieh Mountains and set up his headquarters. His advance columns, however, continued forward. Sixty miles from Hankow, a Szechuan regiment came out to attack his scouts. A Communist soldier is said to have shouted the words: "Down With Chiang Kai-shek!" Whether he actually shouted out these words or not, we don't know; but at any rate, Chiang's troops downed their arms and came over to Liu's side.

In September, Liu's forces reached the Yangtze River. Small bands of his cadres, disguised as ordinary travelers, crossed into Kiangsi, the province the Reds had left thirteen years before to undertake their famous Long March, and there in the hills began to stir up peasants who had fled from their homes to escape conscription and had become bandits. Within a few days, Liu's forces had interdicted the river with fire so that for a time traffic ceased on China's most important waterway.

No longer could the Kuomintang call this tremendous advance a flight. The navy was summoned from the ocean and sent up the Yangtze. Several billion dollars' reward was offered for Liu's head. Finally, lest Liu flee into the capital of Nanking itself, Chiang was forced to organize a Central China Command and open up a new front.

This confession on the part of the Kuomintang that Liu had succeeded in his plans to open a new front fell in with larger Communist designs to bring other armies out of North China into Central China. Because of this, Liu's troops far from their old bases and without any chance of quick help, fought hard to attract as many of Chiang's soldiers as they could. For the Communists had another shot in their great offensive to establish themselves in Kuomintang territory.

In Liu's path, General Chen Yi sent a number of his troops out of Shantung to link up with guerrillas on the east who had remained in north Kiangsu near the sea. At the same time both Liu and Chen worked east and west along the Lunghai Railway, until they had isolated Kaifeng, Lanfeng and Chengchow, all cities that Chiang had to hold if he was to hold Nanking.

Following Liu, at least six top-ranking Communist generals crossed the Yellow River into Central China. Slowly joining forces, they made connections with agents in Hankow, Nanking and Shanghai and began preparations for another offensive which was to strike Chiang in the spring of 1948.

The atmosphere after the Communists came into Kuomintang territory was melancholy.

Chiang's political structure yielded suddenly on all sides simultaneously. The cry, "The Communists are in the Yangtze Valley," is followed by a number of denunciations of Chiang Kai-shek. The disintegration is not rapid, nor complete, but it is unprecedented. Feng Yu-hsiang, the Christian general who had come to America, refuses to return to China and exhorts his former subordinates to rebel. Li Chi-sen, former head of the generalissimo's headquarters, from Hongkong issues a new call for South China to revolt. The warlords of fabulously rich Szechuan, feeling the pressure of peasant discontent, cry out for a decrease of their rice shipments along the Yangtze to Chiang's hard-pressed armies. Communist money appears for the first time in Pootung, the Brooklyn of Shanghai. In other areas, the value of Communist money skyrockets to thirty and forty times the value of Kuomintang money. Everywhere in the rear, unrest spreads. Guerrillas and bandits take over great areas of Kwangtung in South China far from the fighting fronts. Farmers in desperation, before brutal taxation and conscription that demands they pay three to four million dollars to avoid being kidnaped into the army, take to the hills as bandits. Students grow uneasy, shopkeepers contribute voluntarily to Communist war funds. Boys and girls flee to the Communist areas. Chiang tries to halt the disintegration, he purges the Kuomintang, he outlaws the Democratic League, he erects walls from what is left him of his gestapo, he arrests officers of the operation department of General Sun Lien-chung, head of his war area in Peiping; in vain does he recall to the members of the Kuomintang that they are a revolutionary party; the Kuomintang is now composed of old men and they are tired of revolutions. Such was the turnabout that came in China's civil war.

How did the Communists greet this new situation? They immediately burned all their bridges behind them and abandoned any pretense of making a peace with Chiang Kai-shek. The cry now is: "Chiang must go." Chu Teh, commander in chief of the 8th Route Army, declares the objective of his army is to overthrow Chiang Kai-shek and organize a coalition government. On Christmas Day 1947, Mao Tze-tung announces: the offensive is "a turning point in history. It signals the end of the counterrevolutionary role of Chiang Kai-shek and the end of more than a hundred years of rule of imperialism in China."

Was this Communist leader right? For the moment that question would have to remain unanswered.

After going to Shantung to see the flooded areas, then returning to Honan to see the counteroffensive get underway, I was convinced that a turning point in the war had come, and I immediately started back across the North China Plain, intent on getting to Peiping and telling these events to the outside world.

PART XII

DICTATOR VS. PEOPLE

❦

51. The Republican Party and Chiang Kai-shek

I EMERGED from the Liberated Areas and returned to Nanking and Shanghai to find a sharpening tension in government circles over Chiang Kai-shek's failure to bring the war to a successful and speedy conclusion. These strongholds of the generalissimo were far removed, both physically and spiritually, from the passionate disturbances in the countryside and the growing discontent in the army on the front. Nevertheless, the troubles of the war had produced psychological and material strains within Chiang's governing bureaucracy.

On the surface, however, everything remained much as before. Generals and propagandists in the summer of 1947 were proclaiming that the Communists had been all but wiped out in North China and only mopping-up operations remained. The professors and some of the more daring liberals were raging against corruption and inefficiency. The students were parading for peace. The Americans were conducting behind-the-scenes activities trying to persuade Chiang to remove some of his less-talented generals in favor of men the Americans preferred. But the corruption continued unabated, the voices for war in the highest circles shouted louder than ever and the same inefficient generals held on to their positions at the front.

The exchange which had been seven thousand of Chiang Kai-shek's dollars to one American dollar when I arrived in China was now up to three hundred thousand. People were sleeping in the streets and dying every day. Ricksha boys were operating in gangs, robbing both Chinese and foreigners on the main streets at night. Everything was growing more dear and the homeless in the cities were increasing all the time. But the leavings of the old feast were still plentiful.

Officials rode around in cars bought up at seven thousand dollars American money from American importers who moaned in their Scotch and water at the American Club about the hard times that had come to

China. Sumptuous parties were in progress in the dining rooms of expensive restaurants. Out in the country the peasants were eating millet husks. But here in Shanghai, officials and businessmen, their mouths full of food and curses for both the Communists and Chiang Kai-shek, were eating five bowls of rice at one sitting and complimenting one another on the tastiness of the Mandarin Fish, the Gold Coin Chicken, the fatted Peiping Duck and the specially warmed yellow wine. The war raging in the countryside did not prevent the parties in the foreign correspondents' club atop the eighteen-story Broadway Mansions, where dancing went on under gaily colored lights and where White Russian mistresses mingled with American wives and both cursed the Chinese; it did not prevent the homy gatherings of American Army personnel on China's supposedly sovereign soil, nor did it put a halt to the wild black market speculation or the gambling behind closed doors or the open smoking of opium in every major Chinese hotel in Shanghai.

All remained as before yet nobody felt sure of himself. The storm in the countryside, though distant, nevertheless reverberated in the yamens of the Nanking government. All the Chinese army was aware of it and even the more discerning civilian officials.

The nature and the scope of the dissolution in North China, however, was at this time well concealed from the general public in the Yangtze Valley. The ignorance of people about events that were transpiring in Communist areas surprised me. When I told foreign officials that an offensive had begun, they looked at me as if I were crazy. "Forget it," said one high-ranking Army officer, "the Communists have no weapons and will never be able to launch an offensive." The crossing of the Yellow River to many observers was just a flight, in accordance with Kuomintang propaganda, or merely a raid. The Nanking correspondent of *Time Magazine* declared that the movement of General Liu Po-cheng across the Yellow River was of no significance because an army couldn't fight without bases. A member of a foreign embassy in Nanking told me that my statement that the peasants were joining One-Eyed Liu against Nanking was a lot of Communist "crap." What did the peasants care about the war? American foreign policy—as if that were a magic entity that existed in a vacuum—was all that mattered to some of these specialists and seemingly all they understood.

That no one cared to understand that the Chinese Revolution was the decisive factor in the war seemed to me somewhat obstinate. These men would not expose their minds to the shock of revolution. Whenever I tried to tell US military men about the rising of the peasantry, they interrupted me to inquire about the pay of soldiers in the 8th Route Army, the kind of uniform they wore, the size and shape of their medals or the kind of trees that grew along highways where revolutionists fell. Not willing to expose themselves to new ideas, they could not help but concern themselves with unessentials.

Consciously and unconsciously, some of these men were afraid of becoming tainted with a politically pink tinge. The Communist witch hunt in America and the fact that congressmen were at periodic intervals sounding off about the "Reds" in the State Department made some of the more intelligent observers cautious and understandably so. American diplomats and military observers were willing to report the corruption in the Chiang government, the inefficiency of his generals, the dissidence of various factions in the government, but anything about the revolution in the Communist-held countryside many of them either deliberately side-stepped or hedged about, with all sorts of qualifications, and denunciations. One American official quite frankly told me: "I'm not sticking my neck out." Another one said: "You've been away so long, you don't know what it's like in the States. You either is [a Red] or you isn't. What you tell me may all be true, but I'm not going to report it."

Before going any further I should perhaps state that I do not wish to criticize the professional qualifications of our representatives in China. On the whole, they were decent, forthright and intelligent men, probably as capable agents of this country as could be found anywhere abroad. American diplomats, military attachés, businessmen, correspondents and missionaries must be given full credit for honestly exposing the inefficient, corrupt and despotic nature of the Chiang regime. However, it was impossible for these men entirely to avoid the effects of the proscription of freedom of thought and conscience in the United States itself. It is true that they were not hunted down as many ordinary American citizens have recently been hunted down in the United States in an orgy of denunciation, suspicion, rumor and fear, but they were made to feel uneasy to a point where some of them were inclined to lose their curiosity about the inner workings of the Chinese Revolution. This led a few men to hold up mirrors to the viewpoints of their superiors in America instead of reflecting their own viewpoints as in the past.

Though indirect, the pressures on Americans dealing with Chinese public affairs was sometimes real enough. For example, when I emerged from Communist areas I sent an American national magazine two articles which appear in this book under the titles "Mission Murder" and "Stone Wall Village." These articles were bought by the editors with the words "excellent," "your best." However, in the midst of the artificially created atmosphere of hysteria in the United States, the publisher stepped in, canceled the articles and declared that I identified myself with "mob violence." In early 1949, an intelligence report issued by General Mac-Arthur's headquarters attempted to link Miss Agnes Smedley, a writer who had produced many books about the Chinese Revolution, with a pro-

Russian Japanese spy ring which had operated during World War II. The charges were so fantastic that the Army had to back down, but the bared fangs were clear enough to anyone who tended to scare easily. When the Communists crossed the Yangtze River, a New York newspaper suggested that the FBI investigate all writers who had ever said that China's Reds were not Communists. In other words, an attempt was being made to frighten observers of the China scene with the specter of an American gestapo.

This kind of long-distance and indirect bulldozing of American writers (also American diplomats and missionaries), which was partially instrumental in blurring the picture of the China war, happened in the year 1947 to fit in with a definite political need of Chiang Kai-shek. Because he did not trust his own people and because he needed American help, Chiang did not dare admit how bad his situation was in North China. Yet, in order to get American help, he had to admit defeats somewhere and also find a reason for these defeats that would not discredit him or his ruling group.

The history of all revolutions and civil wars invariably shows that a threatened ruling class finds the cause of its misfortune not in itself, but in foreign agents or powers. The ruling class of China being no more original than other endangered regimes in history now tried to convince itself and the outside world that the cause of its troubles lay in the Soviet Union. Such an attempt, however, strained even the fertile imaginations of Chiang's ruling clique and involved the bureaucracy in serious contradictions. In the first place, Chiang's generals and many of his top ministers knew their lack of success against the 8th Route Army was not due to Russian help given the Communists. In fact, many of these generals blamed Chiang Kai-shek's mistakes and the corruption of the bureaucracy for their own defeats in the field and they had strong desires to reform the army and the government itself. Therefore, any attempts to blame the Soviet Union seemed to these generals like an attempt to whitewash the bureaucracy, to prevent reforms and to strengthen Chiang's hands which they wanted to weaken. In the second place, many of Chiang's supporters had no wish to alienate the Soviet Union in favor of the United States, rather preferring to balance themselves between the two. Thirdly, it was obvious to everyone, including foreigners who had been in the areas, that no Russians or Russian arms were in North China which was separated from the borders of Siberia by over a thousand miles of forests and mountains, not to mention Chiang's troops themselves.

Under these circumstances, for the Chiang Kai-shek government to seek to blame its misfortunes on the Soviet Union was not only difficult but dangerous. A combination of factors, however, led a few party officials to adopt a risky course. In the first place, there was the psychology of the government leaders themselves. Aghast at the peasant uprisings in the north, shaken by the disaffection of generals and oppressed by the insistent and insidiously growing demands for peace on the part of the intellectuals, students and impoverished merchants, the Kuomintang ruling clique had suffered a tremendous loss of self-confidence and had begun to doubt the ability of Chiang Kai-shek to win the war. No longer believing in themselves or their leader, these officials saw their only means of salvation in getting help from the United States. But the corruption in their own ranks and the oppressive nature of the Chiang dictatorship had been so widely publicized that these men also clearly recognized that their only way to get such help was to identify their twenty-year civil war against their own Communists with America's worldwide struggle against the Soviet Union. Ideological identification, however, was not enough, and it became necessary for the Kuomintang to find a formula whereby they could accuse the Soviet Union of interfering in China's civil war in order that they might get American help and save their own skins.

Such a formula was difficult to find. George Marshall, then Secretary of State in President Truman's administration, had publicly stated that there was no evidence of Russian interference in China's civil war. It was obvious, therefore, that the government of the United States had no intention of helping Chiang invent such a formula. There was, however, at this time a powerful group of American interventionists who saw in Chiang's dilemma an identity of interests with their own needs and they quickly came to Chiang's assistance.

The chief proponents of American intervention in China at this time were the *Time-Life-Fortune* publishing group, headed by China-born Henry Luce, the Scripps-Howard newspapers, certain high members of the Republican party, a few lesser lights such as Congressman Walter Judd, Generals Albert Wedemeyer and Claire Chennault and most important of all, Mr. William C. Bullitt, former US ambassador to Moscow and Paris and an important foreign policy spokesman for the Republican party with whom Henry Luce was intimately associated.

Although Bullitt and Luce at various times expressed admiration for Chiang Kai-shek, though Governor Thomas Dewey in his campaign for the presidency of the United States also indicated his sympathy for the generalissimo's government and though all these men were undoubtedly moved by anti-Communist feelings, there is also the fact that the interests of the Republican party and China's dictator coincided at important points. Chiang Kai-shek had to find a scapegoat for his defeats. The only scapegoat could be the Russians and the only place there could be any Russians was Manchuria. The Republican party, facing a presidential election, was under the compelling necessity of discrediting the Democratic administration of President Truman not only at home but abroad. The misfortunes of Chiang Kai-shek furnished influential party members with ammunition to blame the spread of Communism in China on President Roosevelt because of the deal he made at Yalta with Stalin to get Russian troops into the war against Japan in Manchuria.

Although Chiang's strategy had collapsed because he had been unable to beat his way across the North China Plain, Chiang's propagandists continued to maintain the fiction that they were victorious in this area. They adopted just the opposite propaganda tactic in relation to Manchuria. Correspondents were now treated to the spectacle of a government trying to make an admittedly bad situation even worse than it was. All of us were fed inside stories from "authoritative sources" about the imminent evacuation of Manchuria, about lost battles that never took place and many other tales, as interesting as they were unreliable.

Most foreign correspondents saw that the object of all this propaganda was to try to portray Manchuria as the central battleground— the only important battleground—of the China civil war in order that military reverses could be blamed on the Russians. Correspondents in China, however, formed a very ineffective force in getting the facts about the Far East home to the American public.

This was particularly true when Governor Dewey, Senator Vandenberg, Alfred Landon and a host of other prominent Republicans began thundering about the need of aiding Chiang Kai-shek. In the meantime Henry Luce's *Time* and *Life* magazines, while often disregarding their own correspondents' dispatches, also demanded aid to Chiang and dispatched Bullitt to China. The denunciation of all those who had refused to play Chiang's game swelled to a mighty chorus. George Marshall was bitterly assailed for not helping Chiang; the deceased General Stilwell, who despised the generalissimo, was attacked as a gullible liberal, and President Roosevelt was roundly assaulted for "betraying" his country's vital interest to the Soviet Union.

About this time, Bullitt came to China as a correspondent of *Life Magazine*. The former ambassador spent a short time in several Chinese cities and then went home and published a twelve-page article in *Life* entitled "Report to the American People on China." Actually, this piece was not so much a report as an incitement to direct and open military intervention on behalf of Chiang Kai-shek to "keep China out of the hands of Stalin." It declared that General MacArthur should take charge of the program for aiding Chiang, dividing his time equally between China and Japan.

Luce announced this article by placing full-page advertisements in dozens of papers throughout the country. The Bullitt thesis was plugged by Chinese government spokesmen and it had some influence on the Chinese civil war.

Bullitt's argument was very simple. Chiang Kai-shek was a man whose "foresight and wisdom have rarely been surpassed in the annals of statesmanship" and whose only ambition was "to lead the Chinese to the peaceful establishment of democratic institutions and modernization of their ancient civilization." He would have succeeded in his self-appointed mission if not "betrayed" to Stalin at Yalta which made it possible for Russia to threaten the territorial integrity and the "very independence" of China. Therefore the United States had to take immediate action to defend Chiang Kai-shek from the encroachment of the Soviet Union and drive every last armed Chinese Communist out of China. Such a program could be achieved very cheaply at the cost of only a billion dollars to the American taxpayer.

Bullitt's thesis produced a curious reaction in China. In the first place, his proposal that the United States intervene in China's civil war offended the nationalist sentiments of many Chinese intellectuals. Secondly, his praise of Chiang Kai-shek offended democratic sentiments. Thirdly, his suggestion that the United States continue to help China until every last armed Communist had been liquidated offended the peace hopes of middle-of-the-road Chinese. Finally, his idea that China's civil conflict could be decided merely by sending a billion dollars to the national government offended the common sense of the Chinese people.

Nor was Bullitt's thesis accurate in any detail. In concentrating his attention on Manchuria, Bullitt declared that Communist forces in North China were guerrillas. But the plain fact was that both the Communists and the national government had greater regular forces deployed in North and Central China below the Great Wall than they had in Manchuria, outside the Great Wall. In other words, the main Communist armies had come into being and had defeated Chiang Kai-shek in areas where there were no Russians and where there was no contact with them. When Bullitt indicated that Chiang Kai-shek was being defeated primarily because of the Yalta deal, he made no allusion to the fact that General Wedemeyer had advised the generalissimo in 1945 not to go into Manchuria and was now, in 1947, privately saying that Chiang's position beyond the Great Wall was hopeless. In short, Bullitt was advocating a program that was based on wrong assumptions to begin with and on questionable conclusions to end with.

I shall have occasion later to show how the actions of American interventionists played some role in bringing about the collapse of Chiang Kai-shek's power. Here, however, it is necessary to admit that the ceaseless stream of stories about the Soviet Union's interference in China's civil war did for a time have an effect on that war, not so much in China, but abroad. For one thing the constant barrage of anti-Russian propaganda made it difficult for any correspondent to point out the major reasons why Chiang Kai-shek was being defeated. For another thing, the piling up of stories made Manchuria much more important than it was and completely hid the role of the peasants in the war. Finally, the stories affected even us who were there and made us wonder just how much the Russians were really helping the Chinese Communists. I decided to go to Manchuria and see for myself.

52. Loot of Manchuria

ONE of the first men I met in Manchuria was a Western intelligence officer who told me the only funny story I heard during my entire stay in China's northeast. This story which was well known in diplomatic circles in Manchuria had peculiar interest because it symbolized the techniques that a few of Chiang Kai-shek's officials were then using to prove that Russian soldiers were fighting in the ranks of the Chinese Communists beyond the Great Wall.

According to this story, during the withdrawal of the Soviet Union's Red Army from Manchuria, a Russian straggler was cut off from his unit and captured by Chiang Kai-shek's troops. My friend, the foreign officer, hearing of his capture, was able to interview the soldier and had quite a long conversation with him.

The soldier, an affable fellow, admitted his Kuomintang hosts were treating him well, but expressed bewilderment at Chinese habits. "Tell me," he said to the foreigner, "why do Chinese take so many pictures? One day, they stick me in a trench, hand me a tommy gun and photograph me from a dozen different angles. The next day, they dress me in Chinese uniform, give me a rifle and take a dozen more pictures. Then, sometimes, they get Russian civilians to lie down on the ground and they take their pictures, too. I don't understand it."

The foreigner was nonplussed by the soldier's story, but filed it away in his mind for future reference. Some time later, representatives of Chiang Kai-shek's army in the Northeast presented him with a set of pictures they had taken of Soviet nationals that had allegedly been killed by Kuomintang troops in a fight with Chinese Communists. Among these supposedly dead warriors, the foreigner noted some white Russian civilians with whom he was personally acquainted. He was about to mention this when he was handed a photograph of the Russian soldier with whom he had previously spoken. There, just as he had described himself, was the soldier in a trench with a tommy gun. There he was again, in various other pictures, in Chinese Communist uniform and with a Chinese rifle.

The Kuomintang officials carefully explained they had taken the pictures from the dead soldier's pockets, just a few days before.

"He was a Russian," they said, with patriotic indignation.

"I know," said the foreigner, no longer able to control himself. "I talked with him the other day."

That ended the attempt to convince this particular Westerner that Russians were fighting on the Chinese Communist side in Manchuria. It did not, however, end the attempts of some of the American interventionists or a few (not many) of Chiang Kai-shek's officials to convince the outside world that Communist successes were primarily due to Russian interference in China's civil war.

The chief factor in causing some of these men to harp on Russian influence in the Chinese war was probably the military situation in Manchuria itself. Since the beginning of 1947, Chiang had been on the defensive in the northeast. The Communists controlled 90 per cent of Manchuria, two-thirds of the railways, the majority of the soy bean and kaoliang lands, nearly all the timber without which the railways could not be rebuilt and, most important of all, the grudging, but growing respect of the Manchurian people. The only thing Chiang Kai-shek controlled was the big cities and industry, and this last was losing its importance, for what the Russians hadn't looted, Chiang was unable to get going.

Such a colossal failure outside the Great Wall had profound repercussions inside China proper. Many high Kuomintang officials by 1947 had concluded they could not beat the Communists in Manchuria by themselves. Lacking the power to overcome the Communists and harboring few illusions about the loyalty of the Manchurians, who had already become disaffected, these men were waging a war of wits to convince both their own subjects and the outside world that the historic Hun, Mongol and Tartar barbarians had risen again in the person of the Soviet Union. In such a propaganda war, American interventionists, of course, became a useful ally.

Yet no neutral observer believed in this Russian interference. In many months in Communist North China I had seen no evidence of it. Nor did I hear much evidence of it in Manchuria. Although it seems obvious that the Chinese Communists will be closely linked to the Soviet Union in the future, the most that could be said about Russian help to the Communists in the midst of China's civil war was that part of the Japanese arms captured by the Russians might have fallen into the hands of the 8th Route Army. But Chiang Kai-shek had captured far more arms from the surrendering Japanese than the Communists ever did. It is also probably true that in 1948 the Russians gave the troops of Communist

General Lin Piao some trucks in exchange for Manchurian products. The Communists, however, got far more transport from America than they ever got from the Russians. This attempt to blame Chiang Kai-shek's defeat on Roosevelt and the Russians won't do.

Just why, then, were the Communists winning in Manchuria and Chiang Kai-shek losing? There were many reasons. But first it is necessary briefly to examine a few facts of history. When the Japanese invaded Manchuria in 1931, Chiang Kai-shek not only left the Manchurians entirely to their own fate, but at the same time he squashed all patriotic demonstrations inside the Great Wall, censored all books dealing with anti-Japanese sentiments and even banned the singing of China's most popular song, "Arise," which was written in commemoration of the Mukden incident of 1931. This alienated many Manchurians.

Although they had been deserted by China's ruler, some of the more daring Manchurians began to organize resistance bands which became known as the Manchurian Volunteers. All through those years when every foreign nation was recognizing Japan's right to Manchukuo and when Chiang Kai-shek accepted Japanese sovereignty over Manchuria, these small guerrilla bands fought the Japanese. Most of the leaders were killed and in the end the bands could survive only in small numbers.

However, when the Russian Red Army drove out the Japanese in August 1945, the Manchurian Volunteers appeared again and grew swiftly. They took over the rural areas and captured some Japanese arms, while the Russians were taking the railways and the big cities. At the same time a few regular Communist 8th Route Army troops already fighting in southern Manchuria drove north and contacted the Volunteers. A little later, forces of the 8th Route Army operating inside the Great Wall also drove north under Communist general Lin Piao who amalgamated all these elements. There were in the beginning perhaps only fifty thousand regular Communist troops.

While this was going on, the United States rushed nearly two hundred thousand of Chiang's troops into Manchuria by ship and plane. Chiang's officials and officers might have contacted the Volunteers as did the Communists and won them over. However, they adopted just the opposite course. They contacted landlords who had been agents for the Japanese for fourteen years and organized them into armed bands to fight the Volunteers and the Communists. In other words, the Kuomintang, true to its own semifeudal nature, allied itself with the most hated elements in Manchuria and thus laid a basis for a class war. This gave the Communists an opportunity to win rural Manchuria, as they won rural North China.

Strangely enough, the Russians at this time helped Chiang Kai-shek and not the Chinese Communists. For while the Volunteers and General Lin Piao's bands were taking over the countryside, the Russian

Red Army installed Chiang's officials in all the Manchurian cities and protected them for many months. At the same time, Chiang officially asked the Soviet Union to stay in Manchuria longer than originally scheduled so that he could have more time to bring in troops by American transport. Both the Russians and the United States, therefore, helped the generalissimo. Later when the Russians evacuated Harbin and other north Manchurian cities they took with them, at Chiang's request, all the officials whom the generalissimo had appointed to rule those cities. They saved these officials from the Manchurian people and returned them safely to Chiang. In thus relying on both the Russians and the United States, Chiang Kai-shek admitted that he could not control Manchuria without foreign armed help.

With the evacuation of the Russians, Chiang Kai-shek, now having five American-equipped armies in southern Manchuria, began a drive to the north. Held up by a bloody battle at Szepingkai, he managed at last to reach the city of Changchun where his march came to a halt under the terms of the Marshall truce agreements. It has been assumed by some people, especially those with an interest in discrediting George Marshall and the Truman administration, that this truce prevented Chiang from conquering Manchuria. But there is not the slightest evidence to suppose that Chiang's troops, already spread thin, could have continued on for hundreds of more miles and captured Harbin and Tsitsihar on the borders of the Soviet Union. Even supposing they could have, such an operation would have resulted in ultimate disaster, for it would have put Chiang at the end of an even longer supply line than the one he unsuccessfully tried to support in southern Manchuria.

Suppose for a moment we forget that Chiang deserted the Manchurians in 1931, forget that he allied himself with puppet landlords and not the Volunteers, forget that the Russians installed his officials in the cities—forget all this and suppose for a moment that the Russians did help the Communists in Manchuria. Even taking all these assumptions for granted, I found that Chiang Kai-shek had been defeated in the Northeast for reasons entirely unconnected with Russian help.

As in Formosa, another area outside of China proper that was highly developed by the Japanese, the Kuomintang in Manchuria had established a military, economic and political structure that Bullitt, Republican party leaders and some Democratic congressmen, would have done well to study since it indicated that the regime of China's dictator was quite incapable of adding to the substance of a country, but was only capable of devouring it.

By the summer of 1947, when some quarters were proclaiming that Manchuria was being betrayed to Stalin, the Kuomintang could point to three major accomplishments in the Northeast. It had destroyed at least half of the forces and a good part of the effectiveness of seven armies, trained and equipped for them by the Americans. It had ruined, with the aid of prior Russian looting, a powerful agrarian and industrial economy bequeathed it by the Japanese. It had lost the good will of many Manchurians who, instead of revolting against Chiang Kai-shek as did the Formosans, had gone over to the Communists.

The Kuomintang armies that had been bled white in the civil war in Manchuria and cut down to Communist size were not traditional Chinese rabble troops. They were among the best units Chiang Kai-shek ever had, certainly the best-equipped armies in Chinese history. They represented the culmination of a dream General Joseph W. Stilwell had when he was making his forlorn retreat out of Burma in 1942. He could not fly American equipment to China, so he decided to fly Chinese soldiers to American equipment in India, build up an army and retake Burma. This he successfully did. But he soon thought that he was building an army that was going to fight the Chinese Communists after the war and not the Japanese during the war. On this ground, he opposed Chiang Kai-shek, lost out, went home and died a brokenhearted man. Since General Stilwell before his death believed Chiang Kai-shek had lost the mandate of the people and no longer had the right to rule China, he would perhaps from a political standpoint have been happy to see how Kuomintang troops in Manchuria had deteriorated. As an army officer, however, he would have been saddened by the sight of well-tempered combat units that had become little better than gendarmes and garrison troops.

Not only had the army deteriorated physically, but its morale was completely shot. A squabble had broken out between General Tu Li-ming, commander in chief in Manchuria, and General Sun Li-jen, a graduate of Virginia Military Institute. The Americans, who had disliked Tu ever since his failure to launch an attack in Burma in accordance with American orders, sided with Sun and tried to get Tu relieved. In the end, both were relieved.

Changes in command produced no improvement. Nepotism and bribery had rotted the moral fiber of units once famous for their discipline. A colonel I knew had a chance to become a battalion commander, but had to step aside when he could not pay his superiors for the job. Put in charge of a regimental transport unit, he was forced to give the supply depot officer one-seventh of all his gasoline. His superiors took another seventh for their personal graft. He only kept his vehicles rolling by selling lubricants and grease on the black market and buying gasoline. Padding of pay rolls, ended by the Americans in India, had begun again. As a result, when a division went into combat, it often had only 60 per cent of its supposed strength. Worse than that, pay was often not forthcoming and soldiers had to indulge in petty looting.

Garrisoned in towns because of the high command's defensive complex, idle officers were turning to the charms of feminine companionship as a surcease from the rigors of war of which they had long become tired. Chiang's officers kept some Japanese girls who were supposed to be repatriated to Japan locked up in their rooms and forced others into prostitution. Not only in towns did one see Japanese girls consorting with Kuomintang officers, but also riding on supply trains in the company of lieutenants and captains. Standing at the doors of freight cars dressed in foreign-style kimonos, under which they apparently wore nothing, these girls spiced up the scenery for a jaded traveler, but what they contributed to beating the Communists was a mystery.

The slow physical and moral disintegration of Chiang Kai-shek's Manchurian army was a strange contrast to the ever-growing strength of the Northeast United Democratic Army run by the Communist commander Lin Piao. In 1945 and 1946, while American ships and planes were transporting Kuomintang troops to the Northeast, the Communists who were marching overland through the Great Wall passes had only scattered bands of troops, numbering from forty thousand to fifty thousand men. By 1947 this force had grown to nearly three hundred thousand men, of which at least one hundred twenty thousand men were organized into a striking force of six corps of three divisions each. It was very obvious, as I wrote at the time, "Communist forces will eventually drive Chiang's forces out of Manchuria or annihilate them where they stand."

While the Kuomintang was rapidly blunting the edge of the army delivered to them by the Americans, it was at the same time doing even worse damage to the powerful Manchurian economy left them by the Japanese. Chiang's forces then controlled 80 per cent of the industry in the Northeast, but they had only 10 per cent going. Much of this could be put down to Russian looting and some to the war, but a great deal of it could be put down to Kuomintang corruption and inefficiency. I gained numerous examples of this all over Manchuria, but here I shall only mention the conditions obtaining in the Fuhsun coal mines.

About Fuhsun, where was located one of the biggest open coalpits in the world, the Japanese had built a miniature Pittsburgh, with subsidiary industries in shale oil, gas, paraffin, mobile oil, coke, asphalt, high carbon steels, cements and various smaller industries. At the height of their production, the Japanese had mined twenty thousand tons of coal a day. The Chinese had got it up to five thousand, but now it had fallen back below two thousand principally because of army interference in the mine. Ten thousand workers had been conscripted along with eighteen thousand civilians to build defense works. None of these workers were fed or paid by the army. The miners could stand that but they hated the fact that frameworks, steel rods, valuable vanadium, rust-resisting steels and timber supposedly taken from the mines for defense works, seldom went into defense works but went by cart to Mukden for sale.

Chiang's officers and soldiers in Fuhsun city were very arrogant.

They requisitioned houses and buildings and materials without orders. Sometimes they broke the windows of mine managers' homes in the middle of the night, crawled into the houses and threw the managers out. While I was in Fuhsun, I stayed at the mine hospital which provided free medical treatment to its workers. Alongside the hospital was a nurses' home. Soldiers, under orders, tore some of it down to get bricks for defense works. A few bricks went into pillboxes but most into the black market.

I met a Chinese doctor who had been educated in Germany. "Everything is rotten," he said. "Gendarmes come into our hospital, take what they please, even our medicines and sell it on the black market. They don't give a damn for anybody."

I went to see one of the assistant managers who was then in charge of the mine—a man who had been educated in America, an engineer and also a businessman.

"Chiang's gendarmes," he said, "tell us they are here to protect us from the Communists who would take our mines and homes from us, but what's the difference if we lose them to Chiang or the Communists, we lose them anyway."

An even more embittered mine staff member said: "The Communists don't need to come here, everything is divided already."

Somewhat better than conditions in industry were those existing in agriculture. But even here, the same Kuomintang tactics, practiced in China proper had been exported beyond the Great Wall. Soy beans, which were once the greatest export product of Manchuria, were no longer a source of wealth to the natives. The Northeast China Command had dictated that soy beans could only be exported by the Central Trust, a government monopoly, or the army. Though the Central Trust was getting ten cents a pound for its product, the farmer who sold to the trust was getting only three cents a pound. Of this he was allowed to keep little as he was forced to contribute most of his sale money to equipping and clothing local defense units.

Due to lack of transport, war and old-fashioned skullduggery, Manchuria's whole export trade was in bad shape. No banks in Manchuria were allowed to deal in foreign exchange and it was impossible for local firms to do any foreign trade. The central government at Nanking had allowed the Northeast no import quotas and all produce came from ports below the Wall with consequent high extra transport charges. These two regulations were enough to ruin any local firm. Angry Manchurian businessmen said they were made purposely to favor Shanghai trading companies in which Chiang's officers and officials had invested.

Red tape was also stifling trade and giving southern officials a chance to squeeze small Manchurian merchants. No merchants could export goods from Manchuria without a permit from the Foreign Trade Commission. But small, poorly dressed merchants could not even get in the building harboring the trade commission without paying a bribe to the guard at the door. Once in the building the clerks had to be bribed before one could even talk to someone who was empowered to issue a permit. As a result, desperate small traders were buying permits through brokers or trying to smuggle goods through the Great Wall.

It was not only Manchurians who were disgusted, but even many officials in Chiang Kai-shek's own government. I met an English-speaking official in the Trade Bureau in Mukden. "Our government," he told me, "is corrupt, but in the Northeast it's specially corrupt. Everyone around me in my office is robbing and stealing. I have to connive at extortion. I have come to hate my work. I can't stand any more. I'm going to resign and get out of here."

A decade of Japanese rule had inured Manchurians to most anything. But the Japanese, like all capitalist barons, put something into the country at the same time they were robbing it. The Kuomintang, the Manchurians complained, took, but put nothing back.

This trade of Japanese efficiency for Kuomintang corruption wouldn't have been so bad, the Manchurians felt, if at the same time, they had traded in their slavery under the Japanese for freedom under the Kuomintang. However, all the Manchurians received in a political way from the Kuomintang was one-party rule, military law and the secret police.

The lip service the Kuomintang paid to democracy particularly nauseated the Manchurians. People's Political Councils which were merely advisory and had no legislative, executive or judicial functions had been organized in several provinces so that the "voice of the people" could be heard. In Mukden, seventeen councilors were elected in the following fashion. Blank ballots were distributed to Kuomintang district and ward leaders, who handed them out to the people to sign and/or "chop" with their seals. When the ballots were returned, the local party headquarters then filled in the names of the men they wanted elected. In some cases, the ballots were not even distributed. The ward leaders merely collected merchants' seals and stamped the ballots themselves. Many people did not know why their seals were collected and did not even know they were supposed to have voted. A provincial council was "elected" in the same way.

Worse than any lack of democracy was the lack of freedom in the Northeast. There was not even a pretense of a free press, freedom of assembly or free speech. In Mukden, I found all but one newspaper were run by the army or its secret service organs, and that one was subsidized by army and party. Since all printing presses had been seized by the army, it was impossible for a private person to have his say in print. The most liberal publication in the city was the news bulletin put out by the United States Information Service which reprinted articles from American newspapers, some of them about China. Chiang's secret service men often did not like these articles and they called on the USIS in person and raised violent protests. In fact, they at one time became so threatening that the American in charge had secretly to ship out one of his Chinese employees on an American Army plane to Shanghai. Later, however, the Communists in Peiping practiced just as bad measures of intimidation against USIS.

Chief watchdogs of tyranny in the Northeast were skilled SS operators trained by Tai Li, dead but not forgotten chief of Chiang Kai-shek's gestapo. Sent from Sian, long the headquarters of the anti-Communist movement against Yenan, these men were ostensibly concerned with ferreting out Communists. In practice, their job amounted to suppressing all criticism of the government which they did by accusing any critic of Communism. Even worse, Manchurians claimed the operators of the Special Service Section were getting rich by squeezing bankers, merchants, landlords and former high-ranking Manchukuo officials. With funds squeezed from puppets and their rich associates, the SS men were opening small department stores, restaurants, import-export firms and dance halls which they operated clandestinely in cellars.

All the nepotism, extortion and oppression practiced by Chiang's officials and army officers in the Northeast had endeared them to few Manchurians. The natives felt—and rightly, too—that Chiang's southerners had no desire to stay in Manchuria. In several minor Communist offensives, mayors had fled from their posts without orders. When officials cleared out of danger spots in such a precipitate hurry with their wives and mistresses and loaded with so many gold bars the Manchurians but drew the conclusion that the southerners were just in Manchuria to get rich and were leaving as soon as the chance of making money disappeared. The flight of Chiang's officials in time of danger, however, was not without comfort to the local people. When the Communists by-passed the city of Changchun in one of their offensives and cut the railway below the city, instead of being alarmed at being cut off from the outside world, many people breathed a sigh of relief.

"Whew!" they said. "We're cut off. That's good. Now those Kuomintang turtle eggs can't come back."

From all I saw in Manchuria I got the feeling that the people would have driven Chiang Kai-shek's forces from the country immediately if they had the chance. There were three symptoms that clearly showed their sentiments. One was the feeling that the Japanese were, after all, not so bad. They gave the people security, kept the industries going, kept prices down and operated the country on an efficient basis.

The second symptom of anti-Nationalist feeling was the increasing popularity of the Chinese Communists. Because they were Communists, they had to live down the bad name left by the Russians and also the name of bandits given them by Chiang Kai-shek's propagandists. They did this to a startling degree. Distribution of captured food stores increased their popularity with the poor. Because there was no confiscation of business and commercial houses the fears of the town merchants had been somewhat allayed. Ordinary human sympathy also won them respect, if not popularity. In street fighting in the cities, the nationalist commander refused to allow civilians to leave their homes so that many noncombatants were killed. Whenever the Communists occupied a street, however, they allowed the people to escape the fighting and go wherever they pleased—to the Kuomintang side, if they liked. This action made a tremendous impression on the people of Manchuria.

Finally, another proof of Chiang Kai-shek's failure in the Northeast was the revival of the Manchuria-for-the-Manchurians movement. People who backed such a movement wanted a dominion status (like Canada) under the Chinese Republic. They wanted to elect their own officials and not have them appointed from above. "Our ancestors came from China," they said, "but we don't want the rotten traditional system of China put back on top of us." These men also did not want the Communists.

The army and secret police were well aware of this growing feeling of discontent among the Manchurians. They were afraid of another Formosa revolt. Actually, there was no need for a revolt. All those who wanted to oppose the government could let off steam by running over to the Communists in the countryside.

Nevertheless, the government was trying to squash the revolt before it happened. They did not give the people bread, but they did give them circuses. They were rather grim affairs.

You could see them any day in the city of Changchun, then cut off from Mukden by Communist raids against the railway. I flew up there in an American Army plane, over the Communist-held countryside. In this former capital of Manchukuo, which the Japanese built for Emperor Henry Pu Yi, there was near the center of the city a great traffic circle which in Japanese times was known as Universal Harmony Circle. When the Russians came to drive the Japanese out, they erected a monument there, put a plane on top of it and called the place Utopia Circle. Later, the Chinese arrived, put up a large picture of Chiang Kai-shek and embossed it with two chauvinistic slogans: "Up with the country!" "Up with the race!"

On my arrival, this circle was noteworthy for two features. On one side, there was a "flea" market where were sold the goods looted by the people from hospitals and factories and the materials requisitioned by officials from the people. On the other side of the circle, there was a public execution ground.

During the week of my arrival, a "criminal" a day was killed in this circle. All the executions were announced ahead of time in the papers. A rainy spell, however, brought the executions to a halt. Perhaps the authorities did not want to kill without an audience. As far as I know, the executions may still have gone on after I left. The victims? A twenty-year-old girl accused of Communism. A sixteen-year-old boy accused of spying. A fifty-six-year-old woman accused of spreading rumors. At other times, those to be done away with were just —"bandits."

There was a Roman air about it all. The victim's hands were tied behind him. A board inscribed with his crime was fitted against his back. Then he was made to kneel in a cart and drawn to the circle.

As he stepped from the cart, the crowd sighed, and parted to let him through. Then he knelt on the ground, a soldier of the Changchun garrison stepped up close behind him, quickly raised a revolver and pulled the trigger. The crowd grunted. The body fell forward. The people went away.

Far above the execution ground towered the picture of Generalissimo Chiang Kai-shek. His lips, as the artist had painted them, were parted in a smile.

*　　*　　*

I left Manchuria with the feeling that unless Chiang Kai-shek evacuated his troops back below the Great Wall, he would suffer a terrible catastrophe. I wrote so at the time, including many of the facts given above. Not a word of mine was published in America. In the meantime, the interventionists continued to promote the thesis that Chiang could be saved in Manchuria. The support of these men may have been a factor in making Chiang hold on to an untenable position. Thus, the very men who wanted to help him were instruments for effecting his military suicide. For Chiang's position in Manchuria was irretrievable. General Wedemeyer had advised him not to go there in the first place. From the standpoint of grand strategy, Chiang had failed in Manchuria because he had not been able to win the North China Plain and link up his capital and his main bases of supply with the Northeast. His fronts had no unity. His position was very similar to that of von Rundstedt's in Normandy. The German general wanted to get out, Hitler refused. Chiang's generals also wanted to get out; American advisers told him to get out; Wedemeyer said his position was hopeless. But Chiang refused to budge.

The causes of Chiang's defeat in Manchuria, however, went far deeper than any strategy. The spirit of his army was disintegrating in the chemical processes of the Chinese Revolution. Torn from their villages in the south and exported beyond the Great Wall, the soldiers and even the officers felt they were in a foreign country, where their feelings and those of the native population were refracted through entirely different mediums. They could not help but notice the looks of hatred thrown at them like so many knives by the sturdy Manchurian people. A mood of angry frustration, followed by feelings of guilt, burned away at the soldiers' heart.

As the Communists moved in on villages, Chiang's army was torn loose from its social moorings. Psychologically, the soldiers felt completely lost. The further the army got away from the good Chinese earth, the more did it become like a balloon which, rising from the ground, gets ever higher until its internal tensions cause it to burst. In drawing away from the villages, Chiang Kai-shek's Manchurian army was also building up internal tension, and its bursting point was not far off.

A very striking picture of the loss of internal self-confidence in the army was furnished me on the train I traveled on from Mukden to Peiping. At a stop along the way, a Chinese cavalry general entered my compartment and seated himself opposite me. I nodded to him, but gave no indication I spoke Chinese. In a short while, an infantry colonel entered the compartment and engaged the general, who was unknown to him, in conversation. By many subtle remarks, the two officers began feeling out each other's sentiments toward the war. The general would make a slight criticism, the colonel would cap it with a stronger one, and the general would follow with a still more bitter comment. Soon both were denouncing the conduct of the war.

"I am a cavalry commander," said the general. "You can use cavalry for reconnaissance, patrol or a charge, but I'm just guarding a railroad. But how can I guard it? The peasants come and take up the tracks. What can I do about that? I am a Northeasterner; shall I shoot my own Northeastern farmers? I ask for orders. But I don't get orders. Nobody has any idea how we should fight. I often wonder why we are fighting. Fourteen years, the Japanese occupied our woods and rivers and hills, and now here we are killing each other again."

The colonel nodded. The conversation lapsed for a moment. We were drawing near to Shanhaikuan where the Great Wall comes down to meet the sea. The colonel looked out the window, then turned back. "You know," he said, "I don't think the 8th Route needs to take Changchun and Mukden. They'll just take the countryside all around, organize the militia, then they'll come down here by the Great Wall and cut us all off. I don't know what the higher authorities are thinking of. We ought to get out of here or stop fighting."

The colonel sounded so lugubrious and the general looked so sad that I could not help but burst into laughter. They both looked at me. "You understand Chinese then?" said the general. I nodded.

"There's no way," he said. "No way. Useless."

Indeed this general was right. There was no way. The soldiers of

Chiang Kai-shek on Manchurian soil did not wish any longer to fight. They began to fraternize with the Manchurian people and then with the 8th Route Army. It was this fraternization that broke up Chiang Kai-shek's vain hopes to hold on to Manchuria. Slowly his hold on the territory beyond the Great Wall weakened and crumbled away.

In the meantime, inside the Great Wall far to the south and also far from the borders of the Soviet Union, China's dictator was threatened from still another direction. The Chinese people were in almost open revolt against the despot who had ruled them for twenty-two years.

53. Paradise Lost: Massacre at Formosa

WHEN I returned from Manchuria, I found the Kuomintang had declared semi-open warfare on its own people. Nationwide demonstrations against the civil war, against American intervention and against dictatorship had been met by direct and bloody suppression. Thousands of students, businessmen and intellectuals had been beaten, thousands of others imprisoned and still others shot down, bayoneted and murdered. Most of these actions were performed in the name of suppressing bandits, catching spies or uncovering Communist agents. Both the numbers and the prominence of the victims prevented these charges from gaining any wide acceptance, and in order to quiet the anguished howls of criticism that rose from all quarters, the Chinese government was sometimes forced to admit that many of the victims were not Communists, but merely youths who had been led astray by false and foreign doctrines. In order to save China from these pernicious influences, said Chiang Kai-shek, it was necessary that the people return to the virtuous ways of the ancient sages and allow the government to regenerate them.

During 1947 and 1948, on the island of Formosa, an experiment in this "regeneration" of the people by the government of Chiang Kai-shek was carried out on a laboratory scale—beyond the reaches of the Russians, beyond the grasp of the Chinese Communists and even beyond the civil war and therefore very convincing. During February 1947, Chiang's soldiers had killed hundreds of unarmed Formosans, but these events had passed almost unnoticed in the outside world until John W. Powell, the courageous American editor of the *China Weekly Review* visited the island and gave a factual account of what he saw and heard. Although Powell was reviled by the Kuomintang press for "exaggerating" a minor affair, I found things even worse than Powell had described.

To appreciate the nature of the tragic events on Formosa, it is necessary to understand something about the setting in which they occurred. This long oval island, which is about the size of Holland and lies a hundred miles off the coast of China, must be regarded as one of the most attractive places in the Orient. Within its narrow confines there is contained a wealth of scenery that is almost as varied as that offered by the entire United States. Two-thirds of the island is mountainous, with seventy-seven peaks reaching nearly to ten thousand feet. Some of these mountains have a savage and enchanted look, plunging almost perpendicularly from heights of seven thousand feet directly into the Pacific which runs around the island in a belt of pale green water. In the rainy season, torrents come roaring down from the mountains and are important sources of hydroelectric power. Tropical forests cover the lower slopes of the hills, forming jungles that are difficult to penetrate. The lowlands are intensively cultivated and the whole countryside is a vast green and yellow garden of paddy fields, peasant hamlets, well-worn paths and meandering creeks. Necklacing the island are numerous sandy beaches which offer ideal spots for sun-bathing and swimming. The climate is warm and equable; a sea breeze, which sometimes sharpens into a hurricane, keeps the island fresh and cool even on the hottest days. The people on Formosa grow more food than they can use, and rice, fruits and fish are everywhere in abundance. To complete the picture of this natural paradise, there are flowers of many colors which decorate the hill slopes, the paddy fields and also the heads of the pretty Formosan-Chinese women.

Formosa has had a violent history. The Chinese made the first recorded expedition to the island in A.D. 605. Later, when the Manchus conquered China, Ming dynasty expatriates found refuge here and drove the aboriginal tribesmen into the hills. For a time, Formosa became a great pirate lair and buccaneers from headquarters on the island made raids up and down the China coast and also feasted off the hundreds of Western-world ships that were wrecked on her treacherous rocks. Castaways were generally killed. The Dutch and the Portuguese occupied parts of the island at various times and finally in 1895, the decrepit Manchus signed Formosa over to the Japanese. It took the Japanese seven years to pacify the island, but when they had done so they improved the living conditions of the people by developing communications, improving public health, expanding commodity distribution and instituting agricultural planning. They eliminated banditry, developed railways, made the roads safe for travel and gave the Formosans a Spartan kind of justice, but not much social or political freedom.

Because of this last fact, because they considered themselves Chinese, because they did not realize they were culturally more advanced than the people of their own motherland and because they had heard of the

Atlantic Charter, democracy and the New Life Movement of Madame Chiang Kai-shek, the arrival of Chinese troops in the autumn of 1945 created a great stir of enthusiasm among the islanders, and they trooped to the railway stations and the docks in holiday clothes to welcome their "liberators."

Their joy, however, vanished almost overnight, for they found they were not being liberated, but conquered—and by a lower civilization at that.

Chiang's soldiers took goods from the market stalls without paying for them, robbed civilians on the streets at night and killed villagers so that their robberies would not be discovered. Thus, villages and towns, which had never known any thieves under Japanese rule, were forced to organize their own local protective associations.

When Chiang's civilian officials took over from the army, conditions did not improve, but became worse. Carpetbagging bureaucrats confiscated all Japanese property, selling most of it on the black market for private gain, or shipping it over to their own homes on the mainland. Having seized Japanese property, Chiang's officials quickly turned their eyes on the wealth of the Formosans.

When taking over a factory, Chinese gendarmes asked three questions: "How much cash on hand?" "Any motorcar?" "Any house?" Formosan staff members were dismissed and replaced by Kuomintang hangers-on. Though the island had almost as many trained technicians as the whole of China put together, most all of these men were indiscriminately thrown out of their jobs and forced to become cooks, clerks or menial servants for party ward heelers. The head of a pharmaceutical factory, for example, was fired and replaced by an errand boy from a Shanghai drugstore who was a relative of a Chinese official. Technicians from the fisheries were dismissed and took up jobs as houseboys and orderlies. The manager of the Taipeh Gas Company had to become a clerk in a foreign firm. Under these conditions, plus the lack of any real Chinese capital, plus the effects of American air raids, Formosan industry was deprived of its life blood and collapsed like a stuck pig.

The Chinese threw Formosans not only out of business, but also out of government. Even junior and senior clerks had to surrender their jobs to Kuomintang patronage seekers. The highest government job held by any Formosan was that of vice-director of education, and he was later killed.

This dual monopoly of government and business was a perfect get-rich-quick setup for Chiang's carpetbaggers. Licenses for shops and trade were seldom issued without the payment of bribes.

Chinese extortionists were furnished protection by the party secret service and Chiang's government. A procurator of the Chiayi local court succeeded in indicting a Chinese chief of a monopoly bureau for graft, but the government stepped in before the trial and said there was not sufficient evidence. A courageous Formosan judge challenged the government: "You may cut off my head," he said, "but under no circumstances can you interfere with the law." As a result, the indicted Chinese official was shipped back to the safety of the mainland. The judge was later killed.

Chiang's bureaucrats, adopting mainland practices, soon put most businesses from tea to fertilizer under government monopoly, drove the Formosans out of trade and obtained a free hand for private grafting.

Under the attacks of these carpetbaggers, every branch of Formosan life began to collapse. When the American Army first arrived on Formosa, the local dollar was valued at ten American cents and remained stable for six months. Instead of allowing Formosan money to remain on a sound basis, however, the Chinese hooked it up to their own printing press currency with the result that the Formosan dollar declined to a tenth of a US cent. In the words of an American official on the island, this was a "crime against the people of Formosa," deliberately made with the intention of fleecing the islanders and also done with the intention of creating a fluctuating exchange behind which all sorts of illegal manipulations would be carried out.

The profits piled up by Chiang's officials knew few bounds. When UNRRA sold coal to the National Fuel Commission at Taiwan for $5.26 a ton, it appeared later on the black market for $130. UNRRA brought 120,000 tons of fertilizer to Formosa and handed it over to Chiang's officials at eight yen a pound. This fertilizer, paid for by American taxpayers, instead of going directly to the hard-pressed farmers for whom it was intended, appeared on the market for 160 yen a pound.

This exploitation had profound effects on the living conditions of the people. Under the Japanese, the laboring classes had been able to eat fish, eggs and some meat on an average wage of a hundred yen a month. By 1947, workers were receiving an equivalent of only twenty-five yen. Ninety per cent of their pay went for food; they could buy no clothing and soon they began to go barefoot like the peasants. Nor were the middle classes any better off. Unable to live on their salaries, they first sold their furniture, then, as their savings disappeared, some of them sent their daughters into whorehouses and their sons to peddle cigarettes on the streets. Under the Japanese, these children had gone to school. The Chinese said: "That was compulsory education; now you are free." Free to become beggars, the Formosans answered.

The Kuomintang looting of Formosan food went to criminal and even murderous lengths. As indicated before, there is an oversupply of food on the island. Paddy fields are so productive that normally many acres can be left uncultivated for a year or more and there will still be enough for everyone to eat. The Japanese never took any rice out of the island until all the crops were collected and they could decide on an equitable tax. The Chinese, however, arbitrarily assigned a tax in kind on each mow of land, with the result that peasants with a poor crop had to pay taxes that left them little rice. Worse still, when the peasants brought their rice to the tax-collecting stations, military posts along the road would forbid them to pass until they got their own squeeze. Thus, peasants arrived at the tax collectors' with insufficient rice.

It was not only the living conditions of the people that were lowered, but their standard of health, too. Before the coming of Chiang's government, there had not been a case of smallpox in the island for over fifteen years. By 1947, there were 4,193 cases with the death rate 37 per cent in five months. Because of the excellent Japanese quarantine system, there had been no cholera in the island since 1920. The Chinese, however, were conducting a thriving smuggling trade between the island and the mainland and they also smuggled cholera back into Formosa. UNRRA made repeated representations to the medical authorities of Formosa to stop the smuggling and reinstitute cholera controls. Chiang's doctors replied that it was difficult to stop the smuggling, because the smugglers were armed. At this time there were forty thousand soldiers on the island. Later they were used to suppress the Formosan people, but now they could not halt a few armed smugglers.

Under these conditions, it is not surprising that a cholera epidemic broke out in 1946. The epidemic was particularly severe in southern Formosa and the death rate soon rose to 80 per cent of all cases. UNRRA dispatched all of its nurses and doctors to the threatened area, with the intention of putting the isolation hospitals in decent shape and cleaning up foul conditions. At this time there were only one Chinese doctor and five nurses in the cholera hospitals. In a near-by provincial hospital, however, there were fourteen Chinese doctors and thirty nurses to look after only fifteen patients. All of these refused to go into the cholera hospitals. Conditions became so bad that patients were found dead in furnace rooms and in woodsheds behind the hospitals.

Further difficulties were encountered. Cholera is a disease that takes water out of the blood stream. The veins fold together, the blood gets thicker until the veins burst and the heart fails. The usual way of curing cholera is to give intravenous saline injections of Ringer solution. This is a very simple solution to make. Even if it cannot be made, hot water solutions are of some help. At the very height of the epidemic, however, a Chinese medical official issued an order to be sparing in the use of the solutions. UNRRA officials protested violently against this order, which could only result in the death of victims who could be saved. One official answered: "These cholera victims are only poor and unimportant people." One UNRRA doctor, with tears of rage, turned on the official and declared: "You are rich and important, but I pray to God that you yourself get cholera."

When I was in Formosa, UNRRA claimed there were one thousand lepers loose on the island. Formerly they had been in a government leper colony, subsidized by the Japanese, but with the arrival of Chiang Kai-shek's government, no one was prepared to pay their expenses and they had been shipped home. As if all this were not enough, doctors' licenses were being sold for three hundred thousand yen apiece.

Along with the decline in the living conditions and the health of the Formosans, a parallel decline occurred in education and morals. When the Chinese entered the island, they began a determined campaign to stamp out the use of the Japanese language. The common people were extraordinarily eager to learn mandarin Chinese as they were told they thereby could become true Chinese citizens. However, they soon began to feel they were nothing but a colonial population, and no matter how hard they studied, they would never become true nationals of China.

For the first six months in the schools, Kuomintang teachers taught little but the Chinese language and Kuomintang principles. Arithmetic, science and other subjects were forgotten. The Chinese told the Formosans they would teach them the standard national language, but in a camp held for Formosan teachers, five Chinese professors all spoke a different dialect and the poor Formosans had no idea what was the national language of China.

Worse still, language was used as a means of suppression and control. Kuomintang teachers asked mainland girl students to spy on Formosan-Chinese girls and report all those who were speaking Japanese among themselves. Originally, the island girls had been willing enough to learn Chinese, but the prohibition aroused a spirit of rebellion in them and they began to speak Japanese and Formosan dialects to show their disapproval of the Chinese.

Under the Japanese, cheating in an examination had been considered a terrible offense and anyone caught in such an act was immediately dismissed from school. But when a Chinese boy in a Formosan middle school was caught cheating and when the whole student body voted to dismiss him, the boy's father who was an influential Kuomintang official not only succeeded in getting his son reinstated, but in making the principal apologize. Seeing the new rules of society, Formosan students soon began to cheat on a widespread scale themselves.

Bribery of teachers by students, common in China, had been almost unknown till the advent of Chiang's pedants. By 1947, however, students before every exam were bringing money wrapped up in red paper on which were inscribed suitable characters wishing the teacher success. Students who did not bring such bribes had to be super scholars in order to receive even passing grades.

Chiang Kai-shek's officials not only brought corruption, chicanery and cholera in their suitcases to Formosa, they also brought with them Chinese feudal practices that had long since vanished from the island. Concubinage, which had been almost unknown under the Japanese, was reintroduced into the island. Under Japanese rule, Formosan girls would have been ashamed to be second or third wives, but now, because they could not make a living, many of them thought it the best arrangement.

The Chinese were quite heartless in their treatment of Formosan girls. For example, seven young Chinese officials pooled their money, bought a ring and sent one of their number to pay court to a Formosan girl. With the family's permission, the official married the girl, brought her home and spent an enjoyable wedding night with her. On the second night, a different husband came into the girl's bed, and on the third night still another husband. In desperation she fled away. Many Formosan girls who married Chinese later discovered that they were merely "little wives" when the real Chinese wife arrived from the mainland.

As if by a slow wasting poison, the Formosans themselves were corrupted to the level of their Chinese rulers. Concubinage and prostitution spread everywhere. Morality fell to a new low. Noting this tendency, saddened Formosans remarked among themselves: "In a few years we will be the same as the mainland pigs."

With every desire not to bring a subjective note into a discussion of the practices of dictatorship, the writer cannot help remarking that what Chiang Kai-shek's regime did to the Formosan people was nothing but a crime against humanity. Under the Japanese, there had never been a rice shortage, never a food shortage, never an epidemic, never an inflation, never any children who did not attend school, never any beggars on the street. There were hospitals for all, public welfare clinics and public dentists. Now there were none of these things. Despite their suppression of freedom, the Japanese had a public conscience. When they collected taxes, they put the money back into the island again and developed the economy. The Chinese, however, just collected and put nothing back.

In exploiting Formosa, Chiang Kai-shek's officials not only brought themselves into low repute, but their whole country. The very term "Chinese" became a synonym for something both hateful and ridiculous. Whenever something went wrong, the Formosans said: "This is Chinese." Such a phrase covered a multitude of sins—having two wives, taking life easy, getting paid before doing a service, putting relatives in high office. It also became synonymous with the American word "snafu." Fountain pens, electric lights, telephones that wouldn't work—all these were called Chinese. Even the aboriginal tribesmen in the hills said a mountain path that had fallen into disrepair was a Three People's Principles Path.

The Formosans tried to reform Chiang's officials by pleading with them. That did not work. So they resorted to sarcasm. On the walls they put up posters showing a dog (Japs) fleeing from the island and a pig (Chinese) coming in. "The dog can protect the people," said the poster, "but the pig can only eat and sleep." These posters produced little effect on the Chinese bureaucrats, but did serve to give Formosans an idea they were fighting back.

Since they had not taken any part in political affairs for fifty-one years under the Japanese, the Formosans did not know quite how to combat the skilled Chinese politicians. At first, they just met in small groups, talked about Chinese practices and discussed what they ought to do. Everyone was hypnotized by the fact that they had no arms. They decided their only weapon was the pen, so they established newspapers and magazines, published articles about democracy and self-government and then began an open criticism of corruption, graft and despotism in the government. Later, most of those who attacked the government were either arrested or killed on the charge that they were "Communist ruffians."

Few Formosans had originally thought to take any active measures against the Chiang regime, but only to reform the officials. They soon believed this was impossible. Still, they would have done nothing had not conditions become desperate. In September 1946, due to the export of rice from the island, prices went up with alarming speed. Rice lines formed in all the cities. Formosans became thinner every day. As they got poorer, the anger of the Formosans began to rise. Soon the idea spread that they could fight the Kuomintang in April and May 1947 by holding back the rice harvest and rousing the whole island to struggle. In this way they hoped to force Chiang Kai-shek's officials to reform. Proponents of this idea were not prepared to fight earlier. Events, however, moved too swiftly, and what might have been a planned revolt broke out spontaneously, headlessly and with disastrous consequences.

The incident that set off the Formosan revolt was in itself quite inconsequential, but it was the straw that broke the patience of the ordinary island people. One of the biggest complaints of the Formosans against the Chinese had been the trade monopolies by which the Chinese cornered all business in the islands. Police of the monopoly bureau, under the excuse of stopping the illegal sale of cigarettes, began attacking child peddlers and robbing them of their cigarettes. On the night of February 27, an old woman peddler in the capital at Taipeh refused to give up her cigarettes and was shot by a policeman. That night a thousand Formosans marched on the police bureau and demanded satisfaction. They got none.

The next day five thousand people, accompanied by Western business-men who agreed to act as witnesses, marched on the monopoly bureau to make a protest against the shooting. While delegates went into the government building the crowd remained standing outside the door. Soldiers, stationed on the roofs, opened fire and in the first volley wounded eight Formosans. Frightened, but at the same time enraged, the crowd scattered and began to look for Chinese. They halted all cars, stopped all well-dressed Chinese, took their money from them and publicly burned it. At this moment, the crowd had no thought for the future, but simply thought to destroy the wealth which they considered Chinese officials had taken from them.

At this time, a group of students who had gone to the railway station to take a train to the south were arrested by the railway police and beaten—some of them, to death. An enraged crowd of four thousand people marched on this office and were shot upon by gendarmes in full sight of the American consulate.

Now fully aroused, the people in Taipeh soon took control of the whole city except for a few strategically located government buildings. Chen Yi, the governor, frightened by developments, broadcast a speech promising to punish those guilty for the shootings and promising to meet the demands of the people for reform. With this the city calmed down, students and businessmen formed patrols in the streets and kept order. From then on, until the arrival of Chiang Kai-shek's troops, there was absolute peace in the city.

On March 1, the Taipeh City Assembly formed a committee to deal with the incident. Everyone soon agreed that there was no use stopping just at the incident, but that demands must be pressed to satisfy all their other grievances.

Therefore, after a public meeting in the town hall, the committee sent to Governor Chen Yi a list of demands which included appeals for self-government, true democracy and true liberty as guaranteed by the consti-tution which Chiang Kai-shek had ratified when George Marshall was in China. The governor sent this communication back with the statement that it was not legally and properly phrased and would have to be written over again. It became apparent that the governor was stalling for time. That could only mean troops from the mainland.

Formosans realized they were too weak to stand up against armed divisions. They went to the American consulate and asked if the United States could not in some way arbitrate the incident. They also requested that Ambassador Stuart in Nanking try to prevail on Chiang Kai-shek not to send troops into an island that was peaceful. The Formosans were told in effect that this was too small an incident to concern the United States.

In the meantime, the Formosans had taken over nearly the whole island. Branch political associations had taken over police stations and all government buildings and offices in the provinces and town assemblies had begun to function. There were few disturbances. It was one of the most peaceful rebellions in history. Technically speaking, it was not a rebellion, for the Formosans were not trying to overthrow their rulers, but reform them.

Meanwhile, Governor Chen Yi, a wise old Fukien warlord, skilled in the ways of politics, played with the inexperienced Formosans as if they were little children. Because one of the main demands of the Formosans was for adequate representation in the government, Chen Yi asked the people to send him a list of the mayors, town assemblymen and officials they wanted to govern them. Not knowing any better, the Formosans complied and thereby furnished Chen Yi with a black list for subsequent arrests and executions.

On March 8, Chiang's troops arrived in Keelung and that night entered the capital of Taipeh. They immediately dragged many Formosan youths into the street and shot them. Soldiers threw stones through windows, climbed inside and ransacked houses before the eyes of the terrified occupants. They went into the house of a woman primary school teacher, raped her, shot her father, who was a school principal, and her brother.

The next day, Governor Chen Yi abolished the people's committee, and the soldiers occupied the broadcasting station, all government buildings and all schools. Young men and students were ordered into the streets and over a hundred were arrested. Throughout March 9 and 10, firing continued both day and night. A clerk of the Taiwan Power Company went out with three thousand yen in his pocket to buy rice, was robbed and then killed. A primary school principal, carrying thirty thousand yen in school fees, was likewise robbed and killed. Taiwanese found out of doors were bayoneted or shot. Meanwhile a search was carried out for middle school students who were arrested, beaten and also executed. One group of gendarmes went to arrest a city councilman. His wife came to the door with her baby in her arms and barred the way. She was shot. People on the street were held up and robbed, beaten and reviled, while homes were broken into and ransacked.

On March 11, 12 and 13, the killings became more systematic as soldiers and gendarmes, acting on grudge lists supplied by mainland Chinese, searched out personal enemies, particularly newspapermen, schoolteachers, committeemen and businessmen. Often such men were shot on the spot. Others were taken away and never heard of again. If they could not be found, their families were taken as hostages.

Judge Wu Fan-chin, who had sentenced a corrupt Chinese policeman to a jail sentence, was taken from his home, thrown under a bridge and killed. The same thing happened to an official of the tobacco bureau and eight other Formosans who were likewise thrown under the bridge, where their noses were slit, their faces scarred and they were castrated. A graduate of an American university, who wanted to develop a Formosan sugar company and keep Chinese capital out of the island, was shot and killed. Three judges, all of whom had sentenced corrupt Chinese officials, were kidnaped from their homes. A seventy-two-year-old member of the People's Political Council was dragged from a sick bed and murdered with his two sons. He had attacked Chinese corruption in public speeches.

Dozens of bodies of students and others were discovered in shallow mass graves or washed ashore after being dumped in the sea. Bodies indicated death by beating, bayoneting, shooting and execution by sword and mutilation. Wives and sisters of murdered victims were not only numbed with grief, but completely bewildered. Kneeling beside their relatives, they would cry out: "You are not a ruffian; you did nothing; why were you killed?"

The Formosan massacres shocked the Chinese people, and for a brief moment even the rest of the world. They were, however, soon forgotten in the press of other events, and the Chiang Kai-shek government, instead of bowing its head in shame, was able to utter the most sanctimonious statements about the mass murders its soldiers had committed.

Said Chiang Kai-shek: "The trouble was all instigated by Formosan Communists who had been drafted by the Japanese to fight in the south seas."

Said a publicity handout about Governor Chen Yi: "He was a champion of democratic administration. . . . He recruited honest and experienced aides from the mainland, and those who came did so at great personal loss. Because he was too liberal, the Formosans lost control of themselves."

When Chiang's bureaucrats started on the road of demagoguism, they stopped at nothing. In their lexicons, robbery and murder were synonyms for liberalism. The authorities began a New Cultural Movement. Party hyenas, brought over from the mainland to clean up after the tiger Chen Yi, eulogized the government, requested submission to authority and acquiescence to official arrogance. Those who criticized corruption were denounced as traitors, self-seekers, Communists or separatists. Such was the new culture invented by the old feudalism!

Not satisfied with this hypocrisy, the government twisted the knife in the wound. Schools were told to set aside April 26 as a day of thanksgiving when the children could show their gratitude to the Chinese army which had come over and halted the riots and protected the people. Pupils in primary schools were asked to donate five yen and those in middle schools ten yen as a sign of their thanks. In other words, children were to give presents to those who had killed their fathers.

The rebellion and its brutal suppression provided gendarmes with a new method of enriching themselves. Now secret service men and party thugs could secretly arrest some of Formosa's richest men, accuse them of being connected with the rebellion and extort money from them on pain of death. If people were too poor to pay much, they bought themselves free in groups. Thus in Keelung seventeen people were said to have bought themselves out of jail by paying one hundred thousand yen to Chiang's gendarmes. In northern Taiwan, thirteen people were given three days' time to supply four thousand bags of rice in exchange for their lives. As rice was then selling at ten thousand yen, or ten US dollars a bag, this ransom was respectable even by American standards.

Just to make sure that the people were kept on the *qui vive*, the gendarmes every once in a while held a public execution. Thus in Takao, long after the rebellion and its suppression, two brothers, aged twenty-five and thirty-five, were shot in the main square near the railway station in front of their families who were made to watch the executions.

Formosans say twenty thousand people were wounded, killed or disappeared on the island after March 1947. Probably this is an exaggeration. Foreign businessmen and diplomats put the number at five thousand. The figures can't be checked. But the fact remains that there was a terrible slaughter of an unarmed people. Ninety-nine per cent of these killings were unnecessary. Why then did they occur? There is only one answer. The Chiang Kai-shek government used terror as a definite weapon in their rule.

This terror policy worked. The Formosans were almost completely cowed. For the most part, they did not want to have anything to do with politics whatsoever. They did not even want to criticize the government or its corruption. Not openly, anyway. But in private they would talk. In fact, only in private could they talk. The precautions they had to take were fantastic. Anyone seen talking to a foreigner was under suspicion. Thus, when I talked with a Formosan I had to go to a rendezvous a half an hour before time. Then the Formosan would leave a half an hour before me so that there would be no suspicion of our being together.

I found most Formosans in a helpless mood. That was the great difference between them and the people in Communist areas. There, through many years of struggle, the people had learned to fight with only the most meager weapons because they had been given a program and a method of struggle. When I asked the Formosans why they didn't organize guerrilla warfare in their impenetrable mountains, they shook their heads. "No arms. It is impossible." These people no longer believed in themselves.

How could they be otherwise? They were but children in the affairs of the world. Chinese maneuvering and intrigue mystified them and they lost their way in the mazes of Kuomintang double-crossing and triple checking.

"The Japs treated us badly," a Formosan told me, "but at least we knew where we stood. We did not have much liberty, but we had a hard kind of justice. When we went to court, everything was legal and official. The Japs were hard masters, but they never stabbed you in the back. Now we have police, gendarmes, secret agents, the youth corps, the party, the government and so many organizations watching us that we can't count them.

"You have to bribe someone, but you never know where the money goes, and you just hope it reaches the right people and you will be released from jail. Even our police are helpless. They have no right to arrest the Chinese gendarmes or military police who commit crimes, and no right to interfere with the army. Before, when our policemen arrested a thief, the government would pay to bring the thief to court trial in the capital. Now, the policemen never know whether their expenses will be paid, so they let the thieves go and soon the thieves and police are working together.

"What can we hope for? Where can we turn? With so many over us, to whom can we appeal? You can just look to Heaven and cry, that's all."

In these words one may hear the inner despair of a people overcome by a great tragedy. The events on the island of Formosa, however, were not only tragic, but revolutionary, in significance. For on this small island, seemingly isolated from the rest of the world, there was performed a kind of laboratory experiment, almost as though under a microscope, which tested and laid bare the inner processes of Chinese history.

Chiang Kai-shek's government did so much evil in Formosa that Chinese everywhere saw there was no need for the Communists to come to destroy the country; the Reds could never do what had already been done by the feudal bureaucrats of China. On the island of Formosa, it was proved beyond a shadow of a doubt that the very bureaucratic-capitalist structure of the Chiang regime forced it, even against its will, to rob its subjects. Within the framework of this structure reform was impossible and every protest, every criticism, every revolt that threatened the profits of the ruling apparatus could only be met with suppression, brutality and murder.

This experiment on a tiny island in the Pacific was not without its effect on the great Chinese mainland. Many Chinese who had hitherto been sitting on the fence, trying vainly to balance themselves between the struggling forces, now concluded that the civil war was not a war between communism and democracy, but a war between the people and their dictator. After Formosa, many people, especially the intellectuals, turned sharply toward the left—away from Chiang Kai-shek and toward the Communists.

The events on Formosa also held a lesson for the rest of the world. On this small island, it was proven with brutal finality—if any proof were needed—that there is no longer any place to hide. Gone, like Formosa, are the other island paradises celebrated by Gauguin, London and Melville. The old havens have been taken over by the generals, the admirals, the politicians and the gangsters.

Finally, Formosa was the complete answer to those Americans who sought to pin all the troubles of China's dictator on President Roosevelt and the Russians. This tiny island, when Chiang Kai-shek took it over, was a going concern, only partly damaged by the war. A few months later, it was little more than a prison house, a paradise turned into a Devil's Island.

54. The Rising of the Intellectuals

THE chief motive force behind the Communist movement in China was the insurrection of the peasantry. But peasant support, though it was the decisive factor in the civil war, was not sufficient to bring victory to the Communists over Chiang Kai-shek. To win the war and gain control of the state, the party had to wean a good portion of the intellectuals, the businessmen and the army away from the Kuomintang regime. Otherwise, it ran the risk of seeing the whole revolution peter out into a mere peasant uprising that would collapse when it hit the cities.

To find a bridge over to the people in Chiang Kai-shek's areas was difficult. Most of the politically conscious elements in Kuomintang territory were not well disposed toward the Communists. During the early part of the war, the party found few intellectuals as allies. Engineers, writers, physicians, professors and students kept very much aloof from the movement in the countryside. The dearth of speakers, agitators and "leaders" was keenly felt in the schools, in the villages and in the political meetings in the Liberated Areas. It is a plain fact that the great majority of Chinese intellectuals, though they are now expressing their love for the "revolution," did not at first give support to the Communist party and even turned their backs on it. Nevertheless, it was the revolt of many of these intellectuals that hammered the final nail into Chiang Kai-shek's coffin which the bold blows of the peasantry had already hewn into rough shape.

The tremendous economic collapse and the widespread terror practiced by Chiang's gendarmes and gestapo were major factors in convincing the intellectuals that Chiang Kai-shek could not possibly solve their life problems. That made them feel cornered. Still they would not have turned actively toward the Communists had they not caught in the Communist program a glimmer of hope, a road of escape, a path to the future. Upon close examination the means and implements the Communists used in getting this program across to the Chinese people outside their areas seem all out of proportion to the effects they produced. The Communist underground, while very skillful, was quite negligible in numbers when the war began. Their nuclei among the workers in Chiang's areas was almost nil. Their pamphlets and magazines enjoyed a very small circulation. The Kuomintang controlled all of the press in Shanghai, Peiping, Chungking, Hankow, Canton and other large cities. Yet the Communist program in the end took possession of a decisive minority of the people. How?

The explanation is very simple: The Communist slogans—against civil war, against oppression, against dictatorship, against American intervention—corresponded to the urgent demands of the people in Chiang Kai-shek's areas and created all kinds of revolutionary channels for themselves. It would be a very vulgar mistake, however, to suppose that the Communists merely took advantage of discontent by propaganda. The Communists were not demagogues or charlatans in that sense. The Communists definitely guided themselves by the needs, the hopes and the experiences of those they wanted to win over. In fact, there is nothing to show that the slogans I have just mentioned did not originally come from opposition elements in Chiang Kai-shek's areas. These demands of the people the Communists took as their point of departure. That was one of their marks of superiority to Chiang Kai-shek. They listened to the people and learned from them; Chiang stopped up his ears and remained in ignorance.

Nothing could illustrate this more clearly than the question of peace. Whether the Communists or the Kuomintang were responsible for starting the civil war is an academic question that could be of interest only to people who write government white papers. What was important in the struggle for power, however, was the policy each side adopted toward the peace question and the effect that such policies had on the Chinese people. There can be little doubt that the Communists at the end of the Japanese war were determined to struggle toward state power and determined eventually to overthrow Chiang Kai-shek. But the Communists never, until very late in the civil war and then only in a limited form, declared that they wanted to overthrow Chiang at the cost of peace or anything else. They were too wise for that. Also the Communists in all the years of the civil war never suppressed peace movements; in fact, they deliberately fostered them, as the Soviet Union three years later also fostered peace movements. The Chiang government, under pressure from the right wing of the Kuomintang, however, took just the opposite course. And it ruined them.

Because he adopted the line that the Communists were "bandits" and had to be wiped out at any cost—a line that was later to be echoed by Mr. William C. Bullitt—Chiang Kai-shek made the terrible strategic blunder of suppressing the demands of his own people for peace. This brought him into open conflict with the intelligentsia and the left-wing university professors who had a wide following among the students— traditionally the most politically conscious element in an illiterate Chinese society.

The battle between the intellectuals and the rulers of China began shortly after V-J Day when police threw hand grenades into a student peace demonstration in Kunming, killing four students and wounding fourteen. This was only the opening salvo in a campaign of larger proportions. Two and a half months after the Kunming killings, during peace parleys in Chungking several hundred Kuomintang thugs demolished the rostrum of a mass meeting and manhandled more than fifty leaders of a people's organization. The arrival of George Marshall in China brought the demands for peace still more into the open and consequently forced the Chiang regime also more into the open against its own people. In March 1946, a parade to welcome truce teams composed of Americans, Kuomintang and Communist party members was dispersed by Kuomintang troops and forty ringleaders were arrested. Two schoolteachers were said to have been buried alive and eight boy and girl students were drowned in a near-by river, while the rest were imprisoned. On June 25, in Suchow, the local garrison forces of Chiang Kai-shek shot to death twelve and wounded twenty-seven students of the Suchow Middle School. The dean of the school was hit by seven bullets and killed. More than three hundred students fell on their knees in front of machine guns—possibly supplied by the truce-making United States—and pleaded for their lives.

During most of 1946, the Kuomintang terror was consistently aimed at halting the peace demands. Notable social leaders, advocating peace, were subjected to wild beatings by Kuomintang thugs, two professors were assassinated in Kunming after speaking to an anti-civil war rally and the Peiping Committee member of the Democratic League was kidnaped and tortured.

By such methods, the Kuomintang quelled the popular demands for peace throughout the country. It would be idle to think that this suppression did not have effect. After the killing of the intellectuals and the arrest of students, the peace movement assumed a semi-underground character. However, the offensive against the peace movement nurtured its own counteroffensive. For the killings of the intellectuals not only shocked the democratic yearnings of the people, but also brought home clearly to the politically conscious elements of society the fact that Chiang Kai-shek wanted war. Had he been able to finish off the war quickly, the suppressions might have been forgotten. But the desolation brought about by the continuing war made the murders of the leading peace proponents seem doubly unbearable.

The government had begun the war with the promise that it would be over in three months. By the end of 1946, everyone saw that it would probably not come to an end even in three years. People believed that the generalissimo could not fight without American help. They began to talk among themselves about keeping American arms, American advisers and American soldiers and marines out of China. Two days before the end of the year, the rape of a Chinese girl by American marines in Peiping brought these sentiments violently into the open. The indignation of the Chinese led to a monster student demonstration which broke out almost simultaneously throughout the country. The first year of the war thus ended in storm and thunder.

These flashes of popular indignation did not go entirely unheeded by the government. But it was placed in a dilemma. "Hands off China" had become the new rallying slogan of the peace movement. The government did not dare smash the patriotic nature of the new demands. Yet it did not idly look on. Under one pretext or another, in the spring of 1947, Chiang's gendarmes rounded up two thousand civilians in Peiping and another three thousand in Tsingtao and Canton.

Such actions managed for a while to keep the people quiet, but the decline in the opposition to Chiang Kai-shek did not last very long—not longer than a few weeks. As of old, it was the students who rushed to the forefront of the ranks fighting Chiang Kai-shek. This battle between students and dictator, which flared into open warfare in 1947 centered not so much around the question of peace as it did around the question of personal liberty in the schools.

To understand this war on the Chinese campus, it is necessary here to say a few words about Chen Li-fu, Kuomintang party boss, and also minister of education. Chen was a benign-looking man, with a pink and gray face, and an air of moral earnestness. He had studied Western science briefly at the Pittsburgh School of Mines, but quickly forgot his Western ideas when Chiang Kai-shek took power. Becoming the chief promoter of the return to Confucianism—the traditional ideology of despots—he also pumped hard for his own special brand of "vitalism." This was a curious theory that began with the dubious point that "Einstein's discovery of the fourth dimension" was anticipated by the Chinese and then ran the whole gamut of knowledge from an analysis of the atom and hydrogen nucleus, the life principle, the animal, vegetable and mineral kingdoms, the true, the good and the beautiful, the six ages of man, and the six stages of political development—leadership, feudalism, monarchy, democracy, party dictatorship and finally "government of all the people."[1]

These atavistic doctrines Chen shoved down the throats of China's students along with some books advocating "one party, one ideology, one leader," which he copied from Hitler. Books of a liberal sort were banned from the schools, and students caught reading them were often beaten by Chen's thugs or those of Chiang's Youth Corps who were armed with pistols and lived on the campus as students, but were really spies.

By spring of 1947, the nerves of the students were frayed to the raw edges. Campuses all over China were boiling like a kettle. May 4 was Chinese Student Movement Day. The students had intended to mark this day in a general manner: by parades against food reduction, against kidnaping, against intellectual persecution and mass dismissals. It had occurred to many that the government might oppose the parades, but none thought Chiang would take violent action in the larger cities, such as Shanghai and Nanking where there were numerous foreign eyewitnesses. But the nerves of the bureaucrats, like those of the students, were very shaky. They couldn't stand the sight of popular movements, and ordered the parades suppressed. In the capital of Nanking itself, right in front of the diplomatic corps, bayonets and iron bars were brought into play against girl and boy students alike. The student body was enraged. During the following days, a series of strikes began in university classrooms all over China. This was a signal for the police to storm the campus.

The nature of these attacks is probably hard for a Westerner to understand. For an apt comparison, it would be necessary for an American to imagine that in Columbia University the students were peacefully sleeping in their dormitories when heavily armed New York City policemen, in company with scores of gestapo agents of the Democratic party, (i.e. the party in power) suddenly descended on the campus at three o'clock in the morning, killed a few students, arrested many others and threw them in jails where they were held without trial and assumed to be guilty of "treason," "Communism," or just of being "dangerous." That is what sometimes happened in China.

Early in May 1947, the police raided the campus of the Shanghai Law College, killed one co-ed and arrested eleven students. The raids soon spread throughout Shanghai and Nanking until on May 24, 150 students were under arrest. Four days later, one thousand of Chiang Kai-shek's gendarmes broke into Chinan University, arrested seventy-one pupils and wounded or beat over a hundred. On May 30, more than two thousand troops and police surrounded Chiaotung University in the heart of

---

[1] See *The United States and China*, John Fairbanks (Cambridge, Massachusetts: Harvard University Press, 1948), p. 256.

Shanghai. On June 1, the garrison of Hankow (the Chicago of China) raided National Wuhan University with rockets and machine guns, seized five professors and over thirty students. When the whole student body gathered to protect the seized victims, they were machine-gunned, three killed and over fifty hurt. In Chungking, eighty-four girl students of the Women's Normal College were arrested and over three hundred students from Chiang's Japanese wartime capital were thrown in prison. In the fortnight between May 20 and June 2, 1947, 923 known students and teachers were arrested and more than a thousand were believed to have been killed or injured.

These indiscriminate attacks against the educated youth brought the literate of the nation to an angry boiling point. Government authorities tried to tell parents that their children had been corrupted by Communism. The parents would not have it. In a desperate attempt to pacify the students and the parents and at the same time to crack down on all liberalism, the government followed up the mass arrests with mass dismissals. In 1947, several thousand students and 230 professors and lecturers were dismissed from the colleges. Its self-confidence completely shaken, the government followed up these extremities by bringing up secret agents into the classes to spot any remaining suspicious students. The aim, of course, was to insure complete philosophic and political orthodoxy on the campus.

"During the night," writes a student of North China College to the American-owned *China Weekly Review*, "gestapo students inspect dormitories with pistols in their pockets. Anyone can be arrested for being impolite or hated by these students. If we hold a debating meeting to discuss technical problems, we are closely watched by the gestapo students. If we speak one word of criticism, we are reported and our names put on the black list."

This attempt to insure orthodoxy in the schools had a peculiar psychological effect. The gendarmes, the secret service and the youth corps, both on the campus and in the "reformation" camps for arrested students, carried on a ceaseless campaign against the Chinese Communists, painting their evils in lurid colors. This strong weapon of propaganda proved two-edged, for the terrorized students wondered why the news about the Communists came from sources so hateful to them. Why was it that the men who had beaten them talked most loudly about the savagery of the Communists? Why was it that their most liberal-minded teachers, the very ones who had tried to protect them from the clubbings of the youth corps, were just the ones that were accused of being Communists? Why was it that the thirty-year-old students who swaggered around in long gowns with pistols under their belts suddenly leaped up and denounced a student who spent much of his time in the school library as a Communist?

During this period, the Kuomintang developed a new, but still a very old, strategy for dealing with political opponents that ultimately led to their psychological divorcement from the intellectuals of China. In the dictionary of the ruling clique, mass action, student parades, protests against oppression, demands for lowered taxes, tortured screams for liberty, every attempt to avoid exploitation—in a word, every progressive thought or action—became the synonym for Chinese Communism or "8th Route banditry." Does this mean that all these things are Communism? the students would ask themselves. Chiang Kai-shek compelled his people to identify their thoughts and demands, even their secret hopes, with the slogans of the Communist party. If you call a person a Communist long enough, he very well may end up by saying: "Maybe I am a Communist." If this seems nonsensical, such a phenomenon can be observed to a small degree today in the United States where the drive of the Un-American Activities Committee and other organizations for philosophic and political orthodoxy in our schools have forced people either to get down on their knees and slobber out their loyalty or to stand up for their rights, thereby identifying themselves with Communism in which they may not believe at all.

This trend in the United States is not yet out of hand, but it is fast getting so. As I write, news has come to hand that the Oklahoma State Legislature has passed a bill requiring all teachers in the state and all students in state-supported colleges to affirm their loyalty to the US "as a condition of employment or of participation in the activities of the institution." At the same time a bill is before the New York State Assembly which provides that "any person who is a member of the Communist party or who refuses to disclose upon inquiry, whether or not he is a member of the Communist party, or who subscribes to its doctrine, or who espouses or is in sympathy with its cause, shall be ineligible for employment in the teaching profession or in the school systems of this state."

Although such organizations as the American Civil Liberties Union, the New York Teachers Union, the American Labor party and others have opposed this last bill, there are powerful interests which support such bills. The Hearst papers, for example, want the whole nation to adopt such bills in order to protect our schools from Communism because they are the first places Communists infiltrate.

Quite apart from the oft-observed fact that the victim of such bills is generally not Communism, but freedom of thought, apart also from the fact that these bills will make our schools sterile centers of orthodoxy, and also apart from the general threat to liberty, regulations of this kind, if one may judge from the experiences of China, do not protect the schools from Communism, but only create allies for it.

In the first place, forbidden fruit is always attractive, especially to the young, and any attempt to keep Communism out of the schools will make the secret reading of Communist pamphlets a great adventure instead of a dull study. Secondly, the attempt by authorities to prevent Communist doctrines from competing with democratic doctrines in an open arena of discussion, leads naturally to the conclusion that authorities really have no faith in the superiority of democracy at all. Thirdly, such bills create the need for an apparatus of enforcement, which *ipso facto* gives semidictatorial powers to a privileged group, leads to spying and the creation of intellectual gestapos in the schools which breed their own opposition. Fourthly, it allows a privileged group to set itself up as the arbiter of what is Communistic and what is not. This often leads the most courageous and the most free-thinking members of the student-teacher body to defy the school authorities' definition of Communism. In turn, this leads to a new suppression and the creation of a new opposition. Finally, all such bills create a common basis for co-operation between Communists and liberals and are either self-defeating or lead to the suppression of liberty. Such trends if carried to their ultimate conclusion can only result in dictatorship—fascist, communist, American or whatever brand you like.

In China, the government's attempt to insure orthodoxy on the basis of anti-Communism helped to bring about the defeat of Chiang Kai-shek. The attitude that anyone who stood for liberty and democracy was a Communist could not help but lead the Chiang regime into a series of atrocities which brought many of the most passive and non-political people into the fight against the Kuomintang government.

The atrocities reached a new high on July 15, 1948 when the authorities in the city of Kunming, near the borders of Burma and far from the civil war, mobilized more than two thousand policemen and gendarmes, not to dispel a demonstration, but to raid the campuses of Yunan University and Naching Middle School. Armed with pistols, rifles, machineguns, bayonets and water hoses, the gendarmes killed five students, injured more than a hundred and arrested a reported twelve hundred. Three hundred of these were imprisoned in concentration camps where they underwent rigid thought control. Seven hundred were placed in cells and tortured. A girl student named Wu Shou-chin became insane after being treated five times in an electric chair. Torture caused a woman teacher to have a miscarriage. The student prisoners were fed daily with two bowls of rice and a cup of salt water. At midnight they were dragged out of their cells and made to kneel on the gravel. Special guards then waved shining bayonets over their heads and fired their rifles into the air in order to make them say they were Communists. More than thirty prisoners were buried alive. None was given a court trial.

As if they had not subjected the youth of China to enough misery and torture, the Chiang regime, desperate, angry and fearful of the rising tide of public opinion, in August 1948 created a number of special tribunals to purge the schools of students the Kuomintang spies did not like. Writs of arrest were issued for a thousand students throughout the country. The aim of the Kuomintang authorities was evidently to cleanse the campus so thoroughly before the autumn session that no student unrest could possibly occur in the next year.

The special tribunals derived their legal power from "the regulations for the punishment of crimes endangering the republic during the period of bandit suppression." In thus trying to shield themselves from the Chinese people by the questionable authority of a higher law, the Kuomintang compromised the law and the constitution in the eyes of its own people. The effect was doubly compounded when prominent liberals and educators used the law as an excuse for helping the government in the student purges. American life offers somewhat of a parallel in recent events at Washington University, where school authorities made their professors face a court of inquiry concerning their political beliefs.

The political orthodoxy of prominent liberals in China curiously enough did not strengthen the hand of the government but only produced another factor into its decay. For many students and the professors came to believe there was no hope in seeking democratic reforms under the existing structure. They must stand up and fight the Chiang dictatorship openly. And this many of them now did. Students not only rallied to protect their classmates threatened with arrest, but many professors joined hands in Peiping and issued a joint statement accusing the government of deliberately fostering disturbances in the universities.

Intellectual opposition to the government came daily more into the open. From all over China letters poured into the offices of the *China Weekly Review*, one of the few public opinion outlets available to the oppressed Chinese people. "Can such things happen in a democratic country?" inquires a student from North China College. The question more than contains its own answer. The acme of disillusion, however, is expressed by a student writing from Wuhu in Anwhei Province: "A half a year ago I had interest in reading criticisms of the government. . . . Now they seem to me, just as does the government, meaningless. If there are men who still believe in the Kuomintang, they are idiotic."

From complete disillusionment, it is only one step to revolt. Many students no longer tried to live under Chiang Kai-shek. Most all of those for whom the writs of arrest were issued fled over to the Liberated Areas, thereby furnishing intellectual leadership to the peasantry. Such living deeds are more precious testimony than any sociological research into the correlation of forces. For they clearly reveal that the students had lost hope in the old regime and were seeking a way out in the new one. They also bared the basic charlatanism underlying all of the Chiang regime's tactics. As a magician seemingly creates rabbits out of thin air, so China's gestapo created Communists where there apparently had been none. The students' role in both crippling the Kuomintang and bolstering the strength of the Communists can hardly be overestimated. They were in reality the only articulate section of the suffering people in Chiang's areas. Thousands of students who migrated from the Kuomintang regions into the Liberated Areas furnished much-needed brains to the slender ranks of the Communist party. During the Japanese war, more than ten thousand students went to Yenan from the Kuomintang areas to study. Many of them had already become key political and administrative cadres before the civil war broke out in 1946. The mass student migration continued as the Kuomintang persecution was intensified in 1948. Seventeen hundred students were said to have crossed the lines after the Kuomintang announced its black list in August 1948. In October of the same year, during the ten days after the fall of Kaifeng in Central China, forty-five hundred more students trooped over to the Communists.

This migration produced a kind of united front between the students on both sides. New leaders of the students in the Kuomintang areas, succeeding those who entered the Communist areas, kept close underground contact with the latter or followed the path already traversed by their predecessors. There was thus growing up beside Chiang's apparatus of power, a new machinery, a kind of underground state within a state.

There is a revolutionary lesson in these events. And it is simply this: You cannot halt a revolution with tactics alone. In this respect, war and revolution are alike. Tactics should never be anything but the arm of strategy and strategy should be the arm of politics. If it is the other way around you are doomed to failure. Chiang had no policy—except to keep himself in power. Therefore, he subordinated everything to his tactic of anti-Communism. His secret service tried everything—murder, suppression, special laws—and each one of these methods betrayed him.

During these days when up on top, in the fine yamens of the government, there was taking place a loose coalition between the Ministry of Education, the party and Chiang's secret agents against the students, there was taking place underneath the surface of Chinese life, but barely concealed, a union between the students and some of the small businessmen, the native industrialists and a few of the city workers. During student parades, it was noticed that shopkeepers ran out amid the students and pressed money in their hands. "Go to it," they would whisper. "We are with you." Thus, different sections of Chinese society began to reach across the bayonets of Chiang's gendarmes and shake hands with each other.

A factor of primary importance in bringing about this alliance between the intellectuals, the shopkeepers and native industrialists in Chiang's areas was the tremendous economic collapse which whipped up the discontent of the entire Chinese people. As the war went on the food situation in Chiang's cities became worse. The standard of the masses oscillated between hunger and outright starvation. Refugees and landless peasants crowded into Shanghai and cluttered the alleyways with corpses—mute and damning testimony of the utter inability of the Chiang regime to solve the life conditions of its people. The newspapers, despite the heavy censorship, began publishing stories of appalling economic tragedies. The letter columns of the *China Weekly Review* became a kind of wailing wall where the people howled out their anguish. Every class in Chinese society began to disintegrate. The factory workers and the ricksha coolies lost their taste for labor and took to robbery. The administrations in the factories began to fall apart. Property rights under Chiang Kai-shek appeared unreliable. Profits were falling off, dangers growing. Native industrialists were being driven out of business by the Chiang bureaucracy while others were losing their taste for production under conditions of so-called nationalization and the alarming inflation.

This inflation was really fantastic. The printing press money climbed in huge upward spirals from three thousand Chinese dollars for one American dollar to three hundred thousand, then to the unheard of figure of six million. The deterioration assumed such terrific proportions that the value of Chiang's money dwindled to no more than the paper money burned for the dead. A large paper mill in Kwangtung bought up eight hundred cases of notes ranging from hundred dollar to two thousand dollar bills to use as raw material in the manufacture of paper. The phenomenon of money being used for something else besides money frightened everyone almost to the state of hysteria. Naturally prices bounded upward almost beyond computation. In South China, nearly a thousand miles from the civil war areas, rice rose from eighteen million dollars to thirty-six million dollars a picul within a few days. Newspapers estimated that a single grain of rice would cost fifteen dollars and a single match two hundred dollars. But nobody would trade on this basis. Worse—the government paid its civil servants and teachers in small denomination notes. But the Central Bank, the Post Office, the Railway Administration and tax-levying organizations all refused to accept such notes. This, of course, was nothing but direct robbery of the middle classes. The Chiang bureaucracy, however, aimed even higher. Scared by the grumblings from below, Chiang Kai-shek in August 1948 issued a new gold yuan, exchanging three million of the old dollars for one of the new. At the same time it compelled the people, under threat of arrest and by forcible house search, to surrender their gold, silver, Mexican dollars and all foreign currency to the Central Bank. As one commentator put it: "The government holds out a piece of paper in one hand and as if by magic whisks the wealth of the people away with the other."

The new "gold dollar" which was designed to salvage the government's discredited currency only wrecked it further. Production came to a standstill. Prices remained stable for a few brief days and then began climbing back again toward the old levels. The government tried to hold the prices in line by economic decree. Embattled shopkeepers, knowing full well that nothing could hold prices in line for long, fought back by refusing to put goods on sale in their stores. People rushed in mobs to buy whatever they could lay their hands on. Wealthy residents in Shanghai began to buy up the biggest diamonds, the costliest watches, the greenest jade and other articles to get rid of the gold yuan. In Peiping, ricksha coolies bought up expensive French pastries because they could not find anything else on the market. In Canton, housewives were reported buying snakes to eat rather than keep their gold yuan overnight in the hope of finding food on the market. To the Chinese people, the new currency was just so much paper backed by the assets of a government in which they had lost confidence.

In a desperate effort to restore the confidence of the people and halt threatening riots, Chiang Kai-shek sent his Russian-educated eldest son, Chiang Ching-kuo, to Shanghai and set him up with special troops and police as economic dictator over the port. Young Chiang met secretly with his close associates and decided on a policy of striking against the middle classes in order to enlist the support of the city poor. His tactics were patterned after those used by Hitler to seize power. With a demagogic flair that his more austere father could not have equaled, young Chiang appealed to the people of Shanghai for what he called a program of "social revolution."

Dispatching his spies and armed troops into Shanghai's stores, the dictator's son forced shop owners, on pain of arrest, to sell their merchandise at his artificially created prices. With this pistol at their heads, the storekeepers could do nothing but submit. Given a chance to turn worthless money into valuable commodities, Shanghailanders went on a buying bender. For perhaps the first time in modern Chinese history, sales clerks and shop owners deprecated the quality of their merchandise, frantically trying to persuade the customer not to buy. In vain. Customers wanted goods of any shape or size and right away. A coolie grabbed a handful of penicillin from a shelf. When an astonished clerk asked him if he knew its use, the coolie replied: "No, but I know it's worth more than money."

The shelves of Shanghai's stores were swept clean. Within a few days, numerous shopkeepers were ruined. In trying to solve economic problems by political demagoguery, Chiang Kai-shek had revealed the

desperateness of his position to everyone. However, the submission of
the shopkeepers encouraged Chiang Kai-shek and permitted him to turn
his panic into madness. He decided to show an iron energy. The middle
classes had been thoroughly exploited. Now it was the turn of the upper
classes. With a crazy disregard for consequences, young Chiang attacked the bankers and the big city racketeers—the most firm supporters
of his father and the men who had helped him to power and kept him
there for twenty years.

To win support for his neofascist program, young Chiang conducted
a series of raids against the property of the rich. Godowns, stores,
markets, vehicles, ships, airplanes were all pounced on by Chiang's
police. Following the seizure of capital goods, young Chiang turned to
arrest the capitalists themselves. As a warm-up gesture, he shot a
second-rate speculator, Wang Chun-chieh, to scare others into paying
off.

Next, young Chiang arrested the owners of the Sun Shing Textile
Mills, the Wing On Mills and bankers and money changers of the
Chekiang provincial bloc, all of which were basic components of his
father's financial machine. With amazing rapidity, young Chiang knocked
away the props of his father's economic support.

In other words, that classic moment in the life of a dying regime
had arrived when the leaders of the old society organize their own
suicide. In such moments, history has a deplorable habit of turning
artistic. That Chiang's son should be the instrument for weakening one
of his father's last means of support seems like poetic justice. That
this son should have been educated in the Soviet Union seems like a
caricature of a poor novel. The climax of young Chiang's activities,
however, was carried out in the manner of a movie designed for people
of bad taste. In 1927, Chiang Kai-shek had come to power when Tu
Yueh-sen, reputed opium king of Shanghai, had dispatched five thousand
gangsters through the International Settlement against the workers in
the native city. Now, young Chiang turned against his father's bene-
factor and arrested the opium king's son.

After the blows against the Shanghai upper classes, the Chiang Kai-
shek regime survived only some dozen weeks. The terrorism against
the middle and upper brackets of Chinese society in the city played an
important role, but a very different one from that upon which its perpe-
trators had counted. It did not weaken the crisis, but sharpened it.
People talked everywhere of the "economic executions" and the plunder
of the rich. The inference was obvious: even Chiang's supporters have
no weapon of defense against him, but to get rid of him. By autumn
1948, Chiang had destroyed many of his former bases of economic
support. All that was left him were a few landlords in the interior and
utter dependence on the United States. As the circle of Chiang's in-

fluence grew smaller and smaller, the masses, half leaderless, crowded in closer and closer, breathing anger, despair and defiance. For hundreds of thousands of people, the problem of life was no longer one of Communism or dictatorship, but one of survival. Teachers in China, loyal to their trust, had formerly declared that they would rather die of starvation than quit their posts. Faced with actual instead of possible starvation, however, they swiftly changed their minds. On October 24, 1948, eighty-two professors of Peking National University announced a strike, declaring that their monthly salaries were only enough to keep them alive for a few days. Two days later, Tsinghua, Nankai, and Peiyang universities went on strike. Sixteen municipal high schools and 234 primary schools in Peiping followed suit. Beginning on November 13, twenty-eight colleges and high schools in the Hankow area and thousands of professors and students in Kunming, Tsingtao, Nanking, Shanghai, Chengtu, Changsha and other cities joined in the strike wave. Education in a Western sense ceased. Teachers had to spend hours trying to borrow money to buy food. Students queued up for poor professors in the rice lines.

Teachers began to commit suicide. A woman professor of biology in Amoy University swallowed poison, saying she was no longer able to support her children. Professor Tu Su of National Kwangsi University killed himself by jumping from a building because he couldn't pay his hospital bills. A teacher of Han Min Middle School hanged himself because he had been suspected of stealing when he was found on the roadside selling his own clothing. Not only teachers, but even army officers killed themselves. Major General Loh Ying-chao jumped off a ship, leaving behind a note in which he said: I have been in the army thirty years and I am a major general, but still I can't support my family. I cannot bear to watch them die."

Apathy and despair flowed down like rain. But with these emotions, there was a rising anger. Crowds in Shanghai stormed the rice shops, the restaurants, the grocery stores, the coal shops. Police rounded up scores of rioters, but had to release them. The jails were already filled. Moreover, policemen had begun to look the other way when mobs burst into rice shops. "Why should I arrest them?" a policeman asked a reporter. "I may join them myself tomorrow."

In the words of this policeman, one may hear the death knell of the old society. The fact that the armed guardians of the social regime are now ready to join the common people adequately enough indicates the disintegration of the power of the government. As the result of their clearly revealed incapacity to deal with the situation, the members of Kuomintang lost faith in themselves, the party fell to pieces; a bitter struggle of groups and cliques prevailed, hopes were placed in miracles or—American intervention.

But politically active Chinese no longer believed in miracles. They wanted no more of the Kuomintang regime. It would be wrong to think that the majority of the Chinese people revolted against their rulers. Such was not the case at all. But it was true that a decisive minority of the whole people, or a majority of those actively engaged in the political struggle, were now willing to endure sacrifices and take great risks in order to get rid of Chiang Kai-shek.

This change in the political feelings of a great number of people was not only produced by the collapse of life conditions in Chiang's areas, but by the sharp contrast offered by living conditions in Communist areas. The liberal economic policies of the Communists, their protection of private property in commerce, trade and native industry, had served to dispel the fears of many Chinese businessmen and given them the belief that they could exist under the Communists which they could no longer do under Chiang Kai-shek. The lenient treatment of captured Kuomintang generals made Kuomintang commanders think twice before risking their lives for Chiang's sake. The idea that they could surrender to the Communists and then regain their influence by political intrigue within the enemy camp also attracted many others. Students who had fled over to the Liberated Areas reported they were honored leaders in the "new society." Many people in Chiang's areas began to see a path of escape from the cul-de-sac where society had trapped them. From passive opposition to Chiang Kai-shek, not a few Chinese now turned directly to support the Communists.

From Shanghai and Hongkong, a fleet of junks, organized by businessmen, sailed with gasoline, kerosene, tires, automobile spare parts, chemicals and other products to Communist territory along the coast. When General Liu Po-cheng's troops crossed the Yellow River and came into Central China, businessmen immediately began to ship cloth across the lines to make uniforms for Liu's soldiers. Part of this trade was due to the corruption of Chiang's officials, part due to the fact that trade will always find its own channels, but some of it was due to the fact that many Chinese wanted to get rid of their dictator and saw their only hope in the Communists. Chiang Kai-shek had been able to stop UNRRA relief materials from going to the people in the Liberated Areas, but he found himself quite unable to halt the trade which was impudently carried on right under his nose. Shipments to Communist areas were passed by the Shanghai-Woosung Garrison command of Chiang Kai-shek himself. Junks loaded with materials for the Communists sailed with perfect impunity directly under the guns of the Woosung forts guarding Shanghai. Naval patrol vessels at the mouth of the Woosung and the Yangtze rivers were paid off with gold bars carried by the junk commanders. More revealing still, the shipments were insured by Chiang's government banks. Communist agents who walked the streets of Shanghai with forbidden gold bars in their pockets were often armed with special passes from Chiang Kai-shek's secret service, many of whom were fed up with their dictator.

Everywhere the oppositional mood of the people was transmuted into a definitely revolutionary mood. The compensation for Chiang's terror came fast. Driven, persecuted, tortured, murdered, the intellectuals and the students rose more rapidly than ever. Professors in Peiping University now openly lectured on the evils of "American imperialism." Wall newspapers went up proclaiming the glories of the "new democracy" promulgated by Mao Tze-tung. The process of opposition ran from the campuses in Peiping into the provinces, from the cities into the villages. Most resolute of all were the peasants in South China, nearly a thousand miles from the civil war areas. In Kwangtung Province where the Kuomintang revolution had begun a quarter of a century before, peasant guerrillas took over whole counties from Kuomintang officials. In Yunan, near the borders of Burma, the same thing happened, with local heroes fighting on the side of the poor carving out petty domains for themselves. The Chiang government refused to heed these warnings; the landlords remained in power and the peasants continued to revolt.

Seeing the handwriting on the wall, leaders of Chinese society began to withdraw from the crumbling Chiang machine. Warlords from Szechuan stopped sending rice down the Yangtze. Marshal Li Chi-sen, former head of the generalissimo's headquarters, from the safety of British Hongkong organized an opposition Kuomintang and called for a nationwide revolt against Chiang. Southseas Chinese began to halt their remittances to the homeland. Some Chinese leaders in the United States withdrew their support from the generalissimo. In vain did Chiang try to hold back the rising tide against him. His secret service accused everyone in opposition of being a Communist. All to no avail.

With all his former bases of support collapsing, Chiang's army also began to collapse. Hitherto, the Communist land reform had been a powerful agent in helping demoralize the peasant soldiers in the Kuomintang armies. Now, the disaffection of the intellectuals in the rear lines brought about the collapse of morale among the generals, many of whom were on the verge of revolt.

Desperate, angry, fearful, the Chinese people slowly pushed their dictator toward the wall.

PART XIII

COLLAPSE OF A DYNASTY

❦

55. Military Collapse

SWIFT changes in the political allegiances of a decisive portion of the Chinese people were the most immediate cause of Communist success in China. Transformation of civilian psychology, however, was not enough to guarantee that Chiang Kai-shek could be overthrown in a short period of time. For the Reds were not only waging revolution against the old Chinese society, they were also waging war against the army of Chiang Kai-shek. This war was a revolutionary war and, as such, it partook of the nature of both war and revolution. Its tactics therefore were an amalgam of both of these activities. The usual method of waging war is to vanquish the enemy by military means. The common method of waging revolution is to win over a good portion of the enemy by political means. The chief contribution of the Chinese Communists to the arts of war and revolution was that they combined both politics and combat to a degree never before observed in so complete a form, wielding both almost as a single instrument.

It was not, however, the strategy of the war which controlled the revolution, but the strategy of the revolution which dictated the tactics of the war. This was particularly so when the Chinese civil war and the Chinese Revolution reached their most critical periods. The fate of every revolution at a certain point is decided by a shift in the feelings of the army. This is of necessity also true of a revolutionary war which originally deploys weaker forces than its foes. Against the numerous and well-armed troops of Chiang Kai-shek, the poorly armed forces of the Communists at the start of the civil war could not possibly gain a victory. Nor could they ever have gained a decisive victory within a short time had not a large share of Chiang's army come over to the forces of the revolution. The going over of many of Chiang's divisions to the Communists did not happen of itself nor as a result of mere agitation. Rather was it the result of a long molecular process which worked like a ferment within the army, producing a change in its psychology.

In the early part of the war, contradictions within Nationalist forces had revealed themselves most sharply in the conflicts between officers and soldiers, with the Communist land reform playing a large part in whipping up the discontent of the peasant privates and noncoms. Through 1948, however, the discipline and loyalty of the field officers and the generals in the combat areas was badly shaken. Economic chaos, gestapo terror, terrible blunders in strategy at the highest levels had all served to disgust the officers' corps with the way the war was being conducted. The rivalries of different cliques in Nanking produced the same bitter contentions on the front. Numerous cabinet reshuffles left the loyalties of the generals hanging in mid-air. Finally, Chiang's utter dependence on America, his suppression of anti-American demonstrations, the presence of American military men in China, the maintenance of a naval base on China's soil, special treaties signed with the United States—all of which exacerbated the nationalistic feelings of the literate Chinese public—also produced a great discontent in army circles, wounding the officers' patriotic vanity and making him a target for Communist propaganda.

It would be incorrect to represent conditions in the army as being the same throughout the country in all troops and regiments. The variation was considerable. While former warlords and provincial generals were carrying on all sorts of intrigues on the front, Chiang Kai-shek's Whampoa cadets were viciously suppressing any criticism of the "leader." There were many such contrasts between and within units. Nevertheless, the political mood of the officers, as well as the soldiers, was moving toward a single level—peace at any cost.

It is impossible to understand the mechanics of China's civil conflict without fully realizing that the most important task of the war—defeat of Chiang Kai-shek's army—had already been half accomplished by the revolution before the beginning of the conclusive battles in Manchuria and North and Central China in the middle of 1948. The last half of the Communists' quest for power consisted of two parts: to bring Chiang's soldiers from a state of discontent to open revolt, or at least refusal to fight, and to liquidate the remainder in actual combat.

The classic way of winning troops to the cause of revolution is by mass strikes, demonstrations, street encounters, fights at the barricades. This enables revolutionary elements to get in direct contact with wavering troops and infect them with their own mood. If such activities come at a critical moment of the revolution, an insurrection may occur and the state power be seized. At least that is the way the February and October revolutions in Russia reached their climaxes. The unique thing about the mechanics of the Chinese Communist movement as a revolution, however, was that it reached its crisis and gained its greatest victories not by an insurrection in the capital of the country against the summit of state power, but by success on the battlefield. The unique feature of this movement as a war was that it triumphed on the battlefield not only through combat but through insurrections within Chiang's army.

Since they were so weak in the cities and since the Chinese proletariat was such an ineffective force, the Communists could not stimulate Chiang's troops to revolt by mass strikes. In fact, their best method of directly contacting Chiang's troops was on the field of battle. It was principally through contact in combat that the Kuomintang soldiers and officers were aroused to turn over to the Communists. This must be accounted one of the more ludicrous phenomena of the Chinese war. To beat the Communists, Chiang had to attack them, but every time he did so, his troops became infected with the revolutionary mood of the 8th Route soldiers.

It seems that the first break in the army appeared among the provincial forces and former subordinates of the Christian General Feng Yu-hsiang, who had come to America and denounced Chiang Kai-shek. This does not mean that these troops were necessarily more revolutionary than the others. On the contrary, the regiments, close to the old China, had many elements of conservatism. But just for this reason the changes caused by the war were more noticeable in them. Besides, they were always being shifted around, watched by Chiang's spies, given worse equipment than Chiang's favored forces. They were sick of it, and wanted to make peace.

In September 1948, the fall of Tsinan, the capital of Shantung Province, was precipitated by the revolt of General Wu Hwa-wen, commander of the 94th Army and a former follower of Feng Yu-hsiang. More striking still, however, was the fact that General Wang Yao-wu, governor of Shantung Province and a favorite of American military men, when captured by the Communists immediately got on the radio and urged the rest of the Shantung troops to mutiny right at the front or surrender en masse or else not to offer any strong resistance and to lay down their arms at the proper moment. Simultaneously, far to the west, three division commanders of Yen Hsi-shan surrendered outside of Taiyuan, the capital of Shansi Province, without fighting. It is possible to see behind such revolts mere conspiracies. However, other events along the whole length and breadth of the tremendous Chinese front clearly indicate that Chiang's army collapsed in the end, not only as the result of conspiratorial intrigue, but also as a result of revolutionary disintegration. An almost perfect example of this is offered by events in Manchuria.

During the latter half of 1948, Kuomintang commanders in Manchuria drew back into the cities, with orders, it was said, to hold on until Dewey was elected president of the United States and America poured forth her might in aid of Chiang Kai-shek. Some weeks before the presidential election, the 60th and the 7th Kuomintang armies retired on the city of Changchun with their heavy American equipment while a small force of the People's Liberation Army of General Lin Piao took up positions of siege around the city. Here the Communists had an extraordinary opportunity to apply their methods of disintegrating Chiang's army by revolutionary propaganda.

Every squad in Lin Piao's forces organized an "enemy work group." They discussed the misconceptions of the Kuomintang troops facing them. Then a program of propaganda was decided upon and a "shouting war" began.

"Brothers!" the voices called across no man's land, "lay down your arms which you never wanted to take up. Did you join the Kuomintang army? No, you were dragged into it at the end of a rope. Come over to us. If you want, we will send you home. Better still, you can join us and fight to free your homes as we have ours."

A barrage of fire greeted these words. But the words themselves were a red-hot revolutionary medium, a high conductor of ideas, that the rifles could not still. Pretty soon, at scattered places along the front, the rifles ceased firing. At last a squad of seven men led by a soldier named Tang Kuo-hua crossed the lines. The Kuomintang commanders were frightened. They told their troops that the deserters had been disarmed by the Communists and buried alive. This lie was shortlived. For Squad Commander Tang, himself, soon called across the seventy-five yards separating the two forces, and begged his old comrades to follow him into the New China. From a handful, the number of desertions grew to a steady stream.

The Kuomintang tried countermeasures. It scoured Changchun for prostitutes and officers' wives and sent them into the front lines to sing obscene songs and invite the soldiers of the People's Liberation Army to cross over to them. "Brother," called back Lin Piao's soldiers, "how can your officers deceive us, when they can't even deceive you?"

Soon letters were exchanged between the opposing forces. One Kuomintang squad wrote saying its commander was sick and resting inside Changchun, but as soon as he came back, they would come over. Another wrote: "Thanks for the cakes, but we are southerners and would like rice. We also can't understand your dialect, find a southerner to shout to us."

Propaganda bombs with leaflets inside them were thrown across the lines. Even small propaganda boats were set loose on the river and floated down into the city. Inside the city itself, posters and whitewashed slogans appeared on the walls and even on the pillboxes of the Kuomintang soldiers. The Manchurian people were joining in the struggle and showing where their hearts lay.

Within a few weeks thirteen thousand officers and men—over one-tenth of Chiang's forces in the encircled city—crept over to the Communist side. Among them were sixteen colonels and 282 officers of the rank of lieutenant or above. All brought rifles and some even brought radio sets. Most of them turned around to fight against their former comrades.

These dramatic events at Changchun are significant; they reveal the workings of the inner processes of the revolution in the Chinese army, the foundation of which had been laid by the whole past history of the country. The soldiers in Manchuria did not want to live any longer in the Old China. Because they saw no other way out, they joined forces that promised them a New China. This change in the state of mind of the soldiers was one of the most immediate causes of Chiang Kai-shek's military collapse.

Everywhere the story was the same. Even the commanders no longer wanted to fight. In September and October 1948, the provincial cities of Kaifeng, Tsinan, Chefoo and Linyi fell to the Communists almost without a struggle. Overnight Chiang lost three hundred thousand troops, including the 93rd Army, the 60th Army and the 70th Army. Not a single one of these commanders fought to the death as the generalissimo had ordered. Some fifty generals preserved their lives by mutinying, surrendering or allowing themselves to be captured. Eighteen full divisions, nine brigades and fifteen regiments within the space of two months were wiped out. Casualties were few. Everywhere white flags were hoisted.

The darkest hour for Chiang Kai-shek was at hand. With the Kuomintang soldiers facing them in a revolutionary mood, the Communists struck swiftly to take full advantage of the situation. In Manchuria, while the soldiers in Changchun were running out to join his besieging forces, General Lin Piao concentrated his main forces in the south and cut the Liaoning corridor through which Chiang's commanders had hoped, in the event of an emergency, to escape through the Great Wall into North China.

That emergency was now on them and the generalissimo, himself, flew to Manchuria. Into an already disintegrating situation, China's dictator introduced a last element of chaos. Lin Piao had surrounded the city of Chinchow, main Kuomintang supply and transport base. Chiang ordered an army group of twelve divisions under General Liao Yao-hsiang to the relief of the beleaguered city. Chinchow, however, fell and with it 120,000 troops while the Liao Army Group was just a little way out of Mukden.

In desperation, Chiang cabled an order to the 60th and 7th Kuomintang armies in Changchun to leave that city and join his other forces in the Mukden areas. This was a move he should have made a year before. Now, it was too late. Instead of obeying this order, the commander of the 60th Army revolted and turned his guns on the 7th Army. Changchun immediately fell to the Communists without a struggle.

The Liao Army Group, which had come out from behind the fortifications of Mukden, was meanwhile on the road where the Communists liked to fight best. Lin Piao, wheeling up from the south and down from the north caught nearly the whole twelve divisions in a pincer and wiped them out. On October 30, Mukden itself fell and a few days later Changteh, the capital of Jehol and gateway through Inner Mongolia to North China.

A few days after the fall of Mukden, Harry Truman was elected president of the United States. Governor Dewey, the last white hope of Chiang Kai-shek, was defeated. And with him the generalissimo.

The Communists, with all-out victory in sight, never hesitated. Instead of waiting many weeks to repair the railways and amass supplies, General Lin Piao immediately dispatched his soldiers on foot through the Great Wall and south into China proper. Advancing as much as fifty and sixty miles a day, columns of Lin Piao covered eight hundred miles within twenty days and in early December 1948 reached the railway junction of Fengtai near Peiping. General Fu Tso-yi, who had ruled Inner Mongolia for many years and who was considered one of China's better generals, was shaken from his slumbers by the advent of this force which he thought was many miles distant. Although only a few patrols had arrived, Fu was so badly upset that he hastily withdrew behind the walls of Peiping where he started bargaining with the Communists to have his name taken off the list of "war criminals."

In the meantime, the rest of Lin Piao's army poured down through the Great Wall and joined forces with the Communist detachments from Shansi, Shantung and Hopei. Within the space of a few days, North China's greatest port, Tientsin, fell to Lin Piao's fur-hatted Manchurians. Peiping, the ancient capital of the empire, soon followed suit.

Thus, by not retreating from the northeast Chiang Kai-shek had lost not only Manchuria, but all of North China, too.

Eight hundred miles to the south, however, even worse catastrophes were in store for China's dictator. For Generals Chen Yi and one-eyed Liu Po-cheng—the Hammer and the Brain of the Communist armies—had now organized Central China and were about to strike against the bases of Chiang's power in the Yangtze Valley and against the capital of the nation—Nanking.

*   *   *

The depth and extent of the military crisis which overcame China in 1948 was fully foreseen neither by the Communists nor by Chiang Kai-shek. It would seem that the Communists seriously underestimated the collapse of morale on their opponent's side. The politically active masses in Chiang's territory— the intellectuals, the students, the army officers and the lower government officials—were often to the left of even the Communists. While the party was still talking of a five-year war, a large share of Chiang's army was ready to end the war immediately by revolts. Nevertheless, though they did not foresee the speed of Chiang's collapse, the Communists observed events on the whole much more ably than did the national government. For this reason they were able to take advantage of a situation which left Kuomintang leaders gaping with surprise and helplessness.

Part of this was due to the inadequate moral leadership Chiang gave to the war. Where the Communists had adopted a Churchillian strategy of promising their people nothing but "blood, sweat and tears," Chiang had promised his followers immediate victory. At the convening of the national assembly in 1946, he had told the country that he would bring about peace within three months. A year later he lengthened the period to six months. In April 1948 when the revealed bankruptcy of the regime was causing some observers to predict that the government would collapse within six months, Chiang announced: "I can assure you that our Nationalist China will not collapse in six months, six years or sixty years." Concluding a review of the military situation, he declared that he would exterminate the Communists in all of Central China within three to six months.

There was a great deal of madness in such statements. China's dictator had lost touch with his environment and was drifting in a dream world of his own. However, there was also some deceit in the generalissimo's attitude. Suddenly deserted in the north and in Manchuria by his generals, Chiang could not help but be aware that danger was pressing closer on him. When he returned from Manchuria, he called a conference "to seek life in the face of death." After the loss of Mukden, Chiang was said to have had a hemorrhage and continued to have hemorrhages. When General Wu Hwan-wen went over to the Communists and precipitated the fall of Tsinan, the generalissimo in a fit of astonished rage is said to have turned to his subordinates and said: "Let them all desert me." Chiang no longer had faith in his top military men. Like Hitler, who at the last put his faith in his SS troops, Chiang tried to give the dirty end of the military stick to generals unfriendly to him while he pulled out his own personally loyal divisions. He presented the command authority to General Fu Tso-yi in the north and to General Pai Chung-hsi in Central China, planning to withdraw his own troops south of the Yangtze. But it was too late.

Chiang's moves were not based on military calculations, but on a desire to preserve his own power within his collapsing camp. No one dared now to become premier of his government and cabinet after cabinet resigned. Generals Li Tsung-jen, Pai Chung-hsi and Ho Ying-chin became active in trying to force the generalissimo's resignation. In order to prepare the next move and seize the anti-Chiang leadership, certain elements from Chiang's own personal clique began participating in these intrigues.

But China's dictator refused to step down. In a speech on November 8, 1948, he declared: "I have all my life done things with the attitude that once anything is begun it must be carried through to success." The generalissimo comforted his subordinates by saying: "Despite military failures in Manchuria our political military and economic foundations in the rest of China have not been shaken in the slightest. Compared with the Communist bandits our strength is superior."

This statement was a simple lie. Chiang's foundations had collapsed. His superiority no longer existed. Events in Manchuria, and North China, however, were so far away that a blow closer to his power in Nanking was needed to complete the downfall of the generalissimo. This blow was delivered by Communist Generals Liu Po-cheng and Chen Yi around the town of Suchow, 180 miles north of Nanking in November and December 1948. It was to prove catastrophic.

The city of Suchow, which lies at the junction of the east-west Lunghia Railway and the north-south Tientsin—Nanking Railway, is perhaps the most strategic city in modern-day China. Situated at the southern boundaries of the North China Plain, this town and the area adjacent to it form a kind of gateway between the north and the south. Possession of Suchow by a force operating from the south may not be decisive in war, as the rest of the North China Plain must be conquered in order to unify the country. Capture of the town and destruction of its defenders by a force coming from the north—as the Communists came— however, may be crucial, as the loss of Suchow in this event makes Nanking, Shanghai and Hankow almost undefendable.

The terrain in this region is flat as a pavement, but approaching the capital at Nanking, the land is broken up by rivers and creeks and low-lying hills which come down almost to the shores of the Yangtze. The flat nature of the terrain makes it an ideal battleground for a war of maneuver. To fight a static warfare with troops garrisoned in towns, strong points and along rail lines is to invite the enemy to attack you piecemeal and to court disaster. Nevertheless, this was how Chiang Kai-shek tried to fight the Communists. This was a mistake in tactics, but Chiang made an even graver mistake in strategy. When he lost the province of Shantung north of Suchow and when General Liu Po-cheng began operating on his flanks west and south of Suchow, Chiang should have pulled back and concentrated his forces closer to the Yangtze River so that he might cover a retreat across the river to the south or be able to bring up reserves from the south across the river to the north and so influence any battle. Chiang, however, made the same mistake Hitler did in Germany and fought before the Yangtze as Germany's dictator fought before the Rhine until the best part of his army was trapped and wiped out.

The importance of Suchow in the scheme of China's war was clearly recognized by the Communists. As early as January 1947, they told this writer that the war in China would be decided by the outcome of the battle for Suchow. In January 1948, this writer predicted that Chiang was facing a great military catastrophe at Suchow unless he immediately altered his plans. Not a word of mine about this front was printed in the United States either. I say this now not with any desire to play the role of unhonored prophet, but merely to show that anti-Communism has reached such a state in this country that even coldly objective facts about military events will not be printed by scared editors. This ostrich attitude, of course, can only lead to suicide as it led Chiang to suicide.

Chiang Kai-shek had concentrated four hundred thousand men of the 2nd, 12th, 13th, and 16th armies for the defense of Suchow. The strongest of these was the American-trained and equipped Second Army under General Chiu Ching-chuan which was concentrated northwest of the city where Chiang Kai-shek expected Communist General Chen Yi to attack.

Chen Yi, however, chose another road. From the north and east, he launched a surprise attack against the much weaker 7th Army Group under General Huang Po-tao. This force began to crumble when two armies formerly organized by the Christian General Feng Yu-hsiang surrendered without fighting. These surrenders gave Chen Yi's offensive a continuity which might not otherwise have been possible. Quickly the Communist general divided his forces into two columns. With one column he encircled the remainder of the 7th Army Group, which was unable to take any further part in the battle and was thereafter destroyed. The other column he interposed between the isolated army group and Chiang's 13th Army inside of Suchow. When Chen Yi's initial operation had been completed, 180,000 of the four hundred thousand men Chiang had assembled to hold Suchow had become casualties, surrendered or been broken up to a point where they no longer represented an organized military force.

At this point, Chiang Kai-shek took a hand and again, as in Manchuria, introduced chaos into a confused situation. Instead of withdrawing as it was imperative for him to do, the generalissimo, like a gambler who has lost his nerve, began throwing good money after bad.

Seeing the plight of the 7th Army Group, Chiang ordered the still untouched 2nd Army Group to leave its position northwest of Suchow and rush east to break the trap. This group marched, but its movement was reluctant and slow and the force it was to rescue was totally eliminated before it arrived. Meanwhile, its departure from the west enabled the Central Liberation Army under one-eyed Liu Po-cheng to rush into the vacated breach. Liu's troops soon took the town of Suhsien fifty miles south of Suchow.

Liu used part of his troops to deal with Chiang's 12th Army Group, which was not originally one of the forces defending Suchow but had been ordered from Hankow to reinforce the garrison when the situation became critical. Composed of 120,000 men, this force was intercepted by Liu when on the road and surrounded twenty miles west of Suhsien. It continued resistance for a while but was finally wiped out on December 7.

Liu had enough troops to spare during these operations to join Chen Yi's armies coming from the east. The two commanders made contact south of Suchow and ringed the whole area, cutting it off from Nanking. What the Communists had done in essence was to erect a trap into which Chiang obligingly sent all his forces which now could not escape. Moreover, most of them did not want to escape.

Yet they had to escape. Else the government at Nanking was finished. Chiang had ordered them into the trap, now he tried to order them out so that they could get back to the Yangtze and defend Nanking. It was too late. The city garrison in Suchow, which had not yet faced any enemy, was reluctant to venture into open country where Chen Yi and Liu Po-cheng were waiting for it. Only by cutting off all the air-borne supplies on which the troops in Suchow depended was Chiang able to get them to obey his orders.

As soon as Chiang's forces left Suchow in a southerly direction, Chen Yi swung up to meet them. He hit their line of march in several places, driving them in great disorder and panic into a new encirclement fifty miles southwest of the city. Within a short while the 13th Army Group was completely wiped out, with all its troops surrendered.

It was now clear that not only had the strategic Suchow area been lost for good, but none of the great army that had been gathered there would ever be free to defend the capital at Nanking or any other point. The end of this classic battle of encirclement left Chiang Kai-shek with virtually no combat troops in parts of China under his control and wrote finish to his hopes of military comeback, and perhaps of survival itself.

56. Chiang Kai-shek

THE defeat of the Nationalist army and the advance of the Communists to the north bank of the Yangtze River changed everything in the Kuomintang capital at Nanking. It was clear now that Chiang must go. The opportunity to force him out existed for the first time since 1932. Even his old cronies who had ridden with him to power ganged up with Shanghai merchants to drive China's dictator from his capital. Before examining these events we may perhaps pause and have a last look at this man who ruled China almost without interruption for two violent decades of war and revolution.

It has been assumed by no few observers that the personal traits of the generalissimo were responsible for the terrible series of events that have wasted China for the last quarter of a century. General Stilwell, who was Chiang's chief of staff during part of the Japanese war and who had an unparalleled opportunity to watch China's dictator at work, wrote in his diary that the cure for the troubles of China was the elimination of Chiang Kai-shek. This viewpoint was echoed and re-echoed with varying modifications throughout the civil war. Many observers, especially foreigners, even went so far as to attribute Communist victories to Chiang's stupidities or his domineering disposition.

This psychological approach to the problems of history is not one which the writer finds very useful. To say that the causes of the tremendous social upheaval in China lay in the character traits of the generalissimo is as meaningless as to say that the cause of the fall of Roman civilization was that a certain Roman emperor ruled his state badly. The causes of such an event in which millions of people fought one another, peasants turned on landlords, brothers on brothers and wives on husbands, cannot be the fault of one man. No doubt, if Chiang Kai-shek had not been in power at the end of the war with Japan, then China's political structure would have been different and it is possible that war might not have broken out or that some of the events of the war might have taken place in a different order. But it is indisputable in any case that the Chinese Revolution did not result from the character of Chiang Kai-shek and that a dictator with a different name would not have solved its problem. Nor can we see the cause of Communist victories in the incompetence of China's dictator. People are not stupid or clever in themselves, but only in relation to their circumstances. A peasant may seem like the smartest man in the world by coaxing crops from unfertile ground, but he may appear like a perfect idiot when asked to cope with a complicated machine. Napoleon at Austerlitz is a genius; at Moscow, a fool. Just so Chiang Kai-shek, when he rode to power during the counterrevolution of 1927, appeared to personify the wisdom of his age; when he was constantly defeated during the revolutionary upheavals of 1945 to 1949 he seemed like a blundering madman.

The forces that brought about China's civil war and revolution were superpersonal in character and so were the forces that swept the Communists toward power. One of these forces was dictatorship or despotism. This institution by its very nature is bound up with the personal. But it was not the personality of Chiang Kai-shek that shaped the nature of the despotism, but the nature of the dictatorship that shaped Chiang Kai-shek. Moreover, the character of this despotism was itself shaped by much larger forces—that is, the semifeudal, semicolonial quality of Chinese civilization.

This dual nature of Chinese society resulted in a dual sovereignty—the rule of the native landlords and the merchant-industrial class tied to foreign capital. In his role of dictator, Chiang personified the union of these two ruling groups, with the party and the army adhering to them and sometimes sitting on top of them. The bourgeois and feudal elements in Chinese society were always at war with each other and so were the comprador and landlord elements in Chiang's character always fighting one another. The Chinese bourgeoisie, tied to foreign capital, was infected with feelings of inferiority and antiforeignism. In the same way, Chiang hated foreigners even while he depended on them. The landlords, the dying ruling class of China, were pervaded by premonitions of early death and were mortally afraid even while they tried to maintain their own attitude of superciliousness. So Chiang Kai-shek was afraid and tried to rid himself of his fears by an outward show of arrogance.

Because the comprador element dominated the feudal element in the Kuomintang, it also dominated in the character of the country's ruler. The primary traits of a comprador are: 1. Dependence on foreigners, and 2. Lack of character. Like any common compradore, who has illusions about making himself independent of his foreign boss, Chiang also cherished such dreams, but when it came to a showdown, he was seldom able to fight any of his bosses, but maneuvered among Japan, Russia, the United States and England, serving first one power and then another. Because a comprador is not engaged in production, like an ordinary capitalist, he has nothing to sell but tricks. It was the same with Chiang. He was sharp, quick, ruthless and did not hesitate to spend money in huge bribes to win his ends. A comprador is always maneuvering between landlords and foreign businessmen, trying to make money from both, and he can never be independent and never have any real character of his own. Chiang operated in the same way, trying to maneuver between both feudal China and foreign countries. Because he could be loyal neither to the old China nor to the new China, Chiang was disliked by foreigners and by old-style Chinese.

Chiang's compradorism was complicated by the feudal nature of Chinese life. Scratch the despot in Chiang and underneath you would find a medieval clan leader. He was smarter than the old-style warlords, yet politically he was descended from them. He ruled the countryside through village loafers, dog legs, and bailiffs who were the agents of the landed gentry. He ruled the cities through gangsters and secret societies. Feudal tyrant, bourgeois comprador, village suzerain, secret society member and party leader—Chiang was both the product and the uncrowned head of a society in transition. His philosophy, personality, thoughts and even daily actions were molded by this fact.

The figure of Chiang Kai-shek is a little depressing, a little ridiculous, at all times contradictory, and sometimes tragic. One of the chief elements of tragedy lies in the relation of the free will to necessity. The tragedy of Chiang Kai-shek was that he tried to do the impossible. He attempted to create capitalism through feudalism, Christianity through Confucianism, democracy through despotism, nationalism through chauvinism. In the end, he created only chaos—both within the nation and within his own soul.

Born in Chekiang Province, not far from Shanghai, Chiang reportedly claimed kinship with an ancient king of China. With his eyes looking back and up, it became inevitable that China's dictator noticed neither the lowly peasant at his feet nor the gigantic strides this simple man was taking forward. As a result, he fell before the peasant's onslaught hardly knowing what hit him.

In morals, as well as politics, Chiang claimed to be a Confucianist. But it is doubtful if he had any principles at all. As Harold Isaacs put it in *No Peace for Asia,* Chiang's "motivations are in terms of himself. Ideas he must borrow. . . . He has used communism, Anglo-Saxon democracy, Christianity, European fascism." Chiang embraced some of the tenets of Christianity, but none of its basic concepts. He knew little charity or mercy and less about the sanctity of the individual or the equality of man. He spoke of Christ, but burned offerings to the dead; he spoke of democracy, but practiced the Confucian doctrine of the "princely man" —the "Superior Man." His faith was that of filial piety and he believed that a son should obey his father, a younger brother an elder brother, and a subject his ruler. He was the ruler.

His governmental principles were those of the Han despots—political authority centralized in one man, reinforced by a graded bureaucracy. The sanction for government was the possession by the ruler and his ancestors of a magical[1] property called "virtue." Benevolence, Righteousness, Wisdom, Fidelity and Politeness—these insured the prosperity of the country. "As the wind blows so will the grass incline," said the ancients. Chiang echoed them. But somehow, the more he blew, the more the people inclined in the opposite direction.

When he was unable to cure the ills of a mortally sick China with this philosophy borrowed from Chinese medicine men, Chiang blamed it on the loss of the ancient goodness. The peasants revolted because they were "unfilial." The intellectuals criticized him because they were not "sincere." A general turned over to the Communists because he had forgotten "loyalty." This attempt to monopolize moral goodness inevitably led the people of China to consider Chiang, himself, immoral. The inferior man was tired of the Superior Man.

Chiang has been compared by his admirers with Napoleon. But the two men had little in common. To be sure, both came to power by means of a *coup d'état* and both turned their guns on the revolution. But the French emperor was a military genius, an efficient organizer and a creative administrator. China's dictator was an atrocious strategist, a bad organizer and a worse administrator. Napoleon was the very personification of the bourgeoisie and he brought down European feudalism with the artillery of the French Revolution. Chiang was not a true representative of the bourgeoisie in China and he never came to grips with the relics of feudalism in his own land. Napoleon was a great conqueror of foreign countries; Chiang was a servant of foreign nations. Finally, what did a party mandarin like Chiang have in common with the man who gave Europe the Napoleonic Code?

Chiang has also been compared to Hitler because of his unstable character and his air of injured nobility. Before foreigners, Chiang put on a face of expressionless calm. With his own subordinates, however, he went into rages, screamed like a shrew, threw teacups, pounded on tables. So did Hitler. These two dictators were alike in their distrust of everybody due to a distrust of themselves. But Hitler had some style and some originality. Chiang had little style and not much originality. Hitler was vastly more colorful; there was an element of passion, almost of greatness in Hitler's rantings, however foully conceived. Chiang never said anything—at least publicly—with the slightest emotional appeal. Hitler inspired the bruised and defeated soul of the German people. Chiang stirred no one—not even his most ardent supporters—to any real depth of feeling unless it was fear. Hitler was a religious fanatic who devoutly believed in his mission. Chiang was a confused Machiavellian

---

[1] In ancient China, kings derived sanction for their rule from the possession of a quality known as *"teh"* or "magical power." Later, Confucian scholars gave the word the moral connotation of virtue. When the magic virtue was lost, the ruler was destroyed. That is why Chiang tried to monopolize this commodity for himself.

with none of the clarity of thought or well-conceived tactical principles of the Italian. Hitler was the Devil himself and his evil was thorough and black. But Chiang was merely an inefficient "leader" who wanted to become a sage.

Chiang was not only unstable, but treacherous. When Marshal Chang Hsueh-liang saved his life during the Sian kidnaping of 1936, Chiang repaid this deed by imprisoning the Young Marshal when that commander flew in all trust to Nanking. This was fear of a rival and also a kind of revenge on a man who had shown himself a better judge of the political temper of his officers than had Chiang.

Chiang may not have been personally cruel. But he let others do his dirty work for him and thus avoided direct responsibility, and he seldom condemned those who performed murders in his name. At the very dawn of his reign, gangsters slaughtered the Shanghai workers and Chiang made the gang leader one of the pillars of his regime. In fact, Kuomintang papers called this gangster king "the well-known philanthropist." Toward the end of his reign, when his soldiers massacred the Formosans, Chiang castigated the murdered islanders, but not his murdering troops. Yet, when Tai Li, the head of his secret service, whose men performed their duties with hatchet, poison and pistol, died in an airplane accident, the generalissimo is said to have wept. This ruler who could weep for the death of a hatchet man, but could remain unmoved by the killings of professors, is somehow more awful than the most ignorant and bloodthirsty peasant. The peasant killed in the name of an honest passion and a strong personal desire for revenge. Chiang let others do the killings, then gave a lecture on Jesus Christ and Confucius, prayed in the Methodist Church and bowed to his ancestral tablets. This simultaneous calling on the gods of the feudal landlords and the Western powers was, of course, but the spiritual reflection of the dual nature of Chiang's material bases of power.

Underneath Chiang's instability, it is hard not to see a gnawing fear. He was vain and touchy to the point of hysteria. He had the supersensitivity of an omnipotent nobody and felt at ease only among mediocre people. Public soothsayers, fortunetellers and village witches said him well. But during his twenty-year reign, scarcely one Chinese writer of any standing had anything good to say about him. Not sure of his talents, Chiang took refuge in being noble. When dealing with rare characters like T. V. Soong or General Stilwell who refused to kowtow and scrape before him, he got rid of them. He selected his ministers and commanders on a principle of loyalty and moral supineness. Men of brain and character he summoned only in an emergency.

Chiang's basic feelings of inferiority led him to indulge his vanity to the point of meanness. Even the smallest incidents of everyday life furnished him with an excuse for an arrogant display of his power.

In 1944, General Stilwell, a man with a vinegar tongue and a sharp eye for detail, accompanied the generalissimo to graduation exercises at the Military Academy and noted down in his diary this description of the ruler of China as he appeared before the future defenders of the country:

> As the Peanut [Chiang] mounted the rostrum, the band leader counted 1-2-3. The Peanut was furious, stopped the band, bawled out the leader. "Either start playing on 1 or start on 3. Don't start on 2." Then a speaker pulled his notes out of his pockets. This infuriated the Peanut. He bawled him out and told him that in foreign countries you could put a handkerchief in your pants pocket, but not papers. Papers go in lower coat pockets and if secret in upper coat pockets. Then someone stumbled on procedure and the Peanut went wild screaming that he ought to be shot. . . .[2]

It is impossible to imagine the president of the United States acting in such a fashion before a graduating class of West Point cadets. Yet Mr. William C. Bullitt declared that Chiang was a "far-sighted statesman" who bulked larger than any living American. For ourselves we cannot call Chiang a statesman unless this word be synonymous with what is mean and invidious in public life. And we think Stilwell was much closer to an accurate portrait than Bullitt when he referred to Chiang as "the Peanut," "little bugger," "tribal chieftain," "Big Boy," "the all-wise," "the rattle snake."

Chiang was not a statesman. He was a despot, benevolent or otherwise, and he felt all the effects of one. In the field of political tactics, he was a master; in strategy—an opportunist; in government—a fumbler; in war—a fool.

With intrigue, treachery, blackmail, terror and Confucian maxims, he rode to power. A *coup d'état* against the Kuomintang of Dr. Sun Yat-sen brought the party to his feet in 1926. The slaughter of the Shanghai workers delivered the whole nation into his hands in 1927. A series of slow-burning intrigues and comic-opera wars further consolidated his control. Well did China's dictator know how to coax the Christian General Feng Yu-hsiang into the fold and then win all his soldiers from him; how to lure Warlord Han Fu-chu to a meeting in a railway train and execute him; how to persuade Marshal Chang Hsueh-liang to fight, not the Japanese who were in his Manchurian homeland, but the Communists who were advocating war against Japan.

Once in power, Chiang kept there by playing one opponent off against another: right against left, reactionary against liberal, warlord against Communist, secret service against student, gestapo against merchant, party against government, T. V. Soong against H. H. Kung, General Chennault against General Stilwell, and the United States against Russia.

[2] *The Stilwell Papers,* ed. Theodore H. White (New York: William Sloane Associates, 1948).

To stamp, to rage, to threaten, to breach his opponent's strategy with quotations from the Master, to win by stealth and destroy with rewards —for Chiang everything lay in this—to plot, plot, plot incessantly—and he put his faith in this method for he understood the cupidity, the weakness and the cowardice of men. It was a formidable method and one which united to the desperate times in which he was born, made this austere lord of the Orient invincible in Chinese politics for nearly a quarter of a century.

But times changed, and this method which overwhelmed warlords and was irresistible in the limited wars of his early career, where intention rather than execution ruled, suddenly was no longer applicable to the people's war and the revolution which the Communists hurled like a club at Chiang's head. In these spheres, mass passions were king and it was these passions that Chiang failed to understand and that overwhelmed him.

Whether history forced Chiang into despotism or he chose the road voluntarily himself is a question best answered by philosophers, but this fact is plain—the very logic of dictatorship prevented him from foreseeing the dark forces that whirled up from the countryside against him.

No one told Chiang Kai-shek the truth. No one dared. Chiang flew into a rage if anyone argued against him. He was not willing to listen to anything unpleasant. So everybody told him pleasant things. "The only way to handle him," remarked a close associate, "is to tell him he is the most wonderful man in the world." Foreign correspondents never could interview Chiang successfully because official interpreters were too scared to ask questions posed by reporters. In his presence, petty officials were seized with fits of trembling. His conferences were sterile of arguments and questions. His dinner parties were icy affairs where nothing but platitudes were served and everyone, as Stilwell remarked, sat stiffly waiting to be addressed from the throne.

Chiang handled his government officials as a titled lady handles her household servants. Occasionally a wave of public criticism or disgusted American pressure would force some cabinet change. Then the generalissimo, in the words of White and Jacoby[3] would make cabinet changes "almost the way American children play musical chairs; on the given signal everyone would rush for someone else's seat." There were usually the same number of chairs and the same number of players, and outsiders rarely got into the game.

Because he distrusted everyone, Chiang had to consider himself infallible. He wrote orders by the thousands and everyone said yes to his orders, but the generalissimo seldom knew what had been done. He seems never to have been aware—until too late— that he could not order events

[3] Theodore H. White and Annalee Jacoby, *Thunder Out of China* (New York: William Sloane Associates, 1947), p. 114.

on a nationwide scale in the same manner that a landlord could order events within a village. Almost to the end of his reign, he persisted in the delusion that he was a god who could control every happening.

Two thousand miles from the front, he wrote endless instructions to his commanders, telling them to take actions that bore no relation to existing conditions. "I have to lie awake nights," he told Stilwell, "thinking what fool things they [the generals] may do. Then I write and tell them not to do these things. . . . This is the secret of handling them . . . you must imagine everything that they can do that would be wrong and warn them against it."[4] The result of this, of course, was that division commanders became vitally interested in doing what they thought Chiang wanted them to do and not what the situation required.

From this it might appear that Chiang had unlimited power over his subordinates. But even the most despotic rulers cannot arbitrarily control either men or events. Leo Tolstoy understood this very well when he said: "The strongest, most indissoluble, most burdensome, and constant bond with other men is what is called power over others, which in its real meaning is only the greatest dependence on them." These words might have been written about Chiang himself. He was utterly dependent on other men. Even in the heyday of his career, China's dictator had to balance himself between the clandom in the countryside and the compradors in the cities. Since he had enemies in both camps, he tried to build up an independent apparatus in the army, the party and above all in a secret service loyal to him personally. For a while he was able to control affairs with some degree of accuracy. But as his sun declined toward the west, his machinery of power began to creak and break down. The old organizers of society deserted him; his despotism became more isolated, the circle of loyal supporters grew less and the dangers increased all the time. China's dictator lost the ability to predict what was going to happen. In this respect, the institution of despotism itself proved an unbearable handicap. Surrounded by lickspittles and spies, the generalissimo was alert to the slightest tremor in the ranks of his graded bureaucracy, but when the arena of struggle was enlarged to a national war against a foreign foe such as the Japanese, or a mass rebellion such as that led by the Communists, Chiang, being isolated by a wall of misinformation and lies and compounding his own isolation by acts of fear and favor, was unable to predict the course of events accurately and staggered around like a blind man who has suddenly been deserted by his seeing-eye dog.

At the start of the Japanese war, Chiang's advisers indicated the Western powers would interfere if he fought in Shanghai, and instead of massing his troops in the interior and taking advantage of his magnificent back country, he put seventy-eight divisions under Japan's naval guns, until the better part of his army was wiped out and he had to

4 *The Stilwell Papers*, p. 117.

flee fifteen hundred miles to Chungking. At the start of civil war the rightist clique in the party said they could wipe out the Communists in six months and Chiang, having no better information, tore up the Marshall truce agreement and launched an ill-conceived offensive. An American-educated Chinese general thought it would be best to get out of Manchuria, but Chiang's spies hinted that this man was plotting with the Americans to take over his position in China and he clung on till he was liquidated. His air force declared it had achieved a big victory at Suchow in November 1948 and Chiang held onto the city, while Communists were striking at his rear until two army groups were surrounded, practically annihilated and his very capital at Nanking threatened. His party bosses said the mammoth student parades for peace were mere Communist plots and he never interfered with the breakup of the parades and the clubbing of the students. His secret service declared that professors writing articles against inflation were Communists and he let them be arrested. Foreign correspondents reported that his soldiers had shot down and killed unarmed bankers, lawyers, teachers, students and farmers on the island of Formosa, and the generalissimo reproved the reporters for making misstatements that might alter the friendly relations between the Chinese people and America.

This supercilious, despotic attitude, this unwillingness to give credence to any reports but those of his own loyal spies, this blindness to the mighty social convulsions that were shaking China, led the generalissimo into weird realms of thought that can hardly be described as anything else but insanity. As the war went against him, Chiang lost touch with his material environment and lived in a world of his own making. "Those whom the gods will destroy, they first make mad," said the Greeks, and it is hard not to believe them.

Chiang was well born, but late born. "Fifty or a hundred years ago," said Stilwell, "he might have been an acceptable leader in China. But his lack of education handicapped him under modern conditions." When events refused to bend to his will, be became bewildered, then angry. Like Miniver Cheevy, Chiang sighed for what was not and "grew lean while he assailed the seasons."

He wanted to be a moral potentate, a religious leader, a philosopher. But he had little culture. "The picture we see clearly," said Stilwell, "is dark to him. . . . He hurdles logic by using his intuition, dismisses proven principles by saying Chinese psychology is different."[5]

Chiang had no scientific knowledge, yet tried to direct forces equipped with American arms. Under the circumstances he would have been much better off to fight on purely Chinese terms, as did the Communists. Because he knew little of foreign culture or foreign morality, he dealt with foreign powers as if he were dealing with local warlords, followed

[5] *Ibid.*

the ancient dictum of using "barbarians to control barbarians" and tried to play one power off against the other until he had alienated almost every chancellory in the world.

Chiang's intellectual deficiencies had serious effects on his character. Noted in his early days for his boldness and resolution, Chiang lost both qualities in the wars against Japan and the Communists. In the one case he was up against an enemy that could not be blackmailed, bribed or bullied; in the other case he was up against a mass rebellion of common people. In both cases, since he had to deal with the unfamiliar, his intelligence lost its original force, and Chiang became only the more timid the more he became aware of the danger of irresolution which held him spellbound. Thus we find him caught in the horrible slaughterhouse at Shanghai in 1937, unwilling to retreat, unable to come to a decision and vacillating so long that he lost the flower of his army. Thus we find him in 1947 and 1948 plunging forward stubbornly in Shantung, then halting, then wavering, then holding on, refusing to advance, refusing to retreat, until in disgust some of his generals turned over to the Communists.

Chiang was not a weak man, but in him strength of character often led to a degenerate form of it, obstinacy. Hardened by years of struggle, he sometimes fell into the error of proceeding with plans from a feeling of opposition instead of from a conviction or a higher principle. It was stubbornness that made him disregard the warnings of the Young Marshal, Chang Hsueh-liang, that his Manchurian soldiers no longer wanted to fight the Communists, and resulted in his being kidnaped at Sian in 1936; it was ignorant obstinacy that made him countermand General Stilwell's order in 1942 for Chinese troops to evacuate Burma by way of India so that many were lost under the fastnesses of Tibet where they died; it was conceited mulishness that made him go into Manchuria in 1945 against the advice of General Wedemeyer; and finally, it was blind obstinacy and a crazy faith in his own rightness that made him disregard the warnings of his generals that the war could only be settled by political means until in the end politicians refused to head the government, generals refused to take command in the field and foreign powers refused to send him any more aid. You may call this resolute determination, if you will, but then call Hitler resolute for directing von Paulus to hold on at Stalingrad, von Rundstedt to hold on in Normandy and the German Army of the west to hold on at the Rhine so that all were wiped out and the war lost.

In the end, Chiang divorced himself not only from the mass of the people, but even from his own supporters. In vain might the army officers beg him to retreat, the intellectuals plead for freedom, the students parade for democracy, Ambassador Leighton Stuart tell him to liberalize his government. The army officer would be relieved, the intellectual shot, the student beaten and Ambassador Stuart given a Confucian maxim. Being vain, Chiang could not change. Being "superior," he could not get in touch with the poor. Being "virtuous," he could understand benevolence, sincerity and fidelity, but not the people's need for charity, sympathy and hope. Professing Christianity, he had little compassion in his make-up. Asserting he was revolutionary, he kept his face turned toward the past. On the battlefield, he lacked boldness; in politics he lacked creativeness; in government, he lacked justice. He could neither unite broad masses of troops in great sweeping maneuvers, make bold political plans, nor create any major reforms. In short, Chiang, caught in an age entirely too modern for his intellect, was in a job much too large for his talents.

Not entirely lacking in imagination, nor completely impervious to the needs of his country, as were Czar Nicholas of Russia and Louis XVI of France, when they were ground beneath the wheels of revolution, Chiang Kai-shek was not dominated by a strong wife as were those rulers. Yet he was much under the influence of the madamissimo, as foreign diplomats called his consort, and this influence increased with the years and the difficulties and Chiang's dependence on the United States. Together the gissimo and the missimo constituted a kind of unit —and this combination was almost an exact parody of the union of the Occident and the Orient in Chinese life and the subsidiary union between the feudal and bourgeois elements of the ruling social structure. But first we must speak of Madame Chiang herself.

This first lady of China was a member of the fabulous Soong family, consisting of three sisters and several brothers, all of whom bulked large on the pages of recent Chinese history. The father of the Soongs was a Chinese Christian who waxed moderately wealthy on the word of God and was able to send his children to school in the United States. In America the Soongs absorbed the teachings of Western culture with such rapidity and acumen that they were able to return to their native land and almost immediately assume an important role in Chinese government and politics. The first Soong to come into prominence was the gifted and idealistic Soong Ching-ling who married Dr. Sun Yat-sen, the father of the Chinese Republic. Soong Mei-ling went her sister one better and married Chiang Kai-shek, the assassin of the republic. A third sister married Dr. H. H. Kung, the financier of the republic, who became premier of China and retired to the United States. A brother, T. V. Soong, became one of the richest men in China and also was at one time premier of the national government. All the Soongs had a finger in public Chinese life and they conducted war and politics as if it were a family affair. Like all families, the members had their differences. Madame Sun Yat-sen was the idealist of the family; Madame Chiang loved power;

Madame Kung liked money. T. V. Soong, combining all the qualities of his sisters, was idealistic and ambitious.

In one respect, Madame Chiang was very much like the consorts of Czar Nicholas and Louis XVI. Not actually foreign born like Alexandra and Marie Antoinette, the madamissimo was nevertheless somewhat of an alien among her own people. Educated in the United States, she took on all the trappings of an upper-middle-class American woman. Twenty years ago, a reporter was unkind enough to refer to her as an "American flapper." This statement was an exaggeration, but in it there was an element of truth. Madame Chiang had a taste for luxury and excitement. Her clothes betrayed an expensive state of mind. She had numerous fur coats, fine wraps and carefully fitted printed dresses. She wore toeless shoes with spiked heels, carried smart handbags, and decorated her ears with diamond clips.

With such trappings, Madame Chiang went far. When she visited the United States during World War II to plead for immediate help to China, she had no trouble winning the sympathy of American congressmen. So devastating was her effect on aging senators that George Marshall, who was trying first to finish off the war in Europe, was moved to tell correspondents that Madame Chiang was the most powerful advocate he had ever had to face. An American reporter who came under her spell wrote: "Her eyes are limpid pools of midnight inkiness; her teeth are visual symphonies of oral architecture; her hands are lotus fronds swaying in a summer breeze."

Madame was somewhat of an actress. With missionaries, she was reserved. With photographers, she was temperamental. With General Stilwell, a blunt and forthright man, she also was blunt and forthright. She tried to feed General Stilwell's vanity. "We're going to make you a full general," she would say. Another time, she told Stilwell: "Your star is rising." As the years passed, Madame Chiang came more and more to play the role of China's first lady. "Madame Empress," foreign diplomats called her. Or else: "Queen Marie." Stilwell had another name for her: "Snow White."

Nevertheless, Stilwell had a great deal of admiration for Madame Chiang. What the General seems to have admired most was the Occidental mind that existed in Madame Chiang's Oriental body. "A clever brainy woman," said Stilwell. "She sees the Western viewpoint and can appreciate the mental reactions of a foreigner." This was true to a certain extent. The tragedy was that Madame Chiang couldn't appreciate the mental reactions of any but a narrow clique of her own people.

Western education gave the madamissimo a touch of masculinity. She told Stilwell she wished that she had been born a man. She was direct, forceful, energetic and loved power like a man, but ate up flattery like a woman. She craved action. Stilwell thought it would be a good idea to make her a minister of war.

Her long residence abroad gave Madame Chiang an understanding of the world, but deprived her of an understanding of her own country. She could imitate the fireside chats of the Roosevelts, but not the warm and democratic humanity of Mrs. Roosevelt, nor even that of her sister Madame Sun Yat-sen who broke with Chiang Kai-shek for what she considered a betrayal of her husband's doctrines. And while Madame Chiang could act as a translator between her husband and such highly placed persons as General Marshall and President Roosevelt, she could not interpret between him and the Chinese people.

Some social psychologist ought to draw an analogy between the marriage of China's ruling pair and the marriage between her two ruling classes, the landlords and the comprador bourgeoisie. Just as the merchant-industrial class, a product of Western trade, could never cut the cords that bound them to feudal China and even fashioned new ties with the landlords, so Madame Chiang, a product of Western culture, could never completely break away from the old China and tied herself to its crowned representative. That these unions took place almost simultaneously is not strange. In 1927, the Chinese bourgeoisie, blinded by its own narrow class interest, turned on its supporters, disavowed its principles and allied itself with the landlords. Almost at the same time, Madame Chiang threw in her lot with the generalissimo.

People thought the bankers and industrialists would break with Chiang Kai-shek, just as they predicted Madame Chiang would divorce her husband within a year of her marriage. Both unions, though strained and uneasy, however, lasted until the year 1949 when the merchant-industrial class in the cities broke with the feudal countryside and Madame Chiang left her husband and came to the United States.

Madame Chiang was sometimes at war with her husband as the businessmen were at war with the feudal elements. This was due not only to a difference in temperament, but to a difference of interests and intellectual attainments. As the bankers and industrialists of China were far more intelligent than the landlords, so Madame Chiang was more intelligent than her husband. Bankers used to complain to Americans about the stupidity of feudal generals and feudal-minded party members, so Madame Chiang, on occasion, came running in despair to General Stilwell to report: "I've prayed with him; I've done everything but murder him."[6]

The historic tragedy of China was refracted through the personalities of her ruling couple. Still less than any peasant and his wife were the generalissimo and the Madame able to escape from the effects of the breakup

[6] *Ibid.*

of ancient China. Their characters were definitely molded by this mighty event. To some degree, they were also molded by association with each other, Madame pulling Chiang toward the West and modernity, Chiang pulling his wife toward the East and backwardness. Stilwell thought the influence of Madame on her husband was along the right lines. By this we suppose he meant that Madame softened her husband's medievalism, modernized his thinking and turned him toward the West. However, in another way, it is just as safe to assume that Madame Chiang influenced her husband along the wrong lines. For in trying to change her husband she added an element of personal confusion to a mind which had already been turned into a squirrel cage by conflicting historical cultures.

If Madame was leading China's ruler in the right direction, why did the people of the country pay her so little respect? The answer is simple. While trying to maintain her position as China's first lady, Madame Chiang adopted the habits and customs and even the God of the West in that very period when the Chinese people were making mighty efforts to free themselves from alien domination. Madame Chiang was probably sincerely patriotic. But it was noted that whenever she struggled against the feudal elements in Chinese life, she generally did so on behalf of the business elements—her brother T. V. Soong and her sister's husband, H. H. Kung—who were allied with foreign capital. Having risen to the heights of Chinese despotism, this lady did not want to step down. A few days before her husband was forced from his capital at Nanking, Madame Chiang, being unable to plead with the Chinese people, who certainly would not have listened to her, came to the United States to plead with the president of this country to save her husband's regime. There is perhaps nothing that indicates more clearly where Chiang's power lay or where the interests of his wife resided than this final attempt to save a tottering dynasty.

57. The Last Rulers of Old China

IT MAY have occurred to the reader of these pages, as it occurred to many people in China, to ask why the Kuomintang leaders who wanted to save themselves from the Communists did not get rid of Chiang Kai-shek and create a revolution of their own. Some wanted to, but did not dare. Others found Chiang a useful screen behind which to conduct their own personal struggle for power and riches. Still others cynically let the Communist-led revolution take its course, while piling up wealth by means of war and leaving the back door open for flight abroad. Finally, many drifted with events or were held spellbound in the grip of a suicidal feeling.

Nevertheless the idea of throwing out the nation's dictator and instituting reform was one that attracted many officials in Nanking as well as members of the American embassy and the American State Department from the second year of the war right up until the day Chiang abdicated his capital. That this thought was never transmuted into action until very late in the civil war is proof of the weakness of the opposition inside the ruling group and also proof that the forces which defeated the generalissimo came primarily from below and not from within his own ranks.

What went on in government circles, however, was by no means without effect on the course of events. In the end, the Kuomintang fell to pieces and a bitter struggle of cliques prevailed at the summit of power. This was one of the premises of Communist victory, though a passive one. It was also one of the reasons Chiang was able to hold on to many of the strings of power beyond a period of normal expectancy. Chiang had always operated successfully on the principle of divide and rule. But this tactic which was so effective in normal times, when the question of power was limited to who ruled the Kuomintang, was fatally defective during a period of revolutionary upsurge, when the question of power was broadened to who ruled the state and who ruled the new society growing up within the old social order. Under these last circumstances, the principle of divide and rule not only divided Chiang's enemies within the Kuomintang, it also divided the enemies of the Communists.

A sense of the danger of employing his favorite tactic does not seem to have awakened in Chiang until very late in the civil war. He never could get it into his head that he was facing a revolution and not a conspiracy. As for his enemies within the Kuomintang, the danger to Chiang was not so much that they would seize him as they would walk away from him.

The simplest method of the ruling groups to rid themselves of Chiang would have been to kill him, kidnap him or imprison him. But though the malice against the generalissimo penetrated the highest circles and though the Communists after their great military victories even called on opposition Kuomintang leaders to seize Chiang, there is no evidence that a determined plot against the person of China's dictator ever existed. Certainly the United States which was anxious to get rid of Chiang in order to reform the government was never party to such intrigue. Direct action of this kind was contrary to American tradition. It was, however, not contrary to Chinese tradition. Chinese history is filled with instances of such corrective practices effected against unpopular rulers: this type of operation was last carried out in the kidnaping of

Chiang Kai-shek in 1936. It is by no means certain, therefore, that a seizure of the generalissimo's person by his old comrades would have offended Chinese public opinion. On the contrary, such a deed might have transformed even the most odious of the Kuomintang leaders into a kind of national hero. But no one in the ruling group had stomach for such an action. Of course, many were afraid that a bullet directed against Chiang would also reach the heart of the Kuomintang and deliver it into the hands of the Communists. This fear was probably correct. But dread of the Communists was not the only thing that kept the bureaucrats from taking aim at their dictator.

Those with the best opportunity of getting rid of Chiang were the men closest to him. But the immediate camarilla surrounding China's leader was a contradictory crew—an indigestible mixture of YMCA secretaries, Shanghai gangsters, ambitious sycophants, disillusioned visionaries, party thugs, tired revolutionaries, wistful liberals, palace eunuchs, feudal clowns, corrupt bureaucrats, Confucian mystics and sick psychopaths. "The Grand Eunuch," "Rasputin," "Little Lord Machiavelli"—these were some of the names foreign diplomats fastened on the leaders of Kuomintang society and they adequately bespeak the low prestige in which the government was held both at home and abroad. Most of these men were tied to Chiang Kai-shek by reason of interest, habit and fear. They had no belief in their own cause; in fact, they did not have a cause.

In a sense, the older leaders of the Kuomintang were adventurers. In their youths, they rebelled against the traditions of their times. They helped overthrow the Manchu emperor, they founded the republic, fought against the warlords and united in a common brotherhood dedicated to the overthrow of Western imperialism which had dominated their country for a hundred years. But the subtle tragedy that William Bolitho says lies in wait for all adventurers had overcome these men: they had ceased to be adventurers.

Chiang Kai-shek, a stock market gambler, a consort of Shanghai gangsters, a bold maker of *coups d'état,* turned into a mealymouthed despot, given to prayers and moral exhortations. Madame Chiang, the little Christian who had thrown in her lot with a then disreputable militarist, became a middle-class woman given to respectable airs. Wang Ching-wei, the brilliant Kuomintang leader who in his youth plotted to assassinate the Manchu emperor and then became premier of China was so affected by a desire to conserve his wealth and power that he became the chief puppet of the Japanese and ended up his days behind guarded walls, a prisoner of his greed and his fear. T. V. Soong, a man of courage, intelligence and imagination, one of the few who ever dared stand up to Chiang Kai-shek, a bold constructor of banks and financial systems, a man of conscience who searched his soul with Vincent Sheehan after the massacres of 1927, turned into a nervous, banal millionaire. Chen Li-fu, the party leader, in his youth staked out his claims for adventure in the domains of the mind, studying Western science with the zeal of a true rebel. But his intelligence lost its curiosity and he gave himself up to the mouthing of moth-eaten doctrines. Sun Fo, the son of Dr. Sun Yat-sen, father of the republic who dreamed of a China freed from the domination of foreign powers, found the great adventure of building an independent nation too much for him and ended up by begging the United States to establish military and naval bases on China's soil.

It is fascinating but depressing to follow the lives of Kuomintang leaders and see them first facing the future then turning toward the past, wooing the unknown then taking refuge in the known, eagerly seizing power and wealth then trying to conserve both while fear crept in and deadened their sensibilities. Even the greed of some Kuomintang leaders which was one of their strongest motivations to action lost its pristine magnificence. During the Japanese war and the early days of the civil war the Kuomintang bureaucrats turned to squabble among themselves over the wealth of the country which was fast diminishing. During the latter days of the civil war their acquisitive instincts turned into conservative instincts. They wanted to hold on to what they had. "When pirates count their booty," says William Bolitho, "they become mere thieves." It is hard not to apply this statement to many of the leaders of Nationalist China.

Behind the greed of many Kuomintang leaders, one notes another factor: disappointed hopes. Among the older men who had known Dr. Sun Yat-sen and followed the generalissimo with revolutionary enthusiasm to power there lurked a strange feeling of guilt. They had begun as revolutionists seeking to construct a new order, but they had become oligarchs defending an old order, or rather, their power. Memory of youthful dreams, however, sometimes persists to poison the will. Kuomintang leaders were suffering from a mortal sickness of the soul. Sworn to end warlordism, they had ended up in the train of one of the biggest warlords in Chinese history. Sworn to establish democracy, they had created a despotism which made the ancient emperors of China look like fumbling amateurs. Promising to improve the "livelihood of the people," they made it worse than it had been in the memory of living man. Dedicated to freeing China from foreign powers they had become dependent on them.

So these men had no cause. They no longer believed. Many of them had forgotten how to dream. Moreover, Chiang's terror had ripped out the souls of many bureaucrats so that they could do little more than blindly follow their leader on the road to destruction. Moral contamination affected the capacity for action of others. There is no need to go into their bizarre activities here in any detail, but we may mention in passing the official's daughter who carried a whip with her to beat ricksha coolies; the division commander who asked an American doctor in Shanghai to kill his son because he had inherited his father's syphilis; the official's wife who loaded dogs onto a plane in place of her fellow-countrymen who were fighting to escape Hongkong after Pearl Harbor; and the general who in the summer of 1948 seduced the eight-year-old daughter of a minor official in Nanking, infected her with gonorrhea and then threatened to arrest the girl's father and his neighbors if they pressed suit against him.

How could such people summon the moral energy to throw off the dictator whose very existence guaranteed that they might continue in such actions? The answer is, they could not. But they could not summon much energy to defend Chiang either. Moreover, their greed and their fright before the collapsing situation did not necessarily unite them; it often divided them. Each man tried to save himself in his own way.

Madame Sun Yat-sen, who deserted the generalissimo twenty years ago because she believed he had betrayed her husband's principles, refused to have anything to do with him right to the end and refused even to join oppositional elements within the Kuomintang who were heading a peace movement. Her sister, Madame Chiang, fled to the United States to plead with President Truman to save her husband. Dr. H. H. Kung, descendant of Confucius, Yale University alumnus and financial wizard, combining the wisdom, gusto and foresight of all three, also came to the United States where he could enjoy his wealth in safety and muse on the days when he had been premier and finance minister in Chiang's government. Wong Wen-hao, an economist summoned to the premiership in the spring of 1948, resigned four or five times and finally let it be known that he spent his days at home "reading and writing poetry" because he "no longer feels interested in national affairs." Tai Chi-tao, an "elder statesman" of the Kuomintang, committed suicide in Hongkong, Chen Pu-lei, personal secretary of the generalissimo and famous feudal literatus, wrote a letter to Chiang in which he quoted the words of a classical poem—"the oil is exhausted; the light is dying—" then he, too, killed himself. With an owl scream in the dark, feudalism paid its last tribute to China's despot.

So it went. The old Nationalist revolutionaries could not steel their hearts to overthrow their despot. But they could run away from him. With such an attitude prevailing it is no wonder that the movement against Chiang in the upper circles often reduced itself to vicious snarls, gallows jokes and muttered imprecations. "Our government is a fascist dictatorship," a minister would remark to a foreign correspondent. And you would wait there thinking you were in the company of a desperate revolutionist. But it would all end up with a sepulchral laugh. Nor did any iron opposition within government circles show up at the other end of the political spectrum—among the liberals. George Marshall had seen the salvation of China in a movement by government and minority party liberals to take power "under the leadership of Chiang Kai-shek." But this type of salvation was little better than a pious hope. Liberals in China were unarmed and a Chinese liberal without a gun was no more effective than a watchdog without a bite or a bark. And who were these liberals? By Western tradition a liberal is one who has respect for another's viewpoint. But such men, due to the effects of the authoritarian Confucian tradition, were so few as to be practically nonexistent in China, either in the Kuomintang, the Communist party, minority parties or anywhere else. Furthermore, except for the already mentioned intellectuals and students who stood up courageously against Chiang, there were few liberals—certainly not within the government—willing to show their colors so openly. Within the ruling classes, for every courageous critic who wanted to get rid of Chiang, there were two who wanted to "reform" his character. During the civil war, in the midst of one of the terror campaigns against the students, a university professor, a member of the government, was sent to me by an American with the recommendation that I write an article about "an ardent opponent of Chiang Kai-shek, one of the better type of men in whom the salvation of China lies." A long conversation revealed that this particular savior of China had visited the generalissimo as spokesman for a Christian group, had praised the dictator as a "great man" and had ended up by reading a poem about George Washington. The implication was that Chiang should try like George to become the revered "father of his country."

With poesy the liberals wanted to soothe the savage breast of China's dictator. But iambic pentameter, even when translated into Chinese, could not lure Chiang into making reforms, much less into abdicating his seat of power. It is true there were some phrase makers who cried out: "if we don't put down Chiang Kai-shek, we will go down with him." The idea of making a revolution from above in order to forestall a revolution from below held an irresistible charm for Chinese intellectuals as well as pale-faced college men in the halls of foreign embassies. But such ideas hung in the air as mooded despair. They never developed into a hard plot. The heart of Chinese liberalism was literary, but rather weak. In any case it was quite willing to surrender the honor of getting rid of the generalissimo to the old Kuomintang provincial militarists of whom it had been so contemptuous. These leaders were more hardheaded and for that reason a little more resolute. They now re-entered the political picture and offered the most determined opposition to Chiang within his own party.

We have already remarked at the beginning of this book that when Chiang Kai-shek started the civil war against the Communists he had rendered ineffective nearly every warlord or provincial military man who had ever opposed him. Now it is a curious fact that the very powerlessness of these men was just what enabled them in the long run to make a comeback in Chinese politics. This seeming paradox is explained by a peculiar change which took place in the social structure of the Kuomintang during the Japanese war. In 1937 and 1938, when the Japanese drove the Chinese government away from the coast, Chiang Kai-shek was deprived of most of the nation's industrial plants and the proceeds from foreign trade. As a result, between 1938 and 1945, he was compelled to rely more and more on the feudal barons in the interior to maintain himself in power. This brought about a decline in the economic strength and the political influence of the native industrialists and bankers while the power of the "sedan chair" gentry grew and along with it the feudal elements within the Kuomintang. Within a couple of years, a war of cliques developed within the party for the control of the only real wealth in China's interior—land and the produce of the land and trade communications resulting from that produce.

Politically this struggle was highlighted by the rise in relative economic strength of the right-wing CC Clique, of the Kuomintang. At the conclusion of the Japanese war, compradore interests in the Kuomintang, using their superior administrative capacities and their contacts with American interests, gained most of the spoils from the occupied areas, leaving CC Clique out in the cold. Thus, the CC men, needing continued party dictatorship to strengthen their economic position, became the spearhead of the movement for war against the Communists. This war gave the CC Clique an opportunity to follow in the wake of the army and to organize local party bureaus and also, through their Farmers Bank and Bank of Communications, to organize rural co-operatives with the aid of the landed gentry. At the same time, through its control of the party, the CC men took over numerous newspapers and publications which it used to assault its enemies within the Kuomintang. In addition, they also manipulated the students in movements against rival cliques and various wartime premiers. Because of these struggles the middle elements of the Kuomintang were devoured much as small businessmen are devoured by giant trusts and monopolies. The Kuomintang gradually became more and more polarized between right and left, between those with power and those without power, between those who wanted reform and those who resisted reform. The native bankers grew weaker under pressure from the bureaucrats. Kuomintang leaders, oriented toward the West, became involved in a war for control of help coming from the United States. Those with the least power were pushed aside. Just as the Chinese people disinherited from society had grown in leaps and bounds, so there took place a disinheritance within the Kuomintang itself. At the same time, Communist land reform and Communist military conquests, plus carpetbagging by Chiang's officials, deprived the gentry and local civilian leaders in Manchuria and North and Central China of their economic bases. The comparative opulence and the corruption of Chiang's top bureaucrats along with the increased power of the rightist clique in the Kuomintang now seemed intolerable to these newly dispossessed leaders. As the tenant, with his back against the wall, had turned on the landlord, so the petty party leaders were now ready to turn on the top party leaders.

These twin developments—increased party dictatorship plus the disinheritance of the lower party ranks—gave hitherto powerless Kuomintang militarists a chance to reenter the Chinese political picture. Misery loves company and the old militarists who had long been deprived of power by Chiang now found companions of the road in new malcontents within the Kuomintang. It remained, however, for the generalissimo's oldest enemies within the party to take leadership of the movement against him at the highest levels.

In Chiang's political closet there were many skeletons. Three of the more lively ones were Pai Chung-hsi, Ho Ying-chin and Li Tsung-jen. All of them were old members of the Kuomintang. All of them were generals. And all of them at one time or another had opposed China's dictator. At the conclusion of the Japanese war, the generalissimo isolated these three men by separating them. General Li Tsung-jen was kicked upstairs and made titular head of the generalissimo's bureau in Peiping. General Ho went to the United States. General Pai was appointed defense minister, a post with little meaning. So segregated, the three could not pull together.

But the triumvirate outsmarted the generalissimo. General Li, in Peiping, cultivated the northern generals and also curried United States favor, adopting a liberal coloring and protecting intellectuals and students from Chiang's gendarmes. Pai maneuvered himself into a strategic position in Central China and became commander of the government's defense at Hankow. General Ho, while in the United States, joined the Oxford Movement and talked knowingly of the need for democracy in China.

The three generals formed a loose union among themselves which became popularly known in China as the White Fox Alliance—a term derived from the similarity in sounds between their names and the Chinese characters for an animal with magical powers known as *Paihuli.*

The first opportunity any of the generals had to challenge Chiang's control of the party, and hence of the government, came in April 1948 during the convening of the national assembly in Nanking. Meekly, delegates elected Chiang Kai-shek president of China. Immediately afterward, however, delegates from Manchuria and North China, among whom were bankers, educators and gentry who were disgusted with the way Chiang's bureaucrats had looted their provinces and with Chiang's unwillingness to arm the population, rallied around Li Tsung-jen and backed his candidacy for the vice-presidency against Sun Fo, the generalissimo's choice for the office.

Chiang Kai-shek and the CC Clique, fearful of the implied threat to their control of the party, brought heavy pressure on Li to retire from the race. The night before the balloting Chiang's secret police visited the known supporters of Li and advised them to switch to Sun Fo. Delegates were told this was an order from the generalissimo; if they did not obey, their lives would be in danger. Under this threat Li withdrew his name from the election. He then addressed the assembly with a letter in which he expressed his deep indignation that terror had been employed against delegates to prevent them from exercising their rights to vote freely. The assembly was thrown into a great state of confusion. Some delegates were so aroused that they lost their usual caution and shouted such slogans as "Down with dictator Chiang Kai-shek." In embarrassment, Sun Fo, Chiang's candidate, also withdrew from the race.

Both Chiang and the CC Clique realized they had gone too far. They attempted to remedy the situation by some Oriental maneuvering behind the scenes. The story was circulated that the generalissimo wanted to follow the custom of the United States and name the vice-president himself. Finally the generalissimo then changed his mind, the assembly reconvened, the election was held and Li became the vice-president of the country.

For the first time in twenty years Chiang's control of the party had been challenged and he had been defeated. Despite the break in party ranks, Chiang was able to maintain control in the nation's capital at Nanking until the collapse of his armies at Suchow and the advance of the Communists to the Yangtze River. This changed the temper of all but the most ardent die-hards.

The pressure for peace was severe and came from every quarter. Shanghai merchants, having no desire to see their property sacrificed in a last-ditch defense of China's dictator and fearing an alliance between hungry mobs and still hungrier soldiers, began maneuvering among local garrison commanders and paying off their troops. Shanghai's foreign community, particularly American businessmen (no matter what the United States policy was), also had no desire to see a battle around the port and they too began to add their pettish voices to the chorus demanding that Chiang resign. They wanted peace even at the cost of Communist domination of the government. That meant: get rid of Chiang.

But China's dictator could not be exorcised by mere wishes. He had to be driven out. This was difficult because he controlled the secret service and had the loyalty of the armed forces of General Tang En-po, fellow-provincial of the generalissimo, whom Chiang had pulled out of the front lines and made commander of the Nanking-Shanghai area. Yet Chiang by no means had complete control over the areas still unconquered by the Communists. By the middle of December 1948, after his severe defeats, there were perhaps only a million front line Kuomintang troops to oppose any further advance of the Communists. Nearly all of these troops were scattered at indecisive places throughout China, with no chance of massing them effectively for a military defense of Nanking. One of the biggest concentrations of troops, numbering nearly a quarter of a million soldiers, was at Hankow, the Chicago of China, six hundred miles up the Yangtze River from Shanghai. Some of these troops were loyal to Chiang, but they were under the command of General Pai Chung-hsi, an old opponent of Chiang.

Pai and his associates wanted to get rid of Chiang in order to save something from the wreck of Kuomintang power. Pai suggested that Chiang resign. Chiang answered he would do so when all hope of foreign mediation had vanished. While waiting for Chiang to take this step, Pai froze Nanking's military assets in Central China: he put traffic on the Yangtze River under strict control, recalled troops from the Suchow battle and sent his former chief of staff to Hongkong to contact dissident democratic groups who were in touch with the Communists.

This move and similar ones by other generals, which became known in China as "polite insubordination," placed Chiang in a double dilemma: he had to gain a breathing spell through a truce with the Communists and he had to deal with his recalcitrant generals. Therefore, Chiang allowed peace rumors, which he had heretofore suppressed, to gain momentum, and at the same time he sought desperately to obtain foreign support to bolster his dying prestige.

Chiang first turned toward the United States. Shortly after the collapse of resistance in Manchuria, Dr. Sun Fo, a member of the National Reconstruction Group of the Kuomintang from which Chiang drew much of his party support, urged the United States to establish military and naval bases on the supposedly sovereign soil of China, to take over her greatest inland waterway, the Yangtze River, and to send General MacArthur to China to take command of an aid program. This was nothing but an elaboration of the old Bullitt plan. But to hear the son of Dr. Sun Yat-sen make such a proposal was a distinct shock to the national feelings of many Chinese. The fact that Chiang was to be offered an equal partnership with Hirohito as a kind of subemperor under MacArthur also injured Chiang's prestige. Thus, another element of decay was introduced into Chiang's power.

Shortly after Dr. Sun's appeal, Chiang sent his wife to the United States. A Shanghai newspaper reported that she had a number of "olive leaves" to hold out to American leaders: 1. China's inland shipping rights; 2. Concession of all Formosa as a United States military base; 3. Broadened powers for the joint US Military Advisory Group; 4. Complete handling by American personnel of US aid.

These proposals by Dr. Sun and Madame Chiang were received coldly in the United States for it was plain to American policy makers that Chiang no longer had anything to offer. The political situation in the United States, however, led some of Chiang's intimates to hope that the United States might still interfere in China's civil war to save their personal power.

In December 1948, Chiang is reported to have asked his representatives in the United States whether he should resign. The agents, presumably not disposed to offend Chiang, told him to hang on and wait developments in Congress. But the situation in China would not wait. For the Communist party, which had been keeping a careful eye on the shifts within the Kuomintang, suddenly decided to force matters.

On Christmas Day, 1948, they broadcast a list of forty-three "war criminals." The list included not only Chiang Kai-shek, his wife, his various in-laws and top government officials and diplomats in the United States, but also various provincial politicians and militarists who were carrying on their own maneuvers for peace and power. This Christmas package fell like a sword among the squabbling Kuomintang leaders. Pai Chung-hsi and the Hupeh Provincial Council immediately brought the question of peace before the generalissimo.

The old dictator, caught in a cul-de-sac, tried to wriggle out. On New Year's Day, 1949, he broadcast his own "appeal for peace." This was one of the most curious documents of modern warfare. In essence it was a no-peace-no-war formula designed to gain time. Chiang spoke of the national independence of China, but made no move to dismiss American marines from Chinese soil or to demand the return of naval bases used by the United States. At the same time, the government began to make certain treaties with the Soviet Union in Singkiang Province. Chiang wanted to preserve the constitution under which his regime was legitimized and also the "entity" of the armed forces by which he ruled the country. All in all his conditions of peace were so unrealistic that the Communists could not possibly accept them.

But a breach had been made in the Kuomintang's will for war and the Communists poured in to widen it. On the same day that Chiang issued his peace appeal, the Communists' New China News Agency published an historic editorial called "Carry the Revolution to the Very End." Denouncing the "peace plots" of the Kuomintang "reactionaries" and warning that the American government was trying to organize an opposition within the revolutionary camp "to halt the revolution" or to force it to "take on a moderate coloring so as not to encroach too much on the interests of imperialism," the agency called for a closing of all ranks against the rulers of old China:

The question now confronting the people of China is: are they to carry the revolution through to the end or are they to abandon the revolution in mid-stream? If the revolution is to be carried through to the end, then this means using revolutionary methods to wipe out all reactionary forces. This means the unswerving overthrow of imperialism, feudalism and bureaucratic capitalism. This means overthrowing the reactionary rule of the Kuomintang throughout the entire country and establishing a republic of the people's democratic dictatorship under the leadership of the proletariat with an alliance of the workers and peasants as the main body.
If the revolution should be abandoned in mid-stream, that would be going against the will of the Chinese people, giving in to the will of foreign aggressors and Chinese reactionaries, enabling the Kuomintang to gain a respite, permitting the wounded beast to nurse his wounds and then spring up again one day to throttle the revolution so that the entire country would return to the world of darkness.
The question of the moment is presented just as clearly and sharply as this: there are two roads; which one do you choose?

This might have been the voice of Lenin himself speaking. Or even that of Karl Marx or Engels. For like the authors of the *Communist Manifesto*, the authors of this editorial "scorned to conceal their aims." Gone were the tactical shifts, gone the political double talk, gone the illusions of a mere "reform" government. What the Chinese Communists were saying in essence was: "you are either for us or against us. Choose!"

Kuomintang leaders had no intention of choosing the revolutionary road of the Communists and thus liquidating their own society. Nevertheless, they saw they would have to sacrifice, or appear to sacrifice, the generalissimo. Plead as he would, Chiang could not get the Kuomintang to close ranks and rally behind him. On January 8, 1949, he sent his personal trouble shooter, Chang Chun, to Hankow and Changsha to ask the support of Pai Chung-hsi, Central China political leader, and on the same day appealed to the four governments of France, England, the United States and the Soviet Union to mediate China's civil war. He was turned down—both inside and outside the country.

Chiang's movements were now those of an animal in a cage. One by one he shakes at every locked opening: his old cronies in the Kuomintang, his revived enemies, the United States, even the Soviet Union. All to no avail. With characteristic directness, the Communists moved in to separate Chiang from his protecting followers.

On January 14, Mao Tze-tung, scorning all foreign mediation of China's war, declared that the People's Liberation Army had the power to trample the whole Kuomintang machinery of rule "into dust and extinction." However, for the sake of peace, the Communist party would end the war under the following conditions:

1. Punishment of war criminals.
2. Abrogation of the bogus constitution.
3. Abolition of the Kuomintang's illegal regime and rule.
4. Reorganization of all reactionary armies in accordance with democratic principles.
5. Confiscation of bureaucratic capital.
6. Reform of the agrarian system.
7. Abrogation of treaties which betray the nation.
8. Convocation of a Political Consultative Conference without the participation of reactionary elements and establishment of a coalition government to take over all power from the Kuomintang Nanking government and its lower organs of administration.

Such terms amounted to a demand for unconditional surrender. They could not be accepted by the Kuomintang. Yet Mao's statement completely discredited Chiang's peace appeal. There was no longer any corner in the field of propaganda where he could hide. He had to retire. Such a move would naturally endanger his prestige. But the generalissimo found it politic to leave Nanking in order to quell the rising tide of fear and opposition within the Kuomintang, to gain more time to build up defenses south of the Yangtze and to seek foreign aid behind the screen of continued peace negotiations carried out by other elements of the government.

In this kind of backstage intrigue, Chiang was an experienced hand. On hearing Mao's peace demands, he called together a dozen of his more faithful followers, including Chen Li-fu, Ku Cheng-kang, Huang Shao-ku, Tao Hsi-sheng and others. It was reported that Chiang, though going into retirement, would maintain control over the peace movements. His political cohorts would be protected by the Kuomintang secret police, while the Central Bureau of Investigation and Statistics was empowered to punish all those who did not accept his leadership. The most important political prisoners would be moved to South China.

Chiang spent his last days in Nanking closely guarded by his secret police. Possibly he was afraid that he might be kidnaped again. It was reported that he slept each night aboard a former British warship anchored in the Yangtze River. In the event of an uprising in the capital, he could make a quick getaway. But no uprisings occurred.

At 2 P.M., on January 21, after turning his office over to Li Tsung-jen, the generalissimo boarded a two-engined American plane and flew to his ancestral home in Fenghwa in Chekiang Province, 210 miles from Nanking. For twenty-two years, with one or two interruptions, Chiang had been at the helm of the Chinese state, but his retirement and departure were greeted with indifference by the common Chinese people.

During the three and a half years since the surrender of Japan, Chiang's prestige had dipped to an all-time low. The same man who had been a magnet for a hundred thousand cheering Shanghai Chinese at the victory celebration in Racecourse Park in 1945 now drew neither cheers nor tears as he headed back to his ancestors and perhaps oblivion.

That oblivion, however, would not be a matter of Chiang's own choosing. Behind him the generalissimo left a farewell message that was couched in terms ambiguous enough to leave the road open for his return. On the second day after his departure, an order transmitting instructions from Ku Chu-tung, chief of staff of Chiang's armies, and retransmitted to officers in the field, cleared up all doubts. This message read:

President left Nanking with full advance preparations. Vice President Li Tsung-jen and executive head Sun Fo will take political responsibilities. The international scene is full of changes, and we have every guarantee of victory. We are all students of the President and the Chief of Staff and should keep the troops well in hand.

Thus did the forces of Old China seek to rally around their retired leader.

58. The End of an Era

THE years 1945 to 1949 in China present an extraordinary spectacle of millions of people in constant turmoil. Men leave their customary pursuits, march to and fro across the continent, plunder and slaughter one another, triumph and are plunged in despair, betray and are betrayed, and during this time the whole course of life is altered and probably the very future of Asia itself. What was the primary characteristic of all this terrific commotion?

One is inclined to answer in the largest philosophic terms that what we see before us in China are the phenomena of birth and death. On the one hand, a new society is coming into being; on the other hand an old order is dying out.

In the camp of revolution everything is young, lusty and in the process of growth: peasant bands are becoming armies, village assemblies are becoming regional governments, co-operative societies are enlarging into state banks. But in the camp of reaction just the opposite process is going on: everything is old, feeble and in the process of decay: armies are degenerating into police forces, national governments are becoming provincial assemblies, banks end up as mere chests of gold hidden in secret caches on faraway islands. One gets the impression that the forces generating these processes are inexorable; they can be delayed, they cannot be halted.

This does not mean there was anything predestined about the fall of Kuomintang society and the rise of Communist society. Far from it. The Chinese civil war was only decided in the fighting of it. Nevertheless, the Chinese Revolution by 1949 had created such a wave of power, principle and passion that no one could hold it back any more than a man with a broom can hold back a flood that has burst its dam.

Chiang Kai-shek is a case in point. When he retired from Nanking, the generalissimo tried desperately to hold his deserting supporters together. Because he still controlled the monies of the state treasury, he was able to outbid most of his rival politicians for the support of the secret service and some of the army commanders. And because he still possessed enormous talents for intrigue, he was also able to continue to divide his party opponents. But he had not enough money to hold any large groups of men together and his divisive tactics, though they gave him the upper hand over his top opponents, only succeeded in demoralizing the lower ranks of the party and the army until many of them had no spirit to resist at all.

Chiang probably calculated that the Communists would make peace demands that his rivals in the Kuomintang could not possibly accept. With his opponents discredited, he then could make a comeback with restored prestige. In the meantime, his closest supporters planned to sabotage peace and those who opposed his personal rule. This was a cute strategy. But in sabotaging the reform group in the government and in sabotaging the movements for democracy and peace, Chiang's supporters were in reality sabotaging the ability of his party and government to make war. The efforts to halt the disintegration of Chiang's own support merely increased the over-all disintegration of Nationalist society. And for all his intrigues, Chiang was never wise enough to set in motion any revolutionary policies that alone might have saved him, if saved he could be.

From the shadows of his ancestral tombs in Fenghwa, the generalissimo throughout the spring of 1949 continued to reach out his black hand to control the events in the capital he had abandoned. Newspaper editors who criticized his backstage manipulations were arrested, students who paraded for peace were clubbed, shot and killed on the streets of Nanking and an attempt was even made to kidnap Li Tsung-jen who had taken over the presidency from the generalissimo.

Much more startling was the fact that after Chiang's retirement ninety-two accused traitors and collaborators with the Japanese were released from jail while 260 Japanese war criminals convicted by Chinese courts were sent back to Japan. More revealing still, General Okamura, Japanese staff expert who had made a lifelong study of how to conquer China, who had been commander in chief of Japanese forces in North China and then Central China and who was the author of the "kill all, loot all, burn all" policy, was suddenly, in late January 1949, declared innocent of war crimes by Chiang's judges and allowed to return on an American ship to Japan and the protection of General MacArthur. The continued suppression of his own subjects along with the release of Japanese "war criminals" naturally dropped Chiang's prestige still lower among the common people of China. From this one can only conclude that Chiang had no confidence in his ability to rouse his own people to beat the Communists. He was banking on a third World War and was laying out his lines of alliance to Japan and the American military in Japan.

Despite Chiang's attempts at long-distance control of the Chinese state, his departure from the capital had definitely weakened his authority. The rift within the Kuomintang kept widening. The government was nominally and factually nowhere. In Fenghwa there was a "retired" but not yet resigned president, intriguing for war. In Nanking there was an acting president, intriguing for peace. In Canton there was an Executive Yuan, the Kuomintang cabinet, headed by Chiang's own men. On the island of Formosa there was another group headed by General Chen Cheng, Chiang's right-hand military man known as the "Little Generalissimo," and Chiang's eldest son. These groups accused each other of being warmongers or capitulationists, depending on their point of view.

Peace was an issue underlying the split in the Kuomintang, but it was not the greatest issue. For many of the top leaders, peace was merely a verbal façade behind which they realigned themselves for further resistance to the Communists and further struggles for power and wealth. Hope for United States aid played a great part in the jockeying between contending factions. Wu Te-cheng, the deputy premier and foreign minister in the cabinet at Canton, told seventy-six leading Kuomintang members in a meeting in that city on February 6, 1948, that "a move is underway in the United States Congress to give us an additional military aid of six hundred million dollars, a grant of two to three hundred million dollars' worth of commodities and another two to three million dollars as a fund to stabilize our currency."

The same hope stimulated warlords in the far-off provinces to realign themselves for continued resistance. At an Eight Province Defense Conference in Chungking, General Wang Ling-chi, governor of Szechuan, announced that the southwest provinces would raise a new fighting force of five million men. The general was exaggerating; he could not raise any such force; he probably hoped also to obtain American aid. In this he was encouraged by certain American military commentators who advocated supporting provincial Chinese leaders to stem the Red tide in China. Such a program was nothing but an imitation of a similar policy that had failed thirty years earlier when the Great Powers supported Admiral Kolchak against the newly born Soviet Union. The policy had proved defective then; it would have been equally defective now.

One reason for this was that among the Kuomintang leaders who were breathing defiance of the Communists few had the stomach for fighting further. Their self-confidence was almost completely shot. On the brink of oblivion, they made almost no attempt to save themselves by winning the common people to their cause. On the contrary, they stepped up the robbery of their subjects. After all, why shouldn't they? It was their last chance.

In their haste and greed, the rulers of old China abandoned almost all pretense. The plunder was now open and aboveboard. Take, for example, Kunming, chief city of Yunan Province. This city had been the terminus for the American air supply route over the "Hump" during World War II and it was filled with American dollars left there by American soldiers. On February 10, 1949, a huge amount of purple-colored Gold Yuan notes of fifty-dollar denomination were brought into the city and used by the Central Bank of China to buy up all foreign notes and gold bullion on the open market. The price of gold and all commodities doubled within twenty-four hours. On the second day, the bank announced that all the fifty-dollar notes were counterfeit. Thirty thousand people gathered on Nanping Street where the bank was located and began a run on the bank. The bank closed its doors and a riot ensued. Governor Lu Han arrived in an armored car at the head of several hundred soldiers, dispersed the crowds and indiscriminately arrested 118 people. A court-martial, presided over by Lu, was set up on the road opposite the bank building. The arrested men were questioned briefly and then shot to death, one by one, with thousands looking on. The governor ordered the "trial" to come to an end after twenty-one had been executed and after the executioners pleaded that "all the rest seemed to be accomplices only."[1]

This sorrowful incident was but one of many which darkened the declining days of the Kuomintang. As the tide of civil war turned ever against them, even as the Communists stood poised for a push into South China where the resources were many and the people numbered two hundred million, the Kuomintang bureaucrats sought not so much to transform the huge potential of the masses into a support for their regime as they sought to transform their wealth into gold bullion and foreign exchange easy to be taken abroad. The compulsory conversion of foreign money into Gold Yuan resulted in an estimated 180

[1] As reported by Far Eastern Bulletin, Feb. 19, 1949.

million dollars being taken from the people after August 1948. Forty more million dollars were squeezed out of the commercial banks by an order of Chiang's Finance Ministry which wanted to raise capital deposits in the Kuomintang treasury.

Where was all this wealth going? Many places. On March 2, 1949, the Ta Kung Pao reported that eighty-six hundred cases of China's precious stones, treasures and rare books were transported to America. Trunks and chests of gold, amounting to an estimated four million ounces were sent to the island of Formosa. These caches were kept in such a way that they could be shipped abroad at any time in the event of an emergency. Fifty thousand ounces of gold and fifty million Hongkong dollars, which the Canton Bank had acquired through the Gold Yuan conversion, were deposited in Hongkong, the British safe deposit box. The Philippines also became a refuge for Chinese banking capital, a new paradise for Kuomintang investors with American money and a busy center for trade speculation among fleeing party leaders. Many party bureaucrats were selling their estates in Shanghai to European refugee Jews and then settling the deals in Manila where they set up corporations and factories. Kuomintang leaders were begging Americans to invest in their country and their party's future, but the measure of their self-confidence can be gauged by the fact that they themselves were sending much of their capital abroad for investment.

It has always been characteristic of Chinese warlords that they hold on to their positions to the last, not out of belief in their own destiny, but so that they may tax the people for years ahead, put their wealth in foreign concessions or abroad and then retire or make a deal which will enable them to live handsomely in exile. Kuomintang leaders, though more adroit, were much the same. Perhaps they were not to blame: they were merely following "old Chinese custom."

The spirit of the times, then, was not *fin de siècle*, like the exhausted days of latter nineteenth-century England, but *fin du monde,* like czarist Russia or Bourbon France. In this world of despair, anything went, anything was excusable. Save yourself: that was the code.

So the graph of Kuomintang power, haltingly, but ever declining, approached its steepest drop. Threatened with extinction, it was necessary if they were to survive as a political entity that the Kuomintang leaders give up their old ways, their outmoded techniques of power, their tactics of graft, and get down among the people to fight the Communists on their own terms.

But the Kuomintang leaders could not change. They were compradors and landlords by nature and they were true to themselves to the end. The remainder of their actions have only the interest of a study in vivisection. As of old, the students were beaten and shot, the people taxed to death, the peasants kidnaped from their homes and forced into the army. And, as of old, the same actions produced the same results. Despite the fact that the Communist armies had not crossed the Yangtze River, nevertheless, deep in the Kuomintang rear, farmer guerrilla bands mushroomed suddenly from nowhere and then spread everywhere like a fatal rash across a diseased body. The story was always the same: peasant revolts, led by local intellectuals, against the bailiffs, the landlords and the gendarmes. To the very end, the Kuomintang stubbornly and characteristically refused to come to grips with the gentry and now it was going down with them. Brutally, bloodily, blindly, the rulers of old China moved toward the abyss.

During this period of truce, which the Kuomintang so urgently needed but so ill employed, the Communist party, north of the Yangtze River, used its talents to more effective purpose. Having laid down peace terms which the Kuomintang could not accept, Mao Tze-tung directed his followers to make full war preparations for crossing the Yangtze into South China. These preparations were thorough, but not solely military. In the countryside, the land reform continued at a wiser and less brutal tempo. In the newly conquered cities, the common people were kept quiet by food supplies brought in from the farms. On the other hand, in order to arouse the intelligentsia, the party appealed in Peiping and Tientsin for student volunteers to accompany their southbound armies as political auxiliaries. Because they had been but newly freed from Kuomintang terror and because their fellow-students in the south were still being arrested and killed, the pupils in the north flocked to the Communists as converts gather to a new religious leader. Within a few weeks, ten thousand girls and boys from the universities and middle schools of Peiping and Tientsin had learned the Red techniques for taking over cities and were eagerly awaiting the call to march south.

That call was not long in coming. By the middle of April, the Communists had concentrated one million soldiers of the People's Liberation Army in staging bases along a six-hundred-mile front skirting the north bank of the Yangtze River from the China Sea to river gorges near the Szechuan border. On the south side of the river, secret Communist agents had already organized peasant guerrilla bands to aid in the crossing. With every preparation made to seize the Nationalist capital at Nanking, the Communists sent a last ultimatum to the Kuomintang government.

The terms were stiff. They called among other things for: 1. Nationalist agreement to an unopposed crossing of the Yangtze; 2. Surrender of all war criminals, including some members of the Nationalist government; 3. Formation of a "coalition" government dominated by the Communists.

A deadline was set for the Nationalist answer. Twice the deadline was put ahead. Then, on April 17, the Communists announced that unless the government, headed by Acting President Li Tsung-jen, yielded by April 20, they would force the river barrier. Seven hours before the April 20 deadline, the Nationalists rejected the terms. Mao Tze-tung, chairman of the Communist party and General Chu Teh, commander in chief of the People's Liberation Army, immediately issued a joint order commanding their forces to push south and "liberate all of China." All Kuomintang "reactionaries" who dared resist were to be wiped out.

On the evening of April 20, within a few hours of Mao Tze-tung's order, the People's Liberation Army began to cross the Yangtze River. Landing operations proceeded along a 350-mile front from Kiukiang in the west to Kiangyin in the east. The Yangtze in this section of China is sometimes two miles wide and it is deep enough to allow the passage of ocean-going steamers and warships of nearly every size and description. To negotiate this formidable water barrier, the Communists had only wooden boats, junks, and rafts. Everything they would need in South China, including artillery, ammunition, provisions and supplies of all kinds had to be ferried over the river by these primitive means. To halt the Yangtze crossing, the Kuomintang had a navy and an air force. Outwardly, the odds appeared in favor of Chiang Kai-shek.

But there was almost no resistance to the crossing. The Chinese navy, which had been partially equipped and trained by the United States, showed little stomach for a fight. The air force, which had also been furnished to Chiang by the United States and which might conceivably have turned the crossing into a holocaust, seldom appeared to give battle to the Communists.

The Kuomintang had deployed nearly half a million troops to man the Yangtze, but their fighting power was not to be measured by their numbers. The first break in the river line was made at Tikang on the evening of April 20. Garrisoning this town were the 80th and 88th divisions, the latter a crack outfit and one of the three army units originally known as "Chiang's Own." Both divisions revolted on the eve of the battle. On April 21, the Communists landed at Kiukiang midway between Nanking and Hankow. A day later, forces of the People's Liberation Army were in the Kiangyin fort area, supposedly the strongest point in Kuomintang defenses. The garrison batteries in the Kiangyin fort opened fire, not on the People's Liberation Army, but on Kuomintang gunboats so that the Communists could the more easily cross the river. Everywhere, the story was repeated: insurrection, surrender, disintegration. Formerly, military analysts had made distinctions between the fighting power of Central troops and Irregular troops loyal to the Kuomintang. The Yangtze crossing proved that such distinctions no longer existed. The revolution had brought all to the same level.

The advance of the People's Liberation Army was unbelievably swift.

During the first week after the crossing, Communist troops captured an average of three cities per day. Within twenty-four hours, thirty thousand soldiers were at Wuhu, sixty miles southwest of Nanking. Within three days, they were at the walls of the capital of the republic.

The Kuomintang did not put up any fight for the capital of Chinese nationalism. As the Communists poured across the river, Chiang's officials and generals boarded American-made planes and flew in panic to Shanghai. A foreign diplomat who had come to say good-by noticed among the air-borne generals great piles of household furniture including one piano. With a whole world collapsing, the Kuomintang leaders, true to their nature, think only of saving their property.

When the officials sneaked away from Nanking, the city police took off their uniforms. Defenders of law and order, they had no desire to defend a dead regime. The common people emerged into the streets and began looting. So little affection did the crowds have for their departed rulers that they rushed to the house of President Li Tsung-jen and stripped it bare. In this they were aided by the departed president's housekeeper. Some American apologists for Chiang Kai-shek had often said he was a creative force in China because he had morally regenerated the people. Now, all the world could see just how deeply this regeneration had taken effect.

On April 24, the People's Liberation Army under the command of General Chen Yi and General Lin Po-cheng marched into Nanking. The Communist radio in a jubilant broadcast said: "This is the end of the reactionary rule of the Kuomintang. The government has passed out of existence."

Excited crowds gathered in the streets to see the army that had driven out their former rulers. While the crowds around them listened, the soldiers sang a number of anthems:

"We must think of the common man."

"Down with reactionaries."

"Mao Tze-tung is our savior."

Thousands of other soldiers moved hurriedly through the city without stopping and struck south and east in pursuit of Chiang's fleeing forces. General Chen Yi, conqueror of Nanking, ordered the publication of a seven point policy which promised to protect lives, property, churches and schools, but demanded the confiscation of the bureaucratic capital belonging to the "rebel [sic] Chiang Kai-shek & Co." and prohibited the hoarding of arms and ammunition. Foreigners, including diplomatic personnel, would be protected "unless they indulged in law violations or subversive activities."

The next day, at 6:45 o'clock in the morning, twelve soldiers invaded the United States embassy and entered the bedroom of the American ambassador, J. Leighton Stuart, who was lying in bed, half awake.

After rudely addressing the seventy-two-year-old diplomat, a fluent Chinese scholar and a lifelong resident of China, they pointed to articles in his room and said, "These will soon belong to the people." As they were leaving, they told a servant of the embassy that Stuart should not be allowed to leave the residence compound. These simple soldiers, armed creators of the revolution, were no respecters of persons. They were probably a portent of the shape of things to come in the Orient.

The fall of Nanking was of little military importance. Its political significance, however, was tremendous. For three decades, this metropolis of one million people on the banks of the Yangtze, 235 miles from the China Sea, had been the symbol of the Chinese republic. It was here, on January 1, 1912, that Sun Yat-sen took the oath as president of the republic. It was here, in 1929, that generalissimo Chiang Kai-shek had set up his capital and headquarters for the war against the Communists, then but a small guerrilla band isolated in South China. Now, these same guerrillas, enlarged into an army of nearly three million men had taken his capital and he had not been able even to attempt to defend it. Such was the tremendous turnabout that had occurred in Chinese politics.

From Nanking, the Communists wheeled on Shanghai, long the base of Western imperialism in the Far East. This city of six million people with its former foreign concessions which had stood inviolate during innumerable Chinese civil wars, was now protected only by a wooden fence and mud pillboxes. Behind these stage property defenses—built not for defense but for graft—fifteen thousand Americans, British and Europeans awaited the Communists with no thought of resisting. Twenty-two years earlier, the forerunners of these men had allowed the armed gangsters of Chiang Kai-shek to pass through the foreign concessions and slaughter factory workers in the native city who were adhering to the Communist cause. Now, no such easy solution of Chinese Communism was possible.

During the crossing of the Yangtze River, there occurred an incident which pointed up the significance of the whole China war in a fashion more revealing than a dozen political dissertations. The Yangtze, one of the world's great rivers, which has its source in Tibet and its mouth three thousand miles away in the China Sea, is navigable for its last thousand miles by ocean-going steamers. On this stretch of the river, foreign warships have been maneuvering for nearly a hundred years, with no Chinese government able or willing to keep them out. As the battle over this great waterway began, British naval authorities, with a sublime indifference to the new realities in China, ordered the sloop *Amethyst* to move out of Shanghai with supplies for British embassy officials in Nanking. This action was definitely, though perhaps not purposely, provocative. Later both Kuomintang and British authorities were to declare that the ship had a perfect right on the Yangtze because of treaties concluded with the Chiang government. But it was just these treaties which the Communists were fighting to destroy. As might have been expected, Communist soldiers in the midst of a battle with the Kuomintang fleet and Kuomintang soldiers on the opposite shore opened up with their American-made batteries on the *Amethyst*. She was severely damaged and ran aground fifty miles from Nanking. From that city another British warship, the destroyer *Consort*, headed downstream but was beaten off by Communist guns. Adding folly to arrogance, two other British warships moved upstream from Shanghai; they too were heavily shelled and turned tail and fled. In all, the British suffered forty-four seamen killed, eighty injured.

The significance of this event is tremendous. Thirty years earlier, the mere presence of the British warships on the Yangtze would have been enough to turn the tide of any civil war. Twenty years ago, such an incident would have sent every foreign warship on the China station scurrying up the river to silence the insolent Chinese; diplomats would have sternly demanded apologies; the foreign press would have thundered for revenge and editors would have written philosophic dissertations on the need for "law and order." But 1949 was not 1929.

The crossing of the Yangtze—like the crossing of so many other river barriers in history, from the Rubicon to the Rappahannock or the Rhine —may stand as a decisive date in world history.

It is likely to stand [remarked the New York *Herald Tribune*] as the day on which Chinese Communist gunners, learning how to use American equipment, brushed the Royal Navy contemptuously aside. It is likely to stand as the day when a bankrupt old regime in China was forced finally to confess itself impotent, and when the Western policies, founded upon hopes of its survival, were compelled to admit they could not save that regime and that new and different forces had assumed dominant power over the Chinese millions. It is proof certainly the old order is done, that neither the Chinese monied classes, British imperialism nor the American "open door doctrine" have sufficed to open a pathway through the tangled problems of the times which the Chinese people could follow.

This day is also likely to stand, the newspaper might have added, as the day which sounded the death knell of imperialism in Asia. The crossing of the Yangtze rang down the curtain on an era of history. It was an era that had opened one hundred years ago when the forces of reaction in Europe were crushing the Revolution of 1848 and beginning a ruthless expansion eastward into Asia. It was an era which saw Perry's opening of Japan, the Crimean War, the Indian mutiny, Russian czarist expansion to the Amur. It was an age which witnessed the Taiping and Moslem rebellions in China, the Meji Restoration in Japan and Civil War in the United States and the freeing of the Russian serfs. It was an age in which the British blew down the back doors of China, when the

French grabbed Indo-China and Hainan, the Japanese seized Korea and Formosa and even little Portugal sliced off Macao from China. It was an age during which imperialism forced opium on the Chinese people, set up foreign concessions in China's cities and ruled her by special and unequal treaties. It was an era which saw Western capitalism devour itself in two costly wars, the first resulting in the Russian Revolution and the rise of a rival Asiatic imperialism in Japan, the second bringing about the Chinese Revolution and crushing blows to all imperialism in the Far East.

The Yangtze River crossing ended these days forever. Gone was the era of gunboat diplomacy, gone the treaty port concessions, gone the specially conceded naval bases, the military missions, the ill-disguised interference in Chinese affairs. The China of the imperialists that had existed with only insignificant changes since the middle of the nineteenth century was going up in the smoke of a Communist-led revolution.

For better or for worse, a new day was dawning in China. The weather of this day was uncertain. Many storm clouds were on the horizon. But that a new day was coming up in an ancient land, of that there could be little doubt.

The Communists in crossing the Yangtze River had begun an adventure of terrible proportions, from which there could be no turning back. They had set out to conquer all of China and there could be no compromise. The risks of such an undertaking were enormous. In evolving from country-based guerrillas to aspirants for state power, the Communists were now face to face with the bared fangs of the Western powers. In crossing the Yangtze River, they were leaving the scene of their greatest triumphs where they had built up their strength by close association for thirteen years with the people of the North. There they had bases in the countryside, now they had none, but must create them. Behind them was the turbulent past, ahead of them the uncertain future.

The risks taken by the Communists were great. But the difficulties facing them were greater still. Before them lay a vast territory larger than Europe, of endless variety and almost limitless boundaries. Great cities, such as Hankow, Canton and Shanghai, with their foreign populations, their factory workers, their gangster problems and their international ties, posed terrible challenges to country-bred cadres. Two hundred million people speaking a score of different dialects remained to be won over. The way of conquest was a long and an arduous one. The terrain was far different from the flat lands of the North China Plain. Here, south of the Yangtze River, where the Communists were going, were the hills of Kiangsi whence they themselves had begun their famous six-thousand-mile Long March fifteen years before. Here were the paddy fields of the Canton delta, from which had sprung Sun Yat-sen and the Kuomintang revolution. Here, the far-off province of Yunan with its wild Lolo tribesmen, here the lush fields of the Red Basin in Szechuan, the desert of northwest China, the towering mountains of Tibet and the great and almost impenetrable Yangtze gorges and the winding three-thousand-mile barrier of the river itself. And beyond the soaring boundaries, beyond the Great Wall, to the north and west, lay the wary Soviet Union, and to the south Indo-China and the French, frightened for their empire, and to the east, Hongkong, an English fortress in a Chinese sea.

This final act in the Communist drive for power in China might be long and it might be difficult. But the outcome could scarcely be in doubt. The movement for social revolution had gained too much headway to be halted now. The Kuomintang armies might put up resistance here and there. The great landholders of South China, following the traditions of Tseng Kuo-fan and Tso Tsung-tang who put down the Taiping Rebellion, might raise a gentry-led guerrilla force. Chiang's secret service might plant centers of resistance in every corner. The United States might even funnel many more millions into the China rathole. But it would make little difference. There was little soul left in the Kuomintang any more. Indeed, the "oil was exhausted and the light was dying."

In the meantime, a mighty convulsion is shaking the land of Confucius. For four thousand years the Chinese people have been kowtowing before their ancestral tombs, seeking an answer to life in the past. But now, almost for the first time since Chinese medicine men and despots put their blight on the Chinese mind, the common people of Cathay are beginning to stand erect and seek an answer to their problems in the future. For better or for worse, the Chinese Communists have succeeded in awakening in millions of people a sense of personality. In the wake of this act has come an irresistible discharge of emotional energy that is sweeping the last barbarities of Oriental medievalism along with the more refined barbarities of Occidental imperialism remorselessly toward oblivion. Whether a new barbarism is rising remains for history to decide.

Only four things can possibly halt the onward march of the Chinese Revolution. The first of these is the rising of a new force in South and West China, utterly divorced from Chiang Kai-shek and the old leaders of the Kuomintang, with a land reform program of its own, and with a leadership just as revolutionary as the Communists'. The possibility of this happening is one in a hundred. The second way in which Chinese Communism might be halted would be by interference from the Soviet Union. The possibility of this happening is just as remote. The third possibility is an internal revolt in the revolutionary camp against the Communists. This, too, is unlikely. There remains a third World War. Cornered in South China, the retreating Nationalist armies might conceivably back into Indo-China and Burma and seek to obtain the aid of France and England and through them the United States. In this way, the old leaders of Chinese nationalism might attempt to set themselves up as a bulwark against Communism in southeast Asia.

This occurrence is a distinct possibility. But it is not a probability unless the United States tries to restore the old structure of imperialist empire in the Orient. That the Chinese Communists might become involved in any such event merely brings more sharply into focus the astounding fact that the tiny band of guerrillas who were once outlaws in the interior of China have now become major actors on the stage of world power.

Since there are peasants like the Chinese, more or less similar in every country in the Orient, from Japan to Indonesia, led by intellectuals with a Marxist ideology, these men have become a portent. Statesmen may fear them or wonder at them, and businessmen may try to serve them while philosophers shudder. But whatever one thinks about them or plans to do about them, they cannot be wished out of existence nor can their importance be denied. There they are, vibrant, vital and vigorous, marching across Asia with arms in hand, blood in their eyes and a song on their lips, a new force, a terrible force in an ancient world, a crumbling world.

PART XIV

CHINESE HORIZONS

❦

59. Power

THE movement led by the Chinese Communists has meant different things to different people. Orthodox Marxists have called it reformism. Trotskyists have called it Stalinism. Some American liberals have termed it grass-roots democracy. Chiang Kai-shek has called it a bandit rebellion. Chinese Communism has been all of these things, but it has also been much more. Since it has already resulted in one of the greatest social upheavals in world history, it must be called a revolution. It is true that this revolution exhibits certain basic differences from its Russian counterpart. It is being made in the name of "new democracy," not proletarian dictatorship. It advocates the overthrow of feudalism and the establishment of a mild form of capitalism, not socialism, though that is the eventual goal. Until recently it drew its main and most impassioned support from the farmers, not the city workers. In fact the whole civil war has been a war of the Communist-led countryside against the Kuomintang-led cities. Finally, all the other characteristics of the 1917 Revolution—a *coup d'état* at the top, state ownership of the means of production, nationalization of the land, soviets and even the Cheka—have *so far* been missing from China's Revolution.

These differences have led both critics and admirers to assume that the Chinese Communists are leading a mere reform movement. This would seem to be a fundamental error. Certainly any movement which overthrows property relationships, turns out the governing class, changes the tax system, assaults the cultural and religious patterns, arouses bloody passions among millions of people and produces a social convulsion of continental proportions can hardly be called anything but a revolution.

We shall perhaps need another twenty-five years to see this revolution in its true light. Nevertheless, we may at this moment try to ferret out its main purpose and its main result. The logic of the Chinese Revolution, like any other political event, is not to be found in any ideology, but in facts. The central fact of the Communist-led movement against Chiang Kai-shek is the creation of a new power, the self-styled representative of the people. This power, since it is only just changing over from a process of becoming to a process of being, cannot be analyzed in detail at this time. Yet we must examine something of its nature, for it is the relation between the new power and the existing society that will determine the attitude of China toward property, liberty, religion and even toward the United States, the Soviet Union and the rest of the world.

Perhaps we can obtain a better understanding of the power that the Communists have erected in China by taking a brief glance at the history of other political revolutions. Here we may draw with profit on the very important book, *On Power*, recently written by Bertrand de Jouvenel. Before the English, French and Russian revolutions, notes De Jouvenel, we see the rule of a Charles I, a Louis XVI, a Nicholas II. After the revolutionary storm subsided there was a Cromwell, a Napoleon, a Stalin. In other words, a weak power had been replaced by a strong power.

This indisputable sequence of events has caused De Jouvenel, as well as other observers, to believe that the business of a revolution is not to increase the spread of liberty, but to add to the weight of power. The revolutionary cycle begins with the downfall of an inadequate power only to close with the consolidation of a more absolute power.[1]

Chinese history would seem to confirm this thesis in many respects. As far as I know, China has had only two really great political and social revolutions. The first of these began about six hundred years before Christ, around the time of Confucius, and ended about four hundred years later with the destruction of Sinic feudalism and the formation of the first empire constructed on a system of bureaucratic control. This political system remained fundamentally unchanged until the middle of the nineteenth century when the West broke down the doors of the Manchu Empire and put in motion China's second great revolution. The dominant feature of this revolution, like that of its predecessor, has been a general tendency toward unification and the erection of a strong central power at

[1] Cf. Bertrand de Jouvenel, *On Power* (New York: The Viking Press, 1949), p. 216. De Jouvenel goes much further than this and says that revolutions are not reactions of the spirit of liberty to an oppressor and that no revolution ever overthrew a true despot, but only a weak ruler. It is hard to agree with this viewpoint in its entirety. Naturally, any ruler who is overthrown appears weak. But this is not necessarily an indication of a lack of tyranny—that is the arbitrary, unlawful and unjust use of power—but may indicate a decay of power. If a people never rise against a power that squeezes the life out of them, as De Jouvenel asserts, how explain the Formosa Revolt in 1946. If regimes overthrown by revolutions are not tyrannous, how explain the murder of civilians in Shanghai, 1949, the killings of the students and so on. De Jouvenel also says the function of revolutionaries is only to flout power and not to build or create. The Chinese Revolution of the last thirty-eight years supports this viewpoint, but it is too early to apply it to the Chinese Communists.

the expense of the old social authorities. That Chinese genius for authoritarian and centripetal unity which triumphed in the year 251 B.C. with the formation of the first empire, seems about to triumph again in the year A.D. 1949 with the Revolution. The heart of ancient China is therefore still living in the present.

The modern Chinese Revolution has had two constant policies: to overthrow feudalism and to free China from alien domination, whether it be the Manchus or Western imperialism. These two policies, however, would seem to be facets of one general process—the building of a stable and authoritative power. If we follow the course of Chinese history in China for the last hundred years, we note that the numerous wars and the continuing process of revolution have not resulted in the decrease of power, but in its increase. The alien Manchu rulers of China had so little real power that they were not only unable to oppose the encroachment of the West, unable to dominate the Chinese feudal gentry, but also unable to break into the walls of the clans which kept a tight control over marriage, local justice and many other affairs which are the functions of modern governments. With the fall of the Manchus before the 1911 Revolution, the warlords immediately began the re-creation of power on the basis of naked force. After a sixteen-year interregnum, Chiang Kai-shek and the Kuomintang absorbed or rendered harmless most of the provincial militarists and erected a state apparatus stronger than any that had yet appeared in China. But the Kuomintang Nationalists were never able to build a sovereign power because they never completely smashed the rural authorities, but compromised with them, never broke completely with Western imperialism, but depended on it. The inadequate nature of Kuomintang power is best characterized by the fact that in much of the countryside custom and folkways remained sovereign and large sections of the population continued to live under the despotism of the dead (ancestor worship). The Kuomintang bourgeoisie was never able to legitimize its reign; it could not create a parliament and hence it could not make the government the supreme authority in the land. In fact, state power remained so ineffective that during the twenty-year rule of the Kuomintang, Chiang Kai-shek could not eliminate banditry nor bring one year of peace to the country.

Because Chiang Kai-shek compromised and then allied himself with the remnants of medieval and imperialistic authority, he perpetuated the basic contradictions which have torn Chinese society asunder for the last hundred years and thereby he left the door open for the advance of a new power. Starting where Chiang Kai-shek left off, the Communists have now built a power of such dimensions that it is on the verge of destroying Asiatic feudalism and routing Western imperialism.

To sum up this cursory *tour d'horizon*, it is clear that the Chinese Revolution has resulted in the increase of power. The 1911 Revolution, beginning in the name of democracy, threw out the pusillanimous Manchu despots but immediately brought in the far stronger warlords. The 1927 Revolution, in the name of national unification, liquidated the generals and created the generalissimo. Now, the Revolution, under the banner of the "people" has cast down the Leader, Chiang Kai-shek, and raised up the Saving Star, Mao Tze-tung.[2]

Thus power has passed from the Emperor, to the Militarist, to the Caesar, to the Savior. And at every turn it has grown stronger.

I.

From where did this accretion of power come? Certainly not from any industrial or technological advances. Nor did it come from what a recent writer in *Life* calls "a Western type of discipline alien to Asia." To put it briefly and baldly, this power was the result of a great robbery. The Chinese Revolution stole its forces from the ancient social institutions and enlisted them in the service of power.

When the West broke down China's back door, it also broke up China's self-sufficient feudal economy and with it the force of the old authorities— the family, the landlords, the Buddhist Church, the Confucian bureaucracy and the ancient but strong Chinese traditions. With the walls of the old clan cells shattered, the released prisoners poured into the cities, the factories, the army into the service of power itself. The 1911 Revolution stepped up this process, Chiang Kai-shek carried it still further, and the Communists seem about to complete it. The destruction of the old social command posts is not yet total, but it has gone so far that the Communist party is well on the road to becoming the only real authority in China— social or political.

It is important that the logic of this process be understood, for it explains why Chiang Kai-shek fell and also why the Communists may be able to build the first stable society in China since feudalism was engulfed by the waves of Western capitalism. The only way for China to rid herself of feudalism and Western domination was to build a strong power, but the only way to build this power was to raid the feudal manors and organize the released prisoners. This is what the Communists did and what Chiang failed to do. That is why the generalissimo, though he hated the West, was never able to get rid of it and always relied on foreign guns. To put it in psychological terms, Chiang feared his own people more than he feared foreigners.

The Chiang Kai-shek regime was oppressive. Of that there can be little

[2] *Ling Hsiu*, or leader, was the term given Chiang Kai-shek by right-wing Kuomintang propagandists. *Chiu Hsing*, or Saving Star, was a propaganda term used in rural areas to refer to Mao. In a way, the terms illustrate a difference between the nature of Chiang's authority, which was a kind of semi-Caesarism founded on no real philosophic doctrine, and the authority of Mao which is based on an ethical content.

doubt. Whether Chiang himself was a tyrant is a matter of little concern. In any event his regime exercised power with a rigor not authorized by laws or justice. But this authority could not be wielded in all places at once with the same degree of effectiveness. Moreover, Chiang's despotism was modified by inefficiency. In a sense, he was pulled down, not because of his oppressive power, but because he could never make this power sovereign. He became the enemy of the people because his power was so flabby that he could not prevent intermediate authorities or his own organs of rule from grabbing wealth, levying taxes, committing atrocities, making heavier the ancient social yokes. In the final analysis, Chiang's power never became independent but remained based on a collapsing social hierarchy. When the Communists attacked the remnants of the old social pyramids, Chiang Kai-shek fell because the very foundations of his rule had been eaten away from under him.

The difference between the power formerly wielded by the Kuomintang and that now held by the Communists is one of both degree and kind. Power to many Kuomintang bureaucrats meant wallowing in riches, farming out taxes to the gentry, putting business undertakings in the hands of its supporters or bureaucrats. Power to the Communists has also meant ambition, but not wealth; and so far it has functioned primarily through the services it could perform. The Communists were victorious in China because they were able to win the people to their desires more effectively than the Kuomintang. Chiang Kai-shek remained aloof from the people and he could not inspire them to make great sacrifices. But the Communists were able to create an astonishing amount of force because they conceived the authority of the people to be their "muscle and bone." They looked on the masses as a kind of bank from which they could draw funds to meet their purposes. They nourished themselves on the people, but the Kuomintang found no soil on which it could feed and as a result its power withered and died.

The Communists pulled down the proud and raised up the humble. They freed women from man, the child from the father, the tenant from the landlord. They interfered in every form of private life and burst into a world from which Chiang Kai-shek had been excluded. And from this world they took out the cadres and the resources necessary to erect their power.

The Communists presented themselves as allies of those dominated by the landlords and also as allies of the native capitalists dominated by the bureaucrats and the "imperialists." Their appeal was philanthropic, altruistic, idealistic, even nationalistic, but at the same time there was always the tendency to increase their own power at the expense of the decaying feudal world. Thus the Chinese Revolution, contrary to Marxist Doctrine, has not dismembered state power; on the contrary, it has strengthened it by destroying the traditional institutions which obstructed its advance.

Whether this accretion of power will work for the benefit of Chinese humanity is not a question that readily admits of an answer. Power is essential to the ordering of human life; in itself it is not evil; it is only so when its gets out of control. Up to the present moment—without considering the future—it can be stated that the increase of Communist power has been a tremendous boon to the Chinese people. It has protected the masses from the excesses of society, it has brought order out of chaos and it has guaranteed a living to those who might otherwise have starved.

2.

To grasp another element of Communist power in China, it is necessary that we turn our eyes directly on the volcano of the Revolution itself. The most impressive spectacle in any revolutionary eruption is the sudden blaze of flaming passions. These explosions of overheated emotions have always given middle-class philosophers the shudders. But passion is a far truer guide to the discovery of the wellsprings of revolution than is thought. Any man behaves in the critical hours of his life as people behave in revolutions. In the heat of a revolution, a society reaches the height of its sincerity, clairvoyance into itself. Since man yearns to escape the calamities of his fate, it is only natural when his life conditions reach their lowest ebb that he summon passion to carry him where thought does not dare to go.

Passion gives an energy to a revolution which thought could never give. Passion equalizes men where thought differentiates them. It makes the king the equal of the commoner, the lord of the serf, man of woman. It confounds the aristocratic ethics of the philosopher, denounces the inculcated thought patterns of a ruling class and throws traditions off as so many chains. Passion creates a milieu in which a revolution can thrive because momentarily it makes every man the same.

Man's greatest passion is his intense desire to survive. In China when the collapse of the social order and the excesses of the ruling authorities put the people's backs against the wall, this yearning for survival expressed itself politically as a passion for equality. These egalitarian desires did not spring so much from the propagation of incendiary political principles as they sprang from the desperate need of the disinherited to share in the proceeds of production in order to remain alive. In times when men are dying for want of food, it becomes immoral for some to have more than others. Thus in China the pressing material need for equality often clothed itself in a religious feeling. Even the landlords and the gentry were stirred by the passion for equality because they soon began to feel that they were outside the moral order. What happened from a psychological standpoint was that the two poles of Chinese society originally driven apart by the upheaval of war were after a time inexorably driven toward each other. Distinctions of thought and habit, as well as property, were leveled by the fires of the revolution.

In his book, *On Power,* De Jouvenel notes that the passion for equality inevitably falls into a conspiracy with the passion for power because both have to advance at the expense of the existing social authorities. This is what has been happening in China for the last fifty years but with particular intensity during the last four years. The Chinese people brought so much emotion to the death of the old social order that they did away with many of the old institutions, customs and beliefs that have recently blocked the advance of power.

Because they severed many of the leading strings with which the old society hampered Chiang Kai-shek's control, the Communists have a much more absolute power than did the Kuomintang. The nature of this power is definitely egalitarian. There is no reason to believe that at this moment the Communists do not represent the people. They do not do this in the American sense by being chosen elected representatives, they do it by reflecting the passions of the people, the "popular will." Mao Tze-tung clearly recognized this when he told a foreign correspondent that Chinese Marxism was a "religion of the people."

Perhaps this source of Communist power can be better illustrated by specific examples. When I was talking with Gold Flower, the girl mentioned earlier in this book, she frequently wept when telling me of her life with her husband. At such moments, she would often say: "When I think of my past bitterness, I think of the Communist party which rescued me." Previously, in her life crises, a Chinese woman would dissolve into tears or commit suicide in the village pond. But now she cries out for equality, she cries out for a god of all womankind. This god very often is no other than the Communist party.

Peasants often told me: "The 8th Route Army is just like your own father and mother." The Communist party put it the other way around: "We are descendants of the people; the people are our ancestors." Nothing could illustrate the nature of Communist power more clearly than this. When you look on another force as your own father and mother, you are recognizing that force as the only authority in life. And you are going to fashion all your hopes, actions and ideas on the moral codes set up by this force which claims to represent the general will. A power like this of the Chinese Communists, which claims descent from the masses, therefore tends to become not only egalitarian, not only social, but also total.

3·

Communist power in China is not yet absolute in the way it is in Russia. The Chinese Revolution has not swept away all the checks and balances. It has not formed all the citizens into one class. Inequalities still exist and so therefore do checks on power. Social differentiations, however, are not so marked as in the United States, and from this standpoint the new power in China will not have to break down so many barriers as those facing state power in America.

Calling it "new democracy," the Chinese state is going to try and make all the castles of the feudal system its own. But so far it is not assaulting the nests of a still youthful capitalism. Landlords have been abolished, but private ownership of land has not. Bureaucratic holdings of the Chiang governors have been taken over but native industrialists and businessmen have been allowed to keep their property. It is noteworthy that the Communists are not trying to curry favor with the city workers by paying excessively high wages, and that in private factories they give the last word on production to management.

The very manner in which the Communists are taking power has tended to put a check on the passion for equality and hence the passion for totalitarianism. The Chinese Revolution is strikingly different from European revolutions in that it developed at a slower rate, over a wider territory and in a more diffused manner. Cromwell, Napoleon, and Lenin came to power as the result of sudden blows against a central authority in London, Paris and Petrograd. The Chinese Communists, however, are taking over control of the state not by any sudden *coup d'état* in a single concentrated area, but by a long slow process of development which has given their power a great deal of time to congeal and take counsel of itself, with the result that passions have had a chance to cool, that there has been less need for measures of oppression to insure political control, that there has so far been little need of an apparatus of terror.

There is another important result of this slow development of the Chinese Revolution. Because they did not initiate the Revolution but are deepening a movement begun by the Taiping Rebels and broadened by Dr. Sun Yat-sen, the Communists are entering the state command posts with some of the greatest social barriers to power already half destroyed by their predecessors. This means that they do not have to take on themselves the onus or the shame of destroying great institutions that still command a great deal of popular respect. For example, the greatest spiritual force in China—the Confucian tradition—had already been severely damaged by the the West long before the Communists appeared on the scene. The same applies to the Buddhist Church which has suffered a severe decline in the last fifty years, especially in North China and particularly during the Japanese war. The Christian Church, of course, does not occupy an important enough position in Chinese life to be the subject of either violent attack or defense except in limited localities. Thus, there exists an entirely different situation in China than exists in eastern Europe where the new Communist power finds itself forced to attack the Catholic Church which still wields a great deal of influence due to its ownership of land, control of the schools and great spiritual authority. In their battle for complete power in China, the Communists will not have to attack many intrenched lines of capitalism. What large private interests existed in China were long ago taken over by the Kuomintang bureaucrats and there does not remain much for the Communists to destroy. Native capitalist victims and capitalist opponents will be few. Foreign "imperialists," however, will probably be psychologically hounded, severely taxed, and either driven out of China or forced to kowtow to the "people."

Since the capitalist doctrine of free enterprise never took firm roots in China, not much ideological opposition can be expected on this score, either. Nor is there any strong middle class, save the peasant proprietors, to stay the hand of Communist power. All in all a strong social or spiritual opposition to Communist rule does not exist at the present moment. The obverse of this medal is that the Communists are not inheriting any great material accumulations on which to build a strong authority.

The Chinese Revolution has aimed much lower than many historic European revolutions. Though China's Reds relied to a great extent on the people's passion for equality, they never promised them complete equality as did the French Revolution. They have not promised to abolish classes as did the Russian Revolution. They have never held out the lure of a glittering Utopia to the Chinese people. When Lenin took Petrograd, he said: "Now we shall proceed to build a socialist society." When the Communists took the ancient capital of China in Peiping, they humbly stated: "We must learn."

With no tremendous goals promised, the Communists therefore can proceed to consolidate their power at a slower rate. Undoubtedly they are going to have to share the power in China for some time with other groups. The necessity for doing this was outlined a number of years ago by Mao Tze-tung in the following words:

Some people wonder if the Communists, once in power, will establish a dictatorship of the proletariat and a one-party system, as they have done in the Soviet Union. We can tell these people this: A new democracy of a union of democratic classes is different in principle from a socialist state with the dictatorship of the proletariat. China throughout the period of her new democratic system of government can not and should not have a system of government of the character of one-class dictatorship or one-party monoply of government. Russian history determined the Soviet form of society. In the same way, Chinese history will determine the Chinese system. An unique form—a new democratic state and regime of a union of the democratic classes—will be produced, which will be entirely necessary and rational to us and different from the Russian system.

Despite the democratic picture conjured up by these words, there is every reason to suppose that the Communists are going to strive toward monolithic rule in China. They intend to establish a coalition government, but all indications are that this government will reflect the domestic aims of Mao Tze-tung's "new democracy." This doctrine recognizes the need for class collaboration, but it is improbable that non-Communist groups will be able to express themselves too strongly in opposition to the fundamental Communist program—land reform and mild state capitalism internally and alliance with the Soviet Union externally.

The Communists have indicated that they are going to set up some sort of a representative assembly in order to make their power sovereign. By the time this book sees print such a body may already be in existence. Undoubtedly, it will be more representative of the general Chinese public than anything the Kuomintang had. However, any observer must naturally wonder whether sovereignty will be transformed to a new parliament or whether it will rest with the Communist mass organizations where it now is. Since there are so few organized institutions from the old society, such as banks, universities, church authorities, landlords, businessmen and so on, any parliament runs the risk of being a mere emanation of the revolutionary power instead of representing social forces. If China sets up a one-house parliament to "reflect the will of the people" without establishing another body to represent sectional and hence economic and social interests, the Communist control of the country will tend toward absolutism. The danger then will be that their power, resting merely on "the people," without checks from the courts or regional interests, may become a candidate for tyrannny. Whether the new China avoids this danger or not depends in part on what kind of a representative state institution is set up within the next year.

4.

The Communists took power by making love to the people of China. The rural proletarians and the rural women joined the revolution because they were given human sympathy and material aid. Communist success was founded on empirical psychology and not on any pretentious political philosophy. The Celestial Reds won the people to their cause not by any process of reasoning, but by arousing the hope, trust and affection of the people.

In this way the Communists built up a wholly new power apparatus established by and for the masses. There is every reason to believe that the Communists are sincere when they say they intend to use this power to represent the interests of the common people, but there is also reason to believe that this machine might elude their intentions and tend to exist for its own sake. In other words, there may arise a new elite, a set of managers standing above the Chinese masses.

Most revolutions are characterized by the coming of a leader who generally reduces his former equals to a subordinate position or liquidates them. We saw this a hundred and fifty years ago in France, twenty years ago in Russia, fifteen years ago in Germany and only yesterday in Chiang Kai-shek's China. We might see it tomorrow in Communist Cathay. But here again the slow tempo of the Chinese Revolution and the fact that the Communists are not coming to power by a *coup d'état* militates against the chances of this being carried to grotesque lengths.

However, there is a tendency for the victorious Communist sect to take on the character of a theocracy. Mao Tze-tung, as noted, is often referred to as the "saving star" of the people. Such a phrase has both a religious and an undemocratic ring to a Western ear. Anyone who has risen to be a constellation in the sky would seem to be already far out of reach of the earthly masses. But perhaps Chinese thinking is different than Western thinking in this respect.

Communist power is motivated by a social urge, but it also has an egoist nature. This egoism is definitely self-conscious. The party makes every effort to equate itself in the public mind with democracy and liberty. One of the most popular Communist songs—"In Praise of Mao Tze-tung"—accents this theme:

> Oh, you are the bright symbol and victorious flag,
> Long live our venerable Mao Tze-tung.
> We are fortunate to live in your era and learn your example.
> We will follow you and enter a new world.
> Which is full of liberty and welfare.

Taken by itself, there is nothing wrong in such self-love. A certain assurance of rightness, a belief in one's own virtue is necessary for rulers. The danger is that rulers who are not subject to democratic checks may expand their own private viewpoints into an arbitrary vision of what society should be. Confusing themselves with God, they force their dreams on others, blunder into grave political mistakes and finally plunge into outright tyranny. The Chinese Communists so far have been able to avoid this trap because they have been in extremely close touch with the common people and so have been able to acquire an accurate picture of public requirements. They have depended on experience rather than on logic. Thus, they have made many small errors but no irretrievable blunders. Their mistakes have never been solidified into a dogma. The party, up to now, has been, in fact as well as in theory, an agent of the general welfare. No power, such as theirs, which rose from absolutely nothing, could have conquered on any other basis.

Power that is becoming and power that is in being, however, are entirely different things. Now that they have conquered a large part of the country, the attitude of the Communists seems to be undergoing a change. When Chiang Kai-shek had the power, the limits on it could not be too great; now that they have the power, the limits on it cannot be too little.

Welfare of society is identified in the minds of the Communists with party welfare. Everything of any real account is to be done under the leadership of the party. Mao Tze-tung has continually published anathemas against intellectuals who still labor under the delusion that there is a "third road." He shows no indication of giving up power. If he did, he would cease to be the type of leader he is.

Communism was not the force that overthrew Chiang Kai-shek. Yet to Communist leaders, the party is almost everything. It is a weapon for revolutionary construction of society, including its morality. Only that conduct is good which is helpful in the struggle toward socialism. Mao, for example, in a pamphlet on literature, rejects the idea that literature should be founded on love for mankind. Only what is good for the revolution is good literature. This applies to everything.

Mao's doctrine: "Learn from the masses and then teach them" is a kind of perversion of Loyola's doctrine: "Follow the other man's course to your own goal." Thus, in the past, the Communists applauded liberals, cheered the students, shouted for freedom of speech and abolition of tyranny. Now, they still shout for these things, but freedom is to be given only to the "people" and not to "reactionaries." That a reactionary may be equated with anyone who opposes the dictatorship of the state is very much within the realm of possibility. The dangers are too self-evident to need dilating on here.

Ultimately the Communists may be corrupted by power as was the Kuomintang. Dependence on Marxist philosophy instead of concrete experience, on intelligence instead of touch, theory instead of practice, could conceivably lead the Reds into errors of far greater magnitude than those made by Chiang Kai-shek. The power of the Chinese Revolution was not built by a generalized philosophy but by scattered revolutionaries working on their own initiative and dealing with concrete situations. If China's Reds should forget this, if they now should try to form a picture of what all China needs, which is quite beyond the capacity of human intelligence, if they should rely on the general instead of the particular, they might become the worst despots and the crudest blunderers in Chinese history. However, Cathay's Marxists are practical men,[3] with a profound instinct for self-preservation. They have no intention of immolating themselves on the altar of any doctrine. To do so

[3] Where internal policy is concerned. They are somewhat mystical and arbitrary in regard to foreign policy.

they would probably have to get rid of their present leader, Mao Tze-tung, who a number of years ago remarked: "Dogma is more useless than cow dung."

5.

It is characteristic of a ruling authority that it cannot tolerate for long a power which does not spring from itself, just as it makes every effort to throw off checks on its own power. An indication of this is furnished by recent happenings right in our own country where the power of labor has been checked by the Taft-Hartley Law, where Marxist doctrine cannot be taught in many schools, where liberty is being suppressed under the name of security and where individuals are being made the playthings of different authorities struggling for political domination of the state.

The Chinese Communists have also given many indications that they are not very friendly toward a power which does not issue from themselves. It is true that they are one of the first revolutionary groups in history who tried deliberately to check their own power by limiting party representation in regional assemblies to one-third the total members. But there is something of a conjuror's trick in this policy, because the real and sovereign power in Communist areas did not lie with elected assemblies or with the government but in the machinery of the Revolution itself—the mass organizations. These organizations—youth, women and farmers' associations—all look independent but all came from the Communist party and all are reflections of its policy.

This does not mean that the mass organizations are puppets of the Communist party in the way this word is used in the United States. The revolutionary function that these mass organizations performed was to furnish a medium or an atmosphere in which a new power could take roots and grow. But such organizations would have been utterly impossible had they not met the needs of the people suffering under unbearable conditions. Thus, though it is correct to say that these organs reflect Communist policy, it is also just as correct to say that the Communists reflect the needs of these organs.

When I was in Communist territory there were four big power apparatus: the party, the army, the government and the National Salvation Association. This last organ ran the mass associations. The cadres had a saying: "The government has the right, but the Salvation Association has the power." From all I observed this was quite true and the Salvation Association might perhaps be called the chief organ of the Revolution.

It was this organ that conducted the land reform and led the peasants to establish Farmers Associations in every village. These peasant unions today are generally in the hands of men who took the most active part in struggling against the landlords. They form the base of the Communists' power pyramid. They definitely have a vested interest in the Communist party. However, since it was the 8th Route Army, and not the Communist party, that was the symbol in the villages of the struggle against Chiang Kai-shek, it is barely possible that if a schism should develop in the army that many peasants would follow the army and not party leaders. The symbol of Mao Tze-tung would be an important factor here.

When I was in the Liberated Areas, the Communist party, as such, did not operate on the village level. The lowest Communist cadres were to be found in the *Chu*, the governmental subdivision under the county or district. Here, there was a four-way system of power divided among four cadres—those of the party, the government, the self-defense unit and the Salvation Association. Each of these four cadres had his own chain of command reaching back up through the county to various regional set ups where the party, government, army and Salvation Association were in charge.

In such a setup, the Communist cadre was by no means always sovereign. The local party man could not dictate to the local militia chief for the simple reason that such a leader had the support of armed farmers. Nor could he always dominate the Salvation Association leader who had gained the support of various peasant associations through the land reform.

Frictions between party and government representatives were numerous and existed on nearly every level, as the Communists only too readily admitted to me. In extreme cases, these frictions, plus boredom, led cadres to desert to the Kuomintang side. But frictions between party and non-party organs never reached a serious stage. Party and government each tended to back their own cadres, but each was too wise to support a cadre who was clearly in the wrong.

The peasants were the decisive factor in the civil war. But it is doubtful if they will hold on to many strings of the central power. The intellectuals will be the bosses of the new China. This is not a prospect to be faced with complete equanimity. By tradition and training one who can read and write in China is a priviliged person, a sort of superior grade of being, with all that means in scholarly arrogance and adherence to dogma. Because the Chinese intelligentsia in the past obtained and retained their privileged position in society due to their ability to recite Confucian classics, it is very easy for many of them to fall under the spell of a new dogma. They may use Marxist philosophy, just as they used the old philosophy, as an intellectual mumbo jumbo to keep them from thinking and as a weapon to force their viewpoints on others.

Old-line Communists, who are mostly intellectuals themselves, and their allies who joined them during the Japanese war, avoided this trap to a marked extent because of their close association with the masses and because of the impingement of experience, sensation and events upon them. But the new and younger intellectuals who are rushing to join the Revolution often do not possess an equal amount of tolerance and intellectual curiosity. They are ridden by dogma; they are more "Marxist" than the Communists themselves; they are anti-foreign and chauvinistic on purely doctrinaire grounds; and, though they mouth words about the common people, they display a kind of patronizing superiority to the peasant and a curious lack of interest in the peasant's life. I do not mean to make sweeping generalizations about Chinese intellectuals and it must be admitted that the Chinese Revolution has had a great democratizing influence on Chinese men of letters in those cases where they were forced to struggle for their own existence. But the newest elements that are joining the Communist cause are somewhat different.

The Chinese Reds are not unaware of the dangers inherent in such a situation. They are warning their youthful adherents not to be "narrow minded," otherwise many progressive youths will be scared off and "solidarity with the masses" cannot be obtained. The party is making every effort to gain the support of Chinese youth as a bolster to their power. Failure to do so contributed to the defeat of the Kuomintang. The Communists are not making the same mistake. They have abandoned the Communist Youth Corps and organized a New Democracy Youth Corps. In this way, they hope to obtain a larger democratic base for their rule. This corps has already passed resolutions against "closed-door policy, youth-vanguardism and cliquishness."

The Communists intend to use this Youth Corps as a definite weapon to extend their control over China. It is quite clearly stated in various resolutions that the basic program of the corps is to study "Marxism-Leninism methodically." In addition, the Youth Corps is to lead other youths to join the army and to support agricultural and industrial production. Corps members must help government education officers in reforming school education and mass education for local communities. Besides participating in military, political, economic and cultural activities within China, they are also to participate in "international youth anti-imperialist and democratic peace movements." Thus they are to be a weapon of international Communist policy as well as internal policy.

Undoubtedly the Communists will have much success with the young men and women of China. Instead of trying to suppress or control the students, as did the Kuomintang, they are trying to direct their energies into channels which will serve their interests. The Communist appeal is idealistic and so far it has satisfied the desires of Chinese youth to be of service to society. The fresh enthusiasm with which the young are now greeting the Communists may die out within one or two years, but by that time, the Communists may have an effective apparatus.

In 1949, the center of gravity of the youth movement shifted from the countryside to the cities, the large factories and the most densely populated towns. This was in accord with Communist recognition that the success or failure of their revolution no longer depends on military victories but on what they can accomplish in the complex field of big-city management.

The Communists may have a tough time in the cities. But it should be remembered that they are earnest and determined revolutionists and that one of their chief virtues is that they can recognize a mistake when they see one. At a celebration given in Pieping, a Communist speaker admitted the inexperience of the Reds in big-city rule and then declaimed with passionate fervor, "We must learn, learn, learn."

This inordinate desire for knowledge plus humility about their own ignorance gives the Chinese Communists a good chance to succeed where many observers have predicted they will fail. When they took over Peiping and Tientsin, each a city of two million people, their political workers went from block to block, like canvassers in a public opinion poll, asking questions of all strata of the population. As in the villages, the cadres quizzed the people about their own grievances and also encouraged them to talk about their neighbors. In this way they gathered information about the problems they were up against and also some intelligence on the "enemies of the people."

Undoubtedly, enemies of great authority and experience await the Communists in the big cities. Shanghai, for example, has numerous secret societies. Many gangsters and underground agents of Chiang Kai-shek may try to sabotage Communist rule. More subtle enemies exist in the corrupting influence that the cities themselves may have on the Communists or their non-Communist allies. Already some of the country cadres have begun to backslide and succumb to the allurements of such entertaining places as Peiping and Tientsin. Much of this goes on behind the backs of the Communists, but when they discover such incidents the party press publicly scolds the errant members and warns them to beware of temptation.

The passionate preaching, public confessions of penitents, the Speak Frankness and Speak Bitterness Meetings have all been imported from the country to the city. But this sort of thing does not seem to be going down so well with the more sophisticated town folk. Reports are filtering out from Tientsin that the people are taking a tongue-in-cheek attitude toward the Communists' efforts to reform them. "The Communists' problem," says A. T. Steele, "is to defeat corruption before their own moral standards are undermined. They have made a good start, but it will be a battle against heavy odds rooted in centuries of tradition."[4]

---

[4] *New York Herald Tribune*, May 12, 1949. Copyright, 1949, New York Herald Tribune, Inc.

6.

Are the Chinese Communists who were strong enough to overthrow Chiang Kai-shek strong enough to create a lasting revolution in China? Are they strong enough to become the sole authority throughout the nation?

Many neutral observers do not believe so. Such men think that China's problems are so tremendous that the Communists will not be able to solve them any more than did Chiang Kai-shek. This bolsters them in the belief that the Chinese people will commit another revolution and throw out the Communists.

History, it is true, furnishes numerous examples of a revolutionary force seizing power and then falling almost immediately beneath the wheels of a counterrevolution. But the records of bloody civil upheavals also show that a group which smashes an old master class and assails every form of social authority usually manages to fasten a grip on the positions of state command that cannot easily be broken.

Communist power has an expansionist character and it tends to grow at the expense of all other authority. But this power cannot consolidate itself overnight; it must proceed by gradual steps or run the risk of being scuttled by its own excesses. In the immediate future the Communists are going to have to share some of the social authority and part of the state power with other groups. The factors that will hamper complete Communist control of China and make their power position uneasy for some time can be outlined as follows:

1. Chiang Kai-shek was not defeated in the name of Communism but in the name of independence, democracy and the people's livelihood. The Communists cannot now switch tactics and try to gain complete control of the revolutionary movement without seriously compromising themselves in the eyes of public opinion. The vast majority of those who joined the struggle against Chiang Kai-shek are not Communists and they are not yet completely controlled by the party. The party therefore must go slow.

2. For the first time in their twenty-year history. the Communists have to feed cities which were formerly fed by the Chiang government. Peasants in the Liberated Areas, therefore, will have to give up a larger share of their food than they gave to the Communists before. Since the cities will not be able to recompense the peasants with adequate industrial goods, the benefits of the land reform might prove illusory and the peasants might become discontented. The Communist desire to industrialize the country could accentuate this trend.

3. The insignificant weight of the Chinese cities in the over-all economy of the country leaves China's Reds with a much narrower base of proletarian support than that available to Communist parties

in Europe. The Communists have promised the city workers no great wage increases and they will have to depend on winning proletarian support by ideological methods, pep talks and the elimination of social instead of economic dissatisfaction.

4. Because there are so few city workers the Communists must curry favor with classes that are not traditionally oriented toward Marxism. The political weight of the "middle bourgeoisie" in China, however, is also insignificant, and it is doubtful if it would prove a good conductor to lead Chiang Kai-shek or the Kuomintang back to power. However, the weakness of the city proletariat does give other elements freedom to maneuver.

5. The great extent of China, poor communications and ingrained territorial feelings will force the Communists to make local deals and compromise with regional authorities. Centralized control will be difficult and slow. The conquest of Mohammedan war bands such as those in Inner Mongolia and the Northwest and the consolidation of outlying territories will require many years and cannot be achieved by military means alone. The Communists cannot possibly hold down the amorphous continent of China with their armies, but will have to rely on political and social factors to build a stable society. Thus, it becomes absolutely necessary for them to form an alliance with other groups in order to achieve their ends. Again this means some freedom of maneuver for non-Marxists.

6. The People's Liberation Army is not completely controlled by the Communist party. From 1927 to 1937, this army was known as the Red Army and was politically homogenous. During the next ten years, in the war against Japan, this army became saturated with patriotic elements and its class character was adulterated. In the renewed civil war, the army again changed until now it is filled with thousands of Chiang Kai-shek's former soldiers. The army is thus more representative of the nation but at the same time it poses a problem of control to the Communist party, as such. There have been cases where Kuomintang officers surrendered to the People's Army and then went back to the other side again. Twenty years ago the original Chinese Red Army was formed when a group of officers revolted after Chiang Kai-shek's *coup d'etat*. Though slight, the possibility exists that the same thing could happen again, but this time in reverse. Therefore, the Communists cannot push one party rule too hard or too openly at this time. So, for the moment, the Communists will probably adhere to their idea of coalition government.

7. The continued existence of traditional enemies plus enemies raised by the war and revolution may lead to plotted assassinations, local revolts, gang intrigues and sabotage. The strong desire of the Chinese people for peace and security, however, will probably prevent such movements from gaining headway.

8. The Kuomintang air force and navy can still blockade the coast of China and keep Western ships out of Communist ports. In the long run both the navy and the air force will probably lose all their continental bases and retire to the island of Formosa and possibly Hainan as did the last of the Mings. In the immediate future, however, the blockade of China's coast might lead to international complications and might delay foreign recognition.

9. The lack of trained personnel will hamper Communist development of the country but will not seriously affect the question of power, as the Communists can use the same technicians that the Kuomintang employed.

10. The position of China as a political football between the United States and the Soviet Union places the Communists in an embarrassing position with the rest of the country. Pressure from outside China might force them to adopt unpopular policies inside China. However, the new Chinese government, in the event of continued difficulties with America, can probably obtain aid and encouragement from Great Britain and Australia. Past American intervention in China's affairs can also be used as a whip for internal unity.

11. Chinese economy is so shattered that popular discontent must in some measure redound to the discredit of any new power that seeks to run China. The Revolution that once seemed to open up every possibility for the satisfaction of long-held dreams might then be seen in a different light. This could affect Communist power which has heretofore depended so much on its ability to act for the common good. However, since the Revolution was not made in the name of Communism, the party could shift the blame elsewhere.

12. Finally, the Communists who depended on the libertarian sentiments of the people for so much of their success, now show definite signs of subordinating the individual right to the social right and on this ground they might arouse opposition.

Such, in a general way, are some of the factors that endanger Communist control of China. But does this mean that the Chinese people will soon make another revolution against China's Reds? Not necessarily.

Apart from its wishful thinking, the idea that there will be another revolution in China seems to derive its main force from the belief that the Communists will not be able to solve China's economic problems and therefore will create a mass misery that will lead to a new mass revolt. But revolutions, contrary to common conception, do not take place solely because of economic chaos. To be sure, endangered living conditions play a large part in bringing about revolutions, but in themselves they are not sufficient to cause the overthrow of a social regime. If they were, impoverished masses would always be in revolt. In China, it was only when a sufficient number of people came clearly to realize that the Kuomintang regime could not get them out of their blind alley that economic suffering became intolerable and then the program of the Chinese Communists offered them a way of escape and a hope for a new life. But there does not exist today, either in China or abroad, any group with any program that offers the Chinese people an escape from their historic dilemma as did the Communists. Certainly American interventionists, whose only program is to "wipe out the Communists" and allow American military men and American economists to take charge of the country, are not looked upon by the Chinese people as a hopeful alternative. Moreover, it is interesting to note that many people joined the Communists and deliberately endured greater privations than any they had known before. These people did not revolt for the simple reason that they believed their sufferings were temporary but because they were willing to undergo great hardships in order to achieve what they considered a sacred goal.

There are other reasons for believing no new revolution will take place in China within any foreseeable future. In the first place, few people ever make a great revolution twice within one generation. The Chinese people have been so exhausted by war, their hopes, their energies, their very lives have been so spent that it would seem physically and psychologically almost impossible for them to raise another revolution against the one already made. In the second place, the Communists through their land-reform program have wiped out the main basis for revolution—at least north of the Yangtze River, and there seems no possibility of any other Chinese group taking leadership of this kind of program south of the river. Thirdly, the idea that the Communists who rose to power by the weapon of guerrilla warfare can also be overthrown by guerrilla warfare would seem to be unsound. Partisan war was possible in China only because of rural bankruptcy brought about by the over-all effects of Western, and later Japanese capitalist penetration of China. With the elimination of the basic causes of rural collapse, there may be local peasant revolts but there will not be any widespread people's war. To generate a people's war, it is necessary that there be burning personal reasons for such a war and adequate, courageous leadership. Such do not exist any more in the camp opposed to the Communists. The only conditions under which a widespread counter-guerrilla movement could take place in China would be a counter land-reform program in a well-protected part of the country or a brutal land collectivization by the Communists which would arouse peasant opposition. It is improbable that such conditions will arise in China in any near future. They might arise, however, later on, depending on how well the Communists are able to solve China's economic problems.

7.

The Chinese Communists cannot build a stable society in China by power alone. No society coheres unless there is mutual confidence between men. There must be a community feeling, a generally acknowledged ethic and accepted codes of right conduct. Otherwise the social order disintegrates into a medley of disharmonious behaviors.[5]

China maintained a stable society for two thousand years, not because there was a strong power on the throne at Peking—which there was not —but because she evolved a practical set of rules and a moral way of life that was admirably suited to her particular needs. Community of belief was the most powerful factor in social cohesion. Customs, folkways, the Confucian ethic, ancestor worship, filial piety—in short, a general adherence to an accepted way of life—were what held the country and the people together. It mattered not that China was invaded time and again or that one dynasty was overthrown by another; China never met a superior culture and her folkways remained sovereign and kept order.

When the West with its higher culture broke down the economic patterns of Chinese society, the old folkways, the traditions and the Confucian way of life lost their sovereignty because the codes of conduct which had been made for a patriarchal and an autarchic peasant society no longer applied to the precapitalist mode of life that was introduced into the country. Men were uprooted and, being thrust into new conditions, did not know how to act any more.

Under these circumstances, it became the duty of the creators of a new society to formulate rules that could reharmonize men's behaviors. No one was able to do this. When the Manchus fell before the 1911 Revolution, the warlords tried to bring back order to China by force alone. Their failure was colossal and only resulted in increased disunity and more misery. Dr. Sun Yat-sen and the Kuomintang then sought to glue China together with the Western doctrines of nationalism, democracy and economic welfare. These doctrines proved a poor substitute for the old beliefs because they were not cast in any moral framework and because they were general precepts and not practical codes of action.

Moreover, since these doctrines had been borrowed from the West of the nineteenth and early twentieth century, they were bound up with the capitalist ethic of free enterprise. This ethic proved an admirable moral cement in the young continent of America because the native population could be wiped out and all the immigrants could become early starters in the race for wealth, everyone could become an individual proprietor and, in a sense, an individual capitalist. But in an ancient country like China, where the population was several hundred million and where a graded society already existed, only those with some pre-existing form of authority, prestige or education could make advantageous use of such an ethic which fell with a heavy hand on the lower echelons of the body social. Later, when the top members of the Kuomintang began to monopolize the youthful capitalist enterprises for their personal profit, the free-enterprise

[5] For an extremely intelligent discussion of this idea see Bertrand de Jouvenel's *On Power*, pp. 356-381.

philosophy proved utterly incapable of creating a community feeling among the Chinese people because it resulted in the tremendous increase of the disinherited mass at the bottom, and the elevation of an arrogant plutocracy to the top. Free enterprise seemed immoral because it became a chartered libertinism for the strong and because it resulted in general insecurity and the decrease of liberty. The corruption of the bureaucratic capitalist wing of the Kuomintang ruptured the social contract, and irregularity spread from the top of society to the bottom. With no common interests to defend, the community of sentiments was lost and China became ever more spiritually divided.

The feudal wing of the Kuomintang then tried to halt the cleavage by advocating a return to the ancient folkways, by a reinstitution of the Confucian ethic, by adherence to ancient tradition. But how could a peasant flung into a factory, a squire turned into a big city speculator, a landlord become factory owner apply the old practical rules to this new situation? They could not. And the social disharmony spread ever wider.

Chiang Kai-shek then sought a remedy in pure power. The code of right conduct became obedience to the state. At every turn Chiang emphasized the word "loyalty." His soldiers' undershirts were stamped with the character for loyalty. His army officers rose and fell on the basis of their loyalty. His ministers were hired and fired on the degree of their loyalty. Citizens were adjured to be loyal to their ancestors, to the state, to the Chinese way of life.

But loyalty is not a doctrine that can by itself produce a community feeling in society. When a state emphasizes loyalty above everything else, it is already far gone on the road to dissolution. For it then becomes apparent to the citizens that their rulers have little to offer them but obedience to power.

To secure loyalty, Chiang had to increase the methods of coercion. He multiplied the rules all the time. And as the rules multiplied, he had to multiply the men who would enforce them. He passed antisubversive laws, he put thought police in the schools, he created special tribunals, he increased the numbers of the state police, the party police, the secret service. To no avail. For all the rules he made to hold China together were founded on a conception of society that was false and deadly, all of them were distinctly antisocial and all of them resulted only in increased chaos and divided society into discordant behaviors.

Chiang Kai-shek fell because his regime lost the magic virtue,[6] because it offended the moral law, because it was not able to evolve a rule of life

---

[6] It must be admitted that Chiang understood the sources of his power far better than many of his followers and much better than did his American advisers. Quite rightly, he emphasized the "magic virtue," which is the traditional source of power in China. The trouble was that even if Chiang himself was virtuous, his regime was not.

which his people could follow. On the ruins of Kuomintang virtue, the Communists rose.

Whether the Communists can now accomplish what no one else has been able to accomplish in the last hundred years, whether they can make Chinese society cohere once more, must depend in the final analysis, not on how much help they get from Russia or don't get from the United States, but on how well they can develop a community feeling among the Chinese people. They have already done this to an astonishing extent with the cadres of the Revolution, but it is now necessary that they extend this sense of brotherhood to include the whole population. They must restore confidence to human relations in China or they will fail.

8.

Many people have noted the religious aspect of the Marxist doctrine, and it cannot be denied that the appeal of Chinese Communism definitely borders also on the religious. I cannot handle this subject here in any detail, for it is entirely too complicated, involving as it does various elements of Confucianism, Buddhism, Christianity, ancestor worship, the Oedipus complex, witchcraft, animism, magic and any number of different beliefs and folkways. So I will confine myself to a few general remarks about the ethical content of Chinese Communism and its relation to power.

Every religion, in one way or another, centers around the idea of birth or rebirth. In times of troubles, when prophets spring up, people have a great desire to start life all over again, to wash away both the sins and the sorrows of the past. This idea of rebirth is a strong motive force behind the Communist drive in China. It has nothing in common with Chiang Kai-shek's New Life Movement which concerned itself with external things like keeping one's clothes buttoned or not spitting on the streets. It goes much deeper than that and touches some of the inner chords of men.

The biggest slogan of the Chinese Communists has been *Fan Shen*— literally, "to turn over the body," but sometimes translated as "standing on your own feet." When applied to politics *Fan Shen* means to overturn the landlord system, overturn feudalism, overturn dictatorship. But *Fan Shen* is more than this. It is a distinct and conscious effort to give the Chinese a moral ethic. When applied to the individual, it means to overturn your thoughts, overturn your way of life, overturn your conscience. The philosophy behind such an ethic is of course the philosophy of reform, but it goes even deeper than that for it embraces the idea of rebirth also.

A landlord must overturn his thoughts, not only so he won't rob his tenant of the fruits of his labor, but so that he himself can cease to be a landlord and be born again as an entirely different man. A husband must cease to beat his wife not only for his wife's sake, but so that he may become a new person. A "broken shoe," or a prostitute, must reform so that she can become a young girl again, one capable of finding a husband or a useful place in society.

Another aspect of *Fan Shen* lies in the longing that everyone has to recapture his youth. In times of political and social reawakening, a whole race may be afflicted with the desire to rediscover its childhood. At such periods, forgotten folkways, dances, songs and traditions froth to the surface again. So it has been that the Chinese people have taken the revived *Yangko* songs and dances to their hearts and gone swinging in chanting conga lines down the streets of all the villages and cities in North and Central China. The Communists in this way have satisfied popular yearnings to dance, to laugh, to be carefree once again.

Because group songs and group dances are an expression of a collective spirit as opposed to an individualistic spirit, they always furnish a revolutionary power which bases itself on the "people"—a ready field for propaganda. Singing and dancing have definitely been weapons in building up Communist power and also in creating a fraternal feeling among the masses. Since they reveal the class nature of the Communist appeal, we will quote the words of a few songs here:

Reactionaries who exploit the people deserve to be cut into thousands of
    pieces;
They totally ignore the afflictions of the common people and want only to be
    dictators.
Big landlords, big warlords, big compradors, big families—all conspire
    together, all conspire together.
And, therefore, we poor people suffer.

Another *Yang Ko* song goes:

Papa and Mama are poor and cannot send me to school.
Others read and write while I am illiterate.
We want to learn to read books; want existence; we want freedom.
Let's all go to school together; let's all go to school together.
Collective studying assures better results.

Closely allied with the idea of rebirth is the idea of salvation. The appeal here is on several different planes. One is: "You are doomed; but there is a way out." This is the revolutionary appeal, the redemption of all mankind through the class struggle. The words "class struggle," however, were seldom used by the Chinese Communists in their dealings with the people. The appeal was much more basic and simple than that. It was a case of telling the people: "You are starving, save yourself, band together, join us."

Salvation was also to be achieved by "self-purification." The "broken shoe" was to purify herself of lustful emotions, the intellectual to purge himself of snobbish thoughts, the landlord to cast greed out of his heart, the peasant to rid himself of slothfulness, the cadre to purify himself night and day of the "dogmatic way of handling affairs."

The road to salvation was not easy, but there was a guide—the People's Army and the Communist party. This thought is well expressed by the title of a song, "You Are My Lighthouse." The party thus inculcated the idea that it was the shepherd of the people.

To the evil members of society, the Communists promised salvation through repentance. Husbands should repent for their treatment of their wives, landlords for their bad treatment of tenants, the Kuomintang for the treatment of the people and even the "imperialists" for their treatment of China.

Repentance does not seem to be an idea original with the Communists, for it was also used by the Kuomintang. Obviously, in a semiprimitive country like China, where the means of coercion available to the state are limited, conformity and co-operation can only be achieved by a certain amount of social pressure. Repentance was a method of impressing on people that certain types of conduct were wrong under the new order. Thus, offenders against the social order were to bow their heads, kowtow on the ground and admit all their sins. In this way, the Communists obviously hoped to set up invisible directors inside each man to guide his actions in the new way of life.

Public confession was another way in which the Communists sought conformity. But here again the methods were more Chinese than they were Marxist. People in the West confess their sins in private to the priest or sometimes directly to God. But in China, since the people themselves have been enthroned as God, confessions were made in public.

Thus, Speak Frankness Meetings became forums where individuals confessed their sins against the body social. I shall have occasion later to remark on the threat to liberty contained in such confessions, but here I wish to point out that when a usurer got down on his knees before the assembled village and confessed that he had grown fat on the flesh of others, when a husband confessed that he had treated his wife wrongly, when a village bully confessed that he had coerced women into fornication and when a man confessed that he had stolen melons from his neighbor's field, it was driven home to people that a new morality was coming into being. Once this feeling took possession of the public there was an irresistible drive toward new codes. To profit from others became an offense against natural law. So strongly did this affect many villages that not only did landlords disappear but with them thieves also. And you could find in Communist areas whole villages which did not lock their doors at night.

The reverse of the Speak Frankness Meetings, of course, were the Speak Bitterness Meetings, where people confessed, not their sins, but their sorrows. This had the effect of creating emotional solidarity. For when people poured out their sorrows to each other, they realized they were all together on the same sad voyage through life and from recognition of this they drew closer to one another, achieved common sentiments, took sustenance and hope.

Struggle Meetings were also definite weapons in molding public opinion and regulating morals. Tenants struggled against landlords, wives against husbands, farmers against thieves, the individual against the bad demon inside him. The central idea behind many such meetings was public humiliation.

In any backward society, where law has not become sovereign, it is custom that is sacred. Once custom is upset, people can no longer tell how their associates will act and confidence in society is lost. Under such circumstances, the common way of preserving community feeling is to publicly shame an offender against tradition. Thus, Eskimos punish a violator of the public order by tormenting him with "teases" who dance around him chanting songs of derision. The village assemblies in Communist China resorted to similar methods. Rich peasants who tried to seduce tenants or land-reform cadres with the bodies of their wives were paraded through the streets of towns with dunce caps on their heads. This kind of punishment is no longer effective in the West and is used only against children. But in rural China, public humiliation and teasing were useful in building up an ethic and restoring unity to society. Struggle meetings also contained threats to liberty.

The Chinese Communists are setting out not only to reform Chinese society, but Chinese man. Like Diogenes, they wander around with their probing lamps, uncovering social injustices, rescuing the afflicted and punishing (or saving the soul of) the wrongdoer. They are definitely trying to make each Chinese a good and virtuous man. This, of course, is all very dangerous. But it is effective and it is also pleasing to many more people than you would think.

There is a sense of brotherhood among the people, especially the youth, in Communist areas that you will not notice in Kuomintang China where everyone is engaged in a bitter wrangle over money problems. In the villages, the meetings of the Women's Associations and the Farmers Associations give peasants a chance to settle problems in common and hence to achieve a community feeling they did not have before. The same thing is now going on in city factories where workers for the first time have a chance to discuss mutual problems among themselves and also with management. A moral conversion is taking place among the intellectuals, much of it sincere and much of it undoubtedly merely the suppression of convictions because there is no chance to use them. As for the rest of the population, many of them are bored with the continuous moralizing and depressed by the ceaseless barrage of propaganda.

In general, it may be said that the Communists are trying to unify China by the enthronement of the social right over the individual right. If you want to express your individuality, you do not belong. You must indulge in self-examination. You must come to the group and be criticized. You must acknowledge your errors. You must work for society, not yourself.

The Communists have not stopped with the propagation of general precepts which very few people could apply to particular situations. They have laid down detailed and meticulous rules[7] to guide men in their behavior toward one another. Since these rules are not based solely on loyalty to the state, but on social service, they have created harmony where Chiang Kai-shek's rules only brought on chaos.

To conclude this hasty analysis of the ethical content of Communist power, it is clear that the Communist party has become the only real moral force in China today, because the other authorities in the country —the landlords, the gentry, the scholars, the generals, the financiers, the government bureaucrats—even where they were personally upright and honest men, indulged in activities that destroyed social harmony.

The rulers of twentieth century China did not have any universally acknowledged spiritual authorities that could help them reshape new codes of moral conduct. China has had no universally worshiped supreme god she could call upon to reassert the eternal verities or evolve new ones. The basic codes of life, ancestor worship and filial piety proved poor guides under conditions of modern life. China's famous doctrine of "virtue," to which emperors and notables all had to subscribe, also lost its force because the social authorities in order to resist the pressures of imperialism pushed all the economic burdens back on the weakest members of society. Nobles and clan leaders who had formerly taken responsibility for those under them began to take responsibility only for the increase or preservation of their own wealth. Since it is in the nature of men to doubt moral concepts because of doubts they have about social and spiritual authorities, the rule of virtue also lost its sovereignty over men's minds.

Higher religions have also not been able to offer any practical rules of morality to the common Chinese people. Buddhism, which entered

[7] For example, at one time, soldiers of the New Fourth Army were given these ten points of conduct to follow. 1. When you leave a civilian's house put the doors (which have been used for beds) back in the right place. Put things in order and bind the straw into a bundle and return it to the owner. 2. Sweep the floor. 3. Speak kindly, don't shout. 4. Pay the normal price for goods; don't haggle. 5. Return what you borrow. 6. Pay for what you break. 7. When you relieve yourself, use the toilet. 8. When bathing, don't let women see you. 9. Inside or outside, engage in propaganda work. 10. Don't kill captives.

China from India and then conquered as a proletarian religion, long ago lost most of its spiritual force.

Christianity, which came late to China, was in even worse case. The Christian doctrine had a great chance to conquer China when it became the spark that ignited the proletarian Taiping rebels in the middle of the nineteenth century. But after Western adventurers joined the Chinese nobility and the alien Manchus in suppressing the Taipings, Christianity gradually lost its proletarian character. Later, it became the ethic of China's compradors, the doctrine of men like T. V. Soong, H. H. Kung and Chiang Kai-shek. Under these circumstances, Christianity could not become a religion of the people.

Gods cannot keep their thrones unless they serve the human cause. In times of overwhelming sorrow, of revolutionary upheavals, of war and pestilence, prophets may revive a dying god by bringing him down from heaven to thunder against injustice, to rescue the miserable, to strike down the oppressors of the poor. In this way, they make God a champion of the lowly and give assurance that good will ultimately prevail. But there were no prophets in China except the Communists.

With their own gods long ago beaten into the dust and with the God of the foreigner no longer responding to their needs or their hopes, it is not strange that the disinherited masses of China turned toward Communism, a doctrine opposed to imperialism which had brought ruin to China, and to Christianity which had failed to bring them social justice or spiritual succor.

Thus, for the moment, the Communists find themselves the temporal and the spiritual rulers of China. For hopes hung in heaven, they have substituted hopes fastened to the earth. Faith in God they are seeking to replace with devotion to human ideals. Popular sovereignty has become the idol of the day, socialism the heaven of the future.

60. Property

"THE theory of the Communist," says the *Communist Manifesto*, "may be summed up in one sentence: the abolition of private property." This is the kernel of the Russian practice (in the Soviet Union) as well as theory. But it finds no place among the Communists of China.

Regulations of the Chinese Communist agrarian law, which was not drawn up until September 1947 and then only on the basis of actual experience, specifically state that:

1. Land shall be equally distributed, irrespective of young or old, landlord or tenant, Kuomintang or Communist.

2. The property distributed to each person shall be his personal property and may be freely managed, bought or sold and, under special conditions, rented.

There is a wide gulf between the old Bolshevik attacks on private property and the policy of the Chinese Communists. The Russians left no choice to the individual. He gave up his land or was cast out. But the Chinese Communists, like their Yugoslav counterparts today, do not seek the outright abolition of private property. Although in their minds, they think this villain is the root of all evil, they would not slay him—not now at any rate. They would compromise with him, humor him. They have no anathemas against the holding of land. In fact, just the opposite is the case. Take the land and get rich is the present idea.

The Communists make concessions to private property in their agrarian law, but no concessions are made to the landlord. Regulations specifically state that all landlords are abolished. There is no appeal from this judgment. The landlord either submits or he is done in. He is deprived of all social attributes and the political power he formerly enjoyed. The Communists think that by eliminating the landlords they have ended the most cruel forms of feudal exploitation. Against this, all their wrath is directed. There are no tirades against capitalism.

Here again they differ from original Marxist theory which says: "The middle class owner of property must be swept out of the way." This originally applied not only to the means of production but also embraced the means of distribution.

Such theories were also held with almost dogmatic faith by Chinese Communists back in the late 1920's and early 1930's. An attempt to put them in practice in some measure led to the defeat of Chinese Marxism twenty years ago. These theories at present have gone by the board. Mao Tze-tung has waged a constant battle to uproot them from the thoughts of Communist cadres, both old and new. The middle-class owner of property is deliberately coddled and given concessions. Provisions of the Chinese land reform specifically guarantee that commercial and business enterprises be given a preferred place. So strong is this feeling among the top party group that for a time it insisted on lightening the tax burden on business and trading ventures.[1] Few eco-

---

[1] How long this attitude will last is problematical. The Communists give some indications of wishing to drive Western interests out of China by means of heavy taxes. Thus, the Shanghai-American School has been taxed U. S. $76,000 and is about to close. The Anglican Holy Trinity Cathedral has been presented with a land-tax bill for $56,000. When presented with this bill, the dean of the cathedral remarked: "There must be some mistake." It is doubtful if there is any mistake. The Communists seem determined to get rid of "imperialist" influences.

nomic strictures have been placed on private property. Just the opposite. The private businessman, the coal-mine owner, the match-factory operator, at least during the period of the civil war, have all been regarded as children of fortune.

Certainly it has not been any belief in the sacredness of private property that has moved the Communists to adopt such a mild program. They do not see man fully emancipated under their present policy. Poverty will not vanish from the earth. Economic inequality will not be gone. What has made them come to terms with the devil of private property are the objective conditions of Chinese society and their own twenty years' experience with the land reform. Both of these things have taught the Chinese Communists the wisdom of going slow. They do not care whether they are called bandits or reformers. They see everything in the light of the present task.

Chinese Communism, in its political form, is a technique for getting, holding and extending state power. To Mao Tze-tung, the central problem of the war against Chiang Kai-shek was to win the support of the masses and alienate as few people as possible.

Mao thought this support could best be gained by an equal division of the land. Such a program, he thought, would alienate only 8 to 10 per cent of the population, comprising the landlords and rich peasants, who held 70 to 80 per cent of the land. Therefore, he believed the number of people who would participate in the land reform and the united front would compose 90 per cent of the people.

Personally, I think Mao's figures are much too high, but they are the ones he has given and the ones on which he stated to his party that he was basing his tactics.

Mao advocated two general principles: rely on the poor peasants and unite with the middle peasants. Realizing that his most ardent supporters would come from the tenants, he wished to make the poor peasant leagues the legal organs for dividing the land. Yet he saw the middle peasants as the decisive factor. Concessions must be made to them, he warned. If they did not agree to an equal land division, they must be permitted to retain more land than the average peasant.

In this respect, Mao often had to put a brake on the poor farmers and some of his zealous cadres who got quite out of hand in conducting the reform.

"In many places," Mao noted in April 1948, "many laboring people who did not engage in feudal exploitation were placed in landlord or rich peasant categories. Thus the area of attack was erroneously expanded and forgotten was the extremely important strategic principle that it is possible and necessary to unite around 92 per cent of the rural households and establish a united front against the feudal system."

Not only did Mao have to prevent his lower cadres from alienating the middle peasants, but he had to wage a war against many thugs who had crept into the party and thought that abolishing feudalism meant killing of the landlords.

"Our object," said Mao, "is to eliminate the feudal system of exploitation and to eliminate the landlords as a class but not to eliminate the person of the landlord."

This warning was needed. Many cadres did not interfere with peasant violance because they wanted to follow the slogan: "Do things the way the masses want." Other cadres did not interfere with killings because they thought they were just. Still others used to confide to me that such violence was a "distortion of the land reform."

While Mao was trying to check—successfully at this writing—the violence of the land reform, he at the same time had to wage a battle for his thesis of equality which was not always practiced in the initial stages of the reform. In some places, landlords and rich peasants were left much more land than the average. Mao believed this concession was entirely wrong. On the other hand, he declared that the "ultra-left policy" carried out between 1931 and 1934 of no land to the landlord and poor land to the rich peasant should not be repeated.

"The landlords must be given land and property equal to that of the peasants and they must be helped to work and produce and join the ranks of the national economic life."

Only tyrannical elements with enormous crimes whose guilt had been proved should be punished.

"A policy of leniency toward all men must be carried out prohibiting any indiscriminate violence."

Moderation and going slow were to Mao Tze-tung an important tactical principle.

"Do not attempt to eliminate the whole feudal system of exploitation overnight," he warns.

"In regions not firmly occupied, do not be in too much of a hurry to carry on agrarian reform, but do beneficial work for the people in accordance with existing conditions.

"Distribution of property and land must be done after the environment is comparatively stable and an overwhelming majority of the masses have been fully aroused, otherwise it is adventuristic, unreliable and wholly detrimental."

So much for land reform and the struggle for power. Whether land reform can solve China's ills is another question entirely. Land division, in itself, cannot create a sound agrarian economy in China, it cannot create the capital necessary for industrialization nor can it eliminate the pressure of the excess rural population on the land. These indisputable facts were used by Chiang Kai-shek's agronomes and they are still being used today by foreign experts to prove that the Communist land-reform program was entirely unnecessary. But, as we have already pointed out, land reform was not just a question of land, but also was a question of the whole social system tied to the landlord structure. Without land reform people could be deliberately starved to death, men could be murdered at will and women bought and sold like cattle. It has also been assumed by Chiang's supporters that land reform is a retrograde economic step because it split up large estates. But there is little capitalist farming in China—certainly not in North China where the Communists put their program into practice. Moreover, the tendency was not to make big farms into small ones, but to make small ones into larger ones by co-operative labor.

The present Communist attitude toward private property does not mean that they may not someday nationalize the land. Get a Communist in a corner and tell him that you don't think splitting up the land holdings will solve China's basic need for industrialization of agriculture and hence for larger holdings and he will answer: "Our first problem is to give the peasant a chance to live by freeing him from landlord exploitation. When he gets land, he realizes he is an individual and that everyone has equal rights and then he realizes the need for democracy. After that, as we are already doing in the older Liberated Areas, we will teach the peasants to work each other's land co-operatively. Then he will gradually realize the need for bigger farms. His own private holding will seem less important to him than his general well-being. Gradually the peasant will work out his own forms and we will follow him. It may take ten years to divide the land over all China. Maybe another ten years to introduce co-operative farming. After that we can talk of collectivization. But nationalization of the land may be no good for China. If not, we won't use it. Russia made the peasant the tenant of the state. For the time being we don't want any tenants."

While I was in Communist territory, outside of a few local thugs and some zealous local cadres who unofficially taxed landlords engaged in commerce and business, I did not see any basic violation of the Communists' general policy toward property. Certainly there was no attempt to abolish private property, nationalize commerce or collectivize the land. The spread between practice and theory was very narrow.

As for the immediate future of Chinese economy in the event of a Communist victory, Mao Tze-tung gave his ideas of what it should be in a speech to the central committee of the party on Christmas Day, 1947. His words are a kind of hazy blueprint for a future Chinese society and I paraphrase them here without comment.

The three great economic tasks of the revolution, according to Mao, are to:

1. Confiscate the land of the feudal classes and put it under the ownership of the peasants.

2. Confiscate the monopoly capital headed by China's four big families —Chiang Kai-shek, T. V. Soong, H. H. Kung and Chen Li-fu—and put it under the new democratic state.

3. Protect national industry and commerce.

The "four families," says Mao, during their twenty years have amassed enormous capital worth twenty billion American dollars and monopolized the economic pulse of the entire country. This bureaucratic capital, merged with state power, has become intimately connected with foreign imperialism. It oppresses not only workers and peasants but also the petty and the middle bourgeoisie.

Therefore, the objects which the Revolution is to eliminate are feudalism and monopoly capitalism, the landlord class and the bureaucratic bourgeoisie, not capitalism in general and not the petty and middle bourgeoisie.

Because of the backwardness of China, it will be necessary to permit the existence of capitalist economy.

China's agricultural economy will also be scattered and individual for a long time. Nevertheless, having been freed from feudalism, it can be guided in the direction of co-operatives. For this reason the existence of small and middle capitalist elements is not dangerous, but desirable. For the same reasons the new rich peasant economy that will come into being after the agrarian revolution will also not be dangerous.

The mistakes of 1931-1934, when the party wanted to liquidate commercial and industrial classes, must not be repeated.

There must be no excessively high working conditions for the laborer, no exorbitant income taxes, no infringing on industrial and commercial elements in land reform, no repetition of the shortsighted policy of so-called "welfare of the toilers."

In brief, the economic structure of the new society is:

1. State economy.

2. Agricultural economy developing step by step toward a collective one.

3. The economy of independent, small industrial and commercial business and the economy of small and middle private capital.

The guiding principles of the national economy must be the development of production, the guarding of public and private interests and creating benefits to both capital and labor.

Any other policy would be fatal and erroneous.

Such is Mao's vague plan for the "new democracy."

More specifically, it is safe to say that all heavy industries, such as iron and steel, all defense industries, such as the manufacture of munitions and chemicals, and all manufactures of tools and capital goods will be solely reserved for the state. Private capital, however, will be given unlimited opportunities in light industry. Already Kuomintang businessmen and industrialists have been invited to invest in the Liberated Areas and special assistance has been given them by various Communist-led governments.

So far, private banks and money changers have been allowed to continue their operations in the large cities newly conquered by the Communists. Probably they will be allowed to do so for some time to come. Communist trade policy will undoubtedly be guided by two principles: free trade internally and state control of foreign trade. "The aim of controlled foreign trade," says the Communist magazine, China Digest, is "to import only materials necessary and beneficial to economic reconstruction while banning nonessential imports harmful to home industry." Theoretically this is the same policy adopted by the government of Chiang Kai-shek, but the Communists claim that Nanking trade policy was nothing more than a monopoly by the "Four Big Families" which paved the way for the dumping of American goods. Under such a policy, only the government bureaucrats profited; private firms were driven out of business and the economy of the entire nation was strangled. The Communists claim that their new government will practice state trading to acquire foreign exchange, but at the same time will guarantee profits for the individual exporter. The Chiang Kai-shek regime was never very successful in this policy and that is one reason why it alienated Chinese businessmen. Whether the Communists will succeed where the Kuomintang failed remains to be seen.

61. Liberty

TO ESTIMATE the future of liberty under the Chinese Communists we must first examine the system of liberty that existed in China before the Communists rose.

If we define the essence of liberty as our being exempt from subjection to the will of another;[1] in our being free to do as we please as long as our actions do not injure the basic requirements of social life—then we will immediately see that China's system of liberty until recently was far different from any system we have in the West.

In modern Western society, social order is maintained by a vast administrative machinery, both regional and central, and by a complex body

[1] Webster's New International Dictionary.

of laws. In so far as we do not come in conflict with these laws we have a species of liberty.

In Chinese society, until recently, it was not any state power or political law that harmonized the many individual wills. Rather was it a complicated structure of traditions, ritual and folkways that dictated to men their behaviors. Civil liberties were enjoyed, not by reason of restraints the government imposed, but by checks customs imposed. Protection against the government was not guaranteed by constitution, but by folkways, and also by a kind of divine law which Mencius formulated as the right of the people to rebel against a ruler who had lost the mandate of Heaven.

The rules of everyday life being well outlined, so were the modes of liberty. The code of filial[2] piety, the cult of ancestor worship, an early training in the Confucian virtues, a universal respect for wisdom and the veneration of age, strict modes of propriety and the finest ritual of politeness the world has ever seen, all of these conditioned men to certain ways of acting. Whenever men violated the accepted rules, it was not the state which generally punished them, but the force of public opinion which, in extreme cases, might even exile a man from his village.[3]

Chinese rules of conduct were based, not so much on class as family status. Status within the family was codified in the famous five relationships between ruler and subject, father and son, elder brother and younger brother, husband and wife, friend and friend. Kinship relationships were clearly marked and carried with them compelling responsibilities and rights. The advantage of such a system was that everyone knew his exact place in the family and in society and hence knew how everyone else would act.[4]

Outside the individual family, liberty was naturally most enjoyed by those who were best capable of defending it—that is, by the biggest families. The more brothers, cousins, uncles a man had to avenge or protect him, the greater was his freedom. Even today, in some parts of China, it is common practice for a man to seek justice by summoning his family and their allies to beleaguer the home of the person who wronged him. When a quarrel between families led to the magistrate's court, the

---

[2] Violation of filial piety, "the first of a hundred virtues," sometimes was punished by death within the clan. Failure to worship the ancestors could also be cause for state prosecution. Societies which advocated the abolition of ancestor worship were generally considered revolutionary and hence a threat to the patriarchal state power.

[3] Where a public servant, such as a magistrate or a general, offended the state, he might be banished to the barren territories beyond the Great Wall. Famous operas and plays, generally sympathizing with the banished culprit, have been written around such themes.

[4] See John Fairbanks, *The United States and China* (Cambridge, Mass: Harvard University Press, 1948), p. 34.

number of "brothers" that a man could summon on his behalf often decided the rights of the case. Justice, therefore, also depended on family power.

Another way of defending one's interests in China was to have a friend in the government and that is why families tried to raise at least one son to be a scholar that he might pass the Confucian examinations, enter the bureaucracy and so bring not only honor and prestige to the family, but also a certain amount of protection against the hardships of life. Chinese intellectuals have always been a race of "place hunters," and they have always preferred the chance of obtaining a protected job with the government more than they preferred being protected from the government.

Because China's aristocracy was always weak, her concepts of liberty were always more socialistic than individualistic. Even her philosophers were concerned more with ethical social relations than with the liberty of the individual. Practical Confucianism, which depended so much on ritual, was designed to preserve society, not free the individual. And, it might be added, Confucianism, with its dual nature, acted not only to preserve the state power but also to put limits on it.

Although China had a state despotism, she managed to maintain a fair balance between security and liberty almost to the present day because the rights and duties of different social groupings were almost of the same kind. There were few great accumulations of wealth, one of the primary reasons being that fathers divided their property among all their sons instead of giving it to one son. Because there were no tremendous inequalities, interests and duties were nearly of the same kind and society remained on an even keel, adjustments being made every few centuries by overthrowing the ruling dynasty and redistributing some of the land.

The coming of the West upset this system of liberty in a particularly violent fashion. Men rushed to embrace Occidental freedoms, without considering whether such freedoms were suited to China. To middle-class peasants who became warlords, liberty was less attractive than political authority.

If the new rulers could not fit their freedoms into the old system of folkways, the old authorities showed just as little responsibility. The village elders, who had formerly to assume not only the rights but the responsibilities of their positions, soon turned into absentee landlords, with no other view of responsibility than that of milking their tenants of rents, engaging in usury and amassing land. Village nobles, become factory owners, turned into greedy capitalists who saw their workers as mere pawns in a labor contract. Sons of the gentry, who attended Christian schools, studied English and went abroad, having learned Western concepts of liberty, returned home and put them in practice as compradors, bureaucrats and bank managers. Under the doctrine of free enterprise and the right of the individual, they plundered whole provinces, robbed the people of their gold and silver and even took food out of their mouths. In a word, these men had swallowed the idea of liberty without digesting the responsibilities that it brings.

Under these circumstances, the subjective rights of the individual which had been maintained by the old customs could no longer be maintained because people no longer had rights of a nearly equal kind. No one had any idea how people would act any more.

From that time on, the majority of the Chinese people began more and more to reject the doctrine of individual liberty because they came to believe it was a weapon of the strong to oppress the weak. During the Japanese war and immediately afterward, when the authorities became ever more greedy and callous, the Chinese masses bent their efforts to destroying the individual right and substituting for it the social right— the doctrine of the "common people." In this manner, the multitude of Chinese, and particularly the Chinese Communists, bolstered by their Marxist philosophy, came to disavow the concepts of liberty admired in the West and until a short time ago admired by them.

It is only in such a historic context that the attitude of the Chinese Communists toward freedom can be understood. When they say they do not intend to give freedom of the press, assembly or petition to "reactionaries," they mean they are going to suppress warlords and other "antisocial" elements just as offenders against the code of filial piety were formerly suppressed because they destroyed the social harmony. When they castigate an English-language newspaper in Shanghai for publishing "rumors" about mines in the Yangtze River, they are asserting the rights of power against the individual right. When students rush to study Marxism-Leninism so that they may become political cadres in the army invading South China, they are following in the footsteps of their ancestors who sought "places" by studying the Confucian classics. They are expressing their desire for a great spiritual adventure, but also their desire to wield authority which has nothing to do with the desire to be free of authority.

China has thus turned abruptly aside from the direction leading to individual liberty. If this causes the leaders of the Kuomintang to rage at the subornation of individual rights, they have nobody but themselves to blame. For it was they who by their greed and arrogance reduced the majority of the people to such misery that they were glad to give up their subjective rights in order to find a safe haven under the protection of men who could guarantee them security.

I.

More than any other people, we Americans have made liberty the cornerstone of our civilization. But perhaps, by reason of our peculiar history, we are disqualified from understanding the nature of the struggle for liberty outside the borders of our own land.

Because we had an unsettled country in which we could expand, we adopted the principles of rugged individualism and free enterprise as the ruling doctrines in our country. Even so, we were not able to build our society and hence our system of liberty without eliminating the civilization which was here before we came. To achieve our own liberties, to put into practice our individualistic ideals, we not only had to wipe out the freedom of the Indians, but found it necessary to physically liquidate them.

This method of establishing a new society is not open to any people in the world today. And it should be obvious that in a country of four hundred million people, like China, unrestricted use of individualistic doctrines could only end in complete social disaster.

In overcrowded China, which has the lowest living standard of any great nation in the world and where the margin between life and death is a very slender one, the most valuable liberty that any government can bestow on the people is not freedom of speech, vote or assembly, but simply the freedom to survive.

Without a doubt freedom from starvation is the greatest gift that the Communist-led revolution has given the people in the Liberated Areas. The land reform has not freed the peasant from want, but it has at least equalized poverty and made sure that no one will starve while there is food in the village. This economic justice, won only at the cost of a bitter struggle with the landlords and gentry, has had profound emotional results and given the poor and landless farmer one emotion that was lacking from his life—hope.

Freedom to obtain food may seem to have no relation to liberty—that is, with the subjective right of the individual. But there is a connection. For poor peasants and tenants, subject to the will of the landlords and the usurers, often could be coerced into getting off the land, into giving up their wives and into starving. Freedom from starvation is a subjective right, but it is not an objective guarantee. Droughts and floods may cause famine, and people may starve, but they will not do so, because someone with economic power has driven them from the land or taken their grain stocks, but because there is just not enough food in the village.[5] Land collectivization, of course, might change this liberty.

Many of the Chinese people who allied themselves with the Communists probably did so for reasons of economic security and not liberty. The desire for security, however, became a revolt for liberty, because it had to be made against old masters. This was particularly so of the guerrilla areas where you could find the most libertarian

[5] I speak here only of North China and Manchuria, the only regions where land division has been thoroughly carried out.

spirits in the world. The Japanese war, the civil war and the land reform raised the most audacious men to positions of command and posts of authority. The timid, who ran to cover in the revolutionary crisis, were pushed to the lower rungs of the social and political ladder. But there are several complications here. Many elements of the "dark masses" did not revolt for ideals of liberty itself. They rebelled because they were insecure, because they wanted to acquire control over the fruits of their own labor, because they wanted to deprive others of authority. Now, these men wish to protect what they have, and they rate liberty much cheaper than when they rose.

Bitter class scars and terrible personal tragedies have perverted the thinking of many men. Hardheaded peasants who went through the purgatory of the Japanese war have no pretty intellectual theories about liberty. To them, liberty means the ability to protect themselves, and they have no intention of letting their enemies rise again.

In any and all cases, however, whether the people joined the Revolution for reasons of security or for reasons of liberty, they became accustomed to act in concert for social reasons rather than for purely individual reasons. Even in the guerrilla areas where a great amount of anarchy prevailed, there was always a certain group discipline. The people wanted protection, they wanted peace, they wanted food more than they wanted individual liberty.

Therefore, many of them expect everything from the new political authority, from the social right, but they do not expect so much from liberty in the way this word is used in the West.

2.

The struggle of the Chinese people for liberty in the last hundred years has centered around three main processes. In the first of these, men have been trying to free themselves from imperialism and establish an independent nation. In the second, men have been seeking to control the state power and institute democracy. In the third, men wanted to free themselves from feudal masters, individual exploiters and outworn social institutions.

I cannot dilate on these processes here except to remark that they are all interdependent and cannot be divorced from each other. From the standpoint of personal liberty, the third of these processes has naturally been the most important. But the struggle against individual exploitation and semislavery has always been irrevocably bound up with the struggle for national independence. This is so for the simple reason that the feudal masters—the landlords, the usurers and the bailiffs—were until recently tied to compradors or government bureaucrats who in turn were bound to foreign interests that were protected by special treaties, gunboats, military missions and all the usual accouterments of imperialism. For this reason, men have been trying to build a strong state apparatus to free the nation and many of them have tended to look on power as a savior and not an oppressor.

I have already given numerous examples in this book of how the people in rural China, incited by the Communists, freed themselves from feudal burdens. And I do no more here than emphasize again that in liberating woman from man, the son from the father, the peasant from the usurer, the tenant from the landlord and the soldier from the conscription agent, the Communists did in effect bring many new liberties to the poorer sections of Chinese humanity.

Liberation of this kind, however, has a dual nature. A revolution, which raises disinherited masses to a position of equality with others, cannot help but interfere with the liberty of many people. In China, the Communists' revolutionary (as distinct from the Kuomintang's evolutionary) freeing of women has not only put checks on the will of man but in some cases definitely interfered with his personal liberty. Freedom of marriage has limited the autocratic will of the parents and subverted the doctrine of filial piety. Freeing of the native industrialists from domination by Kuomintang leaders has resulted in the suppression of big capitalists. In a word, the liberty of the slaves has had to be paid for by the liberty of the masters.

It is in the nature of revolutions to free one class and suppress another. The Chinese Revolution has so far freed the poorer peasantry and the rural proletarians and suppressed the landlords and the compradors.

The danger is that the rising revolutionary class may not only suppress the top dogs, but everyone else, including, in the end, itself. The Chinese Revolution, like any other revolution, has not been able entirely to avoid this danger.

In the early stages[6] of the land reform, not only were landlords suppressed as a class, but often as people, too. In the tide of passion that swept the villages, many innocent people (not only landlords) were killed and many more were mocked, reviled, stripped of decency and deprived of normal human rights. Necessity is the god of any revolution and this god, quite independent of the Communists, often arrogated to himself all rights, all privileges and all temporary laws.

Mao Tze-tung[7] strove to hold back the whirlwind he had created, but often his words were lost in the uproar of the storm. Moreover, many

[6] After 1947, the land reform was conducted at a much slower and more moderate pace than I have described in this book.

[7] Mao, who seems to be one of the most outspoken and frank political leaders in the world, openly admitted murders committed during the land reform and inveighed against them. In many instances, he came out against the doctrine of "following the masses."

party members, under the impulse of subordinating everything to the struggle for power, directly gave instructions that were quite contrary to generally accepted ideas of human liberty.

In the Shansi-Hopei-Chahar Border Region I saw a newspaper which criticized land-reform cadres for not ridding themselves of "bourgeois" thoughts in dealing with the landlords and the rich peasants. The paper held up as an example for all to follow a village which refused to let the landlord participate in the Farmers Association, refused to allow him to leave home without written permission and encouraged the village children to taunt the landlord's children and to refuse to play with them. Thus, everyone was to be made aware of what a sin it was to be a landlord and even the second generation was to suffer for the wrongs of the first.

I met a cadre once—a mayor of a city—who used to dream that at war's end he would get a job in the Foreign Office and hand out passports night and day to anyone and everyone who wanted to go abroad. Since Chiang Kai-shek, like Stalin, let none but a selected few of his subjects leave the country, this daydream to my friend seemed like a wonderful symbol of the liberty which the victorious Revolution would bring. Yet, in the face of the fact that some men were not even being allowed to leave their villages, what a nightmare this dream might turn out to be.

In justice, it must be said that not everywhere were conditions the same. It is impossible to generalize. In Liu Po-cheng's areas, I know, cadres fought hard for the ex-landlords' rights. But this dependence on the benevolence of local cadres and the good intentions of the party hierarchy is an inadequate guarantee of liberty. What has been needed and what has been lacking in Communist areas are makeweights against power, a good body of laws, a new court system, and checks on popular sovereignty.

3.

The Chinese Communists, in the process of raising a people's rebellion, freed the peasants from feudal burdens and the nation from domination by the West. But it is very doubtful if they have liberated the people from the encroachments of state power. They will be freer of arbitrary authority and brutal masters than they were under Chiang Kai-shek, but probably less independent of power itself.

Such a result has not sprung from any Marxist ideology, but from the mechanics of the revolutionary process itself. Because the poorest farmers, who were the backbone of the rural rebellion, often looked on the Communists or at least the 8th Route Army as saviors who could intervene on their behalf, they tended to endow mass organization with the fullest authority. By creating a power of their own that could free them from bondage to old institutions and old masters, they have now raised a new institution and a new master that is far more egocentric and egoistic than the others.

This master is none other than the "people" themselves. In Communist China, today, the people are considered to hold the power. Everything belongs to them and everything is being done in their name. Loudly and clearly the Communists proclaim the sovereignty of the people. And loudly and clearly they claim that they themselves are "descendants of the people."

Because the power rests on the people, it might be thought that the future of individual liberty is assured. But the trend is in just the opposite direction. For any power which bases itself on the general will must, by definition, end up by subjecting the individual will. This is what is happening in China today and the Communists proudly declare that it is their aim to make the social right supreme over the individual right.

Many supporters of the Chinese Communists have made what Montesquieu called the mistake of confusing the power of the people with the liberty of the people. China's Communists, who are refreshingly frank, seldom made this mistake. When they told me the people were their "tissue and bone," they made it abundantly clear that they were speaking of the source of their power and not about ideas of individual liberty.

During the Japanese war and during the early days of the civil war there was a tremendous amount of individual liberty in Communist areas. And there was a great deal of truth in speaking of a people's war, a people's democracy, people's government and sovereignty of the people, for the simple reason that any number of persons in guerrilla bands and guerrilla governments had the chance to share in power and control their own destinies.

Because they were actually engaged in shaping power, the people saw no reason to be suspicious of organs that represented themselves. Therefore, under the banners of the popular will, they attributed everything to authority. The 8th Route Army was the people and the people were the 8th Route Army. "We are all from one family," said the Communists. And it was true, as long as power was confined to a narrow region where the people had control over it.

But to speak of the sovereignty of the people now that the Communists wield command over an area containing nearly two hundred million people hardly seems correct. The people may have been able to direct a country militia outfit, they may have been able to direct land reform in a particular village, but they cannot direct the nation of China. Sovereignty means command and obviously everyone cannot command.

The Communists' use of the word "people" sounds somewhat mystical to a Western ear. The Chinese emperor used to call himself the Son of Heaven. Now the Chinese Communists call themselves Sons of the People. In other words, the people have replaced God and the Communists have replaced the emperor. The emperor used to rule because he had the command of Heaven; the Communists rule because they have the command of the people. In old China, the people lived under the despotism of the dead and had to pay obeisance to their ancestors. Now, the Communists say the people are the ancestors and obeisance should be paid to them. To put this in Western terms, the sovereign emperor has been replaced by the sovereign people; and the divine will has been replaced by the general will.

If all wills must submit to the supreme will, then it follows that the individual must also bow down to the people. And in some instances this is just exactly what happens. When men come late to mass meetings, they are sometimes bidden to kowtow to the whole assembly. This is called "apologizing to the mass." That is, bending the neck to the sovereign.

In proclaiming the power of the common people, many of the followers of Mao Tze-tung put forth doctrines more characteristic of the Middle Ages than of Marxism. "Follow the masses," they say, proclaiming that the people are always good, that the people can do no wrong. Thus they pave the way to absolutism, for obviously if the people can do no wrong, then the power that represents the people can also do no wrong.

Mao Tze-tung has fought against these theories, but since the Communists continue to refer to the "people," it is apparent that the individual part of the populace must subordinate itself to the whole populace. By setting up the people as a transcendent principle, above all and beyond all, the Communists have created an atmosphere in which their power can expand without inhibition. Everything must be rendered to the people, that is to the sovereign, to power itself.

Individual liberty in the Western sense is not the cornerstone of the Chinese Revolution. You may examine Mao Tze-tung's writings and find very little mention made of man's rights. His words are touched with wit, irony, cogent analysis, but there is little mention made of the individual.

Mao Tze-tung has always emphasized the "democratic dictatorship" of the people. His followers generally speak of the rights of the people, not the rights of the individual. The Communists do not care for complicated motives. They don't want confusion. They don't want to awaken sympathy for the opposition. They want to awaken the idea of service and they want everyone to think in a social manner.

The Communists believe that individualistic doctrines are selfish and have caused many of China's troubles. Informal meetings and study groups emphasize this theme. The techniques are illustrated by a meeting of the staff members of the Nanking power plant in which the deputy chief engineer, Chang Lan-ko, a graduate of Cornell, made these remarks:

"I am a man over fifty and have studied abroad," said Chang. "Due to polite flattery by younger people, I considered myself sufficiently educated. I even read books sometimes, but this was motivated by the prospect of personal advancement. Now I study for a different purpose. I realize now that only through the advancement of the whole society is there a chance for individual advancement. It was individualism among other things that led to bribes, corruption and private influence in the Kuomintang regime."[8]

The Communists' main slogans—overturn, struggle, repent, reform, purify yourself, we are from one family—all of these have the purpose of creating solidarity, unity, oneness. This is social brotherhood, however, this is not individual liberty.

China's modern leaders have all stressed democracy and slurred over liberty. Mao wrote a whole book on the "new democracy" and made little mention of the individual. Sun Yat-sen made democracy one of his Three People's Principles, not liberty (except for the nation). It is probable that the Chinese have made the mistake of thinking that Western man derived his liberty from his congresses and parliaments, when actually they came from judicial institutions which act as a bulwark against executive and legislative power.

Therefore, even though the Communists have instituted elections in their villages, there is no reason to believe that these elections will in themselves guarantee personal liberty. Only when there are safeguards for the individual can unrestricted democracy work hand in hand with liberty. In China, there are few traditional safeguards. In fact, the tradition is to surrender the ordering of public affairs to a benign sovereign.

Whether a "people's dictatorship," based on the social right instead of the individual right, will bring the Chinese people more happiness than they had before is a question best left to history. In any event, it is perfectly clear that the Communists' doctrine of the "common people" is going to result in an entirely different solution of the problem of liberty than that reached in the West.

4.

Freedom to assemble peaceably and freely to criticize the government was not a liberty that existed in Chiang Kai-shek's areas, except in a few large cities, where even there it was curtailed, but it has existed to some extent in Communist areas. Farmers Associations and the Women's Associations are extremely active forces in the countryside and are con-

[8] Henry R. Lieberman, *New York Times*, July 12, 1949.

stantly meeting, discussing, speaking openly and sometimes criticizing the way things are run in the villages.

A provision of the land reform guarantees that the government shall give peasants and their representatives full rights at all meetings freely to criticize and impeach all cadres of all kinds and levels, and rights to remove and elect all cadres of the government and peasant organizations. Unfortunately, politically immature peasants do not always exercise this privilege as often or as freely as they might. Yet there are some astonishing instances of peasants exercising their prerogatives against 8th Route Army officials. While I was in Hopei, a farmer militaman, armed with a summons from his native village, walked fifty miles to the North China University and demanded that a highly placed 8th Route Army cadre who was then occupying a professor's chair be handed over to him for trial before a court in his village. Despite the fact that his colleagues objected, the professor was immediately given into the militiaman's care and then sent to his village which "struggled against" him for some previous wrongdoing. Not punished, but much disgraced, he returned to the university with hanging head. Such affairs as these made many of the intellectuals in the Liberated Areas frightened of the peasants and their new democracy.

Freedom of speech is a new liberty for many sections of the populace in Communist areas. Previously, as noted, poor peasants in certain sections of North China had no right to talk. They did not dare criticize the landlord openly. If a peasant spoke back to a landlord, he always ran the risk of being shut in a dungeon, killed or exiled from his village. Now that is all gone and the poor man dares speak as freely as anyone else.

Free speech is also a new concept to many of North China's[9] rural women. They no longer have to sit at the table with bowed heads and speak only when spoken to. They have equal rights with men, they may go out of doors when they please, assemble freely, engage in political affairs and assume control over the conduct of affairs in their villages.

Freedom of speech against the government allows much room for complaints, grumbling and grousing, but there seems to be no freedom to get up and denounce the Communist party.

Freedom of the press exists to some extent in Communist areas. But Shanghai officials have openly stated that they don't believe in press freedom for "reactionaries." It is only fair to state that nearly all papers in China have been organs of the army, the party or the government so that when the Communists closed many papers, they were only doing what we did in Germany and Japan. There were a few independent papers in Shanghai and Tientsin which at times served as a check on

[9] North China women have had much less freedom than women in South and Central China because the remnants of feudalism were much deeper in the north.

the Chiang government by arousing public opinion. The Communists have allowed these papers to continue publication, as they have also allowed foreign papers to continue publishing, but their basic attitude toward the press arouses skepticism as to just how much press criticism of their regime they will allow.

Though it is by no means a universal opinion in the Communist party, it is nevertheless the belief of the leaders and their propaganda agents that all writing should serve the cause of the Revolution. Mao Tze-tung believes that literature should be subordinated to politics. One famous writer in the Liberated Areas disagreed with Mao and said that politics should be subordinated to writing. Some party members felt quite insulted, but the writer was allowed to express his opinions unmolested. Because Mao keeps declaring that there is no "third road," we now find propaganda officials echoing him with statements that no writing can be neutral. That, they say, is all a "camouflage."

Even though the Communists used their press for political purposes, freedom of information, at least during the civil war, was very extensive throughout all their areas. Communist leaders, and nonparty guerrilla commanders and county magistrates often remarked to me: "Everything here is *kung kai*—open to public view. This, I believe, with few exceptions, was absolutely true. It had to be. You could not make a revolution, the way the Communists did, from the bottom up, village by village, without complete freedom of information. The Communists needed this freedom, not only to get their own viewpoints across, but to find out what the peasants were thinking.

One of the reasons this book is so filled with violence is that I deliberately looked for it. I did not do this with any desire to discredit the Communist party, but because the material was intrinsically more interesting. Far from denying me access to this material, everyone went out of his way to try and find it for me. Most all the information I have presented in this book on the land reform came from village and county land-reform cadres, from peasants and from what I saw myself. Little or no information was obtained from the Communist party hierarchy, which did not have many of the details which I have collected here. To gather material, it was necessary for me to go from cadre to cadre, from village to village, much as a student might travel from classroom to classroom where every lesson was different. From what I saw, the Communist party, even though it had twenty years' experience behind it, had to learn about the problems of the land reform in much the same way. The subject was entirely too vast to allow any other approach.

For this reason, though the land reform was filled with numerous distortions, mistakes and injustices, chief among which was an inclination to follow the mob, these mistakes were not solidified into a dogma.

Freedom of information is the lifeblood of any revolution and the Chinese Revolution was no exception in that respect.

Freedom of information during a revolution is one thing. Freedom of information after that revolution is made is another thing. Now that the Communists are moving toward state power, it is unlikely that information will circulate as freely in their areas as it did before. Undoubtedly this will be particularly so in the field of foreign news.

5.

The struggle of the Communists to restore harmony to Chinese society must arouse in the mind of any honest observer a great deal of sympathy and respect. Men in China, due to the shattering impact of capitalist civilization on the feudal way of life, forgot the correct way of acting. Habits and traditions could no longer insure obedience to a way of life so that conformity had to be secured by repression.

Chiang Kai-shek's instrument of repression was the police and the gestapo. But since there never could be as many policemen as citizens, he was overthrown. The Communists are now trying to constrain the populace with appeals to social conscience, using the methods of mass propaganda and suggestion. Some observers call this the totalitarian way of securing cohesion by wiping out differences. But it is possible that no other way exists of restoring social harmony to China.

In setting out to reform all of Chinese society, the Communists are riding the horns of a grave dilemma. They must not only transform China's social and economic patterns, but the very habits, customs and thoughts of the people. Under normal circumstances, people change their subjective outlook on life in a gradual manner as a result of slowly changing material conditions. But history, which heretofore allowed China to develop at a slow pace, has taken that privilege away from her. And the Chinese Communists, in order to overthrow feudalism, to abolish imperialism and to gain real and complete independence for the country, have been forced to attack habit patterns with an energy so vigorous and a zeal so religious that threats to individual liberty are inevitably engendered.

China's Communists are men of high moral character. But it is their very virtue that is frightening. They believe they are right and that everyone who is opposed to their basic philosophy of life is wrong. They are not fanatics in the way this word is understood in America. They do not rant or rage; they seldom (with noted exceptions) use force to inflict their opinions on others; they solicit criticism; they are patient beyond understanding in explaining their program. Nor are they Utopians. They see no ideal society in China in the near future. They are practical men (about their own country). Nevertheless, the Communists believe that they alone understand historical necessity. And it is this belief that drives them to try to mold men into images of themselves, with resultant threats to liberty.

The slogan of *Fan Shen*, with its underlying philosophy of character reform, is a good example of the way in which a high moral concept may end up by cutting down both evil and liberty at the same time. *Fan Shen* has been a great instrument in the regeneration of local bullies,[10] loafers and opium smokers, and it cannot be denied that many former scavengers on Chinese society have been made into useful human beings. But on the other hand, this doctrine of reform, when used by professional do-gooders, sometimes turns into a weapon of intellectual oppression, and young students often wield it in such a fashion as to control the liberties of others.

Furthermore, when it becomes the duty of citizens to denounce corrupt practices, to expose reactionaries, to reform other people, then, in a sense, the danger exists that everyone will become a spy on everyone else. This has not yet gone to unmanageable lengths in Communist territory as yet, but the trend exists.

The use of the "struggle" technique is also a dangerous weapon in the hands of unscrupulous cadres. In fact, the word "struggle" has in some places acquired such a sinister meaning that mere mention of it is enough to silence opposition.

China's Reds pride themselves on their methods of "self-criticism." And rightly so. For it was only by constantly re-examining themselves that they were able to correct their mistakes and avoid the dangers of dogma. But very often "self-examination" or "purification-of-thought" meetings were conducted not only to correct dogmatic attitudes of the cadres toward the masses, but to change individual convictions that were not in line with party policy. Many intellectuals who fled over from Chiang Kai-shek's areas privately told me they at first hated these criticism groups, but afterward came to like them because they helped their "outlook." This system of thought control has not yet been carried to its logical conclusion, but there is a risk that intellectual curiosity may be stultified and thought and action become based solely on party policy.

How it could be otherwise in a country like China where there is no strong middle class, where codes of right conduct have been lost, and where all other groups have shown themselves morally incompetent, is not a question that opponents of the Communists have been able to answer.

After all, the West has had a hundred years to bring a better way

[10] There are said to be fifteen to twenty million "loafers" and "rascals" in China. They terrorize villages, sleep with what women they please, eat off of others and do no work. Up to now, everyone has despaired of reforming them.

of life to China. Chiang Kai-shek had twenty years. It is now the turn of the Communists to try to make society in their own image.

6.

All discussions of liberty must eventually be stricken with a certain amount of intellectual futility, because the thing itself is indefinable. Obviously, liberty, like religion, means different things to different people. The god of the peasant is not the same as the god of the philosopher, and the liberty of the poor man is not the same as the liberty of the capitalist. A facile observer might prove anything he wished about the system of freedom existing under the Chinese Communists, either for it or against it. And I am not under any illusion that I have been able to explore the subject successfully or to strike a fair balance.

In general, there are two great misconceptions in this country about the state of liberty under China's Communists. The greatest liberty that has been crushed in their areas is simply the freedom of the previous social regime to murder its own citizens, either directly by the gestapo, the gang or the gendarmerie, or indirectly by inflationary robbery, iniquitous taxation or villainous corruption.

On the other hand, it is overlooked by some American supporters of the Chinese Communists that power of the people is not necessarily liberty of the people.

Both sides also forget that the main business of a revolution—even the American Revolution—is not the creation of liberty but the creation of a new power. Both sides fail to consider that a revolution in being and a revolution accomplished are entirely different things. And finally, both sides ignore the fact that the revolution led by the Communists in China is not finished and that at this stage no system of liberty could have been definitely established.

Within the limits of these factors, and recognizing that everything is still in a process of change, we may attempt to recapitulate the status of freedom in Communist areas. The Communists have given the people, particularly those in the rural areas, these freedoms they did not have before:

Freedom from starvation, freedom to bear arms, freedom of marriage, freedom to vote, and partial freedom to assemble peaceably and criticize the government.

The Communists have guaranteed the security of private property, outside of bureaucratic holdings, but they have taken away the freedom to rent land, except under special conditions.

Freedom to come and go is widespread in their areas, but freedom to travel abroad is unlikely to exist in the future. Freedom of opinion and its expression are more widespread than before, particularly in relation to social authorities, but it is doubtful if there will be freedom of expression such as obtains in the United States. There is still some freedom of the press but many newspapers are organs of the political power.

In the villages, the people have freed themselves from feudal masters and assumed a great deal of control over their own affairs. Peasants can no longer be dispossessed by landlords, ground to death by usurers or kidnaped from their families by draft agents. Women cannot be beaten by men, soldiers by officers or people by soldiers. Everyone, whether in the country or the city, has been freed from fear of pillage and plunder by marauding troops.

The Communists have not yet established a completely totalitarian regime. They have not taken over all industry, commerce and agriculture and put them under the state—that is, the party and the leader. They have not ground all private property to dust and removed the disharmony of society by removing all the distinctions.

They have not killed prisoners of war. They have had no motorized tumbrels, mobile tribunals or executions in the streets. The party has not yet made terror into a system and the top leaders have fought against violence, though not always with success.

The Communists have not yet instituted any loyalty checks against government employees. They have no regional antisubversive laws. They have set up no Un-Chinese Activities Committees. They have not barred the members of the their chief opposition party, the Kuomintang, from holding government jobs. They have not hauled writers up before special boards and demanded to know their party affiliations. They have treated most of their former opponents with studied kindness. They made laws guaranteeing Kuomintang army officers a share in the land from the villages.

On the other side of the fence, the Communists are making a strong drive to establish an economic, social, political and cultural imperium. The barrage of mass propaganda and mass suggestion is intensive. Study groups instituted in factories and schools, though awakening social consciousness in individuals, have the effect of creating an intellectual unity that may be deadening. The party shows indications of eventually assuming some form of control over literature, art, drama and science. Ideological opposition to the party, as such, or criticism of its fundamental policies, is at a minimum. Members of different parties and groups are to be allowed in the government, but "no anti-Communists."

The drive for intellectual indoctrination will probably be carried on more intensively than under the generalissimo. The rewriting of history, particularly that concerning United States activity in the Orient, has already begun.

Freedom of conscience is promised, but the party has given every indication that it intends to look into the moral, philosophic and psychological outlook of the unreconstructed citizens. The party is an eternal busybody and its cadres enter into realms of life unknown to the Chiang regime. Since those who can read and write in China will be the rulers, moral indoctrination falls more heavily on the intellectual than anyone else. The ceaseless talk of reform and repentance, purification and self-examination, may end up in a new orthodoxy. But so far intellectual oppression is at a minimum.

Freedom of person under habeas corpus, the right of trial by a jury divorced from the state power[11] and many other liberties until recently taken for granted by Westerners are all in doubt.

There has never been a decent independent court system in China and the Communists will have to create one out of almost nothing. The people's courts at the moment are often organs of power. Struggle Meetings and Speak Frankness Meetings are sometimes mere weapons for private revenge. Individuals are sometimes made to revile themselves, make confessions and kowtow before the "people" with little chance for defense. At the moment, law under the Communists expresses the will of the people on the march, the needs of an expanding power. Unless the Communists establish an independent court system, law cannot become sovereign. Government, as under Chiang Kai-shek, might continue to be by men, not by laws, and individual liberty may founder.

It would be a mistake to suppose that the system of liberty in Communist China will be the same as the system of liberty in the United States. For better or for worse, it would not be the same, no matter what kind of a government existed in China. Liberty is not only a matter of government, it is also a matter of geography, of tradition, of habit, belief and feeling.

China's Communists do not act or talk like men who believe in personal liberty the way it is understood here. They expect nothing from liberalism. They have only contempt for capitalist society. They wish to lead China toward socialism. And they seem determined to make the social right supreme over the individual right.

[11] This principle was not observed in the United States, itself, during the Judith Coplon espionage trial when six jurors were members of the government.

INDEX

Selected Modern Reader Paperbacks